Conference of the North American Chapter of the Association for Computational Linguistics: Human Language Technologies (NAACL HLT 2022)

Industry Papers

Online
10 – 15 July 2022

ISBN: 978-1-7138-5619-1

Printed from e-media with permission by:

Curran Associates, Inc.
57 Morehouse Lane
Red Hook, NY 12571

proceedings.com

Some format issues inherent in the e-media version may also appear in this print version.

Printed with permission by Curran Associates, Inc. (2022)

For permission requests, please contact the Association for Computational Linguistics at the address below.

Association for Computational Linguistics
209 N. Eighth Street
Stroudsburg, Pennsylvania 18360

Phone: 1-570-476-8006
Fax: 1-570-476-0860

acl@aclweb.org

Additional copies of this publication are available from:

Curran Associates, Inc.
57 Morehouse Lane
Red Hook, NY 12571 USA
Phone: 845-758-0400
Fax: 845-758-2633
Email: curran@proceedings.com
Web: www.proceedings.com

NAACL-HLT 2022

The 2022 Conference of the North American Chapter of the Association for Computational Linguistics: Human Language Technologies

Industry Papers

July 10-15, 2022

Introduction

We welcome you to NAACL-HLT Industry Track 2022.

The industry track was first introduced to a major NLP conference at NAACL-HLT 2018 in New Orleans and has since become a standard track at the NAACL conferences. The Industry track provides a forum for researchers, engineers, and application developers to exchange ideas, share results and discuss use cases of successful deployment of language technologies in real-world settings. It also inspired industry tracks at other conferences such as COLING and EMNLP.

Each conference year is unique, and 2022 was no exception. The roll-out of COVID vaccines made it possible to return to in-person or at least hybrid conferences. Yet the unpredictability of this pandemic meant that even at the time of writing this preface, we do not know how many people will be comfortable attending in-person and who will prefer remote attendance.

Another big change in 2022 was the transition of the main track to ACL rolling review (ARR). Since the criteria for Industry track papers differ from those used in ARR, we needed to organize a separate review process. However, we used the OpenReview platform to streamline the author experience. This decision came with a steep learning curve for us, and we are grateful to all authors and reviewers for being flexible and working with us as we were learning the ropes. We are also very thankful to the OpenReview support, who were always available to answer our questions.

Finally, we introduced senior area chairs. We selected ten experienced researchers with a broad range of industry and academic experience who wrote meta-reviews for each paper and helped us make the final decisions.

This year we received 128 paper submissions. Five submissions were rejected without review due to incompleteness, non-compliance with format requirements, or submission policies (such as the double submission policy). Our program committee reviewed the remaining 123 papers with a rich representation of the present spectrum of NLP researchers and professionals. Each submission was reviewed by at least three members of the program committee. Reviews solicited committee opinions along two primary aspects: Focus on real-world applications and lessons offered by the paper. Reviews also considered clarity, methodological rigor, ethical use of datasets, and compliance with conference guidelines. The area chairs then reviewed each paper and the reviews and provided their recommendation along with a short metareview. Finally, we accepted 40 papers based on committee recommendations as well as alignment of the papers with the goals of the industry track (acceptance rate of 32%).

This year, the Industry Track program will consist of two oral sessions (10 papers in total) and one poster session (30 posters). Each oral session will have a diverse set of talks covering the areas of Text Mining, Question Answering, Interactive or Dialog Systems, Summarization, Translation, Speech Technologies, Green NLP, Bias, Fairness, and Ethics. The work presented in the poster session paints a rich picture of the many real-world applications of language technologies and the challenges associated with these applications.

NAACL-HLT 2022 Industry Track also features the now traditional "Careers in NLP" panel discussion. This year we are expanding the range of careers discussed in the panel by introducing a career in product. The panel will be moderated by Yunyao Li, and we expect the conversation to include trends in NLP careers, emerging skills, main challenges and opportunities for cross-functional collaboration as NLP professionals in today's organizations, and more.

It has been a privilege chairing the Industry Track this year. We thank the conference general chair, Dan Roth, for inviting us to the organizing committee. Thanks also to Program Chairs Marine Carpuat, Marie-Catherine de Marneffe and Ivan Vladimir Meza Ruiz, and all members of the organizing committee. Yunayo Li and Owen Rambow served as advisors for the Industry Track to provide continuity for this new track. We were generously helped by every member of this committee over the past year, and organizing this track was possible only with their advice and efforts. We once again recognize and thank every member of the industry track program committee for volunteering their time. Finally, thanks to the authors and attendees of the industry track for embracing this initiative and offering a reason to continue the industry track at NAACL-HLT conferences.

Anastassia Loukina, Bonan Min, Rashmi Gangadharaiah

Program Committee

Industry Track Co-chairs

Anastassia Loukina, Grammarly
Rashmi Gangadharaiah, AWS AI, Amazon
Bonan Min, Raytheon BBN Technologies

Senior Area Chairs

Alborz Geramifard, Meta
Marjorie Freedman, USC/ISI
Debanjan Ghosh, Educational Testing Service
Siddharth Patwardhan, Apple
Mathias Lambert, Meta
Weiwei Guo, Pinterest
Yang Liu, Amazon
William Hartmann, Raytheon BBN Technologies
Aoife Cahill, Dataminr
Roy Schwartz, Hebrew University of Jerusalem

Program Committee

Tong Guo
Rylan Conway
Jangwon Kim
Shihao Ran
Ralph M. Weischedel
Abhijit Mishra
Alex Acero
Alex Marin
Alexey Romanov
Alok Baikadi
Amar Prakash Azad
Ankush Gupta
Anmol Goel
Annemarie Friedrich
Antonie Lin
Aoife Cahill
Aparna Elangovan
Avinesh P.V.S
Byung-Hak Kim
Beata Beigman Klebanov
Benjamin Han
Benjamin Vladimir Rozonoyer
Brian Lester
Budhaditya Deb
Chanjun Park
Charith Peris

Chinnadhurai Sankar
Chris Brew
Christine Doran
Christopher Hidey
Ciprian Chelba
Constantine Lignos
Damianos Karakos
Daniel Dickinson
David Uthus
Deborah A. Dahl
Deepak Muralidharan
Derrick Higgins
Deyi Xiong
Ehud Reiter
Emre Barut
Fabio Mercorio
Feifei Pan
Frederic Mailhot
Geewook Kim
Heba Elfardy
Honglei Guo
Hyeonseok Moon
Hyung Won Chung
Igor Shalyminov
Ioannis Partalas
J. William Murdock
Jaegul Choo
Jaime Lorenzo-Trueba
Jangwon Kim
Jean-Philippe Fauconnier
Jiangning Chen
Jinseok Nam
Jinyeong Yim
Joel R. Tetreault
John Chen
Joo-Kyung Kim
Judith Gaspers
Jun Seok Kang
Juntao Li
Kai Yu
Kalpa Gunaratna
Kartik Mehta
Kasturi Bhattacharjee
Keith Trnka
Kevin Stowe
Kyle Williams
Laura Chiticariu
Lee Becker
Lei Chen
Lei Shu
Li Dong

Liangming Pan
Ling Tsou
Lingjia Deng
Long Qin
Lynette Hirschman
Manuel Rafael Ciosici
Marek Suppa
Margot Mieskes
Marina Danilevsky
Matthew Mulholland
Matthew T. Dunn
Michael Flor
Michal Shmueli-Scheuer
Mingyue Shang
Minhua Chen
Minkai Xu
Mohammad Kachuee
Olga Golovneva
Oliver Ferschke
Pablo Duboue
Petr Lorenc
Prasanna Muthukumar
Radhika Gaonkar
Radityo Eko Prasojo
Rahul Divekar
Rajasekar Krishnamurthy
Ramy Eskander
Ryan Georgi
Rylan Conway
Sachin Agarwal
Saleh Soltan
Saloni Potdar
Sangameshwar Patil
Sanjeev Kumar
Sarah C Campbell
Satwik Kottur
Shang-Yu Su
Shashank Gupta
Shuangyong Song
Shuyan Dong
Song Feng
Sopan Khosla
Sourish Chaudhuri
Sudarshan R. Thitte
Sugyeong Eo
Tariq Alhindi
Tilman Becker
Tong Guo
Tong Wang
Trung Bui
Varun Kumar

Varun Nagaraj Rao
Vinayshekhar Bannihatti Kumar
Wei Zhu
Wenhao Yu
Weiwen Xu
Wonseok Hwang
Yannis Katsis
Yoav Katz
Young-Suk Lee
Youngja Park
Yuta Koreeda
Yuval Marton

Careers in NLP Panel

Yunyao Li, Apple Knowledge Platform
Yang Liu, Amazon, Alexa AI
Timo Mertens, Grammarly
Thamar Solorio, University of Houston and Bloomberg LP
Luke Zettlemoyer, University of Washington and Meta

Table of Contents

Program

Monday, July 11, 2022

13:15 - 14:15 *Careers in NLP Panel*

Tuesday, July 12, 2022

08:00 - 09:00 *Oral session 1*

CREATER: CTR-driven Advertising Text Generation with Controlled Pre-Training and Contrastive Fine-Tuning
Penghui Wei, Xuanhua Yang, ShaoGuo Liu, Liang Wang and Bo Zheng

Augmenting Poetry Composition with Verse by Verse
David Uthus, Maria Voitovich and R.J. Mical

FPI: Failure Point Isolation in Large-scale Conversational Assistants
Rinat Khaziev, Usman Shahid, Tobias Röding, Rakesh Chada, Emir Kapanci and Pradeep Natarajan

ReFinED: An Efficient Zero-shot-capable Approach to End-to-End Entity Linking
Tom Ayoola, Shubhi Tyagi, Joseph Fisher, Christos Christodoulopoulos and Andrea Pierleoni

15:45 - 14:15 *Oral session 2*

Self-supervised Product Title Rewrite for Product Listing Ads
Xue Zhao, Dayiheng Liu, Junwei Ding, Liang Yao, Mahone Yan, Huibo Wang and Wenqing Yao

Local-to-global learning for iterative training of production SLU models on new features
Yulia Grishina and Daniil Sorokin

Medical Coding with Biomedical Transformer Ensembles and Zero/Few-shot Learning
Angelo Ziletti, Alan Akbik, Christoph Berns, Thomas Herold, Marion Legler and Martina Viell

CTM - A Model for Large-Scale Multi-View Tweet Topic Classification
Vivek Kulkarni, Kenny Leung and Aria Haghighi

Self-Aware Feedback-Based Self-Learning in Large-Scale Conversational AI
Pragaash Ponnusamy, Clint Solomon Mathialagan, Gustavo Aguilar, Chengyuan Ma and Chenlei Guo

Aspect-based Analysis of Advertising Appeals for Search Engine Advertising
Soichiro Murakami, Peinan Zhang, Sho Hoshino, Hidetaka Kamigaito, Hiroya Takamura and Manabu Okumura

Tuesday, July 12, 2022 (continued)

17:45 - 16:15 *Poster session*

Scalable and Robust Self-Learning for Skill Routing in Large-Scale Conversational AI Systems
Mohammad Kachuee, Jinseok Nam, Sarthak Ahuja, Jin-Myung Won and Sungjin Lee

AB/BA analysis: A framework for estimating keyword spotting recall improvement while maintaining audio privacy
Raphael Petegrosso, VasistaKrishna Baderdinnni, Thibaud Senechal and Benjamin Bullough

Temporal Generalization for Spoken Language Understanding
Judith Gaspers, Anoop Kumar, Greg Ver Steeg and Aram Galstyan

An End-to-End Dialogue Summarization System for Sales Calls
Abedelkadir Asi, Song Wang, Roy Eisenstadt, Dean Geckt, Yarin Kuper, Yi Mao and Royi Ronen

Controlled Data Generation via Insertion Operations for NLU
Manoj Kumar, Yuval Merhav, Haidar Khan, Rahul Gupta, Anna Rumshisky and Wael Hamza

Easy and Efficient Transformer: Scalable Inference Solution For Large NLP Model
Gongzheng Li, Yadong Xi, Jingzhen Ding, Duan Wang, Ziyang Luo, Rongsheng Zhang, Bai Liu, Changjie Fan, Xiaoxi Mao and Zeng Zhao

Efficient Semi-supervised Consistency Training for Natural Language Understanding
George Leung and Joshua Tan

Distantly Supervised Aspect Clustering And Naming For E-Commerce Reviews
Prateek Sircar, Aniket Chakrabarti, Deepak Gupta and Anirban Majumdar

CULG: Commercial Universal Language Generation
Haonan Li, Yameng Huang, Yeyun Gong, Jian Jiao, Ruofei Zhang, Timothy Baldwin and Nan Duan

Constraining word alignments with posterior regularization for label transfer
Thomas Gueudre and Kevin Martin Jose

Scalable and Robust Self-Learning for Skill Routing in Large-Scale Conversational AI Systems

Mohammad Kachuee, Jinseok Nam, Sarthak Ahuja, Jin-Myung Won, Sungjin Lee
Amazon Alexa AI
Seattle, WA
{kachum, jinseo, sarahuja, youngone, sungjinl}@amazon.com

Abstract

Skill routing is an important component in large-scale conversational systems. In contrast to traditional rule-based skill routing, state-of-the-art systems use a model-based approach to enable natural conversations. To provide supervision signal required to train such models, ideas such as human annotation, replication of a rule-based system, relabeling based on user paraphrases, and bandit-based learning were suggested. However, these approaches: (a) do not scale in terms of the number of skills and skill on-boarding, (b) require a very costly expert annotation/rule-design, (c) introduce risks in the user experience with each model update. In this paper, we present a scalable self-learning approach to explore routing alternatives without causing abrupt policy changes that break the user experience, learn from the user interaction, and incrementally improve the routing via frequent model refreshes. To enable such robust frequent model updates, we suggest a simple and effective approach that ensures controlled policy updates for individual domains, followed by an off-policy evaluation for making deployment decisions without any need for lengthy A/B experimentation. We conduct various offline and online A/B experiments on a commercial large-scale conversational system to demonstrate the effectiveness of the proposed method in real-world production settings.

1 Introduction

Large-scale intelligent conversational systems such as Apple Siri, Amazon Alexa, Google Assistant, and Microsoft Cortana are an integral part of the transition from traditional human-machine interactions to seam-less and natural interactions. A conversational system is a complex interplay of multiple components ranging from the hardware and signal processing blocks to machine learning models. Figure 1 shows an overview of the major processing steps to handle a user request: (i) the automated speech recognition (ASR) block transcribes the utterance along with generating a transcription confidence signal and other voice features such as user's emotion (ii) the natural language understanding (NLU) generates a set of ranked interpretations in terms of user intent as well as named entity resolution and slots corresponding to each interpretation, (iii) a skill routing system uses NLU and ASR outputs as well as other contextual signals to select a skill and NLU interpretation to serve the request, (iv) the selected skill handles the request and generates a response for the user (Sarikaya, 2017).

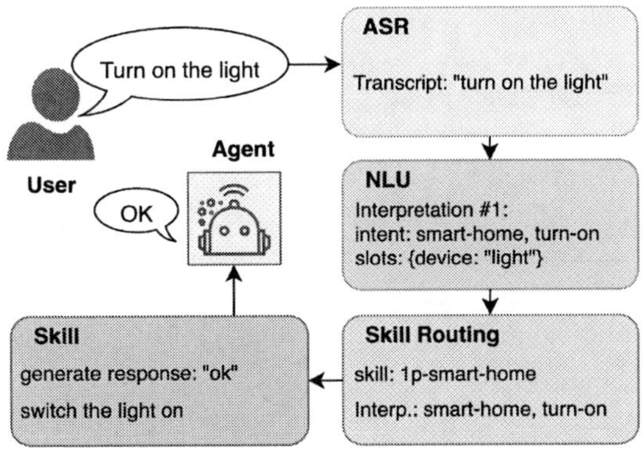

Figure 1: An overview of the major processing steps to handle a user request in a conversational system.

To provide the supervision necessary for training skill routing models, different approaches such as replicating a rule-based system, using human annotation, and relabeling based on user paraphrases have been suggested in the literature (Park et al., 2020b; Sarikaya, 2017; Sammut, 2001). Using human annotations is very expensive and suffers from high turn-around times, making it impractical for real-world large-scale systems in which new skills are being introduced frequently. On the other hand, relabeling methods such as the one introduced by Park et al. (2020b) are limited to cases where we observe enough rephrases with high precision.

Proceedings of NAACL-HLT 2022: Industry Track Papers, pages 1 - 8

From the scalability and turn-around time perspective, the traditional approach of training models then conducting long A/B experiments before each model deployment results in a limited model update frequency, often insufficient for keeping up with the introduction of new skills and other traffic changes. An alternative would be to formulate the problem as a contextual bandit and directly aim to maximize the user satisfaction (Karampatziakis et al., 2019). This approach can be more scalable in terms of supervision as user satisfaction is already an established metric in conversational systems (Kachuee et al., 2021). Also, off-policy evaluation can be used to reduce the need for conducting A/B experiments. However, in a large-scale production system relying solely on the user satisfaction maximization may cause instabilities due to bandit exploration or even estimation errors in the off-policy learning (Sachdeva et al., 2020; Joachims et al., 2018).

This paper presents a novel *self-learning* approach based on contextual bandit learning to continuously explore alternative decisions, get user feedback, and learn to improve the skill routing decisions. As frequent model refreshes are a part of the self-learning loop, we suggest a hybrid policy architecture aimed to control policy deviations ensuring consistent and robust improvements to the user experience i.e., not causing an abrupt policy change that results in a broken user experience on certain use cases. The suggested method is simple and yet effective as it supports different levels of robustness-sensitivity for each NLU intent. Furthermore, the proposed approach relies on off-policy evaluation followed by extensive tests rather than the traditional A/B analysis. This approach enables low turn-around time model refreshes in the real service settings, while maintaining the best user experience for business-critical use-cases. To validate the effectiveness of the proposed method, we conduct extensive offline and online A/B experiments on real customer traffic in a real-world large-scale commercial dialogue system.

2 Related Works

The first generation of skill routing in conversational systems used a rule-based system to serve a user's request. These rules can be defined at multiple levels and on different signals such as pre-recorded voice, utterance transcript, or NLU interpretation (Sarikaya, 2017; Sammut, 2001). However, rule-based implementations suffer from the inability to generalize and understand natural language variations. Another important drawback of rule-based routing systems is scalability issues arising when dealing with a large number of competing skills and rules (Jadhav and Thorat, 2020; Agostaro et al., 2005).

Model-based conversational systems use machine learning models to understand the user's utterance and select the best skill to serve the request. A model-based system can generalize beyond the capability of a rule-based system as a machine learning model can potentially understand the semantic meaning of a request (Park et al., 2020b). Note that despite the promise of better generalization and scalability, in a real-world large-scale system, the transition from a rule-based to a model-based approach is challenging as complex models are known for lack of robustness and interpretability (Li et al., 2021).

Providing supervision for model training is an important consideration in training skill routing models. A rule-based system can be used to provide a supervision signal to a model, hoping the model to generalize beyond the provided training examples. This kind of replication objective is relatively simple and desirable when considering the robustness aspects; however, in practice, it may not generalize much beyond the rule-based approach (Li et al., 2021).

Another line of work is based on relabeling samples by detecting rephrase utterances (Park et al., 2020b) as users tend to rephrase and repeat when the agent fails to properly respond. However, such a relabeling only covers correction patterns for a subset of traffic presenting only a limited routing improvement opportunity. For example, a user may decide to abandon the dialogue rather than paraphrasing the same request.

Considering user satisfaction being a major goal of dialogue systems one can use satisfaction as a supervision signal to guide the routing decisions. User satisfaction measurement and prediction in dialogue systems has been studied extensively in the literature (Kachuee et al., 2021; Park et al., 2020a; Bodigutla et al., 2019; Jiang et al., 2015). One possible approach is to formulate the skill routing problem as a contextual bandit problem aiming to maximize the user satisfaction (Karampatziakis et al., 2019). It enables an active exploration of alternative candidates guided by the user experience in user-agent interactions. However, in a real-world production system, it is critical to control the agent behavior changes as excessive exploration or off-policy estimations errors in bandit learning may cause unexpected behavior.

3 Proposed Method

3.1 Problem Definition

We consider the general problem of skill routing in conversational systems. Specifically, we define different pairs of NLU interpretation (e.g., domain, intent, slots, etc.) and skill (e.g., weather skill or shopping skill) as routing candidates, i.e. the action space of our policies. Given a set of routing candidates and their corresponding contextual signals, encoded in vector space as $X = \{\mathbf{x}_1 \dots \mathbf{x}_T | \mathbf{x}_i \in \mathcal{R}^d\}$, the skill routing agent is tasked to select a routing candidate, $a \in \{1 \dots T\}$, to serve the user.

Furthermore, we assume there exists a current, not necessarily optimal, policy denoted by $\Pi_0(a|X)$. The task is to learn from the experiences collected from the current policy interactions in an off-policy setting to train a new policy parameterized by θ, $\Pi_\theta(a|X)$, aiming to improve user satisfaction. Here, after taking an action, the agent observes a reward signal, r, that is a measure of user satisfaction. The reward signal itself consists of multiple components such as implicit/explicit user feedbacks and machine learning models.

3.2 Self-Learning Process

Figure 2 shows an overview of the proposed self-learning process. First, a batch of logged interactions is collected from the current policy (denoted by HP_i in the figure). Then, we use off-policy learning to update the policy using a split of the logged traffic (Section 3.4 and Section 3.5). The new policy is evaluated before and after the actual deployment enabling the use of guardrail metrics for making a deployment decision as well as tracking the actual online performance of the new model (Section 3.6).

3.3 Model Architecture

Figure 3 shows an overview of the model architecture. Inputs to the model consist of NLU interpretation and skill for each candidate as well as ASR transcription and a diverse set of contextual signals (e.g. ASR confidence, device type, device status, etc.) shared among candidates.

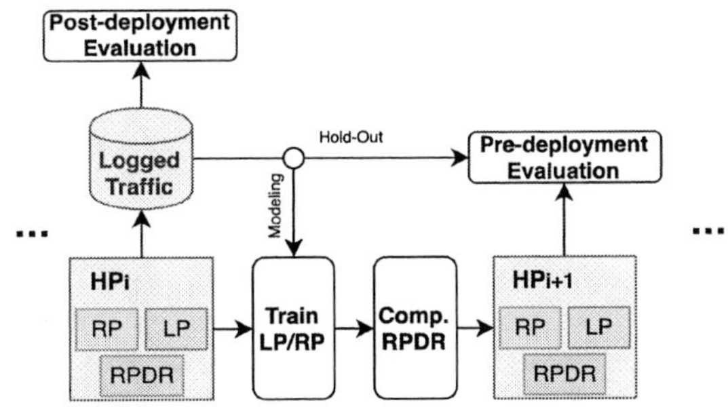

Figure 2: An overview of the self-learning process: model training, RPDR computation, pre-deployment evaluation, and post-deployment evaluation.

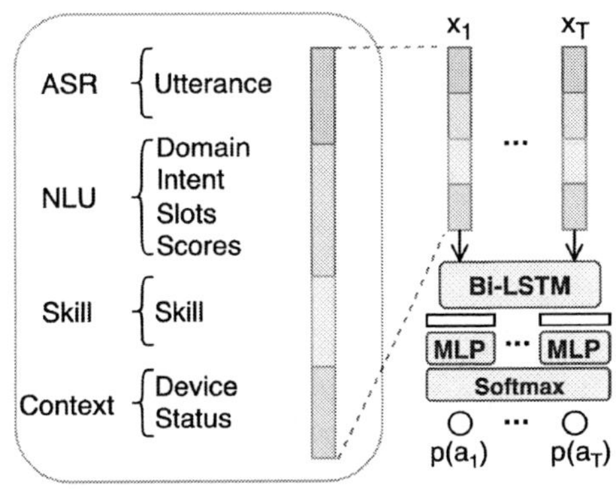

Figure 3: An overview of the proposed model architecture: a set of hypothesis are encoded as vectors $(\mathbf{x}_1 \dots \mathbf{x}_T)$ and fed to a bi-directional LSTM which is followed by a shared MLP and a softmax layer to normalize the predicted candidate selection probabilities.

We encode categorical features using an embedding matrix with a feature size proportional to the square root of the number of unique values. Utterance text is encoded using word vectors and a bi-directional LSTM. The sequence of embedded vectors is reduced via a summation operation, and contextual signals are concatenated to get the final representation i.e. $\mathbf{x} \in \mathcal{R}^d$. Finally, the set of encoded hypotheses, X, is sorted based on the NLU interpretation confidence and fed through a bi-directional LSTM, two fully-connected layers, and a softmax activation to output action probabilities for the $\Pi_\theta(X)$ policy.

3.4 Model Training

We define two training objectives: replication policy (RP) and learning policy (LP). RP objective tries to train models that replicate the logged actions. Specifically, we define the RP loss function to minimize:

$$L_{RP} = \mathbb{E}_{X,a \sim \mathbb{D}} \sum_{i=1}^{T} -\mathbf{1}[a = i] log(\Pi_{\theta}(a|X)). \quad (1)$$

In short, (1) is a cross-entropy loss encouraging the new policy to assign the highest scores to actions that replicate the logged actions. We also explored other alternatives such as KL-divergence or soft-distillation objectives but found that the simple cross-entropy objective is very stable and shows an excellent replication performance.

We define the LP loss function to be an off-policy contextual bandit objective such as the inverse propensity scoring (IPS) objective:

$$L_{LP} = \mathbb{E}_{X,a,r \sim \mathbb{D}} = r \frac{\Pi_{\theta}(a|\mathbf{x})}{\Pi_{0}(a|\mathbf{x})}, \quad (2)$$

r is the observed reward for taking action a logged in the dataset. The objective of (2) trains a policy aimed at maximizing the expected reward. Here, for simplicity, we use the vanilla IPS estimator; however, any other off-policy bandit objective (e.g., doubly-robust estimator) can be used instead.

3.5 Hybrid Policy

In a production system, any policy update directly impacts the user experience. Training new policies with a general reward maximization goal, without any control on the changes in behavior, imposes various practical risks. For example, a new model may reduce the quality of skill routing for tail domains while showing a better average performance. As another example, the new policy may explore alternatives aggressively which, considering the turnaround time in the off-policy setting, may cause a widespread negative experience until the next model refresh. To mitigate this issue and limit the changes in the policy behavior in a single model update, we introduce the idea of using a hybrid policy (HP). An HP consists of two internal models trained using the RP and LP objectives. Since the RP replicates the current behavior and the LP tries to maximize the reward, by stochastically selecting RP or LP, we can create a balance between replication of the current behavior and potential improvement in the reward function by making alternative decisions.

Specifically, to create an HP model, we start by training two individual models using the RP and LP objectives. Then, we use the validation set to

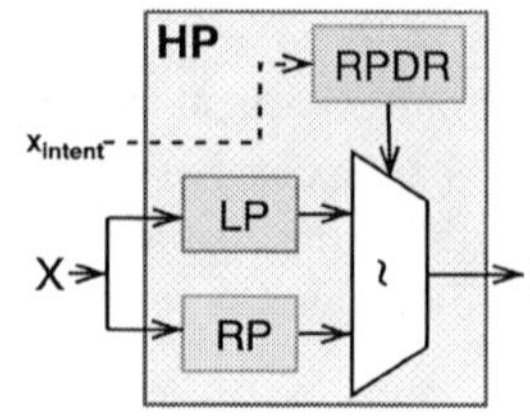

Figure 4: The hybrid policy consists of the LP and RP models as well as the pre-computed RPDR values. At the inference time, the RPDR value corresponding to the NLU top intent used to stochastically decide which model handles that sample.

compute the rate at which LP replicates the current policy for each data segment, computed as:

$$\kappa_j = \mathbb{E}_{X \sim \mathbb{D}_j}[1 - \frac{|\Pi_{\theta}(X) - \Pi_{0}(X)|_1}{2}], \quad (3)$$

where j is the index of each data segment and κ_j is the expected rate at which the new LP policy replicates the current policy. In this work, we define data segments to be based on the highest scoring NLU intent. Furthermore, we set a desired minimum replication rate ($\tilde{\kappa}$) for all data segments (e.g. $\tilde{\kappa} = 99\%$). To achieve the desired level of replication, we define the reference policy decision rate (RPDR) as:

$$RPDR_j = \begin{cases} 0 & \text{if } \kappa_j \geq \tilde{\kappa} \\ \frac{\tilde{\kappa} - \kappa_j}{1 - \kappa_j} & \text{otherwise} \end{cases}. \quad (4)$$

Intuitively, assuming RP is a good replication model, by using RPDR to stochastically decide whether LP or RP should handle each sample, we can achieve the desired level of minimum replication for each segment. The final HP model consists of the LP, RP, and a dictionary of pre-computed RPDR values for each intent. See Figure 4 for an illustration of the HP.

To update the HP, depending on the LP/RP update frequency, each time one of the models is trained on the modeling data split, followed by computing the RPDR values (see Figure 2). We update LP models more frequently than RP (e.g., LP is updated daily while RP is updated weekly). The reason behind this decision is to limit the changes in the routing behavior for longer periods. The less frequently updated RP model act as a moving average filter, gradually absorbing the LP behavior.

3.6 Pre/Post- Deployment Evaluation

After creating a new HP, the off-policy evaluation (OPE) is used to evaluate the new policy before

Metric	Description
Replication (defect/non-defect)	rate of Π_θ making actions similar to Π_0
L1-distance	average of L1-distance between Π_0 and Π_θ
STD of L1-distance	std of L1-distance between Π_0 and Π_θ
Expected reward	IPS weighted reward for Π_θ (counterfactual estimation)
Expected IPS weight	average IPS weight (ideally equal to 1.0)
Stochastic exploration (defect/non-defect)	the rate of not selecting the highest scoring candidate

Table 1: The summary of main metrics used in the pre-deployment evaluation.

the deployment. Table 1 shows a summary of main metrics reported for each data segment (here, domain-intent of the top NLU interpretation) by the OPE analysis. In the pre-deployment evaluation, a set of expert-defined guard-rails is applied to the evaluation results to ensure robust model updates, especially for business-critical cases. If a new model fails the guard-rail conditions, the deployment will be aborted, and a human expert is tasked to investigate the issue. Otherwise, the self-learning loop will continue to optimize the policy behavior incrementally based on the user feedback, as new models are trained and deployed automatically. This automated process effectively unblocks the self-learning system from the high turn-around times required for unnecessary human intervention or A/B experimentation.

OPE provides valuable insights about the performance of a model prior to the deployment; however, OPE estimates may suffer from an estimation bias due to weight clipping usually used to bound the IPS weights and high variance due to the log dataset coverage issues (Swaminathan et al., 2016; Joachims et al., 2018; Sachdeva et al., 2020). Therefore, it is essential to track the post-deployment performance of deployed polices and measure the empirical replication and user experience metrics.

4 Experiments

4.1 Setup

To evaluate the proposed self-learning skill routing method, we conducted extensive online and offline experiments in real-world production settings. In this section, we use the term baseline to refer to an implementation of a policy similar to the relabeling approach suggested by Park et al. (2020b).

We conducted online A/B experiments involving about 6M unique customers where the baseline policy served the control, and the self-learning models served treatment customers. We trained four consecutive self-learning HPs (denoted by HP1 to HP4) with the cadence of one HP per week. Each model was trained on a traffic window of two weeks of treatment data, except the first treatment model (HP1) which was trained on logged data from the baseline collected prior to the experiment. Due to A/B slot availability limitations in production, we decided not to update the RP in this A/B experiment and used OPE analysis to evaluate the performance of trained RP models. Therefore, we used a fixed RP model that replicates the baseline policy and focused on updating LPs throughout the experiment. We set the desired level of minimum replication for individual intents ($\tilde{\kappa}$) to 90%.

Additionally, we had an initial A/B experiment consisting of seven LP and two RP model updates over 49 days, demonstrating stable, steady improvements over a long period of time. However, due to certain deployment issues, the schedule of model updates was impacted and we decided to present those results in the appendix.

4.2 Results

Figure 5 shows the percentage of the difference between the treatment and control for the A/B tested models. From the figure, the proposed self-learning model improves the average reward showing a general trend of improvement over iterations. Note that in a highly-optimized production system a 1% improvement is considered a significant improvement in the user experience. Here, we use bootstrapping method with eight re-samples to find 95% confidence intervals and show them with filled regions in the figure. Note that each reported value is the average of about 40M utterances collected over a week. Comparing the performance of the HP3 and HP4 models, we can see a regression with the forth model refresh that was predicted by OPE. However, since the reward regression did not exceed our pre-deployment guard-rail tolerance values, the deployment was proceeded.

Table 2 shows OPE results comparing the four trained HPs. In addition to the reward, in this table,

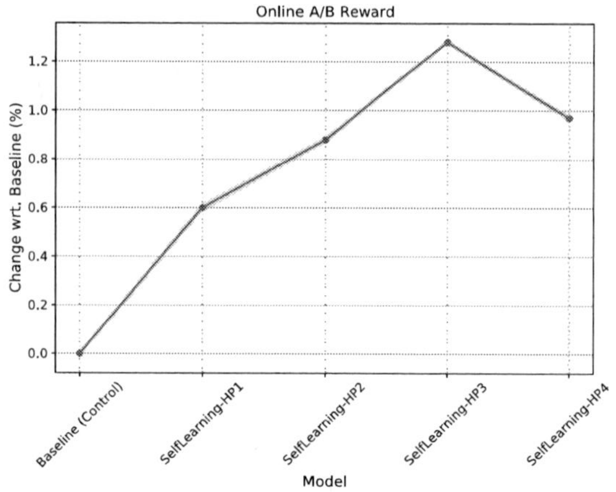

Figure 5: The comparison of the online reward measured for the baseline policy and four iterations of the self-learning model. We report the percentage of change normalized wrt. the baseline control policy.

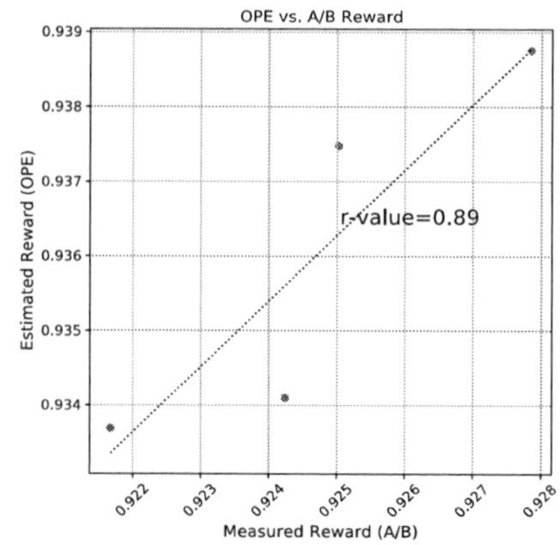

Figure 6: A calibration plot showing the correlation between the OPE reward estimates and online A/B reward measurements.

Metric	HP1	HP2	HP3	HP4
Reward (%)	93.37±0.02	93.41±0.02	93.88±0.02	93.75±0.04
Replication (%)	98.06±0.02	98.01±0.02	97.75±0.02	97.71±0.03
L-1 Distance	3.6e-2±4e-4	3.7e-2±3e-4	4.7e-2±5e-4	4.5e-2±5e-4
Stch. Explr. (%)	0.26±0.01	0.28±0.01	0.14±0.00	0.13±0.01

Table 2: OPE results comparing the performance of the four HP models on the expected reward, replication rate, L-1 distance, and the rate of stochastic exploration.

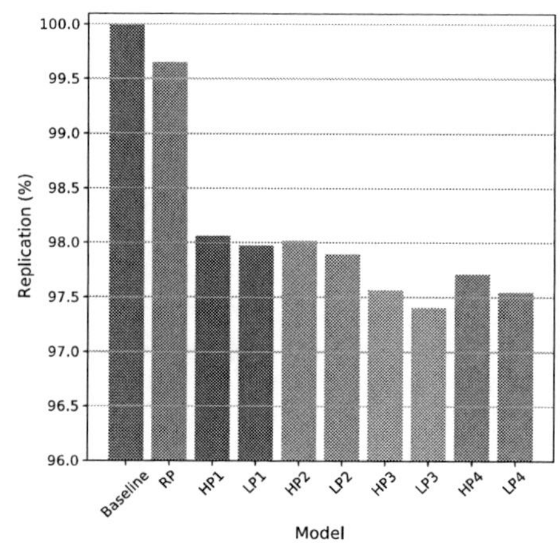

Figure 7: The comparison of the replication rates with respect to the baseline policy for the trained RP, LP, and HP models.

we report the rate of replication (i.e., the models making similar actions to the baseline) as well as the average L-1 distance of action propensities between each model and the baseline. Also, we report the rate at which the policy takes actions that are different from its highest-scoring action due to sampling of the softmax policy outputs. The general trend in Table 2 indicates that with each model refresh the new policy, on average, shows more reward and deviates more from the baseline policy. Also, the rate of stochastic exploration appears to be reduced with the consecutive updates perhaps as the model gets more confident.

Figure 6 compares the empirically measured reward values using online A/B experiments with OPE estimates. From the calibration plot, the OPE estimates tend to have different absolute values but show a high correlation (r-value=0.89) compared to the empirical measurements. Accordingly, OPE is capable of providing insight into how the performance of a new model would compare to the current model if we were to deploy the new model.

In Figure 7, we compare the replication rates with respect to the baseline policy for the trained RP, LP, and HP models. From this result, RP shows very high replication rates. When comparing the HP and LP replication rates, we can see HP shows a higher replication rate as the RPDR logic is adjusting the replication rate for individual intents to be no less than the desired threshold.

In addition to the presented quantitative results, we present a qualitative comparison of the baseline and self-learning models in the appendix.

5 Conclusion

We presented a novel self-learning approach for the skill routing problem in large-scale conversational AI systems. It leverages the user satisfaction signal to constantly improve routing decisions while maintaining frequent robust policy updates via a hybrid architecture and extensive offline analysis. The suggested hybrid architecture provides a fine-grained balance of replication and policy improvement for each NLU intent providing controlled model updates, especially for business-critical use-cases. We demonstrated the effectiveness of the proposed approach using extensive offline and online experiments in a commercial conversational system.

References

Francesco Agostaro, Agnese Augello, Giovanni Pilato, Giorgio Vassallo, and Salvatore Gaglio. 2005. A conversational agent based on a conceptual interpretation of a data driven semantic space. In *Congress of the Italian Association for Artificial Intelligence*, pages 381–392. Springer.

Praveen Kumar Bodigutla, Lazaros Polymenakos, and Spyros Matsoukas. 2019. Multi-domain conversation quality evaluation via user satisfaction estimation. *arXiv preprint arXiv:1911.08567*.

Komal P Jadhav and Sandeep A Thorat. 2020. Towards designing conversational agent systems. In *Computing in Engineering and Technology*, pages 533–542. Springer.

Jiepu Jiang, Ahmed Hassan Awadallah, Rosie Jones, Umut Ozertem, Imed Zitouni, Ranjitha Gurunath Kulkarni, and Omar Zia Khan. 2015. Automatic online evaluation of intelligent assistants. In *Proceedings of the 24th International Conference on World Wide Web*, pages 506–516.

Thorsten Joachims, Adith Swaminathan, and Maarten de Rijke. 2018. Deep learning with logged bandit feedback. In *International Conference on Learning Representations*.

Mohammad Kachuee, Hao Yuan, Young-Bum Kim, and Sungjin Lee. 2021. Self-supervised contrastive learning for efficient user satisfaction prediction in conversational agents. In *Proceedings of the 2021 Conference of the North American Chapter of the Association for Computational Linguistics: Human Language Technologies*, pages 4053–4064.

Nikos Karampatziakis, Sebastian Kochman, Jade Huang, Paul Mineiro, Kathy Osborne, and Weizhu Chen. 2019. Lessons from contextual bandit learning in a customer support bot. *arXiv preprint arXiv:1905.02219*.

Han Li, Sunghyun Park, Aswarth Dara, Jinseok Nam, Sungjin Lee, Young-Bum Kim, Spyros Matsoukas, and Ruhi Sarikaya. 2021. Neural model robustness for skill routing in large-scale conversational ai systems: A design choice exploration. *arXiv preprint arXiv:2103.03373*.

Dookun Park, Hao Yuan, Dongmin Kim, Yinglei Zhang, Matsoukas Spyros, Young-Bum Kim, Ruhi Sarikaya, Edward Guo, Yuan Ling, Kevin Quinn, et al. 2020a. Large-scale hybrid approach for predicting user satisfaction with conversational agents. *arXiv preprint arXiv:2006.07113*.

Sunghyun Park, Han Li, Ameen Patel, Sidharth Mudgal, Sungjin Lee, Young-Bum Kim, Spyros Matsoukas, and Ruhi Sarikaya. 2020b. A scalable framework for learning from implicit user feedback to improve natural language understanding in large-scale conversational ai systems. *arXiv preprint arXiv:2010.12251*.

Noveen Sachdeva, Yi Su, and Thorsten Joachims. 2020. Off-policy bandits with deficient support. In *Proceedings of the 26th ACM SIGKDD International Conference on Knowledge Discovery & Data Mining*, pages 965–975.

Claude Sammut. 2001. Managing context in a conversational agent. *Linkoping Electronic Articles in Computer & Information Science*, 3(7).

Ruhi Sarikaya. 2017. The technology behind personal digital assistants: An overview of the system architecture and key components. *IEEE Signal Processing Magazine*, 34(1):67–81.

Adith Swaminathan, Akshay Krishnamurthy, Alekh Agarwal, Miroslav Dudík, John Langford, Damien Jose, and Imed Zitouni. 2016. Off-policy evaluation for slate recommendation. *arXiv preprint arXiv:1605.04812*.

A Appendix

A.1 Qualitative Results

Table 3 shows a qualitative comparison of the baseline (relabeling approach) and self-learning (bandit-based HP) decisions. We provide the actual user utterance transcription and the selected skill using each method. The green color shows the skills providing the best user experience.

A.2 Additional A/B Experiment Results

Figure 8 shows the trend of change in the reduction of user dissatisfaction rate over a 49-day long A/B experiment. During the A/B experiment, we updated the LP model seven times and the RP model two times. As this long-running A/B was one of our initial proof-of-concept experiments on the production system, we faced several deployment and technical issues that impacted the schedule of LP and RP updates. Nonetheless, from the results, we can see consistent and statistically significant improvements in user satisfaction.

		Selected Skill	
Example	**Utterance**	**Baseline Model**	**Self-Learning Model**
win-1	*what is the best seasoning for mahi-mahi*	shopping	knowledge (Q&A)
win-2	*show me wildlife photography*	shopping	photos (gallery)
win-3	*give me n. b. c. news*	knowledge (Q&A)	daily briefing (news)
win-4	*get some cheeto puffs*	knowledge (Q&A)	shopping
win-5	*set up [DEVICE NAME]*	pairing (Bluetooth)	setup (home automation)
loss-1	*what is the best song in the world*	knowledge (Q&A)	find music
loss-2	*play announcement*	announcement	get message

Table 3: A few examples of skill routing for the baseline and self-learning models. The green color is used to indicate skills providing the best user experience.

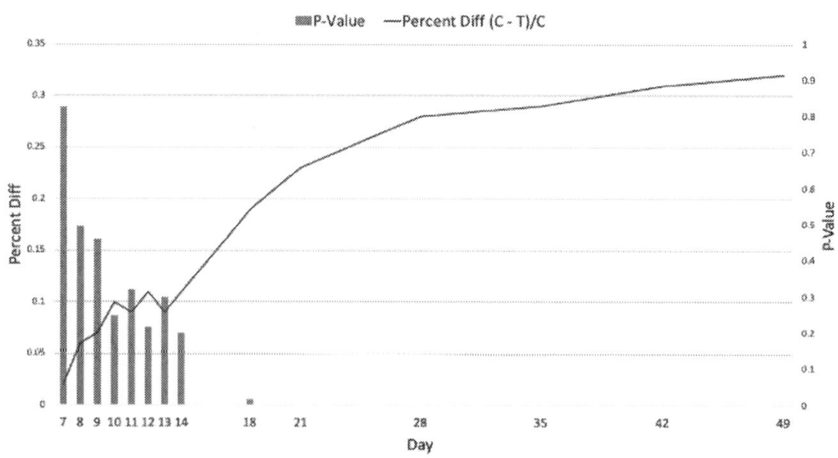

Figure 8: The percentage of difference for the measured reward between the control (relabeling baseline) and treatment (self-learning) slots over a 49-day initial proof-of-concept A/B experiment.

CREATER: CTR-driven Advertising Text Generation with Controlled Pre-Training and Contrastive Fine-Tuning

Penghui Wei, Xuanhua Yang, Shaoguo Liu*, **Liang Wang** and **Bo Zheng**
Alibaba Group
{wph242967,xuanhua.yxh,shaoguo.lsg,liangbo.wl,bozheng}@alibaba-inc.com

Abstract

This paper focuses on automatically generating the text of an ad, and the goal is that the generated text can capture user interest for achieving higher click-through rate (CTR). We propose CREATER,[1] a CTR-driven advertising text generation approach, to generate ad texts based on high-quality user reviews. To incorporate CTR objective, our model learns from online A/B test data with contrastive learning, which encourages the model to generate ad texts that obtain higher CTR. To alleviate the low-resource issue, we design a customized self-supervised objective reducing the gap between pre-training and fine-tuning. Experiments on industrial datasets show that CREATER significantly outperforms current approaches. It has been deployed online in a leading advertising platform and brings uplift on core online metrics.

Figure 1: An illustration that shows the creative of an online advertisement in news feed on mobile.

1 Introduction

For businesses that want to promote their items and services, running online advertisements on advertising platforms is an effective way to achieve their marketing goals. With the aim of attracting users to know more about the displayed items, advertisers design ad creative (such as text, image and video). Figure 1 is an illustration that shows the creative of an ad in news feed, which contains a text and an image.

An appropriate creative design capturing user interest accurately can improve the ad's click-through rate (CTR). CTR is a key metric that quantifies the effect of an ad, because click is the precondition for any further actions such as sharing and purchase taken by users. Thus designing ad creatives that can achieve higher CTR is crucial for ad delivery.

Traditionally, advertisers need to manually design the creative of each ad, and then resort to online A/B test results to continually refine initial creative for catching user interests. Such trail-and-error process is labor-intensive and usually inefficient. In terms of the text in a creative, due to the variation characteristic of language expressions, it may need to be polished multiple times for obtaining an ideal one. To improve the efficiency of ad delivery for advertisers, especially for small advertisers that may not afford to hire professional writers, this paper focuses on automatically generating the text for an ad, and the goal is that the generated text can capture user interest for achieving higher CTR.

There are several challenges to achieve this goal. **(I)** First, it is important to choose a suitable source for generating ad texts. A straightforward source is the corresponding item's title in landing page. However, a title is usually a mixture of item attributes while may not reflect user preference. In contrast, an ad text should contain insightful and informative contents that can arouse purchasing desire of users. **(II)** Second, most of current natural language generation (NLG) models are optimized using cross-entropy criterion, which is discrepant to the CTR metric we concern. To encourage the model to generate texts achieving higher CTR, there is a great need to incorporate CTR objective into training. **(III)** Last but not least, a well-trained NLG model usually need a large amount of paired data. However it is costly to collect sufficient human-written ad texts, especially for small advertisers, thus we are faced to low-resource problem.

*Corresponding author.
[1]**CTR**-driv**E**n **A**dvertising **TE**xt Gene**R**ation

Proceedings of NAACL-HLT 2022: Industry Track Papers, pages 9 - 17
July 10-15, 2022 ©2022 Association for Computational Linguistics

In this paper we propose CREATER, a CTR-driven advertising text generation approach, to address the above challenges. **(I)** First, we choose high-quality user reviews as input source for generation. Compared to titles, user reviews intuitively contain contents that reflect real experience after purchasing. We also introduce an aspect term as input control code to improve the informativeness of generated text. **(II)** Second, to explicitly incorporate CTR objective during optimizing NLG models, we make use of collected user feedback through online A/B test. Advertisers always perform online A/B test to compare two different texts of a same ad, where online CTR metric reflects the distinction between a relatively "good" text and a "bad" one. We employ contrastive learning for model optimization, which encourages our model to generate texts that can achieve high CTR. **(III)** Finally, to alleviate the low-resource problem, we make use of large-scale unpaired reviews to perform pre-training that provides warm-starting. We design a novel self-supervised objective customized to our scenario, which reduces the gap between pre-training and fine-tuning.

CREATER has been deployed online in a leading advertising platform and it achieves significant improvement on core online metrics. The main contributions of this work are summarized as follows:

- We propose CREATER for generating ad texts that capture user interest based on high-quality user reviews. We make use of online A/B test data to perform contrastive learning, which encourages the model to generate texts that achieve higher CTR.
- We propose a novel self-supervised objective to provide warm-starting with unpaired reviews, which is customized to our scenario and reduces the gap between pre-training and fine-tuning.
- Experiments on industrial datasets show that CREATER outperforms previous approaches on both automatic and human evaluation, and online results verify that it brings significant uplift on core metrics.

2 Problem Formulation

Given a source x and a control code c for an ad, where the source is a high-quality user review of the ad item, the control code is an aspect term of such review to guide generation, we aim to learn a generation model $p_\Theta(y \,|\, x, c)$ that can produce an appropriate ad text y (where Θ denotes trainable parameters of the model). Our goal is that the generated ad text can capture user interest and attract users to know more about the ad item.

3 Proposed Approach: CREATER

Figure 2 illustrates the workflow of our CREATER, and it consists of two stages. The first stage is *Controlled Pre-Training*, which learns from unpaired user reviews to provide warm-starting for low-resource scenario. The second stage is *Contrastive Fine-Tuning*, which further learns from online A/B test data that reflects user feedback, aiming to encourage the model to generate ad text that can achieve higher CTR.

3.1 Stage 1: Controlled Pre-Training

We construct a large set of user reviews as the pre-training corpus $\mathcal{D}_x$. Based on $\mathcal{D}_x$, we extract a set of aspect terms $\mathcal{D}_c$ using an off-the-shelf unsupervised model ABAE (He et al., 2017), and each aspect term is typically represented as a word.

Recall that we aim to learn a generation model $p_\Theta(y \,|\, x, c)$, while the pre-training stage only makes use of *unpaired* user reviews $\mathcal{D}_x$. To ensure that the model benefits from pre-training, we propose a novel self-supervised objective customized to our scenario, which reduces the gap between pre-training and fine-tuning. The core is that, for each review $x \in \mathcal{D}_x$, we construct an aspect-based *pseudo-target* $\tilde{y}$ from the review x and mask this segment in x. The self-supervised objective is to perform aspect-controlled generation, which aims to recover the segment $\tilde{y}$ given the masked review with the guidance of corresponding aspect term.

Aspect-Controlled Masking For a review $x \in \mathcal{D}_x$, we tokenize it as a list of segments $[x_{\text{seg\_1}}, x_{\text{seg\_2}}, ...]$ based on punctuations and dependency parser, where each segment $x_{\text{seg\_i}}$ is a sub-sequence of x. Given an aspect term $c \in \mathcal{D}_c$ existed in the review x, we compute the matching score between c and each $x_{\text{seg\_i}}$ with a matching function $f(c, x_{\text{seg\_i}})$.[2] We then select the segment with highest matching score as the *pseudo-target* $\tilde{y}$ for the given pair of (source x, control code c):

$$\tilde{y} = \arg\max_{x_{\text{seg\_i}} \in x} f(c, x_{\text{seg\_i}}) \qquad (1)$$

For each triple (source x, control code c, pseudo-target $\tilde{y}$), our aspect-controlled masking strategy masks the review x by replacing its pseudo-target $\tilde{y}$ with a special word "`[MASK]`". Thus we transform each triple $(x, c, \tilde{y})$ to a masked one $(\tilde{x}, c, \tilde{y})$, where the masked review $\tilde{x}$ is specific to the aspect term c.

[2]The function $f(\cdot,\cdot)$ can either be a lexical-based one (such as similarity of sparse TF-IDF vectors) or an embedding-based one (such as similarity of averaged word embeddings).

Figure 2: Overview of our proposed approach CREATER for CTR-driven advertising text generation.

Aspect-Controlled Generation Given a masked review $\tilde{x}$ with an aspect term c, our self-supervised objective is to recover the masked segment (i.e., pseudo-target $\tilde{y}$) of original review x with the controlling of c:

$$\min_{\Theta} -\log p_{\Theta}(\tilde{y} \,|\, \tilde{x}, c). \quad (2)$$

Such aspect-controlled generation enforces the model to understand the context of input masked review better. Compared to general pretraining models (Zhang et al., 2020; Lewis et al., 2020; Raffel et al., 2020), the proposed objective is customized to our scenario. The input information $\tilde{x}$ does not contain the content to be generated, improving the ability of generating abstractive contents other than simply copying from input only.

Formally, we first prepend the control code c to the masked source $\tilde{x}$, and add a special word "`[SEP]`" between them. We then feed the concatenated sequence $[c, \texttt{[SEP]}, \tilde{x}]$ into CREATER to generate the pseudo-target $\tilde{y} = [\tilde{y}_1, \tilde{y}_2, \ldots, \tilde{y}_{\tilde{T}}]$ (where $\tilde{T}$ denotes the length), where the model architecture is a Transformer encoder-decoder (Vaswani et al., 2017) and it is optimized via teacher-forcing:

$$\begin{aligned} \tilde{\boldsymbol{h}}_1, \tilde{\boldsymbol{h}}_2, \ldots, \tilde{\boldsymbol{h}}_{\tilde{N}} &= \mathsf{Enc}([c, \texttt{[SEP]}, \tilde{x}]) \\ p(\tilde{y}_t \,|\, \tilde{y}_{0:t-1}, \tilde{x}, c) &\sim \mathsf{Dec}\left(\tilde{y}_{0:t-1}, \tilde{\boldsymbol{h}}_{1:\tilde{N}}\right) \\ \min_{\Theta} \sum_{t=1}^{\tilde{T}} &-\log p_{\Theta}(\tilde{y}_t \,|\, \tilde{y}_{0:t-1}, \tilde{x}, c) \end{aligned} \quad (3)$$

where $\tilde{N}$ is the length of the sequence $[c, \texttt{[SEP]}, \tilde{x}]$, and $\tilde{\boldsymbol{h}}_i$ is the i-th word's representation.

3.2 Stage 2: Contrastive Fine-Tuning

To incorporate CTR objective during generation, we make use of existing online A/B test data that reflects user preference. Specifically, we construct a dataset $\mathcal{D}$, where each sample is a tuple (source x, control code c, positive target y^+, negative target y^-). Both y^+ and y^- are human-written ad texts (given x and c), while y^+ achieves higher CTR than y^- during online A/B test.

Next, we start from describing a vanilla fine-tuning objective that only considers y^+. We then introduce two contrastive fine-tuning objectives which take good advantage of online A/B test data.

Vanilla Fine-Tuning A straightforward objective is to maximize the generation probability of positive target y^+:

$$\mathcal{L}_{ft} = -\log p_{\Theta}(y^+ \,|\, x, c). \quad (4)$$

Obviously, this learning objective omits the utility of negative targets.

To enhance the model's discriminative ability of ad texts with different CTR, we propose to expose the decoder to both positive and negative ad texts via modeling their distinctness. Specifically, we leverage the paradigm of contrastive learning, where the positive/negative target (i.e., ad text with higher/lower CTR) is used to construct positive/negative paired instance, and introduce two contrastive learning based objectives to fine-tune the pre-trained model.

i. Margin-based Contrastive Fine-Tuning We first propose to directly maximize the margin of generation probabilities between the positive target y^+ and the negative target y^-. This yields the following loss function:

$$\mathcal{L}_{cont} = \max\{0, -(\log p_\Theta(y^+ | x, c) - \log p_\Theta(y^- | x, c)) + \gamma\} \quad (5)$$

where the margin γ is a hyperparameter. Through this loss, the optimization procedure is encouraged to maximize the probability gap of ad texts having distinct CTR.

ii. InfoNCE-based Contrastive Fine-Tuning From the perspective of representation learning, we propose a contrastive loss based on InfoNCE (Oord et al., 2018), which maximizes the similarity between source and positive target, and minimizes that between source and negative target:

$$\mathcal{L}_{cont} = -\log \frac{\exp(\text{sim}((c,x), y^+)/\tau)}{\exp(\text{sim}((c,x), y^+)/\tau) + \exp(\text{sim}((c,x), y^-)/\tau)} \quad (6)$$

where τ is temperature. $\text{sim}(\cdot, \cdot)$ is similarity function of encoder and decoder representations.

We adopt mean-pooling to the top layer of the encoder/decoder as their representations. Let $\boldsymbol{h}$, $\boldsymbol{z}^+$ and $\boldsymbol{z}^-$ denote encoder representation, decoder representations for positive and negative targets. We then add two fully-connected layers to the encoder and the decoder side respectively, transforming them to the same vector space. Thus an inner product operation is used to obtain the similarity scores:

$$\begin{aligned} \text{sim}((c,x), y^+) &= (\mathbf{W}_e \boldsymbol{h})^\top (\mathbf{W}_d \boldsymbol{z}^+) \\ \text{sim}((c,x), y^-) &= (\mathbf{W}_e \boldsymbol{h})^\top (\mathbf{W}_d \boldsymbol{z}^-) \end{aligned} \quad (7)$$

where $\mathbf{W}_e$ and $\mathbf{W}_d$ learnable parameters.

Objective The final loss of contrastive fine-tuning stage is the sum of $\mathcal{L}_{ft}$ and contrastive loss:

$$\mathcal{L}_{ft}(y^+) + \mathcal{L}_{ft}(y^-) + \alpha \mathcal{L}_{cont} \quad (8)$$

where α is a trade-off hyperparameter, and $\mathcal{L}_{cont}$ can either be margin-based or InfoNCE-based.

Comparison The advantage of margin-based loss is that it does not add extra parameters, directly incorporating CTR objective to generation probabilities. InfoNCE-based loss considers encoder representations to learn better decoder representations. Although it adds a few parameters (i.e., two fully-connected layers), they are pruned at inference. The construction of positive-negative pairs in CREATER is designed for CTR objective via user feedback, unlike recent work tackling other issues (Cao and Wang, 2021; Pan et al., 2021; Lee et al., 2021)

Dataset	Pre-training ($\mathcal{D}_x$)	Fine-tuning ($\mathcal{D}$)
# Samples	1,471,106	43,985
Avg. length of reviews	25.05	25.31
Avg. length of ad texts	N/A	13.06

Table 1: Statistics of the datasets used in our experiments. "Avg. length" means the average number of characters in a sequence (review or ad text).

4 Experiments

4.1 Experimental Setup

Datasets To our knowledge, there is no available public dataset that contains ad texts coupled with CTR information, thus we collected data on a leading advertising platform. We construct a dataset $\mathcal{D}$ where each sample is a tuple of (user review, aspect term, positive ad text$_1$, negative ad text$_2$), in Chinese, through online A/B test. Overall the user reviews are ensured to be high-quality based on rules and filtering models. Each ad text is written by human editors given the review and aspect term, covering 4,047 advertisers. More details about data preprocessing and filtering can be found in **Appendix** A.1.

We also produce a large-scale review corpus $\mathcal{D}_x$ for constructing pre-training dataset via aspect-controlled masking (§ 3.1). Table 1 lists the statistics. We split $\mathcal{D}$ with 7:1:2 to obtain the training/development/test set.

Comparative Approaches We choose two types of comparative approaches in our experiments. The first type contains *non-CTR-driven approaches*: (1) SEGEXT (Segment extraction) employs unsupervised aspect-controlled masking (§ 3.1) to return a segment of source as the ad text. If the returned segment is too short to display, we add its left or right segment based on matching score. (2) PGNET (Pointer-generator) is an RNN-based approach via copying mechanism (See et al., 2017); (3) C-PGNET improves PGNET by adding control code during decoding, which imposes on the generation gate; (4) TRM (Transformer) is the state-of-the-art architecture for text generation; (5) C-TRM improves TRM by adding control code at both encoder and decoder sides, with the help of fusion layers; (6) C-TRM-RL fine-tunes the C-TRM with reinforcement learning (RL), where an extra CTR regression model (trained on $\mathcal{D}$) is the reward estimator that produces click probability of a generated text (Hughes et al., 2019). Negative targets are used to train the reward estimator, and are not explicitly used for optimizing generation model.

The second type contains *CTR-driven approaches*. They exploit negative target y^- during training to explicitly incorporate CTR information: (1) QUALITYMODEL employs click behavior as a quality measure for paired samples (Wang et al., 2019). It first builds a CTR latent space to represent source and target, and then computes the cosine similarity between them as the quality score of the sample. Quality scores are used to weight the cross-entropy objective and reduce the probability of generating low-quality texts; (2) CONTRAMODEL is a variant of CREATER, which removes the controlled pre-training stage; (3) BART+CONTRAMODEL performs pre-training from scratch using the self-supervised objective of BART other than our proposed one, and then performs fine-tuning with CONTRAMODEL.

4.2 Implementation Details

Both the encoder and the decoder of CREATER contain four layers, and the dimension of hidden representations produced by each layer is set to 512. For fair comparison, all comparative approaches that based on Transformer employ the above architecture. For text preprocessing, we tokenize sources and targets to word sequences, and thus our CREATER generates ad texts at word-level. We restrict the max length of input as 128 words. The overall parameter size is 129M. At the pre-training stage, we employ Adafactor optimizer (Shazeer and Stern, 2018), with a mini-batch size of 4096 for training 10 epochs. Models are trained on 8 Tesla V100 32GB GPUs. We implement our approach with *PyTorch*[3] and *Transformers*[4].

In terms of the model for extracting aspect term set, during early experiments we found that the performance of CREATER is not sensitive to it and thus we employ the representative model ABAE. For matching function $f(\cdot,\cdot)$ (Equation 1) used in aspect-controlled masking for building pre-training data, we try a lexical-based (similarity of sparse TF-IDF vectors) and an embedding-based one (similarity of averaged word embeddings), and found that the performance of fine-tuned model is not sensitive to them. Thus we choose the former for simplicity.

At the fine-tuning stage, we set the mini-batch size to 1024 for 20 epochs. When the margin-based contrastive loss is used, the margin parameter γ is set to 1.0. Or if we the use InfoNCE-based contrastive

[3]https://github.com/pytorch/pytorch

[4]https://github.com/huggingface/transformers

Approach	BLEU-4	RG-1	RG-2	RG-L
Non-CTR-driven Approaches				
SEGEXT	13.54	31.11	7.71	23.66
PGNET	24.85	44.79	16.76	35.21
C-PGNET	37.69	55.09	31.70	46.62
TRM	33.36	50.58	26.23	42.44
C-TRM	48.66	61.73	42.43	54.82
C-TRM-RL	50.11	62.59	42.26	55.43
CTR-driven Approaches				
QUALITYMODEL	49.89	62.67	43.85	55.84
CONTRAMODEL	51.47	63.47	43.94	56.93
BART+CONTRAMODEL	53.35	65.04	46.20	58.51
CREATER	**54.56**	**65.93**	**47.44**	**59.77**

Table 2: Main results. "RG" stands for ROUGE. Both BLEU and ROUGE scores are multiplied by 100.

loss, the temperature parameter τ is set to 1.0. We set the trade-off hyperparameter α to 1e-3 (which is searched from {1e-2, 1e-3, 1e-5}). We choose the checkpoint that has lowest perplexity on validation set as the final model. At inference time, we use beam search algorithm to generate texts, where the beam size is set to 5. The BLEU metric is evaluated using *NLTK*[5], and the ROUGE metric is evaluated using *pyrouge*[6]. All reported results of different approaches are run based on the same random seed.

4.3 Performance Comparison

Table 2 shows the comparison results, and we report BLEU-4 and ROUGE-1/2/L (positive targets are regarded as gold-standard).[7] It is natural that the approaches considering aspect terms outperform those that do not perform controlling.

CTR-driven approaches usually outperforms non-CTR-driven ones, demonstrating that exposing the model to both positive and negative targets improves generation quality. QUALITYMODEL and CONTRAMODEL represent two paradigms to incorporate CTR information. CONTRAMODEL is superior to QUALITYMODEL, which indicates that directly modeling the distinctness as an auxiliary objective is more effective than weighting the original loss.

BART+CONTRAMODEL performs better than CONTRAMODEL by adding a pre-training stage. CREATER proposes a customized controlled pre-training objective and achieves the best result. This verifies that designing a suitable self-supervised objective is crucial to improve generation.

[5]https://github.com/nltk/nltk

[6]https://github.com/bheinzerling/pyrouge

[7]Our CREATER performs significantly better than the second best comparative approach at the level of $p < 0.05$.

Variants of Pre-training	BLEU-4	RG-1	RG-2	RG-L
CREATER ($p(\tilde{y}\,\vert\,\tilde{x},c)$)	**54.56**	**65.93**	**47.44**	**59.77**
w/o masking ($p(\tilde{y}\,\vert\,x,c)$)	51.24	63.65	43.74	56.94
w/o control code ($p(\tilde{y}\,\vert\,\tilde{x})$)	53.11	64.64	45.91	58.28
w/o whole pre-training	49.92	62.20	41.91	55.09

Table 3: Comparison of pre-training objectives.

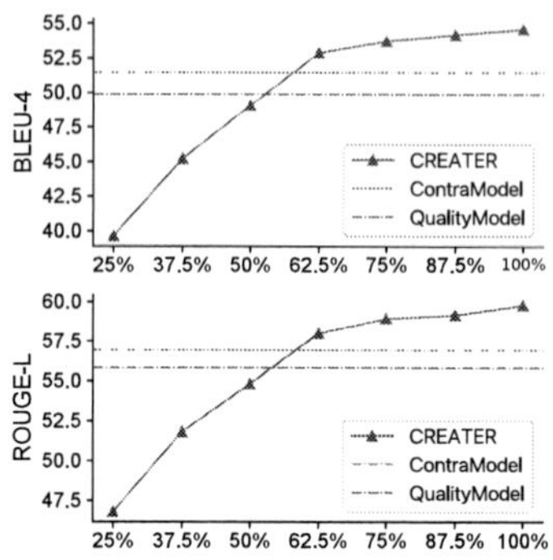

Figure 3: Results with limited fine-tuning data. Dashed lines are two strongest baselines trained on whole data.

4.4 Discussion

Effect of Aspect-Controlled Masking During pre-training, aspect-controlled masking ensures the ability of generating abstractive contents other than simply copying from source. Besides, the model takes aspect terms as control codes to generated masked contents (pseudo-targets). Both the two mechanisms reduce the gap between pre-training and fine-tuning. We verify their effectiveness by removing one of two mechanisms, and the fine-tuning stage keeps unchanged. Results are shown in Table 3. The two variants are inferior to the full model, demonstrating that both of them can improve pre-training to provide better warm-starting. Aspect-controlled masking brings improvements over 3 BLEU score and 2 ROUGE score. Thus, our novel controlled pre-training objective indeed enhances the performance of advertising text generation via effective self-supervised learning on unpaired corpus.

Benefit in Low-Resource Scenario We further verify the effect of controlled pre-training when there are only limited paired data for fine-tuning. We change the size of data (from 25% to 100% of the whole training set), and compare to two strongest baselines (QUALITYMODEL and CONTRAMODEL, without pre-training) that are trained on the whole training set. As shown in Figure 3, with only half of fine-tuning data, CREATER performs on par with QUALITYMODEL, verifying the benefit of our controlled pre-training in low-resource scenario.

Variants of Contrastive Loss		BLEU-4	RG-1	RG-2	RG-L
Pre-Train	Contrastive Loss				
✓	InfoNCE-based	**54.56**	**65.93**	**47.44**	**59.77**
✓	Margin-based	54.26	65.93	47.23	59.57
✓	No	53.70	65.38	46.57	58.94
×	InfoNCE-based	49.92	62.20	41.91	55.09
×	Margin-based	**51.47**	**63.47**	**43.94**	**56.93**
×	No	50.37	62.27	42.19	55.36

Table 4: Comparison of contrastive learning objectives.

Approach	Gram.	Info.	Suit.	Avg. Rank (↓)
SEGEXT	**4.97**	2.19	1.92	4.53
C-TRM	4.95	2.69	2.44	3.65
QUALITYMODEL	4.96	2.81	2.49	3.19
CREATER	4.96	**3.21**	**3.05**	**2.09**
Human-written (high-quality)	4.99	3.60	3.22	1.48

Table 5: Human evaluation results. "Gram.", "Info.", "Suit." and "Avg. Rank" stand for grammaticality, informativeness, suitability and average rank, respectively.

Analysis of Contrastive Fine-Tuning Our CREATER exposes the model to both positive and negative targets for incorporating CTR information. Table 4 shows the comparison of two contrastive objectives. For with and without pre-training, the best-performing model is based on contrastive learning.

An interesting point is that when we perform pre-training, InfoNCE-based model achieves best performance, while margin-based model outperforms other variants if we do not pre-train the model. We suggest that InfoNCE-based loss is designed from the perspective of representation learning, and pre-training can provide better text representations compared to no pre-training. Thus in this situation the utility of InfoNCE-based model is highlighted.

4.5 Human Evaluation

An ad text will be measured from the three views: grammaticality, informativeness (whether its content reflects the key points of aspect term and the source) and suitability (whether it is suitable to be displayed). Each view is ranging from 1 to 5 (5 is the best). We randomly choose fifty samples and invite three human judgments.

Table 5 shows that CREATER performs well on most views and achieves the best ranking results among four comparative approaches, possessing the ability of generating fluent, informative and suitable ad texts. We found that the reason why the informativeness and suitability of CREATER are not as high as human-written ones is that the faithfulness of generated texts is not always ideal. We leave the improvement in future work.

Approach	**Source**: 水果很新鲜, 口感很好吃着非常甜, 价格优惠, 下次还会光顾 (The fruit is fresh, and it tastes delicious and sweet. The price is favorable. Will buy it next time.) **Control code**: 口感 (taste)
SEGEXT	水果很新鲜, 口感很好吃着非常甜 (The fruit is fresh, and it tastes delicious and sweet.)
C-TRM	他家的水果挺新鲜, 口感挺值的 (The fruit in this shop is really fresh, and the taste is worth the price.)
QUALITYMODEL	超喜欢他家水果, 品质好, 口感很好 (Really like the fruit in this shop, which is of good quality and tastes well.)
CREATER	份量很足, 水果新鲜, 口感甘甜很解渴 (The fruit is a big portion and fresh. It tastes sweet, quenching your thirst.)

Table 6: Case analysis. Texts in parentheses are the corresponding contents translated to English.

Approach	CTR (↑)	CPC (↓)
BASE	-	-
QUALITYMODEL	+4.5%	-4.1%
CREATER	**+6.9%**	**-6.1%**

Table 7: Online results (relative improvement).

4.6 Case Analysis

We further show the generated ad texts from different approaches for case analysis. Table 6 is a case analysis that the input contains a source review with an aspect term. By comparing these generated results, We can see that the ad text generated by CREATER is more suitable to attract users. The generated phrase "`sweet, quenching your thirst`" is more attractive than other results like "`tastes well`". On the whole, the overall quality of the ad texts generated by CREATER is better than other competitive approaches.

4.7 Online Experiments

We have deployed CREATER to a leading advertising platform. Our online experiment is conducted for one-week, and all ads are displayed in mobile news feed. For the ad that containing more than one generated texts (because there may be multiple control codes), we randomly choose one of them to display. The experiment traffic covers over 12,000 advertisers, and results are computed based on over ten million impressions to ensure the confidence of online metrics.

We compare performance among the ad texts generated by CREATER, QUALITYMODEL, and those provided by advertisers (as BASE). Core metrics are CTR and cost per click (CPC): CTR $= \frac{\#\text{click}}{\#\text{impression}}$ reveals attractiveness; CPC $= \frac{\text{total cost of advertisers}}{\#\text{click}}$ reflects ad delivery efficiency. Table 7 shows that CREATER achieves significantly improvements on both CTR and CPC, verifying its effectiveness of improving delivery efficiency.

5 Related Work

Most studies focus on generating ad texts given landing page contents (Thomaidou et al., 2013). Hughes et al. (2019) employ a CTR model as reward estimator with self-critical RL, and Kamigaito et al. (2021) consider fluency, relevance and quality rewards to capture the characteristics of effective ad texts. Kanungo et al. (2021) incorporate masked language modeling with self-critical learning to improve the generation for multiple products. Wang et al. (2021) design model-based RL system that mimics real user feedback.

To model user click behavior, Wang et al. (2020) take click as a measure of text fitness and design click-based reward. Wang et al. (2019) build a CTR space to obtain sample quality that weights cross-entropy loss. Unlike these work, we directly model the distinctness of positive and negative targets, and propose a customized pre-training objective.

6 Conclusion

We propose CREATER for generating ad texts, which employs contrastive learning to encourage the model to generate texts achieving higher CTR. We design a novel self-supervised objective customized to our scenario, reducing the gap to further fine-tuning. Experiments verify that CREATER brings significant uplift on core metrics.

In future work we will take a next step to improve faithfulness, and extend the model to handle multiple aspects (Chan et al., 2021) and multiple reviews (which may be conflicting) with graph neural networks (Wei et al., 2021).

Acknowledgments

We thank all the anonymous reviewers to their valuable comments for improving this work.

Ethical Considerations

When we apply large-scale corpora from the Web, alleviating bias issues is necessary. We make efforts from two perspectives: (1) For input reviews, we have filtering steps to remove harmful contents, and ensure that they do not have user privacy information like age and gender ("Data Collection and Filtering" of § A.1); (2) For output ad texts, we are cautious before online deployment with a risk control procedure ("Post-Processing before Deployment" of § A.1). (3) Our model does not use user privacy information like age and gender.

References

Shuyang Cao and Lu Wang. 2021. CLIFF: Contrastive learning for improving faithfulness and factuality in abstractive summarization. In EMNLP.

Hou Pong Chan, Lu Wang, and Irwin King. 2021. Controllable summarization with constrained markov decision process. Transactions of the Association for Computational Linguistics.

Ruidan He, Wee Sun Lee, Hwee Tou Ng, and Daniel Dahlmeier. 2017. An unsupervised neural attention model for aspect extraction. In ACL.

J Weston Hughes, Keng-hao Chang, and Ruofei Zhang. 2019. Generating better search engine text advertisements with deep reinforcement learning. In KDD.

Hidetaka Kamigaito, Peinan Zhang, Hiroya Takamura, and Manabu Okumura. 2021. An empirical study of generating texts for search engine advertising. In NAACL.

Yashal Shakti Kanungo, Sumit Negi, and Aruna Rajan. 2021. Ad headline generation using self-critical masked language model. In NAACL.

Seanie Lee, Dong Bok Lee, and Sung Ju Hwang. 2021. Contrastive learning with adversarial perturbations for conditional text generation. In ICLR.

Mike Lewis, Yinhan Liu, Naman Goyal, Marjan Ghazvininejad, Abdelrahman Mohamed, Omer Levy, Veselin Stoyanov, and Luke Zettlemoyer. 2020. BART: Denoising sequence-to-sequence pre-training for natural language generation, translation, and comprehension. In ACL.

Aaron van den Oord, Yazhe Li, and Oriol Vinyals. 2018. Representation learning with contrastive predictive coding. arXiv preprint arXiv:1807.03748.

Xiao Pan, Mingxuan Wang, Liwei Wu, and Lei Li. 2021. Contrastive learning for many-to-many multilingual neural machine translation. In ACL.

Colin Raffel, Noam Shazeer, Adam Roberts, Katherine Lee, Sharan Narang, Michael Matena, Yanqi Zhou, Wei Li, and Peter J Liu. 2020. Exploring the limits of transfer learning with a unified text-to-text transformer. Journal of Machine Learning Research.

Abigail See, Peter J Liu, and Christopher D Manning. 2017. Get to the point: Summarization with pointer-generator networks. In ACL.

Noam Shazeer and Mitchell Stern. 2018. Adafactor: Adaptive learning rates with sublinear memory cost. In ICML.

Stamatina Thomaidou, Ismini Lourentzou, Panagiotis Katsivelis-Perakis, and Michalis Vazirgiannis. 2013. Automated snippet generation for online advertising. In CIKM.

Ashish Vaswani, Noam Shazeer, Niki Parmar, Jakob Uszkoreit, Llion Jones, Aidan N Gomez, Łukasz Kaiser, and Illia Polosukhin. 2017. Attention is all you need. NeurIPS.

Xiting Wang, Xinwei Gu, Jie Cao, Zihua Zhao, Yulan Yan, Bhuvan Middha, and Xing Xie. 2021. Reinforcing pretrained models for generating attractive text advertisements. In KDD.

Yongzhen Wang, Heng Huang, Yuliang Yan, and Xiaozhong Liu. 2019. Quality-sensitive training! social advertisement generation by leveraging user click behavior. In WWW.

Yongzhen Wang, Jian Wang, Heng Huang, Hongsong Li, and Xiaozhong Liu. 2020. Evolutionary product description generation: A dynamic fine-tuning approach leveraging user click behavior. In SIGIR.

Penghui Wei, Jiahao Zhao, and Wenji Mao. 2021. A graph-to-sequence learning framework for summarizing opinionated texts. IEEE/ACM Transactions on Audio, Speech, and Language Processing.

Jingqing Zhang, Yao Zhao, Mohammad Saleh, and Peter Liu. 2020. PEGASUS: Pre-training with extracted gap-sentences for abstractive summarization. In ICML.

A Appendix

A.1 More Details of Dataset Construction

Data Collection and Filtering As mentioned in § 4.1, we construct the dataset $\mathcal{D}$ where each sample is a tuple of (user review, aspect term, positive ad text, negative ad text). The construction procedure of $\mathcal{D}$ mainly contains the following steps:

1) Collecting a set of high-quality user reviews $\mathcal{D}_x$. Firstly, a large size of reviews of e-commerce and retail items are collected. We then filter out low-quality ones via a set of rules (e.g., length constraint, repeat term constraint and harmful/abusive word vocabulary) and a spam detection model (trained based on both text contents and fraud behavior features). After this step, we obtain a review corpus $\mathcal{D}_x$ containing 1,471,106 reviews, which is also utilized to pre-training.

2) Building an aspect term set $\mathcal{D}_c$, utilized to guide generation and ensure the relevance between review contents and ad texts. According to business demands, we first construct a seed set provided by advertisers. We then expand this small set via an unsupervised extraction model ABAE (He et al., 2017), trained on the review corpus $\mathcal{D}_x$. Each aspect term is typically represented as a word. After a simple filtering

rule based on IDF to remove noise, we obtain an aspect term set $\mathcal{D}_c$ containing 991 terms.

3) Professional editors write two distinct ad texts for each given (user review, aspect term) pair. Because writing high-quality ad texts is time-consuming and labor-intensive, this procedure collects around 50,000 samples. We check the correlation between input and output via randomly sampling a fraction of all tuples written by the same editor, and remove low-quality ones. Besides, we ensure that in a paired sample the ad text does not match word-for-word to the original review.

4) Conducting online A/B test to collect user preference (i.e., CTR) on these ad texts. Traditionally, advertisers resort to this step to polish their ad texts for catching user interests. In this work we make use of these data to train contrastive learning based generation model.

5) Filtering out invalid tuples to obtain the final dataset $\mathcal{D}$. We remove outlier samples during online A/B test, e.g., the ads that do not have sufficient impressions or obtain anomalously high CTR. We also use Z-test to ensure that the CTR difference between two ad texts of same ad is significant. As a result, this dataset contains 43,985 samples and covers 4,047 advertisers.

No personal identifiable information is included in our dataset: (1) During collection, only review texts are saved, and other meta-information (such as original authors) is not collected. (2) To exclude identifying information which may be contained in texts, we employ regular expression for replacement by placeholders.

Post-Processing before Deployment Before online deployment, we have a risk control procedure to cautiously perform post-processing on the ad texts generated by models, aiming to ensure the suitability of ad texts before displaying. For instance, text contents that contain false, useless or harmful information cannot be displayed to users. Specifically, this procedure removes the texts containing non-compliant words (e.g., harmful words), and performs manual-checking on generated texts. Overall, the passing rate of generated texts is around 90% to 95%, which means that the generation models can be deployed online in industry.

Augmenting Poetry Composition with Verse by Verse

David Uthus and **Maria Voitovich** and **R.J. Mical**
Google Research
{duthus, mvoitovich, gameman}@google.com

Abstract

We describe Verse by Verse, our experiment in augmenting the creative process of writing poetry with an AI. We have created a group of AI poets, styled after various American classic poets, that are able to offer as suggestions generated lines of verse while a user is composing a poem. In this paper, we describe the underlying system to offer these suggestions. This includes a generative model, which is tasked with generating a large corpus of lines of verse offline and which are then stored in an index, and a dual-encoder model that is tasked with recommending the next possible set of verses from our index given the previous line of verse.

1 Introduction

There has been a lot of growing interest in poetry generation (Gonçalo Oliveira, 2017). Some of these approaches have even shown quality approaching that of humans (Lau et al., 2018). However, much of this has been in the view of letting an AI write a full poem by itself, thus writing in a closed system. Only recently have some approaches started to explore human interaction when composing a poem (Ghazvininejad et al., 2016, 2017; Gonçalo Oliveira et al., 2017; Zhipeng et al., 2019).

Verse by Verse[1] is our experiment in augmenting the creative process of poetry composition with an AI. Unlike past approaches that focused on generating a full poem, we are interested on how we can use AI to offer suggestions to a user as they compose a poem. This is a much more challenging task, as one needs be able to offer suggestions with minimal latency while meeting constraints of the poem structure and handle the challenges of user input. Additionally, to make this a more educational experience, we wanted to generate the verses in the style of various classic American poets.

In this paper, we describe the underlying system that powers Verse by Verse. Our main contributions are:

- A novel approach using multiple models that allows us to split local verse knowledge (how to generate a line of verse) and global poem knowledge (what line of verse would best follow a previous line of verse).
- A novel way of determining rhyme phonemes for verses that is robust with user input.
- The first approach that we know that incorporates techniques to help reduce possible learned biases within a poetry system.

2 Verse by Verse Overview

As mentioned, Verse by Verse is an interactive application that allows users to compose a poem while getting suggestions from the system. To use this application, users first pick a few classic American poets to act as their muses. They will then pick the structure of the poem (quatrains, couplets, or free verse), and optionally syllable count and rhyme schema (when applicable). Afterwards, they can begin to compose a poem.

While the user composes a poem, the poets will make suggestions of next possible lines of verse given the previous verse (as shown in Figure 1). Users may either use these suggestions (including being able to edit the suggestions to make them more personal) or continue writing verses of their own. This goes on until a user is satisfied with their poem, in which they can then optionally add a title[2]

[1] https://sites.research.google/versebyverse/

[2] We had initially designed the system to start with a poem title, but feedback from our initial user subject studies showed that our poet enthusiasts preferred adding a title after a poem had been written. Having the title first made users feel forced to fit the poem to the title, while having the title last allowed them more freedom of creativity during composition.

Proceedings of NAACL-HLT 2022: Industry Track Papers, pages 18 - 26
July 10-15, 2022

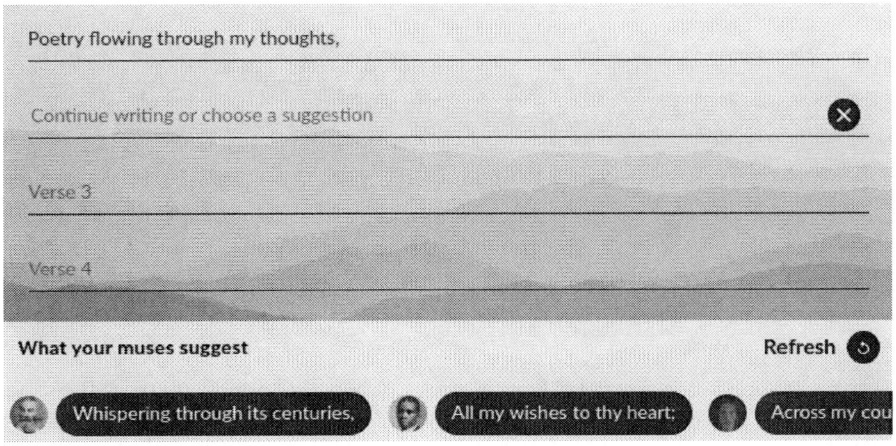

Figure 1: UI of Verse by Verse, with a user composing a poem and the AI making suggestions.

and save the final poem as text or as an image.

Figure 2 shows an overview of how we suggest verses to the user. Our system first receives from the user as input: the previous verse, poem structure metadata (such as syllable count and selected poets), and, if needed, a verse to rhyme with. When a rhyming verse is provided, the system will find the rhyming syllables for this verse. The rhyming syllables along with the poem structure metadata will then be used as filters on the generated verse suggestions. With the previous verse input, the system will then encode the verse using a feed forward network. This encoding will be used in a search against pre-generated and pre-encoded verses, taking the dot product of each pair of encodings. It will then output a list of the n-best[3] possible verses per poet to suggest as the next verse based on the dot product scoring.

The next few sections will cover the various parts of the system: verse generation, verse retrieval, and determining rhyme syllables.

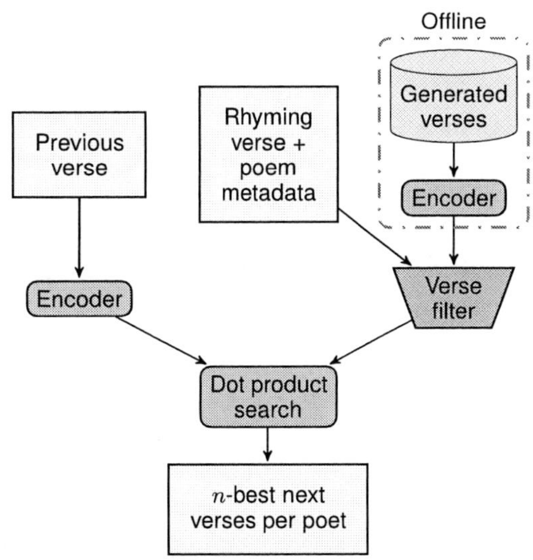

Figure 2: Overview of underlying system that handles user input and suggests next possible lines of verse.

3 Offline Verse Generation

We generate our verses offline and store them for later retrieval, which differs from past approaches of poetry generation. This allows for faster serving (Henderson et al., 2017), especially when used in a dual encoder network as described in Section 4.

Our verse generation is done in a pipeline composed of multiple steps. Figure 3 shows an overview of this. It takes original poetic sources and creates new verses (Section 3.1); then filters out poorly-generated verses (Section 3.2); and finally adds metadata for each verse such as the rhyme syllables and syllable count (Section 3.3).

3.1 Generating Novel Verses

In our approach, we present users the option to choose from 22 American poets to act as their muses. These poets are restricted to those in which there is substantial enough material available to use that is no longer under copyright, with most material found on Project Gutenberg[4].

[3] The value of n is controlled by the UI, which considers two factors: whether the user is on desktop or mobile (we can show more suggestions when viewing on desktop) and how many poets the user has selected to act as their muses.

[4] http://www.gutenberg.org/

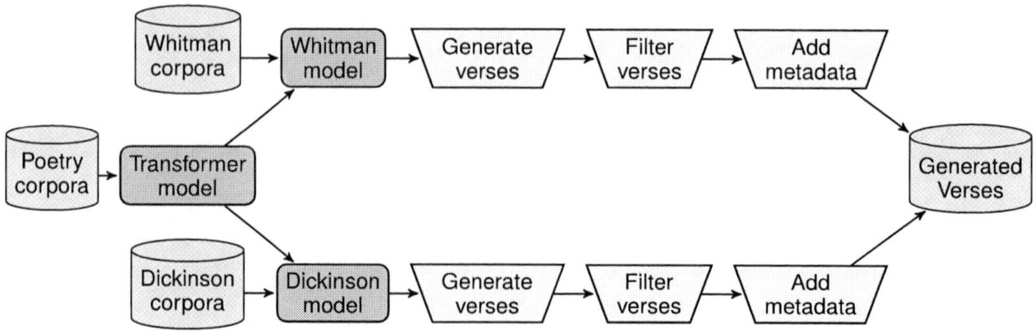

Figure 3: Overview of how we generate our lines of verses offline. We begin with the full corpora of English poetry and train a transformer model. We then copy this model and fine tune it for each of our poets on their individual corpora, using Whitman and Dickinson as examples here. These models are then used to generate novel verses, which are filtered for quality and amended with metadata. All these generated verses are then added to our generated verses index, which is used for serving lines of verse to our uses.

3.1.1 Architecture and Training

We use a decoder-only Transformer model (Vaswani et al., 2017) for generating these verses. This model is trained to predict the next single subword token given the previous tokens in a line of verse. It is composed of 8 multi-head attention layers with 8 heads each. The layers had a hidden dimensionality of 128 and feed-forward dimensionality of 512.

We first pretrain the model on a large corpus (1,116,297 lines of verse) of English-speaking poems from Project Gutenberg, including the above mentioned 22 American poets. This is done for 400 epochs. Following this, we make 22 copies of the model and fine-tune each one on a given poet, training for 50 epochs per poet. This fine-tuning then allows us to capture the style of each poet. For both phases of training, we use a batch size of 128, dropout rate of 0.1, and the same learning rate as described in the Transformer paper (Vaswani et al., 2017).

3.1.2 Generation

After the generative models have been trained, we next start generating all feasible lines of verse per poet. This involves taking a set of starting tokens and then extending with all the suggestions of the model given a certain threshold is met. The set of starting tokens is composed of the original starting tokens of the lines of verse by a given poet combined along with tokens that were common across the 22 poets. The extra starting tokens are particularly beneficial for poets whose corpus is small and might not have as many tokens to start a verse with. But to help to avoid introducing uncommon tokens that may be part of a poet's style, we restrict to tokens that have been used by at least 12 poets.

For each partial verse (any verse that does not yet contain an end-of-line token), we expand it by considering all tokens whose normalized score (probability of being the next token normalized against the maximum probability) are above a threshold of 0.925. An expansion that results in an end-of-line token will then be included in that poets' generated corpus. Any incomplete verses will be considered for another iteration of expansion. This continues on for 10 iterations. To help contain the exponential growth as we generate the lines, for each iteration, we only carry over the 100M best partial verses seen that iteration. This is determined by summing the scores seen so far for a given partial verse.

3.1.3 Quality vs Quantity

As mentioned in the previous section, we had used a threshold of 0.925 for the verse generation. We had experimented with different values, and found this to give us the best balance of quantity vs quality. Intuitively, having a higher threshold would result in much better quality of verses, though allowing for only a smaller set of generated verses. And for a closed system, where topics can be more restricted, this would have sufficed. But as we need to handle any possible topic presented by the user, we needed to loosen quality in order to allow for a wider variety of verses.

3.2 Quality Control Filtering

After we have generated our collection of verses, we then run them through various filters to remove those of poor quality (especially as discussed in previous section we have lowered the quality threshold to allow for a wider variety of verses). This includes: making sure parenthesis and quotation marks are balanced, filtering out verses of syllable counts not supported in the application, removing verses which contain words that we do not want to serve to the user (e.g., offensive words), and filtering out any verse that matches one of the original verses written by the given poet.

An additional filter we implemented is filtering by part-of-speech. Using the large corpus of English-speaking poems, we go through each line of verse and get a POS "fingerprint," which is a concatenation of POS tags representing a line of verse. Then, for every generated verse, we check to see if that line of verse's POS matches that of one of the fingerprints from the original verses. If so, we keep the line of verse, otherwise it is removed from our collection. The reasoning behind this is that since we are doing a deep search of many possible verses with our generative model, it will sometimes generate lines of verse of very poor grammar.[5] By utilizing the POS used by our real poets, we can then help to improve the quality of the generated verses.[6]

After the filtering, we are left with a total of 26.9M generated verses for our 22 poets. But as our poets all have different styles, along with a different amount of available past works available, some poets will have a resultant larger set of generated verses than others, ranging from 60K for our smallest to 8.3M for our largest.

3.3 Metadata

All generated verses that are of good quality are finally labeled with metadata. This metadata includes the poet source this was generated from, syllable count and rhyming phoneme (to be discussed later in Section 5), and any other fields we may need to filter upon for serving to our users.

[5]While poets may compose lines of verse that purposely break the rules of grammar, we are more focused on filtering out lines of verse that are unreadable due to their poor grammar.

[6]Alternatively, we had experimented with language model classifiers prior to implementing the POS fingerprint filtering. These classifiers did not work very well, oftentimes removing too many good verses or allowing too many poor quality verses to pass through, especially for our poets with small bodies of work available.

4 Next Verse Prediction

We use a dual encoder network architecture for suggesting the next line of verse of a poem. We will discuss training of the network, the indexing of possible verses, and the retrieval of verses.

4.1 Dual Encoder Model

We use a dual-encoder architecture that is similar to what was used in Gmail's Smart Reply (Henderson et al., 2017). In the original work, the authors would encode the user input with one encoder and all possible replies with the other encoder. In our model, one encoder is used to encode a parent (previous) verse and the other encoder is used to encode a child (next) verse. Then, same as in the original work, the model optimizes for a given verse's dot-product score with the true following verse to be higher than with random negatives from the batch.

Our network does differ though from the original work with respect to the composition of the encoders. For the two encoders in our network (as shown in Figure 2), they both take in an input and feed that into a SentencePiece model (Kudo and Richardson, 2018), consisting of a vocab size of 128K. This then feeds into a set of Transformer layers (Vaswani et al., 2017). The Transformer consists of 4 layers, each with 4 attention heads, a hidden size of 1024, and a feed-forward size of 4096. Finally, these then feed into a set of 2 fully-connected layers, with ReLU activation on the first layer and Softsign activation on the second. These deep layers consist of a hidden size of 500 each. In terms of weights, the Transformer layers for the two stacks share weights while the fully-connected layers do not.

4.2 Training

We use two collections of data for training data. One is a mixture of poems (such as those used for poetry generation) and other similar mediums, which we call *poetic*. This set's purpose is to train the model to predict the next line of verse given the previous. The other is composed of comments from internet discussion forums, which we call *comments*. For this, we train to predict a comment given the previous comment. Doing so allows us to expose the model to a larger vocabulary and more noisy data than what would normally be seen in the *poetic* corpus, which is important when dealing with user input.

To train the dual encoder, we first pretrain the

model on our *comment* data for 20M steps with a learning rate of 0.01. After this, we will fine-tune the model on the *poetic* corpus for an additional 10M steps with a learning rate of 0.001. We use dropout for both the Transformer attention and ReLU layers of 0.1. We use a training batch size of 100. Additionally during training, we use the parent (previous verse or comment) as extra negative examples, which helped train the model not to repeat itself.

4.3 Verse Indexing and Retrieval

After we have trained the dual-encoder model, we can then use it to start to encode all our generated verses from the previous section. Each generated verse will be encoded using the encoder for the child verse. These are then stored in an index. During retrieval, instead of using an exhaustive search across all possible verses, we use a hierarchical quantization approach for allowing for fast search (Guo et al., 2016; Wu et al., 2017).

When composing a poem, the system will receive the previous verse and various metadata for filtering, as shown in Figure 2. We first encode the previous verse using the parent encoder. We then take the dot product of this verse and all possible verses, filtering out verses based on what the user needs. Afterwards, the system will return the n-best possible next verses.

In the end, this architecture allows us to do a lot of the expensive process offline and allows for fast retrieval and filtering when users are composing a poem. Additionally, this adds the capability of filtering verses by their respective metadata, so that we can match the requirements of what a user desires for the structure of their poem.

5 Rhymes and User Input

As we allow users to enter their own verses or edit candidate verses, we then have to take this into account for next-verse suggestion when dealing with rhyme. In many past approaches that are generating a poem in full, they can use various heuristics to help meet requirements for rhyme, such as restricting what words are available. Or in some cases, such as with Deep-speare, learn a model for rhyme (Lau et al., 2018). Since we were creating an interactive approach, we then had to take a different route for dealing with rhymes.

5.1 Text Normalization

For rhyme syllables (and syllable count), we initially used the CMU pronunciation dictionary[7], which has been used in past approaches such as Ghazvininejad et al. (2016) and Hopkins and Kiela (2017). This was unfortunately problematic – its use is limited when dealing with words with multiple pronunciations (e.g., past and present tense of "read"), and failed when handling irregular spelling and out-of-dictionary words both from what poets used in their writings (e.g., "W'en daih's chillun in de house," by Paul Laurance Dunbar) and when handling user input. We also considered training a model for rhyme, similar to what was done for Deep-speare (Lau et al., 2018). While this would help alleviate some of the dictionary issues, it would still be fragile when handling user input.

To overcome these issues, we used the Kestrel text normalization system (Ebden and Sproat, 2015) for determining the rhyming syllables and syllable counts of a verse. It is able to determine correct pronunciations of words like "read" with respect to tense, and is able to suggest phonemes for out-of-dictionary words. Furthermore, it can handle more extreme situations, such as "In my pocket there is $.50". In this case, the system is able to understand that it needs to find a word that rhymes with "cents".

5.2 Perfect and Imperfect Rhymes

This work uses both perfect and imperfect rhyming. For the imperfect rhyming, we loosely follow the steps as described by Ghazvininejad et al. (2016), with slight modifications to accommodate the difference between their use of the CMU dictionary and our use of Kestrel.

Expanding beyond their work, we also allow for imperfect rhymes on single-syllable words. For this, we find similar consonant phonemes for the last phoneme of the word where the logs-odd scoring is 0 or greater from the work by Hirjee and Brown (2010).

When a user is composing a poem and we need to suggest a rhyming line of verse, the system will attempt to show a mixture of both perfect and imperfect rhyming verses. Only if it is unable to find any verses that rhyme, a possibility given the wide range of possible inputs, it will then show non-rhyming verses.

[7] http://www.speech.cs.cmu.edu/cgi-bin/cmudict

	Human	Verse by Verse
Judged human	82.7%	47.0%
Readability	3.8	2.9
Relevance	3.9	3.2
Evocative	3.4	2.7
Aesthetic	3.7	3.0

Table 1: Human evaluations comparing poems written by classic poets with those generated with Verse by Verse. "Judged human" represents the percentage of quatrains that the evaluators had judged as having been written by a human. The four proceeding metrics were judged on a scale of 1-5.

6 Evaluation

We ran comparative evaluations of Verse by Verse against poems written by classic poets. While Verse by Verse is meant to be used in an interactive setting to aid a user in writing a poem, we felt it was still worth evaluating how well it works on its own in writing a poem given a first line of verse.

To do so, we gathered a collection of 100 quatrains written by the 22 classic poets. Then, for each quatrain, we would take the first line of verse, and use that as the first line of verse for Verse by Verse. It would then take the top suggestion (using the same poet as that who wrote the poem), to pick the subsequent 3 lines. When possible, it would try to follow an ABAB rhyme pattern.

We built upon the work of Hopkins and Kiela (2017) for evaluating. We would show evaluators one poem at a time. They then needed to classify if the poem is human- or AI-written (they are shown the full quatrain and asked to evaluate on the last 3 lines), and rate on a scale of 1-5 for readability (to what extent is the quatrain easy to read? does it make sense?, relevance (given the first line, how relevant are the subsequent lines of verse?), evocation (how much does the quatrain evoke emotion when reading it?), and aesthetic (how much does the quatrain sound nice to read, such as in rhythm?). Each poem was evaluated by 3 evaluators.

Table 1 shows the results of these evaluations. As shown, while Verse by Verse does not do as well as the poems written by classic poets, it still was able to do well enough. More importantly, almost half the poems written by Verse by Verse were thought of to have been written by humans, which shows the feasibility of our approach. A couple of the highly rated poems can be seen in Figure 4.

Her eyes, twin pools of mystic light,
Forever in her radiance white—,
She sought the bosom of the Night.
Away it came, that mystic sight!

Whether I travel by land or by sea,
Just while I travel with its fairy tide,
Leaving a gleam that I may never see,
Although I travel close upon your side.

Figure 4: Example quatrains rated highly by evaluators. The first line is by a poet and the subsequent 3 lines are generated by Verse by Verse.

7 Related Work

Poetry generation is a growing field of research, with many diverse approaches for generating full-length poems of various forms (Gonçalo Oliveira, 2017). Some related areas to touch upon are user interaction and verse generation.

7.1 Interactive Generation

There have been some recent work that have looked at interactive approaches to composing poetry or song lyrics.

Jiuge (Zhipeng et al., 2019) is a similar interactive approach to writing Chinese poetry. Users would input keywords, text or images, and from there the system would extract keywords to use within a generative model for writing the poems. Users could then edit or make use of suggestions.

Hafez (Ghazvininejad et al., 2016, 2017) offered a variety of inputs for users to dictate how a poem was generated (e.g., topic; desired words; control for sentiment, alliteration, etc.), and then automatically generated a full poem given these inputs. Users could then further tweak the controls until a poem was generated to their liking. Underneath, given these set of input values, it would initiate with a candidate set of rhyming words, and then use a Finite State Acceptor to guide a Recurrent Neural Network for generating new verses.

Co-PoeTryMe (Gonçalo Oliveira et al., 2017), which was built on PoeTryMe (Gonçalo Oliveira, 2012), would generate full poems given some inputs (e.g., keywords, number of syllables). Users were then allowed to edit lines and use suggested lines as seeds for further generation of suggestions.

DopeLearning (Malmi et al., 2016) was focused on generating rap lyrics. It allowed for interactive rap composition – for each verse, a user could either pick from a list of candidates or enter their own input. For determining its suggestions, DopeLearning treated their approach as an information retrieval task, ranking the best response given the previous verse. DopeLearning was restricted though in only reused existing rap verses, as it did not generate any novel verses.

7.2 Verse Generation

There have been many different approaches to how a line of verse is generated. Earlier works included template-based approaches (Colton et al., 2012; Gonçalo Oliveira, 2012) while most recent works have been neural-based approaches (Ghazvininejad et al., 2016, 2017; Hopkins and Kiela, 2017; Lau et al., 2018; Van de Cruys, 2020; Yi et al., 2018; Zhang and Lapata, 2014).

As with recent approaches, ours is also considered a neural-based approach. Our approach is closest to the work of Liao et al. (2019), which involved a Transformer-based approach using GPT. Both their approach and ours used pre-training and fine-tuning of the models, though the type of data used differs. Our model used poetry data for both phases, while their approach first pre-trained on a news corpus, then fine-tuned on Chinese poetry. An additional difference is how the models are used – they used their model for generating a whole poem while we use our model for offline verse generation of single lines of verse and instead rely on a dual-encoder model for determining the next line of verse in a poem.

8 Conclusions

We have described the underlying system of Verse by Verse. It is composed of two primary models, one for verse generation and one for verse recommendation. Results show that this approach works well for an interactive setting, generative novel verses that do well in human evals and meet the more challenging demands of human interaction.

Ethical Concerns

As this system is intended to be deployed to a general audience of all ages, there are concerns of how the tool can accidentally suggest offensive verses. We have taken some steps to help alleviate this: augmenting the training data and filtering out problematic verses.

Augmenting Training Data

We have augmented some of the *poetic* data to help reduce bias using the techniques described in Sheng and Uthus (2020). In their work, they had used a style transfer model to augment some of the data to make the sentiment more positive, with particular focus for the case when the parent verse contained a demographic mention. In do so, this then helps move the model to suggest verses of more positive sentiment when the previous verse of a poem contains a demographic mention.

As with their work, we augment all child verses that have parent verses containing demographic mentions and about 50% of those without a parent verse containing a demographic mention. While we followed much of their described approach, we use a different style transfer model though for our augmentations, using TextSETTR (Riley et al., 2021) as a replacement. TextSETTR was shown to yield better results in transforming sentiment while preserving fluency (important aspects for our work). As described in the TextSETTR paper, we use the model that had been fine-tuned on English Common Crawl data. To change sentiment, we gave the model 10 examplars each of negative and positive lines, and then used this to change the sentiment of negative lines of verse using the techniques described in Sheng and Uthus (2020).[8]

We note that even though we have changed some of the sentiment to make the system as a whole more positive, it does not prevent users from writing negative poetry. If a user writes a negative verse, the system can still suggest negative verses. Additionally, the system does allow users to edit suggestions, so a user can also edit a verse to make it more negative if that is their desire.

Verse Filtering

We also filter out verses that can potentially be offensive. This includes filtering out verses that contain obscene words (especially as what was acceptable in the past might not be acceptable today), along with verses that may contain groups of words

[8] For positive examplars, we used: "The food was great!", "I really loved it.", "Absolutely my favorite book.", "I am filled with love.", "The seas are calm.", "She delights me", "He understands me,", "My soul is full of light,", "The scene is full of heroes", "This cup of tea tastes delightful". For negative examples, we used: "The food was awful!", "I really hated it.", "I regret reading this book.", "I am filled with hatred.", "The seas are violent", "She annoys me", "He ignores me,", "My soul is full of darkness,", "The scene is full of villans", "This cup of tea taste horrible".

that, when put together, can be offensive.

One of the advantages of our system, where we generate and store our verses offline in an index, is that it makes it easier to explore how the filters would impact what verses we have available. We can see if certain grouping of words are present in the index, and if such, filter out such verses. More importantly, this allows us to further check if filtering out a group of words may filter out too many verses that would not be offensive, and thus allow us to better refine the word filtering as needed.

References

Simon Colton, Jacob Goodwin, and Tony Veale. 2012. Full-FACE poetry generation. In *Proceedings of the 3rd International Conference on Computational Creativity*, pages 95–102.

Peter Ebden and Richard Sproat. 2015. The Kestrel TTS text normalization system. *Natural Language Engineering*, 21(3):333–353.

Marjan Ghazvininejad, Xing Shi, Yejin Choi, and Kevin Knight. 2016. Generating topical poetry. In *Proceedings of the 2016 Conference on Empirical Methods in Natural Language Processing*, pages 1183–1191. Association for Computational Linguistics.

Marjan Ghazvininejad, Xing Shi, Jay Priyadarshi, and Kevin Knight. 2017. Hafez: an interactive poetry generation system. In *Proceedings of ACL 2017, System Demonstrations*, pages 43–48. Association for Computational Linguistics.

Hugo Gonçalo Oliveira. 2012. PoeTryMe: A versatile platform for poetry generation. In *Proceedings of the ECAI 2012 Workshop on Computational Creativity, Concept Invention, and General Intelligence*.

Hugo Gonçalo Oliveira. 2017. A survey on intelligent poetry generation: Languages, features, techniques, reutilisation and evaluation. In *Proceedings of the 10th International Conference on Natural Language Generation*, pages 11–20. Association for Computational Linguistics.

Hugo Gonçalo Oliveira, Tiago Mendes, and Ana Boavida. 2017. Co-PoeTryMe: a co-creative interface for the composition of poetry. In *Proceedings of the 10th International Conference on Natural Language Generation*, pages 70–71, Santiago de Compostela, Spain. Association for Computational Linguistics.

Ruiqi Guo, Sanjiv Kumar, Krzysztof Choromanski, and David Simcha. 2016. Quantization based fast inner product search. In *Proceedings of the 19th International Conference on Artificial Intelligence and Statistics*, volume 51 of *Proceedings of Machine Learning Research*, pages 482–490, Cadiz, Spain. PMLR.

Matthew Henderson, Rami Al-Rfou, Brian Strope, Yun-Hsuan Sung, László Lukács, Ruiqi Guo, Sanjiv Kumar, Balint Miklos, and Ray Kurzweil. 2017. Efficient natural language response suggestion for smart reply. *CoRR*, abs/1705.00652.

Hussein Hirjee and Daniel Brown. 2010. Using automated rhyme detection to characterize rhyming style in rap music. *Empirical Musicology Review*.

Jack Hopkins and Douwe Kiela. 2017. Automatically generating rhythmic verse with neural networks. In *Proceedings of the 55th Annual Meeting of the Association for Computational Linguistics (Volume 1: Long Papers)*, pages 168–178. Association for Computational Linguistics.

Taku Kudo and John Richardson. 2018. SentencePiece: A simple and language independent subword tokenizer and detokenizer for neural text processing. In *Proceedings of the 2018 Conference on Empirical Methods in Natural Language Processing: System Demonstrations*, pages 66–71, Brussels, Belgium. Association for Computational Linguistics.

Jey Han Lau, Trevor Cohn, Timothy Baldwin, Julian Brooke, and Adam Hammond. 2018. Deep-speare: A joint neural model of poetic language, meter and rhyme. In *Proceedings of the 56th Annual Meeting of the Association for Computational Linguistics (Volume 1: Long Papers)*, pages 1948–1958. Association for Computational Linguistics.

Yi Liao, Yasheng Wang, Qun Liu, and Xin Jiang. 2019. GPT-based generation for classical chinese poetry. *CoRR*, abs/1907.00151.

Eric Malmi, Pyry Takala, Hannu Toivonen, Tapani Raiko, and Aristides Gionis. 2016. DopeLearning: A computational approach to rap lyrics generation. In *Proceedings of the 22nd ACM SIGKDD International Conference on Knowledge Discovery and Data Mining*, KDD '16, pages 195–204, New York, NY, USA. ACM.

Parker Riley, Noah Constant, Mandy Guo, Girish Kumar, David Uthus, and Zarana Parekh. 2021. TextSETTR: Few-shot text style extraction and tunable targeted restyling. In *Proceedings of the 59th Annual Meeting of the Association for Computational Linguistics and the 11th International Joint Conference on Natural Language Processing (Volume 1: Long Papers)*, pages 3786–3800, Online. Association for Computational Linguistics.

Emily Sheng and David Uthus. 2020. Investigating societal biases in a poetry composition system. In *Proceedings of the Second Workshop on Gender Bias in Natural Language Processing*, pages 93–106, Barcelona, Spain (Online). Association for Computational Linguistics.

Tim Van de Cruys. 2020. Automatic poetry generation from prosaic text. In *Proceedings of the 58th Annual Meeting of the Association for Computational

Linguistics, pages 2471–2480, Online. Association for Computational Linguistics.

Ashish Vaswani, Noam Shazeer, Niki Parmar, Jakob Uszkoreit, Llion Jones, Aidan N. Gomez, Łukasz Kaiser, and Illia Polosukhin. 2017. Attention is all you need. In I. Guyon, U. V. Luxburg, S. Bengio, H. Wallach, R. Fergus, S. Vishwanathan, and R. Garnett, editors, *Advances in Neural Information Processing Systems 30*, pages 5998–6008. Curran Associates, Inc.

Xiang Wu, Ruiqi Guo, Ananda Theertha Suresh, Sanjiv Kumar, Daniel N Holtmann-Rice, David Simcha, and Felix Yu. 2017. Multiscale quantization for fast similarity search. In I. Guyon, U. V. Luxburg, S. Bengio, H. Wallach, R. Fergus, S. Vishwanathan, and R. Garnett, editors, *Advances in Neural Information Processing Systems 30*, pages 5745–5755. Curran Associates, Inc.

Xiaoyuan Yi, Maosong Sun, Ruoyu Li, and Wenhao Li. 2018. Automatic poetry generation with mutual reinforcement learning. In *Proceedings of the 2018 Conference on Empirical Methods in Natural Language Processing*, pages 3143–3153, Brussels, Belgium. Association for Computational Linguistics.

Xingxing Zhang and Mirella Lapata. 2014. Chinese poetry generation with recurrent neural networks. In *Proceedings of the 2014 Conference on Empirical Methods in Natural Language Processing (EMNLP)*, pages 670–680, Doha, Qatar. Association for Computational Linguistics.

Guo Zhipeng, Xiaoyuan Yi, Maosong Sun, Wenhao Li, Cheng Yang, Jiannan Liang, Huimin Chen, Yuhui Zhang, and Ruoyu Li. 2019. Jiuge: A human-machine collaborative Chinese classical poetry generation system. In *Proceedings of the 57th Annual Meeting of the Association for Computational Linguistics: System Demonstrations*, pages 25–30, Florence, Italy. Association for Computational Linguistics.

AB/BA analysis: A framework for estimating keyword spotting recall improvement while maintaining audio privacy

Raphael Petegrosso, Vasistakrishna Baderdinni,
Thibaud Senechal*, Benjamin L. Bullough*
Amazon / USA
{petegrr,vbaderdi,thibauds,bullough}@amazon.com

Abstract

Evaluation of keyword spotting (KWS) systems that detect keywords in speech is a challenging task under realistic privacy constraints. The KWS is designed to only collect data when the keyword is present, limiting the availability of hard samples that may contain false negatives, and preventing direct estimation of model recall from production data. Alternatively, complementary data collected from other sources may not be fully representative of the real application. In this work, we propose an evaluation technique which we call AB/BA analysis. Our framework evaluates a candidate KWS model B against a baseline model A, using cross-dataset offline decoding for relative recall estimation, without requiring negative examples. Moreover, we propose a formulation with assumptions that allow estimation of relative false positive rate between models with low variance even when the number of false positives is small. Finally, we propose to leverage machine-generated soft labels, in a technique we call Semi-Supervised AB/BA analysis, that improves the analysis time, privacy, and cost. Experiments with both simulation and real data show that AB/BA analysis is successful at measuring recall improvement in conjunction with the trade-off in relative false positive rate.

1 Introduction

Keyword spotting (KWS) is the task of identifying if one of a set of keywords, also called wakewords, is present in a speech segment. It is the gatekeeper component that enables hands-free interaction with many smart assistants using voice-enabled smart devices, such as Amazon Echo, Google Home, and Apple HomePod. Extensive work has been done to develop and improve KWS performance, including improvements in architecture (Chen et al., 2014; Sun et al., 2017; Shan et al., 2018; Wu et al., 2018; Gao et al., 2020), training efficiency (Tucker et al., 2016; Raju et al., 2018), as well as audio front-end (AFE) algorithms (Chhetri et al., 2018).

With many lines of research aiming to improve the quality of the KWS, there is also growing interest in techniques to measure if such new technologies are able to improve the customer experience, but less research attention has been given to this evaluation topic. One challenge is that KWS systems are designed to maximize user privacy by only collecting data when the keyword is identified. As a result, evaluations done using this biased dataset do not allow direct measurement of gains in recall metrics to determine if a new model is better than a baseline. Alternatively, evaluations can also make use of datasets not collected by the KWS, such as media recordings, background noise, and environmental sounds. However, these datasets may not be fully representative of the user experience from the evaluation point of view.

Prior research, such as from (Gao et al., 2020; Sainath and Parada, 2015), has made use of datasets with positive and negative labels in order to evaluate, respectively, gain invariant KWS models and CNN for small-footprint KWS. However, the negative data essentially consists of either negative labels obtained from data accepted by the previous models, or datasets composed of just background noise and noise from environment. In a different application context, (Miller et al., 2018) estimates the recall and the derivative of the precision with respect to the recall by modeling the unseen data distribution according to underlying assumptions. This distribution, however, is not clearly defined in the context of KWS when a variety of sounds, noisy conditions, and reverberation can occur.

In this paper, we present a new evaluation framework called AB/BA analysis. To the best of our knowledge, our work is the first to explore the problem of estimating recall improvement when only accepted data is available, such as in a KWS system

*Corresponding authors

Proceedings of NAACL-HLT 2022: Industry Track Papers, pages 27 - 36
July 10-15, 2022

with rigorous privacy settings, in conjunction with the trade-off with false positive rate, without underlying assumptions on the data distribution. We show that the AB/BA analysis is a cross-model offline evaluation framework. In this framework, data is collected from two KWS models, say a baseline, A , and a candidate, B. By running offline model A through data collected by model B, and model B through data collected by model A, we are able to calculate relative metrics without the need for data not seen by individual models. We also present assumptions that can be applied to the relative metrics calculation that result in a lower variance estimator, even if the number of false positive is small. We additionally describe a Semi-Supervised formulation of AB/BA analysis which provides improvements in the analysis time, cost, and data privacy by utilizing soft machine-generated labels instead of human annotations from the models being evaluated. We present experiments using simulation data, real data, and also experiments comparing the performance of AB/BA and Semi-Supervised AB/BA.

2 Methods

In this section, we describe the proposed method for estimation of recall improvement. Basic metrics concepts can be found in Appendix A.1.

2.1 AB/BA Analysis

The AB/BA analysis framework is composed of four main steps, as depicted in Figure 1: Online data collection, Offline decoding, Labeling, and Metrics computation.

In order to collect data, given two KWS models, say A and B, the models are deployed simultaneously to two populations of users, also called A and B, as shown in Figure 1 (A). The percentage of users in each model is usually based on the presumed risk of deploying each model, as well as the statistical significance desired for the metrics computed, as shown later. It is important, though, that models are deployed simultaneously, with random assignment, similar to a conventional A/B-Test. Notice that the data collected by the models will only contain samples where the keyword is detected in order to preserve user privacy.

The collected data is then used for offline decoding, in which models are run offline on the data collected online. As shown in Figure 1 (B), the data collected by model A is used by model B for keyword spotting, and model B is run on the data collected by the model A. A detailed review on keyword spotting can be found in (López-Espejo et al., 2021). Running a keyword spotter on an utterance i will produce a score s_i representing how likely it is to have detected the keyword.

The data that is collected and decoded offline by the KWS systems will also require labeling in order to be used for metrics estimation. This step, shown in Figure 1 (C), is usually done by either human annotation, or machine-generated. The process to use machine-generated labels is described in more detail in Section 2.2.

Human annotation is an expensive and time consuming process, in addition to being susceptible to error. Therefore, it is desirable to carefully select which utterances to annotate. Stratified sampling can be used to provide more annotations on models disagreement to reduce the need for human annotations (details in Appendix A.2). The labeled data is then used to compute metrics that represent the relative improvement of model B with respect of a baseline model A, as shown in Figure 1 (D).

AB/BA analysis utilizes two relative metrics: False Positive Rate Ratio and Recall Ratio. The Recall Ratio (rRecall) is a relative metric used for comparing two models to determine which model yields better recall. Given two KWS models A and B with datasets containing utterances collected by the same models online, and labeled as $L \in \{0, 1\}$, using the Bayes' theorem, the rRecall can be defined as:

$$\begin{aligned} rRecall &= \frac{P(B=1|L=1)}{P(A=1|L=1)} \\ &= \frac{P(B=1|A=1,L=1)}{P(A=1|B=1,L=1)}, \end{aligned} \tag{1}$$

where $P(B=1|A=1,L=1)$ indicates the probability model B found the keyword when run offline ($B=1$) on true positives from model A used online ($A=1, L=1$).

Therefore, a key aspect of AB/BA analysis is that the rRecall can be computed using terms $P(B=1|A=1,L=1)$ and $P(B=1|A=1,L=0)$ that are directly observable.

Concretely, we can compute rRecall using the following quantities:

$$rRecall = \frac{NTP_{BA\_on\_A}}{NPos_A} * \frac{NPos_B}{NTP_{AB\_on\_B}}, \tag{2}$$

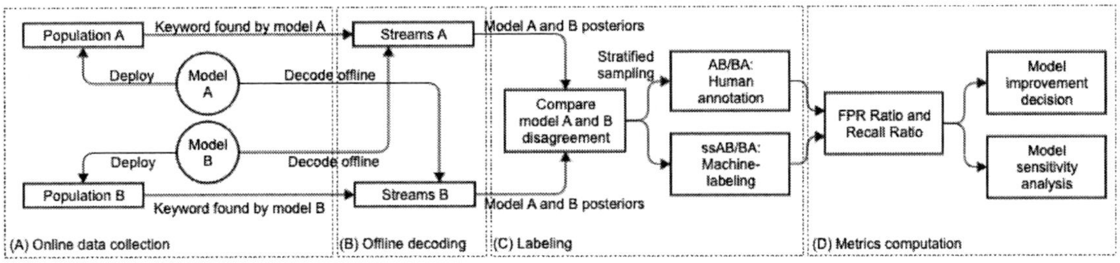

Figure 1: **The four main components of the AB/BA analysis**

where $NTP_{AB\_on\_B}$ is the number of TPs of model A and B on data collected by model B and $NPos_B$ is the number of positive labels on the data collected by B.

Similarly, the FPR Ratio (rFPR) between two models A and B can be calculated as:

$$rFPR = \frac{NFP_{BA\_on\_A}}{NNeg_A} * \frac{NNeg_B}{NFP_{AB\_on\_B}}, \quad (3)$$

where $NFP_{AB\_on\_B}$ is the number of FPs of model A and B on data collected by model B and $NNeg_B$ is the number of negative labels on the data collected by B.

Notice that the number of FPs can be small, leading to large variance in the rFPR estimation. Therefore, assuming that keywords and confusing sounds (those that induce FPs) generated by population A and population B are randomly drawn from the same distribution, we propose to assume that the ratio of TPs and FPs in the streams accepted by both models is the same, represented as:

$$\frac{NFP_{BA\_on\_A}}{NTP_{BA\_on\_A}} \approx \frac{NFP_{AB\_on\_B}}{NTP_{AB\_on\_B}} \quad (4)$$

Then, by introducing the following variables:

$$\begin{aligned} NTP_{AB} &= NTP_{BA\_on\_A} + NTP_{AB\_on\_B} \\ NFP_{AB} &= NFP_{BA\_on\_A} + NFP_{AB\_on\_B} \\ \alpha &= \frac{NTP_{BA\_on\_A} + NFP_{BA\_on\_A}}{NTP_{AB} + NFP_{AB}} \\ \beta &= \frac{NTP_{AB\_on\_B} + NFP_{AB\_on\_B}}{NTP_{AB} + NFP_{AB}} \end{aligned} \quad (5)$$

We can find rFPR and rRecall using:

$$\begin{aligned} rFPR &= \frac{\alpha(NFP_B + \beta NFP_{AB})}{\beta(NFP_A + \alpha NFP_{AB})} \\ rRecall &= \frac{\alpha(Nmiss_A + \beta NTP_{AB})}{\beta(Nmiss_B + \alpha NTP_{AB})}, \end{aligned} \quad (6)$$

where $Nmiss_A$ is the number of TPs accepted by model B but not accepted by A. With this estimator, uncertainties on NFP_{AB} have less impact on the rFPR uncertainty. This is shown in the simulation on Section 3.1.1.

2.2 Semi-Supervised AB/BA Analysis

Semi-Supervised AB/BA (ssAB/BA) analysis is a technique to estimate rFPR and rRecall metrics, while avoiding the need to label utterances by human annotation, which are instead estimated in a semi-supervised way. Because of that, the technique has lower cost and is faster to run than AB/BA analysis. The process also improves audio privacy, since no audio is listened to by annotators. However, since it relies on a machine-labeling process, the technique is more susceptible to errors due to bias.

There are several lines of research on Semi-Supervised Learning models, such as Teacher models (Li et al., 2017; Tarvainen and Valpola, 2017), which provide posterior probabilities as soft labels in order to train Student models.

Assuming that we have a Label Machine $\mathcal{M}$, we apply this machine on utterance i to produce a score m_i. However, if m_i produces a soft label m_i, a mapping function $\phi_{\mathcal{M}}(m_i) = p_i$ can be used to convert the machine-generated score m_i from machine $\mathcal{M}$ to a probability of true accept p_i. Appendix A.4 illustrates this process using a polynomial mapping.

When only soft labels are available, representing a probability of true label, we can apply the Bayes' theorem on Equation (1) to calculate rFPR using:

$$rFPR = \frac{\frac{P(L=0|B=1,A=1)*P(B=1|A=1)}{P(L=0|A=1)}}{\frac{P(L=0|A=1,B=1)*P(A=1|B=1)}{P(L=0|B=1)}}, \quad (7)$$

which results in:

$$rFPR = \frac{\sum_{i=0}^{N_A} p(L_i = 0|A_i = 1, B_i = 1)}{\sum_{i=0}^{N_A} p(L_i = 0|A_i = 1)} * \frac{\sum_{i=0}^{N_B} p(L_i = 0|B_i = 1)}{\sum_{i=0}^{N_B} p(L_i = 0|B_i = 1, A_i = 1)}, \tag{8}$$

Equations (3) and (8) are, therefore, equivalent if $p(L_i = 0)$ is a hard ground-truth label (either 0 or 1).

Similarly, in Semi-Supervised AB/BA the rRecall can be written as:

$$rRecall = \frac{\sum_{i=0}^{N_A} p(L_i = 1|A_i = 1, B_i = 1)}{\sum_{i=0}^{N_A} p(L_i = 1|A_i = 1)} * \frac{\sum_{i=0}^{N_B} p(L_i = 1|B_i = 1)}{\sum_{i=0}^{N_B} p(L_i = 1|B_i = 1, A_i = 1)}, \tag{9}$$

where $p(L_i = 1) = 1 - p(L_i = 0)$ is the probability of TP for a given utterance i.

2.3 Threshold selection

Another important aspect to consider during a KWS model evaluation is the model sensitivity. In order to determine if a given utterance will be considered an accept or reject by the model, assuming high model scores s_i are given to higher chance of detection, the utterance i will be considered an accept by the model X, i.e., $X_i = 1$, if $s_i > t_X$, where t_X is a threshold attributed to model X sensitivity.

Notice that t_X directly impacts the rFPR and rRecall. Essentially, as we increase t_X, it will make the model more restrictive, so both FPR and Recall are reduced. Appendix A.3 gives an example where the threshold t_B of the candidate model B is found according to the trade-off between rFPR and rRecall.

3 Experiments

In this section we present experiments to show the performance of AB/BA and ssAB/BA on simulation and real data.

3.1 Simulations

This section presents the simulations performed.

3.1.1 AB/BA analysis simulation

We created a simulation to show how the calculations from the AB/BA formulas (Equations (2) and (3)) are equivalent to the direct computation of rFPR and rRecall, but without the need for data not accepted by the models. We also show confidence intervals on those metrics as a function of the number of labels. Assume we have a source that emits positive utterances with a probability of 0.3. The model A has a Recall of 0.8 and FPR of 0.1. We consider two pairs of values for model B: Recall and FPR of $(0.82, 0.075)$ leading to rRecall and rFPR of $(1.025, 0.75)$, and Recall and FPR of $(0.84, 0.05)$ leading to rRecall and rFPR of $(1.05, 0.5)$. In addition, data accepted by model A has a probability of being accepted by B of 0.95 and 0.5 for TPs and FPs respectively. We run the simulation considering half of the data is collected by A, half by B. The simulation assumes that the model that does not collect the data is run only on the accepts of the model that does. We report estimated rFPR, rRecall in 3 scenarios, using AB/BA direct estimation, AB/BA with the introduced assumption Equation (6), and using a classic A/B test (only estimating rFPR in this case).

Table 1 shows the rRecall and rFPR, along with 95% confidence interval from 1000 bootstrapping replicates. We can notice in the table that we can detect improvement as small as a 5% Recall improvement and 50% FPR reduction by labeling less than 5000 utterances. We can also see that using the assumption of same TPs and FPs between the models, represented as Approx. AB/BA in the table, to estimate 25% rFPR improvement, the confidence intervals shrink from $-25\%(-52\%, +16\%)$ to $-26\%(-48\%, +2\%)$, while keeping median estimation equally accurate, showing that this is a helpful assumption. The table also shows that the rFPR predicted by regular A/B-Test on the model accepted data also gives close estimation according to the simulated parameters. However, this approach leads to higher confidence interval than the proposed approach and cannot estimate the rRecall.

3.1.2 Semi-Supervised AB/BA analysis simulation

One important point when working with ssAB/BA is with respect to the quality of the label generation process. Therefore, we start with a simulation showing this effect.

In our experiment, we do a Monte Carlo simulation by generating data that can be used to compute

Streams	Labeled	Expected rRecall / rFPR Improv.	rRecall / rFPR Direct AB/BA	rRecall / rFPR Approx. AB/BA	rFPR AB-Test
10K	500	1.025 / 0.75	1.025 [0.963, 1.103] / 0.75 [0.48, 1.16]	1.025 [0.964, 1.102] / 0.74 [0.52, 1.02]	0.74 [0.43, 1.19]
100K	5K	1.05 / 0.5	1.051 [1.028, 1.075] / 0.5 [0.45, 0.55]	1.051 [1.028, 1.075] / 0.49 [0.45, 0.54]	0.49 [0.41, 0.58]

Table 1: **Simulation of AB/BA analysis**

the rRecall and rFPR metrics. Data is generated such that models A and B collect, respectively, 40% and 20% as TPs. The probability that FPs and TPs from model A are also accepted by model B are, respectively, 0.3 and 0.9, and the probability that FPs and TPs from model B are also accepted by model A are, respectively, 0.6, and 0.8. Then, we simulate three soft label machines $\mathcal{M}_1$, $\mathcal{M}_2$, and $\mathcal{M}_3$ using a Beta distribution.

Among the three machines, $\mathcal{M}_1$ is simulated to generate soft-labels with $\mathcal{B}(2, 1000|L = 0)$ and $\mathcal{B}(300, 5|L = 1)$ to have the same accuracy for both models A and B that will be evaluated in ssAB/BA. Then, $\mathcal{M}_2$ is simulated with $\mathcal{B}(5, 100|B = 1, L = 0)$ and $\mathcal{B}(300, 5|B = 1, L = 1)$ to make more mistakes in the form of higher TP probability on the FPs collected by model B, and $\mathcal{M}_3$ with $\mathcal{B}(2, 1000|B = 1, L = 0)$ and $\mathcal{B}(100, 10|B = 1, L = 1)$ to make more mistakes in the form of lower TP probability on the TPs collected by the model B. Notice that we keep the accuracy of the machines on model A data constant, since B is a candidate model with new data never seen before.

Notice that based on the parameters chosen the expected AB/BA rRecall for the simulation is 1.12, since $P(B = 1|A = 1, L = 1)/P(A = 1|B = 1, L = 1) = 0.9/0.8 = 1.12$. Similarly, the expected rFPR is 0.5. Results of the simulation, along with 95% confidence interval from 1000 bootstrapping replicates, are shown in Table 2.

	rRecall	rFPR
AB/BA	1.12[1.10,1.14]	0.50[0.48,0.52]
ssAB/BA $\mathcal{M}_1$	1.12[1.10,1.13]	0.51[0.49,0.53]
ssAB/BA $\mathcal{M}_2$	1.08[1.05,1.10]	0.51[0.49,0.53]
ssAB/BA $\mathcal{M}_3$	1.12[1.10,1.15]	0.56[0.54,0.57]

Table 2: **Simulation comparing AB/BA and ssAB/BA analysis according to label quality**

From Table 2, as expected, $\mathcal{M}_1$ results are almost exactly the same as in AB/BA, since $\mathcal{M}_1$ mean TP probabilities are 0.2% for $L = 0$ and 98.4% for $L = 1$, which are close to ground-truth. When using $\mathcal{M}_2$, however, we can see that the rRecall measured drops from 1.12 to 1.08, as this model makes more mistakes on the FPs collected from model B, increasing the machine TP probability on this data from 0.2% to 4.8%. In this case, we can see that the rFPR is unchanged at the reported precision. Similarly, in the case of $\mathcal{M}_3$ we see a change in the reported rFPR, which increases from 0.51 to 0.56 as this model makes more mistakes on the TPs collected from model B, dropping the TP probability on this data from 98.4% to 90.9%. In this case, the rRecall is mostly unchanged. This results show that, although the label-generation process by machine can be imperfect, it gives good approximations on the Recall Ratio and FPR Ratio in order to make deployment decisions.

3.2 AB/BA Analysis on Real Application

Next, we show how AB/BA performs when applied to real customer data in order to guide the decision on how much customer experience is being improved with the deployment of new KWS models. Comparison between AB/BA and ssAB/BA analysis on real data is show in Appendix A.5.

3.2.1 Comparison between deployments with different threshold t_b

We show results from two real deployments, called D_1 and D_2. In D_1, the AB/BA analysis ratio metrics are used to compare a baseline model to a candidate model with high threshold (more restrictive), while in D_2 the same baseline is compared to the same candidate model with low threshold (more permissive). The two deployments use about 5000 annotated utterances per model. Results are show in Table 3.

As we can see in Table 3, D_1 resulted in loss of Recall by 5% relative, but improving the rFPR in 43% relative. By deploying the candidate model

D	rRecall	rFPR
D_1	0.95 [0.94-0.96]	0.57 [0.46-0.68]
D_2	1.07 [1.05-1.09]	1.33 [1.17 - 1.44]

Table 3: **AB/BA Analysis results when deploying models with different thresholds**

Dataset	rRecall	rFPR
Test set	1.03	0.5
AB/BA	1.16[1.15-1.19]	0.21[0.14-0.26]

Table 4: **AB/BA Analysis Recall Ratio comparison to test set metrics**

with low t_B threshold (D_2), the AB/BA analysis then shows $7\%(5\%, 9\%)$ relative improvement in Recall, with a trade-off of $33\%(17\%, 44\%)$ relative increase in FPR. AB/BA analysis correctly found that the D_1 model is a more conservative model, and D_2 a more sensitive model than the baseline model.

3.2.2 Comparison between AB/BA analysis and the evaluation a test dataset

New candidate models are evaluated on offline test datasets to decide if they can be deployed to customers. However, offline test datasets are composed of utterances collected by the current or older deployed models, and recall improvement of those candidate models may be under-estimated. Here we show measurements from offline evaluation and AB/BA analysis in a real deployment. The AB/BA analysis was performed with approximately 7000 annotated utterances per model.

As we can see in Table 4, the rRecall estimation from the offline test set resulted in 3% relative improvement at the same FPR. That was significantly less than the 16% relative improvement measured during AB/BA, in which data from model B is used in the analysis. Similar observation can be made in terms of rFPR, where evaluation on the test set resulted in a 50% relative improvement at the same Recall, but by also accounting for data collected by the B model in AB/BA, we see that the improvements was 79% relative. This shows the importance of techniques such as AB/BA analysis to better assess the customer experience on the model being deployed.

4 Conclusion

In this paper, we presented a new framework called AB/BA analysis for recall improvement estimation of KWS under high privacy settings. We have shown that by running a candidate model offline on data collected by a baseline, and the baseline model offline on data collected by the candidate model, we were able to compute the relative Recall and relative FPR ratios using only utterances accepted by both models and use it to indicate if a candidate model is better than the baseline. We have also shown that reasonable assumptions can be used to construct an estimator with low variance, even when the number of FPs is small. Finally, we saw that a Semi-Supervised formulation of AB/BA can be used with machine-generated labels representing the probability of a true accept. This techniques brings further improvements to AB/BA analysis, especially regarding privacy on the audio collected, which does not need to be listened to and annotated.

In the past few years, much improvement has been made on the KWS systems. Evaluation metrics, however, are typically based on previously collected data from similar KWS models or data from other sources, resulting in evaluations that do not necessarily translate to customer experience, as it fails to show improvements in data never collected due to privacy constraints. Given that not much attention has been paid to this research topic, we believe that AB/BA analysis is a valuable contribution, and we hope it helps bringing interest in this line of research.

References

Richard E Barlow and Hugh D Brunk. 1972. The isotonic regression problem and its dual. *Journal of the American Statistical Association*, 67(337):140–147.

Guoguo Chen, Carolina Parada, and Georg Heigold. 2014. Small-footprint keyword spotting using deep neural networks. In *IEEE International Conference on Acoustics, Speech and Signal Processing, ICASSP 2014, Florence, Italy, May 4-9, 2014*, pages 4087–4091. IEEE.

Amit S. Chhetri, Philip Hilmes, Trausti Kristjansson, Wai Chu, Mohamed Mansour, Xiaoxue Li, and Xianxian Zhang. 2018. Multichannel audio front-end for far-field automatic speech recognition. In *26th European Signal Processing Conference, EUSIPCO 2018, Roma, Italy, September 3-7, 2018*, pages 1527–1531. IEEE.

Paul HC Eilers and Brian D Marx. 1996. Flexible smoothing with b-splines and penalties. *Statistical science*, 11(2):89–121.

Yixin Gao, Noah D. Stein, Chieh-Chi Kao, Yunliang Cai, Ming Sun, Tao Zhang, and Shiv Naga Prasad Vitaladevuni. 2020. On front-end gain invariant modeling for wake word spotting. In *Interspeech 2020, 21st Annual Conference of the International Speech Communication Association, Virtual Event, Shanghai, China, 25-29 October 2020*, pages 991–995. ISCA.

Jinyu Li, Michael L Seltzer, Xi Wang, Rui Zhao, and Yifan Gong. 2017. Large-scale domain adaptation via teacher-student learning. *arXiv preprint arXiv:1708.05466*.

Iván López-Espejo, Zheng-Hua Tan, John Hansen, and Jesper Jensen. 2021. Deep spoken keyword spotting: An overview. *CoRR*, abs/2111.10592.

Benjamin A. Miller, Jeremy Vila, Malina Kirn, and Joseph R. Zipkin. 2018. Classifier performance estimation with unbalanced, partially labeled data. In *International Workshop on Cost-Sensitive Learning, COST@SDM 2018, San Diego, California, USA, May 5, 2018*, volume 88 of *Proceedings of Machine Learning Research*, pages 4–16. PMLR.

Anirudh Raju, Sankaran Panchapagesan, Xing Liu, Arindam Mandal, and Nikko Strom. 2018. Data augmentation for robust keyword spotting under playback interference. *CoRR*, abs/1808.00563.

Tara N. Sainath and Carolina Parada. 2015. Convolutional neural networks for small-footprint keyword spotting. In *INTERSPEECH 2015, 16th Annual Conference of the International Speech Communication Association, Dresden, Germany, September 6-10, 2015*, pages 1478–1482. ISCA.

Changhao Shan, Junbo Zhang, Yujun Wang, and Lei Xie. 2018. Attention-based end-to-end models for small-footprint keyword spotting. In *Interspeech 2018, 19th Annual Conference of the International Speech Communication Association, Hyderabad, India, 2-6 September 2018*, pages 2037–2041. ISCA.

Michael Stolberg. 2006. Inventing the randomized double-blind trial: the nuremberg salt test of 1835. *Journal of the Royal Society of Medicine*, 99(12):642–643.

Ming Sun, David Snyder, Yixin Gao, Varun K. Nagaraja, Mike Rodehorst, Sankaran Panchapagesan, Nikko Strom, Spyros Matsoukas, and Shiv Vitaladevuni. 2017. Compressed time delay neural network for small-footprint keyword spotting. In *Interspeech 2017, 18th Annual Conference of the International Speech Communication Association, Stockholm, Sweden, August 20-24, 2017*, pages 3607–3611. ISCA.

Antti Tarvainen and Harri Valpola. 2017. Mean teachers are better role models: Weight-averaged consistency targets improve semi-supervised deep learning results. *arXiv preprint arXiv:1703.01780*.

George Tucker, Minhua Wu, Ming Sun, Sankaran Panchapagesan, Gengshen Fu, and Shiv Vitaladevuni. 2016. Model compression applied to small-footprint keyword spotting. In *Interspeech 2016, 17th Annual Conference of the International Speech Communication Association, San Francisco, CA, USA, September 8-12, 2016*, pages 1878–1882. ISCA.

Minhua Wu, Sankaran Panchapagesan, Ming Sun, Jiacheng Gu, Ryan Thomas, Shiv Naga Prasad Vitaladevuni, Björn Hoffmeister, and Arindam Mandal. 2018. Monophone-based background modeling for two-stage on-device wake word detection. In *2018 IEEE International Conference on Acoustics, Speech and Signal Processing, ICASSP 2018, Calgary, AB, Canada, April 15-20, 2018*, pages 5494–5498. IEEE.

A Appendix

A.1 Basic Evaluation Concepts

During our discussion we assume that we have a classification model, $\mathcal{M}(x) \rightarrow y$, which gets an arbitrary input x and output $y \in \{0, 1\}$, where 1 and 0 represent, respectively, a positive and negative label.

A.1.1 Precision and Recall

The Precision and Recall metrics help to distinguish between Type-I and Type-II errors. They are defined as the following:

$$Precision = \frac{TP}{TP + FP} \tag{10}$$

$$Recall = \frac{TP}{TP + FN} = \frac{TP}{P} \tag{11}$$

Precision measures the proportion of correct positive predictions with respect to everything the model believes is a positive, where lower precision represents more Type-I errors. On the other hand, Recall measures the proportion of correct positive predictions with respect to all the data that is actually positive, where lower recall represents more Type-II errors.

As illustration, in a case where 90% of the data has label 1 and the model always gives output 1, this model will have 100% recall, and 90% precision.

A.1.2 False Positive Rate and False Discovery Rate

There are also multiple ways to evaluate a model with respect to the number of False Positives (FPs) it makes. Two of them, which are explored in this paper, are False Positive Rate (FPR) and False Discovery Rate (FDR). They are defined as:

$$FPR = \frac{FP}{N} \tag{12}$$

$$FDR = 1 - Precision = \frac{FP}{TP + FP} \tag{13}$$

Therefore, we can see that the FPR is similar to Recall in the sense that the reference is only one class of the data, which in this case are the negative samples. It measures the proportion of negative samples that are miss classified by a model. The FDR, however, is the complement to the Precision, measuring the number of false positives among all samples that the model classifies as positive.

Considering again the example where 90% of the data has label 1 and the model always gives output 1, its FPR is 100%, while its FDR is 10%.

A.1.3 A/B Test

Another related concept to our proposed method is the A/B test. The A/B test is a frequently used technique in multiple areas, such as medicine (Stolberg, 2006), marketing, political campaigning, product pricing, among others. The technique consists of doing a hypothesis test by giving two randomized and unbiased set of populations, called A and B, two different versions of the subject being compared. For example, in the context of marketing, one could choose to give two different versions of user interface to users in order to measure differences in engagement, which is measured through statistical tests.

In the context of model evaluation, the A/B test can be explored by given two different models to users. After data collection, metrics can be computed for each population, such as metrics presented in Section A.1, and statistical tests, such as t-test, can be used to compare the metrics in the different populations.

The A/B test has, however limitations, when used to evaluate keyword spotting with audio privacy settings. Given that only data where the keyword is detected is collected by the models, the amount of negative data is highly biased towards the false positives from the models that collected the data. Therefore, metrics that rely on negative data, such as Recall and FPR, cannot be computed and compared using A/B test. This limitation is explored in this paper with our proposed AB/BA technique in order to tackle this challenge of Recall improvement estimation.

A.2 Stratified Sampling

To decide if a model is better than the other one, we could simply annotate the utterances where the two models disagree. However, if it is also desirable to calculate absolute metrics, such as False Positive Rate (FPR), then annotation of model agreements is also needed. In order to reduce the amount of annotations for this task, we propose to use stratified sampling, with two strata, agreement and disagreement, such that different number of annotations are done per strata.

Our stratified sampling strategy uses the Neyman allocation principle. The optimal number of annotations N_j for a strata j can be found using:

$$N_j^* = \frac{N w_j \sqrt{p_j(1-p_j)}}{\sum_{i=1}^{L} w_i \sqrt{p_i(1-p_i)}}, \tag{14}$$

where N is our annotation budget, w_j is the proportion in each strata, and p_j is the expected model FPR, assumed to be estimated, for example, from previously annotated data.

The efficiency improvement of the stratified sampling strategy compared to a random sampling strategy, in terms of variance in the FPR, is:

$$\begin{aligned} Eff &= 1 - \frac{\mathbb{V}(fpr^*)}{\mathbb{V}(fpr)} \\ &= 1 - \frac{\frac{1}{N}(\sum_j w_j \sqrt{p_j(1-p_j)})^2}{\frac{1}{N}p(1-p)}, \end{aligned} \tag{15}$$

For the purpose of illustration, assume we have a 10% disagreement between models, with FPR of 20% in this strata, whereas the agreement strata has a FPR of 5%, and the overall FPR of 8%, Equation (14) gives us, for the disagreement strata:

$$\begin{aligned} \frac{N_j^*}{N} &= \frac{0.1\sqrt{0.2(1-0.2)}}{0.1\sqrt{0.2(1-0.2)} + 0.9\sqrt{0.05(1-0.05)}} \\ &\approx 17\%, \end{aligned} \tag{16}$$

indicating that the disagreement strata should optimally be 17% of the annotation budget, without affecting the FPR variance. The efficiency gain of this method is:

$$\begin{aligned} &Eff = \\ &1 - \frac{(0.1\sqrt{0.2(1-0.2)} + 0.9\sqrt{0.05(1-0.05)})^2}{0.08(1-0.08)} \\ &\approx 24\%, \end{aligned} \tag{17}$$

indicating that the annotation budget can be reduced by approximately 24%, without affecting the overall FPR variance.

A.3 Threshold Selection Example

Given two models A and B, where A is a baseline and B a candidate, we assume that A has a known t_A, previously obtained according to the desired FPR and Recall trade-off. Therefore, in order to determine if the candidate model B is better, we can calculate the FPR Ratio and Recall Ratio for multiple thresholds t_B. Next, the decision will be guided towards the goal of model B. Say, for example, that the goal of model B is not to improve FPR, but only Recall, then we select $t_B = t$ such that when applying this threshold it results in $FPR\_Ratio = 1$. One example, illustrating this process, is given in Table 5.

t_B	FPR Ratio	Recall Ratio
0.1	1.5	1.20
0.2	1.0	1.05
0.3	0.8	1.01
0.4	0.7	0.98

Table 5: **Threshold selection:** The table shows an example of how FPR Ratio and Recall Ratio change, as a function of t_B. It shows that, by selecting $t_B = 0.2$, model B has the same FPR Ratio as model B, but improves Recall in 5%.

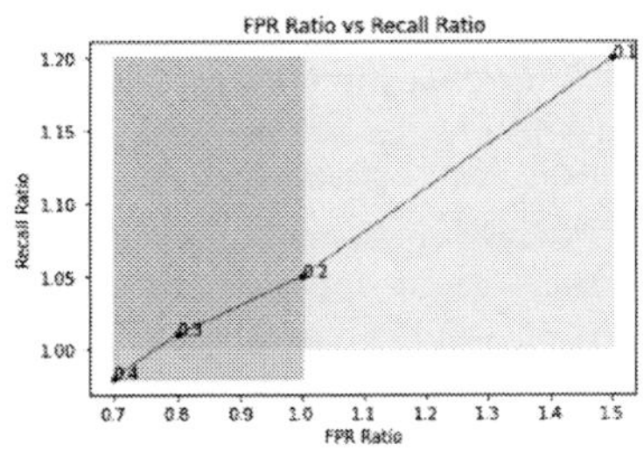

Figure 2: **Model sensitivity selection:** The green area in the figure shows the region where the recall is improved, and the red area where the FPR improves. We can see that 0.2 and 0.3 are potential thresholds for t_B to improve the performance of model A.

Table 5 shows the FPR Ratio and Recall Ratio as a function of t_B, similar to the data behind a traditional DET curve, but using the proposed ratio metrics. We can see that, by selecting $t_B = 0.2$, model B has the same FPR Ratio as model B, but improves Recall in 5% relative. It is also interesting to see that using $t_B = 0.3$ causes improvement in both FPR Ratio and Recall Ratio. Using $t_B = 0.1$ has 20% relative improvement in Recall, but with a high trade-off in FPR and, similarly $t_B = 0.4$ has 30% relative improvement in FPR, but with degradation in Recall.

We see, therefore, that the model threshold can be selected according to the goal in the trade-off between FPR Ratio and Recall Ratio. It is clear though that the model B is superior than model A, since it has a threshold region that improves both FPR and Recall, as shown in Figure 2.

A.4 Soft-Label Score Calibration

Given a set of utterances composed of N machine-generated soft labels $m \in \mathbb{R}^N$ and human labels $y \in \mathbb{R}^N$, we propose to learn $\phi(m_i)$ using a polynomial of degree 3. Notice that, as the target variable is binary, and we expect to have more TAs as m increases, the polynomial should be a monotonic increasing function between $[0, 1]$. Although not guaranteed, our experiments show this to be an empirically good choice. One example is shown in Figure 3. However, since the polynomial is not guaranteed to have probabilities bounded between $[0, 1]$, we have also explored to use a B-Spline Logistic Regression with monotonic constraints (Eilers and Marx, 1996; Barlow and Brunk, 1972). However we have not seen significant difference and have decided to use the polynomial approach for simplicity.

Once we have soft-labels for the utterances from model A and B to be compared, we can use Equations (8) and (9) in order to estimate the FPR Ratio and Recall Ratio trade-off.

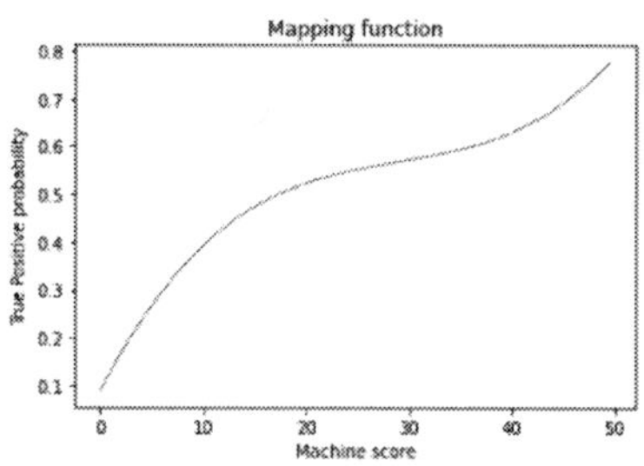

Figure 3: **Probability mapping function:** Using a polynomial of degree 3, arbitrary for this illustration, we can see that scores from a model between 0 and 50 are mapped to a probability of True Positive.

A.5 Semi-Supervised AB/BA Comparison to AB/BA on Real Data

Next we show real data examples where we used both AB/BA and ssAB/BA, in order to see if the ratios reported are similar. In this case, machine-generated scores were generated by a cloud-side verification system, and its scores converted to a TP probability according to a polynomial mapping function learned from other existing labeled datasets, following the process described in Section 2.2. Results are shown in Table 6.

Results in Table 6 show that ssAB/BA is able to well-approximate the AB/BA results, having results with overlapping margin of error in most cases. It is important to notice, however, that there is a risk of using ssAB/BA related to the quality of labels generated. In the Example 3, we can see that ssAB/BA results suggest a Recall loss of 1% relative, while AB/BA suggests a Recall improvement of 1% relative, although the confidence intervals overlap. That represents the case where, when the recall improvement is small, the uncertainty of the machine-label generation may limit its applicability. It is important, therefore, to monitor the quality of the label machines in order to know how trustworthy they are, and to also use other auxiliary metrics that help reducing the risk of trusting the ssAB/BA results by itself.

Example	ssAB/BA rRecall at rFPR	AB/BA rFPR at rRecall
1	1.03 [1.03-1.03]	1.04[1.04-1.05]
2	1.01 [1.01-1.01]	1.0[0.97-1.05]
3	0.99 [0.98-1.01]	1.01[0.99-1.04]

Table 6: **Semi-Supervised AB/BA and AB/BA analysis comparison on real data:** The table shows three examples comparing AB/BA and Semi-Supervised AB/BA on real customer data

Temporal Generalization for Spoken Language Understanding

Judith Gaspers, Anoop Kumar, Greg Ver Steeg, Aram Galstyan
Amazon Alexa AI

Abstract

Spoken Language Understanding (SLU) models in industry applications are usually trained offline on historic data, but have to perform well on incoming user requests after deployment. Since the application data is not available at training time, this is formally similar to the domain generalization problem, where domains correspond to different temporal segments of the data, and the goal is to build a model that performs well on unseen domains, e.g., upcoming data. In this paper, we explore different strategies for achieving good temporal generalization, including instance weighting, temporal fine-tuning, learning temporal features and building a temporally-invariant model. Our results on data of large-scale SLU systems show that temporal information can be leveraged to improve temporal generalization for SLU models.

1 Introduction

Spoken Language Understanding (SLU) models play an important role in voice-controlled devices, such as Alexa or Google Home. Two common SLU tasks are intent classification (IC) and slot filling (SF). Given a user request, IC aims to extract the user's intent, while SF is a sequence labeling task which assigns a slot label to each of the tokens. For example, the user request "play volbeat" should be classified as *PlayMusic* by the IC task, while SF should assign the labels *O* and *Artist* to "play" and "volbeat", respectively. State-of-the-art approaches typically model the two tasks jointly via DNNs (Do and Gaspers, 2019; Chen et al., 2019).

In deployed industry SLU systems, new data continuously flows into the system, and the underlying data distributions keep drifting over time. In this paper, we focus on the setting of temporal *covariate drift*, where the distribution of utterances may change, but the correct label for an utterance or token remains fixed (i.e., no concept drift) (Schölkopf et al., 2012). Such data drifts happen, for example, because customer usage patterns change over time, as new movies are being released or new artists and songs become popular. Another cause of data drifts are seasonal changes or changes related to (re-)occurring events. For instance, the utterance "will it snow tomorrow" is more likely to appear during the winter than the summer season, and the utterance "put on the Christmas lighting" is likely uttered around Christmas.

To accommodate for temporal distributional changes, industry SLU models are typically retrained and redeployed over time; in the following sections, we also refer to this process as *model release*, and we assume that model releases are executed at fixed time intervals, e.g., once per month. We further assume that for each release, new labeled data become available, which were collected since the previous release, yielding data belonging to different time periods.

The common approach to utilize new data is to simply combine them with all previously available data, and subsequently split them into training, validation, and test datasets. We can then build and evaluate a model on these datasets, which we also refer to as *offline* data in this paper. In industry applications, SLU models are subsequently deployed to customers and have to perform well on incoming customer requests, which we also refer to as *online* data. Importantly, aiming to provide the best possible experience for our customers, our main goal is building models which perform well on the online rather than the offline data. Since the online data are not available for model building and evaluation, we need to utilize the offline data to build a model which generalizes well to unseen online data from the upcoming time period.

In this paper, we study this temporal generalization task assuming that data from several consecutive time periods, i.e., months in our case, are available, and we aim to build a SLU model which yields high performance on data from an upcoming

Proceedings of NAACL-HLT 2022: Industry Track Papers, pages 37 - 44
July 10-15, 2022 ©2022 Association for Computational Linguistics

time period. We aim to improve performance over the common approach of simply combining all offline data, which ignores the temporal nature of the data and implicitly assumes that data from all time periods are equally useful for model training. Instead, relating back to the previous examples, we assume that modeling the temporal nature of the data may be beneficial and that data from certain time periods may be particularly valuable. For instance, data from recent time periods may better reflect upcoming trends, and w.r.t. seasonality patterns, data from the same period in previous years may be particularly valuable.

To tackle the task, we explore four directions: i) instance weighting based on our assumptions about the task, ii) temporal finetuning, iii) learning temporal features and iv) building a temporally-invariant model. We present extensive experiments on real-world SLU data of German and Portuguese voice-controlled devices. Our results indicate that temporal information can be leveraged to improve temporal generalization of SLU models. We also show that simple temporal fine-tuning is not very effective and in fact leads to performance drop in certain cases.

2 Related Work

To the best of our knowledge, the temporal generalization scenario studied in this paper has not yet been explored for SLU in the literature, which may be due to the fact that common Academic SLU datasets are rather small and do not have a temporal notation. In general, work addressing the temporal nature of SLU datasets has been limited. Kim et al. (2017) address temporal data drift by adapting from stale to current data with an adversarial domain adaptation approach, treating the stale and current dataset as source and target domain, respectively. Contrasting with our work, they assume the availability of data from the target and they focus on two time periods only. Other work has explored short-term temporal information, e.g., the utterance context provided by a couple of prior utterances to resolve ambiguities (Lin et al., 2021).

In NLP, previous research has explored the significance of temporal drift for several tasks, such as headline generation (Søgaard et al., 2021), sentiment analysis (Lukes and Søgaard, 2018) and named entity recognition (NER) (Rijhwani and Preotiuc-Pietro, 2020), providing evidence that model performance drops when training data age increases compared to the test data. However, despite this evidence, the vast majority of NLP research does not take the temporal nature of data into account for evaluation (Lazaridou et al., 2021).

Lazaridou et al. (2021) show that (downstream task) performance of pre-trained language models suffers when performance is measured on future data. Since (re-)training of larger language models is costly, the authors propose to update model parameters by executing few steps of gradient decent on new data. Other approaches to mitigate temporal drift include predictive feature selection for sentiment analysis (Lukes and Søgaard, 2018), and selecting data based on frequent n-grams for NER (Chen et al., 2021). The most similar to our work is the study conducted by Rijhwani and Preotiuc-Pietro (2020) who tackle temporal drift for a small-scale NER task, i.e., including only 3 named entities. They consider data from several consecutive years and aim to build a model which performs well on data of the following year, focusing – in line with the previously described work – on the effects of data receny. The best performance is achieved by using instance weighting of recent data and temporal finetuning for a Bi-LSTM-CRF with Flair and GloVe embeddings, respectively. By contrast, we study temporal generalization in the context of a large-scale SLU production system covering a large numbers of labels. We focus on smaller time periods, i.e., spanning one month instead of a year, and we consider cyclic/seasonal changes in addition to data recency. For this purpose, we include methods which have not yet been explored in temporal generalization tasks, such as building models that leverage temporally-invariant representations.

3 Method

Given labeled SLU data from several consecutive time periods, our goal is to build a model which generalizes well to unseen data from an upcoming time period. In the following, we first provide a formal definition for our tasks and subsequently present the modeling approaches.

3.1 Learning scenario

We assume that labeled data are available, which span N consecutive time periods, i.e., $D = [D_1, \ldots, D_N]$ with $D_i \in D = \{(x_{i,j}, y_{i,j})\}_{j=1}^{|D_i|}$, where $x_{i,j_1}, \ldots, x_{i,j_n}$ is an utterance with n tokens which was observed during time period D_i. For the SF task, a slot label is available for each token in

$x_{i,j}$, and $y_{i,j}$ is a sentence-level intent label for the IC task. In this work, each $D_i \in D$ comprises data of one month.

The goal is to build a model using $[D_1, \ldots, D_{N-1}]$ which generalizes well to the unseen data D_N. $[D_1, \ldots, D_{N-1}]$ corresponds to the offline data in a release scenario, while D_N corresponds to the online data.

Note that this learning scenario corresponds to the task of domain generalization (DG) (Wang et al., 2021) when considering the time periods as individual domains. In DG, one aims to build a model given several different but related domains (datasets) which works well on data of a new (unseen) domain during testing. However, in work addressing DG, typically the domains under consideration are more distant than the datasets of different time periods in our scenario, which are in fact drawn from the same overall source (domain), and contrasting with our scenario, the domain datasets in DG usually do not have a natural order.

Note further that DG differs from domain adaptation (DA) in that DA assumes the availability of some (unlabeled) data of the target domain, which can be utilized for adaptation.

3.2 Basic SLU model

Our basic SLU model is a common state-of-the-art SLU architecture for joint intent classification and slot filling. It is comprised of a BERT encoder, an intent decoder and a slot decoder. The BERT encoder's outputs at sentence and token level are used as inputs for the intent and slot decoders, respectively. The intent decoder is a standard feed-forward network including two standard dense layers and a softmax layer on top. The slot decoder uses a CRF layer on top of two dense layers to leverage the sequential information of slot labels. As loss we use a weighted sum of the loss of IC L_i and the loss of SF L_s, i.e.

$$L = \lambda_i L_i + \lambda_s L_s, \quad (1)$$

where λ_i and λ_s are weights. We use cross-entropy and CRF loss for IC and SF, respectively.

3.3 Instance weighting

Instance weighting assigns a weight to each training data instance. In a DA task, a weight may be selected such that it reflects the instance's similarity to the target (Jiang and Zhai, 2007). However, since we do not assume the availability of data from the target time period, we cannot compute such similarity scores. Instead, we simply weight instances based on our assumptions about the task.

We assume that recent data, i.e., data from the period prior to the target period, may be particularly valuable, because this period may better reflect recent and upcoming trends, Moreover, instance weighting of data from a recent year has already been shown to improve performance on data of a future year for a small-scale NER task (Rijhwani and Preotiuc-Pietro, 2020). On the other hand, with respect to seasonal changes, data from the same period in previous years could also be of particular value. Thus, taken together, we explore three instance weighting strategies based on recency, seasonality, and combination of both:

1. Reweight each data instance in the period prior to the target period by a weight $w > 1$ (i.e., reweight D_{N-1}),
2. Reweight each data instance from the same calendar month as the target data by $w > 1$,
3. Reweight all instances from either the same calendar month as the target data or from the period prior to the target data by $w > 1$.

Given an utterance and a corresponding weight, we weight the losses of both IC and SF.

The described instance weighting techniques do not require any temporal information during the application phase and no architectural changes.

3.4 Temporal finetuning

We explore temporal finetuning, as it has been previously shown to improve performance on other temporal tasks. In particular, Rijhwani and Preotiuc-Pietro (2020) i) trained Bi-LSTM-CRF models for a small-scale NER task on data from several years, and ii) fine-tuned these models on data of the most recent year, yielding improved performance over the initial models when evaluated on data of a future year. Similarly, we first train a model on all offline data, i.e., on $D_1 \cup \ldots \cup D_{N-1}$, and subsequently we finetune it on data of the most recent offline time period, i.e., on D_{N-1}.[1]

[1]We do not explore sequential temporal finetuning, i.e., first train on D_1, then on D_2, etc. This approach degraded performance on the small-scale NER task explored by Rijhwani and Preotiuc-Pietro (2020), and we expect it to not perform well for our task either, as it corresponds to a life-long learning scenario in which catastrophic forgetting of previously acquired knowledge is a known issue.

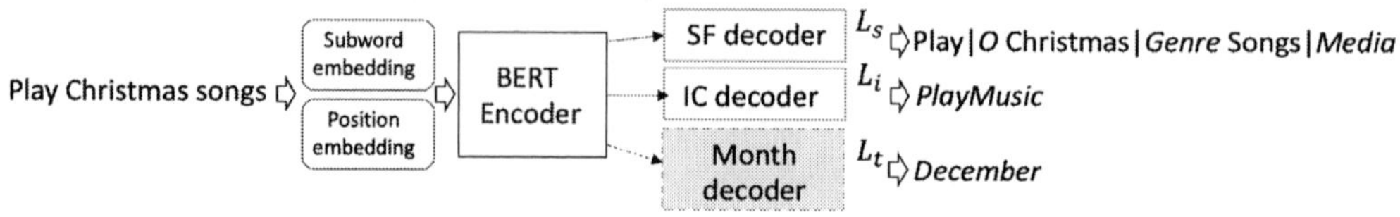

Figure 1: SLU architecture for joint IC and SF with an auxiliary task for predicting the month of an input utterance. While the model is trained by alternating across tasks, during inference only the SF and IC decoders are used.

This technique does not require any temporal information during the application phase and no architectural changes.

3.5 Learning temporal features

We hypothesize that learning temporal features could be beneficial for our SLU task and therefore aim to build a temporally-aware model. For this purpose, we explore two established techniques for injecting auxiliary information, i.e., i) via additional input features, and ii) via an auxiliary task. The training of an auxiliary prediction task to improve embeddings is sometimes called self-supervised learning, and has also been shown to improve generalization in vision tasks (Albuquerque et al., 2020).

3.5.1 Using additional input features

We define a special token for each month, e.g., "[JAN]", ... "[DEC]". For each utterance, information about the month in which it was observed is added before model training and inference using the corresponding special token. E.g., "[DEC] play Christmas songs" indicates that the utterance "play Christmas songs" was observed in December.

While this technique does not require any architectural changes, temporal information is needed during the application phase, which, however, should be easily accessible in most cases.

3.5.2 Using an auxiliary task

We extend the basic SLU model described in section 3.2 by an auxiliary task which predicts the month given an utterance. Specifically, we apply a multi-task model which is comprised of a joint IC and SF task and an additional classification task; the overall architecture is illustrated in Fig. 1. The auxiliary task decoder is a standard feed-forward network comprising two standard dense layers and a softmax layer on top. We optimize the model by alternating across the two subtasks (joint SF and IC vs month prediction), and we use a combined loss

$$L = \lambda_i L_i + \lambda_s L_s + \lambda_t L_t \quad (2)$$

where L_i, L_s and L_t are the losses of the IC, SF and month prediction tasks, respectively, and λ_i, λ_s and λ_i are weights. We use cross-entropy loss for the IC and month prediction tasks and CRF loss for the SF task.

For inference, we apply only the joint SF and IC task, and temporal information is not required during the application phase. The intuition is that via the joint training, temporal information is acquired by the model which can then influence the SF and IC predictions during inference.

3.6 Building a temporally-invariant model

Relating back to section 3.1, our learning scenario corresponds to the task of DG when considering the time periods as individual domains. We selected a popular direction explored in DG (Wang et al., 2021) and DA (Ramponi and Plank, 2020), i.e., invariant representation learning. The intuition is that by removing information which is specific to individual domains, the model should generalize better to an unseen target domain. Thus, contrasting with the approaches described in the previous section which aim to learn temporal features, in this approach we aim to build a temporally-invariant model by removing features which are specific to certain time periods.

Note that both approaches may be reasonable, as there may be different kinds of temporal features and artifacts related to our data, out of which we may want to leverage some, but abstract away from others. For instance, it may be beneficial if the models learn a notation of seasonality and/or recency, but we may want to abstract away from artifacts related to out-dated trends, annotation inconsistencies across time, etc.

One established approach to domain-invariant representation learning is adding an auxiliary domain classifier to a main task predictor, and then optimizing for an accurate task predictor while applying an adversarial training strategy to confuse the auxiliary domain classifier by making the features from source and target domain indistinguishable, thus yielding domain-invariant features. A gradient-reversal layer can be applied for this purpose (Ganin and Lempitsky, 2015; Ganin et al., 2016). We adapt the approach from Ganin and Lempitsky (2015) to build a temporally-invariant model, i.e., we apply it with our SLU model as the main task predictor and using an auxiliary month classifier instead of the domain classifier (and BERT as the feature extractor).

As in case of learning temporal features using an auxiliary task, for inference we apply only the main task, and thus temporal information or architectural changes are not required during the application phase.

4 Experiments

4.1 Data

We use data from large-scale industry SLU systems comprising user requests to voice-controlled devices; all requests were de-identified, annotated with intent and slot labels, and marked with a time stamp. We collected data for two languages, i.e. German and Portuguese, and three domains, i.e. *Music*, *Video* and *Shopping*. The data range from May 2019 to December 2020, and we split them into one dataset per month based on timestamps, resulting in 20 datasets $D_1, \ldots, D_{20}$ for each domain and language. Thus, one dataset is available per month, domain and language. For each domain and language, D_{20} is used for testing, and for $D_1, \ldots, D_{19}$ we create training and validation datasets. For German, for each domain we have more than 100,000 data instances available, while for Portuguese for each domain the data amounts are on the order of tens of thousands.

Qualitative data analyses indicate that both gradual and seasonal drifts are indeed present in the data, but there are domain-specific differences. Due to confidentiality reasons, a detailed data analysis is beyond the scope of this paper.

4.2 Experimental setup

For each domain and language, we use the $D_1, \ldots, D_{19}$ training datasets for model training, and D_{20} for testing. Since we do not have access to target period data, we study two options for creating an offline validation dataset:

1. val_a comprises the offline validation data from $D_1, \ldots, D_{19}$. This corresponds to the common approach.
2. val_r comprises only recent offline validation data, i.e., the validation data of D_{19}.

We train and evaluate our modeling approaches on the described setup. As baseline, we train a model, i.e., the basic SLU model described in section 3.2, following the common approach of simply training on the combined offline data (without leveraging any temporal information). In the following, we refer to this approach as *concat*.

We measure performance using a semantic error rate, which measures intent classification and slot filling jointly and is defined as follow:

$$\mathit{SemER} = \frac{\#(\text{slot+intent errors})}{\#\text{slots in reference} + 1} \tag{3}$$

4.3 Settings

We used pre-trained multilingual BERT (Devlin et al., 2019) (size 768, 110M parameters)[2], and max-pooling for sentence representations. Each of our decoders has 2 dense layers of size 768 with gelu activation. The dropout values used in IC, SF and month decoders are 0.5, 0.2 and 0.5, respectively. We used equal weights for λ_s and λ_i (1.0:1.0) and Adam optimizer with a learning rate of 0.1 and a Noam learning rate scheduler. We trained our models for 20 and 25 epochs for German and Portuguese, respectively, with a batch size of 32. These hyper-parameters were used for all models (where they apply). The best models were selected on offline validation data (val_{all} or val_{rec}). We tried $w \in [2, 5]$ and we varied λ_t from 0.2 to 0.6. Each model was trained on a single GPU.

5 Results and discussion

The results on the "online" test data for using either all offline validation data val_{all} or recent validation data val_{rec} to select the best model are shown in Table 1. For confidentiality reasons, we report the relative change in SemER compared to the *concat* baseline using val_{all}. In the following, we discuss the results w.r.t. different research questions.

[2]The model is taken from https://github.com/google-research/bert/blob/master/multilingual.md (Apache 2.0) and was used for experiments only, not for production cases.

Method	German						Portuguese					
	Music		Video		Shopping		Music		Video		Shopping	
	val_a	val_r	val_a	val_r	val_a	val_r	val_a	val_r	val_a	val_r	val_a	val_r
Concat	0	-1.48	0	-3.0	0	-4.59	0	-1.67	0	**-11.0**	0	-0.54
Weight prev. period	-1.48	-0.67	**-2.96**	**-4.47**	**-8.68**	-7.06	-1.89	-0.33	-4.85	-4.86	-1.99	-5.87
Weight same month	-1.75	-0.47	0.84	-1.48	1.49	-5.09	0.39	-0.78	-4.56	-8.73	-0.09	-3.07
Weight both	1.34	-0.2	-1.96	-2.96	-4.47	**-9.31**	-1.83	-0.39	**-7.15**	-5.14	-2.8	-5.78
Temporal finetuning	-0.2	-0.2	-1.76	-3.04	4.84	-2.73	0.06	2.33	-3.05	0.11	3.43	0
Month feature	-0.94	-1.28	1.045	1.52	-1.61	-0.99	-1.1	1.0	-3.38	-1.69	-2.35	3.61
Auxiliary task	-1.75	**-1.75**	-1.72	-2.32	-2.98	-7.94	**-3.06**	**-2.22**	-5.96	-2.37	**-8.57**	-6.23
Temp.-invariant	**-3.63**	-0.74	-0.92	1.76	-4.84	-5.58	-2.44	-0.67	-6.65	-1.19	-3.88	**-9.2**

Table 1: Results on the "online" test data for using either all offline validation data (val_a) or recent offline validation data (val_r). We report the relative change in SemER compared to the *concat* baseline using val_a.

RQ 1: Can temporal information be leveraged to improve temporal generalization for SLU? Across all domains and languages, improvements in SemER on future data can be achieved by taking the temporal nature of data into account. The best methods differ across domains and languages, which is expected, given that there are domain and language specific differences w.r.t. seasonal and gradual shifts. However, two of the methods yield consistent gains across all domains and languages, i.e., instance weighting of the previous time period and using an auxiliary task yield improved performance compared to the baseline for all considered conditions. Using an auxiliary task achieves the best performance most often.

RQ 2: What is the impact of seasonality and reoccurring events vs recency effects? Previous work in NLP on temporal adaptation and generalization has focused on larger time periods and the effects of data recency, showing strong performance for instance weighting of recent data and temporal finetuning on a small-scale NER task (Rijhwani and Preotiuc-Pietro, 2020). By contrast, our domain datasets cover smaller time periods, with different seasonal effects and re-occuring patterns.

On our task, temporal finetuning gives mixed results, with decreasing performance in several cases. We assume that the models may overfit to the recent data, and some previously acquired knowledge related to older time periods might have been forgotten. However, unlike in the NER task which included only the three named entities *PER*, *LOC*, and *ORG* and in which there might be mostly gradual temporal trends, in our task seasonal drifts exist, potentially making certain older knowledge more relevant. By finetuning on recent data, the models may lose too much relevant seasonal knowledge, harming performance for domains with changes related to seasons or re-occurring events. Instance weighting of recent data gives consistent improvements, which is in line with previous findings, while instance weighting of the same time period gives mixed results, i.e., it helps in some cases, but decreases performance in others. To some extent this may be due to domain-specific differences. However, an issue might also be that there can be conflicting seasonal and gradual drifts. In particular, weighting is performed at the dataset level and a dataset from a year ago might include relevant seasonal data instances, but also less useful data instances such as data related to older (already outdated) trends. The negative effects can be mitigated to some extent by selecting the best model on recent validation data, which yields consistent gains in performance across all domains and languages. Future work may explore how to disentangle these effects, and in temporal DA scenarios one may select utterances based on the similarity to the target. However, in our scenario which does not assume the availability of target period data, modeling seasonal and re-occurring patterns indirectly via an auxiliary month prediction task appears to be a better choice in most cases, yielding consistent – and in most cases higher – gains.

How to create a validation dataset without having access to target data? For half of the domain-language pairings, performance is improved by using a recent offline validation dataset. The choice of the best validation dataset may be both method-specific and domain-specific, as drifts differ across domains.

Interestingly, performance of the concat baseline model, which ignores the temporal nature of the data, is consistently improved across domains and languages when using recent validation data. This shows that model performance can also be improved by taking the temporal nature of the data into account for creating a validation dataset instead of model building.

Should we aim for a temporally aware or invariant model? In this paper, we have explored both building temporally-aware and temporally-invariant models, since there may be different kinds of temporal features and artifacts related to our data, out of which we may want to leverage some, but abstract away from others. Our results show consistent gains for temporally-aware models using an auxiliary month classifier as well as gains in all but one case for temporally-invariant models, with temporally-aware models giving better performance in most, but not all cases. Thus, both directions appear to be generally promising.

Future work may explore different approaches to learning temporally aware or invariant models, for instance, by exploring others DG approaches in the latter case. One potentially interesting direction is to learn disentangled representations that separate temporally-invariant and seasonal components.

6 Conclusion

We studied a temporal generalization task in which we used offline data of time periods spanning one month each to build a model that performs well on future online data. We explored four directions to leverage temporal information which are rather easy to apply in production, i.e., i) instance weighting based on our assumptions about the task, ii) temporal finetuning, iii) learning temporal features and iv) building a temporally-invariant model. Our results on real-world SLU data covering two languages and three domains each show that temporal information can be leveraged to improve temporal generalization for SLU. While several of the explored methods provide consistent gains across all domain-language pairings, the best methods differ, as different domain datasets have different gradual and seasonal drifts. Moreover, our results indicate that methods, such as temporal finetuning, which have been previously shown to provide strong performance on small-scale academic tasks with longer time periods and mostly gradual temporal drifts, do not necessarily yield the best performance in our large-scale SLU task including seasonality patterns.

Acknowledgements

We would like to thank Yannick Versley and the NAACL reviewers for helpful feedback for revising the paper.

References

Isabela Albuquerque, Nikhil Naik, Junnan Li, Nitish Shirish Keskar, and Richard Socher. 2020. Improving out-of-distribution generalization via multi-task self-supervised pretraining. *CoRR*, abs/2003.13525.

Q. Chen, Z. Zhuo, and W. Wang. 2019. Bert for joint intent classification and slot filling. *arXiv:1902.10909*.

Shuguang Chen, Leonardo Neves, and Thamar Solorio. 2021. Mitigating temporal-drift: A simple approach to keep ner models crisp. In *SOCIALNLP*.

Jacob Devlin, Ming-Wei Chang, Kenton Lee, and Kristina Toutanova. 2019. BERT: Pre-training of deep bidirectional transformers for language understanding. In *Proceedings of the 2019 Conference of the North American Chapter of the Association for Computational Linguistics: Human Language Technologies, Volume 1 (Long and Short Papers)*, pages 4171–4186, Minneapolis, Minnesota. Association for Computational Linguistics.

Quynh Ngoc Thi Do and Judith Gaspers. 2019. Cross-lingual transfer learning for spoken language understanding. *Proceedings of the 2019 IEEE International Conference on Acoustics, Speech and Signal Processing, ICASSP*.

Yaroslav Ganin and Victor Lempitsky. 2015. Unsupervised domain adaptation by backpropagation.

Yaroslav Ganin, Evgeniya Ustinova, Hana Ajakan, Pascal Germain, Hugo Larochelle, François Laviolette, Mario Marchand, and Victor Lempitsky. 2016. Domain-adversarial training of neural networks. *J. Mach. Learn. Res.*, 17(1):2096–2030.

Jing Jiang and ChengXiang Zhai. 2007. Instance weighting for domain adaptation in NLP. In *Proceedings of the 45th Annual Meeting of the Association of Computational Linguistics*, pages 264–271, Prague, Czech Republic. Association for Computational Linguistics.

Young-Bum Kim, Karl Stratos, and Dongchan Kim. 2017. Adversarial adaptation of synthetic or stale data. In *Proceedings of the 55th Annual Meeting of the Association for Computational Linguistics (Volume 1: Long Papers)*, pages 1297–1307, Vancouver, Canada. Association for Computational Linguistics.

Angeliki Lazaridou, Adhiguna Kuncoro, Elena Gribovskaya, Devang Agrawal, Adam Liska, Tayfun Terzi, Mai Gimenez, Cyprien de Masson d'Autume, Sebastian Ruder, Dani Yogatama, Kris Cao, Tomás Kociský, Susannah Young, and Phil Blunsom. 2021. Mind the gap: Assessing temporal generalization in neural language models. *Proceedings of NeurIPS*, abs/2102.01951.

Tzu-Hsiang Lin, Yipeng Shi, Chentao Ye, Yang Fan, Weitong Ruan, Emre Barut, Wael Hamza, and

Chengwei Su. 2021. Contextual domain classification with temporal representations. In *Proceedings of the 2021 Conference of the North American Chapter of the Association for Computational Linguistics: Human Language Technologies: Industry Papers*, pages 41–48, Online. Association for Computational Linguistics.

Jan Lukes and Anders Søgaard. 2018. Sentiment analysis under temporal shift. In *Proceedings of the 9th Workshop on Computational Approaches to Subjectivity, Sentiment and Social Media Analysis*, pages 65–71, Brussels, Belgium. Association for Computational Linguistics.

Alan Ramponi and Barbara Plank. 2020. Neural unsupervised domain adaptation in NLP—A survey. In *Proceedings of the 28th International Conference on Computational Linguistics*, pages 6838–6855, Barcelona, Spain (Online). International Committee on Computational Linguistics.

Shruti Rijhwani and Daniel Preotiuc-Pietro. 2020. Temporally-informed analysis of named entity recognition. In *Proceedings of the 58th Annual Meeting of the Association for Computational Linguistics*, pages 7605–7617, Online. Association for Computational Linguistics.

Bernhard Schölkopf, Dominik Janzing, Jonas Peters, Eleni Sgouritsa, Kun Zhang, and Joris Mooij. 2012. On causal and anticausal learning. In *Proceedings of the 29th International Coference on International Conference on Machine Learning*, pages 459–466.

Anders Søgaard, Sebastian Ebert, Jasmijn Bastings, and Katja Filippova. 2021. We need to talk about random splits. In *Proceedings of the 16th Conference of the European Chapter of the Association for Computational Linguistics: Main Volume*, pages 1823–1832, Online. Association for Computational Linguistics.

Jindong Wang, Cuiling Lan, Chang Liu, Yidong Ouyang, and Tao Qin. 2021. Generalizing to unseen domains: A survey on domain generalization. In *IJCAI*.

An End-to-End Dialogue Summarization System for Sales Calls

Abedelkadir Asi[1], Song Wang[2], Roy Eisenstadt[1],Dean Geckt[1], Yarin Kuper[1], Yi Mao[2], Royi Ronen[1]
[1]Microsoft Dynamics,
[2]Microsoft Azure
{abeasi,sonwang,reisenstadt,t-deangeckt, yarinkuper,maoyi,royir}@microsoft.com

Abstract

Summarizing sales calls is a routine task performed manually by salespeople. We present a production system which combines generative models fine-tuned for customer-agent setting, with a human-in-the-loop user experience for an interactive summary curation process. We address challenging aspects of dialogue summarization task in a real-world setting including long input dialogues, content validation, lack of labeled data and quality evaluation. We show how GPT-3 can be leveraged as an offline data labeler to handle training data scarcity and accommodate privacy constraints in an industrial setting. Experiments show significant improvements by our models in tackling the summarization and content validation tasks on public datasets.

1 Introduction

An integral part of salespeople daily routine is summarizing sale calls. The summarization process aims to distill salient information from sales dialogues into succinct highlights, which are then leveraged by salespeople for productivity and coaching purposes. Manually curating a call summary is considered as one of the biggest time wasters for B2B sellers (Zhang et al., 2020). It distracts salespeople from nurturing the relationship with their next customer. Recently, this practice has become more demanding due to the emerging landscape of remote selling where virtual meetings become the new norm (Gavin et al., 2020).

Dialogue summarization induces a variety of unique challenges compared to summarization of documents such as news or scientific papers (Zhu and Penn, 2006). Information density is a key challenge in dialogue text; information is scattered over multiple utterances and participants, leading to frequent coreferences and topic alternations. Spoken dialogues, usually transcribed by speech recognition engines, impose additional challenges such as

Figure 1: A customer-agent call transcript with corresponding summary highlights. Challenges imposed by automatic speech recognition engine can be observed.

redundancies and misrecognized words. The length of these dialogues, e.g. $50K$ tokens in a 45 minutes call, imposes another challenge to state-of-the-art summarization models as it exceeds their input limits (Zhang et al., 2021). Figure 1 illustrates parts of the challenges imposed by automatically transcribed sales dialogues.

Developing a production system which is both fully automatic and agnostic to the input text genre is an extremely difficult task given the current state-of-the-art technology. To this end, we present a pragmatic solution that enables users to interactively edit machine-generated summary for customer-agent sales calls as appears in Figure 2. Our solution summarizes the call into a collection of abstractive highlights to accurately capture the various details of the call. The machine-human interaction is enabled through a designated human-in-the-loop user experience (Ostheimer et al., 2021). It enables users to modify the generated summaries, yet, the intervention is designed to be minimal so that the overall time consumption of users is significantly reduced.

Overall, our contributions are listed as follows:

Proceedings of NAACL-HLT 2022: Industry Track Papers, pages 45 - 53
July 10-15, 2022

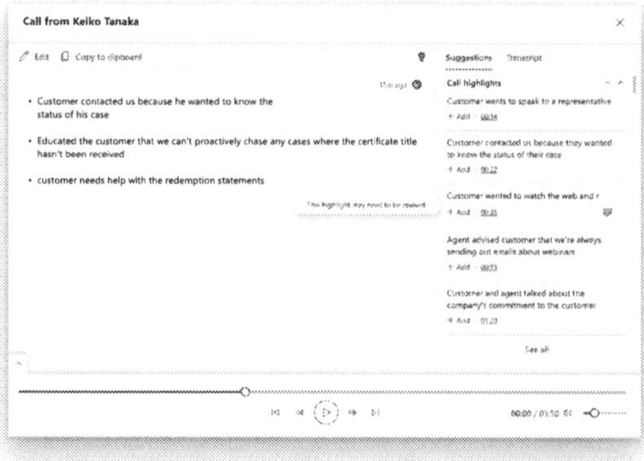

Figure 2: Illustrating human-in-the-loop experience which enables users to interactively handle summarization challenges by adding relevant summary highlights to the editing canvas and modify them, if necessary.

1. **Dialogue summarization system**. We introduce an innovative production summarization system for summarizing call transcripts with a human-in-the-loop setting. Our system uses an advanced summarization model to generate abstractive summaries for dialogues. Additionally, it employs a novel model for quantifying the coherence of the summaries to compensate for the summarization model limitations.

2. **GPT-3 as an offline label generator**. We present a technique for leveraging GPT-3 model to generate pseudo labels without the need to deploy and maintain it in production. This enables us to (i) efficiently generate labels in low-resource setting, (ii) distill GPT-3 knowledge into lighter models, and (iii) accommodate data privacy constraints.

3. **Custom evaluation metric**. We examine the importance of leveraging a comprehensive evaluation metric which takes into account various quality aspects of the generated summary. The metric is utilized to focus our efforts on potential candidate models during the development phase. The suggested metric goes beyond lexical overlap and help us validate that our production model is optimized for generating summaries which are fluent, relevant and factually reliable.

2 Related Work

Document Summarization Summarization methods can be categorized into two classes: extractive and abstractive. Early works focused on extractive methods (Hovy and Lin, 1997; Marcu, 1997), followed by rule-based approaches for abstractive summarization (Barzilay and Elhadad, 1997; Barzilay et al., 1999). Advancements in capabilities of deep neural models led to works such as Rush et al. (2015) where a seq-2-seq attention-based model is used for abstractive summarization. See et al. (2017) overcomes some of the former work's limitations by introducing a pointer generator network that has the ability to copy words from the source document. A major advancement in the field of deep neural models was the introduction of Transformer architecture (Vaswani et al., 2017), which is the basis for current state-of-the-art summarization approaches. Recently, several powerful Transformer-based models have been developed and showed remarkable results on various benchmark summarization tasks (Lewis et al., 2020; Zhang et al., 2019a; Raffel et al., 2020) .

Dialogue Summarization The task of dialogue summarization has been witnessing many commonalities as document summarization as well as new techniques for handling unique structures of various dialogue types. Early works in the domain suggested tackling the problem using extractive methods (Murray et al., 2005; Riedhammer et al., 2008). Shang et al. (2018) used a pure unsupervised graph-based method for keyword extraction and sentence compression. Goo and Chen (2018) proposed to explicitly model relationships between dialogue acts using attention-based sentence-gated mechanism. Chen and Yang (2020) extracted Transformer-based representations for different views of dialogues, conditioned on view representations, to generate summaries using a second Transformer. Zhu et al. (2020) presented a hierarchical Transformer architecture to encompass the structure of dialogues.

3 Method

While most existing methods summarize a call transcript as a single paragraph, our system provides a collection of sentences that summarize the entire dialogue in a chronological order. Given a call transcript, the system utilizes word embeddings to break the transcript into semantically coherent segments (Alemi and Ginsparg, 2015). Each segment is summarized independently capturing key information such as: customer's issue, agent's solution or the underlying topic of the discussion. Finally, the grammatical coherence of highlights is analyzed using a dedicated model before suggesting them to the user. Figure 3 provides a high-level overview of the system's flow.

Next, we introduce the key components of our dialogue summarization system in details.

3.1 DialogBART: Dialogue Summarization Model

Unlike general documents, conversation transcripts have unique structures associated with speakers and turns. In sales calls, participants can either be a customer or an agent and these roles impose a unique language style that can be leveraged by the model. Motivated by this observation, we propose an encoder-decoder model called DialogBART, which adapts the well-known BART (Lewis et al., 2020) model with additional embedding parameters to model both turns and speakers positions (Zhang et al., 2019c; Bao et al., 2020). For speaker embeddings, we introduce designated vectors to represent each speaker which can be easily generalized to multi-participant dialogues. Additionally, we leverage another set of vectors to model turn position embeddings. During inference, the model determines the speaker and turn indices by leveraging a special token that separates the dialogue's turns.

As shown in Figure 4, DialogBART's input is calculated as the sum of the corresponding token, position, speaker and turn position embeddings. These parameters are randomly initialized, however, the remaining parameters are initialized with weights from a pretrained[1] BART-like encoder-decoder models (Lewis et al., 2020; Shleifer and Rush, 2020). All these weights are further fine-tuned on dialogue summarization tasks.

3.2 Acceptability Validation

Despite the human-in-the-loop user experience, customers still expect high quality summaries which require minimal modifications by them. We propose a novel model that determines the quality of each summary highlight in terms of coherence, fluency and its acceptability in general.

Grammatical acceptability, a property of natural language text, implies whether a text is accepted or not as part of the language by a native speaker. The notion was widely investigated through vast work done in automatic detection of grammatical errors (Atwell, 1987; Chodorow and Leacock, 2000; Bigert and Knutsson, 2002; Wagner et al., 2007) and on acceptability judgment of neural networks (Lau et al., 2017; Warstadt et al., 2019). And yet, we are not aware of works that observe the acceptability of neural generated summaries for validation purposes. To determine a highlight's acceptability, we compute the perplexity of each highlight given by a Pretrained Language Model (PLM). This PLM is fine-tuned on summaries from DialogSum dataset (Chen et al., 2021a) and in-domain proprietary data in a traditional self-supervised manner. Recall that the perplexity of a sequence $W = w_0 w_1 ... w_n$ is defined as:

$$PP(W;\theta) = \sqrt[n]{\prod_{k=1}^{n} \frac{1}{p_\theta(w_k|w_0 w_1 ... w_{k-1})}} \quad (1)$$

where θ are the language model specific parameters and p_θ is the probability function corresponding to distribution over vocabulary tokens induced by the same model.

Based on the perplexity score, the system determines whether a given highlight should be filtered out, presented to the user, or presented with an indication that its revision may be required. Figure 2 illustrates how the system helps users focus their efforts on modifying borderline acceptable highlights based on the perplexity score.

4 GPT-3 as an Offline Labeler

Training a dialogue summarization model requires a large amount of labeled examples. Manually annotating data for abstractive summarization is a time-consuming and labor-intensive process, let alone the data privacy constraints. In this work, we provide a method to automatically pseudo label examples to overcome these challenges. We leverage GPT-3 model (Brown et al., 2020) to generate pseudo labels in a zero-shot setting for each call segment. GPT-3 is a large auto-regressive language model with 175 billion parameters that achieves promising results on various NLP tasks, including question answering. We treat the problem of label generation as a question answering task. For each segment, we concatenate a question-based prompt with the segment's content while expecting the GPT-3 model to provide the answer as appears

[1]https://huggingface.co/sshleifer/distilbart-xsum-12-3

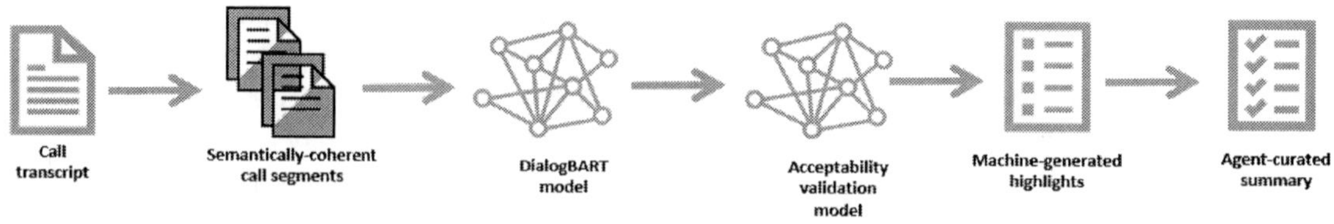

Figure 3: A high-level overview of the system's flow

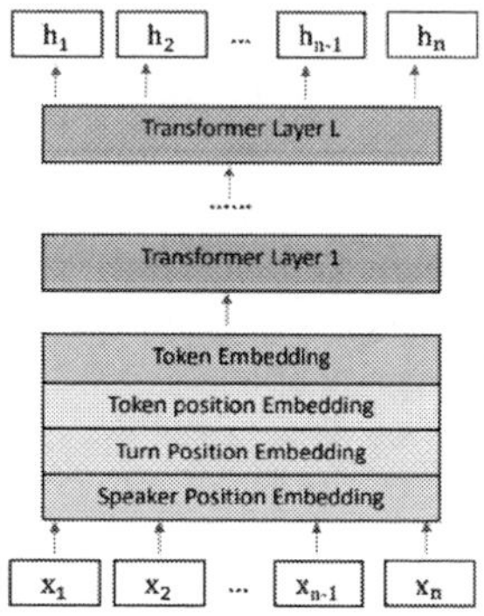

Figure 4: Input representation of DialogBART's encoder.

in Figure 5. These answers are used as pseudo labels for the corresponding segments. This formulation provides the flexibility of defining multiple questions per segment to summarize the segment from different perspectives. Finally, these pseudo labels, combined with proprietary human labeled data, are used to fine-tune the DialogBART model on conversational text.

```
Segment_text = <....>
GPT3_prompt = Segment_text + "Q: Why did the customer contacted the agent?\n"
Answer_prefix = "A: The customer contacted the agent in order to"
.................................................................................
GPT3_label = 'The customer contacted the agent in order to get a mortgage offer.'
```

Figure 5: Utilizing GPT-3 model to generate task-oriented summaries in an offline manner.

5 Custom Evaluation Metric

Common evaluation metrics for text summarization task, i.e. ROUGE and METEOR, have salient limitations as both metrics track lexical overlap between the summary and the original text. This kind of assessment falls short when the summary content perfectly aligns with a reference text but does not necessarily contain any lexical overlap, e.g. abstractive summaries.

In an industrial setting, one needs to consider various quality perspectives to guarantee that the summary's quality does not introduce productivity blockers for users or negatively affect business decisions. We introduce a custom evaluation metric, *SumSim*, that relies on lexical overlap as well as other quality aspects to ensure that summaries are fluent, coherent and factually reliable. SumSim aims to cover the following quality perspectives:

- **Coverage** - how many units from the reference text are covered by the summary (S_r)
- **Relevance** - measures semantic consistency between the summary and the reference text (S_b)
- **Informativeness** - how well it captures predefined keywords which are critical to the business (S_i)
- **Factuality** - how factual the summary is with respect to the original text (S_f)

Our metric uses *ROUGE-L* (Lin, 2004), *BertScore* (Zhang et al., 2019b), exact match of keywords and *FactCC* (Kryscinski et al., 2019) to capture the above quality aspects, respectively. The quality of a given summary is calculated as follows:

$$S_0 = \alpha \cdot S_i + \frac{1-\alpha}{2} \cdot (S_r + S_b) \qquad (2)$$

$$SumSim = \beta \cdot S_f + (1-\beta) \cdot S_0 \qquad (3)$$

where α and β are determined empirically based on the business scenario sensitivity.

6 Experimental Results

In this section we evaluate the performance of our proposed models on various datasets: DialogSum (Chen et al., 2021b), SAMSum (Gliwa et al., 2019), CoLA (Warstadt et al., 2019) and a proprietary data from the sales domain. We also show the potential of $SumSim$ metric compared to traditional evaluation metrics on the text summarization task. We use Huggingface Transformers (Wolf et al., 2020) as a training framework in all of our experiments.

6.1 DialogBART

In the following experiments we show the performance of DialogBART model in summarizing dialogues by examining two factors: (i) speaker/turn position embedding parameters, and (ii) data augmentation by GPT3-labeled data. For comparison purposes, we leverage two baseline models, *BART-large* and *distilBART*, which achieved state-of-the-art results on the summarization task (Lewis et al., 2020; Shleifer and Rush, 2020). All models, including the baseline models, were initially fine-tuned on XSum dataset (Narayan et al., 2018).

First, we examine the contribution of DialogBART's position embeddings on DialogSum and SAMSum datasets. All models were fine-tuned using the relevant training sets and evaluated on the test sets of the corresponding datasets. Table 1 shows that the suggested speakers/turns positions embeddings provide better results when compared to the baseline models.

Model	R1	R2	RL
		DialogSum	
distilBART	35.93	11.71	28.86
+ embeddings	**46.97**	**21.34**	**39.45**
BART-large	46.48	20.89	38.12
+ embeddings	**46.68**	**21.46**	**38.32**
		SAMSum	
distilBART	41.93	19.17	34.05
+ embeddings	**50.21**	**25.89**	**41.99**
BART-large	52.45	28.08	43.84
+ embeddings	**52.91**	**28.39**	**43.90**

Table 1: Effectiveness of DialogBART's speaker and turn embedding parameters using ROUGE metrics.

Second, we examine the implications of fine-tuning DialogBART model using different data types: human-labeled ($20K$ samples) and GPT3-labeled ($21K$ samples) data [2].

We evaluated the models on the test subset of: (i) DialogSum (500 samples), (ii) SAMSum (819 samples), and (iii) proprietary data (100 samples). The evaluation on the public datasets was conducted without fine-tuning the models on the corresponding training sets. Table 2 shows that DialogBART model outperforms the baseline models on public datasets even in out-of-domain setting. Additionally, results show that DialogBART fine-tuned on a mixture of human and pseudo labels outperforms its counterparts which were fine-tuned on either fully human labels or fully pseudo labels. We note that fine-tuning DialogBART on pseudo labels yielded higher ROUGE scores compared to human labels. This could be explained by human tendency to generate variable summaries which induces disagreements between human annotators (Clark et al., 2021). While a model fine-tuned on pseudo labels is less variable in its generations, a model fine-tuned using human data produces text that is, in turn, more variable and leads to less lexical overlap with test references as measured by ROUGE metrics[3] .

6.2 Acceptability Validation

We examine mutiple candidate PLMs with language model objective for this task. Initially we fine-tune the candidate PLM on summaries from DialogSum dataset and later on positive examples from the train subset of our internal acceptability benchmark consisting of in-domain summaries (100 samples). As candidate PLMs, we experiment with GPT-2 (Radford et al., 2019), DistilGPT-2 Sanh et al. (2019) and a RoBERTa encoder (Liu et al., 2019) with a language model head, *RoBERTa-LM*. Table 3 shows comparison results between the examined models and leaderboard competitors on the development set of CoLA as well as on the test subset of an internal benchmark.

We observe that all of the models trained using our method, in the bottom half of the table, which were not trained on CoLA data yield competitive results compared to models explicitly fine-tuned for the task, top half of Table 3. We also found that the RoBERTa-LM model achieves highest results on the internal set. Additionally, we fine-tuned DeBERTa, the strongest CoLA competitor, in a classification setting on the internal benchmark. We observe that results achieved by our models are significantly better. We hypothesize, this phenomenon is due to the fact that valid in-domain highlights, as generated by DialogBART, share a unique structure and can be viewed as forming a specific language which properties are better captured by a language model rather than a classifier.

[2]The anonymized data was collected and used based on a data sharing agreement with customers from different business domains. The human-labeled data is composed of anonymized agent's notes which were captured as part of the daily routine of the agents and not in a crowdsourcing setting.

[3]`https://github.com/google-research/google-research/tree/master/rouge`

Model	DialogSum			SAMSum			Proprietary		
	R1	**R2**	**RL**	**R1**	**R2**	**RL**	**R1**	**R2**	**RL**
distilBART	17.1	3.6	13.5	20.3	4.1	15.5	16.3	1.1	13.1
BART-large	17.7	3.9	13.7	24.9	5.5	18.9	16.9	1.5	13.3
DialogBART									
+ human	21.7	4.5	19.1	18.9	3.0	16.8	20.2	5.3	19.2
+ pseudo	28.0	5.9	22.2	26.0	5.1	20.6	28.5	10.5	24.8
+ human & pseudo	**33.5**	**9.0**	**24.5**	**30.4**	**7.5**	**22.4**	**33.1**	**13.0**	**26.3**

Table 2: Results of fine-tuning DialogBART model on human labels, pseudo labels and mixture of them.

Model	CoLA$_{dev}$	Internal
TinyBERT (Jiao et al., 2020)	54	-
Synthesizer (Tay et al., 2021)	53.3	-
DeBERTa (He et al., 2021)	**69.5**	54.5
DistilGPT-2	61.7	63.6
GPT-2	62.5	60.6
RoBERTa-LM	64.2	**66.7**

Table 3: Accuracy of acceptability validation models.

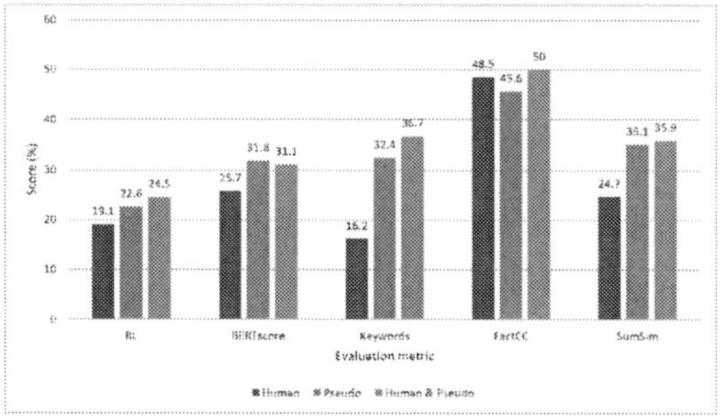

Figure 6: The capacity and limitation of various quality metrics. The bars' colors represent three different models which were fine-tuned on human labels, pseudo labels and a mixture of them, respectively.

6.3 Custom Evaluation Metric

We leverage the DialougSum test set to show the potential of the $SumSim$ metric. Table 2 shows that DialogBART fine-tuned on pseudo labels, M_{pseudo}, outperforms its counterpart that was fine-tuned on human labels, M_{human}. However, Figure 6 shows contradicting insights when comparing the performance of these two models by different quality aspects, i.e., lexical overlap (ROUGE) and factual reliability (factCC).

This observation emphasizes the need for non-standard quality measures for evaluating the performance of abstractive summarization models. This need is critical for customer-facing enterprise products where business decisions can be affected by the generated summary. Figure 6 shows the strengths and weaknesses of different quality metrics in evaluating three DialogBART variants. The M_{pseudo} model outperforms the M_{human} in all quality dimensions except of factuality. This observation is consistent with recent studies which report that large size language models are less truthful than their smaller peers (Lin et al., 2021).

7 Conclusions

In this paper, we present an end-to-end system for abstractive summarization of agent-customer calls. We employ a two-stage strategy to summarize long call transcripts by (i) splitting the dialogue into semantically coherent segments, and (ii) generating summaries using our DialogBART summarization model. We demonstrate how a pragmatic solution that combines a content selection model with a human-in-the-loop user experience can help compensate on generative models' limitations. We show how GPT-3 model can be leveraged as an offline data labeler to train lighter models and accommodate data privacy constraints. Experiments show that the introduced embedding parameters combined with fine-tuning on in-domain data significantly improve the quality of the generated summaries with respect to publicly available BART-based summarization models. We emphasize the need for non-standard evaluation metrics and show how common metrics fall short when evaluation of abstractive summaries is considered.

References

Alexander A. Alemi and Paul Ginsparg. 2015. Text segmentation based on semantic word embeddings. *CoRR*, abs/1503.05543.

Eric Steven Atwell. 1987. How to detect grammatical

errors in a text without parsing it. In *Third Conference of the European Chapter of the Association for Computational Linguistics*, Copenhagen, Denmark. Association for Computational Linguistics.

Siqi Bao, Huang He, Fan Wang, Hua Wu, and Haifeng Wang. 2020. PLATO: Pre-trained dialogue generation model with discrete latent variable. In *Proceedings of the 58th Annual Meeting of the Association for Computational Linguistics*, pages 85–96, Online. Association for Computational Linguistics.

Regina Barzilay and Michael Elhadad. 1997. Using lexical chains for text summarization. In *Intelligent Scalable Text Summarization*.

Regina Barzilay, Kathleen R. McKeown, and Michael Elhadad. 1999. Information fusion in the context of multi-document summarization. In *Proceedings of the 37th Annual Meeting of the Association for Computational Linguistics*, pages 550–557, College Park, Maryland, USA. Association for Computational Linguistics.

Johnny Bigert and Ola Knutsson. 2002. Robust error detection: A hybrid approach combining unsupervised error detection and linguistic knowledge. In *Proc. 2nd Workshop Robust Methods in Analysis of Natural language Data (ROMAND'02), Frascati, Italy*, pages 10–19. Citeseer.

Tom Brown, Benjamin Mann, Nick Ryder, Melanie Subbiah, Jared D Kaplan, Prafulla Dhariwal, Arvind Neelakantan, Pranav Shyam, Girish Sastry, Amanda Askell, Sandhini Agarwal, Ariel Herbert-Voss, Gretchen Krueger, Tom Henighan, Rewon Child, Aditya Ramesh, Daniel Ziegler, Jeffrey Wu, Clemens Winter, Chris Hesse, Mark Chen, Eric Sigler, Mateusz Litwin, Scott Gray, Benjamin Chess, Jack Clark, Christopher Berner, Sam McCandlish, Alec Radford, Ilya Sutskever, and Dario Amodei. 2020. Language models are few-shot learners. In *Advances in Neural Information Processing Systems*, volume 33, pages 1877–1901. Curran Associates, Inc.

Jiaao Chen and Diyi Yang. 2020. Multi-view sequence-to-sequence models with conversational structure for abstractive dialogue summarization. In *Proceedings of the 2020 Conference on Empirical Methods in Natural Language Processing (EMNLP)*, pages 4106–4118, Online. Association for Computational Linguistics.

Yulong Chen, Yang Liu, Liang Chen, and Yue Zhang. 2021a. DialogSum: A real-life scenario dialogue summarization dataset. In *Findings of the Association for Computational Linguistics: ACL-IJCNLP 2021*, pages 5062–5074, Online. Association for Computational Linguistics.

Yulong Chen, Yang Liu, Liang Chen, and Yue Zhang. 2021b. Dialogsumm: A real-life scenario dialogue summarization dataset. *CoRR*, abs/2105.06762.

Martin Chodorow and Claudia Leacock. 2000. An unsupervised method for detecting grammatical errors. In *ANLP*.

Elizabeth Clark, Tal August, Sofia Serrano, Nikita Haduong, Suchin Gururangan, and Noah A. Smith. 2021. All that's 'human' is not gold: Evaluating human evaluation of generated text. In *ACL/IJCNLP*.

Ryan Gavin, Liz Harrison, Candace Lun Plotkin, Dennis Spillecke, and Jennifer Stanley. 2020. The b2b digital inflection point: How sales have changed during covid-19.

Bogdan Gliwa, Iwona Mochol, Maciej Biesek, and Aleksander Wawer. 2019. Samsum corpus: A human-annotated dialogue dataset for abstractive summarization. *CoRR*, abs/1911.12237.

Chih-Wen Goo and Yun-Nung (Vivian) Chen. 2018. Abstractive dialogue summarization with sentence-gated modeling optimized by dialogue acts. *2018 IEEE Spoken Language Technology Workshop (SLT)*, pages 735–742.

Pengcheng He, Xiaodong Liu, Jianfeng Gao, and Weizhu Chen. 2021. Deberta: Decoding-enhanced bert with disentangled attention. In *International Conference on Learning Representations*.

Eduard Hovy and ChinYew Lin. 1997. Automated text summarization in SUMMARIST. In *Intelligent Scalable Text Summarization*.

Xiaoqi Jiao, Yichun Yin, Lifeng Shang, Xin Jiang, Xiao Chen, Linlin Li, Fang Wang, and Qun Liu. 2020. TinyBERT: Distilling BERT for natural language understanding. In *Findings of the Association for Computational Linguistics: EMNLP 2020*, pages 4163–4174, Online. Association for Computational Linguistics.

Wojciech Kryscinski, Bryan McCann, Caiming Xiong, and Richard Socher. 2019. Evaluating the factual consistency of abstractive text summarization. *CoRR*, abs/1910.12840.

Jey Han Lau, Alexander Clark, and Shalom Lappin. 2017. Grammaticality, acceptability, and probability: A probabilistic view of linguistic knowledge. *Cognitive science*, 41 5:1202–1241.

Mike Lewis, Yinhan Liu, Naman Goyal, Marjan Ghazvininejad, Abdelrahman Mohamed, Omer Levy, Veselin Stoyanov, and Luke Zettlemoyer. 2020. BART: Denoising sequence-to-sequence pre-training for natural language generation, translation, and comprehension. In *Proceedings of the 58th Annual Meeting of the Association for Computational Linguistics*, pages 7871–7880, Online. Association for Computational Linguistics.

Chin-Yew Lin. 2004. ROUGE: A package for automatic evaluation of summaries. In *Text Summarization Branches Out*, pages 74–81, Barcelona, Spain. Association for Computational Linguistics.

Stephanie C. Lin, Jacob Hilton, and Owain Evans. 2021. Truthfulqa: Measuring how models mimic human falsehoods. *ArXiv*, abs/2109.07958.

Yinhan Liu, Myle Ott, Naman Goyal, Jingfei Du, Mandar Joshi, Danqi Chen, Omer Levy, Mike Lewis, Luke Zettlemoyer, and Veselin Stoyanov. 2019. Roberta: A robustly optimized bert pretraining approach. *ArXiv*, abs/1907.11692.

Daniel Marcu. 1997. From discourse structures to text summaries. In *Intelligent Scalable Text Summarization*.

Gabriel Murray, Steve Renals, and Jean Carletta. 2005. Extractive summarization of meeting recordings. In *INTERSPEECH*.

Shashi Narayan, Shay B. Cohen, and Mirella Lapata. 2018. Don't give me the details, just the summary! Topic-aware convolutional neural networks for extreme summarization. In *Proceedings of the 2018 Conference on Empirical Methods in Natural Language Processing*, Brussels, Belgium.

Julia Ostheimer, Soumitra Chowdhury, and Sarfraz Iqbal. 2021. An alliance of humans and machines for machine learning: Hybrid intelligent systems and their design principles. *Technology in Society*, 66:101647.

Alec Radford, Jeffrey Wu, Rewon Child, David Luan, Dario Amodei, Ilya Sutskever, et al. 2019. Language models are unsupervised multitask learners. *OpenAI blog*, 1(8):9.

Colin Raffel, Noam Shazeer, Adam Roberts, Katherine Lee, Sharan Narang, Michael Matena, Yanqi Zhou, Wei Li, and Peter J. Liu. 2020. Exploring the limits of transfer learning with a unified text-to-text transformer. *Journal of Machine Learning Research*, 21(140):1–67.

Korbinian Riedhammer, Benoit Favre, and Dilek Hakkani-Tur. 2008. A keyphrase based approach to interactive meeting summarization. In *2008 IEEE Spoken Language Technology Workshop*, pages 153–156. IEEE.

Alexander M. Rush, Sumit Chopra, and Jason Weston. 2015. A neural attention model for abstractive sentence summarization. In *Proceedings of the 2015 Conference on Empirical Methods in Natural Language Processing*, pages 379–389, Lisbon, Portugal. Association for Computational Linguistics.

Victor Sanh, Lysandre Debut, Julien Chaumond, and Thomas Wolf. 2019. Distilbert, a distilled version of bert: smaller, faster, cheaper and lighter. *arXiv preprint arXiv:1910.01108*.

A. See, Peter J. Liu, and Christopher D. Manning. 2017. Get to the point: Summarization with pointer-generator networks. In *ACL*.

Guokan Shang, Wensi Ding, Zekun Zhang, Antoine Tixier, Polykarpos Meladianos, Michalis Vazirgiannis, and Jean-Pierre Lorré. 2018. Unsupervised abstractive meeting summarization with multi-sentence compression and budgeted submodular maximization. In *Proceedings of the 56th Annual Meeting of the Association for Computational Linguistics (Volume 1: Long Papers)*, pages 664–674, Melbourne, Australia. Association for Computational Linguistics.

Sam Shleifer and Alexander M. Rush. 2020. Pre-trained summarization distillation.

Yi Tay, Dara Bahri, Donald Metzler, Da-Cheng Juan, Zhe Zhao, and Che Zheng. 2021. Synthesizer: Rethinking self-attention in transformer models. *ArXiv*, abs/2005.00743.

Ashish Vaswani, Noam Shazeer, Niki Parmar, Jakob Uszkoreit, Llion Jones, Aidan N Gomez, Łukasz Kaiser, and Illia Polosukhin. 2017. Attention is all you need. In *Advances in neural information processing systems*, pages 5998–6008.

Joachim Wagner, Jennifer Foster, and Josef van Genabith. 2007. A comparative evaluation of deep and shallow approaches to the automatic detection of common grammatical errors. In *Proceedings of the 2007 Joint Conference on Empirical Methods in Natural Language Processing and Computational Natural Language Learning (EMNLP-CoNLL)*, pages 112–121, Prague, Czech Republic. Association for Computational Linguistics.

Alex Warstadt, Amanpreet Singh, and Samuel R. Bowman. 2019. Neural network acceptability judgments. *Transactions of the Association for Computational Linguistics*, 7:625–641.

Thomas Wolf, Lysandre Debut, Victor Sanh, Julien Chaumond, Clement Delangue, Anthony Moi, Pierric Cistac, Tim Rault, Remi Louf, Morgan Funtowicz, Joe Davison, Sam Shleifer, Patrick von Platen, Clara Ma, Yacine Jernite, Julien Plu, Canwen Xu, Teven Le Scao, Sylvain Gugger, Mariama Drame, Quentin Lhoest, and Alexander Rush. 2020. Transformers: State-of-the-art natural language processing. In *Proceedings of the 2020 Conference on Empirical Methods in Natural Language Processing: System Demonstrations*, pages 38–45, Online. Association for Computational Linguistics.

Jingqing Zhang, Yao Zhao, Mohammad Saleh, and Peter J. Liu. 2019a. Pegasus: Pre-training with extracted gap-sentences for abstractive summarization.

Tianyi Zhang, Varsha Kishore, Felix Wu, Kilian Q. Weinberger, and Yoav Artzi. 2019b. Bertscore: Evaluating text generation with BERT. *CoRR*, abs/1904.09675.

Xinyuan Zhang, Ruiyi Zhang, Manzil Zaheer, and Amr Ahmed. 2020. Unsupervised abstractive dialogue summarization for tete-a-tetes. *CoRR*, abs/2009.06851.

Yizhe Zhang, Siqi Sun, Michel Galley, Yen-Chun Chen, Chris Brockett, Xiang Gao, Jianfeng Gao, Jingjing Liu, and Bill Dolan. 2019c. Dialogpt: Large-scale generative pre-training for conversational response generation. *arXiv preprint arXiv:1911.00536*.

Yusen Zhang, Ansong Ni, Tao Yu, Rui Zhang, Chenguang Zhu, Budhaditya Deb, Asli Celikyilmaz, Ahmed Hassan Awadallah, and Dragomir Radev. 2021. An exploratory study on long dialogue summarization: What works and what's next. In *Findings of the Association for Computational Linguistics: EMNLP 2021*, pages 4426–4433, Punta Cana, Dominican Republic. Association for Computational Linguistics.

Chenguang Zhu, Ruochen Xu, Michael Zeng, and Xuedong Huang. 2020. A hierarchical network for abstractive meeting summarization with cross-domain pretraining. In *Findings of the Association for Computational Linguistics: EMNLP 2020*, pages 194–203, Online. Association for Computational Linguistics.

Xiaodan Zhu and Gerald Penn. 2006. Summarization of spontaneous conversations. In *Ninth International Conference on Spoken Language Processing*.

Controlled Data Generation via Insertion Operations for NLU

Manoj Kumar[1], **Haidar Khan**[1], **Yuval Merhav**[1], **Wael Hamza**[1]
Anna Rumshisky[1,2] **Rahul Gupta**[1]
[1]Alexa AI, Amazon
[2]Department of Computer Science, University of Massachusetts Lowell
{abithm,khhaida,merhavy,waelhamz,gupra}@amazon.com
arum@cs.uml.edu

Abstract

Use of synthetic data is rapidly emerging as a realistic alternative to manually annotating real data for industry-scale model building. Manual data annotation is slow, expensive and not preferred for meeting customer privacy expectations. Further, commercial natural language applications are required to support continuously evolving features as well as newly added experiences. To address these requirements, we propose a targeted synthetic data generation technique by inserting tokens into a given semantic signature. The generated data are used as additional training samples in the tasks of intent classification and named entity recognition. We evaluate on a real-world voice assistant dataset, and using only 33% of the available training set, we achieve the same accuracy as training with all available data. Further, we analyze the effects of data generation across varied real-world applications and propose heuristics that improve the task performance further.

1 Introduction

One of the common challenges to deploying natural language understanding (NLU) techniques at scale in commercial applications is the necessity for continuous annotation of user data. Models can then be re-trained and updated to capture new usage patterns. This process is expensive, labor intensive, and time-consuming.

At an age when user privacy is becoming the focus of increased concern in all AI applications, manual review of user data normally required for such annotation becomes highly undesirable. Consequently, multiple initiatives are undertaken towards minimizing the amount of human annotations needed for training NLU models.

Data augmentation (DA) refers to strategies that aim at increasing the diversity of training samples without explicitly collecting new data. In this work, we present a generative model that is used to generate labeled synthetic data. Given a set of utterance templates [1] that we construct from a limited amount of labeled data, our goal is to generate synthetic utterances and augment the original (reduced) training data, with the objective of improving the model robustness and performance.

We focus on the special case where the synthetic data must retain a specific fine-grained interpretation of the original utterance, such as token-level annotation. For example, we would like to control the composition of entities (and their combinations) in the training data when expanding to new features while maintaining NLU model performance. In our proposed approach, we control the desired annotation by re-framing the generation process as insertion rather than left-to-right generation. We preserve the desired entities in the synthetic example by including them in the model's input during generation and introduce methods to explicitly prevent entity corruption during the generation process.

Our contributions are as follows: (i) We propose a novel synthetic data generation technique using insertion transformers that allows for token-level control over the generated synthetic utterance. (ii) We demonstrate the usefulness of the proposed approach for NLU model building. Our model which is trained using a limited fraction of user data combined with synthetic data matches the performance of a model trained with the entire real data. (iii) We apply domain-specific heuristics to improve the quality of synthetic data, which would further improving task performance.

2 Background

Our NLU models are responsible for interpreting the corresponding domain, intent and actionable slots of customer utterances. These categories are modularized, i.e., utterances belonging to a partic-

[1]For the purposes of this work, we define a *template* as the sequence of intent label, slot labels and slot values.

Proceedings of NAACL-HLT 2022: Industry Track Papers, pages 54 - 61

Input Template

PlayMusicIntent AlbumName(*shake it off*) ArtistName(*taylor swift*)

Generated Output

PlayMusicIntent [**can you play**] AlbumName(*shake it off*) [**by**] ArtistName(*taylor swift*)[**now**]

Figure 1: An input template to GIT with its generated labeled utterance. The output maintains the original template but inserts new phrases (shown within brackets) between the slots.

ular domain (e.g., Books) are supported by a specific set of intents (e.g., PlayBook) and actionable slots (e.g., BookName), and served by the domain-specific intent classification (IC) and named entity recognition (NER) models. In this work we experiment and evaluate IC and NER tasks across multiple domains. We explore the use of synthetic data as an additional source for training the models of these domains.

While a number of data augmentation techniques for natural language have been proposed, ranging from token-level perturbations (Wei and Zou, 2019) to paraphrase generation (Chen et al., 2020; Jolly et al., 2020) and auto-regressive models (Ding et al., 2020; Malandrakis et al., 2019; Anaby-Tavor et al., 2020; Kumar et al., 2020), these techniques can not be directly applied to token labeling tasks such as NER. Specifically, synthetic data generation for NER involves two additional challenges: (1) **Label preservation**: producing correct token-level annotation in the generated utterances, e.g., in Figure 1 "shake it" may be incorrectly labeled as *AlbumName* instead of "shake it off" (2) **Entity control**: controlling slot-type and slot-values in the synthetic data. e.g., we would like to generate requests for other artists and albums. The first challenge is typically addressed by a label projection approach (Ehrmann et al., 2011) or semi-supervised learning, however this is known to introduce errors in the resulting annotation. To handle the second challenge, methods such as (Jolly et al., 2020; Malandrakis et al., 2019) input the desired slot types and values to the model but cannot force the generator to include these slots in the synthetic example.

3 Methodology

3.1 Synthetic Data Augmentation with GIT

Our approach, dubbed generative insertion transformer (GIT) is based on non-autoregressive insertion transformer model introduced in (Stern et al., 2019). Previously, it has been shown that these models can be used effectively for generating annotations; given an utterance generate the correct NLU interpretation (intent and slots) using insertion operations (Zhu et al., 2020). In this work, we extend the idea to solve the inverse NLU problem; given a template produce a valid labeled utterance that matches the annotation (Figure 1).

The insertion transformer is a generative model in which the decoder generates a sequence by inserting tokens between previously generated tokens. We adopt this idea to insert carrier tokens (token without an entity label) between the labels in the template in an iterative manner. (An example of template is provided in Figure 1, and the insertion process is illustrated in Figure 2). The insertion process at each position in the utterance is independent of every other position and stops when the EOS token is generated at all positions, resulting in a fully annotated synthetic utterance that can be directly augmented with real data for model building purpose. We now describe the stages involved in building and deploying GIT.

Pre-Training: We pre-train GIT using BERT encoder (Devlin et al., 2019) and KERMIT (Chan et al., 2019) objective on an unsupervised LM task: given a sentence with masked tokens, GIT is trained to insert the masked tokens. We test two configurations (1) Pre-training using only English Wikipedia[2] (**wiki**), and (2) Pre-training using an internal corpus of 800M unlabeled utterances randomly sampled from de-identified Alexa requests, using English Wikipedia pre-trained models as initialization (**wiki+in-domain**).

Fine-Tuning: We fine-tune the pre-trained GIT models for each domain (e.g., Books) using annotated real data (reduced). Table 1 shows a few data samples and derived templates. For each utterance, we provide the template as model input and the complete (annotated) utterance as output. During training, at each insertion slot, we have multiple candidate tokens from the ground truth unlike autoregressive generation which entails a single token per generation step. For example, in Figure 2 the tokens "can", "you" and "play" can be inserted between "PlayMusicIntent" and "Album(". Hence, we cannot use the traditional cross-entropy loss

[2] `https://en.wikipedia.org`

Table 1: Representative examples for labeled utterances and derived templates from 3 domains. Carrier tokens (slot label "|Other") are removed from the labeled utterance and intent names added to create a template

ID	Domain	Intent	Labeled Utterance	Derived Template
1	Recipes	SearchRecipe	find|Other breakfast|Meal recipe|InstructionType please|Other	breakfast|Meal recipe|InstructionType
2	Books	NavigateBooks	skip|Other to|Other chapter|SectionName one|SectionNumber	chapter|SectionName one|SectionNumber
3	Home	GetSettingsDetails	what's|Other the|Other heat|Setting set|Other at|Other	heat|Setting

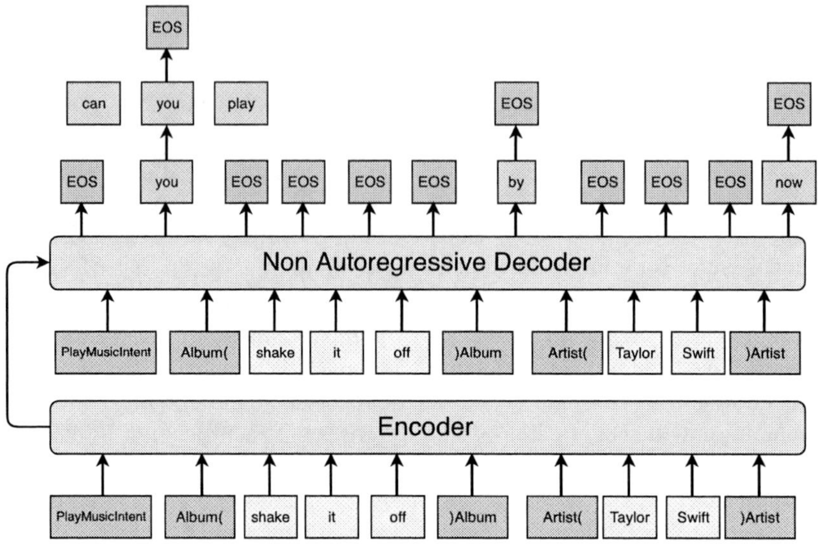

Figure 2: A generation example with GIT. An utterance template is provided as input to the decoder. The decoder generates one or more (carrier) tokens between every two input tokens and stops the generation process when the End of Sequence (EOS) token is generated (we set maximum number of non-EOS generated tokens to three). The model learns to only generate EOS tokens within entity tokens (e.g., "shake it off") but this is not enforced. We discard generated examples when it is not the case (<0.01%).

and instead compute KL divergence between the predicted token distribution and the ground truth distribution at each position, and use the mean divergence over all insertion slots as the training loss (Zhu et al., 2020). The ground truth distribution sets non-candidate token probabilities to 0 and uniformly weighs all candidate token probabilities.

Generation: To generate synthetic data for NLU, we first construct a template that contains the desired intent, slot types, and slot values for the synthetic example. This priming sequence is provided as an input to the decoder, which inserts carrier tokens in an iterative manner to form a coherent utterance. The generation process is shown in Figure 2 and addresses both the label projection and entity control challenges. Templates used in inference are constructed from the reduced real data.

4 Experimental Setup

In order to study the effectiveness of synthetically generated data, we evaluate NLU model performance in reduced data regime. For each domain, we build multiple IC-NER models using all real data, a reduced set of real data and combination of real and synthetic data. All models within a domain share the same training hyper-parameters, including architecture and encoder. They differ only in training data composition. Similar to (Ding et al., 2020), we limit the focus of this work to synthetic data generation and defer hyper-parameter optimization to future work. We use Apache MXNet (Chen et al., 2015) to build both GIT and IC-NER models in this work.

Full: This baseline is trained using all real data and default training hyper-parameters for each domain. This setup reflects the current performance of NLU models in production and serves as an estimate for lower bound in error metric for all other models.

Reduced: We train another baseline using **one-third** of real data. Our reduction of two-thirds of the data is motivated by a privacy control feature allowing customers to delete their data. Given the trends, we estimated a worst case drop of 67% in our annotated data before it can be refilled with more human annotations. To simulate this worst case scenario, we randomly downsample across all utterances.

Duplicate: To reduce the impact of hyper-parameters we also train a model with the **Reduced** set duplicated to reach the full training size. We refer to it as **Duplicate**. We note that duplication has been used as a baseline for data augmentation in (Estabrooks et al., 2004; Kumar et al., 2019; Wei and Zou, 2019)

EDA: Easy Data Augmentation (EDA) consists of four simple operations: synonym replacement, random insertion, random swap, and random deletion. EDA has shown to be a strong baseline, out-performing complex model-based baselines particularly for small datasets (Wei and Zou, 2019). Similar to GIT, EDA can provide control and flexibility over the type of data generated, which is a key requirement from our users.

GIT: (ours). We use the **Reduced** set to fine-tune domain-specific GIT models and also as input templates during inference, with fixed hyper-parameters. During inference, we control the number of generated synthetic utterances which is augmented with **Reduced** set. We test two configurations: in **GIT_50**, the fraction of synthetic to real data is set to 50% while with **GIT_200**, the fraction of synthetic to real data is set to 200%. In the former, synthetic data size is kept smaller than real data while in latter, we add enough synthetic data to compensate for removed data.

4.1 Confidence filtering of synthetic data selection

Not all synthetic utterances may be useful for model training, such as duplicates of real utterances, semantically incorrect samples ("play album" instead of "buy album" for BuyAlbumIntent), etc. A handful of previous approaches have investigated filtering synthetic utterances before augmentation: using influence functions (Yang et al., 2020), reinforcement learning (Bhattarai et al., 2020), etc. In this work, we use the confidence score obtained using **Reduced** models to filter synthetic utterances. Assuming M represents **Reduced** model, we predict labels $\hat{y}$ for a synthetic utterance $\mathbf{x}$ using M, i.e

$$\hat{y}, c = M(\mathbf{x}) \quad (1)$$

Here, c is a confidence score derived as the unweighted mean of IC and NER scores and scaled to (0,1). We select $\mathbf{x}$ for augmentation if (i) $\hat{y} = y$ and (ii) $c \in (t_{low}, t_{high})$, where y is the ground truth label of $\mathbf{x}$ available from its template, and t_{low} and t_{high} are threshold hyper-parameters >0.5. Hence, we select those synthetic samples which are correctly labeled by M and avoid incorrect utterances (t_{low}) and duplicates (t_{high}). We consider $y = \hat{y}$ if the predicted intent label and all slot labels exactly match with the ground truth.

4.2 Evaluation

We evaluate the models on each domain's test set. For each model, we use weighted semantic error rate (SemER$_w$ Su et al. (2018)) to jointly evaluate IC-NER performance. SemER is defined as the ratio of Leveshtein distance between reference and hypothesis labels, and total count of reference labels. We concatenate the intent and slot labels to arrive at an utterance-level label. We weigh each domain's SemER by its test utterance count and report the mean SemER (SemER$_w$) for each model. We report relative performance gains with respect to **Full** baseline: we only report relative performance as we are not allowed to publish absolute performance numbers.

5 Results

Table 2 shows relative SemER$_w$ across different methods (lower is better). We can see that SemER$_w$ for **Reduced** model increases 2.42%. Interestingly, Sports domain improves in SemER (>5%) when reducing real data (**Reduced** vs **Full**; Figure 3): We found that Sports is a relatively smaller domain and tends to have noisier training data (Section 6.3). While **Duplicate** and **EDA** do not improve over **Reduced**, **GIT_50 (wiki+in-domain)** achieves the same error rate as training with all available data. Not surprisingly, using in-domain data during pre-training **GIT_N (wiki+in-domain)** improves results significantly over pre-training only on Wikipedia **GIT_N (wiki)**.

6 Discussion

While the overall regression appears modest, there exists significant variation among domains (Figure 3). We can see that GIT improves SemER only among certain domains when compared to **Reduced** (e.g., Music but not Sports). In general, domains with relatively higher traffic exhibit moderate regression (<5%). Recall that for simplicity we use the same hyper-parameters across all domains.

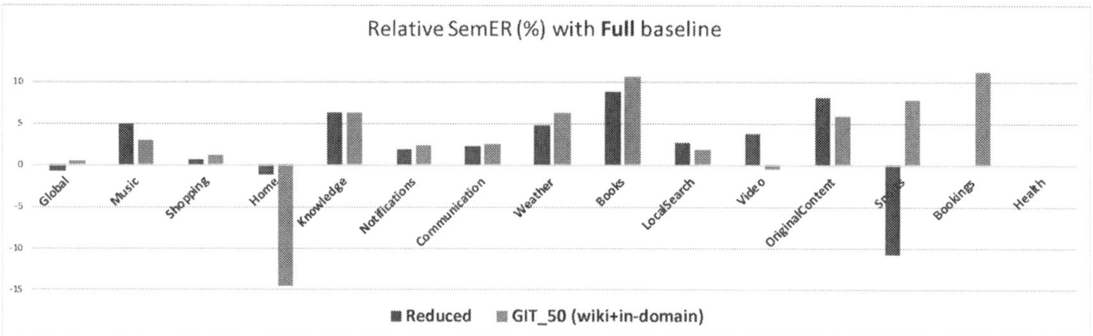

Figure 3: Relative change in per-domain SemER comparing **Reduced** and **GIT_50_wiki+in-domain** to **Full**. Domains are sorted according to decreasing traffic volume

Table 2: Relative SemER$_w$ (weighted mean, by traffic volume) for baselines and GIT models for different pre-training corpora and synthetic data sizes. All results are reported relative to **Full** baseline

Full	Reduced	Duplicate	EDA	GIT_200 (wiki)	GIT_50 (wiki)	GIT_200 (wiki+in-domain)	GIT_50 (wiki+in-domain)
0%	+2.38%	+2.57%	+3.07%	+9.94%	+1.27%	+2.66%	**-0.05%**

6.1 Value of Synthetic Data

While we observe that **GIT_50 (wiki)** and **GIT_50 (wiki+in-domain)** configurations provide overall improvements over **Reduced**, we investigate whether data reduction effects are related to improvements with synthetic data addition. Specifically, using the null hypothesis that the relative SemER (%) between data reduction (**Full** $\rightarrow$ **Reduced**) and data addition (**Reduced** $\rightarrow$ **GIT**) are not related, we estimate the Pearson correlation between them using two-tailed t-distribution. In Table 3, we present the correlation coefficients (**r**) along with significance information. We notice in all configurations that a domain's SemER improvement with added synthetic data is inversely proportional to the regression with data reduction. In other words, domains which are most affected by data reduction benefit from adding synthetic data and vice versa, irrespective of the source and quantity of synthetic data.

Table 3: Pearson correlation coefficient ($p < 0.01$**) for domain-level relative SemER between (Full $\rightarrow$ Reduced) and (Reduced $\rightarrow$ GIT)

Method	**r**
GIT_200 (wiki)	-0.711**
GIT_50 (wiki)	-0.751**
GIT_200 (wiki+in-domain)	-0.234
GIT_50 (wiki+in-domain)	-0.700**

6.2 Confidence Filtering

Among domains where **GIT_50 (wiki+in-domain)** performance is worse than **Reduced**, we notice that there exist real utterances which lack the appropriate context necessary for GIT inference and are more error-prone, such as those without an entity slot (E.g., "stop|Other", "turn|Other off|Other"). As described in Section 4.1, we implement confidence filtering for the top 5 domains with highest SemER degradations for GIT (Figure 3) and present results in Table 5. Based on empirical observations, we choose (t_{low}, t_{high}) = (0.5, 0.85). We find that confidence-filtering results in consistent SemER improvements across domains compared to **GIT**, with upto 12.85% relative improvement for Bookings. When combined with confidence filtering, **GIT** marginally improves over the **Reduced** baseline for these 5 domains.

6.3 Synthetic Data Diversity

In this section, we analyze the generated synthetic data using quantitative metrics and qualitative examples. We use the distinct-n metric (introduced by Li et al. (2016)), which measures the fraction of unique n-grams to the n-gram count (higher metric indicates more diverse utterances). We compare distinct-2 and distinct-3 metrics between real and synthetic utterances for domains with highest (Bookings, Books, Sports) and lowest (Home, Video, Health) relative SemER in Table 6. We notice a clear decrease in token diversity in synthetic data among former domains and increase in token diversity among latter domains. This hints at the usefulness of distinct-n as a measure for predicting value of synthetic data for IC-NER model building.

Table 4: Some representative utterance templates and generated synthetic utterances. Tokens in orange represent carrier tokens which are replaced by tokens in blue during synthetic data generation by GIT

<table>
<tr><th>Domain</th><th>ID</th><th>Real utterance</th><th>Synthetic utterance</th></tr>
<tr><td rowspan="4">Video</td><td>1</td><td>youtube|AppName denis|VideoName daily|VideoName half|VideoName hour|VideoName song|MediaType</td><td>search|Other youtube|AppName for|Other denis|VideoName daily|VideoName half|VideoName hour|VideoName song|MediaType</td></tr>
<tr><td>2</td><td>youtube|AppName baby|VideoName car|VideoName</td><td>search|Other on|Other youtube|AppName for|Other baby|VideoName car|VideoName</td></tr>
<tr><td>3</td><td>find|Other pineola|VideoName lucinda|ArtistName william|ArtistName</td><td>search|Other for|Other pineola|VideoName by|Other lucinda|ArtistName william|ArtistName</td></tr>
<tr><td>4</td><td>show|VisualModeTrigger the|Other video|MediaType nursery|VideoName rhymes|VideoName</td><td>show|VisualModeTrigger me|Other a|Other video|MediaType of|Other nursery|VideoName rhymes|VideoName</td></tr>
<tr><td rowspan="3">Sports</td><td>1</td><td>can|Other you|Other give|Other me|Other the|Other sports|Other news|Other of|Other the|Other day|Other</td><td>tell|Other me|Other a|Other sports|Other updates|Other</td></tr>
<tr><td>2</td><td>can|Other you|Other give|Other me|Other the|Other latest|SortType sports|Other headlines|Other</td><td>what's|Other the|Other latest|SortType in|Other sports|Other update|Other</td></tr>
<tr><td>3</td><td>what's|Other the|Other latest|SortType in|Other the|Other sports|Other program|Other</td><td>what's|Other the|Other latest|SortType in|Other sports|Other update|Other</td></tr>
</table>

Table 5: Relative SemER (compared with **Full**) results using confidence-filtered synthetic utterances for 5 domains with highest regressions

Domain	Reduced	GIT	+ Conf. filtering
Bookings	0%	11.1%	-3.1%
Books	8.8%	10.5%	7.7%
Sports	-10.8%	7.8%	-1.3%
Weather	4.8%	6.3%	3.8%
Knowledge	6.3%	6.3%	6.3%
Total (Weighted)	6.3%	8.4%	5.6%

Table 6: Quantitative estimate of n-gram diversity of real and synthetic utterances as measured with distinct-2 and distinct-3 metrics for each domain. Relative diversity is provided for comparison purposes.

Domain	Distinct-2			Distinct-3		
	Real	Syn	Rel(%)	Real	Syn	Rel(%)
Bookings	0.119	0.108	-9.1	0.194	0.174	-10.4
Books	0.097	0.055	-43.9	0.197	0.116	-40.81
Sports	0.024	0.006	-77.26	0.047	0.010	-78.27
Health	0.076	0.086	13.23	0.139	0.154	10.95
Video	0.072	0.095	31.42	0.158	0.188	18.88
Home	0.018	0.021	18.47	0.045	0.050	10.33

We further discuss two domains which show the highest magnitude of diversity change.

Sports: Similar to typical real-world tasks, Sports domain contains class-imbalanced training data (ranging from $\mathcal{O}(10^2)$ to $\mathcal{O}(10^4)$ samples per intent), ambiguous short utterances ($\sim$65% of utterances in a minority intent contain a single-token and repeat in a majority intent) and 95.3% of utterances do not contain any tokens with slot labels. In addition to reduced token diversity, these factors contribute to shorter synthetic utterances on average (Mean utterance length: real = 3.73 vs syn = 2.32). Representative examples are provided in Table 4: utterances 2 and 3 result in the same synthetic utterance even though their tokens are different.

Video: From Table 4, we observe that GIT enhances the semantics of real utterances by appropriate carrier token insertions, specifically for utterances that search for video titles. In example 1, GIT inserts the tokens "search" and "for" which convey the meaning of the utterance more clearly and disambiguate tokens representing the application and video title. Similarly, in example 3 GIT inserts the correct preposition "by" between "peneola" and "lucinda william" using their slot label information. We hypothesize that such synthetic utterances are a better representation of token-level labels when compared to corresponding real utterances, and better assist NLU model building.

7 Limitations

Since our primary focus in this work was developing insertion transformers for DA, we did not explore extensive hyper-parameter optimization while building IC-NER models using combination of real and synthetic data. For example, we observed that adding the same fraction of synthetic data results in significant performance variations across domains, suggesting that per-domain parameter optimization may be yield improved performance.

8 Conclusion

We demonstrated DA using GIT as a feasible data generation technique to mitigate reduced annotation volumes for IC and NER tasks. We showed that NLU models trained on 33% real data and synthetic data perform similar to models trained on full real data. Further, on domains with highest SemER regressions we improved the quality of synthetic data by filtering them with model confidence scores. Among domains which benefit from synthetic data, we showed that appropriate carrier token insertion enhances utterances' semantics and their value as training samples. In the future, we would like to explore data generation with entities replaced through knowledge base sampling. Such finer control over entities better supports new feature expansion and enhances customer privacy.

9 Ethical Considerations

Risk: In this work, we have not controlled the entities in utterance templates during generation. This presents a risk of private information propagating into the synthetic data. We note that the entities themselves are not introduced during generation, but carried over from real data. As mentioned in Section 8, entity control methods such as considered in the present work with GIT can prevent such identifiable information from being exposed to model training.

Data Protection: There are multiple guardrails to safeguard customer data in our organization. In addition, we remove all metadata and personal identifiable information (PII) from utterances before using them for NU model building and synthetic data generation with GIT in this work.

References

Ateret Anaby-Tavor, Boaz Carmeli, Esther Goldbraich, Amir Kantor, George Kour, Segev Shlomov, Naama Tepper, and Naama Zwerdling. 2020. Do not have enough data? Deep Learning to the rescue! In *Proceedings of the AAAI Conference on Artificial Intelligence*, volume 34, pages 7383–7390.

Binod Bhattarai, Seungryul Baek, Rumeysa Bodur, and Tae-Kyun Kim. 2020. Sampling strategies for GAN synthetic data. In *2020 IEEE International Conference on Acoustics, Speech and Signal Processing (ICASSP)*, pages 2303–2307.

William Chan, Nikita Kitaev, Kelvin Guu, Mitchell Stern, and Jakob Uszkoreit. 2019. Kermit: Generative insertion-based modeling for sequences. *ArXiv*, abs/1906.01604.

Hannah Chen, Yangfeng Ji, and David Evans. 2020. Finding Friends and flipping frenemies: Automatic paraphrase dataset augmentation using graph theory. In *Findings of the Association for Computational Linguistics: EMNLP 2020*, pages 4741–4751. Association for Computational Linguistics.

Tianqi Chen, Mu Li, Yutian Li, Min Lin, Naiyan Wang, Minjie Wang, Tianjun Xiao, Bing Xu, Chiyuan Zhang, and Zheng Zhang. 2015. Mxnet: A flexible and efficient machine learning library for heterogeneous distributed systems. *CoRR*, abs/1512.01274.

Jacob Devlin, Ming-Wei Chang, Kenton Lee, and Kristina Toutanova. 2019. Bert: Pre-training of deep bidirectional transformers for language understanding. In *Proceedings of the 2019 Conference of the North American Chapter of the Association for Computational Linguistics: Human Language Technologies*.

Bosheng Ding, Linlin Liu, Lidong Bing, Canasai Kruengkrai, Thien Hai Nguyen, Shafiq Joty, Luo Si, and Chunyan Miao. 2020. DAGA: Data augmentation with a generation approach for low-resource tagging tasks. In *Proceedings of the 2020 Conference on Empirical Methods in Natural Language Processing (EMNLP)*, pages 6045–6057. Association for Computational Linguistics.

Maud Ehrmann, Marco Turchi, and Ralf Steinberger. 2011. Building a multilingual named entity-annotated corpus using annotation projection. In *Proceedings of the International Conference Recent Advances in Natural Language Processing 2011*, pages 118–124.

Andrew Estabrooks, Taeho Jo, and Nathalie Japkowicz. 2004. A multiple resampling method for learning from imbalanced data sets. *Computational intelligence*, 20(1):18–36.

Shailza Jolly, Tobias Falke, Caglar Tirkaz, and Daniil Sorokin. 2020. Data-efficient paraphrase generation to bootstrap intent classification and slot labeling for new features in task-oriented dialog systems. In *Proceedings of the 28th International Conference on Computational Linguistics: Industry Track*, pages 10–20, Online. International Committee on Computational Linguistics.

Varun Kumar, Ashutosh Choudhary, and Eunah Cho. 2020. Data augmentation using pre-trained transformer models. In *Proceedings of the 2nd Workshop on Life-long Learning for Spoken Language Systems*, pages 18–26. Association for Computational Linguistics.

Varun Kumar, Hadrien Glaude, Cyprien de Lichy, and Wlliam Campbell. 2019. A closer look at feature space data augmentation for few-shot intent classification. In *Proceedings of the 2nd Workshop on Deep Learning Approaches for Low-Resource NLP (DeepLo 2019)*, pages 1–10. Association for Computational Linguistics.

Jiwei Li, Michel Galley, Chris Brockett, Jianfeng Gao, and Bill Dolan. 2016. A diversity-promoting objective function for neural conversation models. In *Proceedings of the 2016 Conference of the North American Chapter of the Association for Computational Linguistics: Human Language Technologies*, pages 110–119.

Nikolaos Malandrakis, Minmin Shen, Anuj Goyal, Shuyang Gao, Abhishek Sethi, and Angeliki Metallinou. 2019. Controlled text generation for data augmentation in intelligent artificial agents. In *Proceedings of the 3rd Workshop on Neural Generation and Translation*, pages 90–98. Association for Computational Linguistics.

Mitchell Stern, William Chan, Jamie Kiros, and Jakob Uszkoreit. 2019. Insertion transformer: Flexible sequence generation via insertion operations. In *International Conference on Machine Learning*, pages 5976–5985. PMLR.

Chengwei Su, Rahul Gupta, Shankar Ananthakrishnan, and Spyros Matsoukas. 2018. A re-ranker scheme for integrating large scale nlu models. In *2018 IEEE Spoken Language Technology Workshop (SLT)*, pages 670–676. IEEE.

Jason W. Wei and Kai Zou. 2019. EDA: easy data augmentation techniques for boosting performance on text classification tasks. *CoRR*, abs/1901.11196.

Yiben Yang, Chaitanya Malaviya, Jared Fernandez, Swabha Swayamdipta, Ronan Le Bras, Ji-Ping Wang, Chandra Bhagavatula, Yejin Choi, and Doug Downey. 2020. Generative data augmentation for commonsense reasoning. In *Findings of the Association for Computational Linguistics: EMNLP 2020*, pages 1008–1025. Association for Computational Linguistics.

Qile Zhu, Haidar Khan, Saleh Soltan, Stephen Rawls, and Wael Hamza. 2020. Don't parse, insert: Multilingual semantic parsing with insertion based decoding. In *Proceedings of the 24th Conference on Computational Natural Language Learning*, pages 496–506, Online. Association for Computational Linguistics.

Easy and Efficient Transformer: Scalable Inference Solution For Large NLP Model

Gongzheng Li[1]*, Yadong Xi[1]*, Jingzhen Ding[1], Duan Wang[1], Ziyang Luo[2],
Rongsheng Zhang[1], Bai Liu[1], Changjie Fan[1], Xiaoxi Mao[1]†, Zeng Zhao[1]†
[1] Fuxi AI Lab, NetEase Inc., Hangzhou, China
[2] Department of Computer Science, Hong Kong Baptist University, Hong Kong SAR, China
{ligongzheng,xiyadong,maoxiaoxi,hzzhaozeng}@corp.netease.com

Abstract

Recently, large-scale transformer-based models have been proven to be effective over various tasks across many domains. Nevertheless, applying them in industrial production requires tedious and heavy works to reduce inference costs. To fill such a gap, we introduce a scalable inference solution: **Easy and Efficient Transformer (EET)**, including a series of transformer inference optimization at the algorithm and implementation levels. First, we design highly optimized kernels for long inputs and large hidden sizes. Second, we propose a flexible CUDA memory manager to reduce the memory footprint when deploying a large model. Compared with the state-of-the-art transformer inference library (Faster Transformer v4.0), EET can achieve an average of 1.40-4.20x speedup on the transformer decoder layer with an A100 GPU.

1 Introduction

In recent years, transformer-based models have achieved impressive performance across variant domains, such as natural language processing (Vaswani et al., 2017; Devlin et al., 2019; Raffel et al., 2020; Brown et al., 2020), computer vision (Jiang et al., 2021; Dosovitskiy et al., 2020) and speech processing (Baevski et al., 2020, 2021). The scaling law proposed by Kaplan et al. (2020) indicates that the validation PPL of a neural language model scales as a power-law with model sizes, dataset sizes, and the amount of training computation. Such law is corroborated empirically by many following works (Brown et al., 2020; Zhai et al., 2021).

However, the mega-sized models are notoriously expensive for deployment in the industry. For example, GPT-2 medium model (700M parameters (Radford et al., 2019)) spends up to 10s to generate 512 tokens given a prompt with the length of 512 on an RTX 2080ti GPU, which is not allowed in the industrial application. Multiple approaches have been proposed to solve such problems, including knowledge distillation (Hinton et al., 2015; Jiao et al., 2020), model pruning (Voita et al., 2019), and quantization (Shen et al., 2019). Apart from these works, much attention has also been paid to optimizing CUDA implementation of a transformer layer for better hardware utilization. Previous works (e.g.: TensorRT (NVIDIA, 2021b), LightSeq (Wang et al., 2021) and Faster Transformer (FT) (NVIDIA, 2021a)) have implemented many optimization techniques, including kernels fusion, gemm optimization, quantization, etc. However, these works still have several limitations. TensorRT only contains the multi-head attention(MHA) operation, lacking a complete transformer model. LightSeq cannot support the model hidden size and input sequence length over 1024. FT contains some performance flaws which need to be improved.

In this paper, we propose a novel transformer inference acceleration library, **Easy and Efficient Transformer (EET)** . First, we implement custom CUDA kernels to avoid explicit matrix addition of attention and padding masks with attention weights. As a result, the attention mask matrix is no longer required, while FT spends overhead to initialize an attention mask on the CPU and push it to CUDA. In addition, compared with FT, padding masks are no longer needed in computation, leading to additional performance improvement. Second, we propose a new method, *thread block folding*, to extend all kernels to support a larger model size up to 12288 and a longer sequence up to 4096. For FT, it directly assigns the thread number in a CUDA block, which may hurt the parallel efficiency. Finally, we design a dynamic CUDA memory management mechanism to reduce the CUDA memory occupation for the same model size, while FT needs to manually allocate memory usage.

We have conducted comprehensive experiments

* Equal contribution
† Corresponding Author

Proceedings of NAACL-HLT 2022: Industry Track Papers, pages 62 - 68
July 10-15, 2022 ©2022 Association for Computational Linguistics

to compare EET with Fairseq,[1] LightSeq and FT. In our experiments, EET achieves about 4.48-20.27x and 4.30-27.43x speedup over Fairseq on 2080ti and A100 respectively. When we set the model size to 768 and 1024 on 2080Ti, EET makes 0.82-2.46x speedup over LightSeq. Compared to FT(v3.1), EET achieves about 1.21-6.30x and 1.62-8.16x speedup on 2080ti and A100 respectively. Compared to FT(v4.0), EET achieves about 1.40-4.20x speedup on A100. The remarkable experimental results corroborate the effectiveness of our EET.

2 Custom Kernels

FT (NVIDIA, 2021a) has implemented highly optimized CUDA kernels for transformer inference. To make further optimization, we design our custom kernels with the considerations below:

• Because padding tokens do not affect the final results, preventing padding tokens from participating in MHA instead of simply applying padding masks can significantly reduce the computational overhead.

• Although an attention mask is essential for MHA in text generation, constructing a mask that varies with the input length is time-consuming.

• The hidden sizes and input lengths of the large-scale pre-trained models can easily exceed 1024. It is necessary to extend these kernels to support large hidden sizes and input lengths elegantly and efficiently.

To remove previously mentioned masks in computation, we redesign the kernels and call the mechanism *mask fusion*. To extend all the kernels to support the model size or sequence length greater than 1024, we improve the CUDA thread structure and call the method as *thread block folding*. Next, we describe these two methods in detail.

2.1 Mask Fusion

The attention mask indicates the attention boundary for each token to prevent the attention from looking forward. The padding mask indicates where the padding tokens are. Thus they both characterize the position information of the tokens in a sequence. Meanwhile, each CUDA thread also has a unique positional index. So we can map each token in the MHA to a thread or block in the CUDA kernels. The function of the attention mask is achieved by comparing whether the CUDA position of the query token being processed is larger than the CUDA position of the key token. The function of the padding mask is achieved by starting the valid calculations from the padding offset when sequentially processing each token. Therefore, we transform the mask computation to logical operation with CUDA thread index comparison. Thus there is no need to store any explicit functional parameters of the masks and the computation overhead of masking operation is saved. The algorithm pseudo-code is shown in Algorithm 1.

Algorithm 1 MHA with *mask fusion*

```
Input: qk, paddingLen, seqLen, batch, headNum
Output: the attention weights back to qk
CUDA Initialize grid ← (batch * headNum)
CUDA Initialize block ← (seqLen)
batchId ← blockIdx.x/headNum
padLen ← paddingLen[batchId]
qkOffset ← blockIdx.x * seqLen * seqLen
qkOffset ← qkOffset + paddLen * seqLen
s ← padLen                              ▷ start at first non-pad
e ← seqLen                              ▷ end at last token
reduceMax ← −inf
reduceSum ← 0
for i = s to e do
    position ← qkOffset + threadIdx.x
    data ← qk[position]
    u ← padLen                          ▷ upper boundary
    l ← i                               ▷ lower boundary
    if l < threadIdx.x < u then
        reduceMax ← blockReduceMax(data)
        reduceSum ← blockReduceSum(data)
        data ← softmax(reduceMax, reduceSum)
    end if
    qk[position] ← data
end for
```

2.2 Thread Block Folding

Large-scale models often have model sizes and input lengths larger than 1024. For example, the standard GPT-3 has a model size of 12288 and an input length of 2048. However, the CUDA block only supports a maximum thread number of 1024, most inference frameworks, such as FT(v3.1) and LightSeq, have implemented kernels that restrict the model size and input length up to 1024, leading to limited availability.

To deal with large model sizes and sequence lengths, we propose to use several blocks to simulate a large block, shown as Figure 1. Imagine a virtual block large enough to hold all the tasks, then we can fold it once to create two blocks, with each block having half the size of the original block. We can repeat the process until the sub-blocks size satisfies the CUDA constraint. Then, the large model sizes or input lengths can be handled correctly, and a new CUDA thread dimension is created to man-

[1] https://github.com/pytorch/fairseq

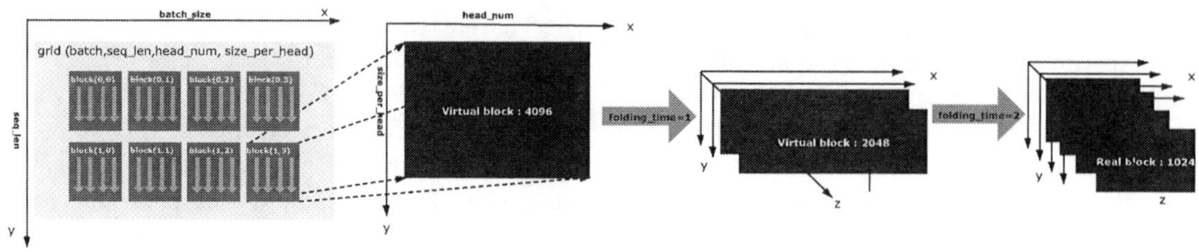

Figure 1: The schematic diagram of *thread block folding*.

age the folding procedure. We call this method *thread block folding*, which allows us to extend any kernel to any model size and any sequence length with minimum changes and non-degraded performance. For instance, assuming the model size is 1280, we fold it once and create two half-size blocks, then the data can be assigned into two separate blocks with 640 threads in each.

We introduce a folding coefficient to characterize the number of folding. Given the model size h, the folding coefficient t and the number of threads n in one block is defined as:

$$t = 2^{\lceil \frac{h}{1024} \rceil - 1}; \quad n = \frac{h}{2^t}$$

As for simplicity, *thread block folding* only adds a new dimension for the block, which slightly impacts the basic CUDA thread grid structure. As for efficiency, the minimum thread number is 512 when the model size or input length is larger than 1024 and makes full use of thread parallelism. The sequence expansion process is similar to the model expansion process. Finally, we support the model size no larger than 16384 and sequence length no longer than 4096.

3 Dynamic Memory Manager

The inference is much more sensitive to latency compared to training. As a result, model parallelism (Shoeybi et al., 2020) and pipeline parallelism (Huang et al., 2019) are undesirable for inference. Their communication overhead introduced by tensor slicing or layer split is significant even with the support of NVLink and GPUDirect. To reduce the latency and hardware requirements for online service, minimizing the memory footprint is of exceptional value when loading very large models. Thus we propose a dynamic memory management strategy for this issue.

Except for the model weights, the memory footprint includes the caches and the buffers. It is hard to reduce the memory footprint of weights because they are inherent to the model. Similarly, The K/V caches for MHA are also hard to compress because they are pre-allocated to avoid runtime memory requests, the size of which depends on the model size, maximum batch size, and maximum sequence length. Whereas the activation cache and the buffers used to store the operator's results are compressible. Hence our dynamic memory management strategy mainly focuses on the activation caches and the operation result buffers.

3.1 Cache Reuse

The caches include K/V caches and activation caches. In incremental decoding, the keys and the values for every step are stored for the next step's attention computation. The maximum size of K/V caches is predictable because we can determine the maximum batch size and decoding steps at the start of the running instance. We allocate the maximum required memory in advance to reduce the forward latency, avoiding malloc overhead and memory corruption.

Different from K/V caches, the activation results are useless after we have calculated and passed them to the next layer. The memory for these activations can be reused across different layers and different operators. We could reuse the activation caches in the following cases.

- The embedding operator shares the cache with the feed-forward operator and the final output. Yet the attention operator holds another cache because of the residual connection.
- The cache for input sequences can be reused by the decoded tokens. The maximum size is determined by the maximum input length.
- The cache can be reused across different layers.

We use the following notations: b, the maximum batch size; s, the maximum sequence length; p, the maximum prompt length; h, the hidden units; l, the layer number. The total activation cache size is:

$$2 * b * h * p$$

The total K/V cache size is :

$$2 * b * h * s * l$$

3.2 Buffer Reuse

The continuous CUDA kernels are not always fused, especially when it comes to Cublas GEMM calls. So we need some buffers to store the returns for those non-fused kernels. Managing the buffers manually like FT is complicated and inefficient. We develop a dynamic buffer manager to avoid the tedium of manual design and achieve a highly efficient memory allocation.

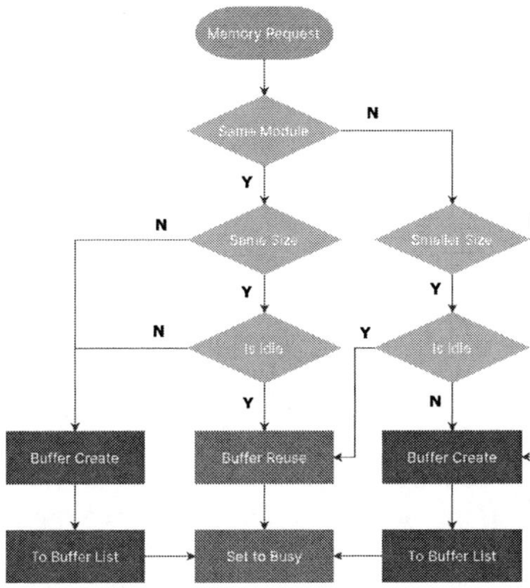

Figure 2: The schematic diagram of buffer decision strategy.

We maintain a list of buffers and use different strategies within and across modules to improve memory utilization. When within modules, we reuse the buffer only when the request size is identical to an idle buffer in the list, preventing memory fragmentation. When across modules, we reuse the buffer when the request size is smaller than any idle buffer in the list, avoiding duplicated malloc. The decision process is demonstrated in Figure 2. In our design, the developer only needs to request a buffer of a specified size and mark it as idle when it is useless, without concerning how to reuse memory exactly. The total buffer size is:

$$b * p * (6 * h + n * p)$$

where b is the batch size, p is the input length, h is the hidden size, and n is the head number.

4 Experiments

During inference, many factors can affect the actual performance, including model size, prompt length, sequence length, padding ratio in a batch, and hardware feature. Completely traversing all combinations requires a huge amount of works. Because the dataset has no effect on the experiment results, we adopt the fake inputs for convenience. To compare fairly and reduce our works, we define some typical experiment settings. If there is no special instruction, the experiment is conducted based on Configuration A in Table 1. Fairseq is an intuitional baseline because it is implemented using pure PyTorch code.

Table 1: Configuration A and B

	CONFIG A	CONFIG B
BATCH SIZE	4	8
MODEL SIZE	1024	2048
MAX PROMPT	1024	1024
MAX SEQUENCE	1024	1024
DATATYPE	FP16	FP16

4.1 Speedup for GPT-2 Layer with Different Sequence Lengths

We first apply EET over GPT-2 on NVIDIA 2080ti and A100. Figure 3 and 4 reveal that EET achieves about 4.48-20.27x and 4.30-27.43x speedup than Fairseq and about 1.21-6.30x and 1.62-8.16x speedup than FT(v3.1), on 2080ti and A100 respectively. For Fairseq and FT(v3.1), the incremental decoding processes the input tokens one by one, while EET improves the tokens parallelism by processing input tokens all at once. As a result, the speedup grows with the increase of the input length.

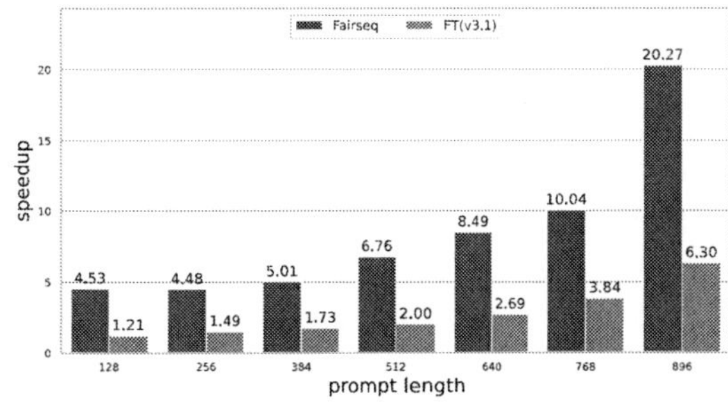

Figure 3: Inference speedup of EET with different prompt lengths on 2080ti compared to Fairseq and FT(v3.1).

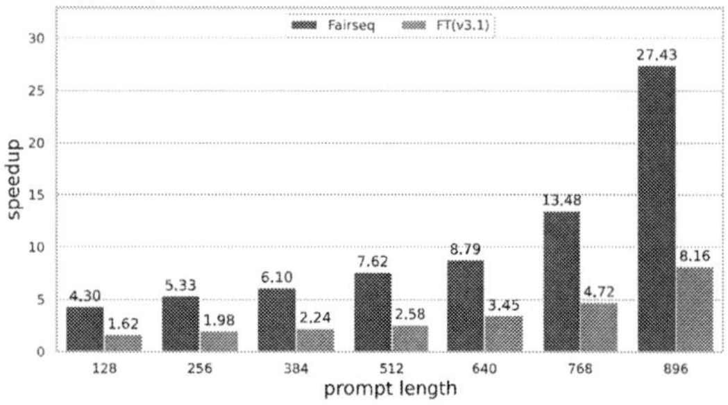

Figure 4: Inference speedup of EET with different prompt lengths on A100 compared to Fairseq and FT(v3.1).

The recent version of FT(v4.0) also introduces the parallel decoding of the input sequences for text generation as we did, so the performance of EET and FT(v4.0) is getting closer with the input length increasing. However, EET still has some performance advantages, which are attributed to our operation kernel optimization. Figure 5 shows that EET achieves about 1.40-2.54x speedup compared to FT(v4.0) with the configuration B in Table 1.

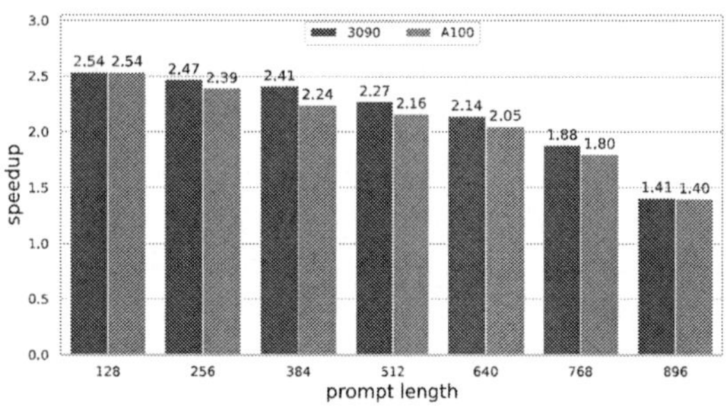

Figure 5: Inference speedup of EET with different prompt lengths on A100 and 3090 over FT(v4.0).

When processing a batch of inputs, the length of them may be uneven. The FT(v4.0) uses the minimum length of the prompts for full decoding, while the EET uses the maximum length. For example, if there is a batch containing sequences of different length like [5, 2, 4, 10], the final prompt length used for parallelism is 2 in the FT. In contrast, it is 10 in the EET. Figure 6 shows that we make 2.74-4.42x speedup with the prompt fixed to 512 and other configurations keeping the same as the configuration B in Table 1.

Unlike Fairseq and FT(v4.0), LightSeq only supports model sizes that are smaller than 1024, we also make a comparison here as a supplement. Figure 7 shows that we make 0.82-2.46x speedup when we set the model size to 768 and 1024.

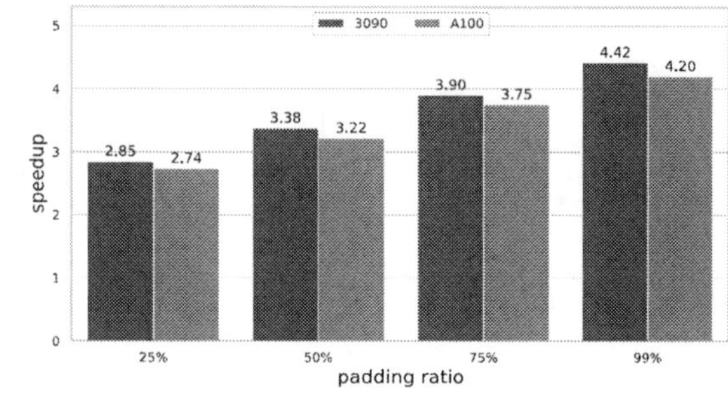

Figure 6: Inference speedup of EET with different padding ratio on A100 and 3090 compared to FT(v4.0)

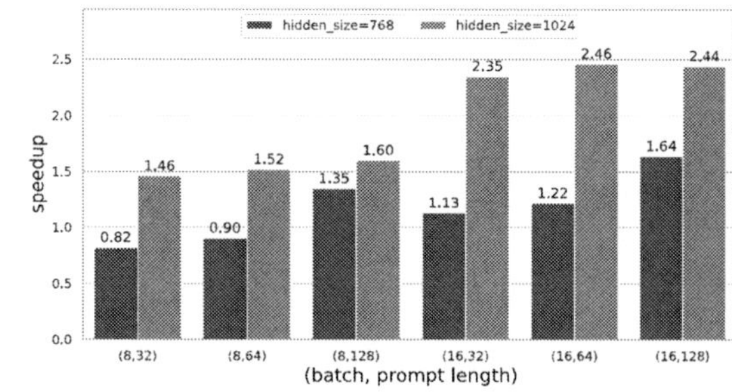

Figure 7: Speedup compared to LightSeq.

4.2 Speedup for Transformer Decoder Layer with Different Model Sizes

To prove the scalability of our EET, we evaluate the performance on different model sizes with configuration C in Table 2. Figure 8 and Figure 9 reveal that EET achieves about 2.25-7.50x speedup than Fairseq and about 1.71-4.61x speedup than FT(v4.0). The acceleration ratio decreases as the model size increases due to the increased ratio of matrix multiplication in the inference. Nevertheless, with the help of *thread block folding*, EET can still deliver significant speedup with very large model sizes, compared to Fairseq and FT(v4.0).

Table 2: Configuration C

	CONFIG C
BATCH SIZE	4 / 8
PROMPT	512
MAX SEQUENCE	1024
DATATYPE	FP16

4.3 Speedup for Bert Layer on 2080ti

We conduct experiments to validate the performance of the Bert encoder layer in EET on 2080ti. It is worth noting that the padding tokens take up

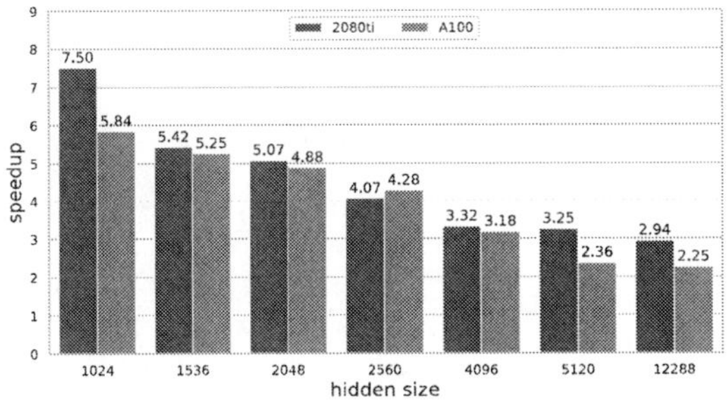

Figure 8: Speedup with different model sizes on 2080ti and A100 compared to Fairseq.

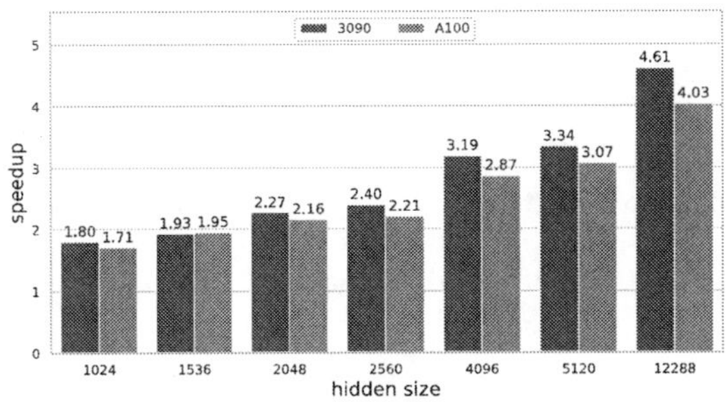

Figure 9: Speedup with different hidden sizes compared to FT(v4.0).

half of the total tokens. The result is shown in Figure 10. Deprecation of the padding masks with the *mask fusion* trick brings in 0.99-1.27x speedup. As for Bert, its hidden size is fixed to 1024 and it has no sequence mask, which kicks off the optimization of thread-block folding and sequence mask fusion, then the speedup is not as significant as GPT2.

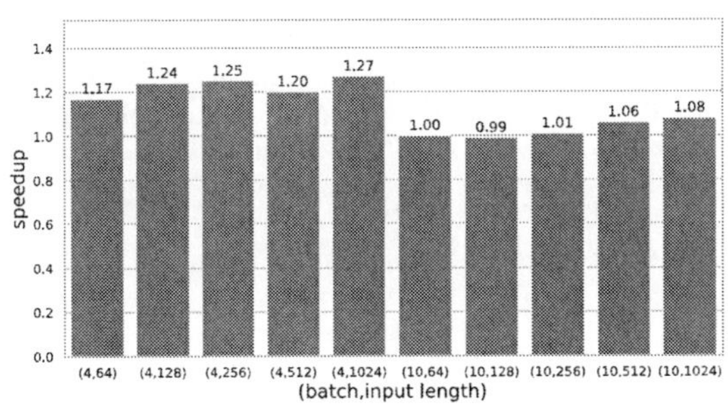

Figure 10: Performance speedup for Bert layer on 2080ti compared to FT(v4.0).

4.4 Memory distribution

Given the batch size 16, the maximum sequence length 1024, the vocab size 13672, we plot the memory distribution of the hidden size of 1024 and 4096 with layer numbers 24 and 40 respectively, as shown in Figure 11. Regardless of the hidden size, we can find that model weights and K/V caches occupy most memory. The activation caches and the buffers only take up a small part, which shows the effectiveness of our dynamic memory management strategy.

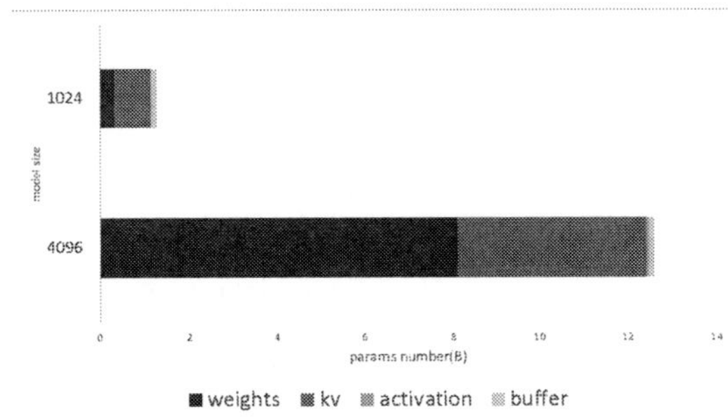

Figure 11: Memory distribution for 1024/4096 hidden sizes.

Given the batch size 4, the maximum sequence length 1024, we plot the memory occupancy of different model parameter sizes, see Figure 12. Compared with the 10 billion of PyTorch's maximum model parameter sizes, it is up to 18 billion for our EET, which proves that we can place much larger models onto one GPU, thus avoiding unnecessary waste of GPU resources and inter-GPU communication overhead on multiple cards.

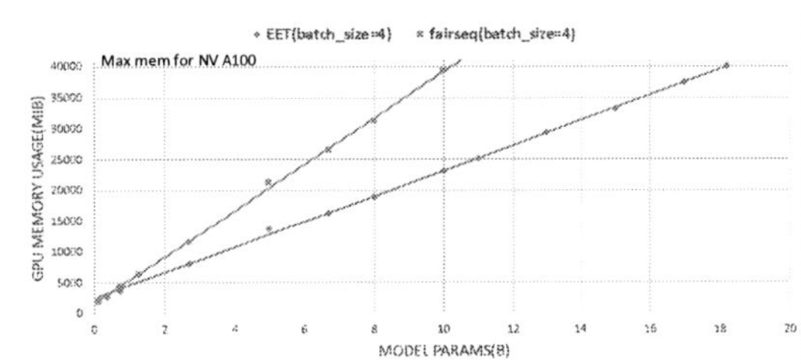

Figure 12: Memory occupancy for different model sizes.

5 Conclusion

This paper comprehensively describes a series of optimization techniques for transformer inference acceleration exploiting both algorithmic and GPU hardware features. These techniques are packed into the EET, a library dedicated to inference acceleration for large transformer-based models and long input lengths. EET has a 1.40-4.42x speedup for the GPT-2 layer and a 0.99-1.27x speedup for the Bert layer compared to the state-of-the-art transformer inference library FT. To make EET easier to apply to a specific task, we provide operation level and model level API, meanwhile integrating web service with dynamic batching. We will continue to improve and keep it up-to-date.

Acknowledgments We would like to thank all the users of EET and the anonymous reviewers for their excellent feedback. This work is supported by the Key Research and Development Program of Zhejiang Province (No. 2022C01011).

References

Alexei Baevski, Wei-Ning Hsu, Alexis Conneau, and Michael Auli. 2021. Unsupervised speech recognition. *arXiv preprint arXiv:2105.11084*.

Alexei Baevski, Henry Zhou, Abdelrahman Mohamed, and Michael Auli. 2020. wav2vec 2.0: A framework for self-supervised learning of speech representations. *arXiv preprint arXiv:2006.11477*.

Tom B. Brown, Benjamin Mann, Nick Ryder, Melanie Subbiah, Jared Kaplan, Prafulla Dhariwal, Arvind Neelakantan, Pranav Shyam, Girish Sastry, Amanda Askell, Sandhini Agarwal, Ariel Herbert-Voss, Gretchen Krueger, Tom Henighan, Rewon Child, Aditya Ramesh, Daniel M. Ziegler, Jeffrey Wu, Clemens Winter, Christopher Hesse, Mark Chen, Eric Sigler, Mateusz Litwin, Scott Gray, Benjamin Chess, Jack Clark, Christopher Berner, Sam McCandlish, Alec Radford, Ilya Sutskever, and Dario Amodei. 2020. Language models are few-shot learners.

Jacob Devlin, Ming-Wei Chang, Kenton Lee, and Kristina Toutanova. 2019. Bert: Pre-training of deep bidirectional transformers for language understanding.

Alexey Dosovitskiy, Lucas Beyer, Alexander Kolesnikov, Dirk Weissenborn, Xiaohua Zhai, Thomas Unterthiner, Mostafa Dehghani, Matthias Minderer, Georg Heigold, Sylvain Gelly, Jakob Uszkoreit, and Neil Houlsby. 2020. An image is worth 16x16 words: Transformers for image recognition at scale.

Geoffrey Hinton, Oriol Vinyals, and Jeff Dean. 2015. Distilling the knowledge in a neural network.

Yanping Huang, Youlong Cheng, Ankur Bapna, Orhan Firat, Mia Xu Chen, Dehao Chen, HyoukJoong Lee, Jiquan Ngiam, Quoc V. Le, Yonghui Wu, and Zhifeng Chen. 2019. Gpipe: Efficient training of giant neural networks using pipeline parallelism.

Yifan Jiang, Shiyu Chang, and Zhangyang Wang. 2021. Transgan: Two transformers can make one strong gan.

Xiaoqi Jiao, Yichun Yin, Lifeng Shang, Xin Jiang, Xiao Chen, Linlin Li, Fang Wang, and Qun Liu. 2020. Tinybert: Distilling bert for natural language understanding.

Jared Kaplan, Sam McCandlish, Tom Henighan, Tom B. Brown, Benjamin Chess, Rewon Child, Scott Gray, Alec Radford, Jeffrey Wu, and Dario Amodei. 2020. Scaling laws for neural language models.

NVIDIA. 2021a. "faster transformer".

NVIDIA. 2021b. "tensorrt".

Alec Radford, Jeffrey Wu, Rewon Child, David Luan, Dario Amodei, Ilya Sutskever, et al. 2019. Language models are unsupervised multitask learners. *OpenAI blog*, 1(8):9.

Colin Raffel, Noam Shazeer, Adam Roberts, Katherine Lee, Sharan Narang, Michael Matena, Yanqi Zhou, Wei Li, and Peter J. Liu. 2020. Exploring the limits of transfer learning with a unified text-to-text transformer. *Journal of Machine Learning Research*, 21(140):1–67.

Sheng Shen, Zhen Dong, Jiayu Ye, Linjian Ma, Zhewei Yao, Amir Gholami, Michael W. Mahoney, and Kurt Keutzer. 2019. Q-bert: Hessian based ultra low precision quantization of bert.

Mohammad Shoeybi, Mostofa Patwary, Raul Puri, Patrick LeGresley, Jared Casper, and Bryan Catanzaro. 2020. Megatron-lm: Training multi-billion parameter language models using model parallelism.

Ashish Vaswani, Noam Shazeer, Niki Parmar, Jakob Uszkoreit, Llion Jones, Aidan N. Gomez, Lukasz Kaiser, and Illia Polosukhin. 2017. Attention is all you need.

Elena Voita, David Talbot, Fedor Moiseev, Rico Sennrich, and Ivan Titov. 2019. Analyzing multi-head self-attention: Specialized heads do the heavy lifting, the rest can be pruned.

Xiaohui Wang, Ying Xiong, Yang Wei, Mingxuan Wang, and Lei Li. 2021. Lightseq: A high performance inference library for transformers.

Xiaohua Zhai, Alexander Kolesnikov, Neil Houlsby, and Lucas Beyer. 2021. Scaling vision transformers. *arXiv preprint arXiv:2106.04560*.

Aspect-based Analysis of Advertising Appeals for Search Engine Advertising

Soichiro Murakami[1,2], **Peinan Zhang**[1], **Sho Hoshino**[1], **Hidetaka Kamigaito**[2], **Hiroya Takamura**[2], **Manabu Okumura**[2]

[1]CyberAgent, Inc., [2]Tokyo Institute of Technology

{murakami_soichiro,zhang_peinan,hoshino_sho}@cyberagent.co.jp, kamigaito@lr.pi.titech.ac.jp, {takamura,oku}@pi.titech.ac.jp

Abstract

Writing an ad text that attracts people and persuades them to click or act is essential for the success of search engine advertising. Therefore, ad creators must consider various aspects of advertising appeals (A^3) such as the *price*, *product features*, and *quality*. However, products and services exhibit unique effective A^3 for different industries. In this work, we focus on exploring the effective A^3 for different industries with the aim of assisting the ad creation process. To this end, we created a dataset of advertising appeals and used an existing model that detects various aspects for ad texts. Our experiments demonstrated that different industries have their own effective A^3 and that the identification of the A^3 contributes to the estimation of advertising performance.

1 Introduction

Search engine advertising (SEA) displays an ad text that consists of a title and a description that are relevant to search queries in search engines, as illustrated in Figure 1. SEA plays an important role in sales promotion and marketing as it allows advertisers to approach users who are interested in specific search queries effectively (Fain and Pedersen, 2006). Ad creators write an ad text that attracts the attention of users and persuades them to click or act by introducing various aspects of advertising appeals (denoted as A^3 in this paper for short), such as *special deals*, as shown in Figure 1. However, products and services exhibit unique effective A^3 for different industries. For example, *limited offers* may be attractive to users in the e-commerce (EC) industry, whereas the *quality of products* may be more important in the automobile industry.

Thus, we argue that the suggestion of effective A^3 for various industries can offer assistance to ad creators. Therefore, we need to discover the effective aspects. However, although aspect-based text analysis has attracted significant attention in the review analysis for products and services (Akhtar et al., 2017; Chen et al., 2019), it has received less focus in the advertisement field.

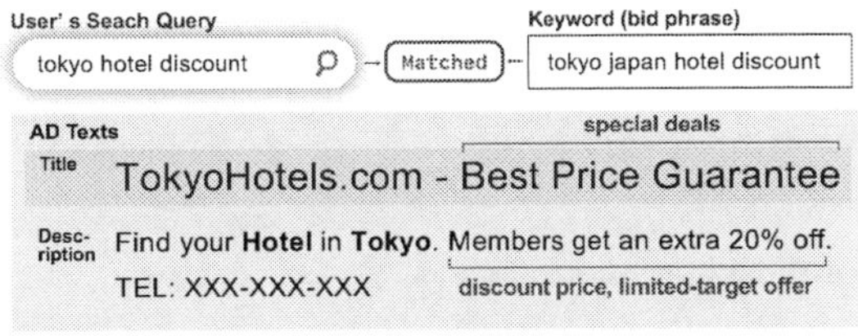

Figure 1: Example ad text and its corresponding A^3.

In this work, to deal with this problem, we defined the A^3 and constructed a dataset of ad texts that are annotated with A^3 in various industries as a first attempt towards assisting ad creators with A^3. Subsequently we developed an aspect detection model to identify different A^3 and performed correlation analysis between A^3 and the click-through rate (CTR), which is used for supporting ad creation, as an advertising performance metric to explore the effective aspects in different industries. Furthermore, we investigated the effectiveness of A^3 in CTR prediction as a potential application for ad creation support.

Through correlation analysis in our experiments, we found that different industries exhibit unique effective A^3. Furthermore, we found that the identification of the A^3 contributes to the CTR prediction.

2 Related Work

Ad Creation Support Attempts have been made to perform automatic generation of ad texts and keywords (Ravi et al., 2010; Hughes et al., 2019; Kamigaito et al., 2021) as well as the estimation of advertising performance metrics such as the CTR (Richardson et al., 2007; Zhang et al., 2014; Mishra et al., 2021) to support the ad creation process. In this work, we tackle the discovery of the effective A^3 for various industries and apply the A^3 to CTR prediction with the goal of improving the efficiency

Proceedings of NAACL-HLT 2022: Industry Track Papers, pages 69 - 78
July 10-15, 2022

Labels	#spans	Labels	#spans
(1) Special deals	343	(12) Limited offers	52
(2) Discount price	120	(13) Limited time	61
(3) Reward points	85	(14) Limited target	114
(4) Free	430	(15) First-time limited	25
(5) Special gift	126	(16) Track record	75
(6) Features	1,360	(17) Largest/no. 1	141
(7) Quality	65	(18) Product lineup	258
(8) Problem solving	17	(19) Trend	99
(9) Speed	142	(20) Others	182
(10) User-friendliness	337	(21) Story	98
(11) Transportation	89		

Table 1: A^3 and statistics of annotated dataset, where "#spans" represents the number of span texts annotated with each label.

of the ad creation process.

Aspect-based Text Analysis Although aspect-based text analysis has attracted significant attention, the majority of studies have been limited to specific domains such as hotels, restaurants, and home appliances (Pontiki et al., 2016; Akhtar et al., 2017; Chen et al., 2019). Moreover, as the product review analysis focuses on the aspects of each product, the defined aspects are extremely fine grained (e.g., the *modes*, *energy efficiency*, and *noise* for refrigerators (Li et al., 2020)). These aspects are not suitable for ad creation because ad creators must deal with ad texts for various products in multiple industries. Therefore, ad creators are required to consider numerous A^3. In this study, we carefully designed labels that cover the A^3 for the general purpose of exploring these in a wide range of industries. Furthermore, we explored methods for aspect detection, as in the previous work (Bagheri et al., 2013), as well as the identification of the effective aspects in terms of advertising performance metrics such as the CTR.

3 Construction of A^3 Dataset

3.1 Data Collection

We constructed a dataset of advertising appeals to understand the A^3 in ad texts. Many A^3 exist in real-world advertisements, including product features, price, and campaigns. We collected 782,158 ads from March 1, 2020 to February 28, 2021 through Google Ads,[1] which is an online advertising platform, to cover the expressions of advertising appeals in a wide range of industries. In this work, we used ads in Japanese. Each ad consists of a title, a description, and a landing page (LP), which is a web page for a specific advertising campaign. We used the meta-description[2] of each LP as the LP content. We sampled 5,000 ad texts for each advertiser to alleviate the bias owing to a different quantity of ad texts for the advertisers. Moreover, we excluded ad texts that comprised less than 15 characters or more than 200 characters. The aforementioned two steps yielded 34,952 ad texts. Furthermore, we excluded duplicates and highly similar texts using the normalized Levenshtein distance metric (Levenshtein, 1966; Greenhill, 2011), because the majority of the ad texts were created from templates for the sake of cost efficiency (Fujita et al., 2010). As a result, we collected 2,738 ad texts consisting of 666 titles, 1,532 descriptions, and 440 LP contents from 13 types of industries.[3] We provide the detailed statistics of the collected ad texts in Appendix A.

3.2 Label Types and Annotation Scheme

Owing to the existence of various A^3, we believe that the systematic organization of the A^3 can aid the ad creation process. We manually defined aspect labels in the following two phases. First, we conducted a preliminary analysis of the collected ad texts and found that approximately eight aspects appeared: *special deals*, *quality*, *problem solving*, *speed*, *user-friendliness*, *limited offers*, *product lineup*, and *trend*. Second, we presented these aspects and the collected ad texts to experienced ad creators and asked for their opinions on the A^3 with the aim of refining the aspect labels. Consequently, the ad creators suggested that we further subdivide *special deals* and *limited offers*. For example, *special deals* was subdivided into *discount price*, *reward points*, *free*, and *special gift*. The reason for this is that there are differences in the strength of the aspects between *free* and *special gift*, even though they appear to be similar. Furthermore, *largest/no.1* was added as another aspect label because it attracts a lot of users.

Table 1 lists the A^3 that we manually defined. Detailed descriptions and examples are provided in Appendix B. Finally, we carefully designed a hierarchical scheme for A^3 to help ad creators and annotators to understand the differences between

[1]https://ads.google.com/

[2]A meta-description is an HTML attribute that provides a brief summary of a web page, such as an LP.

[3]*EC*, *Media*, *Finance*, *VOD&eBook*, *Cosmetics*, *Human resources*, *Education*, *Travel*, *Automobile*, *Entertainment*, *Real estate*, and *Beauty&health*

the labels. The aspect hierarchy consists of five types of coarse-grained labels including *special deals*, which are underlined in Table 1, and 16 types of fine-grained labels such as *discount price*.

Because an ad text often contains multiple expressions of advertising appeals, as depicted in Figure 1, we defined an advertising expression as a span text to be annotated. For example, annotators provide the aspect label (e.g., *special deals*) for the span text "*best price guarantee*." Each span was annotated during the annotation work. Moreover, we allowed the annotators to provide multiple labels for each span because an expression of advertising appeals may contain multiple aspects. For example, the advertising expression "*members get an extra 20% off*" contains two aspects *discount price* and *limited-target offer*, because it means that only users belonging to a membership program can receive an extra 20% discount.

3.3 Annotation Process

We recruited six participants who worked at an advertising agency. We separated 2,738 collected ad texts into two sets consisting of 1,100 and 1,638 texts, and assigned three participants to each set. We presented a one-hour lecture to the participants to explain the detailed definitions of the labels and to provide annotation examples. Furthermore, we asked them to annotate 30 ad texts that were separated from the collected dataset as a practice session. After the session, we answered questions from the participants. During the annotation, we answered any additional questions from them and shared information when a difficult case appeared, which was relatively rare.

3.4 Annotated Dataset Statistics

Table 1 displays the statistics of the annotated dataset. We adopted annotated spans only if at least two of the three annotators for each span text agreed with their boundaries and labels. The annotation work for the 2,738 ad texts required a total of 42 hours; thus, the average time per ad text was 55.2 seconds. A single ad text contains 1.54 spans on average. Furthermore, we calculated the Cohen's Kappa coefficients (κ) between the tokens annotated by different pairs of annotators to determine the inter-annotator agreement. Moreover, following the previous work (Brandsen et al., 2020), we also report the F_1 scores that were calculated between the spans annotated by different pairs of annotators, where we considered one annotation

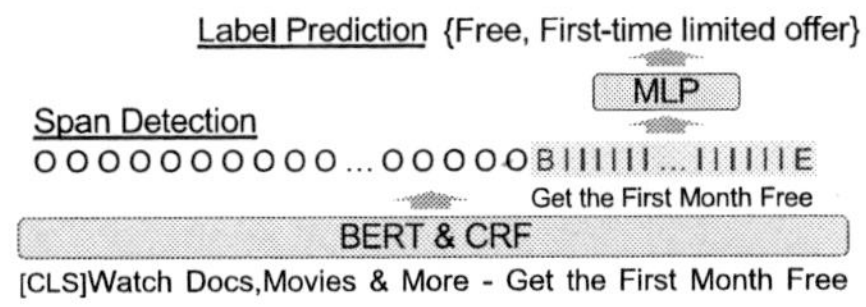

Figure 2: Overview of the span-based model.

as the ground truth and another as the prediction. We obtained relatively high agreement among the annotators: $\kappa = 0.612, F_1 = 0.451$.

4 Aspect Detection Model

We investigate two existing models for aspect detection, i.e., the span-based (Zheng et al., 2019) and document-based (doc-based) models (Devlin et al., 2019). These models receive an ad text $\boldsymbol{x} = (x_i)_{i=1}^{|\boldsymbol{x}|}$ as an input and predict aspect labels $\boldsymbol{y} = (y_i)_{i=1}^{K}$, where x_i and y_i represent a token of an ad text and a binary label for each aspect label, respectively. As each span may contain multiple aspects, both models perform label prediction in the form of multi-label classification (Kurata et al., 2016). K is the number of aspect labels defined in Table 1. We consider an expression of the advertising appeals in an ad text, such as "*best price guarantee*" in Figure 1, to be a *span*. We use $S(i, j)$ to represent the span from i to j, where $1 \leq i < j \leq |\boldsymbol{x}|$. The span-based model consists of two steps: (i) extracting a span $S(i, j)$ from $\boldsymbol{x}$ and (ii) predicting the aspect labels $\boldsymbol{y}$ for each span. In contrast, the doc-based model predicts the aspect labels $\boldsymbol{y}$ for an entire ad text $\boldsymbol{x}$. We employed a pre-trained BERT (Devlin et al., 2019) for both models owing to the limited amount of the annotated dataset.

4.1 Span-Based Model

Figure 2 presents an overview of the span-based model. The task of extracting a span from an ad text can be considered as named entity recognition, and we introduce the boundary-aware neural model proposed by Zheng et al. (2019). We consider characters as a unit (token) in the span-based model. We use the BIOE scheme to create boundary labels $\boldsymbol{l} = (l_i)_{i=1}^{|\boldsymbol{x}|}$ for the input tokens $\boldsymbol{x}$. We feed $\boldsymbol{x}$ into the BERT to obtain a vector h_i for x_i for span detection. Subseqently, we obtain the distribution of the boundary labels $v_i \in \mathbb{R}^L$ by applying a multilayer perceptron (MLP) $v_i = \mathtt{MLP}(h_i)$, where L is the number of boundary types (BIOE). We also use a linear-chain conditional random field (CRF)

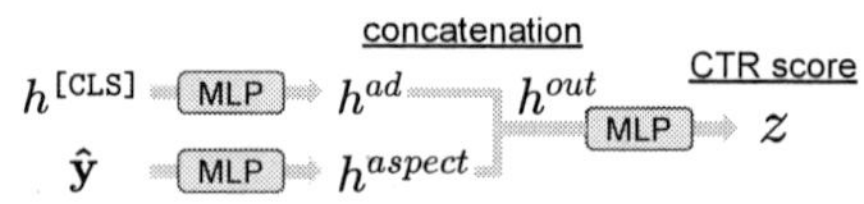

Figure 3: Overview of the CTR prediction model.

(Lafferty et al., 2001) to model the dependencies of the boundary labels (e.g., label E must appear after B or I). As a result, we can obtain the boundary labels $\boldsymbol{l}$ that are predicted by viterbi decoding for the input $\boldsymbol{x}$.

For label prediction, we create a vector representation $h^{avg}_{(i,j)}$ for a span $S(i,j)$ using the average of the output vectors of the BERT (i.e., $h_i, h_{i+1} \cdots h_j$). Thereafter, we obtain the probability that each span $S(i,j)$ belongs to the aspect labels $\boldsymbol{y}$ by applying an MLP and a sigmoid function $\boldsymbol{m} = \texttt{Sigmoid}(\texttt{MLP}(h^{avg}_{(i,j)}))$, where $\boldsymbol{m} = (m_k)_{k=1}^{K}$ and $m_k = p(y_k = 1|S(i,j))$. For example, in Figure 2, the expression "*Get the First Month Free*" is detected as a span, and the model predicts two aspect labels *free* and *first-time limited offer* for the detected span.

4.2 Doc-Based Model

Although the span-based model offers the advantage of detecting a specific expression using span detection, we are concerned that errors in span detection could affect label prediction. Therefore, we also introduce the doc-based model as an alternative to the span-based model.

The doc-based model is a BERT-based classification model. Following the original BERT-based classifier (Devlin et al., 2019), the doc-based model consists of a BERT and an MLP, which take an entire ad text $\boldsymbol{x}$ as an input and outputs labels $\boldsymbol{y}$. Specifically, we first input the ad text $\boldsymbol{x}$ into the BERT and obtain the vector representation $h^{[\text{CLS}]}$ for a [CLS] token. Subsequently, we feed the vector $h^{[\text{CLS}]}$ into the MLP to obtain the probability that the ad text $\boldsymbol{x}$ belongs to the aspect labels $\boldsymbol{y}$ as a multi-label classification task $\boldsymbol{m} = \texttt{Sigmoid}(\texttt{MLP}(h^{[\text{CLS}]}))$, where $\boldsymbol{m} = (m_k)_{k=1}^{K}$ and $m_k = p(y_k = 1|\boldsymbol{x})$.

5 CTR Prediction with A^3

Within the context of ad creation support, the estimation of advertising performance for an ad text (e.g., the CTR) plays a key role in both the improvement and cost efficiency of the ad creation because it helps us understand the user's interest. Therefore, we also investigate whether the A^3 contributes to the prediction of the advertising performance. For this task, we input an ad text $\boldsymbol{x}$ consisting of a title and description, an industry type of the ad $\boldsymbol{t}$ (e.g., EC), and keywords $\boldsymbol{k}$ (e.g., *tokyo* and *hotel*). We also introduce the predicted aspect labels $\hat{\boldsymbol{y}}$ (e.g., *features*) for $\boldsymbol{x}$ as additional features, which were detected by either the span-based or doc-based model. In this case, we use the CTR $z \in [0, 1]$ as the advertising performance (CTR = clicks ÷ impressions).

Figure 3 presents an overview of the regression model. Similarly to recent work (Mishra et al., 2021), we design this regression model based on the BERT. In the model, we feed the three types of tokens $\boldsymbol{x}$, $\boldsymbol{t}$, $\boldsymbol{k}$ into the BERT to obtain the vector $h^{[\text{CLS}]}$ for a [CLS] token. Subsequently, we input $h^{[\text{CLS}]}$ and the aspect labels $\hat{\boldsymbol{y}}$ for the ad text $\boldsymbol{x}$ into the following MLP. Thereafter, we obtain the concatenated vector $h^{out} = [h^{ad}; h^{aspect}]$, where ";" is a concatenation operator. The final MLP then predicts a CTR score z from h^{out} as $z = \texttt{Sigmoid}(\texttt{MLP}(h^{out}))$.

6 Experiments

We conducted experiments on three tasks: (1) aspect detection for the A^3, (2) correlation analysis between the A^3 and CTR, and (3) CTR prediction.

6.1 Experimental Settings

Dataset We used the annotated dataset in Table 1 for the aspect detection. We separated the dataset into 1,857 samples for training, 465 for development, and 410 for testing after excluding 6 ad texts that we determined were inappropriately annotated. We collected 168,412 pairs of ad texts, keywords, and industry types from March 1, 2020 to February 28, 2021 through Google Ads for the CTR prediction. We carefully separated the dataset into 136,352, 16,084, and 15,976 samples for training, development, and testing, respectively. The detailed statistics of the dataset for the CTR prediction are presented in Appendix C. We used the training dataset for the CTR prediction for the correlation analysis between the CTR and A^3. We used the campaign ID of each ad for data division to prevent leakage between the datasets.

Implementation We used the character-level BERT[4] for the span-based model, and the word-

[4] https://huggingface.co/cl-tohoku/bert-base-japanese-char

Labels	Span-based Pred	Span-based Orac	Doc-based
(1) Special deals	0.11	0.19	0.70
(2) Discount price	0.00	0.00	0.57
(3) Reward points	0.62	0.74	0.75
(4) Free	0.68	0.88	0.94
(5) Special gift	0.28	0.40	0.65
(6) Features	0.50	0.70	0.72
(7) Quality	0.00	0.00	0.44
(8) Problem solving	0.00	0.00	0.00
(9) Speed	0.51	0.66	0.92
(10) User-friendliness	0.46	0.59	0.56
(11) Transportation	0.91	1.00	0.53
(12) Limited offers	0.38	0.53	0.62
(13) Limited time	0.00	0.00	0.47
(14) Limited target	0.26	0.57	0.44
(15) First-time limited	0.00	0.00	0.00
(16) Performance	0.27	0.50	0.48
(17) Largest/no. 1	0.67	0.80	0.82
(18) Product lineup	0.42	0.67	0.67
(19) Trend	0.41	0.56	0.47
(20) Others	0.00	0.00	0.39
(21) Story	0.32	0.83	0.53
Macro average	0.32	0.46	0.56

Table 2: Results of the aspect detection (F_1 scores)

level BERT[5] for the doc-based model and CTR prediction. We fine-tuned the models on the dataset and applied an early stopping strategy with 10 epochs. The training was stopped if there was no improvement in the validation loss for three consecutive epochs in all experiments. Further implementation details are described in Appendix D.

Evaluation Metrics We calculated the F_1 scores of the aspect labels for the aspect detection. For the span-based model, a detected label was considered as a true positive if both its span and label were correctly detected. We used the area under the receiver operating characteristic curve (AUC) (Fawcett, 2006), which is a widely used metric in the field of CTR prediction (Zhou et al., 2018; Xiao et al., 2020). Moreover, we used the root-mean-squared error (RMSE) and mean absolute error (MAE) to measure the differences between the ground-truth and predicted scores.

6.2 Aspect Detection

In this experiment, we evaluated two models, the span-based and doc-based models. As errors in the span prediction may affect the label prediction in the span-based model, we also introduced the `Oracle` model, which predicts their labels, provided with *oracle* spans, in addition to the `Pred` model, which predicts both the spans and labels.

[5] `https://huggingface.co/cl-tohoku/bert-base-japanese`

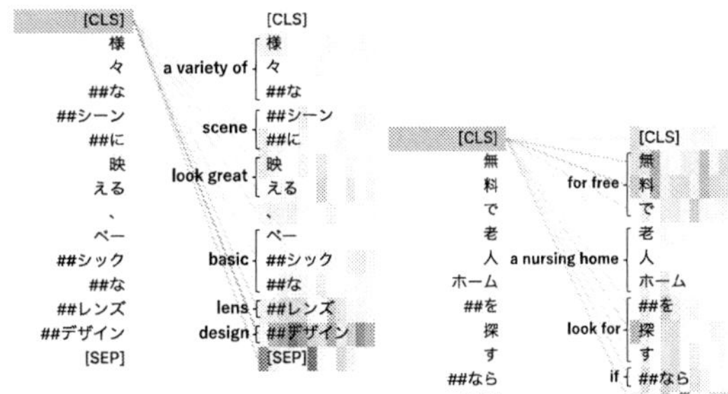

"Simple-designed eyeglass lenses that look great in a variety of scenes"

(a) Ad text labeled as *features*

"Find a nursing home for free"

(b) Ad text labeled as *free*

Figure 4: Visualization of attention weights in the doc-based model. Each example consists of the original Japanese ad text with the literal translation for each subword and the corresponding English ad text.

The evaluation results for the aspect detection are presented in Table 2. The doc-based model outperformed the span-based model, including the `Oracle` model, for most A^3. As the `Pred` model is required to predict both the spans and labels correctly, its task is relatively more difficult than that of other models. In fact, we found that the F_1 score for the span detection is 0.69 for the `Pred` model. Therefore, we conclude that it is the reason why the macro-average F_1 score of `Pred` was lower than those of the doc-based and `Oracle` models.

In the comparison between the `Oracle` and doc-based models, the doc-based model outperforms the `Oracle` model. We hypothesize that its training objective for the span-based model is more difficult as it is more fine grained than the doc-based model.

We observed that the scores for *free*, *speed*, and *largest/no. 1* are high in the doc-based model. This implies that the advertising expressions for these aspects are relatively monotonous and easy to detect compared to the other aspects. For example, the advertising expression *"free shipping,"* which belongs to *free*, often occurs frequently in ad texts for a wide range of industries. The aspect detection was difficult for several aspects in which the numbers of annotated cases were limited, such as (8) and (15), as indicated from Tables 1 and 2. Hence, they exhibited an F_1 score of 0.00.

We also conducted an analysis of the attention in the doc-based model to understand to which signals the model attended in the aspect detection. Figure

Labels	eBook	EC	Fin	HR	Travel
(1)	0.229	0.011	-0.171	–	0.017
(2)	-0.135	-0.166	-0.128	–	-0.176
(3)	0.183	0.000	**0.443**	–	**0.377**
(4)	-0.126	-0.163	-0.052	0.116	–
(5)	0.086	0.122	**0.339**	-0.024	**-0.332**
(6)	-0.128	-0.121	-0.094	-0.040	0.050
(7)	-0.001	-0.081	-0.034	–	–
(8)	–	–	–	–	–
(9)	-0.017	0.065	-0.109	0.024	–
(10)	-0.236	0.053	**-0.252**	-0.004	0.205
(11)	–	–	–	–	–
(12)	-0.036	-0.149	-0.044	0.003	0.221
(13)	-0.090	0.186	0.014	-0.006	-0.184
(14)	-0.020	-0.162	-0.011	0.023	–
(15)	-0.165	–	–	–	–
(16)	0.108	-0.161	-0.099	0.237	-0.148
(17)	**0.283**	-0.073	0.143	0.102	–
(18)	-0.206	0.044	-0.005	-0.159	-0.195
(19)	-0.074	-0.007	0.157	–	–
(20)	0.022	-0.083	0.134	-0.042	**0.268**
(21)	-0.093	–	–	–	–
#cases	30,536	20,671	20,183	10,823	8,093

Table 3: Point-biserial correlation coefficient **r**, where "# cases" denotes the number of ad texts for each industry type and "–" indicates that the corresponding labels were not found.

4 depicts the visualized attention patterns with respect to the `[CLS]` token of the final layer of the BERT. We found that many of the attention heads attend to the words "*design*" and "*for free*" for the ad text (a) and (b), respectively. This suggests that the doc-based model classified the ad text (a) and (b) as *features* and *free*, respectively, because these words were related to the aspects.

6.3 Correlation between Aspects and CTR

To realize the ad creation process considering the A^3, we analyzed which A^3 were effective in each industry through correlation analysis between the CTR[6] and the aspect labels that were predicted by the doc-based model. Because the aspect labels are binary for each aspect (e.g., whether or not each aspect is included in an ad text) and the CTR is continuous, we used the point-biserial correlation coefficient **r** for the analysis. Table 3 lists the point-biserial correlation coefficients **r** between the aspect labels and the CTR. We investigated the correlation among the industry types *VOD&eBook (eBook)*, *EC*, *Finance (Fin)*, *Human resources (HR)*, and *Travel*. As indicated in **bold text** in Table 3, we observed a weak correlation

	AUC (↑)	RMSE (↓)	MAE (↓)
BERT	0.683	0.220	0.142
+ $\mathbf{l}_{span}$	0.709	0.218	0.137
+ $\mathbf{l}_{doc}$	**0.713**	**0.217**	**0.136**

Table 4: Results of CTR prediction

($0.25 < |\mathbf{r}| < 0.5$) between the CTR and the labels, such as (3) *reward points* for *Finance*. This implies that ad texts that include effective A^3 tend to attract more attention from users. However, there was no correlation with regard to the other aspects. This may be because (1) *features*, for example, is considered to be a general-purpose aspect and can be used in any situation.

Based on the above insights, we also investigated the expressions for the effective A^3 in our annotated dataset. For example, regarding the *VOD&eBook* industry, we found that the expression "*one of the largest websites in Japan*" (国内最大級サイト) was annotated as (17) *largest/no. 1*. Furthermore, the expressions for *Finance* "*get* `[N]` *points for new membership*" (新規入会&利用で`[N]`ポイント) and "*earn* `[N]` *points per* `[N]` *yen*" (`[N]`円につき`[N]`ポイント貯まる) were labeled with (3) *reward points*.[7] We believe that the presentation of these effective expressions to ad creators may provide actionable insights and aid in the ad creation process.

6.4 CTR Prediction

We investigated whether the identification of the A^3 contributes to the estimation accuracy of the CTR. Table 4 presents the results of the CTR prediction. For comparison with a baseline (BERT), that does not use A^3, we introduced two models that consider A^3 predicted by the span-based model (+$\mathbf{l}_{span}$) or the doc-based model (+$\mathbf{l}_{doc}$). It can be observed that the aspect-aware models that leverage the A^3 outperformed the baseline model in terms of all evaluation metrics. This suggests that the identification of the A^3 that are included in ad texts can contribute to the improvement of CTR prediction. In the comparison between the two models, +$\mathbf{l}_{doc}$ improved the performance of the CTR prediction more than the +$\mathbf{l}_{span}$. This is likely because the doc-based model predicted the aspect labels more accurately than the span-based model, as indicated in Table 2. We believe that improving the aspect detection with more refined methods will lead to

[6]We used the *actual* CTR for each ad rather than the *predicted* CTR.

[7]Numbers (e.g., price, points) are masked with `[N]`.

better correlation and prediction for the CTR.

7 Conclusions

In this work, we have explored the effective A^3 by means of aspect detection and correlation analysis towards ad creation support with the A^3. Our experimental results demonstrated that each industry exhibits unique effective A^3 and that identification of the A^3 can contributes to CTR prediction.

We demonstrate two possible directions for future studies. First, we will investigate whether introducing the effective A^3 in the ad creation process can help ad creators write effective ad texts in real-world applications. Second, we will develop an aspect-aware model to automatically generate ad texts to support the ad creation process. For the latter, we will train the model with a dataset that includes pairs of ad texts and their corresponding aspect labels predicted using aspect detection.

References

Nadeem Akhtar, Nashez Zubair, Abhishek Kumar, and Tameem Ahmad. 2017. Aspect based sentiment oriented summarization of hotel reviews. *Procedia Computer Science*, 115:563–571. 7th International Conference on Advances in Computing & Communications.

Takuya Akiba, Shotaro Sano, Toshihiko Yanase, Takeru Ohta, and Masanori Koyama. 2019. Optuna: A next-generation hyperparameter optimization framework. In *Proceedings of the 25rd ACM SIGKDD International Conference on Knowledge Discovery and Data Mining*.

Ayoub Bagheri, Mohamad Saraee, and Franciska de Jong. 2013. An unsupervised aspect detection model for sentiment analysis of reviews. In *Natural Language Processing and Information Systems*, pages 140–151.

Alex Brandsen, Suzan Verberne, Milco Wansleeben, and Karsten Lambers. 2020. Creating a dataset for named entity recognition in the archaeology domain. In *Proceedings of the 12th Language Resources and Evaluation Conference*, pages 4573–4577.

Qibin Chen, Junyang Lin, Yichang Zhang, Hongxia Yang, Jingren Zhou, and Jie Tang. 2019. Towards knowledge-based personalized product description generation in e-commerce. In *Proceedings of the 25th ACM SIGKDD International Conference on Knowledge Discovery & Data Mining*, pages 3040–3050.

Jacob Devlin, Ming-Wei Chang, Kenton Lee, and Kristina Toutanova. 2019. BERT: Pre-training of deep bidirectional transformers for language understanding. In *Proceedings of the 2019 Conference of the North American Chapter of the Association for Computational Linguistics: Human Language Technologies*, pages 4171–4186.

Daniel C. Fain and Jan O. Pedersen. 2006. Sponsored search: A brief history. *Bulletin of the American Society for Information Science and Technology*, 32(2):12–13.

Tom Fawcett. 2006. An introduction to ROC analysis. *Pattern Recognition Letters*, 27(8):861–874.

Atsushi Fujita, Katsuhiro Ikushima, Satoshi Sato, Ryo Kamite, Ko Ishiyama, and Osamu Tamachi. 2010. Automatic generation of listing ads by reusing promotional texts. In *Proceedings of the 12th International Conference on Electronic Commerce: Roadmap for the Future of Electronic Business*, pages 179–188.

Simon J. Greenhill. 2011. Levenshtein distances fail to identify language relationships accurately. *Computational Linguistics*, 37(4):689–698.

J. Weston Hughes, Keng-hao Chang, and Ruofei Zhang. 2019. Generating better search engine text advertisements with deep reinforcement learning. In *Proceedings of the 25th ACM SIGKDD International Conference on Knowledge Discovery & Data Mining*, pages 2269–2277.

Hidetaka Kamigaito, Peinan Zhang, Hiroya Takamura, and Manabu Okumura. 2021. An empirical study of generating texts for search engine advertising. In *Proceedings of the 2021 Conference of the North American Chapter of the Association for Computational Linguistics: Human Language Technologies: Industry Papers*, pages 255–262.

Gakuto Kurata, Bing Xiang, and Bowen Zhou. 2016. Improved neural network-based multi-label classification with better initialization leveraging label co-occurrence. In *Proceedings of the 2016 Conference of the North American Chapter of the Association for Computational Linguistics: Human Language Technologies*, pages 521–526.

John D. Lafferty, Andrew McCallum, and Fernando C. N. Pereira. 2001. Conditional random fields: Probabilistic models for segmenting and labeling sequence data. In *Proceedings of the Eighteenth International Conference on Machine Learning*, pages 282–289.

Vladimir Iosifovich Levenshtein. 1966. Binary codes capable of correcting deletions, insertions and reversals. *Soviet Physics Doklady*, 10(8):707–710.

Haoran Li, Peng Yuan, Song Xu, Youzheng Wu, Xiaodong He, and Bowen Zhou. 2020. Aspect-aware multimodal summarization for chinese e-commerce products. In *Proceedings of the AAAI Conference on Artificial Intelligence*, volume 34, pages 8188–8195.

Shaunak Mishra, Changwei Hu, Manisha Verma, Kevin Yen, Yifan Hu, and Maxim Sviridenko. 2021. Tsi: An ad text strength indicator using text-to-ctr and semantic-ad-similarity. In *Proceedings of the 30th ACM International Conference on Information & Knowledge Management*, pages 4036–4045.

Maria Pontiki, Dimitris Galanis, Haris Papageorgiou, Ion Androutsopoulos, Suresh Manandhar, Mohammad AL-Smadi, Mahmoud Al-Ayyoub, Yanyan Zhao, Bing Qin, Orphée De Clercq, Véronique Hoste, Marianna Apidianaki, Xavier Tannier, Natalia Loukachevitch, Evgeniy Kotelnikov, Nuria Bel, Salud María Jiménez-Zafra, and Gülşen Eryiğit. 2016. SemEval-2016 task 5: Aspect based sentiment analysis. In *Proceedings of the 10th International Workshop on Semantic Evaluation*, pages 19–30.

Sujith Ravi, Andrei Broder, Evgeniy Gabrilovich, Vanja Josifovski, Sandeep Pandey, and Bo Pang. 2010. Automatic generation of bid phrases for online advertising. In *Proceedings of the Third ACM International Conference on Web Search and Data Mining*, pages 341–350.

Matthew Richardson, Ewa Dominowska, and Robert Ragno. 2007. Predicting clicks: Estimating the click-through rate for new ads. In *Proceedings of the 16th International Conference on World Wide Web*, pages 521–530.

Thomas Wolf, Lysandre Debut, Victor Sanh, Julien Chaumond, Clement Delangue, Anthony Moi, Pierric Cistac, Tim Rault, Rémi Louf, Morgan Funtowicz, Joe Davison, Sam Shleifer, Patrick von Platen, Clara Ma, Yacine Jernite, Julien Plu, Canwen Xu, Teven Le Scao, Sylvain Gugger, Mariama Drame, Quentin Lhoest, and Alexander M. Rush. 2020. Transformers: State-of-the-art natural language processing. In *Proceedings of the 2020 Conference on Empirical Methods in Natural Language Processing: System Demonstrations*, pages 38–45.

Zhibo Xiao, Luwei Yang, Wen Jiang, Yi Wei, Yi Hu, and Hao Wang. 2020. Deep multi-interest network for click-through rate prediction. In *Proceedings of the 29th ACM International Conference on Information & Knowledge Management*, pages 2265–2268.

Yuyu Zhang, Hanjun Dai, Chang Xu, Jun Feng, Taifeng Wang, Jiang Bian, Bin Wang, and Tie-Yan Liu. 2014. Sequential click prediction for sponsored search with recurrent neural networks. In *Proceedings of the Twenty-Eighth AAAI Conference on Artificial Intelligence*, pages 1369–1375.

Changmeng Zheng, Yi Cai, Jingyun Xu, Ho-fung Leung, and Guandong Xu. 2019. A boundary-aware neural model for nested named entity recognition. In *Proceedings of the 2019 Conference on Empirical Methods in Natural Language Processing and the 9th International Joint Conference on Natural Language Processing*, pages 357–366.

Guorui Zhou, Xiaoqiang Zhu, Chenru Song, Ying Fan, Han Zhu, Xiao Ma, Yanghui Yan, Junqi Jin, Han Li, and Kun Gai. 2018. Deep interest network for click-through rate prediction. In *Proceedings of the 24th ACM SIGKDD International Conference on Knowledge Discovery & Data Mining*, pages 1059–1068.

A Collected Ad Texts for Annotation

Table 7 lists the detailed statistics of the collected ad text. We collected 2,738 ad texts comprising 666 titles $\boldsymbol{x}^{title}$, 1,532 descriptions $\boldsymbol{x}^{desc}$, and 440 LP contents $\boldsymbol{x}^{lp}$ from 13 industries: *EC*, *Media*, *Finance*, *VOD&eBook*, *Cosmetics*, *Human resources*, *Education*, *Travel*, *Automobile*, *Entertainment*, *Real estate*, and *Beauty&Health*.

B Descriptions and Examples of A^3

Table 5 lists the detailed descriptions and examples of A^3 that we have defined. For example, the expression "*enjoy free shipping*" is labeled with (4) *free*, as it represents free offers for products or services. In the table, "#spans" represents the number of span texts annotated with each label.

C Dataset for CTR Prediction

Table 8 lists the detailed statistics of the datasets used for CTR prediction. We carefully separated the dataset into 136,352, 16,084, and 15,976 samples for training, development, and testing, respectively. For correlation analysis between the CTR and aspect labels of advertising appeals, we used the training dataset for CTR prediction.

D Additional Implementation Details

Table 6 lists the implementation details, e.g., hyperparameters, for the aspect detection and CTR prediction models. We developed our models using pre-trained BERT models, which are publicly available from the Transformers library (Wolf et al., 2020).[8] The framework is available under the Apache 2.0 license. We trained the models with a Tesla V100 GPU on the Google Cloud Platform, which is the cloud computing infrastructure. Moreover, we performed a hyperparameter search, using Optuna (Akiba et al., 2019) with default parameters for the aspect detection models on the validation set. In the experiment, the hyperparameter search is limited to 30 trials. Therefore, we performed our experiments in a single run.

We used CRF and binary cross-entropy (BCE) loss for span detection and label prediction in the span-based model, respectively. We used the mean squared error (MSE) as an objective function to train the CTR prediction model. Furthermore, we applied an early stopping strategy to all the models. Specifically, we stopped training if there was no improvement in the validation loss after three consecutive epochs.

[8] `https://huggingface.co/cl-tohoku`

	Aspect labels	Description & Example	#spans
(1)	Special deals	Expressions representing special deals (e.g., *Compare hotels and save money*)	343
(2)	Discount price	Specific discount rate or amount (e.g., *Buy 1 get 1 50% off*)	120
(3)	Reward points	Customers can earn points (e.g., *Use our app to earn points*)	85
(4)	Free	Free offer for products or services (e.g., *Enjoy free shipping*)	430
(5)	Special gift	Special gifts or presents for customers (e.g., *Join today and get a free brush set*)	126
(6)	Features	Features of services or products (e.g., *Ergonomically designed to protect children*)	1,360
(7)	Quality	Top-quality or high-grade services (e.g., *Find premium kitchen appliances*)	65
(8)	Problem solving	Solutions to customer problems (e.g., *Get bright, clear skin*)	17
(9)	Speed	Speed of delivery and services (e.g., *Fast & free shipping*)	142
(10)	User friendliness	Usability of services and products (e.g., *Quick, simple, and easy to use*)	337
(11)	Transportation	Convenience of transportation (e.g., *Centrally located in the heart of Tokyo*)	89
(12)	Limited offers	Limited availability of services and products (e.g., *Limited to 1,000 items per day*)	52
(13)	Limited-time offer	Offers available for a limited time only (e.g., *Three days only at 20% off*)	61
(14)	Limited-target offer	Offers available for target customers only (e.g., *Discount for members only*)	114
(15)	First-time limited offer	Limited offers for first-time customers (e.g., *Take 15% off your first order*)	25
(16)	Track record	Track records of services or companies (e.g., *45M+ users worldwide*)	75
(17)	Largest/no. 1	Largest/No. 1 products or services (e.g., *Boston's no. 1 hair salon*)	141
(18)	Product lineup	Wide range of products or stores (e.g., *Large selection of hotels*)	258
(19)	Trend	Popularity or favorable reputation (e.g., *Top trending shoes and boots*)	99
(20)	Others	Other advertising appeals (e.g., *An experience like no other*)	182
(21)	Story	Synopsis of a movie or drama (e.g., *After Peter Parker is bitten by a$\cdots$*)	98

Table 5: A^3 and statistics of annotated dataset.

	Aspect Detection Model		CTR Prediction Model
	Span-based	Doc-based	
Pre-trained model	`bert-base-japanese-char`	`bert-base-japanese`	`bert-base-japanese`
Number of heads	12	12	12
Number of hidden layers	12	12	12
Hidden layer size	768	768	768
Dropout probability	0.1	0.1	0.1
Vocab size	4,000	32,000	32,000
Batch size	10	10	30
Max sequence length	512	512	512
Number of epochs	10	10	10
Learning rate	8.6×10^{-5}	5.5×10^{-5}	2.0×10^{-5}
Optimizer	Adam	Adam	Adamax
Loss	CRF loss, BCE loss	BCE loss	MSE loss

Table 6: Hyperparameters and implementation details.

Industry	Title	Desc.	LP	Sub-total
EC	131	314	87	532
Others	137	272	123	532
Media	119	250	27	396
Finance	105	203	56	364
VOD&eBook	38	112	78	228
Cosmetics	43	110	20	173
Human resources	72	75	8	155
Education	58	50	10	118
Travel	23	62	18	103
Automobile	18	32	5	55
Entertainment	14	36	3	53
Real estate	5	12	2	19
Beauty&Health	3	4	3	10
Total	766	1,532	440	2,738

Table 7: Statistics of collected ad texts.

Industry	Train	Dev	Test
VOD&eBook	30,536	3,823	3,812
EC	20,671	2,584	2,583
Finance	20,183	2,521	2,521
Others	15,526	1,936	1,936
Human resources	10,823	1,348	1,348
Media	10,434	1,295	1,274
Education	9,592	1,344	1,228
Travel	8,093	1,002	1,042
Cosmetics	5,584	231	232
Entertainment	2,455	0	0
Automobile	1,697	0	0
Beauty&Health	445	0	0
Real estate	313	0	0
Total	136,352	16,084	15,976

Table 8: Statistics of dataset for CTR prediction.

Self-supervised Product Title Rewrite for Product Listing Ads

Xue Zhao, Dayiheng Liu, Junwei Ding, Liang Yao,

Yao Yan, Huibo Wang, Wenqing Yao
Alibaba Group

{xue.zx,liudayiheng.ldyh,djw99219}@alibaba-inc.com
{yaoliang.yl,yanyao.yy}@alibaba-inc.com
{huibo.whb,wenqing.ywq}@alibaba-inc.com

Abstract

Product Listing Ads (PLAs) are primary online advertisements merchants pay to attract more customers. However, merchants prefer to stack various attributes to the title and neglect the fluency and information priority. These seller-created titles are not suitable for PLAs as they fail to highlight the core information in the visible part in PLAs titles. In this work, we present a title rewrite solution. Specifically, we train a self-supervised language model to generate high-quality titles in terms of fluency and information priority. Extensive offline test and real-world online test have demonstrated that our solution is effective in reducing the cost and gaining more profit as it lowers our CPC[1], CPB[2] while improving CTR[3] in the online test by a large margin. It is also easy to train and deploy, which can be a best practice of title optimization for PLAs.

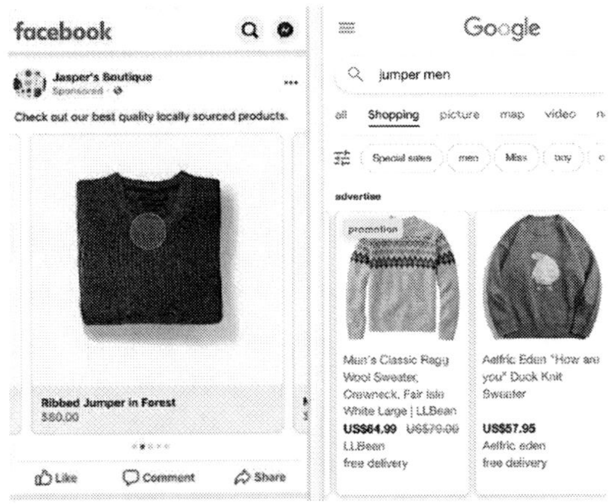

Figure 1: Product Listing Ads from different channels

1 Introduction

Product Listing Ads (PLAs) are crucial online marketing tools for merchants to attract more customers and encourage them to click their ads. They have different names in various ads channels, for example, Dynamic Product Ads in Facebook and Instagram, Shopping Ads on Google, as shown in Fig 1. PLAs usually have a limit on display text length, for instance, in Google Shopping Ads, users can see only the first 70 or fewer characters of the title[4]). Therefore, PLAs titles are expected to reveal the product type and core attributes earlier so that users can clearly identify the product, as illustrated in Table 1. However, to trigger ads more often and affect the user's purchase intention more positively, sellers list as many attributes as possible in the title without considering the fluency and readability, most importantly, the information priority. as illustrated in Table 2. These titles fail to highlight the core information and make it difficult to comprehend as a whole.

Existing work has made the attempt to generate titles from keywords(de Souza et al., 2018) and product images(Zhang et al., 2019), or generate description text(Shao et al., 2021) for products, however, little work has investigated the title optimization for PLAs. At first, we explored the rule-based method by assigning weight to attribute words and reordering the words/chunks by weight. However, the rule-based method heavily relies on the accuracy of attribute detection, phrase boundary detection, and the appropriateness of attribute weights. It is hard to optimize rules without exhausting human effort. Therefore, we attempt to use language models in our title rewrite task.

The biggest obstacle of model-based method is the lack of high-quality titles regarding fluency and information order as labels for supervised learning. In this work, we solve the problem by performing self-supervised learning. Instead of writing high-quality titles as labels, we design a multi-level shuf-

[1]Cost Per Click
[2]Cost Per Buyer
[3]Click Through Rate
[4]https://support.google.com/merchants/answer/6324415?hl=en

Proceedings of NAACL-HLT 2022: Industry Track Papers, pages 79 - 85
July 10-15, 2022 ©2022 Association for Computational Linguistics

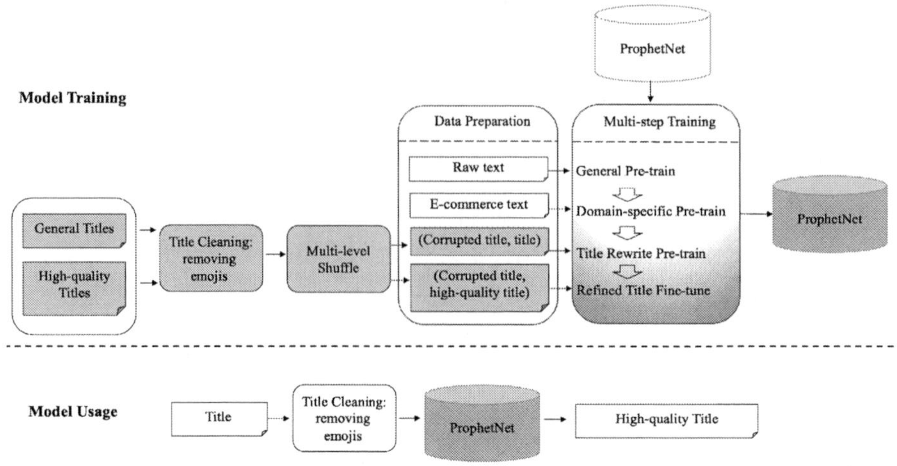

Figure 2: The framework of our product title rewrite solution. The upper part shows model training details: title cleaning, multi-level shuffling, data preparation, and multi-step training. The multi-level shuffle module creates (pseudo title, title) pairs for self-supervised training. The lower part illustrates the model usage: the input title is cleaned and then input to the trained ProphetNet to generate a high-quality one.

Priority	**Attribute Type**	**Attribute Value**
1st	Product Type	phone case
2nd	Core	with magsafe, for iphone13, leather
3rd	Common	new style, golden brown, 6.1 inches

Quality	**Title Example**
good	iphone13 leather phone case with magsafe new style golden brown 6.1 inches
bad fluency	with magsafe new style golden brown 6.1 inches phone case for iphone13 leather
bad priority	new style golden brown 6.1 inches phone case for iphone13 leather with magsafe

Table 1: Examples of attribute priority for a phone case and possible titles. Small case is used in the paper.

title	suitable for apple 12pro mobile phone case iphone12 protective case genuine leather drop-resistant new style all-inclusive silicone ultra-thin 11pro max high-end for men and women limited
optimized	mobile phone case silicone ultra-thin genuine leather protective case drop-resistant suitable for apple 12pro iphone12 11pro max all-inclusive new style high-end for men and women limited.

Table 2: Example of product title optimization.

fle module that uses titles to generate low-quality pseudo titles. Then the language model is trained on (pseudo title, title) pairs, during which it can learn to reorder the words to recover the original titles. Moreover, we propose a multi-step training procedure consisting of pre-train and fine-tune to enable the model to generate good titles.

The overall framework of our solution is illustrated in Fig 2. Moreover, for the sake of information accuracy, we only focus on ***information reordering*** and avoid any word insertion, deletion, and modification to the original title.

2 Method

We first introduce our multi-level shuffle module, which creates the (pseudo title, title) pairs for self-supervised training. Then we elaborate on the multi-step training procedure. It is worth noting that our solution can be built upon any language models, such as BART (Lewis et al., 2019) and GPT2 (Radford et al., 2019). We use the ProphetNet (Qi et al., 2020) framework in practice as it is superior to BART and GPT2 and has achieved new state-of-the-art in multiple text generation tasks(Dayiheng Liu and Duan, 2020).

2.1 Multi-level Shuffle Module

We overcome the absence of a learning target by thinking about the problem from an interesting perspective. The only available titles are seller-created: accurate, informative while uneven in quality, where good titles can train the model to generate better while the bad ones can also be good learning targets in terms of wording and phrasing of attributes, grammar, and the semantic context of the words. If we shuffle the word order of titles as input, even the bad titles become good supervision as they have better fluency than the corrupted ones. In light of these considerations, we build a multi-level shuffle module to mimic the problematic titles and generate low-quality pseudo titles as model input. Specifically, we have three strategies to cover almost all the word order issues in the titles.

Chunk-level We use the chunking tools[5] to split the title into chunks, then we randomly swap two or more chunks to obtain low-quality titles. From Table 1, the good title can be split into *"iphone13 leather phone case | with magsafe | new style | golden brown | 6.1 inches"*. After shuffling, the title may become the bad ones in Table 1.

Span-level We create the text spans by combining the random number of adjacent chunks arbitrarily into a larger text span without overlapping, then we randomly exchange the position of two or more spans. This strategy generates the easiest case for the model to learn because most of the words are still in proper order after shuffling.

Token-level After tokenization, the title is split into a list of tokens. We switch the position of two or more tokens to mimic the word order issue with the highest severity since it needs a more complicated adjustment to recover.

In practice, we make sure to keep 15% titles unchanged. We apply chunk-level strategy to 55% titles, span-level strategy to 25% titles, and process only the rest 5% titles with token-level strategy because such messy corruption hardly happens in titles while a large portion of such hard cases will delay the model convergence.

2.2 Model Training

We introduce the training objective, and the multi-step training in detail.

2.2.1 Training Objective

As mentioned before, we use ProphetNet(Qi et al., 2020) as our language model, which is trained with a novel self-supervised objective called future n-gram prediction. Given the training data (X, Y), where $X = \{x_i\}$, $i \in [1, M]$ is the M-length input and $Y = \{y_i\}$, $i \in [1, T]$ is the T-length output. Typically, the language model is trained to maximize the probability of the next token y_t conditioned on X and all the precedent tokens in Y. ProphetNet is different as it also predicts the future n-grams:

$$L(\theta; X) = -\alpha_0 \cdot \left(\sum_{t=1}^{T} \log p(y_t | y_{<t}, X; \theta) \right) - \sum_{j=1}^{n-1} \alpha_j \cdot \left(\sum_{t=1}^{T-j} \log p(y_{t+j} | y_{<t}, X; \theta) \right) \quad (1)$$

The first part of equation is the original language model loss while the second part is the loss from predicting the future n-grams. The parameters α and other model parameters are all consistent with open-source ProphetNet[6].

2.2.2 Multi-step Training

We propose a multi-step training procedure which allows the language model gradually acquire the generation ability of high-quality titles.

General Pre-train Pre-training is a successful technique to boost the generation quality of language models (Dong et al., 2019). ProphetNet has different open-source pre-trained versions for different languages. For example, ProphetNet-EN is pre-trained with 160GB English raw texts, including Wikipedia, news, and web texts, etc. For convenience, we use a pre-trained ProphetNet (Qi et al., 2020).

Domain-specific Pre-train The pre-trained ProphetNet has a strong ability to generate fluent text in various contexts, but we hope it can focus more on the e-commerce domain. Therefore, we collect 20GB of e-commerce data consisting of the titles and the attribute keywords for domain-specific pre-training, for instance, the title and the attribute values in Table 1. We concat the keywords as model input X, and use product title as model output Y, continuously train the model by minimizing Eq. 1 until reaching convergence.

Title Rewrite Pre-train Our task is to rewrite the seller-created titles into better quality. To

[5] https://alinlp.alibaba-inc.com/

[6] https://github.com/microsoft/ProphetNet

help reduce the gap between the pre-trained language model and our task, we continue pre-training ProphetNet with product titles. We create (pseudo title, title) pairs with tens of millions of titles we have as (X, Y), and pre-train ProphetNet by minimizing Eq. 1. As stated before, all the titles, including the bad ones, can be used as the learning target, since even the bad titles have basic knowledge about titles and still maintain a better fluency compared to the corrupted ones.

Refined Title Fine-tune In particular, the model should learn from high-quality titles about information priority. Intuitively, titles from brand owners or high-rating sellers are more reliable than the others. Online CPC, CPB performance can also be a good indicator of title quality. We combine these rules and select about 10% of all titles, which is millions, as high-quality for refined fine-tuning. We sampled 500 of them and found the portion of good titles reaches 98.0%. Similarly, we create the title pairs then train our model by minimizing Eq. 1.

We start the multi-step training from the domain-specific pre-train step and use 2 32GB Tesla V100 GPUs running for 7 days until convergence.

3 Experiment

We conduct offline and online test to evaluate the generated title in terms of accuracy, information order, fluency, and real-world profits.

3.1 Offline Accuracy

We evaluate token-level accuracy and investigate how much the multi-level shuffle module helps in model training.

Token-level Accuracy Given the golden label (original title) $\bar{Y} = \{\bar{y}_i\}, i \in [1, m]$ and the generated title $Y = \{y_i\}, i \in [1, n]$, we calculate a token-level accuracy as Eq. 2.

$$Acc = \frac{\sum_{i=0}^{\min(m,n)} \mathbb{1}(y_i == \bar{y}_i)}{\min(m, n)} \tag{2}$$

where $\mathbb{1}$ is an indicator function which equals 1 when $y_i == \bar{y}_i$, 0 otherwise. In general, if the prediction mistake happens in the earlier steps, it will propagate the error and affect the future word prediction. Therefore, a title with a wrong beginning and necessarily wrong future tokens will obtain a very low token-level accuracy. Comparably, in PLAs, the beginning of the title is more important. Therefore, the metric somehow shows the quality of generated text as a PLAs title.

Model	Acc_u	Acc_c	Acc_m
Model+ unchanged	**100.0%**	38.88%	34.92%
Model+ random shuffle	92.41%	62.35%	54.61%
Model+ multi-level	93.26%	**73.32%**	**64.50%**

Table 3: Generation accuracy using different shuffle modules. **Acc** is accuracy; **u**, **c**, **m** means test data unchanged, chunk-level shuffled, and multi-level shuffled.

Baselines To examine the effectiveness of the multi-level shuffle module, we train three versions of the model using the original title as output while using different shuffled data as input: unchanged (not shuffled), random shuffle (shuffle the tokens by chance), and multi-level shuffle.

Test Data With 5,000 selected high-quality product titles (separated from the training data beforehand), we create three versions of input data for testing: **u**nchanged, **c**hunk-level shuffled, and **m**ulti-level shuffled, and obtain the (unchanged/corrupted title, title) as the test data. We test the models and calculate the token generation accuracy on three test dataset, by which we can have a more reliable result. However, it is more convincing if a model can recover the original titles from the corrupted ones with higher accuracy.

Result From Table 3 we can observe that ProphetNet trained with multi-level shuffled data outperforms the other models on the shuffled test datasets by a large margin. The multi-level shuffle strategy achieves higher accuracy than random shuffle on all test datasets, so it does help the model generate better. Moreover, the model achieves 100% accuracy when trained and tested on the unchanged data, yet becomes the worst when tested on the corrupted titles because the model only learns making no change to the input.

3.2 Information Priority and Fluency

We examine the information order and fluency via human GSB evaluation, which means to judge the generated title as Good, Same or Bad compared to the original one. We have three PLAs marketing experts from e-commerce online marketing team. Given 1,000 pairs of the original and generated title, every rater votes every pair with one of the GSB labels. We also provide the product image, brand, and category information to help raters resolve the core information from the title. As shown in Table 4, the generated product titles have obtained +25% and 21.9% GSB improvement compared to original titles and rule-based titles, respectively.

Baseline	Good	Same	Bad	GSB
Original	47.5%	30%	22.5%	+25%
Rule-based	37.5%	46.9%	15.6%	+21.9%

Table 4: Human evaluation. GSB=Good Rate-Bad Rate

3.3 Online Test

We run the test on Google Shopping Ads in three countries (MY, PH, SG) for two months. Before the test, we split the items into the control group and test group, then upload them to GoogleAds. In this way, the traffic of the two groups is almost even and with fairly close cost and impressions. We make sure traffic is large enough to keep stable and influential (over 100MM daily impressions). In the first month, we run campaigns and observe the gap of core metrics between the two groups. Then we update the titles into generated titles in the test group and continue running campaigns normally for another month. At last, we assess the **gap change** brought by the generated titles after online for a month.

Country	1st CPB	2nd CPB	CPB
MY	1.75%	-15.23%	**-16.98%**
PH	-0.19%	-12.14%	**-11.95%**
SG	-0.80%	-12.44%	**-11.65%**
Country	**1st CPC**	**2nd CPC**	**CPC**
MY	+1.81%	-1.01%	**-2.82%**
PH	+5.15%	+3.53%	**-1.62%**
SG	-0.19%	+0.17%	**+0.36%**
Country	**1st CTR**	**2nd CTR**	**CTR**
MY	-0.58%	+9.93%	**+10.51%**
PH	+0.10%	+7.01%	**+6.91%**
SG	+2.52%	+7.85%	**+5.33%**

Table 5: Online test result on Google Shopping Ads. 1st means the original metric gap between control and test groups; 2nd is the gap after running generated titles. The gap change is considered as the final metric.

Our core metrics are CPC, CPB, and CTR . From Table 5 we learned that the generated titles are profitable in view of lowering the cost and bringing more conversions[7]. For example, the generated titles have brought 5.33%~10.51% CTR increment, and 11.65%~16.98% CPB drop while saving the cost of PLAs about -2%. We can see a slight CPC fluctuation in SG with a +0.36% increment, which is not hurtful given the significant positive change of CPB and CTR.

[7]Google Shopping Ads charge by clicks, dropping CPC means saving the cost.

4 Discussion

Besides titles, merchants usually also have a great deal of information such as product categories, attributes, etc. We experiment further on how such information helps in model training.

4.1 Category-specific Models

To explore if a category-specific model trained only for the target category can generate better than the model trained on all categories, we train and test the model only on the "Electronics" category, one of our largest categories. In specific, **Model+EL Finetune** is ProphetNet fine-tuned only on the Electronics titles without any pre-training step, which is a basic category-specific model. **Model+Pretrain+EL Finetune** is a more advanced category-specific model, which is first pre-trained on our raw text and keywords and title pairs and titles from all categories then fine-tuned only on the Electronics titles. **Model+Pretrain+Finetune** is our standard multi-step training on all titles. As shown in Table 6, the category-specific model is weak at the generation when only fine-tuned without pre-training. However, the model trained on all categories achieves better accuracy in the target category than the model pre-trained and fine-tuned only for the target category. This may be because training on all categories can facilitate the representation learning of words shared by different categories.

Model	Acc_u	Acc_c	Acc_m
Model+ EL Fine-tune	77.35%	42.14%	38.34%
Model+ Pretrain+ EL Finetune	91.44%	76.33%	68.07%
Model+ Pretrain+ Finetune	**93.69%**	**77.35%**	**68.92%**

Table 6: Generation accuracy of category-specific model and proposed model.

4.2 Attribute-guided Shuffle

The most frequent circumstance in bad titles is the attribute priority. Therefore, we design an

S1-title	olympia dz-220btx series electronic calculator
S1-gen	olympia electronic calculator dz-220btx series
S2-title	27mm aeroforce hammer with double colour handle
S2-gen	aeroforce hammer with double colour handle 27mm
S3-title	household multifunctional plastic multi-clip folding drying rack underwear socks clip drying rack baby hanger
S3-gen	multi-clip folding drying rack household multifunctional plastic underwear socks clip drying rack baby hanger
S4-title	(6 months warranty) replacement toshiba satellite t115-s1100 laptop ac power adapter charger
S4-gen	laptop ac power adapter charger replacement toshiba satellite t115-s1100 (6 months warranty)
S5-title	reflective colorful angel wings laser car stickers six-pointed star beauty body free stickers modified cool decorative
S5-gen	angel wings laser car stickers six-pointed star beauty body free reflective colorful cool decorative stickers modified
S6-title	100% authentic otterbox case symmetry series case for iphone 8 & iphone 7 (not plus)
S6-gen	otterbox case for iphone 8 & iphone 7 (not plus) symmetry series case 100% authentic
S7-title	suitable for lenovo ideapad 320s notebook charging cable 310s-14isk 15ise power adapter
S7-gen	power adapter suitable for lenovo ideapad 320s notebook charging cable 310s-14isk 15ise
S8-title	moon japanese and korean ins fresh flowers for huawei mate40pro phone case internet celebrity mate30/p40
S8-gen	phone case for huawei mate40pro mate30/p40 ins fresh flowers moon japanese and korean internet celebrity

Table 7: Samples of the original titles and the generated titles by the proposed solution.

attribute-guided shuffle strategy that creates low-quality pseudo titles by changing the positions of attributes. We expect this kind of corruption can train models to concentrate more on attribute words and then learn to arrange them better. Surprisingly, as shown in Table 8, the attribute-guided shuffle is comparative but not superior to the multi-level shuffle module, which may be because multi-level shuffle can cover various types of title issues, not only the attribute positions.

Model	Acc_u	Acc_c	Acc_m
Model+ attribute	91.14%	71.92%	63.17%
Model+ multi-level	**93.26%**	**73.32%**	**64.50%**

Table 8: Generation accuracy of different shuffle strategies.

4.3 Why the Optimized Titles Work in PLAs

We sample the generation titles to get a clear view of the generation quality, as displayed in Table 7. First, the core information is prioritized by putting it at the beginning of the title, especially the information that helps users quickly identify the product. For example, S1 moves the model "dz-220btx" to the behind and makes sure the product type " electronic calculator" is visible to users. Similarly, S2, S4, S7, S8 put the product type first. The model is not moving product type to the first blindly. From S3, S6 we can see that model keeps the core attributes in front of the product type to maintain better fluency. Second, the long titles become more fluent and readable. For example, S7 generates a more natural title as a sentence. S5 and S8 properly reveal the product types earlier so that users understand immediately what is selling and make the complicated attribute list more comprehensible. Therefore, the model considers both information priority and fluency to make the product title easier to read and the visible part in PLAs more clear. It is worth mentioning that the trained model fits the titles data perfectly and only predicts the words in the original titles. Hence, the information in the generated titles is usually accurate and complete.

5 Conclusion

We present a practical solution of product title optimization for PLAs which consists of multi-level shuffling for pseudo title production and multi-step training to generate high-quality titles. It can help merchants conveniently build their own profitable title optimization systems.

References

Yeyun Gong Weizhen Qi Hang Zhang Jian Jiao Weizhu Chen Jie Fu Linjun Shou Ming Gong Pengcheng Wang Jiusheng Chen Daxin Jiang Jiancheng Lv Ruofei Zhang Winnie Wu Ming Zhou Dayiheng Liu, Yu Yan and Nan Duan. 2020. Glge: A new general language generation evaluation benchmark. *arXiv*, abs/2011.11928.

José GC de Souza, Michael Kozielski, Prashant Mathur, Ernie Chang, Marco Guerini, Matteo Negri, Marco Turchi, and Evgeny Matusov. 2018. Generating e-commerce product titles and predicting their quality. In *Proceedings of the 11th International Conference on Natural Language Generation*, pages 233–243.

Li Dong, Nan Yang, Wenhui Wang, Furu Wei, Xiaodong Liu, Yu Wang, Jianfeng Gao, Ming Zhou, and Hsiao-Wuen Hon. 2019. Unified language model pre-training for natural language understanding and generation. *arXiv preprint arXiv:1905.03197*.

Mike Lewis, Yinhan Liu, Naman Goyal, Marjan Ghazvininejad, Abdelrahman Mohamed, Omer Levy, Ves Stoyanov, and Luke Zettlemoyer. 2019. Bart: Denoising sequence-to-sequence pre-training for natural language generation, translation, and comprehension.

Weizhen Qi, Yu Yan, Yeyun Gong, Dayiheng Liu, Nan Duan, Jiusheng Chen, Ruofei Zhang, and Ming Zhou. 2020. Prophetnet: Predicting future n-gram for sequence-to-sequence pre-training. In *Proceedings of the 2020 Conference on Empirical Methods in Natural Language Processing: Findings*, pages 2401–2410.

Alec Radford, Jeff Wu, Rewon Child, David Luan, Dario Amodei, and Ilya Sutskever. 2019. Language models are unsupervised multitask learners.

Huajie Shao, Jun Wang, Haohong Lin, Xuezhou Zhang, Aston Zhang, Heng Ji, and Tarek Abdelzaher. 2021. Controllable and diverse text generation in e-commerce. In *Proceedings of the Web Conference 2021*, pages 2392–2401.

Jianguo Zhang, Pengcheng Zou, Zhao Li, Yao Wan, Xiuming Pan, Yu Gong, and Philip S. Yu. 2019. Multi-modal generative adversarial network for short product title generation in mobile E-commerce. In *Proceedings of the 2019 Conference of the North American Chapter of the Association for Computational Linguistics: Human Language Technologies, Volume 2 (Industry Papers)*, pages 64–72, Minneapolis, Minnesota. Association for Computational Linguistics.

Efficient Semi-supervised Consistency Training for Natural Language Understanding

George Leung
Amazon Alexa AI, USA
leu@amazon.com

Joshua Tan
Amazon Alexa AI, USA
jshtan@amazon.com

Abstract

Manually labeled training data is expensive, noisy, and often scarce, such as when developing new features or localizing existing features for a new region. In cases where labeled data is limited but unlabeled data is abundant, semi-supervised learning methods such as consistency training can be used to improve model performance, by training models to output consistent predictions between original and augmented versions of unlabeled data.

In this work, we explore different data augmentation methods for consistency training (CT) on Natural Language Understanding (NLU) domain classification (DC) in the limited labeled-data regime. We explore three types of augmentation techniques (human paraphrasing, back-translation, and dropout) for unlabeled data and train DC models to jointly minimize both the supervised loss and the consistency loss on unlabeled data. Our results demonstrate that DC models trained with CT methods and dropout-based augmentation on only 0.1% (2,998 instances) of labeled data with the remainder as unlabeled can achieve a top-1 relative accuracy reduction of 12.25% compared to fully supervised model trained with 100% of labeled data, outperforming fully supervised models trained on 10x that amount of labeled data. The dropout-based augmentation achieves similar performance compare to back-translation-based augmentation with much less computational resources. This paves the way for applications of using large scale unlabeled data for semi-supervised learning in production NLU systems.

1 Introduction

Deep learning, especially transformer-based language models (Vaswani et al., 2017), have achieved state-of-the-art performance in many tasks and are widely used in NLU systems. A challenge in deep learning is that it often requires large amounts of labeled training data in order to reach a desirable performance level. This is especially a problem for NLU systems in commercial production as the cost of labeling data scales with the expanding number of supported features and languages.

Recent research in semi-supervised learning (SSL) demonstrated that it is possible to combine a small amount of labeled data and a large amount of unlabeled data to match or even outperform purely supervised learning (Xie et al., 2020; Gao et al., 2021). One of the most promising approaches in SSL is called consistency training (Bachman et al., 2014; Rasmus et al., 2015; Tarvainen and Valpola, 2017; Verma et al., 2019). In short, consistency training is a technique that regularizes model predictions to be invariant to augmentations of unlabeled data. Examples of augmentations include applying noise to input features (Sajjadi et al., 2016; Miyato et al., 2018) or hidden states (Bachman et al., 2014).

In this paper, we experimented with consistency training in a major NLU task: Domain Classification (DC). We tested three different types of data augmentations: paraphrasing by user feedback, back-translation, and dropout. As a testbed for our approach, we applied our experiments to BERT (Devlin et al., 2019)-based models using a real-world dataset collected from Portuguese users of a voice-controlled assistant. We found that all three types of augmentations can be effectively used alongside consistency training to improve model performance compared to a baseline model trained without consistency training. For the scenario where labeled data was limited to only 0.1% of all available labeled data, the best top-1 accuracy, which was -9.14% compared to fully supervised model trained with 100% labeled data, was achieved by consistency training on data augmented using back-translation. If we use dropout-only augmentation, the relative top-1 accuracy change was -12.25%. Lastly, we observed a relationship between the amount of labeled data

Proceedings of NAACL-HLT 2022: Industry Track Papers, pages 86 - 93
July 10-15, 2022

used for training and the size of CT benefits, with larger benefits for smaller sets of labeled data. Our results demonstrate the possibility of using consistency training to drastically reduce the amount of labeled data needed for an NLU system while retaining a reasonable accuracy. This can be done on large unlabeled datasets without using computationally expensive back-translation or financially costly human-authored augmentation.

2 Background

2.1 Consistency training

Consistency training (Bachman et al., 2014; Rasmus et al., 2015; Tarvainen and Valpola, 2017; Verma et al., 2019) is a Semi-Supervised Learning technique that utilizes unlabeled data to enforce consistency of the model output given similar inputs. The general schematic of this method is shown in Figure 1. In summary, consistency training is multitask learning with two objectives: minimizing the supervised loss for labeled data and the consistency loss for unlabeled data. The supervised loss is a regular cross-entropy loss for the labeled data. For the consistency loss, the unlabeled data is first paraphrased with data augmentation methods. Then the original data x and the augmented data x' will be passed through the same encoder model M to generate two output distributions respectively $p_M(y|x)$ and $p_M(y|x')$. The consistency loss is defined by the Kullback–Leibler divergence between the two output distributions $D(p_M(y|x)||p_M(y|x'))$. Finally the consistency loss and supervised loss are combined and back-propagated to update the model parameters. In this way consistency training forces the model to be insensitive to the noise introduced by data augmentation.

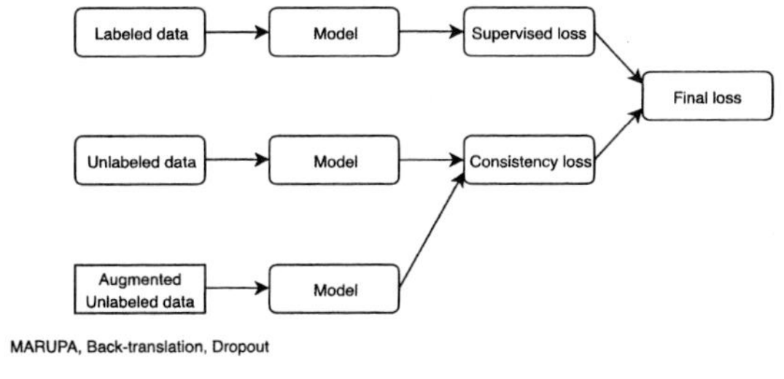

Figure 1: Training objective for consistency training. Note that the three *model* blocks in this figure represent the same encoder model with the same set of parameter.

2.1.1 Paraphrasing by user feedback

MARUPA (Falke et al., 2020) (Mining Annotations from User Paraphrasing) is a tool to leverage real-world user implicit feedback to collect paraphrased utterances. Sometimes when a user is having a failed interaction with the system, the user will paraphrase the utterance and retry. MARUPA collects these utterances fully autonomously without the need for human annotators using paraphrase detection, friction detection and label projection models. This dataset is filtered to make sure it is relevant to the main task (Domain classification). In our experiment, we use the MARUPA dataset without the labels as the augmented unlabeled dataset for the consistency training.

2.1.2 Paraphrasing by back-translation

Back-translation a common approach for data augmentation in NLP (Xie et al., 2020; Edunov et al., 2018). Recent development of Neural Machine Translation (NMT) (Vaswani et al., 2017), has produced models with impressive accuracy in translating text. Back-translation leverages this to generate augmented data by translating example text sequences from an original language to an intermediate language and then back to original language. This method allows us to generate paraphrases while retaining semantic meaning, and has been shown to improve performance in question-answering tasks (Yu et al., 2018; Dong et al., 2017). In our experiment, we leverage a commercially available cloud-based translate service to paraphrase the unlabeled dataset using back-translation.

2.1.3 Dropout as data augmentation

Dropout (Srivastava et al., 2014) is a technique to prevent overfitting in training deep neural networks by randomly dropping units inside the network. In recent research, dropout is also shown to be an effective method for data augmentation (Bouthillier et al., 2015; Gao et al., 2021). The underlying idea is to pass the same input sequence to the encoder twice with different dropout masks. The two resulting embeddings are then used to compute the consistency loss. This method outperforms several deterministic augmentation approaches such as word deletion and replacement (Gao et al., 2021). Another advantage of dropout-based augmentation is that no extra paraphrase process is needed and we can directly use the unlabeled data for consistency learning.

3 Experiment

We designed our experiments to explore the performance impact of incorporating consistency training using each type of data augmentation. We also investigated how performance changes as the amount of labeled data or unlabeled data used for training is varied.

3.1 Consistency-training (CT) models

All the models were based on a distilled (Hinton et al., 2015) Portuguese BERT (Devlin et al., 2019) language model. This model had 4 transformer layers and feedforward hidden dimension of 1200 compare to 12 and 3072 in the BERT-Base model. All experiments were trained on Amazon Web Services EC2 p3.16xlarge instances. We implemented CT using a multi-task learning framework that trained models to jointly minimize the sum of supervised cross-entropy error on labeled data and the consistency loss on unlabeled data. All models were configured to train for up to 20 epochs. During training, CT models alternated between computing loss on the supervised task and the consistency-loss task. The task sampling rates were set such that both tasks would finish iterating through their associated data at approximately the same time. We compare the CT models against a set of baseline models that only performed supervised training.

3.2 Augmentations

We experimented with a total of five CT models varying in type of data augmentation used for consistency regularization: paraphrase by humans (MARUPA), back-translation, and dropout.

For *MARUPA CT* models, augmentations were comprised of paraphrase data. We leveraged the MARUPA paraphrase dataset as unlabeled pairs of augmented data. This dataset consisted of 2,258,828 utterance pairs (4,517,656 total).

For *Back-translate CT* models, augmentations were comprised of back-translated utterances. We used a cloud-based translation service to translate from Portuguese to an intermediate language and back to Portuguese, generating a total of 2,998,782 pairs. For some pairs the original and back-translated utterances were the same, and in that case we switched to a different intermediate language until a different back-translated utterance was obtained. The list of intermediate language was *English, French, Japanese, Korean, Chinese, Hindi* and *Hungarian*.

For *Dropout CT* models, we used dropout to generate an equivalent of data augmentation on the embedding space. Our dropout augmentation involved applying dropout to the same data instance twice with different dropout masks using the same dropout probability. Dropout layers were located in each BERT transformer blocks and fully connected layer with dropout probability set to 0.1. The unlabeled data used in *Dropout CT* was the same as the original data in the back-translation dataset.

We also tested two combinations of augmentations. In *Dropout+MARUPA CT* models, we combined dropout and paraphrase augmentations. Specifically, we applied independently sampled dropout to both utterances in a paraphrase pair, and then compute the consistency loss between the dropout-augmented pair. For *Dropout+Back-translate CT* models, we combined dropout with back-translation pairs in a similar fashion.

3.3 Training data

We experimented with six different labeled-data sizes: 0.1%, 1%, 2%, 5%, 25%, and 100% of the available training data. We randomly sampled three sets of data for each labeled-data size less than 100%. Within each sample, we used a randomly selected 90% as the training data and use the remaining 10% as the validation set. Unless otherwise stated, for each model we experimented with we trained three separate instances, each using a different data split.

We also experimented with different unlabeled data sizes. For this set of experiments we limited our exploration to Dropout CT models that were trained with 0.1% of the available labeled data. For all Dropout CT models, we treated the remaining labeled data as the set of available unlabeled data (i.e., for a model trained using 0.1% of the labeled data, we take the remaining 99.9% and removed the label). We experimented with models that used 25%, 50%, 75%, and 100% of the available unlabeled data. As before, we created three random samples for each unlabeled-set size less than 100% and trained a separate model on each split.

3.4 Evaluation

We evaluated our models using a held-out test set. We considered two different types of testing scenarios. In the first, we tested against the full test set of 191,762 utterances, approximating the distribution of a real-world application scenario. In the second, we tested against a test set that had been filtered to remove all utterances appearing in the training set. This filtered set contained 46,211 utterances and was intended to examine how well our models were able to generalize to unseen utterances.

Our experiments were performed using a production BERT-based domain classification model. Models with differing architectures or for different ML tasks may not yield the same results. Similarly, our results may not generalize to industry applications of NLU in other domain areas, using different spoken languages, or with access to substantially larger amounts of labeled training data.

4 Results

Here we present the results of our consistency-training experiments and illustrate how model performance changed as we varied the underlying training data.

4.1 Metrics definition

All metrics are reported as relative change, including Top-1 accuracy, Top-1-Unseen accuracy, false accept rate and false reject rate. The relative change is defined by

$$(\mu - \mu_r)/\mu_r$$

where μ is the experiment metric and μ_r is the reference metric achieved by the fully supervised model trained on 100% of labeled data.

4.2 Size of labeled data

Our results show that consistency training on augmented data can lead to significant improvements in performance in limited-data settings. As shown in Table 1, when restricting models to use only 1% of the available labeled data as training data, the baseline supervised model achieves a top-1 accuracy of -67%. For the Dropout CT model trained on the same 1% of labeled data, we saw a top-1 accuracy of -4%. The difference in performance was even more apparent in models trained using only 0.1% of the labeled data. For models trained with 0.1% of the labeled data, the baseline model achieved an top-1 accuracy of only -99%. The Dropout CT model trained on the same amount of labeled data achieved a top-1 accuracy of -12.25%. This improvement in top-1 accuracy demonstrates the utility of consistency training on unlabeled data when labeled data is extremely limited. Table 1 also compares the top-1 accuracy of the baseline and Dropout CT model when tested on utterances

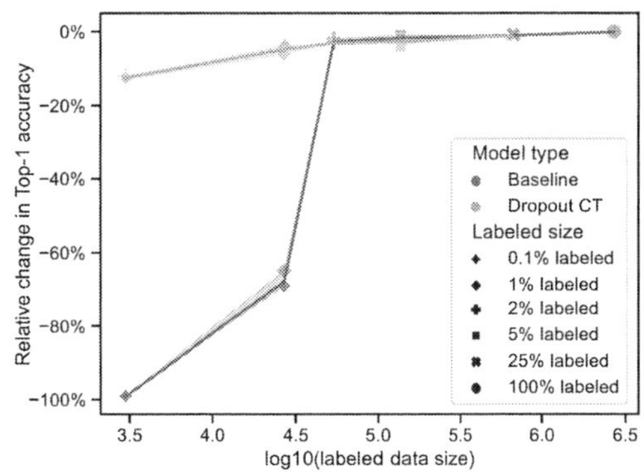

Figure 2: Comparison of top-1 accuracy relative change for baseline and Dropout CT models trained on different amounts of labeled data. Data points are shown for all three experiments run for a given model differing only in training sample (often overlapping).

not seen during training. Given the same model the top-1-unseen accuracy was lower than the top-1 accuracy, as expected since this represents a more difficult task. However, we still saw a performance improvement in top-1-unseen accuracy when applying consistency training.

In Figure 2 we plot the top-1 accuracy of the baseline and Dropout CT model as we varied the amount of labeled training data. While both the baseline and Dropout CT models benefited from training with additional labeled data, the benefit was much greater for the baseline model. Figure 2 also sheds light on the difficulty of the domain classification task. We see that a baseline model trained on 2% of the labeled data has comparable perfomance to a baseline model trained on all the labeled data.

4.3 Size of unlabeled data

Results on varying the size of the unlabeled training data our Dropout CT model trained with 0.1% of the available labeled data are shown in Figure 3. We see that even when using only 25% of the unlabeled data (742k instances), consistency training with dropout-based augmentations achieved a top-1 accuracy of -23%. Increasing the amount of unlabeled data generally led to improved performance.

4.4 Types of augmentation

Table 2 shows our experiments comparing CT models that used different types of data augmentations, where each model was trained on only 0.1% of the labeled data. Overall, every data augmenta-

		Top-1		Top-1-Unseen	
% Labeled data	Count	Baseline	Dropout CT	Baseline	Dropout CT
0.1%	2998	-98.96%	-12.25%	-98.16%	-26.66%
1%	26989	-67.33%	-4.16%	-67.67%	-9.09%
2%	53978	-2.40%	-2.71%	-14.73%	-5.62%
5%	134945	-1.52%	-2.50%	-3.12%	-4.64%
25%	674725	-0.60%	-0.64%	-1.39%	-1.39%
100%	2698903	0%	-	0%	-

Table 1: Top-1 accuracy relative change for baseline models trained on different amounts of labeled data.

		FAR			FRR		
	Top-1	Video	Shopping	Music	Video	Shopping	Music
Baseline	-98.96%	-100%	-100%	-100%	137%	766%	2877%
Dropout CT	-12.25%	308%	344%	71%	59%	346%	543%
MARUPA CT	-22.42%	1145%	2844%	14%	64%	191%	1760%
Back-translate CT	-9.14%	370%	733%	106%	27%	20%	132%
Dropout+MARUPA CT	-21.79%	839%	3372%	14%	73%	236%	1695%
Dropout+Back-translate CT	-9.66%	267%	567%	131%	32%	14%	91%

Table 2: Top-1 accuracy, false acceptance rate (FAR), and false rejection rate (FRR) relative change for the supervised baseline model and the consistency-training models using different underlying data augmentations. All models are trained with 0.1% labeled data. Metrics are reported as relative change compared to a fully supervised model trained using 100% of labeled data. The ground truth test data included 44,221 Music utterances, 2,145 Shopping utterances, and 904 Video utterances.

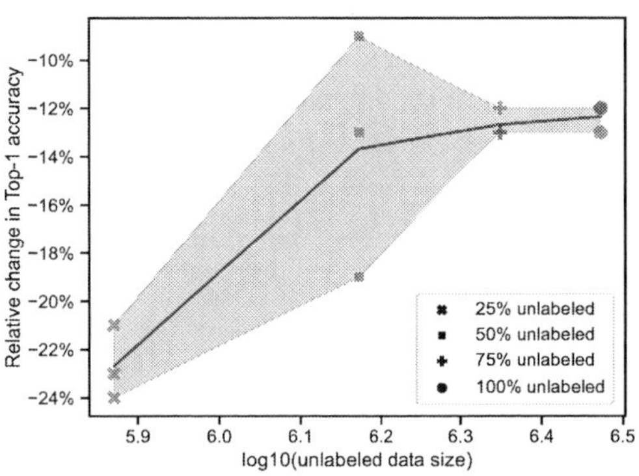

Figure 3: Comparison of top-1 accuracy relative change for Dropout CT models trained on different amounts of unlabeled data. All models were trained using 0.1% of the labeled data.

tion method helped CT to perform better than the baseline model. Out of all the augmentation methods we tested, Back-translate CT performed best. The Back-translate CT model achieved an average top-1 accuracy of -9.14%, followed by the Dropout+Back-translate CT model with a top-1 accuracy of -9.66%. MARUPA models in general performed worse than Back-translate models, but still had significant improvement over the baseline.

We found mixed results on the performance benefit of combining types of augmentations together for consistency training. While the Dropout+MARUPA CT model had a slightly higher top-1 accuracy than the MARUPA CT model (-21.79% vs. -22.42%), the Dropout+Back-translate CT model performed slightly worse than Back-translate CT (-9.66% vs. -9.14%).

We note that the Dropout CT methods, although slightly less performant than Back-translate CT models, have a greater advantage from an operations perspective. Dropout augmentation does not require any kind of domain expertise, pre-computation, or external translation models, which can greatly reduce data-preprocessing time and operational costs.

In addition to top-1 accuracy, Table 2 shows false acceptance and false reject rates for three differently sized domains. The baseline model incorrectly rejected all utterances for which the ground truth domain was one of Video, Shopping, or Music. More interestingly, for a pair of models the better performing model in terms of top-1 accuracy was not always the better performing model in terms of false acceptance or rejection rates for a given domain. For example, although the Dropout CT model had a higher top-1 accuracy than the MARUPA CT model (-12.25% vs. -22.42%), if lowering the false reject rate for the Shopping domain is the highest priority, then the MARUPA CT model may be more appropriate.

5 Related work

5.1 Data Augmentation in NLP

Hedderich et al. (2021) provide a survey of NLP techniques for training models in low-resource scenarios. One of the most common techniques to address this is data augmentation, which produces new input instances by applying transformations to existing data.

In our study, we applied hidden-space augmentations by using independently sampled dropout masks for the same instance. Prior work has also proposed dropout as a data augmentation technique. Bouthillier et al. (2015) demonstrate that the effect of dropout on a neural network can be replicated by projecting dropout noise back into the input space and training a model on the generated data. Zhao et al. (2019) show that dropout can be viewed as equivalent to data augmentation whenever the input space dimension is equal to or higher than the output space.

5.2 Consistency training

Consistency regularization, also known as *consistency training* (Chen et al., 2021), is a popular technique in Semi-Supervised Learning. The underlying idea is that model predictions for a given data instance should not change much when that data instance is perturbed. Xie et al. (2020) proposed UDA, a framework for leveraging data augmentation in SSL settings by jointly minimizing a standard supervised loss with consistency-based loss on data and its augmentations.

5.3 Contrastive learning

The goal of contrastive learning (Chopra et al., 2005), which is very similar to consistency learning, is to learn a data representation such that similar data instances are located near to each other in the representation space and dissimilar instances are pushed apart. Wang and Isola (2020) showed that optimizing a contrastive metric can lead to better *alignment* and *uniformity* of features in the embedding space. Gao et al. (2021) show that standard dropout noise can outperform other types of data augmentation for contrastive learning of sentence embeddings.

6 Conclusion

With the aim of developing a strategy to efficiently leverage large amounts of unlabeled data in deployed NLU systems, we examined three different augmentation techniques for consistency training using real-world data. Back-translation performed the best, dropout was slightly behind and paraphrase by human users was the worst-performing technique. From an operations perspective dropout is more favorable because it doesn't require any extra system resources and is quick to compute. Paraphrasing by back-translation requires a machine-translation model that can translate to an intermediate language and back. This adds extra cost and processing time for unlabeled data which scales linearly with the amount of unlabeled data. For industry-scale NLU applications with massive amounts of data, dropout-based consistency training can provide performance gains over purely supervised methods with minimal additional resource overhead.

References

Philip Bachman, Ouais Alsharif, and Doina Precup. 2014. Learning with pseudo-ensembles. *Advances in neural information processing systems*, 27:3365–3373.

David Berthelot, Nicholas Carlini, Ian Goodfellow, Nicolas Papernot, Avital Oliver, and Colin A Raffel. 2019. MixMatch: A holistic approach to semi-supervised learning. *Advances in Neural Information Processing Systems*, 32.

Xavier Bouthillier, Kishore Konda, Pascal Vincent, and Roland Memisevic. 2015. Dropout as data augmentation. *arXiv preprint arXiv:1506.08700.*

Jiaao Chen, Derek Tam, Colin Raffel, Mohit Bansal, and Diyi Yang. 2021. An empirical survey of data augmentation for limited data learning in NLP. *arXiv preprint arXiv:2106.07499.*

Ting Chen, Simon Kornblith, Mohammad Norouzi, and Geoffrey Hinton. 2020. A simple framework for contrastive learning of visual representations. In *Proceedings of the 37th International Conference on Machine Learning*, volume 119, pages 1597–1607. PMLR.

Sumit. Chopra, Raia Hadsell, and Yan LeCun. 2005. Learning a similarity metric discriminatively, with application to face verification. In *2005 IEEE Computer Society Conference on Computer Vision and Pattern Recognition (CVPR'05)*, volume 1, pages 539–546 vol. 1.

Jacob Devlin, Ming-Wei Chang, Kenton Lee, and Kristina Toutanova. 2019. BERT: Pre-training of deep bidirectional transformers for language understanding. In *Proceedings of the 2019 Conference of the North American Chapter of the Association for Computational Linguistics: Human Language Technologies, Volume 1 (Long and Short Papers)*, pages 4171–4186, Minneapolis, Minnesota. Association for Computational Linguistics.

Li Dong, Jonathan Mallinson, Siva Reddy, and Mirella Lapata. 2017. Learning to paraphrase for question answering. In *Proceedings of the 2017 Conference on Empirical Methods in Natural Language Processing*, pages 875–886.

Sergey Edunov, Myle Ott, Michael Auli, and David Grangier. 2018. Understanding back-translation at scale. In *Proceedings of the 2018 Conference on Empirical Methods in Natural Language Processing*, pages 489–500.

Tobias Falke, Markus Boese, Daniil Sorokin, Caglar Tirkaz, and Patrick Lehnen. 2020. Leveraging user paraphrasing behavior in dialog systems to automatically collect annotations for long-tail utterances. In *Proceedings of the 28th International Conference on Computational Linguistics: Industry Track*, pages 21–32, Online. International Committee on Computational Linguistics.

Tianyu Gao, Xingcheng Yao, and Danqi Chen. 2021. SimCSE: Simple contrastive learning of sentence embeddings. *arXiv preprint arXiv:2104.08821*.

Michael A Hedderich, Lukas Lange, Heike Adel, Jannik Strötgen, and Dietrich Klakow. 2021. A survey on recent approaches for natural language processing in low-resource scenarios. In *Proceedings of the 2021 Conference of the North American Chapter of the Association for Computational Linguistics: Human Language Technologies*, pages 2545–2568.

Geoffrey Hinton, Oriol Vinyals, and Jeff Dean. 2015. Distilling the knowledge in a neural network. *arXiv preprint arXiv:1503.02531*.

Takeru Miyato, Shin-ichi Maeda, Masanori Koyama, and Shin Ishii. 2018. Virtual adversarial training: A regularization method for supervised and semi-supervised learning. *IEEE Transactions on Pattern Analysis and Machine Intelligence*, 41(8):1979–1993.

Antti Rasmus, Mathias Berglund, Mikko Honkala, Harri Valpola, and Tapani Raiko. 2015. Semi-supervised learning with ladder networks. *Advances in Neural Information Processing Systems*, 28:3546–3554.

Mehdi Sajjadi, Mehran Javanmardi, and Tolga Tasdizen. 2016. Regularization with stochastic transformations and perturbations for deep semi-supervised learning. *Advances in neural information processing systems*, 29:1163–1171.

Nitish Srivastava, Geoffrey Hinton, Alex Krizhevsky, Ilya Sutskever, and Ruslan Salakhutdinov. 2014. Dropout: A simple way to prevent neural networks from overfitting. *The Journal of Machine Learning Research*, 15(1):1929–1958.

Antti Tarvainen and Harri Valpola. 2017. Mean teachers are better role models: Weight-averaged consistency targets improve semi-supervised deep learning results. *Advances in Neural Information Processing Systems*, 30.

Ashish Vaswani, Noam Shazeer, Niki Parmar, Jakob Uszkoreit, Llion Jones, Aidan N Gomez, Łukasz Kaiser, and Illia Polosukhin. 2017. Attention is all you need. *Advances in neural information processing systems*, pages 5998–6008.

Vikas Verma, Alex Lamb, Juho Kannala, Yoshua Bengio, and David Lopez-Paz. 2019. Interpolation consistency training for semi-supervised learning. In *International Joint Conference on Artificial Intelligence*, pages 3635–3641.

Tongzhou Wang and Phillip Isola. 2020. Understanding contrastive representation learning through alignment and uniformity on the hypersphere. In *Proceedings of the 37th International Conference on Machine Learning*, volume 119 of *Proceedings of Machine Learning Research*, pages 9929–9939. PMLR.

Qizhe Xie, Zihang Dai, Eduard Hovy, Thang Luong, and Quoc Le. 2020. Unsupervised data augmentation for consistency training. *Advances in Neural Information Processing Systems*, 33.

Adams Wei Yu, David Dohan, Minh-Thang Luong, Rui Zhao, Kai Chen, Mohammad Norouzi, and Quoc V Le. 2018. QANet: Combining local convolution with global self-attention for reading comprehension. In *International Conference on Learning Representations*.

Dazhi Zhao, Guozhu Yu, Peng Xu, and Maokang Luo. 2019. Equivalence between dropout and data augmentation: A mathematical check. *Neural networks*, 115:82—89.

A Appendix

A.1 Ablation studies

The training of our CT models depends on a few hyperparameters, including: training signal annealing (TSA) schedule, softmax temperature control, and a confidence threshold for computing consistency loss. We explored the impact of each hyperparameter on resulting model performance. For these experiments, we used the Dropout CT model trained on 0.1% of labeled data. We did not train multiple models for each random data split.

	Top-1 relative change
Dropout CT*	-11.84%
confidence thresh= 0.6	-11.01%
confidence thresh = 0.3	-11.42%
confidence thresh = none	-32.37%
TSA schedule = log	-13.70%
TSA schedule = exp	-85.69%
TSA schedule = none	-14.22%
softmax temp = 0.7	-13.70%
softmax temp = 0.9	-12.87%
softmax temp = none	-11.94%

Table 3: Ablation studies related to confidence-based thresholding (confidence thresh), training-signal-annealing (TSA) schedule, and softmax temperature. In this table Dropout CT is the base model that each subsequent model modifies. We report the Dropout CT score only for the model trained on the same 0.1% data sample as used for the ablation-study experiments. All reported numbers are Top-1 accuracy relative changes compared to the performance of a baseline model trained with 100% labeled data. *For the base Dropout CT configuration, we used a linear TSA schedule, a consistency-loss softmax temperature of 0.85, and consistency-loss confidence threshold of 0.45.

Distantly Supervised Aspect Clustering And Naming For E-Commerce Reviews

Prateek Sircar
India Machine Learning
Amazon
sircarp@amazon.com

Aniket Chakrabarti*
Alexa AI
Amazon
chakanik@amazon.com

Deepak Gupta
India Machine Learning
Amazon
dgupt@amazon.com

Anirban Majumdar
India Machine Learning
Amazon
majumda@amazon.com

Abstract

Product aspect extraction from reviews is a critical task for e-commerce services to understand customer preferences and pain points. While aspect phrases extraction and sentiment analysis have received a lot of attention, clustering of aspect phrases and assigning human readable names to clusters in e-commerce reviews is an extremely important and challenging problem due to the scale of the reviews that makes human review infeasible. In this paper, we propose fully automated methods for clustering aspect words and generating human readable names for the clusters without any manually labeled data. We train transformer based sentence embeddings that are aware of unique e-commerce language characteristics (eg. incomplete sentences, spelling and grammar errors, vernacular etc.). We also train transformer based sequence to sequence models to generate human readable aspect names from clusters. Both the models are trained using heuristic based distant supervision. Additionally, the models are used to improve each other. Extensive empirical testing showed that the clustering model improves the Silhouette Score by 64% when compared to the state-of-the-art baseline and the aspect naming model achieves a high ROUGE-L score of 0.79.

1 Introduction

The aspect mining based insights and its polarity extraction from reviews is a critical task for e-commerce services that enables seller to understand fine-grained customer preferences and improve product offerings. Extracting important keywords and analyzing their sentiment is a very well studied area. However, the sheer scale of e-commerce services poses important novel challenges. Firstly, review phrases/keywords about the same aspect category need to be grouped together, since each product may have thousands of reviews and there are millions of products. Such aggregation will enable downstream individual aspect analysis by sellers. Secondly, each review phrases/keyword group needs to be assigned an interpretable aspect name to enable easy analysis. Finally, both steps have to be done without human annotations, as human review at e-commerce scale is infeasible. Note that, in this paper, we would refer to the terms, "phrase", "review phrase" and "snippet" interchangeably to denote subsets of a review text, obtained by splitting a multi-context review into smaller sentences of single context. For example, if review text is "The headphone has a good sound quality but not so good bass quality. It is useful for playing music while working out." then the corresponding review phrases would be "The headphone has a good sound quality", "not so good bass quality" and "It is useful for playing music while working out." We have used some syntactic/lexical rules for context splitting.

For unsupervised aspect grouping, extant methods use clustering (Bancken et al., 2014) (eg. k-means) and topic modeling (Brody and Elhadad, 2010) (eg. LDA) approaches. LDA based topic models assume the words are independently generated given the topic and consequently can't leverage the full context of the review sentences. k-means based techniques can overcome the drawback by using contextual embeddings typically generated by transformer based models (Devlin et al., 2018). However, these general purpose transformer language models fail to capture the nuances of e-commerce reviews' language characteristics, such as code mixed sentences including vernacular, incomplete sentence formation, spelling errors. Consequently, these models fail to generalize to e-commerce domain.Another ma-

*work done while author was at India Machine Learning, Amazon

Proceedings of NAACL-HLT 2022: Industry Track Papers, pages 94 - 102
July 10-15, 2022 ©2022 Association for Computational Linguistics

jor drawback of the LDA/k-means based methods is that these techniques are not able to generate a human interpretable name for the aspects (topics/clusters).

In this paper, we propose a practical framework for grouping aspect phrases from reviews into clusters and generate meaningful aspect names for the clusters at scale without any human labeled data. Specifically, the contributions of this paper are as follows:
(1) The proposed framework is able to cluster reviews into clusters by training a transformer model that is aware of the nuances of e-commerce review language characteristics.
(2) The proposed framework is able to generate human readable aspect names for the clusters by training a transformer based conditional natural language generation model.
(3) The proposed framework uses a heuristic distant supervision, thereby avoiding the need for manually labeled data.

To arrive at aspects, we first cluster the phrases by clustering the phrase embeddings generated by the state-of-the-art general purpose semantic matching SBERT model (Reimers and Gurevych, 2019). We fine-tune the transformer based conditional natural language generation (NLG) model T5 (Raffel et al., 2019) for aspect name generation that is distantly supervised using a heuristic TF-IDF distance based algorithm using the above clustering. Finally, to improve the aspect clustering, we train a transformer on the reviews corpus using masked language model (MLM) and subsequently fine-tune it Siamese style using the pairwise triplet loss. The training data (relevant and irrelevant pairs of phrases) for triplet loss is generated using a novel distant supervision strategy that leverages the earlier clustering output and the name generation model outputs. Consequently, the learned text embeddings are very robust to nuances of the e-commerce reviews domain. We empirically evaluate our framework at scale on reviews from a popular e-commerce service. The distantly supervised semantic embedding based clustering model is able to improve Silhouette Score by 64% over a baseline technique using a state-of-the-art general purpose semantic embedding model. Our distantly supervised aspect name generation model is able to improve the Rouge-L score by 16%.

2 Related Works

Aspect phrase extraction from text corpus is a widely researched topic (Quan and Ren, 2014; Qiu et al., 2011; Zhang et al., 2020; Xu et al., 2019, 2018; Wei et al., 2020; He et al., 2017; Vargas et al., 2020). In this paper we explore two tasks after aspect phrase extraction, (1) aspect grouping into clusters, and (2) aspect name generation, that are specifically important to the e-commerce reviews domain due to its large scale and lack of annotation requiring unsupervised techniques. Aspect grouping is done typically by clustering/topic modeling approaches once the aspect phrases have been extracted. Topic modeling approaches include LDA, pLSA, NMF based aspect extraction (Titov and McDonald, 2008; García-Pablos et al., 2018; Mukherjee and Liu, 2012; Chen et al., 2014; W. Xu and Gong; C. Ding and Peng). A number of clustering approaches have also been explored (Zhai et al., 2010; Chen et al., 2016; Zhai et al., 2011; Bancken et al., 2014; Pessutto et al., 2020). One limitation of extant topic modeling/clustering approaches is that these techniques fail to leverage the semantic context of the entire text while clustering. Recently, pre-trained models capable of capturing contextual representations have been developed (Peters et al., 2018; Devlin et al., 2018). However, vanilla pre-trained embeddings doesn't lead to coherent groupings of aspects as the e-commerce review language is significantly different from general English/web text on which these embeddings models are pre-trained. In this paper, we propose a transformer language embedding model that captures the semantics of e-commerce reviews, thereby leading to robust clustering. Note that our generated embeddings may be used with any existing clustering techniques to improve their quality.

3 Proposed Solution

The proposed framework for aspect grouping and naming has two main components: (i) phrase clustering, and (ii) aspect name generation. Our goal is to develop a phrase embedding model that captures the nuances of e-commerce reviews, and a conditional NLG model that generates meaningful names for the aspects without any manually labeled data. To achieve this, we propose a novel distant supervision scheme that uses the two components to improve the other along with some heuristic based automated supervision. Note that

Table 1: Sample output of the aspect insights framework on headphones

Aspect Name	Example Review Snippets
sound quality	['its just like mentioned in description very good quality of sound', 'i must say that i dont regret my decision as its sound quality is too good', 'i can definitely say its sound quality is very good', 'definitely very nice choice its sound is very nice']
value for money	['just go for it on this price bracket it is the complete value for money', 'nothing to dislike as such in this amount of money this is the best thing u get', 'nothing more 1 can ask and to top it all at an amazing price point', 'go for these guys for the price range these are the best']
bass quality	['build quality is pretty good and yeah it does have a punchy bass', 'this must be a nice purchase if you are bass lover', 'just go for it if you are a bass lover', 'just go for it if u are bass lover', 'it is the king of bass so i strongly recommended']

we get the review phrases extracted by the existing pipeline at a popular e-commerce service. Figure 1 shows an overview of the proposed framework

Figure 1: workflow diagram for clustering and naming

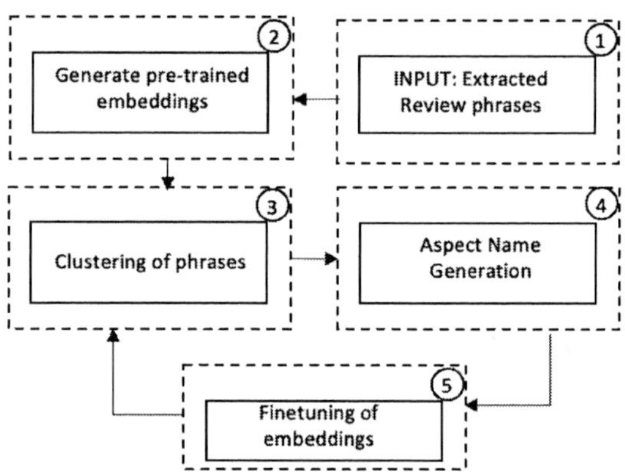

and table 1 shows a snapshot of the final output for a headphone.

3.1 Initial Phrase Clustering

Recently advances in language modeling have resulted in text embedding models (Devlin et al., 2018) such that the embeddings are able to capture the semantics of the text and consequently similar text phrases are mapped to similar vectors. Since our goal is to semantically group review phrases into clusters, we chose the state-of-the-art transformer based semantic text embedding model SBERT-STS (Reimers and Gurevych, 2019) that was trained for the semantic textual similarity (STS) task (Wang et al., 2018). Once each review phrase embedding is generated, we use agglomerative clustering to cluster the review phrases into aspect groups. We chose agglomerative clustering technique instead of k-means as agglomerative clustering is parameterized by only the distance threshold that is easier to tune and interpret in our usecase. While SBERT-STS is a state-of-the-art general purpose semantic embedding model, it fails to generalize to e-commerce reviews. The underlying reason is the nuances of e-commerce reviews, such as the phrases often being short incomplete sentences, presence of code mixed phrases including regional words, presence of spelling and grammar errors. To improve the text embeddings to capture the characteristics of reviews, we propose a novel distant supervision strategy to finetune the SBERT-STS model. We describe this strategy in section 3.3.

3.2 Initial Aspect Name Generation

The goal of this component is to generate a name that represents the common theme of a cluster. We use a sequence-to-sequence based NLG model to generate meaningful aspect names. The main challenge with sequence to sequence models is that they require a significant amount of training data for a stable model. We designed a heuristic based distant supervision strategy that enables us to generate labeled data at scale without human annotation. We chose T5 (Raffel et al., 2019) as the base model as it has been pre-trained on a huge amount of data on multiple NLP tasks, making it a great candidate for transfer learning and stable NLG capabilities. We use k randomly selected review phrases concatenated as the input to T5. We choose the most descriptive n-gram from a cluster of review phrases that satisfy certain linguistic rules as the distantly supervised label (aspect name) for that cluster as follows:We first collect all n-grams (n=1,2,3,4) from the corpus of reviews in a cluster. Next, we eliminate "ineligible phrases" based on POS-tag based rules. We use SPACY (Honnibal et al., 2020) for POS-tagging. Based on the ngrams, we employ the below rules to eliminate ineligible ngrams. Let t be a ngram whose eligibility we would evaluate. Let pos_t be a set of POS tags for each corresponding word in t. t is an ineligible n-gram if either of the following is satisfied:

1. $len(pos_t) > 1$ and last element of pos_t $\in$ ['DET', 'ADP', 'CCONJ', 'ADV', 'PRON', 'AUX', 'SCONJ', 'PART']
2. $len(pos_t) > 1$ and first element of pos_t $\in$ ['ADV', 'AUX', 'PART', 'PRON', 'ADP', 'CCONJ', 'DET']
3. $pos_t \in$ {['ADP', 'NOUN'], ['ADP', 'PROPN'], ['DET', 'NOUN'],['AUX'], ['ADV'], ['INTJ'], ['DET'], ['VERB'], ['CCONJ']}
4. if first or last word of t is "i".

t is an eligible n-gram overriding the above criteria if either of the following is satisfied:

1. $len(pos_t) > 1$ and last element of $pos_t \in$ ['ADJ'] and first element of $pos_t \in$ ['NOUN','PROPN']
2. First word of t is "not".

For an eligible set of n-grams, we propose the following two heuristic algorithms for training label (cluster name) generation:

(1) TF-IDF-based Naming: We derive TF-IDF scores for each n-gram and weight the TF-IDF score by n (in n-gram), i.e. providing higher weight to longer n-grams. This allows us to get more descriptive names. The candidate n-gram with the highest weighted TF-IDF score is the cluster name.

(2) Distance-Based Naming: For each n-gram we compute the mean cosine distance with each member phrase of the cluster. The n-gram with the minimum distance is considered as the cluster name.

For generating the distantly supervised training labels for our model, we choose high confidence cluster names by setting high thresholds for the aforementioned scores.

3.3 Improving Clustering & Name Generation

Next, we use the initial versions of the reviews phrase clustering and aspect name generation model to distantly supervise and improve each other. One of the main limitations of the initial clustering model was the usage of general purpose semantic embeddings from SBERT-STS that fails to capture the distinct characteristics of e-commerce reviews language. Consequently, many phrases could not be assigned a cluster even though they were relevant to certain aspect of a product and in many cases different clusters were formed for the same aspect. To overcome this limitation, we finetune the transformer based text embedding model with reviews text. We use the unsupervised masked language model (MLM) on the reviews text and couple it with distant supervision signal generated from the T5 based aspect name generation model. Below is the algorithm for training our transformer based text representation model.

We first train the transformer using the standard MLM loss (as described in BERT (Devlin et al., 2018)) on reviews text. This enables the model to learn a robust language model specific to the reviews domain. Furthermore, to enhance the semantic matching capabilities, we finetune our model Siamese style using the following triplet loss:

$$loss = max(||e_a - e_p|| - ||e_a - e_n|| + m, 0) \quad (1)$$

where e_a, e_p and e_n are embeddings of anchor phrase, positive phrase and negative phrase, respectively. m is margin. Negative samples should be at least margin further apart from the anchor than the positive. The anchor and positive phrases refer to the same aspect, whereas anchor and negative phrase refer to different aspects. Minimizing this loss would ensure that embeddings of the phrases mentioned in "anchor phrase" and "positive phrase" are close, while the phrases mentioned in "anchor phrase" and "negative phrase" is far away. The methodology to generate triplet data is described below:

(1) Positive Pairs: We hypothesize that clusters with the same/similar names are talking about the same aspect. Therefore, any randomly selected phrase from one cluster could act as a positive pair for another randomly selected phrase from another. For this, we find the cluster names for each cluster by leveraging the T5 based aspect name generation model. We also find the medoid of each cluster. Medoid is defined as an element in a cluster which has the least average distance from the remaining elements in the cluster. We use the initial SBERT-STS embeddings to generate embeddings of the cluster names and medoids and pick positive samples from clusters where (a) cosine distance between cluster names <= 0.08, or (b) cosine distance between cluster medoids <= 0.05 or (c) cosine distance between cluster names <= 0.1 and cosine distance between medoids <= 0.1 as positive pairs. These thresholds were tuned empirically. We sample a small number of anchor phrases with code-mixed or fully regional phrases, and we added their English translation as a positive pair to enable the model's semantic matching robustness in the presence of vernacular.

(2) Negative Pairs: If names of 2 clusters have a distance higher than a particular threshold (0.4), then the phrases from one cluster qualify to be negative pair to phrases of another cluster.

Once the text embedding model is trained and fine-tuned for e-commerce review text, we again use the same agglomerative clustering technique (as described in section 3.1) to generate robust and high quality aspect grouping. After re-clustering using the fine-tuned embeddings, we then use the T5 based aspect name generation model that was developed in section 3.2 to generate the aspect names for these new clusters. Even though the aspect name generation model wasn't re-trained in this step, but still the aspect name generation improves due to the new clusters being more coherent.

4 Experiments

4.1 Baselines

We use the following baseline algorithms to compare with our proposed framework.

(1) SBERT-STS-Clustering: We use the state-of-the-art sentence transformers (Reimers and Gurevych, 2019) model trained the STS task [1] for phrase embedding and agglomerative clustering to create aspect groups. We use this baseline to compare with our aspect grouping model that uses distant supervision.

(2) DS-Clustering: This is our proposed final clustering model as described in section 3.3.

(3) Heuristic-Name-Generation: We use the heuristic algorithm (used for distant supervision) using TFIDF scores and distance threshold as described in section 3.2 as a baseline for aspect name generation.

(4) DS-BART-Name-Generation: We train the state-of-the-art conditional language generation model, BART (Lewis et al., 2019) with our distant supervision strategy as a baseline for aspect name generation model.

(5) DS-T5-Name-Generation: This is our proposed final aspect name generation model as described in section 3.3 using T5 (Raffel et al., 2019).

4.2 Experimental Setup

We use the sentence-transformers [2], HuggingFace [3] and Pytorch [4] libraries to train our reviews phrase embedding model. Training was done on a single Nvidia V100 GPU. Batch size was set to be 16. Learning rate was set to be $2X10^{-05}$ with 10% of total training iterations as warmup steps and a linear decay schedule. We used the ADAM optimizer with parameters (beta1: 0.9, beta2: 0.999, epsilon: 10^{-8}). We train the phrase embedding model for 10 epochs. We use the python SKLearn library for agglomerative clustering. For DS-Clustering, we used a cosine distance margin of 0.5. For the baseline SBERT-STS-Clustering, we use the SBERT-STS model for phrase embedding and the agglomerative clustering threshold was set to 0.2. We train the T5 model using HuggingFace and Pytorch libraries for our aspect name generation model, DS-T5-Name-Generation. Batch size was set to be 2. Learning rate was set to be $5X10^{-05}$. We used the ADAM optimizer with parameters (beta1: 0.9, beta2: 0.999, epsilon: 10^{-8}). We train DS-T5-Name-Generation for 3 epochs. For our BART based baseline training, we set batch size to be 2, learning rate to be $5X10^{-05}$. The baseline was trained for 3 epochs. All the heuristic thresholds described in section 3 were hand-tuned experimentally.

4.3 Results

Dataset: To evaluate the proposed framework at scale, we collect customer reviews and return comments of a random sample of 1500 products

[1]https://huggingface.co/sentence-transformers/stsb-bert-base

[2]https://www.sbert.net

[3]https://huggingface.co

[4]https://pytorch.org

of a popular e-commerce service. The total number of reviews and return comments were around 40 million. These 40 million reviews/comments were broken down into review phrases. The review phrases were on an average 5.5 words long. Language of the corpus is a mix of English and common vernacular languages in India e.g. Hindi. Some phrases have mix-coded tokens from English and Hindi Language. A sentiment model was applied to remove the neutral phrases, resulting in 33 million phrases. Neutral phrases were removed in this exercise, as the intention was to understand the likes and dislikes of a customer for the product. Our goal is to cluster these phrases into coherent aspect groups and subsequently generate human readable names for these clusters.

Phrase Clustering: To evaluate aspect cluster quality, we use the popular Silhouette Score. Intuitively, it measures the closeness of samples to its own cluster as compared to other clusters. Silhouette Score computation doesn't require ground truth labels and consequently can be computed at scale. We also did a human annotation driven evaluation. We define the following two metrics: (i) intra-cluster accuracy: probability that a pair randomly selected from a cluster refers to the same aspect, and (ii) inter-cluster accuracy: probability that a pair randomly selected from different clusters refers to different aspects. We generate a random sample of intra-cluster phrase pairs and inter-cluster phrase pairs from the output of the DS-clustering and the baseline methods. The annotation team marked each pair as similar (pair belongs to same aspect) or dissimilar (pair belongs to different aspects). We estimate intra-cluster accuracy as the fraction of intra-cluster sampled pairs that were similar. Similarly, we estimate inter-cluster accuracy as the fraction of inter-cluster sampled pairs that were dissimilar. We report the clustering metrics in Table 2. Table 3 shows qualitative examples of clustering.

Table 2: Comparison of aspect clustering methods. Method A: SBER-STS-Clustering, B: DS-Clustering w/o MLM, C: DS-Clustering

	A	B	C
Silhouette Score	0.33	0.52	0.54
intra-cluster accuracy	0.88	0.88	0.91
inter-cluster accuracy	0.90	0.98	0.98

We see from table 2 that DS-Clustering improves over all baselines across all metrics. DS-Clustering improves by upto 64% over the baselines on Silhouette Score. On annotation driven inter/intra cluster accuracy, DS-Clustering is able to improve by upto 9%. DS-Clustering is able to improve over the baselines as our distantly supervised text embedding model is able to capture the unique language characteristics of e-commerce reviews where the general purpose text embedding models such as SBERT-STS fail to generalize. Examples of such cases are shown in table 3.

Table 3: Example review phrases that are correctly clustered by DS-Clustering inspite of presence of spelled errors(isound) and code mixing (paisa vasool translates to value for money). Baseline fails to cluster these.

Review Phrase	Cluster Name
isound quality is amazing	sound quality
fully paisa vasool.	value for money
truly value for each paisa spent	value for money

Aspect Name Generation: The name generation models in section 4.1 generate cluster names, which are on an average 2.7 words long. We measure the quality of the generated names by annotating 53K clusters generated by DS-Clustering. The annotation team reviewed sample phrases from each cluster and created a name that best described the aspect of the cluster as per their judgement. We treat this as ground truth and evaluate how close is the name generated via our model and the baselines to the ground truth. We measure closeness using ROUGE-F scores. The summary of metrics can be seen in table 4. We see that DS-T5-Name-Generation model outperforms both the Heuristic-Name-Generation as well as the DS-BART-Name-Generation models in all metrics showing that our model generates names that are most similar to that of human annotation team. Consequently, DS-T5-Name-Generation is able to generate human readable names using our novel distant supervision tech-

Table 4: Comparison of aspect name generation methods. Method A: Heuristic-Name-Generation, B: DS-BART-Name-Generation, C: DS-T5-Name-Generation

	A	B	C
ROUGE-1-F score	0.70	0.71	0.79
ROUGE-2-F score	0.46	0.47	0.63
ROUGE-L-F score	0.68	0.71	0.79

nique. DS-T5-Name-Generation is able to improve by 37% over Heuristic-Name-Generation on ROGUE-2 score even though distant-supervision was created through similar heuristics. This shows that the transfer learning capabilities of T5 combined with our heuristics based distant supervision results in a robust conditional NLG model without any manual labeling. Additionally, we analyzed cases where DS-T5-Name-Generation generated different names when compared to annotated names (i.e. ROUGE-L = 0) in table 5. Our model is able to perform well even in these cases. The ROUGE-L score is 0 as there is no word overlap, however, the generated names are semantically similar to the annotated names showing the semantic language understanding capabilities of our T5 based sequence to sequence model. In table 5, we report such examples. In the first example, a spelling error ("dimesions") in human annotation is leading to a Rouge score of 0, whereas our naming model generates names with correct spelling. In the second example, both the names are semantically similar.

Table 5: Examples where model generated names do not match annotated names. A: DS-T5-Naming. B: Manual Annotation

Cluster Phrases	A	B
['the dimensions too are incorrect','dimensions not appropriate for my usage']	wrong dimensions	inaccurate dimesions
['creating pain in foot', 'hurts feet on walking', 'itspainful for foot']	hurts the feet	Getting foot pain

5 Conclusion

In this paper we presented a practical aspect clustering and naming framework for e-commerce reviews. Our models leverage distant supervision thereby avoiding the need of manually labeled data. Extensive evaluations show improvement in clustering by 64% and naming by 16%. Survey results in appendix show that the approach generates more interpretable aspects when compared to an existing e-commerce baseline. We hypothesize that our novel distant supervision paradigm is generalizable across domains and in future we wish to explore the application of our novel distant supervision scheme to other domains. We also plan to explore principled approaches to handle multi-context phrases (phrase talking about multiple aspects) without needing manual annotations.

References

Wouter Bancken, Daniele Alfarone, and Jesse Davis. 2014. Automatically detecting and rating product aspects from textual customer reviews. In *Proceedings of the 1st international workshop on interactions between data mining and natural language processing at ECML/PKDD*, volume 1202, pages 1–16. CEUR-WS. org.

Samuel Brody and Noemie Elhadad. 2010. An unsupervised aspect-sentiment model for online reviews. In *Human language technologies: The 2010 annual conference of the North American chapter of the association for computational linguistics*, pages 804–812.

T. Li C. Ding and W. Peng. Nonnegative matrix factorization and probabilistic latent semantic indexing: equivalence, chi-square statistic, and a hybrid method. *Proceedings of the American Association for Artificial Intelligence (AAAI), 2006.*

Lu Chen, Justin Martineau, Doreen Cheng, and Amit Sheth. 2016. Clustering for simultaneous extraction of aspects and features from reviews. In *proceedings of the 2016 conference of the north American chapter of the Association for Computational Linguistics: human language technologies*, pages 789–799.

Zhiyuan Chen, Arjun Mukherjee, and Bing Liu. 2014. Aspect extraction with automated prior knowledge learning. In *Proceedings of the 52nd Annual Meeting of the Association for Computational Linguistics (Volume 1: Long Papers)*, pages 347–358.

Jacob Devlin, Ming-Wei Chang, Kenton Lee, and Kristina Toutanova. 2018. BERT: pre-training of deep bidirectional transformers for language understanding. *CoRR*, abs/1810.04805.

Aitor García-Pablos, Montse Cuadros, and German Rigau. 2018. W2vlda: almost unsupervised system for aspect based sentiment analysis. *Expert Systems with Applications*, 91:127–137.

Ruidan He, Wee Sun Lee, Hwee Tou Ng, and Daniel Dahlmeier. 2017. An unsupervised neural attention model for aspect extraction. In *Proceedings of the 55th Annual Meeting of the Association for Computational Linguistics (Volume 1: Long Papers)*, pages 388–397.

Matthew Honnibal, Ines Montani, Sofie Van Landeghem, and Adriane Boyd. 2020. spaCy: Industrial-strength Natural Language Processing in Python.

Mike Lewis, Yinhan Liu, Naman Goyal, Marjan Ghazvininejad, Abdelrahman Mohamed, Omer Levy, Veselin Stoyanov, and Luke Zettlemoyer.

2019. BART: denoising sequence-to-sequence pre-training for natural language generation, translation, and comprehension. *CoRR*, abs/1910.13461.

Arjun Mukherjee and Bing Liu. 2012. Aspect extraction through semi-supervised modeling. In *Proceedings of the 50th Annual Meeting of the Association for Computational Linguistics (Volume 1: Long Papers)*, pages 339–348.

Lucas Rafael Costella Pessutto, Danny Suarez Vargas, and Viviane P Moreira. 2020. Multilingual aspect clustering for sentiment analysis. *Knowledge-Based Systems*, 192:105339.

Matthew E. Peters, Mark Neumann, Mohit Iyyer, Matt Gardner, Christopher Clark, Kenton Lee, and Luke Zettlemoyer. 2018. Deep contextualized word representations. In *NAACL*.

Guang Qiu, Bing Liu, Jiajun Bu, and Chun Chen. 2011. Opinion word expansion and target extraction through double propagation. *Computational linguistics*, 37(1):9–27.

Changqin Quan and Fuji Ren. 2014. Unsupervised product feature extraction for feature-oriented opinion determination. *Information Sciences*, 272:16–28.

Colin Raffel, Noam Shazeer, Adam Roberts, Katherine Lee, Sharan Narang, Michael Matena, Yanqi Zhou, Wei Li, and Peter J. Liu. 2019. Exploring the limits of transfer learning with a unified text-to-text transformer. *CoRR*, abs/1910.10683.

Nils Reimers and Iryna Gurevych. 2019. Sentence-bert: Sentence embeddings using siamese bert-networks. *CoRR*, abs/1908.10084.

Ivan Titov and Ryan McDonald. 2008. Modeling online reviews with multi-grain topic models. In *Proceedings of the 17th international conference on World Wide Web*, pages 111–120.

Danny Suarez Vargas, Lucas RC Pessutto, and Viviane Pereira Moreira. 2020. Simple unsupervised similarity-based aspect extraction. *arXiv preprint arXiv:2008.10820*.

X. Liu W. Xu and Y. Gong. Document clustering based on non-negative matrix factorization. *Proceedings of the 26th annual international ACM SIGIR conference on Research and development in information retrieval, 2003*.

Alex Wang, Amanpreet Singh, Julian Michael, Felix Hill, Omer Levy, and Samuel R. Bowman. 2018. Glue: A multi-task benchmark and analysis platform for natural language understanding. *ArXiv*, abs/1804.07461.

Zhenkai Wei, Yu Hong, Bowei Zou, Meng Cheng, and Jianmin Yao. 2020. Don't eclipse your arts due to small discrepancies: Boundary repositioning with a pointer network for aspect extraction. In *Proceedings of the 58th Annual Meeting of the Association for Computational Linguistics*, pages 3678–3684.

Hu Xu, Bing Liu, Lei Shu, and Philip S Yu. 2018. Double embeddings and cnn-based sequence labeling for aspect extraction. *arXiv preprint arXiv:1805.04601*.

Hu Xu, Bing Liu, Lei Shu, and Philip S Yu. 2019. Bert post-training for review reading comprehension and aspect-based sentiment analysis. *arXiv preprint arXiv:1904.02232*.

Zhongwu Zhai, Bing Liu, Hua Xu, and Peifa Jia. 2010. Grouping product features using semi-supervised learning with soft-constraints. In *Proceedings of the 23rd International Conference on Computational Linguistics (Coling 2010)*, pages 1272–1280.

Zhongwu Zhai, Bing Liu, Hua Xu, and Peifa Jia. 2011. Clustering product features for opinion mining. In *Proceedings of the fourth ACM international conference on Web search and data mining*, pages 347–354.

Denghui Zhang, Zixuan Yuan, Yanchi Liu, Zuohui Fu, Fuzhen Zhuang, Pengyang Wang, Haifeng Chen, and Hui Xiong. 2020. E-bert: A phrase and product knowledge enhanced language model for e-commerce. *arXiv preprint arXiv:2009.02835*.

6 Appendix

6.1 Comparison with a e-commerce baseline

We also compare the performance of our framework with the existing system at a popular e-commerce service that uses a non-negative matrix factorization (NMF) based topic modeling approach [5] on the "document-term" matrix created from the review corpus to extract aspects. A sample output of the framework is shown in table 7.The NMF based system is not able to distinguish semantically different aspects, resulting in incoherent clusters. E.g. "money, refund, wastage, value" are grouped together. Our proposed framework, howerver, is able to distinguish and capture the nuanced aspects. For example it is able to capture "value for money" as a separate aspect.

We use a human annotation driven approach to compare our proposed framework with the existing baseline. For each product type we get the aspect names generated by the topic modeling approach as well as our proposed framework. In each solution, for each aspect, we asked 3 "yes/no" questions to the annotation team.

(1) Does this aspect name describe the aspect of a product?

[5] Details can't be disclosed due to proprietary information

Table 6: User Responses to Survey. Improvement in Favorable Response quantifies how many more favorable responses were received for the DS-clustering + DS Naming framework as compared to the NMF framework.

Questions Asked	Improvement in Favorable Response
(a) Does this aspect name describe the aspect of a product?	+34.78%
(b) Is the supplementary information helping in understanding the aspect better?	+42.72%
(c) Does this help in knowing more about the customer likes and dislikes?	+42.22%

(2) Is the supplementary information helping in understanding the aspect better?
(3) Does this help in knowing more about the customer likes and dislikes?
The results of the survey is summarized in table 6. In the table, the "term" aspect refers to a cluster of reviews. "Aspect Name" refers to the name given to the cluster. "Supplementary Information" are the additional information given along with cluster and cluster name. In the case of DS-Clustering, they are a sample of review phrases belonging to the cluster. In the case of NMF Based Topic Modeling, they are the additional words obtained with each topic words. We can see the annotation team found our proposed framework to be significantly more helpful the topic modeling based baseline. Sample output of DS-Clustering + DS-T5-Name-generation is shown in table 1.

Table 7: Results NMF Based topic modeling on reviews of headphones

aspect name	related words
stopped	left, suddenly, 10, usage, earpiece, working, 15, warranty, function
money	value, waste, completely, spend, wastage, spent, want, refund, definitely
working	fine, left, speaker, button, perfectly, microphone, touch, 15, device
sound	clarity, clear, balanced, base, effect, loud, output, average, quality
range	mids, 10, meters, quite, frequency, audio, available, 500
battery	backup, hours, hrs, 10, long, drains, upto, performance, continuously

Local-to-global learning for iterative training of production SLU models on new features

Yulia Grishina and **Daniil Sorokin**
Amazon Alexa AI, Berlin, Germany
{yuliag,dsorokin}@amazon.com

Abstract

In production SLU systems, new training data becomes available with time so that ML models need to be updated on a regular basis. Specifically, releasing new features adds new classes of data while the old data remains constant. However, retraining the full model each time from scratch is computationally expensive. To address this problem, we propose to consider production releases from the curriculum learning perspective and to adapt the local-to-global learning (LGL) schedule (Cheng et al., 2019) for a neural model that starts with fewer output classes and adds more classes with each iteration.

We report experiments for the tasks of intent classification and slot filling in the context of a production voice-assistant. First, we apply the original LGL schedule on our data and then adapt LGL to the production setting where the full data is not available at initial training iterations. We demonstrate that our method improves model error rates by -7.3% and saves up to 25% training time for individual iterations.

1 Introduction

In many real-world NLP systems with ML models, new data becomes available with time and there is a need to refresh the model (Diethe et al., 2018). In some cases it is a passive flow, when new data arrives due to the properties of the application (e.g. daily search queries) or an active act of collecting new data to be incorporated into the system (e.g. a new feature). In this paper, we regard the use case of an active extension of data to incorporate a new customer-facing feature into a production NLP model. We consider a Spoken Language Understanding (SLU) model that is used to interpret user requests in a commercial task-oriented voice-assistant. The model is a joint intent classification (IC) and slot filling (SF) architecture that is used to process utterances in a single domain.[1] We select one data-rich domain for our experiments, Music, and construct a scenario when an existing IC+SF model is extended with a new user-facing feature that comprises a set of intents and slots to be now recognized by the model.

It is conventional to re-train the original ML model on a combination of the old training data and the additional data for the new feature, starting from the same randomly initialized or pre-trained architecture as the previous time. The practitioners tend to use pre-trained models (language modeling and transfer learning are widely used here) to improve the generalization performance of the model. It seems logical also to re-use the previous iteration of the model trained on the old data in the previous model release to warm-start the next iteration. This could result in a reduced training time and a smaller computational and environmental footprint of the model updates in a scenario where new features are added regularly. Yet, in practice it is usually considered 'safer' to start training from scratch or from the same general-purpose pre-trained model every time, the main concern being that repeated warm-starting would lead to overfitting and poorer generalization (Ash and Adams, 2020).

Re-training the same model architecture on nearly the same data with minimal changes, but extending the output space with a new class is a unique problem for industry applications. Many previous works on continual learning have focused on learning from a continuous stream of data (Biesialska et al., 2020) or on an incremental learning of new tasks (Kanwatchara et al., 2021) and languages (Castellucci et al., 2021). Payan et al. (2021) discuss a single-task continual learning setup and simulated a passive data extension

[1] Intent classification model determines the intent class the query belongs to (e.g., *PlayMusic*) and slot filling is responsible for identifying slot instances in the query (e.g., *SongName*).

Proceedings of NAACL-HLT 2022: Industry Track Papers, pages 103 - 111
July 10-15, 2022 ©2022 Association for Computational Linguistics

scenario where new examples are coming in for all output classes on a public dataset. Similarly, Ash and Adams (2020) evaluate a batch-learning setup, where each model iteration is warm-started from the previous step and the whole training data is always available, while some new data is added across all output classes in each batch. In our scenario, we consider active data extension for new features and we do not restrict the access to the old training data. We rely on an offline training paradigm, where each model release is trained on the latest batch of data until convergence.

If each release adds data for new features with the old data being constant, we can view a sequence of model releases as a subclass of curriculum learning, a machine learning paradigm that aims to arrange training data into a meaningful order to improve model training. In our scenario, the data is arranged by feature. Cheng et al. (2019) describe a local-to-global learning (LGL) schedule for a statistical model that starts with fewer output classes and adds more classes with each iteration. We build upon their results in our work, but remove their assumption that the whole data is available in the first iteration.

In this paper, we repeatedly apply a warm-start for training a set of subsequent IC+SF model releases, each one being extended with a new set of features. We define a single feature as a set of new intents and slots to be recognized by the model that are added to the output space. We focus on a real-life production setting and report results on a dataset sampled from a commercial German voice assistant.[2] As our main contribution, we show that warm-start is an effective strategy to reduce training time for later model releases and improve overall model performance in a scenario when the added training data pertains to new features only.

2 Related work

2.1 Spoken language understanding

Recent research in the field of SLU has made significant advancements through the application of deep learning (Mesnil et al., 2013) and the joint modeling of IC and SF (Zhang and Wang, 2016; Chen et al., 2019; Louvan and Magnini, 2020). Semi-supervised learning and paraphrasing are frequently applied to bootstrap new features, overcome the class imbalance problem and improve the overall SLU performance (Cho et al., 2019; Sokolov and Filimonov, 2020). These methods often rely on the assumption that the number of classes is static, while in a real production SLU system, new classes are added on a regular basis, affecting the target data distribution. In contrast, in this work, we propose to focus on the learning schedule of a model that benefits directly from the increasing number of classes and thus can be adapted to the real-world scenario, where new features are added to the system iteratively.

2.2 Local-to-global learning schedule

The main idea of local-to-global learning (LGL) schedule used in this work is to gradually train a neural network starting with a few output classes and subsequently extending to more classes. It was first introduced in the work of Cheng et al. (2019), who applied it to a computer vision problem. LGL does not require any additional annotated training data, instead it utilises the entire training set in each iteration, but only the data for the classes that are being learned in this iteration is annotated. The data for the rest of the classes is added masked (unlabeled). In each LGL iteration, a set of new classes is added and the model weights are transferred from the previous iteration (see Figure 1).

Cheng et al. (2019) compare the LGL schedule to other curriculum learning and self-paced learning strategies. A typical curriculum learning approach relies on prior knowledge about the data to define a training schedule, such as, for example, the input length (Tay et al., 2019). Self-paced learning alleviates the requirement for prior knowledge by assigning a weight to each training sample based on model's loss (Kumar et al., 2010). Yet, it introduces additional model passes to compute the per-sample loss during training and makes self-paced learning approaches challenging to optimize (Cheng et al., 2019). LGL defines a learning schedule based on the target output classes, by focusing the early stages of training only on a subset of classes. We propose to view feature expansion in a production SLU system as a special case of curriculum learning akin to LGL.

LGL can be also considered a form of a task specific pre-training strategy or transfer learning. Numerous transfer learning strategies were suggested for NLP problems (Ruder et al., 2019) and a complete overview is beyond the scope of our work. In that view, the final stage of LGL train-

[2]The data was de-identified prior to the experiment so that any user identifiable information was removed.

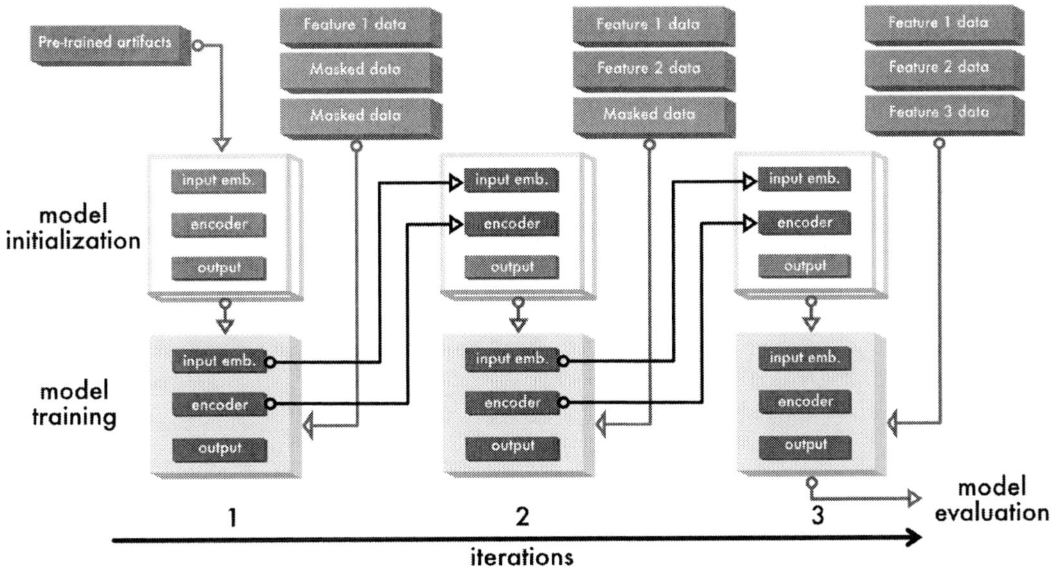

Figure 1: Local-to-Global model training set-up with 3 label batches (3 features) and hence 3 training iterations.

ing with complete annotations would correspond to the usual fine-tuning step. The preceding stages with a subset of classes are pre-finetuning steps, where pre-training is done repeatedly on the same task and with a reduced number of classes. The task-adaptive pre-training approach (Gururangan et al., 2020) uses a similar task to the target task to pre-train the model with a task-specific objective. Pruksachatkun et al. (2020) combine language model pre-training with task-specific pre-training and fine-tuning on the target task to test 110 pre-training task combinations. They conclude that it is still hard to predict, which task would be the most optimal for pre-training. From this perspective, LGL does not have this problem, as it pre-trains on the same task and the same dataset.

A sample LGL training set-up with 3 label batches and 3 training iterations is illustrated in Figure 1. In the first iteration the model is initialized from a pre-trained LM and the first batch of labels are unmasked in the training data, while the rest of data is left masked. In the next iteration, the embeddings and the encoder are initialized from the embeddings and the encoder of the previous iteration model. The second batch of labels is unmasked. In the final iteration, the embeddings and the encoder are initialized from the embeddings and the encoder of the second iteration model, while all three label batches are unmasked. After the last iteration the final model is exported and applied on the test set.[3]

In this work, we focus on applying LGL in a production SLU setup, where new models are released and new classes are added regularly. The experimental setup of Cheng et al. (2019) focuses on improving the final model performance on the full dataset and includes full (partially-masked) training data at each iteration. We first apply LGL to our internal data from a production SLU system. Second, to simulate a real-life situation, we modify this setup and conduct experiments where the data for new classes is not available at the early model training iterations. In Figure 1, this would correspond to not using the masked data batches.

3 Experimental setup

3.1 Dataset

We use a dataset sampled from a commercial German SLU system. The data was de-identified prior to the experiment (so that any user identifiable information was removed), and subsequently annotated across domains, intents and slots. For our experiment, we have selected Music domain, which contains mutually exclusive classes (intents), such as *PlayRadio* or *FindSoundtrack*. The evaluation set comes from the same distribution and was annotated in the same way. The distribution of relative frequencies of intents is typically a heavily skewed one; in the case of LGL, that can result in a large

[3]See Appendix A for an extended definition of LGL.

fraction of the annotated data being masked all at once. However, the main motivation behind LGL is that it is easier to learn fewer classes, while the amount of training data per class may vary (Cheng et al., 2019).

3.2 Model

We use an SLU architecture based on BERT for all of our experiments. Architectures based on pre-trained transformers have recently demonstrated the strongest performance on SLU tasks (Chen et al., 2019; Gaspers et al., 2020; Weld et al., 2021). The model consists of a pre-trained BERT encoder and an intent and slot decoders. The BERT encoder's outputs at sentence and token level are used as inputs for the intent and slot decoders, respectively. The intent decoder is a feed-forward network consisting of two dense layers and a softmax layer on top. The slot decoder uses a CRF layer on top of two dense layers to leverage the sequential information of slot labels. During training the IC and SL objectives are jointly optimized.

3.3 Metrics

We report results with two common metrics used in production SLU: intent classification error rate (ICER) and semantic error rate (SEMER). Both metrics are Recall-based, as they are computing the error rate with respect to the ground-truth domain (annotated manually by language experts). ICER is the ratio of incorrect intents to the total number of utterances (and we will mainly rely on this evaluation metric further for intent classification):

$$\text{ICER} = \frac{(\text{\# incorrect intents})}{(\text{\# total utterances})}. \quad (1)$$

SEMER considers both intent classification and slot classification together. SEMER allows us to measure the effect of improved intent classification on the overall joint model performance. It is computed based on the number of insertions, deletions and substitutions for slots and the intent in a recognised utterance compared to a reference utterance:

$$\text{SEMER} = \frac{(\text{\# slot errors + intent errors})}{(\text{\# reference slots + intents})} \quad (2)$$

4 Results

First, we study the impact of an unmodified LGL method on model training (4.1, 4.2), splitting our training data into several batches and masking parts of the data as described in Section 2. The batches are split per intent, with each batch containing several classes. We train the model in several iterations, gradually unmasking the data. Second, we adapt LGL to SLU production scenario and conduct experiments where the data for new classes is not available at the early model training iterations (4.3). In all experiments, we compare the result against a baseline, which is the same model trained on all classes in a single iteration.

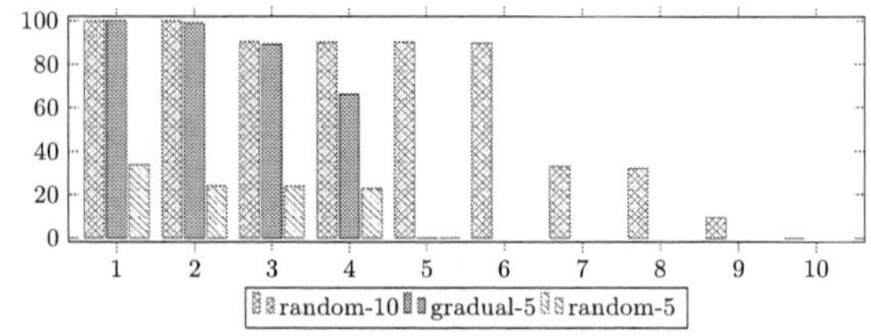

Figure 2: Masked data distribution per iteration (% of the full dataset) for random and gradual orderings in LGL for IC experiment. The last iteration (the 5th or the 10th) contains always only unmasked data.

	ordering, # of batches		
Metric	(r, 5)	(g, 5)	(r, 10)
SEMER	-2.61	-1.98	-2.50
ICER	-3.39	-2.34	-9.11

Table 1: Evaluation results for LGL applied to IC. The relative difference is with respect to baseline model that does not use any form of LGL or other curriculum learning.

4.1 LGL for intent classification

In the first experiment, we apply LGL to intent classification, i.e. only masking intent labels. Specifically, we replace all intent labels in masked batches by a placeholder (*OtherIntent*). We randomly group classes in the dataset into 5 and 10 batches for LGL training, so that each batch contains 5 to 6 intents (we include masked data statistics per batch in Figure 2). To account for the unbalanced class distribution in the dataset, we evaluate two strategies for selecting the order of batches for LGL:

- Random order (*r*). We select the order randomly, which results in 66% of the annotated data being included in the first iteration.
- Gradual order (*g*). We select batches based on the corresponding data size, starting with the smallest one. In that scenario, the first 4

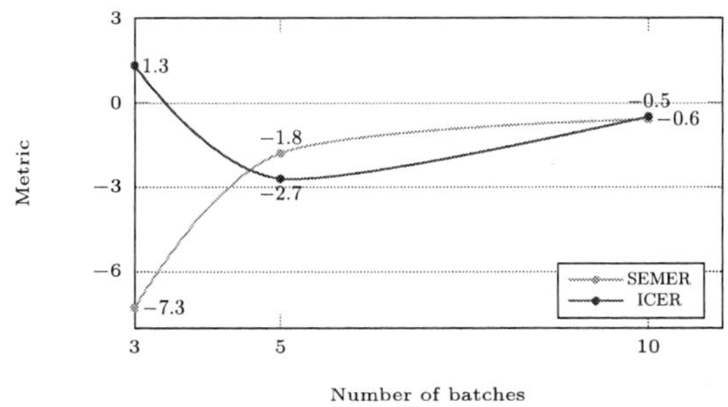

Figure 3: Evaluation results for LGL applied to NER and IC tasks (relative difference). The relative difference is with respect to the baseline model that does not use any form of LGL or other curriculum learning.

> iterations include 33% of the annotated data, while the largest classes are added in the last iteration.

The results of the experiments on a real-life Music dataset are presented in Table 1. We can see that the experimental models trained using LGL outperform the baseline across all metrics, which confirms the results first obtianed in Cheng et al. (2019). For the ICER metric, our best model (LGL (*r*, 10)) improves the error rate by -9.11% compared to the baseline. We conclude that the increasing number of batches has a positive impact on the LGL performance here, as the model trained on 10 batches outperforms the same model trained on 5 batches by 5.72%. The improvement in SEMER is smaller, which is expected as we apply LGL to intent classification only (i.e., the dataset was split into batches based on intents only, and all slots were left unmasked).

The selection strategy (*r* vs. *g*) has a substantial impact on the model performance. The model trained on a random selection of the training classes performs better on both SEMER and ICER metrics than the same model trained on the sets of classes selected gradually (cf. (r, 5) vs. (g, 5) in Table 1). Therefore, we only use the random ordering in the other experiments.

We also experiment with LGL approach without resetting the learning rate. In the current model, we used learning rate scheduler to control the learning rate using the specified steps, where the first step reset the learning rate to 0 for each model iteration. However, since the encoder is initialised from the encoder of the previous model starting from the second iteration, we experimented with keeping the learning rate multiplier constant (0.1) for that and

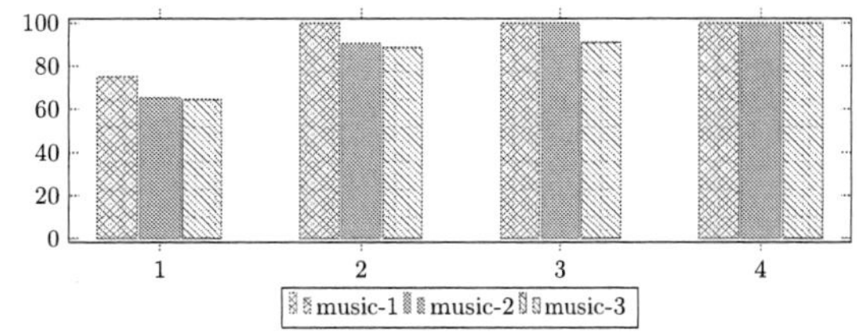

Figure 4: Data distribution per run and iteration (% of the full dataset; the last iteration always contains 100% of the data). Each run represents a different feature grouping and order.

all subsequent iterations. The results with respect to the (LGL (*r*, 5)) approach show only marginal improvement (avg. -0.27 rel. improvement over ICER and SEMER), therefore we conclude that resetting the learning rate does not have significant impact on the LGL training.

4.2 LGL for NER and IC

In this experiment, we apply masking to both intent and slot labels, splitting the training dataset into 3, 5 and 10 batches to further study the impact of the batch size[4]. In addition to intent masking (described in 4.1), slot masking is done as follows: *madonna|ArtistName -> madonna|OtherSlot*.

The results for the Music domain are visualized in Figure 3. As one can see, the best result is achieved when selecting a middle number of batches (between 3 and 5), while a very large number of batches (10) potentially overfits the model. This result differs from the LGL result on IC only (where using 10 batches is superior to using 5 on ICER metric) potentially due to a much larger number of slots that are left masked.

4.3 Gradually adding new features

Having applied LGL to the task of IC and NER, we showed that it is able to improve IC performance by -9.1% relative ICER and -2.5% relative SEMER. However, the downside of LGL for production SLU setup is the increased number of training iterations, which is associated with additional computational cost. In addition, in a real-life scenario, the data for new classes only becomes available with time. Therefore, in the following experiments, we modify the original LGL setup and conduct experiments where the data for new classes is added gradually within several iterations. Note that we select this setup to account for a production scenario when a

[4]We do not include data statistics here for space reasons.

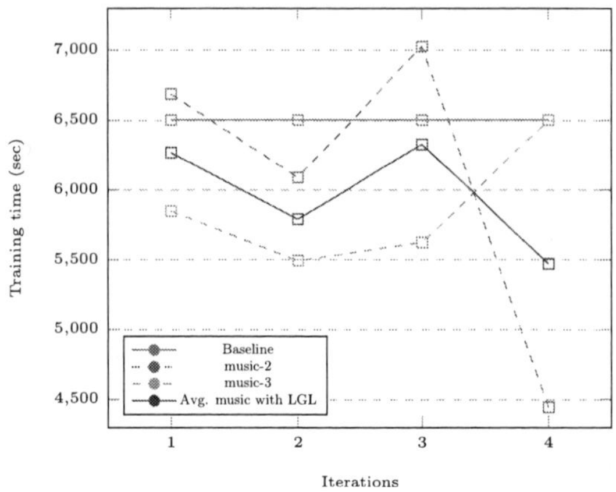

Figure 5: Average training time per LGL iteration compared to the baseline (note that the baseline here is the full model trained once on all available data in each iteration, which represents the upper bound).

model is trained in several iterations within a fixed release cycle (e.g., a period of several weeks); for simplicity, we assume that after each iteration the model is fully retrained on all data to avoid any model drift-related effects (which are out of scope of this work). This would also correspond to a 100% data replay strategy in continuous learning approaches (Payan et al., 2021).

We split the Music domain dataset into 4 batches corresponding to model releases, each one containing a new set of features (another reason for that is best result observed using 3 to 5 batches, cf. 4.2). With each iteration, a new batch of data (comprising several new classes and representing a new feature) is added to the model. We experiment with different feature order when grouping the data into batches (for instance, the first run may contain features represented by *PlaySong* and *PlayAlbum* intents grouped together for the first iteration, *PlayRadio* for the second iteration, while the second run could have *PlayAlbum* as the first iteration, and *PlaySong* and *PlayAlbum* for the second, etc.). We do not apply any masking in this scenario and at every step only the data for the currently supported features is used to train the model. The data distribution per iteration and run is presented in Figure 4.

The results after the final iteration are presented in Table 2 relative to a baseline that was once trained on full data. The experimental models trained using modified LGL setup outperform the baseline across SEMER and ICER in 2 out of 3 cases. In the last case, LGL outperforms the baseline on SEMER (-7.3%), while ICER slightly increases (+2.9%). This could be explained by the different number of classes added to the model – in the last iteration, we add 9.2% of training data, while for other orderings, a much smaller amount is added in the last step.

Run #	ICER	SEMER
music-1	-2.2	-2.3
music-2	-3.2	-2.7
music-3	2.9	-7.3

Table 2: Evaluation results for modified LGL method per run (each run represents a different feature grouping and order). The relative difference is with respect to a baseline model that does not use any form of LGL or other curriculum learning.

Another benefit of the modified LGL method is that it helps reduce training time when new features are added on top. In Fig. 5, we compare the training time for two runs and their average to the baseline model (we use the model trained once on all available data as upper bound; its training time is the same for each iteration). We see that the average training time for each of the iterations is less than the training time of the full model, because we use less training data in the first iterations, and initialise the model from the previous one in subsequent iterations. For individual iterations, we observe up to 25% training time reduction. Overall, we conclude that gradually adding features with warm-starting is beneficial for production SLU, as it helps improve model accuracy and reduces the overall training time spent per release cycle.

5 Conclusion

We applied LGL to the tasks of intent classification and slot filling in the context of SLU and studied the impact of LGL on intent classification error rate and semantic error rate. We conducted the experiments using different class selection strategies and showed that LGL improves intent classification performance for SLU by -9.1% relative ICER, without requiring any new training data or modified model architecture. In addition, we adapted original LGL setup to SLU production scenario when new features are gradually added within fixed release cycle, and showed that it is able to improve model accuracy by up to -7.3% relative SEMER while reducing average training time by up to 25% for individual iterations.

As future work, we would like to further explore

LGL application to feature expansion problem, apply it to other domains and investigate the impact of batch size on the model performance. In addition, we would track the impact of LGL training on model's generalization performance and computational cost over time.

References

Jordan Ash and Ryan P Adams. 2020. On warm-starting neural network training. *Advances in Neural Information Processing Systems*, 33.

Magdalena Biesialska, Katarzyna Biesialska, and Marta R. Costa-jussà. 2020. Continual lifelong learning in natural language processing: A survey. In *Proceedings of the 28th International Conference on Computational Linguistics*, pages 6523–6541, Barcelona, Spain (Online). International Committee on Computational Linguistics.

Giuseppe Castellucci, Simone Filice, Danilo Croce, and Roberto Basili. 2021. Learning to solve NLP tasks in an incremental number of languages. In *Proceedings of the 59th Annual Meeting of the Association for Computational Linguistics and the 11th International Joint Conference on Natural Language Processing (Volume 2: Short Papers)*, pages 837–847, Online. Association for Computational Linguistics.

Qian Chen, Zhu Zhuo, and Wen Wang. 2019. BERT for Joint Intent Classification and Slot Filling. *arXiv preprint arXiv:1902.10909*.

Hao Cheng, Dongze Lian, Bowen Deng, Shenghua Gao, Tao Tan, and Yanlin Geng. 2019. Local to global learning: Gradually adding classes for training deep neural networks. In *Proceedings of the IEEE/CVF Conference on Computer Vision and Pattern Recognition*, pages 4748–4756.

Eunah Cho, He Xie, and William M Campbell. 2019. Paraphrase generation for semi-supervised learning in nlu. In *Proceedings of the Workshop on Methods for Optimizing and Evaluating Neural Language Generation*, pages 45–54.

Tom Diethe, Tom Borchert, Eno Thereska, Borja Balle, and Neil D Lawrence. 2018. Continual learning in practice. In *Proceedings of the NeurIPS 2018 workshop on Continual Learning*.

Judith Gaspers, Quynh Do, and Fabian Triefenbach. 2020. Data balancing for boosting performance of low-frequency classes in spoken language understanding. In *Interspeech 2020*.

Suchin Gururangan, Ana Marasović, Swabha Swayamdipta, Kyle Lo, Iz Beltagy, Doug Downey, and Noah A. Smith. 2020. Don't stop pretraining: Adapt language models to domains and tasks. In *Proceedings of the 58th Annual Meeting of the Association for Computational Linguistics*, pages 8342–8360, Online. Association for Computational Linguistics.

Kasidis Kanwatchara, Thanapapas Horsuwan, Piyawat Lertvittayakumjorn, Boonserm Kijsirikul, and Peerapon Vateekul. 2021. Rational LAMOL: A rationale-based lifelong learning framework. In *Proceedings of the 59th Annual Meeting of the Association for Computational Linguistics and the 11th International Joint Conference on Natural Language Processing (Volume 1: Long Papers)*, pages 2942–2953, Online. Association for Computational Linguistics.

M. Kumar, Benjamin Packer, and Daphne Koller. 2010. Self-paced learning for latent variable models. In *Advances in Neural Information Processing Systems*, volume 23. Curran Associates, Inc.

Samuel Louvan and Bernardo Magnini. 2020. Recent neural methods on slot filling and intent classification for task-oriented dialogue systems: A survey. In *Proceedings of the 28th International Conference on Computational Linguistics*, pages 480–496, Barcelona, Spain (Online). International Committee on Computational Linguistics.

Grégoire Mesnil, Xiaodong He, Li Deng, and Yoshua Bengio. 2013. Investigation of Recurrent-Neural-Network Architectures and Learning Methods for Spoken Language Understanding. In *Interspeech*, pages 3771–3775, Lyon, France.

Justin Payan, Yuval Merhav, He Xie, Satyapriya Krishna, Anil Ramakrishna, Mukund Sridhar, and Rahul Gupta. 2021. Towards realistic single-task continuous learning research for NER. In *Findings of the Association for Computational Linguistics: EMNLP 2021*, pages 3773–3783, Punta Cana, Dominican Republic. Association for Computational Linguistics.

Yada Pruksachatkun, Jason Phang, Haokun Liu, Phu Mon Htut, Xiaoyi Zhang, Richard Yuanzhe Pang, Clara Vania, Katharina Kann, and Samuel R. Bowman. 2020. Intermediate-task transfer learning with pretrained language models: When and why does it work? In *Proceedings of the 58th Annual Meeting of the Association for Computational Linguistics*, pages 5231–5247, Online. Association for Computational Linguistics.

Sebastian Ruder, Matthew E. Peters, Swabha Swayamdipta, and Thomas Wolf. 2019. Transfer learning in natural language processing. In *Proceedings of the 2019 Conference of the North American Chapter of the Association for Computational Linguistics: Tutorials*, pages 15–18, Minneapolis, Minnesota. Association for Computational Linguistics.

Alex Sokolov and Denis Filimonov. 2020. Neural machine translation for paraphrase generation. *arXiv preprint arXiv:2006.14223*.

Yi Tay, Shuohang Wang, Anh Tuan Luu, Jie Fu, Minh C. Phan, Xingdi Yuan, Jinfeng Rao, Siu Cheung Hui, and Aston Zhang. 2019. Simple and effective curriculum pointer-generator networks for reading comprehension over long narratives. In *Proceedings of the 57th Annual Meeting of the Association for Computational Linguistics*, pages 4922–4931, Florence, Italy. Association for Computational Linguistics.

H. Weld, X. Huang, S. Long, J. Poon, and S. C. Han. 2021. A survey of joint intent detection and slot-filling models in natural language understanding.

Xiaodong Zhang and Houfeng Wang. 2016. A Joint Model of Intent Determination and Slot Filling for Spoken Language Understanding. In *Proceedings of the Twenty-Fifth IJCAI*, page 2993–2999, New York, NY, USA.

A Local To Global Learning

The main idea of Local to Global Learning (LGL) algorithm used in this work is to gradually train the neural network starting with a few output classes and subsequently extending to more classes. In the following, we provide a more detiled oevrview of the method following Cheng et al. (2019).

The model training is performed in several iterations. The model for each iteration is initialized from the previous one. During each iteration, the entire training set is used, however, the classes that are not learned during that specific iteration are masked. Thus, the model is learned on a fraction of classes from the complete output space of the training set, while the whole dataset is still exposed. As compared to traditional model learning, the loss function is not minimized across all classes simultaneously, but is minimized iteratively, each time learning a new set of classes in addition to the already known classes. At each step, a set of new classes is added to the training setup by unmasking them in the dataset and the model is trained until convergence. Mathematically, it can be expressed as (we refer to (Cheng et al., 2019) for details):

$$
\begin{aligned}
w_k^* &= \arg\min_w L(w, X_{S_k}, Y_{S_k}; {w^*}_{k-1}) \\
s.t. i^* &= f(w, X_{S_{k-1}^C}, Y_{S_{k-1}^C}; w_{k-1}^*), \\
S_k &= S_{k-1} \cup \{i^*\},
\end{aligned}
$$

where L is the loss function and w^* are the model weight produced by minimizing L. The dataset contains pairs of samples and class annotations $G = \{X, Y\}$, where $K = \{1, 2, ..., K\}$ is a set of available output class labels. The classes are grouped into N batches of equal size and after each training iteration, one batch $i*$ is added. S_k is the set of classes from K that is used in the k-th step. X_{S_k}, Y_{S_k} is the data, which labels are in S_k and S_{k-1}^C is the set of classes not in S_{k-1}. The selection strategy is represented by the function f, which defines how a new batch of classes is selected from the untrained classes.

The set of classes at the current iterations S_k is unmasked in the dataset during the training, while the yet unavailable classes S_{k-1}^C are masked with a placeholder label, but the corresponding data instances $X_{S_{k-1}^C}$ are kept in the training data. Hence, the full data set G is used for training at every iteration. After the model is learned on the first batch, its encoder is used to initialize the encoder for the next training step. Thereby, the final model is learned iteratively through several training runs with an increasing number of output classes. The encoder part of the model is carried further with every iteration and the output layers are re-initialized each time to account for changing output space.

CULG: Commercial Universal Language Generation

Haonan Li[1*] **Yameng Huang**[2*] **Yeyun Gong**[3] **Jian Jiao**[2]
Ruofei Zhang[2] **Timothy Baldwin**[1,4] **Nan Duan**[3]
[1]School of Computing and Information Systems, The University of Melbourne
[2]Microsoft [3]Microsoft Research Asia [4]MBZUAI
haonanl5@student.unimelb.edu.au, tb@ldwin.net
{yamhuang, yegong, Jian.Jiao, bzhang, nanduan}@microsoft.com

Abstract

Pre-trained language models (PLMs) have dramatically improved performance for many natural language processing (NLP) tasks in domains such as finance and healthcare. However, the application of PLMs in the domain of commerce, especially marketing and advertising, remains less studied. In this work, we adapt pre-training methods to the domain of commerce, by proposing **CULG**, a large-scale commercial universal language generation model which is pre-trained on a corpus drawn from 10 markets across 7 languages. We propose 4 commercial generation tasks and a two-stage training strategy for pre-training, and demonstrate that the proposed strategy yields performance improvements on three generation tasks as compared to single-stage pre-training. Extensive experiments show that our model outperforms other models by a large margin on commercial generation tasks.

1 Introduction

Pre-trained language models (PLMs) have achieved impressive success in many NLP tasks across natural language understanding (NLU) and natural language generation (NLG) (Devlin et al., 2019; Yang et al., 2019; Liu et al., 2019; Lewis et al., 2020; Brown et al., 2020; Raffel et al., 2020; He et al., 2020). These successes are usually achieved by pre-training models on large corpora in a task-independent way, and fine-tuning them on a specific downstream task. Researchers have also developed PLMs for specific domains or multiple languages by conducting either pre-training from scratch (Huang et al., 2019; Liu et al., 2020; Xue et al., 2021) or a second phase of pre-training on the basis of existing checkpoints (Howard and Ruder, 2018; Lee et al., 2020; Gururangan et al., 2020). However, PLMs in the domain of commerce, especially for marketing and advertising, remain less studied. On the one hand, adapting PLMs to the advertising domain is challenging because existing pre-training methods usually use open-domain corpora containing largely well-structured text such as books (Zhu et al., 2015), news (Liu et al., 2019), stories (Trinh and Le, 2018), or web text (Radford et al., 2019a) to learn text representations. However, the input text for selecting advertisements is primarily web search queries, which are usually not complete, grammatical sentences. On the other hand, there is no publicly-available PLM in the commercial domain.

This paper introduces **C**ommercial **U**niversal **L**anguage **G**eneration model (CULG), which supports multi-lingual, multi-market, and multi-task ad generation. CULG adopts a transformer-based (Vaswani et al., 2017) encoder–decoder generative framework similar to ProphetNet (Qi et al., 2020), which uses an n-stream self-attention mechanism and supports future n-gram prediction. To adapt to diverse markets, we use the multi-lingual version of ProphetNet — ProphetNet-X (Qi et al., 2021) as our foundation model, and conduct a second phase of pre-training using a self-constructed large-scale commercial corpus.

CULG is trained auto-regressively on four sequence-to-sequence (seq2seq) generation tasks, including: (1) **G**enerate **K**eywords with the **S**ame intent as the query (GKS); (2) **G**enerate **K**eywords that are **R**elevant to a query (GKR); (3) **G**enerate an **A**d **T**itle based on a query (GAT); and (4) **G**enerate an **A**d **D**escription based on a query (GAD). The motivation of these tasks is to infer the user's intention based on the query as well as perform product matching and recommendation. All queries used in this research are real-life search queries that have been submitted to the Bing[1] search engine, and the ground truth targets are created according to either the records of user's click behaviour or labels from hired human annotators. We collected more

*Equal contribution

[1]https://www.bing.com

Proceedings of NAACL-HLT 2022: Industry Track Papers, pages 112 - 120
July 10-15, 2022

than ten million queries from 10 markets in 7 languages, and split them into three classes according to data quality. Given the user query, the gold class is ads that were deemed as relevant to the query by human judges, the silver class is made up of ads clicked on by users, and the bronze class is all ads that been selected by search engine to show to users. Splitting the data into different markets, tasks, and quality classes provides us with flexibility to compare the model's performance under different training setups.

Given that the collected data varies in quality, we split both the pre-training and fine-tuning into two stages, using low-quality data in the first stage and high-quality in the second stage. To demonstrate the effectiveness of this approach, we compare it with alternative combinations of pre-training and fine-tuning. We evaluate CULG on three commercial generation tasks. Experimental results show that splitting pre-training and fine-tuning into two stages not only outperforms the widely-used single-stage pre-train and fine-tune schema, but is also better than other combinations of pre-training and fine-tuning. We further compare CULG with existing pre-trained multi-lingual models (Liu et al., 2020; Qi et al., 2021) and show that it surpasses other models on commercial generation tasks. Finally, we conduct transfer learning experiments on different markets, languages, and tasks by fine-tuning CULG on a market, language, and task that has not been seen during pre-training. The results demonstrate that CLUG also generalizes well to unseen markets, languages, and tasks.

2 Approach

2.1 Model Architecture

CULG adopts the architecture of ProphetNet, an encoder–decoder language generation model with n-stream self-attention mechanism and future n-gram prediction. Instead of optimizing one-step-ahead prediction as with most sequence-to-sequence models, future n-gram prediction aims to prevent overfitting on strong local correlations by simultaneously predicting the next n tokens.

The ProphetNet encoder uses stacked transformer layers with multi-head self-attention, and the decoder uses stacked multi-head multi-stream self-attention layers to enable n-gram prediction. Given the input sequence $x = (x_1, x_2, ..., x_L)$ and output sequence $y = (y_1, y_2, ..., y_M)$, ProphetNet implements future n-gram prediction by replacing the auto-regressive predicting dependency relationship $p(y_t|y_{<t}, x)$ with $p(y_{t:t+n-1}|y_{<t}, x)$. In detail, it first obtains the encoded sequence representation H_{enc} from stacked encoder layers, where $H_{enc} = \textbf{Encoder}(x_1, x_2, ..., x_L)$. Then the decoder predicts n future tokens simultaneously as $p(y_t|y_{<t}, x), ..., p(y_{t+n-1|y_{<t},x}) = \textbf{Decoder}(y_{<t}, H_{enc})$, where n probabilities are generated at each time step and the probability $p(y_{t+i}|y_{<t}, x)$ is generated by the i-th predicting stream. The future n-gram prediction objective can be formalized as:

Code	Language	Code	Country
De	German	Au	Australia
En	English	Ca	Canada
Es	Spanish	Ch	Switzerland
Fr	French	De	Germany
It	Italian	Es	Spain
Nl	Dutch	Fr	France
Sv	Swedish	Gb	United Kingdom
		It	Italy
		Nl	Netherlands
		Se	Sweden

Table 1: Languages and countries contained in our corpus. Throughout this paper, we refer to languages and country names with their ISO codes.

$$\begin{aligned}\mathcal{L} =& -\sum_{j=0}^{n-1} \alpha_j \cdot \left(\sum_{t=1}^{M-j} \log\, p_\theta(y_{t+j}|y_{<t}, x) \right) \\ =& \underbrace{-\, \alpha_0 \cdot \left(\sum_{t=1}^{M} \log\, p_\theta(y_t|y_{<t}, x) \right)}_{\text{language modeling loss}} \\ & \underbrace{- \sum_{j=1}^{n-1} \alpha_j \cdot \left(\sum_{t=1}^{M-j} \log\, p_\theta(y_{t+j}|y_{<t}, x) \right)}_{\text{future } n\text{-gram loss}} \quad (1)\end{aligned}$$

The details of ProphetNet can be found in Qi et al. (2020).

2.2 Data Collection

The corpus was collected from 10 markets across 7 languages (Table 1), where a "market" refers to queries issued from a country in a specific language (and is represented as Language–Country in the remainder of the paper), and the corresponding ads and product information. For each market, three types of data were collected:

Impressed Given a user query, a collection of ads is chosen from the full ads corpus by the Bing

Market	GKS			GKR			GAT/GAD			Total
	Bronze	Silver	Gold	Bronze	Silver	Gold	Bronze	Silver	Gold	
De–Ch	1,129K	140K	2K	15,288K	812K	91K	3,033K	332K	67K	20,898K
De–De	8,847K	2,096K	97K	135,835K	14,000K	413K	18,625K	4,122K	1,711K	185,751K
En–Au	1,992K	383K	75K	25,768K	2,078K	356K	2,820K	580K	1,437K	35,494K
En–Ca	3,412K	586K	58K	24,324K	2,117K	410K	3,081K	640K	619K	35,251K
En–Gb	8,803K	1,741K	137K	89,385K	7,819K	480K	12,416K	2,520K	2,084K	125,389K
Es–Es	1,387K	255K	15K	73,747K	3,792K	103K	11,858K	1,084K	71K	92,317K
Fr–Fr	5,114K	1,259K	105K	102,538K	11,000K	392K	13,239K	2,891K	1,493K	138,035K
It–It	831K	148K	2K	49,352K	2,596K	72K	8,664K	879K	51K	62,600K
Nl–Nl	1,389K	301K	2K	55,619K	3,704K	93K	9,268K	1,177K	77K	71,633K
Sv–Se	409K	88K	2K	11,732K	982K	81K	2,888K	431K	88K	16,703K
Total	33,318K	7,002K	498K	583,593K	48,414K	2,496K	85,897K	14,661K	7,702K	783,585K

Table 2: Statistics of source–target pairs in the CULG corpus partitioned by task, quality, and market.

Figure 1: An illustration of a user query, ad title, ad description, and bidded keyword.

search engine and shown to the user. This decision process is aimed at maximizing the combined utility of users, advertisers, and publishers by taking the query–ad relevance, bidding, and marketplace policy into account. We collect the pairs of impressed ads and user queries in 2020 based on the system log, and treat them as **bronze** quality data. Figure 1 provides an example user query, ad title, ad description, and bidded keyword.

Clicked Among those ads impressed to users, some attract the attention of users and are clicked on for more details. We collect all these clicked ads from the impressed set, and treat them as **silver** quality data.

Labeled We developed detailed guidelines to measure the relevance between queries and keywords, queries and ads (including the ad title, ad description, and displayed URL). We hired and trained a team of judges to measure the quality of keywords and ads, sampling data from the "impressed" data above based on our annotation budget. Those instances that are labeled as "Good" are treated as **gold** quality data.

Table 2 presents the statistics of the CULG corpus. From the data quality perspective, we can see the bronze impressed data is much larger than the silver clicked data, which is in turn larger than the gold labeled data for each market and task. From the perspective of different tasks, the task of GKR contains more data than GKS and GAT/GAD (see below for task details).

2.3 Tasks

We propose four generation tasks for CULG pretraining. Detailed task descriptions are given below, and examples are provided in Table 3.

Query to keywords with exactly the same intent (GKS): Given a user query, generate a list of keywords that have exactly the same intent as the source query. Such a situation usually occurs when advertisers have a clear targeted audience, judging from the search queries.

Query to keywords that are relevant (GKR): Given a user query, generate a list of keywords that is relevant to the query but don't necessarily have exactly the same intent. This happens when advertisers want to reach to a broader slice of users that may be interested in their product.

Query to ad title (GAT): Given a user query, generate an ad title that is relevant to the query. For many electronic business platforms, there are lots of products without ready-made ad titles and descriptions. This task tends to automatically generate titles that attract users.

Query to ad description (GAD): Similar to GAT, generate an ad description that is relevant to a given query. This task helps sellers reduce their copywriting workload. However, as the real product parameters are neither collected nor embedded in the model, we do not evaluate CULG on this task.

Task	Source	Target
	sandstone	sandstones
GKS	kempton park races	kempton park racing
	debenhams ladies clothing	debenhams ladies fashions
	print out boarding pass	boarding pass holder
GKR	perth australia city transport	visiting perth australia
	wood effect gas fire	gas fire repairer prices
	expedia uk	Up to 80% off uk hotels - lowest hotel prices guaranteed
GAT	liverpool	liverpool flights - fly to liverpool
	just eat	official site - just eat
	expedia uk	compare prices on 1000+ sites. the best way to save on your uk hotel!
GAD	liverpool	compare prices on liverpool flights with the edreams official website
	just eat	even more of your favourite restaurants are now on just eat, and just a tap away

Table 3: Examples of the four CULG tasks from the En-Gb market.

2.4 Two-stage Pre-training and Fine-tuning

The model parameters of CULG are initialized from ProphetNet-X, which is pre-trained on the 100Gb wiki-100 corpus and 500Gb of Common-Crawl[2] data. As a state-of-the-art pre-trained NLG model, its NLU and NLG capabilities (including open-domain multi-lingual generation) are roughly comparable to other encoder–decoder models such as BART (Lewis et al., 2020), GPT-3 (Brown et al., 2020), and T5 (Raffel et al., 2020).

To adapt it to the domain of commerce, we conduct a second phase of pre-training on our commercial corpus. Given that data varies in terms of quality and is large in size, we propose splitting the pre-training into two stages and training on data of increasing quality. The same strategy is applied to model fine-tuning. In detail, the proposed stages are as follows:

Pre-train stage I All data including bronze, silver, and gold data from all tasks are used to train the model. As most of the data (> 90%) used in this stage is unlabeled, this stage of training can be considered as unsupervised (in terms of data labeling).

Pre-train stage II The gold data from all tasks is used to train the model. This can be considered to be supervised training, given that all of the gold data has been hand-labeled.

Fine-tune stage I The generative model is fine-tuned on task-specific bronze, silver, and gold data from multiple markets. This stage helps the model to capture the general features of different languages and markets.

Fine-tune stage II The model is fine-tuned on task- and market-specific labeled data to generate high-quality representations, and capture high-level language and market features.

[2]https://commoncrawl.org/

Method	Pre-train		Fine-tune	
	Stage I	Stage II	Stage I	Stage II
1				✓
2			✓	✓
3	✓	✓		✓
4	✓	✓	✓	✓

Table 4: Illustration of settings of different methods.

For pre-training, we argue that the unsupervised stage helps the model to learn general text representations, while the supervised stage improves the quality of the learned latent representations using a small amount of high-quality data. For fine-tuning, general-purpose features can be learned from multi-market and -lingual data during stage I, and specific features can be learned during stage II.

2.5 Training Methods

To validate the effectiveness of the proposed pre-training and fine-tuning strategies, we create four methods using different combinations of the proposed stages in our experiments (Table 4). **Method-1** involves stage II fine-tuning only without CULG pre-training, which means only a small amount of market-specific labeled data is used to fine-tune the model. This is the most commom mode of fine-tuning after pre-training on publicly available checkpoints. **Method-2** adds stage I fine-tuning before method-1, so that multi-lingual and multi-market data is used to force the model to learn general information across markets first. This is the best that can be achieved on publicly available checkpoints. Note that both method-1 and method-2 use task-specific data. **Method-3** and **method-4** add pre-training stages before method-1 and method-2, respectively.

Task	Market	Method 1			Method 2			Method 3			Method 4		
		BLEU-3, 4, AVG			BLEU-3, 4, AVG			BLEU-3, 4, AVG			BLEU-3, 4, AVG		
GKS	De–Ch	6.18	0.00	12.15	21.91	9.32	32.74	21.28	9.10	31.41	24.40	10.98	**34.53**
	De–De	27.38	22.22	35.58	33.73	28.98	40.98	32.12	27.90	39.59	34.94	30.21	**42.08**
	En–Au	34.26	25.83	42.94	40.01	32.19	47.81	38.97	30.89	46.81	41.27	33.62	**48.92**
	En–Gb	32.28	24.17	40.83	37.83	30.46	45.82	36.28	28.48	44.36	38.67	31.03	**46.55**
	Es–Es	31.88	24.53	39.78	50.65	45.60	55.28	46.99	43.12	51.90	52.36	47.20	**56.70**
	Fr–Fr	32.26	25.07	40.69	44.85	38.30	51.73	42.12	35.63	49.13	45.76	39.61	**52.56**
	It–It	13.17	7.79	19.72	34.80	19.28	**43.04**	31.85	20.11	40.23	34.08	18.98	41.92
	Nl–Nl	6.55	0.00	12.42	23.66	12.84	33.93	24.15	14.22	**34.83**	24.97	15.02	34.74
	Sv–Se	6.17	0.00	11.44	22.25	11.55	32.23	21.98	10.39	32.33	22.94	12.15	**32.87**
GKR	De–Ch	25.18	18.56	32.20	29.17	24.66	36.78	28.98	25.58	37.02	29.43	25.19	**37.23**
	De–De	20.90	16.05	27.53	25.07	20.11	32.05	23.46	18.00	30.43	25.02	20.08	**32.09**
	En–Au	21.32	15.13	28.74	24.24	17.85	31.87	24.08	17.21	31.58	24.96	18.44	**32.56**
	En–Gb	16.99	12.45	23.95	20.38	15.98	27.55	19.51	14.39	26.66	20.84	16.09	**27.97**
	Es–Es	23.17	19.28	28.89	27.02	22.11	33.45	26.07	21.18	32.42	27.51	22.83	**33.87**
	Fr–Fr	20.20	14.19	26.90	23.41	17.00	30.40	22.85	16.11	29.92	24.08	17.53	**31.13**
	It–It	26.38	23.82	31.15	31.36	29.00	37.04	30.39	29.19	36.14	31.84	29.54	**37.62**
	Nl–Nl	9.13	2.43	20.85	12.36	4.30	24.66	12.21	4.33	24.37	13.23	4.88	**25.54**
	Sv–Se	20.59	17.34	28.85	25.14	20.99	33.48	26.34	21.96	34.00	25.76	19.53	**33.55**
GAT	De–Ch	6.20	4.02	9.18	8.05	5.86	11.04	7.30	5.10	10.30	8.34	6.14	**11.31**
	De–De	9.05	6.50	12.02	11.92	9.48	15.06	10.92	8.41	14.10	12.62	10.16	**15.75**
	En–Au	6.50	4.11	10.03	9.80	7.22	13.35	8.78	6.20	12.35	10.06	7.50	**13.62**
	En–Gb	5.06	3.06	8.13	7.73	5.86	10.58	6.14	4.27	9.02	8.46	6.51	**11.39**
	Es–Es	9.69	6.84	13.64	13.12	10.24	16.95	11.95	8.99	15.91	13.85	10.95	**17.67**
	Fr–Fr	2.96	1.30	5.62	3.45	1.63	6.41	3.31	1.50	6.23	3.62	1.76	**6.58**
	It–It	24.90	21.24	28.12	26.70	23.03	30.05	25.89	22.09	29.37	26.91	23.24	**30.25**
	NL–NL	5.18	3.29	8.29	8.66	6.60	11.84	7.28	5.15	10.58	9.07	6.94	**12.24**
	Sv–Se	4.28	2.40	7.64	7.27	5.36	10.47	6.39	4.48	9.62	7.76	5.72	**10.98**

Table 5: Main results on GKS,GKR and GAT tasks. BLEU-3, BLEU-4, and BLEU-AVG are reported where "BLEU-AVG" means the average score of BLEU-1, 2, 3 and 4.

3 Experiments and results

Experimental setup For each market dataset, we split it into training, validation, and test set in proportions 80%:10%:10%. The training set is used for CULG pre-training and task-specific fine-tuning.

For pre-training, we fetch the pretrained ProphetNet-X as the basis of CULG, which contains 12 layers in the encoder and decoder respectively, with 1024d hidden size and 4096d feed forward size. The future token prediction length is set to 2, and the max sequence length of the input and output is set to 512. We train the model on all data (stage I) for 1 epoch, and on labeled data only (stage II) for 5 epochs. For training, we use the Adam optimizer (Kingma and Ba, 2015) with a learning rate of 10^{-6} and 10^{-5} and batch size of 1024. We use the sentencepiece tokenizer with the XLM-R (Conneau et al., 2020) 250k vocabulary, which support 100 languages.

CULG is pre-trained on 8×32Gb NVIDIA Tesla V100 GPUs, at a total cost of around 1500 GPU hours.

For fine-tuning, we use a constant learning rate of 10^{-5} and dropout rate of 0.1 for all tasks. We save checkpoints every 10000 steps, and choose the checkpoint with the best performance on the validation set.

3.1 Main results

Table 5 presents the main results on GKS, GKR, and GAT. Several observations can be made. First, method-2 consistently outperforms method-1, and method-4 consistently outperforms method-3. We suggest there are two reasons for this: (a) multilingual and multi-market data helps the model to learn general task features; and (b) during fine-tuning, method-2 and method-4 use $>$ 20 times the amount of data of method-1 and method-3 respectively, for most markets and tasks. Second, method-3 beats method-1 for all tasks and markets, while method-4 beats method-2 for most tasks and markets (with the exception of the GKS task in market It–It). This demonstrates the effectiveness of the pre-training. Third, method-1 and method-3 can be treated as few-shot setups, as the amount of labeled data is much less than the unlabeled data. We find

Task	M-1	M-2	M-3	M-4	mBART
GKS	35.58	40.98	39.59	**42.08**	33.97
GKR	27.53	32.05	30.43	**32.09**	24.29
GAT	12.02	15.06	14.10	**15.75**	13.00

Table 6: Performance comparison between CULG and mBART on the De–De market, based on BLEU-AVG. 'M-i" means method-i.

that method-3 outperforms method-1 by a large margin, demonstrating that our pre-trained model can greatly boost the performance in few-shot settings. Finally, the overall performance on GAT is worse than on GKS and GKR, which appears to be because ad titles usually contain advertiser-specific information, which is difficult to infer from a user query.

3.2 Comparison to mBART

To compare CULG with models that have different architectures and pre-training data, we choose mBART (Liu et al., 2020), a state-of-the-art multilingual encoder–decoder model. mBART is pre-trained on a large-scale monolingual corpus containing many languages, with a denosing objective function. We download checkpoint *mbart.cc25* and fine-tune it on labeled task-specific data.

We compare CULG with mBART on the De–De market (Table 6). We find that even method-1 achieves better results than mBART on GKS and GKR, and comparable results on GAT, which demonstrates the superiority of our model versus mBART. In addition, with ads data pre-training or multi-lingual fine-tuning, each of method-2, method-3 and method-4 exceed mBART by a large margin, verifying the effectiveness of the pre-training and fine-tuning strategies for commercial tasks. For all tasks, method-4 achieves the best performance.

3.3 Transferability

Next, we evaluate the transferability of CULG. Specifically, we use data for a new market, new language, and new task to fine-tune a CULG checkpoint (method-3). For comparison, we choose the publicly available ProphetNet-X checkpoint and fine-tune it using the same data (method-1).

Market Transferability To test the transferability of CULG model over markets, we exclude the data from En–Ca during pre-training and use it for fine-tuning. Table 7 shows the results on the three

Task	M	B-1	B-2	B-3	B-4	B-AVG
GKS	M-1	57.59	39.13	28.04	21.60	36.59
	M-3	60.76	43.94	33.20	26.67	41.14
GKR	M-1	45.45	31.39	21.20	15.25	28.33
	M-3	47.73	34.17	24.20	18.55	31.16
GAT	M-1	11.14	6.61	4.81	3.84	6.60
	M-3	15.74	10.12	7.75	6.43	10.01

Table 7: Evaluation of market transferability on the En–Ca market. "M" and "B" represent method and BLEU, respectively.

Method	B-1	B-2	B-3	B-4	B-AVG
Method-1	14.37	8.06	4.80	2.99	7.56
Method-3	20.52	12.17	7.98	5.54	11.55

Table 8: Evaluation of language transferability on the GAT task for the DA–DK market. "B" represents BLEU.

Method	B-1	B-2	B-3	B-4	B-AVG
Method-1	47.70	42.99	31.46	11.50	33.41
Method-3	50.49	45.17	33.58	13.24	35.62

Table 9: Evaluation of task transferability on the GBK task for the De–De market. "B" represents BLEU.

different tasks. We observe a consistent and substantial improvement by CULG (method-3) versus method-1, which suggests that our model performs well over new markets (in a language that is covered in CULG pre-training).

Language Transferability Data in the En–Ca market is potentially similar to that in En–Us, En–Au, and En–Uk market because of sharing the same language (and having many cultural similarities). It is natural to ask whether our model can also be applied to markets with a language that is unseen in pre-training.

In this experiment, we use data from the Da–Dk (Denmark) market to evaluate language transferability. Note that no Danish data is used during CULG pre-training. At the time of writing this paper, we did not have market data for GKS and GKR, so we will focus exclusively on GAT in this experiment. From the results in Table 8, we see that CULG performs much better than ProphetNet-X, suggesting that our model generalizes to new languages that were not included in pre-training.

Task Transferability The generation model can potentially be applied to many scenarios and downstream tasks. We propose four different tasks for

CULG training but wider demand might be required as products evolve. To test whether CULG can be generalized to a task it has not been trained on, we propose another task, which is to **G**enerate the **B**idding **K**eywords (GBK) for an advertiser automatically given the ad description. Experimental results (Table 9) show that method-3 leads to solid improvements on this task vs. method-1, even though this task is not included in pre-training. This demonstrates that CULG is able to leverage information from other tasks for a new task, suggesting greater scope for its applicability.

4 Related Work

Pre-training for Text Generation Pre-training has been widely used in NLP tasks to learn language representations (Devlin et al., 2019; Liu et al., 2019; Lan et al., 2020; Clark et al., 2020; Yang et al., 2019; Radford et al., 2019b). GPT (Radford et al., 2018) takes plain text as pre-training data to predict the next token in a left-to-right fashion. It performs well on story generation and creative writing. BART (Lewis et al., 2020) uses an encoder–decoder structure to regenerate the original text from a corrupted input using an arbitrary noising function. The denoising training strategy and encoder–decoder structure lead to impressive results on generation tasks. MASS (Song et al., 2019) pre-trains a seq2seq model by masking continuous spans and learn to recover them. T5 (Raffel et al., 2020) investigates different pre-training objectives and model architectures, and pre-trains on a large-scale corpus containing 750Gb of text data. ProphetNet (Qi et al., 2020) introduces a novel self-supervised objective named future n-gram prediction, that explicitly encourages the model to plan for future tokens and prevent overfitting on strong local correlations. In this paper, we use the model structure of ProphetNet, and the same n-gram objective function.

Multi-lingual Model in NLP Building multi-lingual models is becoming more common across NLP tasks. Support for multi-lingual text is either implemented by aligning multi-lingual word embeddings in a universal space (Chen and Cardie, 2018; Lample et al., 2018) or by learning cross-lingual models using a different corpus to exploit shared representations across languages. Models such as mBERT (and), mBART (Liu et al., 2020), XLM-R (Conneau et al., 2020), mT5 (Xue et al., 2021), and ProphetNet-X (Qi et al., 2021) are multi-lingual variants of BERT, BART, RoBERTa, T5, and ProphetNet, respectively.

Domain Adaptive Pre-training In this paper, we adapt the pre-trained ProphetNet-X to a commercial domain by continuing to pre-train. Similar work has been done by researchers in other domains. BioBERT (Lee et al., 2020) is obtained by performing additional BERT pre-training on a biomedical corpora, leading to improvements on a variety of biomedical text mining tasks. Alsentzer et al. (2019) continues pre-training BioBERT on clinical data, and achieves performance gains on three clinical NLP tasks. ULMFit (Howard and Ruder, 2018) introduced task-specific fine-tuning, with the core idea being to continue pre-training language models on task/domain specific data. Chakrabarty et al. (2019) used the approach of ULMFit and continued training it on a Reddit corpus, achieving state-of-the-art performance on four claim detection datasets in doing so. Most recently, Gururangan et al. (2020) continued training RoBERTa across 4 domains and 8 tasks, and showed that both domain adaptive pre-training and task adaptive pre-training lead to performance gains.

5 Conclusion

In this paper, we propose CULG: a large-scale commercial universal language generation model which supports multi-lingual, multi-market, and multi-task ad generation. As part of this, we propose 4 ad generation tasks for CULG pre-training. We then propose a two-stage pre-training and fine-tuning strategy, and demonstrate the effectiveness of the proposed strategy through extensive experiments. We further compare CULG with other multi-lingual generation models, and show the superiority of CULG on commercial generation tasks. Finally, we demonstrate the transferability of CULG in three different settings.

6 Ethical Considerations

This work was conducted while the first author was an intern at Microsoft Research Asia. All data was sourced in strict adherence with the commercial terms of service of the Bing search engine, and no session history or personal data was used in this research.

References

Emily Alsentzer, John Murphy, William Boag, Wei-Hung Weng, Di Jindi, Tristan Naumann, and Matthew McDermott. 2019. Publicly available clinical BERT embeddings. In *Proceedings of the 2nd Clinical Natural Language Processing Workshop*, pages 72–78.

Jacob Devlin and. Multilingual bert readme.

Tom B. Brown, Benjamin Mann, Nick Ryder, Melanie Subbiah, Jared Kaplan, Prafulla Dhariwal, Arvind Neelakantan, Pranav Shyam, Girish Sastry, Amanda Askell, Sandhini Agarwal, Ariel Herbert-Voss, Gretchen Krueger, Tom Henighan, Rewon Child, Aditya Ramesh, Daniel M. Ziegler, Jeffrey Wu, Clemens Winter, Christopher Hesse, Mark Chen, Eric Sigler, Mateusz Litwin, Scott Gray, Benjamin Chess, Jack Clark, Christopher Berner, Sam McCandlish, Alec Radford, Ilya Sutskever, and Dario Amodei. 2020. Language models are few-shot learners. In *Annual Conference on Neural Information Processing Systems*.

Tuhin Chakrabarty, Christopher Hidey, and Kathy McKeown. 2019. IMHO fine-tuning improves claim detection. In *Proceedings of the 2019 Conference of the North American Chapter of the Association for Computational Linguistics: Human Language Technologies*, pages 558–563.

Xilun Chen and Claire Cardie. 2018. Unsupervised multilingual word embeddings. In *Proceedings of the 2018 Conference on Empirical Methods in Natural Language Processing*, pages 261–270.

Kevin Clark, Minh-Thang Luong, Quoc V. Le, and Christopher D. Manning. 2020. ELECTRA: pre-training text encoders as discriminators rather than generators. In *8th International Conference on Learning Representations*.

Alexis Conneau, Kartikay Khandelwal, Naman Goyal, Vishrav Chaudhary, Guillaume Wenzek, Francisco Guzmán, Edouard Grave, Myle Ott, Luke Zettlemoyer, and Veselin Stoyanov. 2020. Unsupervised cross-lingual representation learning at scale. In *Proceedings of the 58th Annual Meeting of the Association for Computational Linguistics*, pages 8440–8451.

Jacob Devlin, Ming-Wei Chang, Kenton Lee, and Kristina Toutanova. 2019. BERT: pre-training of deep bidirectional transformers for language understanding. In *Proceedings of the 2019 Conference of the North American Chapter of the Association for Computational Linguistics: Human Language Technologies*, pages 4171–4186.

Suchin Gururangan, Ana Marasovic, Swabha Swayamdipta, Kyle Lo, Iz Beltagy, Doug Downey, and Noah A. Smith. 2020. Don't stop pretraining: Adapt language models to domains and tasks. In *Proceedings of the 58th Annual Meeting of the Association for Computational Linguistics*, pages 8342–8360.

Pengcheng He, Xiaodong Liu, Jianfeng Gao, and Weizhu Chen. 2020. Deberta: Decoding-enhanced BERT with disentangled attention. *CoRR*, abs/2006.03654.

Jeremy Howard and Sebastian Ruder. 2018. Universal language model fine-tuning for text classification. In *Proceedings of the 56th Annual Meeting of the Association for Computational Linguistics*, pages 328–339.

Kexin Huang, Jaan Altosaar, and Rajesh Ranganath. 2019. ClinicalBERT: Modeling clinical notes and predicting hospital readmission. *CoRR*, abs/1904.05342.

Diederik P. Kingma and Jimmy Ba. 2015. Adam: A method for stochastic optimization. In *3rd International Conference on Learning Representations*.

Guillaume Lample, Alexis Conneau, Marc'Aurelio Ranzato, Ludovic Denoyer, and Hervé Jégou. 2018. Word translation without parallel data. In *6th International Conference on Learning Representations*.

Zhenzhong Lan, Mingda Chen, Sebastian Goodman, Kevin Gimpel, Piyush Sharma, and Radu Soricut. 2020. ALBERT: A lite BERT for self-supervised learning of language representations. In *8th International Conference on Learning Representations*.

Jinhyuk Lee, Wonjin Yoon, Sungdong Kim, Donghyeon Kim, Sunkyu Kim, Chan Ho So, and Jaewoo Kang. 2020. BioBERT: a pre-trained biomedical language representation model for biomedical text mining. *Bioinformatics*, 36(4):1234–1240.

Mike Lewis, Yinhan Liu, Naman Goyal, Marjan Ghazvininejad, Abdelrahman Mohamed, Omer Levy, Veselin Stoyanov, and Luke Zettlemoyer. 2020. BART: denoising sequence-to-sequence pre-training for natural language generation, translation, and comprehension. In *Proceedings of the 58th Annual Meeting of the Association for Computational Linguistics*, pages 7871–7880.

Yinhan Liu, Jiatao Gu, Naman Goyal, Xian Li, Sergey Edunov, Marjan Ghazvininejad, Mike Lewis, and Luke Zettlemoyer. 2020. Multilingual denoising pre-training for neural machine translation. *Transactions of the Association for Computational Linguistics*, 8:726–742.

Yinhan Liu, Myle Ott, Naman Goyal, Jingfei Du, Mandar Joshi, Danqi Chen, Omer Levy, Mike Lewis, Luke Zettlemoyer, and Veselin Stoyanov. 2019. RoBERTa: A robustly optimized BERT pretraining approach. *CoRR*, abs/1907.11692.

Weizhen Qi, Yeyun Gong, Yu Yan, Can Xu, Bolun Yao, Bartuer Zhou, Biao Cheng, Daxin Jiang, Jiusheng Chen, Ruofei Zhang, Houqiang Li, and Nan Duan. 2021. ProphetNet-X: Large-scale pre-training models for English, Chinese, multi-lingual, dialog, and code generation. *CoRR*, abs/2104.08006.

Weizhen Qi, Yu Yan, Yeyun Gong, Dayiheng Liu, Nan Duan, Jiusheng Chen, Ruofei Zhang, and Ming Zhou. 2020. Prophetnet: Predicting future n-gram for sequence-to-sequence pre-training. In *Proceedings of the 2020 Conference on Empirical Methods in Natural Language Processing*, pages 2401–2410.

Alec Radford, Karthik Narasimhan, Tim Salimans, and Ilya Sutskever. 2018. Improving language understanding with unsupervised learning.

Alec Radford, Jeffrey Wu, Rewon Child, David Luan, Dario Amodei, and Ilya Sutskever. 2019a. Language models are unsupervised multitask learners. *OpenAI blog*, 1(8):9.

Alec Radford, Jeffrey Wu, Rewon Child, David Luan, Dario Amodei, Ilya Sutskever, et al. 2019b. Language models are unsupervised multitask learners. *OpenAI blog*, 1(8):9.

Colin Raffel, Noam Shazeer, Adam Roberts, Katherine Lee, Sharan Narang, Michael Matena, Yanqi Zhou, Wei Li, and Peter J. Liu. 2020. Exploring the limits of transfer learning with a unified text-to-text transformer. *Journal of Machine Learning Research*, 21:140:1–140:67.

Kaitao Song, Xu Tan, Tao Qin, Jianfeng Lu, and Tie-Yan Liu. 2019. MASS: masked sequence to sequence pre-training for language generation. In *Proceedings of the 36th International Conference on Machine Learning, ICML*, volume 97, pages 5926–5936.

Trieu H. Trinh and Quoc V. Le. 2018. A simple method for commonsense reasoning. *CoRR*, abs/1806.02847.

Ashish Vaswani, Noam Shazeer, Niki Parmar, Jakob Uszkoreit, Llion Jones, Aidan N. Gomez, Lukasz Kaiser, and Illia Polosukhin. 2017. Attention is all you need. In *Advances in Neural Information Processing Systems*, pages 5998–6008.

Linting Xue, Noah Constant, Adam Roberts, Mihir Kale, Rami Al-Rfou, Aditya Siddhant, Aditya Barua, and Colin Raffel. 2021. mT5: A massively multilingual pre-trained text-to-text transformer. In *Proceedings of the 2021 Conference of the North American Chapter of the Association for Computational Linguistics: Human Language Technologies*, pages 483–498.

Zhilin Yang, Zihang Dai, Yiming Yang, Jaime G. Carbonell, Ruslan Salakhutdinov, and Quoc V. Le. 2019. XLNet: Generalized autoregressive pretraining for language understanding. In *Advances in Neural Information Processing Systems*, pages 5754–5764.

Yukun Zhu, Ryan Kiros, Richard S. Zemel, Ruslan Salakhutdinov, Raquel Urtasun, Antonio Torralba, and Sanja Fidler. 2015. Aligning books and movies: Towards story-like visual explanations by watching movies and reading books. In *2015 IEEE International Conference on Computer Vision*, pages 19–27.

Constraining word alignments with posterior regularization for label transfer

Kevin Martin Jose
Amazon
jskevin@amazon.de

Thomas Gueudre
Amazon
tgueudre@amazon.it

Abstract

Unsupervised word alignments offer a lightweight and interpretable method to transfer labels from high- to low-resource languages, as long as semantically related words have the same label across languages. But such an assumption is often not true in industrial NLP pipelines, where multilingual annotation guidelines are complex and deviate from semantic consistency due to various factors (such as annotation difficulty, conflicting ontology, upcoming feature launches etc.); We address this difficulty by constraining the alignment model to remain consistent with both source and target annotation guidelines, leveraging posterior regularization and labeled examples. We illustrate the overall approach using IBM 2 (fast_align) as a base model, and report results on both internal and external annotated datasets. We measure consistent accuracy improvements on the MultiATIS++ dataset over AWESoME, a popular transformer-based alignment model, in the label projection task (+2.7% at word-level and +15% at sentence-level), and show how even a small amount of target language annotations helps substantially.

1 Introduction

The task of aligning words in parallel sentences (i.e bitexts) originates from statistical machine translation (Brown et al., 1990), where semantic identification was performed based on context similarity in accordance to the well-known *distributional hypothesis*. The most commonly used statistical aligners are built on top of the so-called IBM models (Brown et al., 1993), a series of structured probabilistic models that, while fully unsupervised, often rely on additional assumptions (such as close-to-diagonal alignment) to reach acceptable accuracies. These approaches have since been superseded by neural networks and pretrained embeddings. They nonetheless enjoy a wide popularity across many

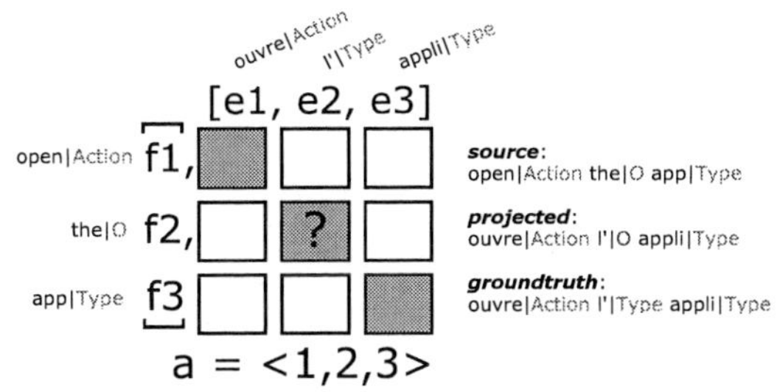

Figure 1: Example of word alignment with notations from English to French. While the identity map is semantically very natural in this example, it conflicts with the ground-truth label. The whole group *l'appli* is labelled as Type in French, possibly to reduce friction with human annotators.

NLP domains owing to their execution speed, data-efficiency and self-contained implementations.

Cheap multilingual word alignments are appealing as they provide a transparent and interpretable way to transfer features from a source language to a target language (see Fig.1). They have been used in the past to transfer costly annotations such as part-of-speech (Yarowsky and Ngai, 2001) or co-reference information from high- to low-resource languages (Postolache et al., 2006). However, the reliability of such a strategy depends on the use case at hand and we argue that it can lead to subtle but systematic failures in downstream tasks. In our industrial use case (that of a voice assistant), multi-lingual named-entity annotation guidelines factor in a great number of aspects (country launches, available features, human-friendly rules for annotators e.t.c) and end up surprisingly riddled with inconsistencies across languages (see table 1). In such cases, even a slight mismatch between semantics and annotation guidelines will lead to systematic errors: annotation guidelines of the source language "bleed" into the target language. This in turn generates friction for NLP pipelines that rely heavily on annotated resources, such as task oriented dialog systems. In this work, we show how to guide word alignments produced by structured

Proceedings of NAACL-HLT 2022: Industry Track Papers, pages 121 - 129
July 10-15, 2022 ©2022 Association for Computational Linguistics

models to conform to the annotation guidelines of the target language, extending them so that they do not solely rely on semantic relatedness. We use the posterior regularization technique of Ganchev et al. (2010), a general framework that allows integrating information coming from a variety of features as optimization constraints. We illustrate our approach using IBM 2 as the base alignment algorithm. To model the label constraints, we construct n-gram tables that count the frequency of labels assigned to n-grams in the target language. These label n-grams, constructed using the same training data, are then used to bias the alignments so they comply with the annotation scheme. We use an EM-like iterative procedure to train the resulting model - label transfer is done by assigning to targets words the label of their aligned source words.

We evaluate our method on two annotated datasets and show that it combines the strengths of both approaches: the inferred alignments produce better labels than either the baseline aligners or the n-gram models alone. It also remains fast, interpretable, self-contained and data-efficient, which makes it easy to integrate into industrial NLP pipelines. However, it has the same drawbacks that IBM model 2 has (no fertility modelling - i.e cannot handle a single source word generating multiple words in the target language, N-1 source-target mapping, danger of local optima during training). We release our implementation as FastLabel[1].

2 Related Work

Statistical word alignment models continue to be widely used to transfer labels from high- to low-resource languages owing to their speed, low memory footprint and interpretability. Their most famous exponents are the IBM models 1 to 4 (Brown et al., 1993; Och and Ney, 2003), a Bayesian models hierarchy of increasing sophistication. fast_align (Dyer et al., 2013) is a fast reparameterization of IBM Model 2 that significantly cuts down training and inference time. Eflomal (Östling and Tiedemann, 2016) augments IBM model 1 with priors on word order and fertility, and uses Markov Chain Monte Carlo (MCMC) to do inference. Much of the recent work depart from the Bayesian modeling tradition by relying on contextual embeddings to perform the alignment (Pourdamghani et al. 2018, Alkhouli et al. 2018, Sabet et al. 2021). AWESoME (Dou and Neubig, 2021) uses multilingual BERT (Devlin et al., 2019) to extract word alignments, and allows fine-tuning the underlying BERT model on parallel corpora to improve alignment quality. While very accurate, they leverage embeddings from computationally expensive neural networks, and as such, they are not self-contained and the errors made by these models are arguably less interpretable than the simpler statistical models presented here.

Mann and McCallum (2007) introduced expectation regularization as a way to encourage unsupervised model predictions to match an expectation from an external prior. Chang et al. (2007) developed the constraint driven learning (CODL) framework that is capable of allowing different levels of constraint violation. Their formulation, however, did not allow for tractable inference and the authors used beam search to solve the optimization problem. The posterior regularization framework introduced by Ganchev et al. (2010) allows constraint violations while remaining tractable.

Applications of statistical word alignment to label projection are numerous. Label projection using word alignments is discussed in Yarowsky, Ngai, and Wicentowski (2001), Hwa et al. (2005), Östling (2016), Das and Petrov (2011) and Duong et al. (2013). The last three models use the stanford POS tagger (Toutanova et al., 2003) on a high resource source-language and transfer the labels to the target language.

3 Model Formulation

We start with the notations and closely follow (Dyer et al., 2013) for clarity. The source (target) sentence is denoted $\mathbf{f}$ ($\mathbf{e}$), of length n (m). The aim is to infer, from bitexts, an alignment $\boldsymbol{a} = \langle a_1, a_2, \cdots, a_m \rangle$ from source to target: each a_i refers to the position of the source sentence word aligned to the ith word in the target sentence (see Figure 1). We will assume that each target target word is associated to at most one source word: this $N-1$ mapping limitation is not a concern in the context of label projection. In the NER (Named Entity Recognition) setup, both source and target sentences may be annotated with NER labels, and we write $\mathcal{L}$ the set of possible labels, and ℓ_{e_i} (resp. ℓ_{f_j}) the label attached to e_i (resp. f_j) ; $\ell_{\mathbf{e}}$ and $\ell_{\mathbf{f}}$ refer to the label sequences of the whole sentences $\mathbf{e}$ and $\mathbf{f}$.

The parameters of the popular IBM models are usually inferred through maximum likelihood (ML)

[1]https://github.com/amazon-research/fast_label

<table>
<tr><th>Dataset</th><th>lang</th><th>example</th></tr>
<tr><td rowspan="7">MultiATIS++</td><td>en</td><td>atis_airfare show me round trip fares from denver to philadelphia O O B-round_trip I-round_trip O O B-fromloc.city_name O B-toloc.city_name</td></tr>
<tr><td>fr</td><td>atis_airfare Me montrer les tarifs aller-retour de Denver à Philadelphie O O O O B-round_trip O B-fromloc.city_name O B-toloc.city_name O</td></tr>
<tr><td>pt</td><td>atis_airfare Mostre tarifas de ida e volta de Denver para a Filadélfia O O O B-round_trip I-round_trip I-round_trip O B-fromloc.city_name O O B-toloc.city_name</td></tr>
<tr><td>de</td><td>atis_airfare Zeige mir Tarife für Hin- und Rück flüge von Denver nach Philadelphia O O O O B-round_trip I-round_trip I-round_trip O O B-fromloc.city_name O B-toloc.city_name</td></tr>
<tr><td>es</td><td>atis_airfare Muéstrame las tarifas de ida y vuelta desde Denver hasta Filadelfia O O O O B-round_trip I-round_trip I-round_trip O B-fromloc.city_name O B-toloc.city_name</td></tr>
<tr><td>zh</td><td>atis_airfare 显示从 丹佛 到 费城 的 往返 票价 O B-fromloc.city_name O B-toloc.city_name O B-round_trip O</td></tr>
<tr><td>hi</td><td>atis_airfare डेन्वर से फिलाडेल्फिया के लिए दोतरफा किराए दिखायें B-fromloc.city_name O B-toloc.city_name O O B-round_trip O O</td></tr>
<tr><td rowspan="6">Internal</td><td>en</td><td>Timer set|o another|o timer|action for|o three|length minutes|length and|o thirty|length seconds|length</td></tr>
<tr><td>fr</td><td>Timer règle|o un|o autre|o minuteur|action pour|o trois|length minutes|length et|length trente|length secondes|length</td></tr>
<tr><td>en</td><td>Weather what|o today's|date temperature|detail</td></tr>
<tr><td>it</td><td>Weather che|o temperatura|date c'|o è|o oggi|date</td></tr>
<tr><td>en</td><td>Appliance turn|action off|action the|o bose|device light|device</td></tr>
<tr><td>pt</td><td>Appliance desligue|action a|o luz|device bose|device</td></tr>
</table>

Table 1: Example training data. The text in teal are word-level labels, and the text in red indicate the overall intent of the sentence. The examples from our internal dataset show some of the discrepancies present in annotation guidelines across languages - for example, the English token-label pair "and|o" corresponds to "et|length" in French. We also observe inconsistencies arising due to word fertility and tokenization choices - "what" corresponds to "che c' è" (i.e 3 different tokens) in Italian and the two words "turn off" corresponds to the single word "desligue" in Portuguese.

$\theta^* = \arg\max_\theta \mathcal{L}(\theta) = \arg\max_\theta P(\mathbf{e}, \mathbf{f}|\theta)$. The parametric family over which inference is performed depends on the IBM models. In what follows, we illustrate our approach on IBM-2 (as used in fast_align), which comes with a diagonal prior and a set of lexical probabilities representing translations:

$$p_{FA}(e_i, a_i|m, n) = \delta(a_i|i, m, n) \times \theta(e_i|f_{a_i})$$
$$p_{FA}(e_i|m, n) = \sum_{j=0}^{n} p_{FA}(e_i, a_i = j|m, n)$$

where $\delta(\cdot)$ models the diagonal prior and the null alignment probability (Dyer et al., 2013). Because alignments are hidden variables, the ML optimization can only be performed approximately, for example with an Expectation Maximization (EM) iterative scheme. EM can be formulated as an ELBO coordinate ascent (Neal and Hinton, 1998):

$$F(q, \theta) = \log \mathcal{L}(\theta) - D_{KL}(q||p_{FA}(\cdot|\mathbf{e}, \mathbf{f}, m, n))$$
$$\text{E-step}: q^{(t)} = \arg\max_q F(q, \theta^t)$$
$$\text{M-step}: \theta^{(t+1)} = \arg\max_\theta F(q^t, \theta)$$

where q is a reference distribution and is used to inject external knowledge into the optimization, and maximization of the E-step is performed over an arbitrary family of alignments probability distribution. For label projection however, we would like to bias the ELBO optimization so as to favor alignments compatible with the target annotation guidelines, without losing information obtained from the bitexts. The posterior regularization (Ganchev et al., 2010) framework offers an elegant solution, by noting that the E-step above can be easily solved over a constrained set of distributions $\mathcal{Q}$, as long as those constraints are defined in terms of moments of $q \in \mathcal{Q}$:

$$\text{E-step (PR)}: q^{(t)} = \arg\max_{q \in Q} F(q, \theta^t)$$
$$Q = \{q : \mathbb{E}_q [\phi(\mathbf{e}, \mathbf{f}, m, n)] = b\}$$

where ϕ is an arbitrary function. In the context of label projection, we wish to match the projected label distribution $P(\ell_\mathbf{e}|\mathbf{e}, \mathbf{f}, m, n)$ to a reference distribution $r(\ell_\mathbf{e})$, that can be defined quite arbitrarily. Given an alignment a, target words receive the same label as their aligned source words $\ell_{e_i} = \ell_{f_{a_i}} \forall i \in [\mathbf{e}]$. We can therefore rewrite such matching condition as:

$$P(\ell_\mathbf{e}|\mathbf{e}, \mathbf{f}, m, n) = \sum_\mathbf{a} P(\ell_\mathbf{e}|\mathbf{e}, \mathbf{f}, \mathbf{a}) P(\mathbf{a}|\mathbf{e}, \mathbf{f}, m, n) \quad (1)$$

$$= \mathbb{E}_q \left[\mathbb{1} \left(\ell_{\mathbf{e}} = \ell_{f_{\mathbf{a}}} \right) \right] \equiv r(\ell_{\mathbf{e}}),$$

$$\mathbb{1} \left(\ell_{\mathbf{e}} = \ell_{f_{\mathbf{a}}} \right) = \begin{cases} 1, & \text{if } \ell_{\mathbf{e}} = \ell_{f_{\mathbf{a}}} \\ 0, & \text{otherwise} \end{cases} \tag{2}$$

The set of contraints, one per label configuration per target sentence, is denoted $\mathcal{C}$. In this case, the E-step admits a dual formulation and the optimal alignment distribution q^* has a simple expression in terms for the unconstrained p_{FA}:

$$q^*(\mathbf{a}) = \frac{p_{FA}(\mathbf{a}|\mathbf{e}, \mathbf{f}) e^{-\sum_{c \in \mathcal{C}} \lambda_c^* v_c^{\mathbf{a}}}}{Z(\{\lambda_c^*\})} \tag{3}$$

$$v_c^{\mathbf{a}} = \mathbb{1} \left(\ell_{f_{\mathbf{a}}} = \ell_c \right) - r(\ell_c) \tag{4}$$

$$\lambda_c^* = \arg\max_{\lambda_c} \left[-\log \left(Z(\{\lambda_c^*\}) \right) \right] \forall c \in \mathcal{C} \tag{5}$$

where $\lambda_c, c \in \mathcal{C}$ is a family of Lagrange multipliers enforcing the constraints over label space. The iterative algorithm closely mimics the classical EM coordinate ascent, with the addition of solving the Lagrange multipliers (see Appendix A).

The value of the Lagrange multipliers λ_c^* are computed through gradient ascent over $Z(\{\lambda_c^*\})$. IBM model 2 enjoys the property that its alignment probability p_{FA} factors over the words of each target sentence. It is therefore convenient to split $\mathcal{C}$ accordingly: to each word e_i and each possible $\ell \in \mathcal{L}$, are attached a Lagrange multiplier $\lambda_\ell^{e_i}$ and the cost $v_\ell^{e_i}$ of labelling e_i with ℓ. In such case, $Z(\{\lambda_c^*\})$ further decomposes:

$$Z(\{\lambda_c^*\}) = \prod_{\mathbf{e} \in \text{corp.}} \prod_{e_i \in s} Z_{e_i}(\{\lambda_c^*\})$$

$$Z_{e_i}(\{\lambda_c^*\}) = \sum_{j=1}^{n} p_{FA} \left(a_i = j | \mathbf{e}, \mathbf{f} \right) e^{-\sum_\ell \lambda_\ell^{e_i} v_\ell^{e_i}}$$

$$v_\ell^{e_i} = \mathbb{1} \left(\ell_{f_{a_i}} = \ell \right) - r(\ell)$$

and its derivative w.r.t $\lambda_\ell^{e_i}$:

$$\frac{\partial Z_{e_i}}{\partial \lambda_\ell^{e_i}} = -\sum_{j=1}^{n} p_{FA} \left(a_i = j | e, f \right) v_\ell^{e_i} e^{-\sum_\ell \lambda_\ell^{e_i} v_\ell^{e_i}}$$

The stationary points is reached when $v_\ell^{e_i} = 0$, selecting alignments for which the transferred label distribution matches $r(\ell)$.

4 Experiments

4.1 Baselines

Eflomal[2] and AWESoME[3] were run using the respective authors' publicly released code. The hyperparameter settings used to run these models are described in Appendix C. Since our work is an extension of fast_align, we ported the original fast_align[4] code to Python and extended it to support posterior regularization. Just like the original fast_align implementation, we did 5 iterations of expectation-maximization to train the model. The trained alignment model (i.e q^* in equation 3) is then evaluated on a held out set of bitexts. For each aligned word pair, the label of the source word (usually from an English sentence) is transferred to the aligned target word. All target words aligned to the "null" token are given a label of "o" (for "other"). We then compare the transferred labels to the true labels of the target sentence to calculate the accuracy. Though the label transfer happens at a word level, we report accuracies at the sentence level as well since perfectly annotated sentences are crucial for our industrial use case. The n-gram classifiers in the tables are simple frequency-based classifiers trained on the target language - for a particular n-gram in the test set, the classifier annotates the nth word with the most frequent label assigned to that n-gram in the training data. For n-grams that were not present in the training data (even after backing-off to unigrams), the classifier outputs the label "o" (for "other"). These simple classifiers are essentially the same models that are used to do posterior regularization in our experiments - when used as classifiers, they only output the most likely label for a given n-gram while during regularization we use their entire label distribution.

Lang	Avg. len.	Avg len. of En translation
	MultiATIS++	
English (en)	11.05	NA
French (fr)	11.72	11.05 (+6.37%)
Portuguese (pt)	11.96	11.05 (+8.17%)
German (de)	11.29	11.05 (+2.13%)
Spanish (es)	11.88	11.05 (+7.62%)
Chinese (zh)	10.95	11.05 (-1.05%)
Hindi (hi)	10.97	11.05 (-0.73%)
	Internal dataset	
Italian (it)	5.29	5.20 (+1.82%)
French (fr)	5.91	5.18 (+14.17%)
Portuguese (pt)	5.42	5.17 (+4.73%)

Table 2: Average sentence lengths (in terms of the number of labelled tokens) for each language present in our datasets. The third column indicates how much longer (or shorter) the sentences in a particular language are compared to their English translations. Unlike MultiATIS++, the English sentences paired with each of languages in our internal dataset are different (i.e the English sentences in the pair en-it are different from those in en-fr), resulting in slightly different average sentence lengths. The translations in both MultiATIS++ and our internal dataset were done by humans.

[2]https://github.com/robertostling/eflomal

[3]https://github.com/neulab/awesome-align

[4]https://github.com/clab/fast_align

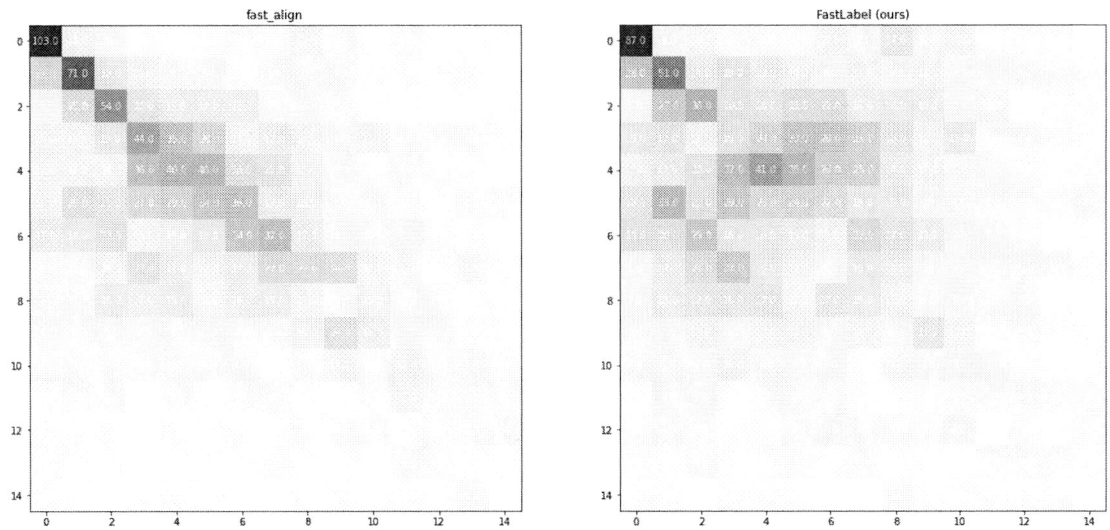

Figure 2: Distribution of word alignments between English-Hindi bitexts in the MultiATIS++ dataset. The left (resp. bottom) axis represents the index of the source (resp. target) word within the source (resp. target) sentence. The left plot shows the distribution of alignments using fast_align. The number inside individual cells represents the frequency of that alignment. The right plot shows the distribution of alignments for the same Engish-Hindi bitexts using FastLabel. We can see from the plots that fast_align has more alignments along the diagonal than FastLabel. Since English and Hindi generally follows different word orders (eg: the Hindi sample present in table 1), the diagonal prior used by fast_align (i.e the assumption that words in target sentence are aligned to the words in relatively the same position in the source sentence) can be problematic. The superior performance of FastLabel (table 3) can be attributed to its ability to overcome fast_align's diagonal prior.

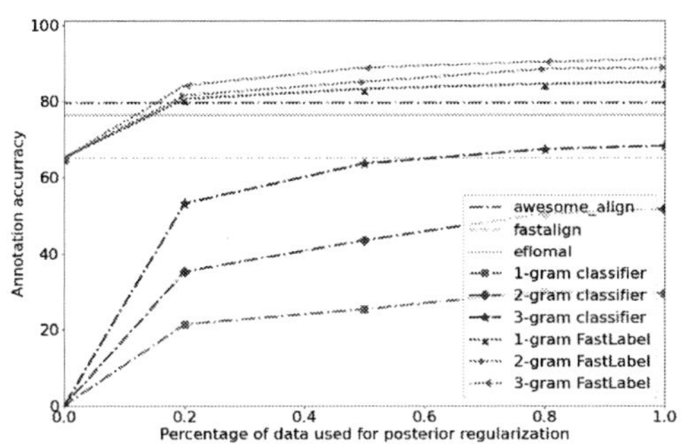

Figure 3: Sentence-level label transfer accuracies between English-German bitexts in MultiATIS++. The amount of German data used to construct the n-gram labels was increased linearly while AWESoMe, eflomal, fast_align, and the word-alignment part of FastLabel were always trained with all available training data.

4.2 Datasets

We ran our experiments on two different datasets - a publicly available corpus of annotated bitexts called MultiATIS++ (Xu et al., 2020) and an internal corpus of annotated bitexts. MultiATIS++ is a multilingual extension of the ATIS (Price, 1990) dataset, which is a transcript of flight information requests to automated airline travel inquiry systems and contains approximately 5000 samples. The queries in ATIS were originally in English and the MultiATIS++ dataset contains annotated human translations of the English queries into six other languages. Our internal dataset consists of queries to a task-oriented dialogue system and contains ten thousand pairs of annotated English-Italian, English-French and English-Portuguese bitexts. The English sentences in the different language pairs in our internal dataset are *not* the same - this means that there is considerable variation in the distribution of intents across different language pairs in this dataset. The scheme for certain type of queries vary across languages (see table 1) as well.

For the set of constraints, we compute a frequency based n-gram model on the annotated monolingual data: the probability of label ℓ_i depends on the word e_i to be labelled, its context of length $n-1$ and the intent of the sentence: $P(\ell_i|\mathbf{e}) = P(\ell_i|e_i, e_{i-1}, \cdots e_{i-n+1}, \textit{intent})$. We include the intent in the counts since labels may strongly depend on it: for example, "play frozen" will be different depending on whether the overall intent is "Music" (resulting in "play|action frozen|album) or "Video" (resulting in "play|action frozen|movie). We construct the n-grams based on the same data that was used to train the word alignment model, and during inference apply the same back-off strategy used by the n-gram classifiers described in the previous section. If an n-gram

	Method	it	fr	pt	de	es	zh	hi
				MultiATIS++				
baselines	fast_align	N/A	48.75 (90.44)	40.14 (90.07)	63.821 (94.54)	52.54 (90.54)	43.04 (83.84)	32.31 (85.17)
	eflomal	N/A	67.17 (94.08)	63.56 (93.71)	76.43 (97.20)	66.10 (93.7)	56.58 (87.8)	73.36 (95.00)
	AWESoME	N/A	74.08 (94.94)	73.23 (95.68)	79.59 (97.83)	72.31 (94.95)	55.47 (89.20)	65.06 (94.69)
	1-gram classifier	N/A	27.88 (86.23)	25.51 (84.43)	29.36 (86.68)	29.05 (85.08)	34.38 (81.81)	33.33 (87.44)
	2-gram classifier	N/A	57.88 (93.35)	57.72 (92.79)	59.66 (93.91)	56.79 (92.1)	66.91 (90.56)	59.64 (94.14)
	3- gram classifier	N/A	66.92 (94.91)	67.78 (94.52)	68.21 (95.42)	67.54 (93.43)	67.28 (91.01)	72.80 (96.06)
ours	1-gram FastLabel	N/A	75.81 (95.96)	69.88 (95.84)	84.97 (98.18)	68.92 (94.69)	73.09 (94.11)	76.85 (96.37)
	2-gram FastLabel	N/A	**79.46** (97.10)	78.25 (97.20)	90.53 (98.90)	76.45 (96.39)	**76.43 (95.13)**	79.03 (97.11)
	3-gram FastLabel	N/A	79.27 (**97.16**)	**78.99 (97.30)**	**91.09 (98.96)**	**76.83 (96.56)**	75.88 (95.11)	**80.34 (97.23)**
				Internal dataset				
baselines	fast_align	x (x')	y (y')	z (z')	N/A	N/A	N/A	N/A
	eflomal	+13.32 (+2.25)	+11.14 (-1.14)	-0.98 (-0.7)	N/A	N/A	N/A	N/A
	AWESoME	+7.49 (+2.07)	+1.4 (+0.02)	+2.4 (+0.55)	N/A	N/A	N/A	N/A
	1-gram classifier	-78.97 (-23.20)	-78.76 (-21.72)	-81.05 (-22.92)	N/A	N/A	N/A	N/A
	2-gram classifier	-76.97 (-22.25)	-76.44 (-20.68)	-78.551 (-22.04)	N/A	N/A	N/A	N/A
	3-gram Classifier	-76.64 (-22.19)	-75.98 (-20.58)	-78.65 (-22.04)	N/A	N/A	N/A	N/A
ours	1-gram FastLabel	+18.48 (+4.36)	+13.62 (+2.89)	+5.08 (+1.48)	N/A	N/A	N/A	N/A
	2-gram FastLabel	**+19.98 (+4.77)**	**+16.72 (+3.42)**	**+8.61 (+2.13)**	N/A	N/A	N/A	N/A
	3-gram FastLabel	+19.65 (+4.67)	+16.10 (**+3.42**)	**+8.61 (+2.10)**	N/A	N/A	N/A	N/A

Table 3: Percentage of perfectly annotated target sentences obtained as a result of label transfer between bitexts - the word level label transfer accuracy is written inside parentheses. Experiments conducted on our internal dataset report accuracies relative to fast_align.

was not observed in the training data, we leave finding the alignment of the corresponding target word unconstrained. Though we stick to simple frequency-based n-gram models for the sake of speed and interpretability, posterior regularization can accommodate any model that can predict a label distribution, including neural networks.

5 Results

Our results are reported in Table 3. Apart from fast_align, we include eflomal, a more sophisticated statistical alignment model, and AWESoME, a strong model that leverages recent advances in pre-trained language models, as additional baselines. On the MultiATIS++ dataset, FastLabel outperforms AWESoME, our strongest baseline, by around 2.7% at word-level label transfer accuracy and gave around a 15% increase in the amount of perfectly annotated target sentences (averaged across all languages). On our internal dataset, FastLabel resulted in an improvement of around 7% (compared to eflomal, which performed better than AWESoME, averaged across all languages) in the amount of perfectly annotated target sentences. The simple n-gram classifiers perform reasonably well on MultiATIS++. After a deeper inspection, we find that most of the words in this dataset receive the label "O", and entities with richer labels (such as city names) are usually present in both the train and test sets, and makes MultiATIS++ easier to annotate correctly. Our internal dataset is more complex, comprising of 185 intents (eg: "Appliance", "Music") and 211 different label types (i.e "o" or "date" or "song") (for comparison, MultiATIS++ has 23 intents and 122 label types). This is reflected in the much poorer performance of the n-gram classifiers on our internal dataset. Though poor as independent annotators, the same n-gram label distributions are beneficial to FastLabel when used for posterior regularization, indicating that our regularization framework is successful in incorporating the right amount of information from the external prior.

We observe a large drop in performance for fast_align when aligning language from different families (such as English-Chinese bitexts), due to the well-known limitations of the diagonal prior assumption. Moreover, as observed in table 2, Hindi and Chinese sentences are usually slightly shorter than their English counterparts, while the sentences from the other European languages tend to be longer. For example, the Italian translation of the phrase "personalize my echo" could be "personalizza il mio echo" - here the two tokens "my echo" generate three tokens in Italian (high word fertility), while a non-Indo-European language might have the opposite problem with respect to English (low word fertility). Despite these challenges, FastLabel performs comparatively well on these languages thanks to its ability to overcome the diagonal prior of the underlying fast_align algorithm. Figure 2 illustrates the effect of posterior regularization on word-alignments. All subplots show alignments between English-Hindi bitexts in the MultiATIS++ dataset. The plot to the left (fast_align) clearly

<table>
<tr><th>id</th><th>source</th><th>fast_align</th><th>ours</th></tr>
<tr><td>1</td><td>track|o a|o wet|attribute diaper|item</td><td>enregistre|o une|o couche|attribute culotte|attribute mouillée|item</td><td>enregistre|o une|o couche|item culotte|item mouillée|attribute</td></tr>
<tr><td>2</td><td>c.|source n.|source n.| source report|o</td><td>le|o compte|source rendu|source de|o c.|source n.|source n.|source</td><td>le|o compte|o rendu|o de|o c.|source n.|source n.|source</td></tr>
<tr><td>3</td><td>show|visual me|o an|o octopus|item</td><td>montre|visual moi|other un|o poulpe|item</td><td>montre| visual moi|visual un|o poulpe|item</td></tr>
</table>

Table 4: Three examples representative of the type of errors in label overcome by posterior regularization. All examples are from the FastLabel evaluated on the English-French bitexts in our internal test dataset. 1) Alignments away from the diagonal - the French word corresponding to "wet" ("mouillée") appear at the end of the sentence. 2) Fertility - "report" is translated into French as "le compte rendu de". 3) Discrepancies in annotation guidelines - though "moi" should be semantically aligned to "me" in the English sentence and hence given the label "o", our internal annotation scheme for French consistently annotates "moi" as "visual" if it follows "montre".

shows a stronger alignment along the diagonal, while this tendency to align along the diagonal is weaker in the plot to the right (FastLabel). Table 4 contains some examples where fast_align made a mistake in transferring the labels from the source sentence, but FastLabel was correct.

How much annotated data is required for FastLabel to improve upon fast_align? Figure 3 reports label transfer accuracy between English-German bitexts in MultiATIS++ using varying amounts of training data to construct the n-gram models. Using only 20% of all available training data to construct the n-gram models gives FastLabel a significant boost over fast_align, demonstrating the applicability of our approach in data-sparse regimes. With growing training data, n-grams become better annotators (to a point where the 3-gram model outperforms fast_align), but a performance gap with FastLabel persists. Although the focus of our work was on maximizing the label transfer accuracy, we also note that posterior regularization resulted in a more semantically accurate translation table (see Appendix B) compared to fast_align.

5.1 Conclusion

We illustrated how to augment existing algorithms (such as fast_align) with information about annotation guidelines, through posterior regularization. Lightweight, self-contained and data-efficient, our approach retains the benefits of statistical aligners while leading to higher quality alignments. It also mitigates semantic inconsistencies that can appear in the annotation guidelines of large scale industrial NLP systems. A natural extension of this work is to use more sophisticated models than n-grams to predict the label distributions. The task of matching the distribution of source labels onto some target through word alignments also bears some similarities with optimal transport. We leave such investigation to the future.

Acknowledgements

We would like to thank Fabian Triefenbach, Markus Boese and Yannick Versley for their feedback on an earlier version of this manuscript.

References

Tamer Alkhouli, Gabriel Bretschner, and Hermann Ney. 2018. On the alignment problem in multi-head attention-based neural machine translation.

Peter F. Brown, John Cocke, Stephen A. Della Pietra, Vincent J. Della Pietra, Fredrick Jelinek, John D. Lafferty, Robert L. Mercer, and Paul S. Roossin. 1990. A statistical approach to machine translation. *Computational Linguistics*, 16(2):79–85.

Peter F. Brown, Stephen A. Della Pietra, Vincent J. Della Pietra, and Robert L. Mercer. 1993. The mathematics of statistical machine translation: Parameter estimation. *Computational Linguistics*, 19(2):263–311.

Ming-Wei Chang, Lev Ratinov, and Dan Roth. 2007. Guiding semi-supervision with constraint-driven learning. In *Proceedings of the 45th Annual Meeting of the Association of Computational Linguistics*, pages 280–287, Prague, Czech Republic. Association for Computational Linguistics.

Dipanjan Das and Slav Petrov. 2011. Unsupervised part-of-speech tagging with bilingual graph-based projections. In *Proceedings of the 49th Annual Meeting of the Association for Computational Linguistics: Human Language Technologies*, pages 600–609, Portland, Oregon, USA. Association for Computational Linguistics.

Jacob Devlin, Ming-Wei Chang, Kenton Lee, and Kristina Toutanova. 2019. BERT: Pre-training of deep bidirectional transformers for language understanding. In *Proceedings of the 2019 Conference of the North American Chapter of the Association for Computational Linguistics: Human Language Technologies, Volume 1 (Long and Short Papers)*, pages 4171–4186, Minneapolis, Minnesota. Association for Computational Linguistics.

Zi-Yi Dou and Graham Neubig. 2021. Word alignment by fine-tuning embeddings on parallel corpora.

Long Duong, Paul Cook, Steven Bird, and Pavel Pecina. 2013. Simpler unsupervised pos tagging with bilingual projections. In *ACL*.

Chris Dyer, Victor Chahuneau, and Noah A. Smith. 2013. A simple, fast, and effective reparameterization of ibm model 2. In *NAACL*.

Kuzman Ganchev, João Graça, Jennifer Gillenwater, and Ben Taskar. 2010. Posterior regularization for structured latent variable models. *J. Mach. Learn. Res.*, 11:2001–2049.

Rebecca Hwa, Philip Resnik, Amy Weinberg, Clara Cabezas, and Okan Kolak. 2005. Bootstrapping parsers via syntactic projection across parallel texts. *Nat. Lang. Eng.*, 11(3):311–325.

Gideon S. Mann and Andrew McCallum. 2007. Simple, robust, scalable semi-supervised learning via expectation regularization. In *Proceedings of the 24th International Conference on Machine Learning*, ICML '07, page 593–600, New York, NY, USA. Association for Computing Machinery.

Radford M. Neal and Geoffrey E. Hinton. 1998. *A View of the Em Algorithm that Justifies Incremental, Sparse, and other Variants*, pages 355–368. Springer Netherlands, Dordrecht.

Franz Josef Och and Hermann Ney. 2003. A systematic comparison of various statistical alignment models. *Computational Linguistics*, 29(1):19–51.

Robert Östling. 2016. A bayesian model for joint word alignment and part-of-speech transfer. In *COLING*.

Robert Östling and Jörg Tiedemann. 2016. Efficient word alignment with Markov Chain Monte Carlo. *Prague Bulletin of Mathematical Linguistics*, 106:125–146.

Oana Postolache, Dan Cristea, and Constantin Orasan. 2006. Transferring coreference chains through word alignment. In *Proceedings of the Fifth International Conference on Language Resources and Evaluation (LREC'06)*, Genoa, Italy. European Language Resources Association (ELRA).

Nima Pourdamghani, Marjan Ghazvininejad, and Kevin Knight. 2018. Using word vectors to improve word alignments for low resource machine translation. In *Proceedings of the 2018 Conference of the North American Chapter of the Association for Computational Linguistics: Human Language Technologies, Volume 2 (Short Papers)*, pages 524–528, New Orleans, Louisiana. Association for Computational Linguistics.

P. J. Price. 1990. Evaluation of spoken language systems: the ATIS domain. In *Speech and Natural Language: Proceedings of a Workshop Held at Hidden Valley, Pennsylvania, June 24-27,1990.*

Masoud Jalili Sabet, Philipp Dufter, François Yvon, and Hinrich Schütze. 2021. Simalign: High quality word alignments without parallel training data using static and contextualized embeddings.

Kristina Toutanova, Dan Klein, Christopher D. Manning, and Yoram Singer. 2003. Feature-rich part-of-speech tagging with a cyclic dependency network. In *Proceedings of the 2003 Conference of the North American Chapter of the Association for Computational Linguistics on Human Language Technology - Volume 1*, NAACL '03, page 173–180, USA. Association for Computational Linguistics.

Weijia Xu, Batool Haider, and Saab Mansour. 2020. End-to-end slot alignment and recognition for cross-lingual nlu.

David Yarowsky and Grace Ngai. 2001. Inducing multilingual POS taggers and NP bracketers via robust projection across aligned corpora. In *Second Meeting of the North American Chapter of the Association for Computational Linguistics*.

David Yarowsky, Grace Ngai, and Richard Wicentowski. 2001. Inducing multilingual text analysis tools via robust projection across aligned corpora. In *Proceedings of the First International Conference on Human Language Technology Research*, HLT '01, page 1–8, USA. Association for Computational Linguistics.

A EM steps with posterior regularization

The iterative algorithm closely mimics the classical EM coordinate ascent, with the addition of solving the Lagrange multipliers:

1. (Start) Random initialization of the IBM 2 model parameters θ_0.
2. Compute p_{FA} as specified by the IBM 2 model, given θ_t.
3. Find the optimal Lagrange multipliers λ_c^* and compute the tilted distribution q^*.
4. Find the optimal parameters θ_{t+1} using q^* in place of p_{FA}.
5. Iterate from step 2 until convergence.

B Excerpt of the translation table for English-French bitexts

In table 5, French words that are not semantic translations of the English source word are highlighted in red. The "count" represents the number of bitexts where the English and French words appeared in the source and target sentences respectively. We observed that posterior regularization using labels improved the quality of the translation table (and consequently, alignments) as well.

fast_align		FastLabel		count
English	French	English	French	
list	courses	list	liste	222
theater	au	theater	theater	22.0
please	te	please	plaît	117.0
closed	est	closed	fermé	5.0
app	application	app	l'	6.0
diaper	culotte	diaper	couche	12.0
don't	ne	don't	pas	11.0
march	le	march	mars	32.0
funniest	la	funniest	drôle	3.0
beauty	la	beauty	belle	4.0
cinema	au	cinema	cinéma	9.0
baby	baby	baby	bébé	11.0
mode	mode	mode	multilangues	4.0
frozen	des	frozen	reine	5.0
snow	des	snow	neige	3.0
oatmeal	d'	oatmeal	flocons	3.0
text	un	text	message	3.0
hip	hop	hip	hip	3.0

Table 5: All disagreements appearing more than thrice between the translation tables produced by fast_align and FastLabel on the English-French bitexts in our internal dataset.

C Hyperparameters

Eflomal was run using the "model3" argument so that the final model makes use of IBM model 1, Hidden Markov Models, and also models fertility. Both the forward and reverse alignments (i.e they were not symmetrized) were used to make the priors.

AWESoME was fine-tuned for 2 epochs in an unsupervised fashion independently on the training split of both MultiATIS++ and our internal data, with the following hyperparameters:

hyperparameter	value(s)
extraction	softmax
training epochs	2
training objectives	Masked Language Modelling (MLM), Translation Language Modelling (TLM), Self-training objective (SO)
gradient accumulation steps	4
learning rate	0.00002
maximum training steps	20000

D Compute

FastLabel, eflomal and fast_align were run on cpu on a consumer-grade laptop. AWESoME was fine-tuned for 2 epochs on a single Nvidia Tesla V100 GPU. Our python re-write of fast_align trains at the rate of approximately 260 samples per second. With posterior regularization using trigrams, the training speed drops down to approximately 80 iterations per second. This translates to a training time of 15 seconds per iteration (MultiATIS++ dataset, 4300 training samples) with fast_align and almost 1 minute per training iteration for FastLabel (with trigrams). Though our rewrite of fast_align (and consequently FastLabel) is faster to train compared to recent models such as AWESoME, it is still slower than the original implementation of fast_align and eflomal (which are written in c) - this is currently a limitation of our work and we intend to address this in a future code release.

Explaining the Effectiveness of Multi-Task Learning for Efficient Knowledge Extraction from Spine MRI Reports

Arijit Sehanobish, McCullen Sandora, Nabila Abraham,
Jayashri Pawar, Danielle Torres, Anasuya Das, Murray Becker,
Richard Herzog, Benjamin Odry, Ron Vianu
Covera Health, New York City, New York
{arijit.sehanobish, mccullen.sandora, nabila.abraham,
jayashri.pawar, danielle.torres, anasuya.das, rherzog,
murray.becker, benjamin.odry, ron.vianu}@coverahealth.com

Abstract

Pretrained Transformer based models finetuned on domain specific corpora have changed the landscape of NLP. However, training or finetuning these models for individual tasks can be time consuming and resource intensive. Thus, a lot of current research is focused on using transformers for multi-task learning (Raffel et al., 2020) and how to group the tasks to help a multi-task model to learn effective representations that can be shared across tasks (Standley et al., 2020; Fifty et al., 2021). In this work, we show that a single multi-tasking model can match the performance of task specific models when the task specific models show similar representations across all of their hidden layers and their gradients are aligned, i.e. their gradients follow the same direction. We hypothesize that the above observations explain the effectiveness of multi-task learning. We validate our observations on our internal radiologist-annotated datasets on the cervical and lumbar spine. Our method is simple and intuitive, and can be used in a wide range of NLP problems.

1 Introduction

Since the seminal work by (Vaswani et al., 2017), Transformers have become the main architecture for almost all Natural Language Processing (NLP) tasks. Self-supervised pretraining of massive language models like BERT (Devlin et al., 2019) and GPT (Brown et al., 2020) has allowed practitioners to use these large language models with little or no finetuning to various downstream tasks. Multi-task learning (MTL) in NLP has been a very promising approach and has shown to lead to performance gains even over task specific fine-tuned models (Worsham and Kalita, 2020; Raffel et al., 2020; Aribandi et al., 2021). However, applying these large pre-trained Transformer models to downstream medical NLP tasks is quite difficult. Medical NLP has its unique challenges ranging from domain specific corpora, noisy annotation labels and scarcity of high quality labeled data. Despite these challenges, a number of researchers and practitioners have successfully finetuned these large language models for various medical NLP tasks. However, there is not much literature that uses multi-task learning in medical NLP to classify and extract diagnoses from clinical text (Peng et al., 2020; Crichton et al., 2017). Moreover, there is almost no work in predicting spine pathologies from the radiologists' notes (Azimi et al., 2020).

In this article, we are interested in extracting information from radiologists' notes on the cervical and the lumbar spine. In a given note, the radiologist discusses the specific, and often multiple pathologies, present in the medical images and grade their severity. Extracting relevant pathologies from these reports can facilitate the creation of structured databases that can be used for a number of downstream use-cases, such as cohort creation, quality assessment and outcome tracking. Single-task learning for information extraction in medical NLP has enjoyed much success in deep learning (Kanakarajan et al., 2021).

However, an ultimate NLP system for a complete understanding of the medical report must be able to perform many diverse information extraction and classification tasks simultaneously and efficiently. Such a system can be enabled by MTL, where one model shares weights across multiple tasks and makes multiple inferences in one forward pass. Such networks can not only be trained with limited resources, but are more scalable and deployable when compared to several single-task models. Moreover, the shared features within these MTL networks can induce more robust regularization and boost performance. Thus there is a lot of interest in the academic and industry research communities to understand when multi-task learning improves performance over single-tasking models (Crawshaw, 2020), and how to group a diverse set of tasks to

Proceedings of NAACL-HLT 2022: Industry Track Papers, pages 130 - 140
July 10-15, 2022

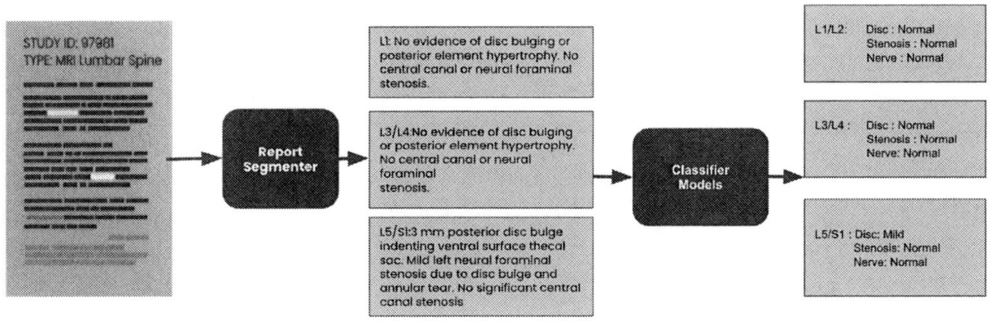

Figure 1: Figure showing how a report looks as it goes through our pipeline.

encourage the model to learn a representation that can be shared across tasks (Standley et al., 2020; Fifty et al., 2021; Bingel and Søgaard, 2017; Zamir et al., 2020). Some of the aforementioned works, most notably in (Shui et al., 2019), define a notion of task similarity via the Wasserstein distance and show that a small Wasserstein distance between tasks aids in MTL.

This work is an extension of our earlier work (Sehanobish et al., 2022) where we used parameter efficient MTL models to extract information from cervical spine. In that work, we defined tasks as a conditional distribution over the classes, and we attributed our success of MTL to smaller Wasserstein distance between tasks. However, computing Wasserstein distance is expensive and suffers from the curse of dimensionality (Cuturi, 2013), which requires the number of samples to be significantly larger than the dimension of the representation (768 for many transformer models) in order for the distance to be accurately estimated. This prevents us from being able to estimate Wasserstein distance for some of our minority classes, which have about 200 examples. Even for majority classes where we have about 5k samples, our work suffers from large error rates. Thus, to alleviate the above drawbacks, in this work, we sought to use methods that are applicable to small data regimes that lie in high dimensional space.

Inspired by the work of (Yu et al., 2020; Chen et al., 2020) and (Kornblith et al., 2019), we hypothesize if the single-task models show similar representations across their hidden layers and the task specific gradients are *aligned* (see Definition 1 in Section 4.2), the multi-task model can match or outperform the task-specific, single-task models. We validate this hypothesis on two multi-task settings on our internal datasets: **(a)** Four of the most common pathologies in the cervical spine - central canal and foraminal stenosis, disc herniation and cord compression, and **(b)** Three pathologies in the lumbar spine - central canal stenosis, disc herniation and nerve root impingement.

In this work, we **(a)** extend our novel pipeline to extract and predict the severity of various pathologies in the lumbar and cervical spine at *each motion segment*, **(b)** compute Central Kernel Alignment (CKA) and show similarity between the transformer layers trained for individual tasks on a given dataset, **(c)** compute dot products between the gradients of the task specific loss functions with respect to various parameters and show that most of the gradients flow along a similar trajectory and **(d)** show how to leverage that information into a simple MTL framework allowing us to achieve significant model compression during deployment and also speed up our inference without sacrificing the accuracy of our predictions.

2 Datasets

We use an internal dataset consisting of radiologists' MRI reports on the cervical and the lumbar spine. Our dataset is heterogeneous and is diversely sampled from a large number of different radiology practices and medical institutions; the cervical MRI data consists of 1578 reports from 97 different radiology practices detailing various pathologies of the cervical spine and our lumbar MRI data contains 2004 reports from 170 different practices.

We annotate the cervical reports with the 4 following pathologies: spinal stenosis, disc herniation, cord compression, and neural foraminal stenosis, and the lumbar reports with the 3 pathologies: disc herniation, spinal stenosis, and nerve impingement. Each of these pathologies is accompanied by an indication of severity. In the cervical reports, the three categories for the central canal stenosis are based on gradation; none/mild are not clinically significant, moderate and severe definitions involve cord compression or flattening. The moderate versus severe gradation refers to the varying degrees of cord involvement. For disc herniation and central canal stenosis, the categories are based on a continuous spectrum and it is a standard practice in radiology for any continuous spectrum to be bucketed in mild, moderate and severe discrete categories. Cord compression severity is binary: compression/signal change versus none. This is because both cord compression and signal change can cause symptoms, and are therefore clinically relevant. Foraminal stenosis is treated as a binary task as well: severe versus non-severe, as severe foraminal stenosis may indicate nerve impingement, which is clinically significant. Similar considerations are taken into account when annotating the lumbar reports. The splits and the details of each category can be found in Table 1. The data distribution is highly imbalanced, and about 25% of these reports are OCR-ed, which leads to additional challenges stemming from bad OCR errors.

Dataset	Pathology	Training Label Distribution	Test Label Distribution
Lumbar	Disc	None/Mild : 1885 Moderate : 1998 Severe : 456	None/Mild : 1068 Moderate :1588 Severe :332
	Stenosis	None/Mild : 3787 Moderate : 350 Severe : 202	None/Mild : 2411 Moderate : 304 Severe : 273
	Nerve	Normal : 3790 Abnormal : 549	Normal : 2376 Abnormal : 612
Cervical	Disc	None/Mild : 2731 Moderate : 2699 Severe : 797	None/Mild : 401 Moderate : 378 Severe : 101
	Stenosis	None/Mild : 5488 Moderate : 561 Severe : 178	None/Mild : 793 Moderate : 68 Severe : 19
	Cord Compression	Normal : 5702 Abnormal : 525	Normal : 806 Abnormal : 74
	Neural Foraminal Stenosis	Normal : 5262 Abnormal : 965	Normal : 789 Abnormal : 91

Table 1: Table showing statistics of our datasets

For a given report, each task is to predict the severity of a pathology for each motion segment - the smallest physiological motion unit of the spinal cord (Swartz et al., 2005). Breaking information down at the motion segment level in this way enables pathological findings to be correlated with clinical exam findings, and can inform future treatment interventions.

Every report is tagged by annotators with labels for relevant pathologies and severities, along with span information indicating which part(s) of the report mentions each pathology. For example, in a report for the lumbar spine, the sentence "L1-L2: There is no disc herniation. No spinal canal or foraminal narrowing" would be given normal or 0 class for each of the 3 pathologies (central canal stenosis, disc herniation and nerve root impingement). Similarly in a cervical spine report, the sentence " C2-3: Normal; no disc herniation or bulge. No central canal stenosis or neuroforaminal narrowing" would be given a normal or 0 class for all the 4 pathologies. An example of a full radiology report can be found in Appendix A.

3 Workflow

In this section, we will briefly describe our pipeline. The reports are first de-identified according to HIPAA regulations. Next, a Spacy (Honnibal et al., 2020) parser is used to break the report into sentences.

A BERT based NER model which we call the *report segmenter* is then used to identify the motion segment(s) referenced in each sentence, and all the sentences containing a particular motion segment are concatenated together. This report segmenter has been shown to achieve an F1 score of .9 on our internal datasets, and the same model is common across both the lumbar and the cervical datasets. More details about the NER model and the hyperparameters used to train it can be found in Appendix B and C. All pathologies are predicted using the concatenated text for a particular motion segment. Finally, the severities for each pathology are modeled as multi-label classification problem, and a pre-trained transformer is finetuned using the text for each motion segment.

For more details about our pipeline and data processing, please see Appendix B. Figure 1 breaks down how a report looks as it is processed through our spine pipeline.

4 Similarity of Representations between Task Specific Models

In this section we will describe our methodology to understand the similarity between the representations of various single task models. For all the experiments in this section, we use the PubMed-BERT (Gu et al., 2020) as the backbone.

4.1 Central Kernel Alignment

We use the linear Central Kernel Alignment (CKA), introduced in (Kornblith et al., 2019). CKA is a scalar similarity index that can be used to compare representations within and across neural networks. (Linear) CKA can be defined by the following:

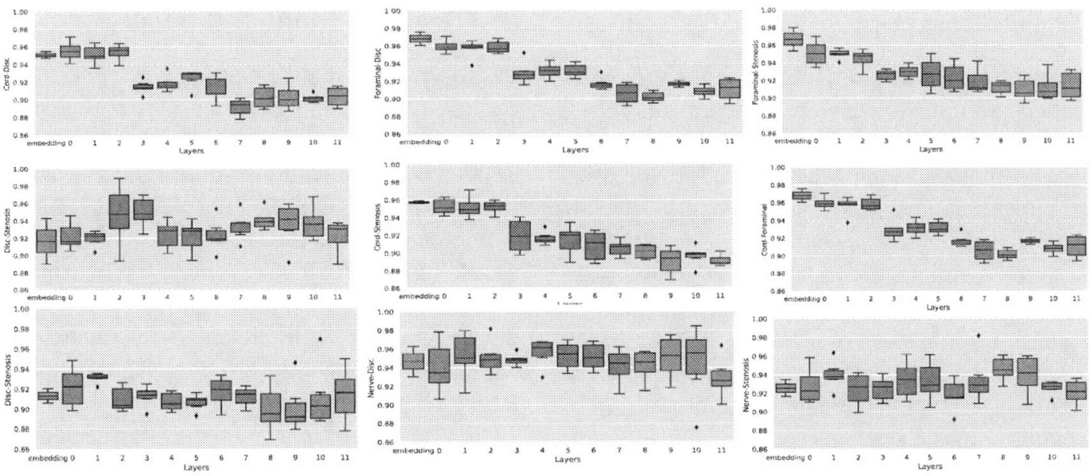

Figure 2: CKA between activation matrices between different finetuned single-task models. The top 2 rows are single-task models trained to predict specific pathologies from cervical dataset and the bottom row for the lumbar dataset. The y-axis is chosen to be between the min and the max values, i.e. in the interval (.86, 1.0)

Given N examples and two activation outputs on these examples, $R_1 \in \mathbb{R}^{N \times d_1}$ and $R_2 \in \mathbb{R}^{N \times d_2}$,

$$\text{CKA}(R_1, R_2) = \frac{||R_1^\top R_2||_F}{||R_1^\top R_1||_F ||R_2^\top R_2||_F} \tag{1}$$

where $|| \cdot ||_F$ is the Frobenius norm.

It is widely believed that similar representations lead to similar performances on downstream tasks (Nguyen et al., 2021). In this work, we compare the representations learned by various single tasking models. For two single task models trained on a specific part of a spine, the CKA between the matrix of activations for each layer of the corresponding models is computed. For illustration purposes, we collect all the CKA values for various activation matrices in a given layer and plot them in a box plot, as shown in figure 2. We observe that for various tasks on both cervical and lumbar spine, all layers of the task specific models learn similar representations.

Additional results on comparing models from the tasks from the lumbar dataset and the cervical dataset can be found in Appendix D.

However, the high value of CKA may also be attributed to the following factors : (i) larger and deeper networks converge to similar solutions (Morcos et al., 2018) and (ii) CKA values do not change drastically when models start from pretrained weights and are only trained for a few epochs (Mirzadeh et al., 2021).

Thus in addition to the above analysis of the activations with the CKA, in the next subsection we look at the gradient level information to understand the trajectory of the task specific learned activations.

4.2 Gradient Alignment

There has been a lot of work in understanding the task specific gradients in the context of MTL. Given tasks $T_1, \cdots T_n$ (for example, they can be classification tasks), one can define n loss functions $\mathcal{L}_{T_j}$ for each task T_j. In our work, all loss functions are cross-entropy losses. Then the task specific gradients are defined to be $\nabla_{\theta_j} \mathcal{L}_{T_j}$ where θ_j are the parameters of the task specific model. More specifically, it is shown in (Chen et al., 2018), that MTL is competitive with single task learners when the norms of the task specific gradients have similar magnitudes. However in (Yu et al., 2020; Javaloy and Valera, 2021), the authors show that the direction of the gradient flow is more important than the magnitude for the success of MTL. More precisely, Theorem 1 in (Yu et al., 2020), shows that the multitask objective converges to the optimum of one of the tasks or a sub-optimal minima in the presence of conflicting gradients. Furthermore, authors in (Javaloy and Valera, 2021) use a synthetic toy example to show the difficulties of optimizing a multi-task loss in the presence of conflicting gradients.

Inspired by the above works, we define the following:

Definition 1 *Two gradient vectors g_i and g_j are aligned if $g_i \cdot g_j > 0$, i.e. the vectors are pointing* *in the same direction.*

To show that the gradients get more aligned as models are trained, we store the gradients for all the parameters for all the mini-batches after every epoch. We then compute the dot products between the corresponding gradients for two tasks. We observe that as the task specific models gets trained, an overwhelming proportion of these gradients are aligned (see Table 2). To illustrate our findings, we take the proportion of these aligned parameters in a given layer and plot them using a box plot in Figure 3. Finally, we compute the proportion of weights across all layers for which the gradients are aligned which we call the Average Proportion of Aligned Gradients (APAG).

$$\text{APAG} = \frac{1}{N_{\text{layers}}}\frac{1}{N_{\text{heads}}}\sum_{\textit{layers}}\sum_{\textit{heads}}\theta\left(g_i \cdot g_j\right) \quad (2)$$

where $\theta(x)$ is the Heaviside step function. This is a scalar value that summarizes the box plot and we show the progression of alignment of the gradients as training progress and the end of the training (Table 2 and Table 6 in Appendix D respectively). Note that, in the above formula, the token embedding layer is included in the computation and it is assumed to have 1 head.

Dataset	Task Comparisons	Epoch 1	Epoch 2	Epoch 3	Epoch 4
Cervical	Cord-Stenosis	.46	.67	.75	.81
	Cord-Disc	.37	.52	.69	.74
	Cord-Foraminal	.49	.61	.77	.83
	Disc-Stenosis	.51	.62	.69	.78
	Disc-Foraminal	.47	.59	.65	.73
	Foraminal-Stenosis	.54	.66	.72	.79
Lumbar	Disc-Stenosis	.44	.53	.59	.68
	Nerve-Stenosis	.51	.57	.66	.73
	Disc-Nerve	.48	.55	.63	.71

Table 2: Results showing the Average Proportion of Aligned Gradients between various task specific models at various epochs.

To summarize: The task specific models not only show similar representations but they arrive at these representations by moving in a similar direction after starting from the pretrained weights. We would also like to point that we observe similar behavior when we run our experiments with the BERT (Devlin et al., 2019) and the Clinical BERT (Alsentzer et al., 2019) models.

5 Results on Multi-Task Models

In this section, we give empirical evidence on the success of MTL for our datasets. The results shown in this section are from our test set.

For our classification task, the PubMedBERT model is used as the backbone. This BERT model is finetuned on the the cervical tasks resulting in 4 task-specific BERT sequence classifier models which provides our baseline results. For the lumbar dataset, the PubMedBERT model is finetuned on the 3 classification tasks resulting in 3 task-specific BERT sequence classifier models.

Now, instead of finetuning the task specific models for extracting various pathology information from the cervical spine dataset, 4 classifier heads (i.e. 4 linear layers) are added to a single PubMedBERT model to create an output layer of shape $[3, 3, 2, 2]$, where the first 3 outputs correspond to the logits for the stenosis severity prediction, the next 3 for the disc severity, the next 2 for the cord severity and the final 2 logits for the foraminal severity. For the lumbar dataset, 3 classifier heads are added to the PubMedBERT model to create an output layer of shape $[3, 3, 2]$, where the first 3 outputs correspond to the logits for the stenosis severity prediction, the next 3 for the disc severity, and the final 2 logits for the nerve severity.

For the experiments, with both the datasets, a dropout of .5 is added to the BERT vectors before passing them to the classifier layers. Each of these classifier heads is trained with a cross entropy loss with the predicted logits and the ground truth targets. All the losses are added up which allows the gradients to backpropagate through the whole model and train these classifier heads jointly.

The results for our experiments are shown in Table 3 for the lumbar dataset and Table 4 for the cervical dataset.

Backbone	Model	Disc	Stenosis	Nerve
BERT BASE	Baseline (single tasker)	$.78 \pm .03$	$.79 \pm .02$	$.8 \pm .03$
	Multi-Tasking	$.77 \pm .02$	$.78 \pm .01$	$.79 \pm .02$
CLINICAL BERT	Baseline (single tasker)	$.81 \pm .03$	$.83 \pm .02$	$.82 \pm .03$
	Multi-Tasking	$.83 \pm .02$	$.8 \pm .04$	$.81 \pm .02$
MSR PubMedBERT	Baseline (single tasker)	$.82 \pm .03$	$.83 \pm .03$	$.81 \pm .04$
	Multi-Tasking	$\mathbf{.84 \pm .01}$	$\mathbf{.84 \pm .03}$	$\mathbf{.86 \pm .04}$

Table 3: Table showing the macro F1 scores over 5 trials of our Baseline and Multi-Tasking Models on the Lumbar Dataset.

For fair comparisons, we also conduct experi-

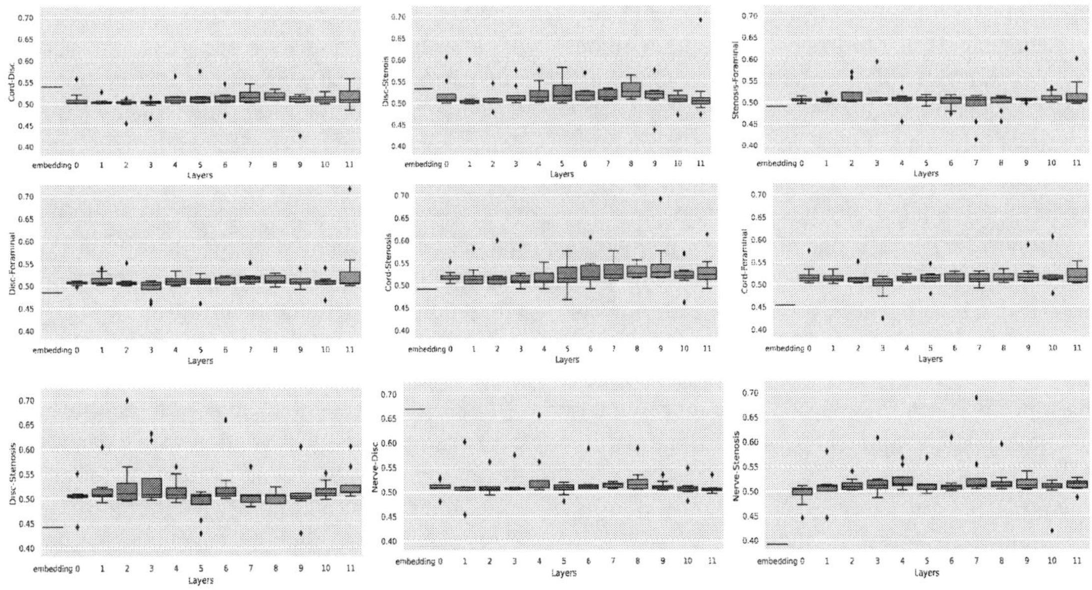

Figure 3: Box Plot showing the proportion of aligned gradients between various task specific models, after training. The top 2 rows are single tasking models trained to predict specific pathologies from the cervical dataset and the bottom row for the lumbar dataset. The y-axis is chosen to be between the min and the max values, i.e. in the interval (.38, .725).

ments with the BERT base and the Clinical BERT models as well. We notice that the PubMedBERT produces slightly better results than both the Clinical BERT and the BERT base. We believe this is due to the fact that the vocabulary for PubMedBERT is tailored for clinical text, unlike that of Clinical BERT, which uses the same vocabulary as that of BERT.

Backbone	Model	Stenosis	Disc	Cord	Foraminal
BERT BASE	Baseline (single tasker)	.62 ± .03	.64 ± .03	.70 ± .03	.79 ± .03
	Multi-Tasking	.62 ± .02	.65 ± .03	.72 ± .02	.78 ± .01
CLINICAL BERT	Baseline (single tasker)	.64 ± .05	.66 ± .02	.71 ± .02	.82 ± .01
	Multi-Tasking	.63 ± .02	.67 ± .01	.75 ± .01	.79 ± .03
MSR PubMedBERT	Baseline (single tasker)	.66 ± .03	.68 ± .04	**.73 ± .05**	**.84 ± .01**
	Multi-Tasking	**.67 ± .01**	**.69 ± .01**	.72 ± .04	.83 ± .03

Table 4: Table showing the macro F1 scores over 5 trials of our Baseline and Multi-Tasking Models on the Cervical Dataset.

The hyperparameters and other training and implementation details can be found in Appendix C.

6 Deployment

We deploy our spine pipeline system on an AWS p3.2x machine with a single NVIDIA V100 GPU. Reports are passed through the pipeline daily and first go through the report segmenter which tags sentences belonging to our set of motion segments. Post-processing is done per report to aggregate sentences belonging to each motion segment group and to filter out any reports that do not contain motion segments. Each grouping of motion segments is individually classified through our MTL model to predict a severity class per pathology. Both the report segmenter and the multi-tasking model are processed in batch mode with latencies of 31ms/report and 56ms/report, respectively. Compared to single pathology models, we observe a 3x improvement in latency per study when using the MTL pathology model. The spine pipeline is routinely evaluated in an offline setting for studies that do not produce any motion segment groupings or fail to capture any sentences for a given motion segment, per report. Our current deployment only supports the lumbar reports and we are in the process of extending our deployment to also support the cervical pathologies.

7 Conclusion and Future Work

In this work, a simple multi-tasking model is presented that is competitive with task specific models. Instead of training and deploying task specific models, only one model is trained and deployed. This allows us to save significant costs during training and faster inference during deployment while achieving significant model compression, without any loss in the quality of performance. Our work opens the possibility of using multi-tasking models to extract information over various different body parts, allowing users to leverage large transformer models using limited compute resources.

Our novel pipeline is one of the very few works that attempts to extract pathologies and their severities from a heterogeneous source of radiologists' notes on lumbar and cervical spine MRIs at the level of *motion segments*. These findings suggest that our approach may not only be more widely generalizable and applicable, but also more clinically actionable.

We believe our analysis with CKA and gradient alignment sheds more light on the success of MTL. This insight has led to our process change from single-task BERT based models to a more cost-effective MTL system. Our analysis is widely applicable for other datasets and tasks.

It is tempting to ask if one can use one multi-task model for both the lumbar and the cervical datasets. This is a work in progress and we have found strong similarity between single task models in the two datasets (most notably between the lumbar disc and the cervical disc models and the lumbar stenosis and the cervical stenosis models). However, unlike in the above analysis, we see low CKA scores between various other task specific models which may make MTL difficult (see Appendix D). We are in the process of using our analysis, along with insights borrowed from (Standley et al., 2020; Yu et al., 2020) to either group tasks from the two datasets or align different task-specific gradients to create an efficient learner.

The biggest drawback of our work is the limited amount of data on which our observations are verified. We are actively addressing this issue as we annotate more reports concerning various pathologies in different body parts.

Ethical Considerations

Because of legal and institutional concerns arising from the sensitivity of clinical data, it is difficult for the NLP community to gain access to relevant data except for MIMIC (Johnson et al., 2016). Despite its large size (covering over $58k$ hospital admissions), it is only representative of patients from a particular clinical domain (the intensive care unit) and geographic location (a single hospital in the United States). Such a sample is not representative of either larger population of patient admissions or other geographical regions/hospital systems. We have tried to address the second issue by collecting data across multiple practices in the US. However, it is impossible to predict whether our models will generalize to the entire patient population without actually evaluating on *all* the different radiology practices. Thus we have to be extra careful about out-of-distribution data since the actionable insights we generate from our models can be potentially faulty and can lead to severe consequences.

Finally, we recognize the need to minimize ethical risks of AI implementation which can include threats to privacy and confidentiality, informed consent, and patient autonomy. We strongly believe that stakeholders should be encouraged to be flexible in incorporating AI technology, most likely as a complementary tool and not a replacement for a physician. Thus, we develop our workflows, annotation guidelines and generate actionable insights by working in conjunction with a varied group of radiologists and medical professionals.

References

Emily Alsentzer, John Murphy, William Boag, Wei-Hung Weng, Di Jindi, Tristan Naumann, and Matthew McDermott. 2019. Publicly available clinical BERT embeddings. In *Proceedings of the 2nd Clinical Natural Language Processing Workshop*, pages 72–78, Minneapolis, Minnesota, USA. Association for Computational Linguistics.

Vamsi Aribandi, Yi Tay, Tal Schuster, Jinfeng Rao, Huaixiu Steven Zheng, Sanket Vaibhav Mehta, Honglei Zhuang, Vinh Q. Tran, Dara Bahri, Jianmo Ni, Jai Gupta, Kai Hui, Sebastian Ruder, and Donald Metzler. 2021. Ext5: Towards extreme multi-task scaling for transfer learning.

Parisa Azimi, Taravat Yazdanian, Edward C. Benzel, Hossein Nayeb Aghaei, Shirzad Azhari, Sohrab Sadeghi, and Ali Montazeri. 2020. A Review on the Use of Artificial Intelligence in Spinal Diseases. *Asian Spine J*, 14(4):543–571.

Joachim Bingel and Anders Søgaard. 2017. Identifying beneficial task relations for multi-task learning in deep neural networks. In *Proceedings of the 15th Conference of the European Chapter of the Association for Computational Linguistics: Volume 2, Short Papers*, pages 164–169, Valencia, Spain. Association for Computational Linguistics.

Tom B. Brown, Benjamin Mann, Nick Ryder, Melanie Subbiah, Jared Kaplan, Prafulla Dhariwal, Arvind Neelakantan, Pranav Shyam, Girish Sastry, Amanda

Askell, Sandhini Agarwal, Ariel Herbert-Voss, Gretchen Krueger, Tom Henighan, Rewon Child, Aditya Ramesh, Daniel M. Ziegler, Jeffrey Wu, Clemens Winter, Christopher Hesse, Mark Chen, Eric Sigler, Mateusz Litwin, Scott Gray, Benjamin Chess, Jack Clark, Christopher Berner, Sam McCandlish, Alec Radford, Ilya Sutskever, and Dario Amodei. 2020. Language models are few-shot learners. In *Advances in Neural Information Processing Systems 33: Annual Conference on Neural Information Processing Systems 2020, NeurIPS 2020, December 6-12, 2020, virtual*.

Zhao Chen, Vijay Badrinarayanan, Chen-Yu Lee, and Andrew Rabinovich. 2018. Gradnorm: Gradient normalization for adaptive loss balancing in deep multitask networks. In *Proceedings of the 35th International Conference on Machine Learning, ICML 2018, Stockholmsmässan, Stockholm, Sweden, July 10-15, 2018*, volume 80 of *Proceedings of Machine Learning Research*, pages 793–802. PMLR.

Zhao Chen, Jiquan Ngiam, Yanping Huang, Thang Luong, Henrik Kretzschmar, Yuning Chai, and Dragomir Anguelov. 2020. Just pick a sign: Optimizing deep multitask models with gradient sign dropout. In *Advances in Neural Information Processing Systems 33: Annual Conference on Neural Information Processing Systems 2020, NeurIPS 2020, December 6-12, 2020, virtual*.

Michael Crawshaw. 2020. Multi-task learning with deep neural networks: A survey.

Gamal Crichton, Sampo Pyysalo, Billy Chiu, and Anna Korhonen. 2017. A neural network multi-task learning approach to biomedical named entity recognition. *BMC Bioinformatics*, 18(1):368.

Marco Cuturi. 2013. Sinkhorn distances: Lightspeed computation of optimal transport. In *Advances in Neural Information Processing Systems 26: 27th Annual Conference on Neural Information Processing Systems 2013. Proceedings of a meeting held December 5-8, 2013, Lake Tahoe, Nevada, United States*, pages 2292–2300.

Jacob Devlin, Ming-Wei Chang, Kenton Lee, and Kristina Toutanova. 2019. BERT: Pre-training of deep bidirectional transformers for language understanding. In *Proceedings of the 2019 Conference of the North American Chapter of the Association for Computational Linguistics: Human Language Technologies, Volume 1 (Long and Short Papers)*, pages 4171–4186, Minneapolis, Minnesota. Association for Computational Linguistics.

Christopher Fifty, Ehsan Amid, Zhe Zhao, Tianhe Yu, Rohan Anil, and Chelsea Finn. 2021. Efficiently identifying task groupings for multi-task learning.

Yu Gu, Robert Tinn, Hao Cheng, Michael Lucas, Naoto Usuyama, Xiaodong Liu, Tristan Naumann, Jianfeng Gao, and Hoifung Poon. 2020. Domain-specific language model pretraining for biomedical natural language processing. ArXiv.

Matthew Honnibal, Ines Montani, Sofie Van Landeghem, and Adriane Boyd. 2020. spaCy: Industrial-strength Natural Language Processing in Python.

Adrián Javaloy and Isabel Valera. 2021. Rotograd: Gradient homogenization in multitask learning.

Alistair E.W. Johnson, Tom J. Pollard, Lu Shen, Li-wei H. Lehman, Mengling Feng, Mohammad Ghassemi, Benjamin Moody, Peter Szolovits, Leo Anthony Celi, and Roger G. Mark. 2016. Mimic-iii, a freely accessible critical care database. *Scientific Data*, 3(1):160035.

Kamal raj Kanakarajan, Bhuvana Kundumani, and Malaikannan Sankarasubbu. 2021. BioELECTRA:pretrained biomedical text encoder using discriminators. In *Proceedings of the 20th Workshop on Biomedical Language Processing*, pages 143–154, Online. Association for Computational Linguistics.

Simon Kornblith, Mohammad Norouzi, Honglak Lee, and Geoffrey E. Hinton. 2019. Similarity of neural network representations revisited. In *Proceedings of the 36th International Conference on Machine Learning, ICML 2019, 9-15 June 2019, Long Beach, California, USA*, volume 97 of *Proceedings of Machine Learning Research*, pages 3519–3529. PMLR.

Seyed-Iman Mirzadeh, Mehrdad Farajtabar, Dilan Görür, Razvan Pascanu, and Hassan Ghasemzadeh. 2021. Linear mode connectivity in multitask and continual learning. In *9th International Conference on Learning Representations, ICLR 2021, Virtual Event, Austria, May 3-7, 2021*. OpenReview.net.

Ari S. Morcos, Maithra Raghu, and Samy Bengio. 2018. Insights on representational similarity in neural networks with canonical correlation. In *Advances in Neural Information Processing Systems 31: Annual Conference on Neural Information Processing Systems 2018, NeurIPS 2018, December 3-8, 2018, Montréal, Canada*, pages 5732–5741.

Thao Nguyen, Maithra Raghu, and Simon Kornblith. 2021. Do wide and deep networks learn the same things? uncovering how neural network representations vary with width and depth. In *9th International Conference on Learning Representations, ICLR 2021, Virtual Event, Austria, May 3-7, 2021*. OpenReview.net.

Adam Paszke, Sam Gross, Francisco Massa, Adam Lerer, James Bradbury, Gregory Chanan, Trevor Killeen, Zeming Lin, Natalia Gimelshein, Luca Antiga, Alban Desmaison, Andreas Köpf, Edward Yang, Zachary DeVito, Martin Raison, Alykhan Tejani, Sasank Chilamkurthy, Benoit Steiner, Lu Fang, Junjie Bai, and Soumith Chintala. 2019. Pytorch: An imperative style, high-performance deep learning library. In *Advances in Neural Information Processing Systems 32: Annual Conference on Neural Information Processing Systems 2019, NeurIPS 2019, December 8-14, 2019, Vancouver, BC, Canada*, pages 8024–8035.

Yifan Peng, Qingyu Chen, and Zhiyong Lu. 2020. An empirical study of multi-task learning on BERT for biomedical text mining. In *Proceedings of the 19th SIGBioMed Workshop on Biomedical Language Processing*, pages 205–214, Online. Association for Computational Linguistics.

Colin Raffel, Noam Shazeer, Adam Roberts, Katherine Lee, Sharan Narang, Michael Matena, Yanqi Zhou, Wei Li, and Peter J. Liu. 2020. Exploring the limits of transfer learning with a unified text-to-text transformer.

Arijit Sehanobish, Nathaniel Brown, Ishita Daga, Jayashri Pawar, Danielle Torres, Anasuya Das, Murray Becker, Richard Herzog, Benjamin Odry, and Ron Vianu. 2022. Efficient extraction of pathologies from C-spine radiology reports using multi-task learning.

Changjian Shui, Mahdieh Abbasi, Louis-Émile Robitaille, Boyu Wang, and Christian Gagné. 2019. A principled approach for learning task similarity in multitask learning. In *Proceedings of the Twenty-Eighth International Joint Conference on Artificial Intelligence, IJCAI 2019, Macao, China, August 10-16, 2019*, pages 3446–3452. ijcai.org.

Trevor Standley, Amir Roshan Zamir, Dawn Chen, Leonidas J. Guibas, Jitendra Malik, and Silvio Savarese. 2020. Which tasks should be learned together in multi-task learning? In *Proceedings of the 37th International Conference on Machine Learning, ICML 2020, 13-18 July 2020, Virtual Event*, volume 119 of *Proceedings of Machine Learning Research*, pages 9120–9132. PMLR.

Erik E. Swartz, R. T. Floyd, and Mike Cendoma. 2005. Cervical Spine Functional Anatomy and the Biomechanics of Injury due to Compressive Loading. *Journal of athletic training*, 40(3):155–161.

Ashish Vaswani, Noam Shazeer, Niki Parmar, Jakob Uszkoreit, Llion Jones, Aidan N. Gomez, Lukasz Kaiser, and Illia Polosukhin. 2017. Attention is all you need. In *Advances in Neural Information Processing Systems 30: Annual Conference on Neural Information Processing Systems 2017, December 4-9, 2017, Long Beach, CA, USA*, pages 5998–6008.

Thomas Wolf, Lysandre Debut, Victor Sanh, Julien Chaumond, Clement Delangue, Anthony Moi, Pierric Cistac, Tim Rault, Remi Louf, Morgan Funtowicz, Joe Davison, Sam Shleifer, Patrick von Platen, Clara Ma, Yacine Jernite, Julien Plu, Canwen Xu, Teven Le Scao, Sylvain Gugger, Mariama Drame, Quentin Lhoest, and Alexander Rush. 2020. Transformers: State-of-the-art natural language processing. In *Proceedings of the 2020 Conference on Empirical Methods in Natural Language Processing: System Demonstrations*, pages 38–45, Online. Association for Computational Linguistics.

Joseph Worsham and Jugal Kalita. 2020. Multi-Task Learning for Natural Language Processing in the 2020s: Where are we going? *Pattern Recognition Letters*, 136:120–126.

Tianhe Yu, Saurabh Kumar, Abhishek Gupta, Sergey Levine, Karol Hausman, and Chelsea Finn. 2020. Gradient surgery for multi-task learning. In *Advances in Neural Information Processing Systems 33: Annual Conference on Neural Information Processing Systems 2020, NeurIPS 2020, December 6-12, 2020, virtual*.

Amir Roshan Zamir, Alexander Sax, Nikhil Cheerla, Rohan Suri, Zhangjie Cao, Jitendra Malik, and Leonidas J. Guibas. 2020. Robust learning through cross-task consistency. In *2020 IEEE/CVF Conference on Computer Vision and Pattern Recognition, CVPR 2020, Seattle, WA, USA, June 13-19, 2020*, pages 11194–11203. IEEE.

A Example of our Dataset

```
'Findings: Osseous structures of the lumbar spine are intact. \nNo fractu
res detected. \nThe conus medullaris is unremarkable. \nNo concerning par
aspinal mass is identified. \nThere is a levoscoliotic curvature to the l
umbar spine. \nT12-L1 through the L2-L3 levels: Unremarkable L3-L4: There
is a small disc bulge. \nThere is mild disc space narrowing. \nNo stenosi
s. L4-L5\n: Left paracentral disc herniation causing posterior displaceme
nt of the left LS nerve root. \nThere is mild left lateral recess stenosi
s. \nSpinal canal and neuroforamen are patent L5-S 1: \nSmall disc bulge.
\nNo stenosis. \nImpression: 1. \nLeft paracentral disc herniation at L4-
L5 level causing posterior displacement of the left LS nerve root and mil
d left lateral recess stenosis. \n2. \nSmall disc bulges at the L3-L4 and
L5-S] levels without stenosis. \n3. \nLevoscoliotic curvature to the lumb
ar spine. \n4. \nNo fractures identified. '
```

Figure 4: An example of a report from our Lumbar Dataset.

In this section, we will show some examples of lumbar and cervical reports from our dataset.

There is mild reversal of cervical lordosis. The vertebral body heights are maintained. No marrow signal abnormalities are identified. Cerebellar tonsils extend up to 2 mm below the foramen magnum on the right. There is no significant crowding at the foramen magnum. Findings are felt most consistent with benign cerebellar tonsillar ectopia Visualized portions of the posterior cranial fossa and brainstem are otherwise unremarkable. The spina cord is normal in caliber and signal intensity within the imaged field-of-view. Paravertebral and paraspinal soft tissues are grossly unremarkable. C1-C2: Intact dens. No spinal canal stenosis. C2-C3: Maintained disc space with mild disc degeneration. No spinal canal stenosis or neural foraminal narrowing. C3-C4: Maintained disc space with mild disc degeneration. Mild disc bulging that impresses on the anterior thecal sac. No significant spinal canal stenosis or neural foraminal narrowing. C4-C5: Maintained disc space with mild disc desiccation. Uncovertebral degenerative changes. No significant spinal canal or neuroforamina

Figure 5: An example of a report from our Cervical Dataset.

B More Details about our Workflow

In this section, we give a more detailed description of our novel workflow. Our main goal is to detect pathologies at the *motion segment* level from radiologists' MRI reports. The motion segments in the cervical reports that we are interested in are C2-C3, C3-C4, C4-C5, C5-C6, C6-C7 and C7-T1 and the motion segments of interest in the lumbar reports are L1-L2, L2-L3, L3-L4, L4-L5 and L5-S1. We first make sure that the reports are de-identified and then use a Spacy (Honnibal et al., 2020) parser to break the report into sentences. Then each sentence is tagged by annotators and they are given

Hyperparameter Type	Single Tasking Models on Cervical Dataset	Multi-Tasking Models on Cervical Dataset	Single Tasking Models on Lumbar Dataset	Multi-Tasking Models on Cervical Dataset	NER
Epochs	5	12	6	11	5
Batch Size	16	16	16	16	16
Sequence Length	512	512	512	512	256
Optimizer	AdamW	AdamW	AdamW	AdamW	AdamW
Learning Rate	2e-5	3e-5	2e-5	3e-5	1e-5
Weight Decay	1e-4	1e-4	1e-4	1e-4	1e-3
Gradient Clip	2	5	2	5	2
Early Stopping	Yes	Yes	Yes	Yes	Yes
Learning Rate Scheduler	Linear	Linear	Linear	Linear	Linear

Table 5: Hyperparameters used for all our experiments

labels of various pathologies and their severities if the sentence mentions that pathology. To detect pathologies at a motion segment level, we use our BERT based NER system to tag the locations present in each sentence. Our BERT based NER model is a binary classifier model (Location Tag vs the Other Tag). It is is trained on both lumbar and cervical MRI reports that can predict the location tags in those reports. Our NER model achieves an F1 score of .9.

We then use an appropriate body part specific rule based system to group all sentences to the correct motion segment. If a sentence does not explicitly have a motion segment mentioned in it, we use a rule based method to assign the sentence to one of the above mentioned motion segments or to a generic category "No motion segments found". Given the disparate source of our data and due to typos and OCR errors, for example, L23, L2L3, L@L3, $L2\_L3$ all may refer to the motion segment L2-L3 and thus our systems are mindful of this diversity of the clinical notes. Finally to use our BERT based models for pathology detection on the level of motion segments for a given report, we concatenate all sentences for a given motion segment and use the [CLS] token for the segment that is used for the downstream classification task.

Since we are interested in predictions at the motion segment level, we do not use the sentences that are grouped under "No motion segments found" to train the classifier models, nor do we evaluate our classifier models on those sentences.

C Hyperparameters and Other Training Details

We create a validation set using 20% of the samples of the training set where the samples are drawn via stratified samples so the data distribution is maintained across splits. The hyperparameters used for training the NER model and various classification models can be found in Table 5.

PyTorch (Paszke et al., 2019) and the HuggingFace library (Wolf et al., 2020) is used to conduct our experiments which are run on 1 NVIDIA V100 16GB GPU.

D Additional CKA Results and Gradient Alignment Results

In this section, we present some additional results on comparing representations between our various models.

We present the average proportion of aligned gradients (APAG) at the end of training in Table 6. We also compute the cosine similarity between the gradients. We then take the average of them for a given layer, thus yielding a scalar value per layer. This yields cosine similarity values which are over 90 % positive. For simplicity, we average those numbers to produce a scalar value that measures the cosine similarity between the gradients of two models. Model level statistics can be found in Table 6.

Dataset	Task Comparisons	Cosine Similarity	Average Proportion of Aligned Gradients
Cervical	Cord-Stenosis	.013	.89
	Cord-Disc	.005	.87
	Cord-Foraminal	.011	.91
	Disc-Stenosis	.012	.88
	Disc-Foraminal	.007	.87
	Foraminal-Stenosis	.005	.84
Lumbar	Disc-Stenosis	.008	.75
	Nerve-Stenosis	.01	.86
	Disc-Nerve	.002	.86

Table 6: Results showing the Cosine Similarity and the Average Proportion of Aligned Gradients between various task specific models after the end of training.

Given some similarities between certain label

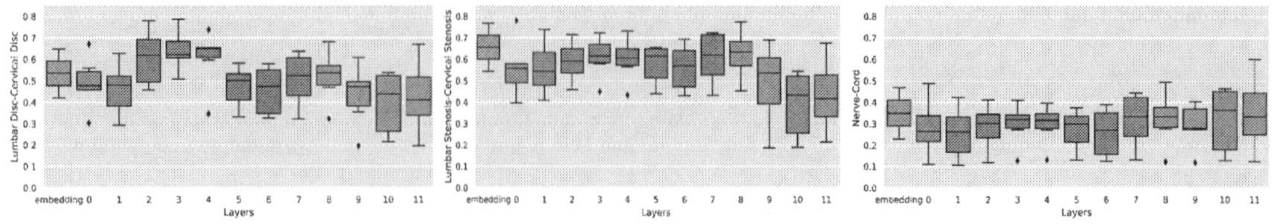

Figure 6: Box plot showing CKA scores between models trained on tasks on the lumbar and the cervical dataset. The y-axis is chosen to be (0,.85). The figure shows the low CKA scores between the cord and the nerve models and high scores between the stenosis models and the disc models.

spaces in the lumbar and the cervical dataset (particularly for the disc herniation and the central canal stenosis labels), we believe that some task specific models between tasks across datasets may show similar representations. To validate this hypothesis, we computed the CKA between lumbar stenosis and the cervical stenosis models and the lumbar disc and the cervical disc models. The natural question is : what happens to the single tasking models that are trained on label spaces that are semantically different? Fig 6 shows low CKA scores between the cord and the nerve models. This is an active work in progress to be able to group similar tasks (Standley et al., 2020) to create a MTL framework that works for both the cervical and the lumbar spine. Another future direction is to use realign gradients using the techniques in (Yu et al., 2020). However to realign the gradients, one has to save the entire computation graph after the backward pass via *loss.backward(retain_graph=True)* which becomes a bottleneck for large transformer models. To mitigate this issue, one can use parameter efficient methods like adapters which we have shown to work in these MTL settings in our previous work (Sehanobish et al., 2022).

E Annotation Process

All data are annotated by our team of inhouse annotators with clinical expertise. All annotators are trained for the given task and provided clear guidelines on the task and performance is measured periodically on a benchmark set and feedback is provided.

FPI: Failure Point Isolation in Large-scale Conversational Assistants

Rinat Khaziev
Amazon Alexa AI
rinatk@amazon.com

Usman Shahid
University of Illinois Chicago
hshahi6@uic.edu

Tobias Röding
Amazon Alexa AI
rodingtr@amazon.com

Rakesh Chada
Amazon Alexa AI
rakchada@amazon.com

Emir Kapanci
Amazon Alexa AI
emirk@amazon.com

Pradeep Natarajan
Amazon Alexa AI
natarap@amazon.com

Abstract

Large-scale conversational assistants such as Cortana, Alexa, Google Assistant and Siri process requests through a series of modules for wake word detection, speech recognition, language understanding and response generation. An error in one of these modules can cascade through the system. Given the large traffic volumes in these assistants, it is infeasible to manually analyze the data, identify requests with processing errors and isolate the source of error. We present a machine learning system to address this challenge. First, we embed the incoming request and context, such as system response and subsequent turns, using pre-trained transformer models. Then, we combine these embeddings with encodings of additional metadata features (such as confidence scores from different modules in the online system) using a "mixing-encoder" to output the failure point predictions. Our system obtains 92.2% of human performance on this task while scaling to analyze the entire traffic in 8 different languages of a large-scale conversational assistant. We present detailed ablation studies analyzing the impact of different modeling choices.

1 Introduction

Conversational assistants have become increasingly prevalent in every-day life. With them, users can control appliances at home, get current weather information, or get help with recipes in the kitchen through simple voice commands. A typical dialog system processes user requests in multiple stages (see Figure 1). First, a voice trigger (or wake word) (Sigtia et al., 2018) model determines whether the user is speaking to the assistant. Following the trigger component, an Automatic Speech Recognition (ASR) (He et al., 2019) module converts user audio stream into a set of discrete text tokens. This text is sent to the Natural Language Understanding (NLU) component, which analyzes what the user request means. The domain classifier (DC) categorizes the user's request into a set of pre-defined topics, the intent classifier (IC) assigns an intent which represents what the user is trying to accomplish, and the entity recognition and resolution component (ERR) recognizes and resolves known entities in the users request. The system generates the best possible response (Result stage) using several subsystems that are specific to each dialog assistant (e.g., dialog management, re-ranking, etc). Finally the response is rendered into a human-like speech using a Text-to-Speech (TTS) system.

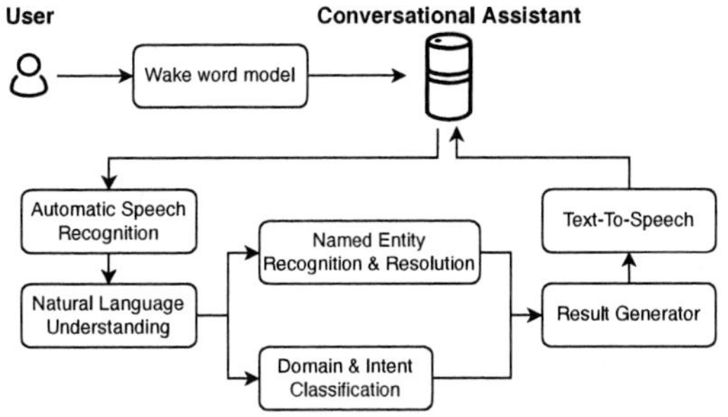

Figure 1: Component-level architecture of a typical conversational assistant.

When such a system makes an error, the complexity of the processing pipeline makes it extremely challenging to isolate the source of a defect. An error in an upstream component (e.g. ASR) can propagate through the system to the final response to the user. In such cases it is likely that multiple components starting from the first source of the error (referred to as "root" or "failure point" hereby) produce erroneous outputs. However, it is critical to identify this error to improve the overall system. Given the large traffic volumes, manual analysis to identify root causes for processing errors is infeasible.

In this work, we develop a machine learning model that predicts which component of a conver-

Proceedings of NAACL-HLT 2022: Industry Track Papers, pages 141 - 148
July 10-15, 2022 ©2022 Association for Computational Linguistics

sational assistant caused the system to fail when processing user requests, a Failure Point Isolation (FPI) model. Our system helps to monitor the performance of the system holistically and improve the components of the dialog assistant that result in defective user interactions. The FPI model takes multiple inputs including the request text, system response, and subsequent turns which together help in capturing implicit feedback from the customer. We leverage recent progress in pre-trained Transformer-based language models to encode this information. We then combine these with encodings of metadata features such as confidence scores from different components in the online system using additional Transformer-based "mixing" layers to output the source of error or mark a request as correctly processed. Our model is trained on a small number of examples annotated with the source of error and then applied on all traffic for failure point isolation.

We present extensive experimental results to characterize the performance of our model and the impact of different modeling choices. Using only encoding of the request text, we achieve an F_1 score of 24.2% for FPI on our test sets. This improves to 40.3% by leveraging the full dialog context and system response. We see a further improvement to 51.4% by including additional metadata features. We also present ablation studies to characterize the impact of different text encoders and architecture choices for the mixing layer that further improve F_1 score to 53.3%. We show that this corresponds to 92.2% of human performance on the FPI task using a "golden" test set created by combining annotations from multiple highly-trained annotators.

2 Related Work

Several works have attempted evaluating dialog systems using deterministic or machine learning-based methods. The majority can be classified into the following groups: word-overlap metrics, user sentiment based approach, or component-specific error attribution.

Word-overlap metrics models like BLUE (Papineni et al., 2002) and ROUGE (Lin, 2004) are not well-suited for evaluating real-world conversational assistants. Liu et al. (2016) has demonstrated that the word-overlap metrics do not correlate wit=[p human judgement. As conversational assistants can also perform real-world functions (e.g., turning on lights), evaluation of such systems based on the textual response alone does not fully capture the set of actions taken by the system. Finally, the deterministic metrics are not fine-grained enough to identify which component of the system was responsible for the defective interaction. Hence, word-overlap metrics have a limited ability to provide prescriptive feedback to developers.

Schmitt et al. (2012) proposed evaluating dialog systems based on the user perception and Interaction Quality (IQ). Here each dialog is assigned a numerical score as evaluated by an annotator. Schmitt and Ultes (2015); Bodigutla et al. (2020); Gupta et al. (2021) developed models that used features derived from the logs of the dialog system to build predictive IQ models. Gupta et al. (2021) demonstrated that transformer-based architectures without log-derived features can outperform previously-developed models. Lowe et al. (2017) proposed a similar to IQ metric, ADEM, and trained a predictive mode. Sinha et al. (2020) developed a transformer-based model, MAUDE. This model is trained using contrastive learning and produces scores that correlates with human judgment. The sentiment or quality-based metrics allow for monitoring real-life dialog systems, however they do not provide actionable insight into the performance of the system components.

Chada et al. (2021) and Sethi et al. (2021) have built systems that attribute errors in the NLU component of a conversational assistant. Chada et al. (2021) focused on building transformer-based models that detect NLU intent and domain classifications errors. Sethi et al. (2021) detect NLU domain and intent errors in the dialog system using confidence scores produced by the NLU models. When attributing NLU errors, they focus on root-causing issues in the training data (e.g., low-resource intent, mislabeling, etc). Though this feedback is actionable, neither of these works attempt to root-cause errors in other components of dialog systems.

These aforementioned approaches have limitations when it comes to failure point isolation in large-scale conversational assistants. Instead of focusing on a small portion of a dialog system, we create an automated error attribution system that can provide insights into the root causes of defective interactions at scale for all of the components of a conversational assistant. Unlike approaches that estimate user satisfaction and dialog quality from the user's perspective, our focus is on understanding whether the system delivered the response that it was designed to deliver and if not, why. In case when the system was designed to perform the action but failed to do so, our model provides clear feedback that can help to improve system performance in the future.

3 Methodology

In this section, we first describe our training and test datasets, and discuss the challenges in constructing them (§ 3.1). Next, we describe the creation of our "golden" test dataset (§ 3.2). Then, we describe the features that we use in our model (§ 3.3). Finally, we present details of the network architecture and model training used to output FPI based on these input features (§ 3.4).

3.1 Training Dataset

To train the FPI model, we created a dataset containing real-world data by extracting a mix of random and targeted samples from a commercial large-scale conversational assistant. Our dataset contains approximately 11.5MM de-identified user requests in 8 different languages. The training dataset was split into train, validation, and dev using a 75/5/20 scheme such that user sessions do not overlap in any split. All requests were manually annotated using internal tools as correct or incorrect. Incorrect requests were further labeled with one of five error types, corresponding to one of the stages of a conversational assistants processing pipeline (see Figure 1). These include:

1. **False Wake (FW)** errors that capture incorrect trigger system predictions
2. **ASR** errors that capture the incorrect transcription of the user speech
3. **NLU** errors that contain domain classification (DC) and intent classification errors (IC)
4. **ERR** errors that capture entity recognition and resolution errors
5. **Result** errors made by the response generation component when the system took an incorrect action even though all previous steps succeeded

When there are several potential errors in a dialog, we only mark one of them as the root cause of the system failure: the first failing stage in the processing pipeline, ordered from Wake Word to Result stages. Figure 2 shows some example turns of what different errors can look like in the processing pipeline. In the first turn, the ASR error would be marked as a fatal error and the root cause of the defective system response. In the second turn, the ASR error would be marked as non-fatal as subsequent components are able to recover from the error and produce a correct system response. In the last turn the system performed as designed, however it could not fulfill user request.

3.2 "Golden" Test Dataset

Given the vast data volumes, failure point isolation in a complex dialog system is a challenging task even for humans. For example, ERR error analysis requires inspecting entity data (such as music catalogs). Further, the definition of the failure point can be ambiguous without subsequently rerunning and correcting each component of a dialog system. As a result, the error attribution labels can have poor quality and consistency across different annotators.

To create a suitable test set for evaluating the accuracy of our model, we leveraged a more sophisticated "golden" annotation workflow. This more labor- and time-intensive workflow does not rely on a single annotator but on a combination of multiple annotators, and an ensemble of machine learning models to make the labeling decision. First, each request gets labeled by the annotators and the ensemble model in parallel. Whenever there is a disagreement on the labels, the request is evaluated by a highly trained annotator who makes the final decision. We annotated approximately 58k sessions through this workflow to create a "golden" test set with higher annotation quality than our training set. The "golden" dataset is not used for training out model, however it is used to report F_1 score of the models we train in this work and compare model performance to humans.

3.3 Feature Engineering

We train our FPI model on a multi-turn dataset, which includes user request, system response (TTS), and the interaction metadata. The interaction metadata is parsed from the logs of the online production system and includes the outputs of the machine learning models executed at each stage of the data processing pipeline and identifiers of the systems that made the final prediction, in the case of multiple models competing for response generation.

We limit user dialog to previous, current, and next user interactions. Using the context of the user interaction, we are aiming to capture implicit customer feedback that a production system might

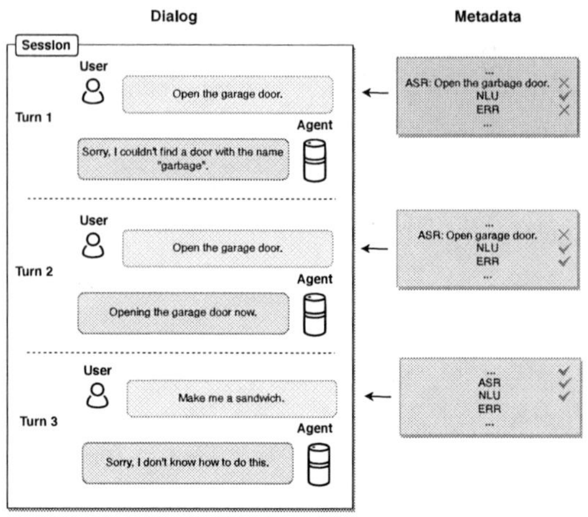

Figure 2: Construction of FPI model features using previous, current and next turn to get features from the whole dialog.

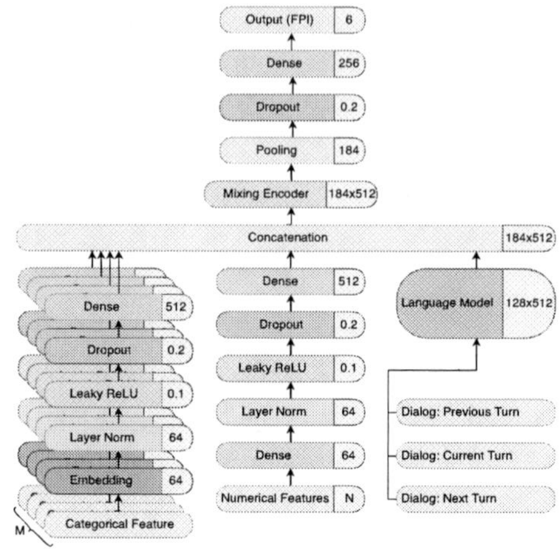

Figure 3: The architecture of the Failure Point Isolation (FPI) model with multi-modal feature embedding networks. M and N are counts of categorical and numerical features respectively.

be lacking. Our feature set includes multiple *categorical features* (e.g., NLU intent predictions), *numerical features* (e.g., confidence scores logged by run-time models, or time difference between user turns), and *text data*, in the form of user request text and system response (TTS) collected from a user session.

Due to a large number of features available in the logs and the complexity of our end-to-end system, we group the categorical and numerical features into 5 major groups for ablation studies: Wake Word (WW) features, ASR features, NLU features, Result features. WW, ASR, and NLU features include the confidence scores produced by the component models. Result features include the details of which sub-system produced response and whether requested action could be fulfilled by the system. We tokenize the text data using the *sentencepiece* tokenizer before inputting them to Transformer-based encoders that we describe in the next section.

3.4 Model Architecture and Training

Executing our model on already processed user sessions gives us two advantages. First, we gather a holistic view into the execution of all asynchronous components by constructing model features from the system logs. Second, there are no latency limitations, which means we can leverage large transformer-based models (Vaswani et al., 2017).

The four main components of our model are: categorical feature embedding networks, a numerical embedding network, a transformer-based language model, and mixing layers built on top of the embedding networks to produce the final predictions. We process all of the numerical features jointly using a single embedding network (see Figure 3). Each of the categorical features are embedded separately. The numerical and categorical features are concatenated with the language model embeddings and are passed to "mixing" layers. Textual features, request text and system response, are processed jointly by multi-lingual transformer-based models (Wolf et al., 2020; Paszke et al., 2019). In order to constrain model latency we use mT5 (Xue et al., 2021) and XLM-R (Conneau et al., 2020) models in their smallest configuration with 170M and 270M parameters. The mixing layer consists of the encoder layers and a final feedfoward block that produces model predictions.

The FPI model is trained using a multi-stage procedure. First, we fine-tune the language models alone on FPI labels without metadata features (Stage 1). This step is necessary for domain-specific adaptation of the models pre-trained on generic datasets. Second, we fine-tune the metadata encoder jointly with textual features on the FPI labels using our training dataset, but do not update the language model during this stage (Stage 2 warm-up). Finally, we fine-tune the whole model on the FPI dataset (Stage 2 fine-tuning). The details of our training setup and computational budget are reported in Appendix A.

4 Results

In this section, we report the results of the experiments with the FPI model. First, we investigate the importance of system response and extended context size (§ 4.1). Second, we illustrate importance of the features derived from logs (§ 4.2). We demonstrate the effect of language model size in (§ 4.3). We perform experiments with fine-tuning language models on the task-specific dataset (§ 4.4) and compare performance of the best performing model to a standard annotator (§ 4.5). The models reported in subsections § 4.1-4.3 were trained using only stage 2 of the training procedure (§ 3.4) with mean-pooling layers unless specified otherwise. F_1 scores are reported from a single training run on the "golden" dataset described in § 3.2.

4.1 Importance of using system response and extended context

context	TTS	F_1 scores						
		FW	ASR	ERR	NLU	Result	Correct	Avg
current	✗	7.8	21.6	1.1	3.1	7.2	87.8	21.4
current	✓	5.8	31.2	10.9	18.9	41.3	90.5	33.1
extended	✓	16.1	40.3	15.5	29.4	48.4	92.1	40.3

Table 1: F_1 scores of models trained with different context (current turn vs extended context) with request text and TTS, as indicated by TTS column. "current" indicates that the model was trained with the current turn, "extended" indicates that the model was trained with previous, current, and next turns.

Table 1 summarizes F_1 results of the experiments that quantify the effect of adding TTS and dialog context on model performance. Thus, adding TTS to the user request improves macro average F_1 score from 21.4% to 33.1%. Further on, we find that extending dialog context to previous and next turn improves F_1 score by another 7.2% absolute to 40.3% . As indicated by consistent gains in Result, ASR, and NLU classes, this set of experiments confirms our hypothesis: extended context captures implicit feedback (e.g., rephrasing) from the customer.

4.2 Importance of features derived from the logs of system components

Based on our experiments (Table 2), adding features derived from the logs of the dialog assistant's online components improves ability to detect errors in those components. For example, NLU, ASR,

component features	F_1 scores						
	FW	ASR	ERR	NLU	Result	Correct	Avg
-	16.1	40.3	15.5	29.4	48.4	92.1	40.3
Result	16.7	42.5	22.9	28.9	48.7	91.7	41.9
NLU	14.4	45.2	22.7	33.7	50.1	92.9	43.2
ASR	17.8	49.4	23.8	30.8	46.4	93.1	43.5
WW	33.3	40.6	18.8	30.3	49.9	92.5	44.2
all	**39.7**	**53.8**	**27.5**	**39.9**	**53.4**	**94.0**	**51.4**

Table 2: F_1 scores of the models trained with full dialog (including TTS) on different sets of features (see § 3.3).

and WW F_1 scores gain 4.3% , 10.1%, and 17.2% absolute when respective feature sets are added to the FPI model. Additionally, adding NLU features leads to improving ASR and ERR scores, and adding ASR features yields improvements in the WW class.

The model trained with the full feature set (bottom row of the Table 2) demonstrates the best performance in this experiment set with a macro-average F_1 score of 51.4%. It benefits from the implicit feedback provided by the dialog text and features derived from logs of all of the system components.

4.3 Performance with a larger language models

component features	F_1 scores						
	FW	ASR	ERR	NLU	Result	Correct	Avg
-	25.9	46.3	20.7	34.6	53.6	93.0	45.7
all	29.7	53.7	27.3	39.7	54.3	93.8	49.8

Table 3: Results of the feature ablation studies with XLM-R model with 270M parameters.

Table 3 presents F_1 scores of the FPI network trained with the XLM-R language model (§ 3.4). Based on the results of our experiments, using bigger models improves F_1 scores of the model trained using dialog as the only features (first row in Table 3) from 40.3% macro-average for a model trained using mT5 to 45.7% for a model trained with the XLM-R model. The advantage of using a larger language models disappears when we leverage a full feature set. Thus, the XLM-R-based FPI model demonstrates 49.8% macro-average F_1 score, which is comparable to the mT5-based model trained with the same feature set (§ 4.2).

4.4 Effect of fine-tuning language models on task-specific data

Pooling layer	F_1 scores						
	FW	ASR	ERR	NLU	Result	Correct	Avg
mean	38.8	52.6	27.2	38.5	52.7	93.8	50.1
max	**40.9**	**55.1**	**30.4**	**42.5**	**57.8**	**94.1**	**53.5**

Table 4: F_1 scores of the FPI models trained with language models fine-tuned on the task-specific data.

The results of training model with stage 1 (language model fine-tuning) and stage 2 are reported in the Table 4. In addition to using fine-tuned language models, we have also varied the pooling method in the "mixing layer" of our network (see additional study in Appendix B). We observe that the network trained with mean-pooling layer did not gain improvements from multi-stage process. However, the network trained with a max-pooling layer demonstrates 53.5% macro average F_1 score, outperforming the model trained only with the stage 2 (§ 4.2).

4.5 Label Quality Analysis

	FW	ASR	ERR	NLU	Result	Correct	Avg
F_1^{FPI}	40.9	55.1	30.4	42.5	57.8	94.1	53.5
F_1^{Human}	57.4	61.5	33.8	44.0	56.1	91.6	57.4
F_1^{FPI} / F_1^{Human}, %	71.2	89.6	89.9	96.7	103.1	102.7	92.2

Table 5: F_1 score comparison of the best FPI model (F_1^{FPI}) and standard annotator (F_1^{Human}).

In order to quantify human performance on FPI task, we compared label produced by a single annotator (non-expert), to the final label corrected by a highly trained annotator in our "golden" dataset (see § 3.2). Our analysis shows (see Table 5) that the task of isolating failure points is easier in the following three categories: ASR (F_1 score of 61.52 %), False Wake (F_1 score of 57.4%) and Result (F_1 score of 56%). Detecting NLU and ERR errors is the most difficult task with 44% and 34% F_1 scores in those classes respectively. We use this analysis to understand reasonable limits for our model which is trained on labels from a single annotator as opposed to the "golden" workflow.

The best FPI model, using the max pooling layer and a fine-tuned language model, on average achieves 92.2% of non-expert human F_1 score on the FPI task (see Table 5). The weakest performance is observed in False Wake detection with 71.2% of human F_1. The model achieves approximately 90% of human performance in ASR and ERR classes, 96.7% in NLU, and outperform humans in detecting Result and Correct errors. We believe that the model demonstrates strong performance in Result and Correct classes, as result errors could be captured by the dialog context, when repeating or restating user request often can lead to the same or similar results for the same user.

5 Limitations

During our research we identified several limitations in the FPI system. First, our training dataset only allows a single failure point, however multiple components of a dialog assistant can fail in a real-world system. Hence, it would be useful to extend FPI task for capturing all critical and non-critical errors regardless of whether they resulted in a defective user session. Second, our system provides only a component-level failure point isolation. Future systems could build on our work to identify the sub-components of a dialog assistant responsible for the failure. Next, it would be useful to develop a framework which would allow joint system-level error attribution and assessment of interaction quality (IQ). Such an approach would not only help developers understand system errors but also cases which result in negative customer interaction. We have not experimented with bigger language models for our application, which might demonstrate stronger performance than the models used in this work.

6 Conclusion

We present an effective machine learning system to detect and isolate failure points in a real-world conversational assistant. Such assistants can have a complex hierarchy of modules making error isolation very challenging. By leveraging pre-trained transformer models to process the request text and contextual metadata features, our system obtains 92.2% of human performance. Given the large volumes of traffic in real-world conversational assistants, the manual process of obtaining human annotations for error isolation is prohibitively time consuming and expensive. While achieving human parity, our system automates this process and scales to a large volume of traffic. We conduct detailed ablation studies of our system and illustrate the key components that led to the highlighted gains.

7 Ethical Considerations

The data used in this paper was collected in accordance with applicable policies, terms of use, privacy notices, and customer privacy settings that disclose to customers how their data may be used. The annotators of the data were compensated for their work consistent with applicable laws and regulations.

Acknowledgements

We would like to thank Mustafa Hameed, Adrien Carre, Vivek Gupta, and Sarah Traylor for managing the program; Adam Berger, Krunal Sheth, Anh Nguyen, Daniel Lawrence, and Emmanuel Gonzalez for software development support; Yan Wang and Claude Paugh for data pipeline support; and Xiao Gong and Matthew Tucker for early exploration work.

References

Praveen Kumar Bodigutla, Aditya Tiwari, Spyros Matsoukas, Josep Valls-Vargas, and Lazaros Polymenakos. 2020. Joint turn and dialogue level user satisfaction estimation on multi-domain conversations. In *Findings of the Association for Computational Linguistics: EMNLP 2020*, pages 3897–3909, Online. Association for Computational Linguistics.

Rakesh Chada, Pradeep Natarajan, Darshan Fofadiya, and Prathap Ramachandra. 2021. Error detection in large-scale natural language understanding systems using transformer models. In *Findings of the Association for Computational Linguistics: ACL-IJCNLP 2021*, pages 498–503, Online. Association for Computational Linguistics.

Alexis Conneau, Kartikay Khandelwal, Naman Goyal, Vishrav Chaudhary, Guillaume Wenzek, Francisco Guzmán, Edouard Grave, Myle Ott, Luke Zettlemoyer, and Veselin Stoyanov. 2020. Unsupervised cross-lingual representation learning at scale. In *Proceedings of the 58th Annual Meeting of the Association for Computational Linguistics*, pages 8440–8451. Association for Computational Linguistics.

Jacob Devlin, Ming-Wei Chang, Kenton Lee, and Kristina Toutanova. 2019. BERT: Pre-training of deep bidirectional transformers for language understanding. In *Proceedings of the 2019 Conference of the North American Chapter of the Association for Computational Linguistics: Human Language Technologies, Volume 1 (Long and Short Papers)*, pages 4171–4186, Minneapolis, Minnesota. Association for Computational Linguistics.

Willian Falcon and The PyTorch Lightning eam. 2020. Pytorch lightning.

Saurabh Gupta, Xing Fan, Derek Liu, Benjamin Yao, Yuan Ling, Kun Zhou, Tuan-Hung Pham, and Chenlei Guo. 2021. Robertaiq: An efficient framework for automatic interactionquality estimation of dialogue systems. In *KDD Workshop: Data-Efficient Machine Learning*, volume 2657. CEUR-WS.

Yanzhang He, Tara N. Sainath, Rohit Prabhavalkar, Ian McGraw, Raziel Alvarez, Ding Zhao, David Rybach, Anjuli Kannan, Yonghui Wu, Ruoming Pang, Qiao Liang, Deepti Bhatia, Yuan Shangguan, Bo Li, Golan Pundak, Khe Chai Sim, Tom Bagby, Shuo-yiin Chang, Kanishka Rao, and Alexander Gruenstein. 2019. Streaming end-to-end speech recognition for mobile devices. In *ICASSP 2019 - 2019 IEEE International Conference on Acoustics, Speech and Signal Processing (ICASSP)*, pages 6381–6385.

Chin-Yew Lin. 2004. ROUGE: A package for automatic evaluation of summaries. In *Text Summarization Branches Out*, pages 74–81, Barcelona, Spain. Association for Computational Linguistics.

Chia-Wei Liu, Ryan Lowe, Iulian Serban, Mike Noseworthy, Laurent Charlin, and Joelle Pineau. 2016. How NOT to evaluate your dialogue system: An empirical study of unsupervised evaluation metrics for dialogue response generation. In *Proceedings of the 2016 Conference on Empirical Methods in Natural Language Processing*, pages 2122–2132, Austin, Texas. Association for Computational Linguistics.

Ilya Loshchilov and Frank Hutter. 2019. Decoupled weight decay regularization. In *International Conference on Learning Representations*.

Ryan Lowe, Michael Noseworthy, Iulian Vlad Serban, Nicolas Angelard-Gontier, Yoshua Bengio, and Joelle Pineau. 2017. Towards an automatic Turing test: Learning to evaluate dialogue responses. In *Proceedings of the 55th Annual Meeting of the Association for Computational Linguistics (Volume 1: Long Papers)*, pages 1116–1126, Vancouver, Canada. Association for Computational Linguistics.

Kishore Papineni, Salim Roukos, Todd Ward, and Wei-Jing Zhu. 2002. Bleu: a method for automatic evaluation of machine translation. In *Proceedings of the 40th Annual Meeting of the Association for Computational Linguistics*, pages 311–318, Philadelphia, Pennsylvania, USA. Association for Computational Linguistics.

Adam Paszke, Sam Gross, Francisco Massa, Adam Lerer, James Bradbury, Gregory Chanan, Trevor Killeen, Zeming Lin, Natalia Gimelshein, Luca Antiga, Alban Desmaison, Andreas Kopf, Edward Yang, Zachary DeVito, Martin Raison, Alykhan Tejani, Sasank Chilamkurthy, Benoit Steiner, Lu Fang, Junjie Bai, and Soumith Chintala. 2019. Pytorch: An imperative style, high-performance deep learning library. In H. Wallach, H. Larochelle,

A. Beygelzimer, F. d'Alché-Buc, E. Fox, and R. Garnett, editors, *Advances in Neural Information Processing Systems 32*, pages 8024–8035. Curran Associates, Inc.

Alexander Schmitt and Stefan Ultes. 2015. Interaction quality: Assessing the quality of ongoing spoken dialog interaction by experts—and how it relates to user satisfaction. *Speech Communication*, 74:12–36.

Alexander Schmitt, Stefan Ultes, and Wolfgang Minker. 2012. A parameterized and annotated spoken dialog corpus of the CMU let's go bus information system. In *Proceedings of the Eighth International Conference on Language Resources and Evaluation (LREC'12)*, pages 3369–3373, Istanbul, Turkey. European Language Resources Association (ELRA).

Pooja Sethi, Denis Savenkov, Forough Arabshahi, Jack Goetz, Micaela Tolliver, Nicolas Scheffer, Ilknur Kabul, Yue Liu, and Ahmed Aly. 2021. Autonlu: Detecting, root-causing, and fixing nlu model errors.

Siddharth Sigtia, Rob Haynes, Hywel B. Richards, Erik Marchi, and John Scott Bridle. 2018. Efficient voice trigger detection for low resource hardware. In *INTERSPEECH*.

Koustuv Sinha, Prasanna Parthasarathi, Jasmine Wang, Ryan Lowe, William L. Hamilton, and Joelle Pineau. 2020. Learning an unreferenced metric for online dialogue evaluation.

Ashish Vaswani, Noam Shazeer, Niki Parmar, Jakob Uszkoreit, Llion Jones, Aidan N. Gomez, Lukasz Kaiser, and Illia Polosukhin. 2017. Attention is all you need. In *Proceedings of the 31st International Conference on Neural Information Processing Systems*, pages 6000–60010. Curran Associates Inc.

Thomas Wolf, Lysandre Debut, Victor Sanh, Julien Chaumond, Clement Delangue, Anthony Moi, Pierric Cistac, Tim Rault, Remi Louf, Morgan Funtowicz, Joe Davison, Sam Shleifer, Patrick von Platen, Clara Ma, Yacine Jernite, Julien Plu, Canwen Xu, Teven Le Scao, Sylvain Gugger, Mariama Drame, Quentin Lhoest, and Alexander Rush. 2020. Transformers: State-of-the-art natural language processing. In *Proceedings of the 2020 Conference on Empirical Methods in Natural Language Processing: System Demonstrations*, pages 38–45, Online. Association for Computational Linguistics.

Linting Xue, Noah Constant, Adam Roberts, Mihir Kale, Rami Al-Rfou, Aditya Siddhant, Aditya Barua, and Colin Raffel. 2021. mt5: A massively multilingual pre-trained text-to-text transformer. In *Proceedings of the 2021 Conference of the North American Chapter of the Association for Computational Linguistics: Human Language Technologies*, pages 483–498. Association for Computational Linguistics.

A Training Parameters

We use AdamW (Loshchilov and Hutter, 2019) optimizer with a fixed learning rate of 5×10^{-5} and batch size of 1024 examples. We train the model for 30 epochs or until we reach early stopping criterion, 5 epochs sequential epochs that do not improve validation loss function. A single training run takes up to 90 hours on NVIDIA V100 GPU.

Our training setup is leveraging PyTorch (Paszke et al., 2019), HuggingFace (Wolf et al., 2020), and PyTorch Lightning (Falcon and eam, 2020). Those libraries were used according to their intended use and distributed under BSD or Apache licenses.

B Experiments with the pooling layer

Pooling layer	F_1 scores						
	FW	ASR	ERR	NLU	Result	Correct	Avg
token	26.7	44.2	3.2	19.9	11.9	91.2	32.8
max	37.5	52.4	21.6	38.5	54.5	93.8	49.7
mean	39.7	53.8	27.5	39.9	53.4	94.0	51.4

Table 6: Performance of FPI models trained with different configurations of the pooling layer. "token" value in the *Pooling layer* column represent first-token pooling layer, "max" represent max-pooling layer, and "mean" represents mean pooling configuration.

Our findings indicate that the structure of the pooling layer makes a significant impact on the model performance. The commonly used first-token embedding (Devlin et al., 2019) performed the worst with the macro average F_1 score of 32.8%. The mean and max pooling layers demonstrated better performance with F_1 score of 51.4% and 49.7% respectively. All of the subsequent experiments were conducted with max and mean pooling layers.

Asynchronous Convergence in Multi-Task Learning via Knowledge Distillation from Converged Tasks

Weiyi Lu[1], **Sunny Rajagopalan**[2,*], **Priyanka Nigam**[1], **Jaspreet Singh**[1], **Xiaodi Sun**[1]
Yi Xu[1], **Belinda Zeng**[1], **Trishul Chilimbi**[1]
[1]Amazon, [2]Google
[1]{weiyilu,nigamp,jazsingh,xiaodisu,yxaamzn,zengb,trishulc}@amazon.com
[2]sunny.rg@gmail.com

Abstract

Multi-task learning (MTL) aims to solve multiple tasks jointly by sharing a base representation among them. This can lead to more efficient learning and better generalization, as compared to learning each task individually. However, one issue that often arises in MTL is the convergence speed between tasks varies due to differences in task difficulty, so it can be a challenge to simultaneously achieve the best performance on all tasks with a single model checkpoint. Various techniques have been proposed to address discrepancies in task convergence rate, including weighting the per-task losses and modifying task gradients. In this work, we propose a novel approach that avoids the problem of requiring all tasks to converge at the same rate, but rather allows for "asynchronous" convergence among the tasks where each task can converge on its own schedule. As our main contribution, we monitor per-task validation metrics and switch to a knowledge distillation loss once a task has converged instead of continuing to train on the true labels. This prevents the model from overfitting on converged tasks while it learns the remaining tasks. We evaluate the proposed method in two 5-task MTL setups consisting of internal e-commerce datasets. The results show that our method consistently outperforms existing loss weighting and gradient balancing approaches, achieving average improvements of 0.9% and 1.5% over the best performing baseline model in the two setups, respectively.

1 Introduction

Over the past few years, large pretrained models have achieved great success on a variety of tasks in natural language processing (Devlin et al., 2019; Yang et al., 2019; Raffel et al., 2020; Brown et al., 2020; Lewis et al., 2020; Clark et al., 2020; He et al., 2021). Most work in this area typically follows the pretraining-finetuning paradigm, in which the model is first pretrained on large text corpora using a self-supervised language modeling objective and then finetuned using supervised data from a target task. In particular, when evaluating on a benchmark that contains multiple tasks such as GLUE (Wang et al., 2018) and SuperGLUE (Wang et al., 2019), a common method is to finetune a separate model for each task in order to achieve the best performance. Although such an approach produces excellent results, it has several drawbacks, including incurring the costs of repeated finetuning efforts and precluding the possibility of knowledge sharing among related tasks. In addition, when it comes to deploying these models for real-world applications, a separate model is deployed for each individual task which can pose challenges for model hosting and maintenance.

An alternative approach is multi-task learning (MTL), which solves multiple tasks together by sharing representations among them. This not only offers benefits in computational and storage efficiency, but also makes it possible to share knowledge among related tasks and encourages the model to learn more robust and generalizable representations (Ruder, 2017; Zhang and Yang, 2017; Crawshaw, 2020). However, one of the biggest challenges in MTL is to balance the convergence schedule across tasks. Differences in task difficulty can result in faster convergence on some tasks over others. As a result, the naive approach which simply adds together the losses of all tasks is typically sub-optimal (Sener and Koltun, 2018; Liu et al., 2019a), since the final model may overfit the tasks that have converged early on during training, while underfitting the others. To tackle this, a large body of work has explored various loss and gradient balancing strategies (Kendall et al., 2018; Sener and Koltun, 2018; Chen et al., 2018; Liu et al., 2019a; Yu et al., 2020; Wang et al., 2021), in order to enforce the same convergence speed across tasks. Despite these efforts, the problem still remains un-

*Work done while at Amazon.

Proceedings of NAACL-HLT 2022: Industry Track Papers, pages 149 - 159
July 10-15, 2022

solved. As we show in our experiments, existing approaches can still fail to balance learning across different tasks in practice.

In this work, we propose a different approach for coordinating the learning across tasks in MTL. Instead of artificially forcing all tasks to converge at the same rate, we allow each task to converge according to its own schedule. We call this asynchronous convergence, as opposed to previous methods which seek to achieve a synchronous convergence schedule across tasks. After each task converges, we avoid overfitting by switching to a knowledge distillation loss for that task for the remaining training steps. The intuition is that continuing to train using the true labels can lead to overfitting. Instead, the knowledge distillation loss encourages the model to maintain its output distribution and thus its performance on the converged tasks at the best level, while the model learns the remaining tasks. We evaluate the proposed method in two different 5-task MTL setups. Our results show that existing loss and gradient balancing approaches fail to produce meaningful improvements over the simple baseline which sums the losses from all tasks or lead to more costly and less efficient training. In contrast, our method achieves consistent improvements. In particular, when comparing the final checkpoint performance, our best performing approach achieves an average improvement of 0.9% over the best baseline model in the first setup and 1.5% in the second setup.

2 Related Work

As already mentioned, one key challenge in MTL is to balance the learning speed across tasks. Some existing methods address this by applying static weights to the losses of different tasks (Kendall et al., 2015; Liao et al., 2016; Kokkinos, 2017), where the weights are usually determined through extensive hyper-parameter search. However, such an approach tends to be sub-optimal (Sener and Koltun, 2018). One line of research improves this by designing algorithms to automatically determine the weights and dynamically adjust them during training (Guo et al., 2018; Kendall et al., 2018; Liu et al., 2019a). Going beyond the loss weighting approaches, there is also work that leverages gradient information and proposes to manipulate the magnitude and/or direction of the gradients from different tasks in order to better coordinate the learning among the tasks (Sener and Koltun, 2018; Chen et al., 2018; Yu et al., 2020; Wang et al., 2021). Recently, Liu et al. (2021) shows improved results by combining loss weighting and gradient manipulation approaches. In all above methods, the goal is to enforce roughly the same convergence speed across tasks, so that the final model fits all tasks well. However, we hypothesize that imposing such an artificial constraint leads to optimization challenges. Instead, we propose a simpler method which allows for asynchronous convergence among the tasks, where each task converges on its own schedule. We focus on avoiding overfitting after a task has converged, which is achieved by distilling from the task's best checkpoint for the remaining training steps.

On the subject of maintaining the performance of converged tasks, a related research area is continual learning (CL) (Parisi et al., 2018; Lange et al., 2021). CL studies the problem of learning tasks in a sequential manner with the goal of avoiding catastrophic forgetting (Goodfellow et al., 2014) of previous tasks while learning new tasks. Replay-based CL approaches are most relevant to our work. The idea is to periodically present the model with examples from past tasks to avoid forgetting (Rebuffi et al., 2017; de Masson d'Autume et al., 2019; Sun et al., 2020a). In particular, Hou et al. (2018) proposes to avoid forgetting by adding a distillation loss formulated using a small subset of examples from previous tasks. In our case, we experiment with a similar setup where we sequentially add one task at a time while using a distillation loss to preserve performance on converged tasks. However, because our focus is on MTL where we have access to the data of all tasks throughout training, we do not down-sample the data of converged tasks. Additionally, our use of the distillation loss is to not only avoid catastrophic forgetting but also overfitting.

Finally, our work is also related to the field of knowledge distillation (KD) (Hinton et al., 2015; Gou et al., 2021), where the goal is to transfer the knowledge of one network to another by training the latter network to mimic the predictions of the former network. It is widely used to distill the knowledge of a large teacher model to a small student model (Hinton et al., 2015; Kim and Rush, 2016; Urban et al., 2017) but has also been applied in MTL (Liu et al., 2019b; Clark et al., 2019) and CL (Hou et al., 2018; Chuang et al., 2020). In particular, Clark et al. (2019) train a multi-task model by distilling from multiple single-task models and show this outperforms directly training a multi-task model. The main difference between this approach and our work is that we do not require separate teacher models per-task, but rather use intermediate checkpoints as teachers as the model converges on each task. Another related work by Wei et al. (2019) also similarly uses intermediate checkpoints for distillation. However, their focus is on training a single machine translation model, whereas we use the technique to train a multi-task model.

3 Proposal: Asynchronous Convergence via Knowledge Distillation

Consider a MTL scenario where we have T tasks and have $\mathcal{D}_t = \left\{\left(x_t^{(i)}, y_t^{(i)}\right)\right\}_{i=1}^{N_t}$ as the training set of task t, with $t \in \{1, \ldots, T\}$ and N_t being the total number of training examples for task t. Let f represent a neural network with parameters θ. In standard supervised training, we would train the network on task t by minimizing a loss $\mathcal{L}_t^{\mathrm{ST}}$ (where ST stands for supervised training) formulated as

$$\mathcal{L}_t^{\mathrm{ST}}(\mathcal{D}_t; \theta) = \sum_{i=1}^{N_t} \ell_t\left(f\left(x_t^{(i)}; \theta\right), y_t^{(i)}\right), \quad (1)$$

where $f\left(x_t^{(i)}; \theta\right)$ denotes the prediction of the model, e.g. probability distribution over all classes for a classification task or predicted score for a regression task, and ℓ_t denotes the corresponding loss function, e.g. cross entropy for classification or mean squared error for regression. As discussed, the challenge of MTL lies in balancing the optimization of the losses across different tasks. In this work, we propose to simply minimize the sum of all task losses, except that after the model has converged on task t, we would change the task's loss from $\mathcal{L}_t^{\mathrm{ST}}$ to a KD loss $\mathcal{L}_t^{\mathrm{KD}}$ formulated against the best checkpoint of task t.

Specifically, let $\widehat{\theta}_t$ denote the parameters of the checkpoint when the model converges on task t. We first use the checkpoint to run inference on the task's training set $\mathcal{D}_t$ to obtain $\widehat{\mathcal{D}}_t = \left\{\left(x_t^{(i)}, \widehat{y}_t^{(i)}\right)\right\}_{i=1}^{N_t}$, where $\widehat{y}_t^{(i)} = f\left(x_t^{(i)}; \widehat{\theta}_t\right)$. Then for the remaining training steps, the model would be trained on task t using a KD loss $\mathcal{L}_t^{\mathrm{KD}}$ formulated as

$$\mathcal{L}_t^{\mathrm{KD}}\left(\widehat{\mathcal{D}}_t; \theta\right) = \sum_{i=1}^{N_t} \ell_t\left(f\left(x_t^{(i)}; \theta\right), \widehat{y}_t^{(i)}\right). \quad (2)$$

Essentially, after the model has converged on task t, we no longer train on the true labels of the task. Rather, we use the KD loss to encourage the model to mimic the predictions from the checkpoint where the best performance is achieved. As we show in our experiments, this method effectively maintains the model's performance on converged tasks without overfitting, while the model continues to learn the remaining tasks. To summarize, we propose to minimize the following loss

$$\mathcal{L} = \sum_{t=1}^{T} \mathcal{L}_t, \text{ where } \mathcal{L}_t = \begin{cases} \mathcal{L}_t^{\mathrm{ST}}, & \text{if task } t \text{ has not converged;} \\ \mathcal{L}_t^{\mathrm{KD}}, & \text{otherwise.} \end{cases} \quad (3)$$

The question of determining when a task has converged still remains. For this, we monitor the validation performance of each task given some patience n_t. If the performance does not improve for n_t consecutive validation steps, we consider the model to have converged on task t. However, one issue with this approach is that, when the patience runs out, we would have already trained the model for some extra steps, and the latest checkpoint could already overfit the task. To resolve this, we rewind back to the checkpoint when the best validation performance is achieved, and use that checkpoint as the best checkpoint $\widehat{\theta}_t$ to formulate $\mathcal{L}_t^{\mathrm{KD}}$. We also rewind and resume training from that checkpoint, effectively discarding the latest steps.

Using this method, we experiment with two different training settings. The first is called **the joint setting**, which is similar to the conventional MTL setup. The model is trained on all tasks together, and we swap in the KD loss as the model converges on different tasks. Training stops when all tasks converge. The second setting is called **the sequential setting** and is inspired by the typical CL setup. Here we start training on a single task and then add one new task at a time after the previous task converges. Following our proposal, we use the KD loss for all converged tasks, while training the model on the true labels of the new task. The process continues until all tasks converge.

One additional hyper-parameter in the sequential setting is the order in which to train the tasks. We experiment with a few different orders, including ordering from (1) the smallest to the largest task by dataset size (**Sequential (Small)**), (2) the largest to the smallest dataset size (**Sequential (Large)**), and (3) the easiest to the hardest (**Sequential (Easy)**). For lack of a better heuristic, Sequential (Easy) uses the order in which the tasks converge in the

Task	Task Type	Size (Train / Val / Test)
Duplicate Detection (Dedup)	Binary classification	3M / 435K / 849K
Perceived Duplicates I (PD-I)	Binary classification	107K / 8K / 29K
Perceived Duplicates II (PD-II)	Binary classification	609K / 30K / 52K
Variations (Var)	Binary classification	5M / 598K / 612K
Unit of Measurement Identification (UoMI)	3-class classification	494K / - / 10K

Table 1: Datasets used in the Related 5-task setup.

Task	Task Type	Size (Train / Val / Test)
Relevant Attribute Identification (RAI)	1359-class multi-label classification	4M / 474K / 474K
Purchase Similarities (SIMS)	Regression	3M / 391K / 390K
Tariff Classification (TC)	93-class classification	28K / - / 3K
Product Type Classification (PTC)	709-class classification	957K / - / 106K
Duplicate Detection (Dedup)	Binary classification	3M / 435K / 849K

Table 2: Datasets used in the Diverse 5-task setup.

joint setting as a proxy for task difficulty ranking. There are potentially better strategies to determine the task order or even strategies that can make the performance invariant of task order. We leave such investigations as future work.

4 Experiments

4.1 Data

We evaluate on proprietary datasets from an e-commerce company. The datasets are in English and include text attributes of product listings, such as title and product description. We experiment with two different 5-task MTL setups. The tasks in the first setup are more similar to each other and are all some form of classification task, while the ones in the second setup are more diverse in terms of application and task type. We evaluate on these two benchmarks to test the effectiveness and robustness of our method in different MTL scenarios. A summary of the tasks used in the two setups is provided in Table 1 and 2, respectively.

The tasks in the first setup, referred to as **the Related 5-task setup**, include (1) **Dedup**, which classifies whether two product listings are duplicates of each other, (2) **PD-I**, which classifies whether two listings have subtle differences but may be perceived as duplicates in search results, (3) **PD-II**, which is the same as PD-I but considers a different set of attributes for defining perceived duplicates, (4) **Var**, which classifies whether two listings are variations of each other along certain set of dimensions (e.g. color, size, flavor, etc.), and (5) **UoMI**, which classifies the unit of measurement of a listing. Among the tasks, the first 4 are closely related, in that they all focus on classifying some sort of similarity between two listings.

The tasks in the second setup, called **the Diverse 5-task setup**, include (1) **RAI**, which classifies whether a listing has any of the 1359 pre-defined attributes, (2) **SIMS**, which predicts how similar two products are in customers' purchase decisions, (3) **TC**, which classifies the tariff category of a listing, (4) **PTC**, which classifies the product type of a listing, and (5) **Dedup**, which classifies whether two product listings are duplicates of each other.

Note that Dedup is used in both setups. Also, UoMI, TC, and PTC do not have separate validation sets, and therefore, we monitor the performance directly on their test sets during training.

4.2 Baselines

We compare our proposal against several baselines, including the naive uniform loss weighting approach, static and dynamic loss weighting methods, and a method which leverages gradient information. Specifically, the baseline models include (1) **Uni. Weight**: This is the uniform weighting baseline where we simply optimize the sum of all task losses. (2) **Muppet**: This is a static loss weighting method proposed in Aghajanyan et al. (2021), which uses a simple heuristic to compute a loss weight for each task such that the losses will roughly be on the same scale after applying the weights. (3) **DWA**: This is the Dynamic Weight Averaging (DWA) method proposed in Liu et al. (2019a), which automatically and dynamically computes the loss weights of different tasks during training. The motivation is to ensure roughly the same decreasing rate across all task losses. (4) **GradNorm**: This is proposed in Chen et al. (2018), which is a method to dynamically adjust the loss weights such that the gradients of different tasks have roughly the same magnitude. See Appendix A for implementation details and hyper-parameters.

4.3 Results

Table 3 shows the results in the Related 5-task setup. Among the baseline approaches, Muppet and DWA

Name	Train Steps	Dedup	PD-I	PD-II	Var	UoMI	Avg
Baselines							
Uni. Weight (Final)	8200	+0.00	+0.00	+0.00	+0.00	+0.00	+0.00
Uni. Weight (Best)		+0.30	+1.00	+1.50	**+1.00**	+0.10	+0.78
Muppet	8200	+0.10	-0.10	+0.10	-0.20	-0.20	-0.06
DWA	8200	+0.10	-0.30	+0.10	-0.10	+0.00	-0.04
GradNorm	8200	-15.50	-15.50	-12.70	-4.80	-2.30	-10.16
This Work							
Joint	8200	**+0.60**	+1.10	**+1.60**	+0.90	-0.30	+0.78
Sequential (Small)	9000	+0.00	-1.20	+1.30	+0.60	+0.10	+0.16
Sequential (Large)	12000	+0.50	**+1.30**	+1.50	+0.90	**+0.30**	**+0.90**
Sequential (Easy)	11000	+0.30	+0.90	+1.50	+0.90	+0.10	+0.74

Table 3: Results in the Related 5-task setup. We report accuracy for UoMI and PRAUC for all other tasks. For all models, we report the performance of the final checkpoint, while for Uni. Weight, in addition to the final performance (Uni. Weight (Final)), we also report the performance using the respective best checkpoint for each task (Uni. Weight (Best)). All results are reported as changes over Uni. Weight (Final). The best performance of each task is in bold, while the second best is underlined.

Name	Train Steps	RAI	SIMS	TC	PTC	Dedup	Avg
Baselines							
Uni. Weight (Final)	10600	+0.00	+0.00	+0.00	+0.00	+0.00	+0.00
Uni. Weight (Best)		+1.10	**+0.10**	**+1.10**	+1.00	+0.10	+0.68
Muppet	10600	-1.00	-0.10	+0.50	+0.70	+0.10	+0.04
DWA	10600	+0.80	+0.00	+0.30	+0.10	+0.00	+0.24
GradNorm	10600	-10.40	-2.10	-1.20	-1.00	-14.30	-5.80
This Work							
Joint	10600	+5.70	+0.00	+0.60	+1.10	-0.40	+1.40
Sequential (Small)	16800	+5.70	**+0.10**	+0.90	**+1.40**	**+0.50**	**+1.72**
Sequential (Large)	37200*	**+7.20**	-0.20	+0.30	+0.80	-2.10	+1.20
Sequential (Easy)	45800*	+4.00	-0.20	+0.50	+1.10	-1.10	+0.86

Table 4: Results in the Diverse 5-task setup. We report accuracy for RAI, TC, and PTC, and PRAUC for Dedup. For SIMS, its labels have been normalized to be between 0 and 1, and we report (1-RMSE)×100. For all models, we report the performance of the final checkpoint, while for Uni. Weight, in addition to the final performance (Uni. Weight (Final)), we also report the performance using the respective best checkpoint for each task (Uni. Weight (Best)). All results are reported as changes over Uni. Weight (Final). The best performance of each task is in bold, while the second best is underlined. *These experiments have a smaller learning rate. See text for more details.

produce similar results as those of the final checkpoint of Uni. Weight, while GradNorm produces much worse results than all other methods. The reason that GradNorm underperforms is because the model still underfits most tasks when training finishes, which suggests that the method is less efficient than others. Overall, there is a substantial gap between the performance of the best checkpoint of Uni. Weight and all other baseline methods, suggesting that none of the methods are able to effectively balance the learning across tasks.

In contrast, both our joint setting and sequential setting are able to achieve the best or second best results across tasks, which shows the effectiveness of our methods. In particular, the joint setting is able to match or surpass Uni. Weight (Best) on all tasks, except for UoMI. Among the experiments with the sequential setting, we can see that task order does impact performance. The exact ordering of tasks in different experiments are shown in Table 7 in Appendix B. Both ordering from the largest to the smallest task and ordering from the easiest to the hardest produce similar results overall, and are comparable with the joint setting and Uni. Weight (Best) in terms of average performance. On the other hand, ordering from the smallest to the largest task produces worst results overall. One possible explanation is that it is easier for the model to overfit the smaller tasks, which not only harms the performance on the tasks themselves, but also provides a sub-optimal initialization point for the later tasks. Finally, comparing the total training steps, we can see that the sequential setting generally takes longer to run, suggesting that the joint setting is a more efficient training method.

In addition to the results in Table 3, we also show the validation plots of different methods in Figure 1 in Appendix C. We can see that all baseline methods show signs of overfitting on some tasks (except for GradNorm which underfits). In contrast, the plots of both our joint setting and sequential setting do not show downward trend in any task, suggesting that our method is indeed effective in maintaining the performance of converged tasks at the best level while the model learns the remaining tasks.

Table 4 shows the results in the Diverse 5-task

setup. This time, the Uni. Weight baseline shows much less overfitting, as can be seen from the validation plot in Figure 2a in Appendix C. Nonetheless, there is still a substantial gap between Uni. Weight (Final) and Uni. Weight (Best) on RAI, TC, and PTC. Muppet is able to almost close the gap on PTC, but it produces worse result on RAI, while DWA almost closes the gap on RAI, but does not improve the other tasks. GradNorm still underfits all the tasks given the same training budget, again showing its lack of efficiency.

Compared to the baseline methods, our joint setting achieves a substantial performance boost on RAI, greatly outperforming even Uni. Weight (Best). It also matches the performance of Uni. Weight (Best) on PTC, and improves over Uni. Weight (Final) on TC. However, the performance on Dedup turns out to be worse. Meanwhile, Sequential (Small), i.e. our sequential setting that goes from the smallest to the largest task, also achieves the same substantial performance gain on RAI, and additionally outperforms or matches Uni. Weight (Best) across tasks. This again validates the effectiveness of our proposed technique in producing better MTL models. For the other two sequential setting experiments with different task orderings, we encountered some issues with training stability when running the experiments, and had to lower the learning rate to 10^{-5} , compared to 10^{-4} used in all other experiments. While fixing the stability issue, this likely prevented the optimizer from fully exploring the loss landscape, which resulted in worse performance on SIMS and Dedup in these two experiments. Nonetheless, they still outperform Uni. Weight (Final) on the other tasks, with Sequential (Large) in particular achieving the highest score on RAI. It is also interesting to note that Sequential (Small) produces the worst results in the Related 5-task setup among the three orders, but actually produces the best results in the Diverse 5-task setup. This could suggest that the effect of task ordering depends on the tasks used, and the optimal ordering strategy differs among the two setups. Another reason why Sequential (Small) outperforms in the Diverse 5-task setup could again be due to the sub-optimal learning rate which we had to use with the other two orders. In the future, we will continue to investigate the effects of task ordering, as well as tackle the training stability issue with smarter learning rate schedules. Also, we can see that the sequential setting again requires substantially more training steps than does the joint setting. This can also potentially be alleviated through a better learning rate schedule. Besides, we will also explore other techniques that can further improve the efficiency of our method, such as reducing the batch proportion of converged tasks.

Name	Train Steps	Dedup	PD-I	PD-II	Var	UoMI	Avg
Exp. 1							
Joint	8200	+0.60	+1.10	+1.60	+0.90	-0.30	+0.78
BAM (M→M)	16400*	+0.40	+1.80	+1.70	+1.00	+0.00	+0.98
Exp. 2							
Sequential (Small)	9000	+0.00	-1.20	+1.30	+0.60	+0.10	+0.16
Continual MTL	10200	+0.00	-0.70	-0.20	+0.50	-0.60	-0.20

Table 5: Results of two additional experiments on the Related 5-task setup. The first experiment compares our joint setting with BAM (M→M) (Clark et al., 2019), while the second experiment compares our sequential setting with Continual MTL (Sun et al., 2020b). All results are reported as changes over Uni. Weight (Final). *Training steps of BAM (M→M) include the training of Uni. Weight. See text for more details.

5 Additional Discussions

In this section, we provide more discussions on the effects of the design choices in both our joint setting and sequential setting. We illustrate the effects through two additional experiments on the Related 5-task setup.

In the first experiment, we compare our joint setting against an alternative approach where we take the respective best checkpoints for each task from the Uni. Weight baseline, and distill them together into a single multi-task model. We call this approach BAM (M→M) as it is the Multi→Multi strategy proposed in Clark et al. (2019). Through this experiment, we seek to compare our way of continued training with a mixture of KD and supervision from true labels against pure KD training. We note that our setting is more challenging as the model needs to learn all tasks from scratch, whereas BAM (M→M) directly transfers previously learned knowledge for each task to the model. Also, we train BAM (M→M) for the same number of training steps as that of our joint setting. However, since we need to obtain the best checkpoint for each task from Uni. Weight, which is also trained for 8200 steps, the total training budget for BAM (M→M) is actually twice as large. The results of this experiment are shown in Table 5 under Exp. 1. We can see that BAM (M→M) has better performance on four out of the five tasks. Nonetheless, our joint setting achieves comparable average performance, despite the fact that our model needs to learn all tasks from scratch and that it receives only half of the training budget.

In the second experiment, we compare our sequential setting with the Continual MTL method proposed in Sun et al. (2020b). It is similar to our sequential setting in that it adds one new task at a time. The main difference is that they always use real labels for training, whereas we use KD to avoid overfitting on converged tasks. Through this experiment, we seek to understand the effects of the KD loss in our sequential setting. Specifically, we choose Sequential (Small) and train Continual MTL using the same task ordering. The results are shown under Exp. 2 in Table 5. We can see that Continual MTL has better performance on PD-I, but is much worse on PD-II and UoMI. Figure 3 in Appendix C shows the validation plots. It is clear that continual MTL suffers from overfitting on PD-II and UoMI, while our sequential setting does not show signs of overfitting. This again validates our assumption that the KD loss is effective in avoiding overfitting on converged tasks.

6 Conclusion

In this work, we propose a new approach to tackle the challenge of task convergence in MTL. In contrast to conventional loss and gradient balancing methods which attempt to enforce a synchronous convergence schedule, we allow the tasks to converge on asynchronous schedules and use a KD loss to maintain the performance on converged tasks while the model learns the remaining tasks. We show that the proposed method consistently outperforms existing loss and gradient balancing approaches. For future work, we will explore strategies to make model performance invariant of task ordering in the sequential setting, or alternatively, explore strategies to optimally determine task ordering. Additionally, we will investigate techniques to improve the efficiency of our method, such as dynamically adjusting the learning rate during training and the batch proportion of converged tasks.

7 Acknowledgments

We would like to thank the M5 Foundational Technologies team within Amazon Search for building the training infrastructure, which enabled the experiments in this work.

References

Armen Aghajanyan, Anchit Gupta, Akshat Shrivastava, Xilun Chen, Luke Zettlemoyer, and Sonal Gupta. 2021. Muppet: Massive multi-task representations with pre-finetuning. In *Proceedings of the 2021 Conference on Empirical Methods in Natural Language Processing (EMNLP)*, pages 5799–5811.

Tom B. Brown, Benjamin Mann, Nick Ryder, Melanie Subbiah, Jared Kaplan, Prafulla Dhariwal, Arvind Neelakantan, Pranav Shyam, Girish Sastry, Amanda Askell, Sandhini Agarwal, Ariel Herbert-Voss, Gretchen Krueger, T. J. Henighan, Rewon Child, Aditya Ramesh, Daniel M. Ziegler, Jeff Wu, Clemens Winter, Christopher Hesse, Mark Chen, Eric Sigler, Mateusz Litwin, Scott Gray, Benjamin Chess, Jack Clark, Christopher Berner, Sam McCandlish, Alec Radford, Ilya Sutskever, and Dario Amodei. 2020. Language models are few-shot learners. In *Advances in Neural Information Processing Systems 33 (NeurIPS)*, pages 1877–1901.

Zhao Chen, Vijay Badrinarayanan, Chen-Yu Lee, and Andrew Rabinovich. 2018. GradNorm: Gradient normalization for adaptive loss balancing in deep multitask networks. In *Proceedings of the 35th International Conference on Machine Learning (ICML)*, pages 794–803.

Yung-Sung Chuang, Shang-Yu Su, and Yun-Nung Chen. 2020. Lifelong language knowledge distillation. In *Proceedings of the 2020 Conference on Empirical Methods in Natural Language Processing (EMNLP)*, pages 2914–2924.

Kevin Clark, Minh-Thang Luong, Urvashi Khandelwal, Christopher D. Manning, and Quoc V. Le. 2019. BAM! born-again multi-task networks for natural language understanding. In *Proceedings of the 57th Annual Meeting of the Association for Computational Linguistics*, pages 5931–5937.

Kevin Clark, Minh-Thang Luong, Quoc V. Le, and Christopher D. Manning. 2020. ELECTRA: Pre-training text encoders as discriminators rather than generators. In *International Conference on Learning Representations (ICLR)*.

Michael Crawshaw. 2020. Multi-task learning with deep neural networks: A survey. In *ArXiv*.

Cyprien de Masson d'Autume, Sebastian Ruder, Lingpeng Kong, and Dani Yogatama. 2019. Episodic memory in lifelong language learning. In *Proceedings of the 33rd International Conference on Neural*

Information Processing Systems (NeurIPS), pages 13132–13141.

Jacob Devlin, Ming-Wei Chang, Kenton Lee, and Kristina Toutanova. 2019. BERT: Pre-training of deep bidirectional transformers for language understanding. In *Proceedings of the 2019 Conference of the North American Chapter of the Association for Computational Linguistics: Human Language Technologies (NAACL-HLT)*, pages 4171–4186.

Ian J. Goodfellow, Mehdi Mirza, Xia Da, Aaron C. Courville, and Yoshua Bengio. 2014. An empirical investigation of catastrophic forgeting in gradient-based neural networks. In *ArXiv*.

Jianping Gou, B. Yu, Stephen J. Maybank, and Dacheng Tao. 2021. Knowledge distillation: A survey. In *International Journal of Computer Vision*, pages 1789–1819.

Michelle Guo, Albert Haque, De-An Huang, Serena Yeung, and Li Fei-Fei. 2018. Dynamic task prioritization for multitask learning. In *European Conference on Computer Vision (ECCV)*, pages 282–299.

Pengcheng He, Xiaodong Liu, Jianfeng Gao, and Weizhu Chen. 2021. DeBERTa: Decoding-enhanced bert with disentangled attention. In *International Conference on Learning Representations (ICLR)*.

Geoffrey E. Hinton, Oriol Vinyals, and Jeffrey Dean. 2015. Distilling the knowledge in a neural network. In *ArXiv*.

Saihui Hou, Xinyu Pan, Chen Change Loy, Zilei Wang, and Dahua Lin. 2018. Lifelong learning via progressive distillation and retrospection. In *European Conference on Computer Vision (ECCV)*, pages 437–452.

Alex Kendall, Yarin Gal, and Roberto Cipolla. 2018. Multi-task learning using uncertainty to weigh losses for scene geometry and semantics. In *IEEE Conference on Computer Vision and Pattern Recognition (CVPR)*, pages 7482–7491.

Alex Kendall, Matthew Koichi Grimes, and Roberto Cipolla. 2015. PoseNet: A convolutional network for real-time 6-dof camera relocalization. In *International Conference on Computer Vision (ICCV)*, pages 2938–2946.

Yoon Kim and Alexander M. Rush. 2016. Sequence-level knowledge distillation. In *Proceedings of the 2016 Conference on Empirical Methods in Natural Language Processing (EMNLP)*, pages 1317–1327.

Iasonas Kokkinos. 2017. UberNet: Training a universal convolutional neural network for low-, mid-, and high-level vision using diverse datasets and limited memory. In *IEEE Conference on Computer Vision and Pattern Recognition (CVPR)*, pages 5454–5463.

Taku Kudo and John Richardson. 2018. SentencePiece: A simple and language independent subword tokenizer and detokenizer for neural text processing. In *Proceedings of the 2018 Conference on Empirical Methods in Natural Language Processing (System Demonstrations) (EMNLP)*, pages 66–71.

Matthias De Lange, Rahaf Aljundi, Marc Masana, Sarah Parisot, Xu Jia, Aleš Leonardis, Gregory G. Slabaugh, and Tinne Tuytelaars. 2021. A continual learning survey: Defying forgetting in classification tasks. In *IEEE Transactions on Pattern Analysis and Machine Intelligence (PAMI)*.

Mike Lewis, Yinhan Liu, Naman Goyal, Marjan Ghazvininejad, Abdelrahman Mohamed, Omer Levy, Veselin Stoyanov, and Luke Zettlemoyer. 2020. BART: Denoising sequence-to-sequence pre-training for natural language generation, translation, and comprehension. In *Proceedings of the 58th Annual Meeting of the Association for Computational Linguistics (ACL)*, pages 7871–7880.

Yiyi Liao, Sarath Kodagoda, Yue Wang, Lei Shi, and Y. Liu. 2016. Understand scene categories by objects: A semantic regularized scene classifier using convolutional neural networks. In *IEEE International Conference on Robotics and Automation (ICRA)*, pages 2318–2325.

Liyang Liu, Yi Li, Zhanghui Kuang, Jing-Hao Xue, Yimin Chen, Wenming Yang, Qingmin Liao, and Wayne Zhang. 2021. Towards impartial multi-task learning. In *International Conference on Learning Representations (ICLR)*.

Shikun Liu, Edward Johns, and Andrew J. Davison. 2019a. End-to-end multi-task learning with attention. In *IEEE Conference on Computer Vision and Pattern Recognition (CVPR)*, pages 1871–1880.

Xiaodong Liu, Pengcheng He, Weizhu Chen, and Jianfeng Gao. 2019b. Improving multi-task deep neural networks via knowledge distillation for natural language understanding. In *Proceedings of the 57th Annual Meeting of the Association for Computational Linguistics (ACL)*, pages 4487–4496.

German Ignacio Parisi, Ronald Kemker, Jose L. Part, Christopher Kanan, and Stefan Wermter. 2018. Continual lifelong learning with neural networks: A review. In *Neural Networks*, pages 54–71.

Colin Raffel, Noam Shazeer, Adam Roberts, Katherine Lee, Sharan Narang, Michael Matena, Yanqi Zhou, Wei Li, and Peter J. Liu. 2020. Exploring the limits of transfer learning with a unified text-to-text transformer. In *Journal of Machine Learning Research (JMLR)*, pages 1–67.

Sylvestre-Alvise Rebuffi, Alexander Kolesnikov, G. Sperl, and Christoph H. Lampert. 2017. iCaRL: Incremental classifier and representation learning. In *IEEE Conference on Computer Vision and Pattern Recognition (CVPR)*, pages 2001–2010.

Sebastian Ruder. 2017. An overview of multi-task learning in deep neural networks. In *ArXiv*.

Ozan Sener and Vladlen Koltun. 2018. Multi-task learning as multi-objective optimization. In *Proceedings of the 32nd International Conference on Neural Information Processing Systems (NeurIPS)*, pages 525–536.

Fan-Keng Sun, Cheng-Hao Ho, and Hung yi Lee. 2020a. LAMOL: Language modeling for lifelong language learning. In *International Conference on Learning Representations (ICLR)*.

Yu Sun, Shuohuan Wang, Yukun Li, Shikun Feng, Hao Tian, Hua Wu, and Haifeng Wang. 2020b. ERNIE 2.0: A continual pre-training framework for language understanding. In *Association for the Advancement of Artificial Intelligence (AAAI)*, pages 8968–8975.

Gregor Urban, Krzysztof J Geras, Samira Ebrahimi Kahou, Özlem Aslan, Shengjie Wang, Abdel rahman Mohamed, Matthai Philipose, Matthew Richardson, and Rich Caruana. 2017. Do deep convolutional nets really need to be deep and convolutional? In *International Conference on Learning Representations (ICLR)*.

Alex Wang, Yada Pruksachatkun, Nikita Nangia, Amanpreet Singh, Julian Michael, Felix Hill, Omer Levy, and Samuel R. Bowman. 2019. SuperGLUE: A stickier benchmark for general-purpose language understanding systems. In *Proceedings of the 33rd International Conference on Neural Information Processing Systems (NeurIPS)*, pages 3266–3280.

Alex Wang, Amanpreet Singh, Julian Michael, Felix Hill, Omer Levy, and Samuel R. Bowman. 2018. GLUE: A multi-task benchmark and analysis platform for natural language understanding. In *Proceedings of the 2018 EMNLP Workshop BlackboxNLP: Analyzing and Interpreting Neural Networks for NLP*, pages 353–355.

Zirui Wang, Yulia Tsvetkov, Orhan Firat, and Yuan Cao. 2021. Gradient vaccine: Investigating and improving multi-task optimization in massively multilingual models. In *International Conference on Learning Representations (ICLR)*.

Hao-Ran Wei, Shujian Huang, Ran Wang, Xinyu Dai, and Jiajun Chen. 2019. Online distilling from checkpoints for neural machine translation. In *Proceedings of the 2019 Conference of the North American Chapter of the Association for Computational Linguistics: Human Language Technologies (NAACL-HLT)*, pages 1932–1941.

Zhilin Yang, Zihang Dai, Yiming Yang, Jaime G. Carbonell, Ruslan Salakhutdinov, and Quoc V. Le. 2019. XLNet: Generalized autoregressive pretraining for language understanding. In *Proceedings of the 33rd International Conference on Neural Information Processing Systems (NeurIPS)*, pages 5753–5763.

Tianhe Yu, Saurabh Kumar, Abhishek Gupta, Sergey Levine, Karol Hausman, and Chelsea Finn. 2020. Gradient surgery for multi-task learning. In *Proceedings of the 34th International Conference on Neural Information Processing Systems (NeurIPS)*, pages 5824–5836.

Yu Zhang and Qiang Yang. 2017. A survey on multitask learning. In *IEEE Transactions on Knowledge and Data Engineering*.

Shuai Zheng, Haibin Lin, Sheng Zha, and Mu Li. 2020. Accelerated large batch optimization of bert pretraining in 54 minutes. In *ArXiv*.

A Implementation Details and Hyper-parameters

For all experiments, we use the same pretrained model, which has a BERT-like architecture (Devlin et al., 2019) and is pretrained using the masked language modeling objective on an internal English corpus consisting of online product listings. The vocabulary is trained on the same corpus using SentencePiece (Kudo and Richardson, 2018) and has 32K tokens. The model has 38 transformer layers, with each layer having 16 attention heads, 1024 hidden dimension, and 4098 intermediate feedforward dimension. The total parameter count is roughly 500M. The model is trained using the LANS optimizer (Zheng et al., 2020) with a batch size of 8192 and a learning rate of 10^{-4}. We had to use a smaller learning rate in two experiments with our sequential setting, which is discussed in Section 4.3. For each batch, we sample heterogeneously from all tasks, and the sampling distribution is roughly based on the dataset sizes, with some manual adjustments to ensure the smaller tasks are not too under-represented.

We validate every 200 training steps. For both our joint setting and sequential setting, we use a patience of 3 validation steps to determine whether a task has converged, and training stops when all tasks converge. For the baseline models, since we lack an aggregated early stopping criterion, for fair comparison, we train for the same number of steps as it takes to train the model in our joint setting. For Muppet, the loss weights for different tasks are shown in Table 6. For DWA, we set the temperature T to 2, which is recommended in Liu et al. (2019a). For GradNorm, we experiment with $\alpha \in \{0.5, 1, 2\}$ and choose the best performing value based on validation performance, which turns out to be 0.5 in the Related 5-task setup and 1 in the Diverse 5-task setup.

Task	Dedup	PD-I	PD-II	Var	UoMI
Weight	3.3	3.3	3.3	3.3	2.1
Task	**RAI**	**SIMS**	**HS**	**PTC**	**Dedup**
Weight	0.32	1	0.51	0.35	3.3

Table 6: Loss weights used in Muppet in both 5-task setups.

For all models, we report the performance of the final checkpoint on all tasks. For the Uni. Weight baseline, we additionally report the performance using the respective best checkpoint for each task, which can be used as a reference for the model's best performance on each task without overfitting.

B Task Order in the Sequential Setting Experiments

	Task Order in the First 5-Task Setup
Sequential (Small)	PD-I → UoMI → PD-II → Dedup → Var
Sequential (Large)	Var → Dedup → PD-II → UoMI → PD-I
Sequential (Easy)	Var → PD-I → PD-II → UoMI → Dedup
	Task Order in the Second 5-Task Setup
Sequential (Small)	TC → PTC → Dedup → SIMS → RAI
Sequential (Large)	RAI → SIMS → Dedup → PTC → TC
Sequential (Easy)	PTC → SIMS → TC → Dedup → RAI

Table 7: Task order in the experiments with the sequential setting in both 5-task setups. Sequential (Small) orders the tasks from the smallest to the largest task by dataset size; Sequential (Large) orders from the largest to the smallest; Sequential (Easy) orders from the easiest to the hardest. For lack of a better heuristic, we use the order in which the tasks converge in the joint setting as a proxy for task difficulty ranking.

C Validation Plots

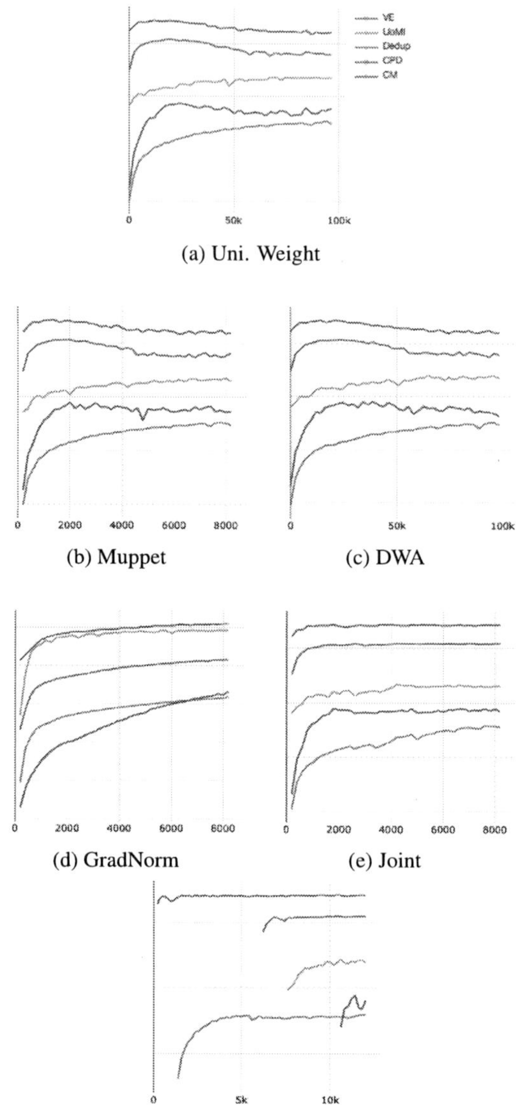

(a) Uni. Weight

(b) Muppet

(c) DWA

(d) GradNorm

(e) Joint

(f) Sequential (Large)

Figure 1: Validation plots of different methods in the Related 5-task setup. For the sequential setting, we only show the plot of Sequential (Large), as it has the best overall performance among different task orderings. Best viewed in color.

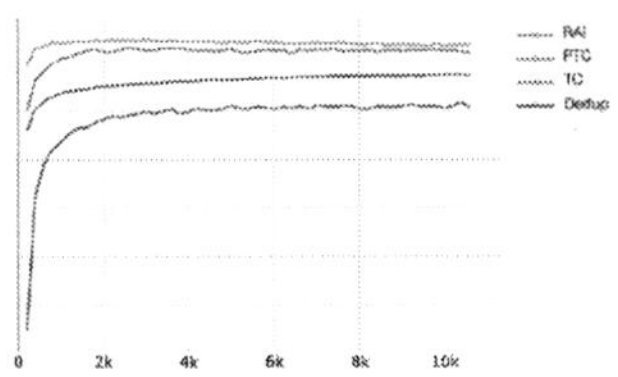

(a) Uni. Weight

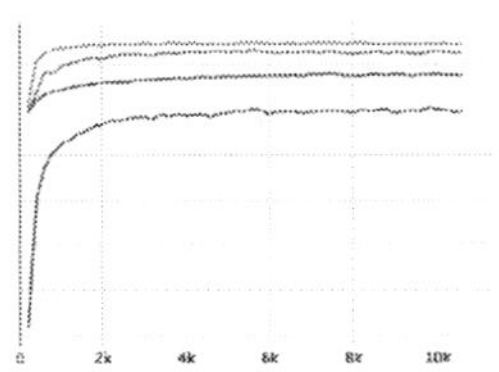

(b) Muppet

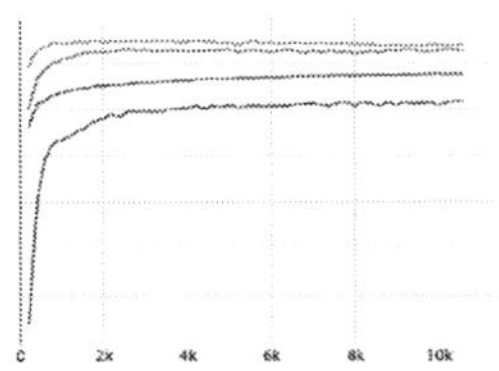

(c) DWA

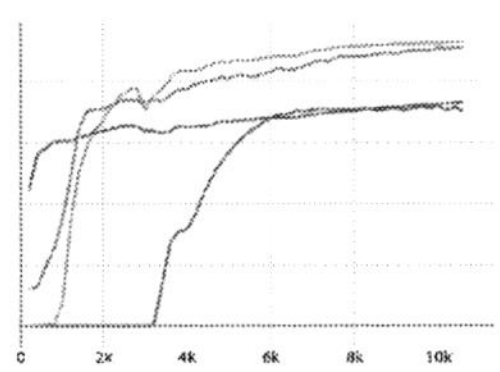

(d) GradNorm

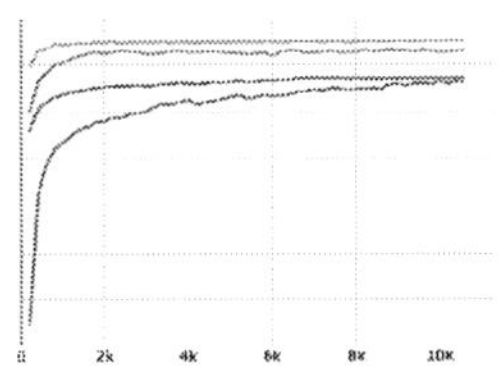

(e) Joint

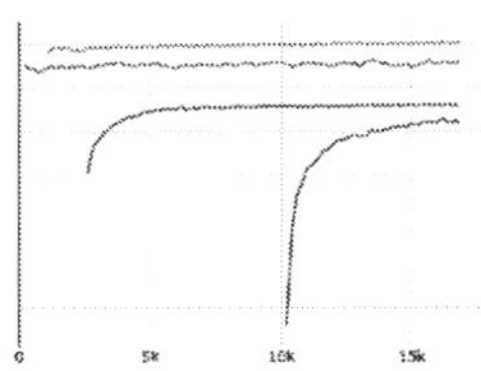

(f) Sequential (Small)

Figure 2: Validation plots of different methods in the Diverse 5-task setup. The plot of SIMS is omitted because its values are on a much smaller scale. For the sequential setting, we only show the plot of Sequential (Small), as it has the best overall performance among different task orderings. Best viewed in color.

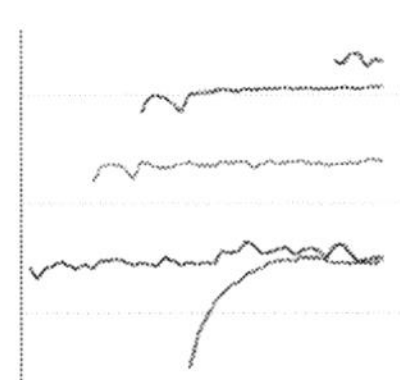

(a) Sequential (Small)

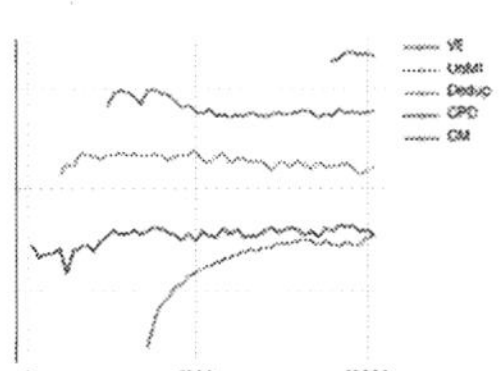

(b) Continual MTL

Figure 3: Validation plots of Experiment 2 on the Related 5-task setup. Best viewed in color.

Augmenting Training Data for Massive Semantic Matching Models in Low-Traffic E-commerce Stores

Ashutosh Joshi[1] Shankar Vishwanath[1] Choon Hui Teo[1]
Vaclav Petricek[1] Vishy Vishwanathan[1] Rahul Bhagat[1] Jonathan May[1,2]
[1]Amazon.com, Inc., [2]Information Sciences Institute, University of Southern California
{jasutos, shavis, choonhui, petricek, vishy, rbhagat}@amazon.com
jonmay@isi.edu

Abstract

Extreme multi-label classification (XMC) systems have been successfully applied in e-commerce (Shen et al., 2020; Dahiya et al., 2021) for retrieving products based on customer behavior. Such systems require large amounts of customer behavior data (e.g. queries, clicks, purchases) for training. However, behavioral data is limited in low-traffic e-commerce stores, impacting performance of these systems. In this paper, we present a technique that augments behavioral training data via query reformulation. We use the Aggregated Label eXtreme Multi-label Classification (AL-XMC) system (Shen et al., 2020) as an example semantic matching model and show via crowd-sourced human judgments that, when the training data is augmented through query reformulations, the quality of AL-XMC improves over a baseline that does not use query reformulation. We also show in online A/B tests that our method significantly improves business metrics for the AL-XMC model.

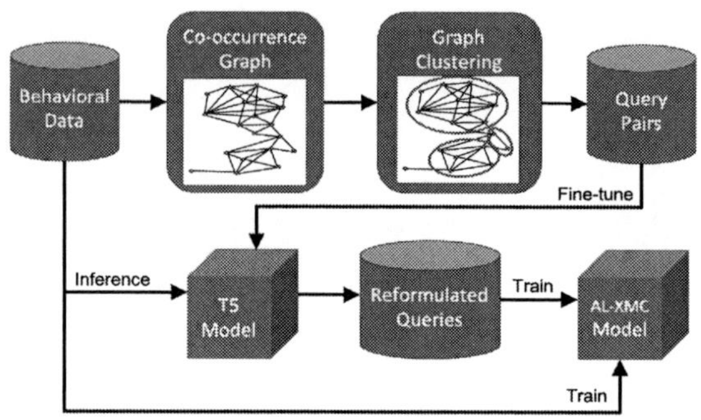

Figure 1: Overview of our approach. We induce query reformulation pairs from behavioral training data to fine-tune a reformulation model (T5). We then augment the original behavioral data with reformulated queries to train an AL-XMC semantic model.

1 Introduction

E-commerce search engines are primarily keyword-based information retrieval (IR) systems comprising two main operations–matching and ranking (Manning et al., 2008). Lexical and/or semantic matching algorithms generate a recall-focused *matchset* which is then ranked based on the match quality of the document (product) to the query (Joachims et al., 2007). Lexical matching algorithms such as Okapi-BM25 (Robertson and Walker, 1994; Robertson and Zaragoza, 2009) score a query-product pair as a weighted sum of overlapping keywords. These approaches, used in many retrieval tasks (Lee et al., 2019; Boytsov and Nyberg, 2020), do not capture customer behavior signals (purchase, stream, etc) and thus do not capture customer preferences.

Semantic matching learns representations of queries and products based on customer behavior and hence captures the products that customers prefer. Semantic matching can be implemented using dual encoders (Nigam et al., 2019; Huang et al., 2013), that separately build query and product representations, then combine the two in a final shared space to determine the similarity of the pair. It is also implemented using extreme multi-label classification (XMC) systems. In particular, Aggregated Label eXtreme Multi-label Classification (AL-XMC) (Shen et al., 2020) partitions the label (product) space by clustering labels into hierarchically granular clusters in a b-ary tree structure. Irrespective of the approach, semantic matching requires a large amount of behavioral data to train. But in newly launched sites or for new products, this behavioral data is not abundant.

In this paper, we propose a method to augment the data available to train semantic models in low-resource e-commerce stores. We use item-to-item collaborative filtering to identify queries that show strong behavioral associations. Such query pairs elicit a similar behavioral response from customers and so represent the same purchase intent. We use these query pairs to fine-tune the text-to-text-transfer-transformer (T5) language model (Raffel

Proceedings of NAACL-HLT 2022: Industry Track Papers, pages 160 - 167
July 10-15, 2022 ©2022 Association for Computational Linguistics

et al., 2020) to generate query paraphrases, which we then use to augment the data available to train the semantic model.

We test our method on an AL-XMC semantic model, though it can be easily used to augment training data for any semantic model. We show, by offline crowd-sourced human judgments as well as online A/B tests, that our data augmentation technique generates reliable training data that improves the performance of the AL-XMC semantic model.

2 Approach

A pipeline diagram of our system is shown in Figure 1. The main goal of this work is to increase good quality query-product pairs with which to train an AL-XMC model; we do this by generating alternative queries from known queries using a fine-tuned T5 model. To fine-tune the T5 model, we identify purchase-intent-preserving query pairs from historical customer data. In Section 3 we describe our approach to constructing the data used to fine-tune the T5 model.

3 Constructing query reformulations

We regard customer interaction data as tuples of the form $\langle q, t, p \rangle$, each consisting of a query q, interaction type t (eg: search, purchase, etc.) and product p. It is generally the case that newer stores do not have sufficient interaction data to train robust semantic models. To increase the data available to train semantic models, we can either increase the number of queries associated with the product, the number of products associated with the queries, or both. In a typical e-commerce site the number of products is usually fixed. It is not usually possible or desirable to artificially augment this set. Instead we fine-tune a language model to generate *query* reformulations and associate the reformulated queries to products using the same interaction type t as the original query. The reformulated queries increase the variance of the tokens, including those from rare queries, in accordance with their distribution in the target store. In order for this to happen, the reformulated queries need to encompass the same purchase intent as the original queries.

For a language model to create high-fidelity reformulations, we need an adequate corpus of intent-preserving query paraphrase pairs. However, generating such a corpus is not trivial. Queries vary widely in specificity, from highly generic (*gifts for teens*) to highly specific (*HP 63XL*). Also, a

```
              fish tank brushes
      fish filter cleaning brush
               filter tube brush
    slson aquarium filter brush
  aquarium tube cleaning brush
        fish tank cleaner brush
```

(a) Similarities of *aquarium filter brush*

```
       cat tag personalized
            gotags dog tags
              heart pet tag
      pet tags engraved cat
               cat name tag
   cat id tags personalized
```

(b) Similarities of *heart name tag for dog*

Figure 2: Top 6 similarities of two example queries, sorted by PMI. While all the top matches to *aquarium filter brush* appear to refer to the same product as the key, many of the top matches to *heart name tag for dog* refer to products that are not good matches.

product can satisfy multiple shopping intents. For example, the same product can be purchased for *kids laptop* and *cheap laptop*. In this section, we describe our methodology to generate high fidelity query reformulations.

3.1 Identifying related queries using Collaborative Filtering

To generate fine-tuning data for a query reformulation model, we need to identify query pairs that have the same purchase intent. We adapt item-to-item collaborative filtering (Linden et al., 2003) to generate query-to-query similarities. In this formulation, we interpret common product interactions of queries as query co-occurrence. For our case, we say two queries *co-occur* iff they *lead to the purchase of the same product*. Given this interpretation, we can then use different measures like pointwise mutual information (PMI) to quantify dependence between queries. Figures 2a and 2b show the top 6 similar queries (or *similarities*) associated with seed queries *aquarium filter brush* and *heart name tag for dog*, respectively. As we can see from these figures, the similarities are generally related to the seeds. However, as seen in Figure 2b, the similarities, while related, do not preserve purchase intent in all cases.

3.2 Clustering the query graph

Since our purpose is to identify queries that have the same purchase intent, for every seed query, we filter out any similarities with a *query specificity* that is not within 10% of the specificity of the seed.

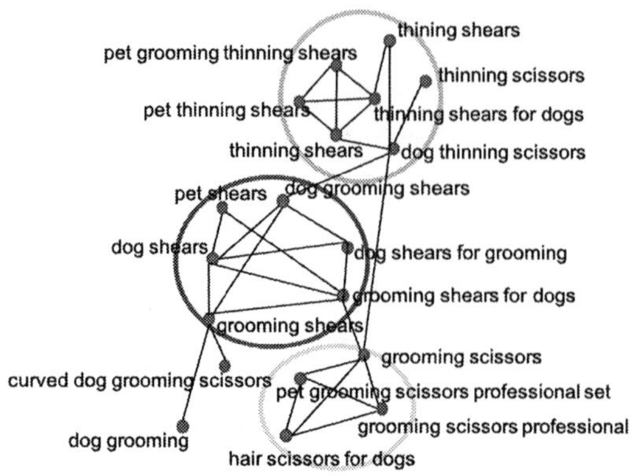

Figure 3: Queries and similarities associated with product *Lily's 8-Inch Japanese 440C Pet Dog Chunker Shears*. This sub-graph shows three clusters that can be visually identified.

We define specificity, $s_Q(q)$, as the inverse normalized click entropy ($H(q)$) of clicks for a query, q.

$$H(q) = -\sum_{p \in c(q)} P(p|q) \log P(p|q)$$

$$s_Q(q) = 1 - \frac{H(q)}{\max_{q' \in Q} H(q')}$$

where $P(p|q)$ is the probability that a customer will click on product p after issuing query q and $c(q)$ is the set of all products clicked by users after issuing q. A very specific query (e.g.: *k-cup coffee pods 72 count*) will have low $H(q)$ and thus high specificity $s_Q(q)$ while broad queries (e.g.: *party dress*) will have high $H(q)$ and low $s_Q(q)$.

Even after specificity filtering, similarities can still show associations that do not preserve query intent (Figure 2b). To further reduce noise, we identify clusters in the query similarities graph. We form this graph by considering every query to be a vertex, and an edge to connect vertices if there is a similarity relation between them. The whole graph, though extremely sparse ($< 0.0001\%$ of the edges of a fully connected graph), can still contain tens of millions of vertices and hundreds of millions of edges for some e-stores. Since our objective is to identify queries that lead to the purchase of similar products, we break the similarities graph into product sub-graphs for each product p as $G_p = (V_p, E_p)$ where $V_p = (V_{Q_p} \cup V_{N_p})$ is the set of vertices formed as follows: V_{Q_p} is the set of queries associated with (i.e. that lead to the purchase of) p, and V_{N_p} is the set of similarities of V_{Q_p}. An edge connecting (v_i, v_j) is in E_p iff $v_i, v_j \in V_p$ and there exists a similarity relation between them. By processing each product sub-graph independently, we can parallelize the clustering problem and operate only on small sub-graphs.

Figure 3 shows the sub-graph of the product *Lily's 8-Inch Japanese 440C Pet Dog Chunker Shears*. The graph naturally separates the queries into multiple sets: thinning shears, grooming shears, and professional grooming scissors, each marked in different colors in the figure.

We cluster each similarities subgraph to identify sets of queries that show high connectivity within the cluster and low connectivity outside it. The aim of clustering is to find groups of behaviorally related queries that satisfy the same customer intent. The subgraph edges already tell us that two queries are related, in that they lead to the purchase of the same product more frequently than would be expected by chance alone. By clustering we can identify groups of mutually related queries. If two queries are behaviorally related to a similar set of queries we can consider them to be related as well.

Graph clustering, though, is an ambiguous problem, with no universal definition of a cluster. Depending on the algorithm used, we can detect one, two, or three clusters in the graph in Figure 4.

Edge clustering (Ahn et al., 2010) combines features of soft clustering, where clusters can share the same members, with hierarchical clustering, where clusters are nested into dendrograms that represent progressive subdivision of a single cluster into a set of singletons. We next describe an edge clustering algorithm that is hierarchical but does not prohibit vertex sharing between clusters.

3.3 Seeding query clusters

Hierarchical clustering recursively merges clusters according to some merge criterion, beginning with each vertex in its own cluster. This imposes a restriction that clusters not share vertices. To avoid this, we let some vertices' base clusters consist of themselves *and* their neighbors (i.e. their similarities). To determine which initial clusters are singleton vertices and which contain vertices and neighbors, we use the *Clustering Coefficient (C3)*, which measures the cliquishness of the neighborhood of a vertex in a graph (Lind et al., 2005). $C3(i)$ is defined as the fraction of the number of triangles observed in the graph out of the total number of possible triangles which may appear. For a vertex i with a degree d_i, the total number of

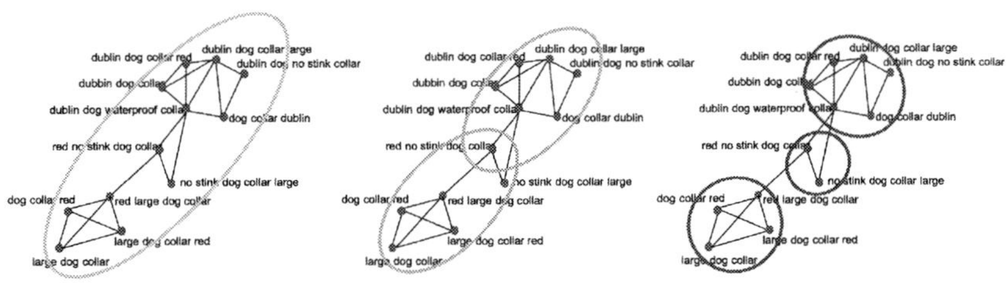

Figure 4: Different ways to cluster a graph

possible triangles is just the number of pairs of neighbors, i.e. $d_i(d_i - 1)/2$. Then $C3$ is given by:

$$C3(i) = \frac{2T_i}{d_i(d_i - 1)} \tag{1}$$

where T_i is the number of observed triangles incident on vertex i.

If a vertex has a high (> 0.33) C3 coefficient, we are assured that the neighborhood has a high internal degree (a large number of edges between vertices in the neighborhood), and so we include its neighbors in its initial cluster. Vertices not meeting this criteria are added as singleton initial clusters.

3.4 Merging query clusters

We then merge clusters hierarchically, based on the size of the vertex intersection between clusters. Starting with the seed clusters (either neighborhoods or singleton vertices), in each round, pairs of clusters are chosen in order by intersection size. A round terminates when for some cluster pair c_i, c_j to be merged, $|c_i \cap c_j| < \theta \times \min(|c_i|, |c_j|)$ for some predefined hyperparameter θ,[1] where $|c_i|$ is the number of vertices in cluster c_i.[2]

3.5 Pruning query clusters

Since we include entire neighborhoods as seed clusters, we may also end up including rogue edges that are tenuously connected to the clusters. After the final merge, we prune the vertices that have an internal-degree to external-degree ratio less than a threshold.[3] This removes noise and bolsters the community structure (high intra-cluster connectivity and low inter-cluster connectivity).

Since query graphs are behavioral, it may not be possible to get semantically distinct clusters. We observe that overly large clusters ($|c| > 10$) include queries with multiple (albeit related) purchase intents. For example, in Figure 5, though mostly semantically grouped, we see a mix of *dog halloween costumes* and *dog sweaters* in one cluster. We thus only consider clusters with fewer than 10 vertices.

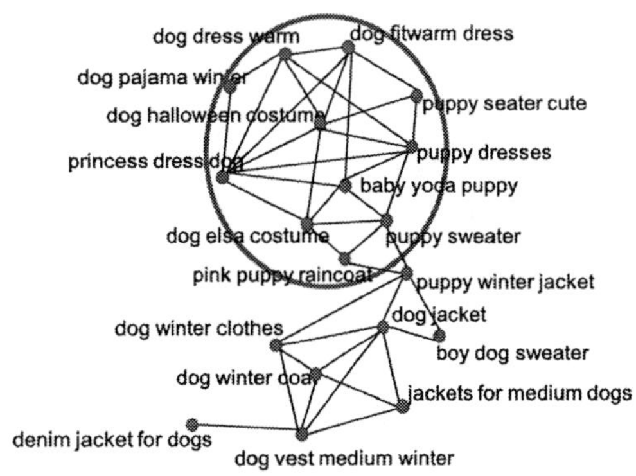

Figure 5: Due to the behavioral nature of the graph, some queries with different intents get grouped together. In this example, 'dog elsa costume' and 'dog dress warm' are grouped together, yet represent different intents.

4 Experiments

From a low resource store we collect 2.4m instances of behavioral association between queries and products. We select behaviors over a threshold level of activity (e.g. clicks and purchases), comprising 0.83m pairs, and use that to train a baseline AL-XMC model; we call this data *local*. To apply query reformulation (*QR*), we first fine-tune a pretrained T5-Base model for a sequence-to-sequence prediction task that uses query pairs from the clusters we generated in Section 3.[4] We fine-tune for two epochs using batches of 32 intent-preserving query pairs and gradient accumulation with a factor of 16, for an effective batch size of 512. We

[1]We use $\theta = 0.4$.

[2]We can interpret the round termination condition as a modified Jaccard similarity, where our condition, $\frac{|c_i \cap c_j|}{\min(|c_i|,|c_j|)} < \theta$, is more amenable to clusters of dissimilar sizes than $\frac{|c_i \cap c_j|}{|c_i \cup c_j|}$, the Jaccard coefficient.

[3]We use 0.5.

[4]We again impose the restriction that the specificity of the target query be within 10% of that of the source query.

size	accuracy
130k	79.67%
460k	86.67%
4m	90.33%
40m	93.00%

Table 1: Impact of data size on fine-tuned T5 reformulation's intent preservation, showing that accuracy generally correlates with data size. The 130k and 460k data points use only reformulated local data, while the 4m and 40m data points use data from other high-resource stores. Our QR experiments use the local-only 460k-tuned T5 model.

optimize with Adam, with a learning rate of $3e-4$. We fine-tune using 8 NVIDIA V100 GPUs; each epoch takes around 24 hours to run.

We use the fine-tuned T5 model to reformulate the query for each of the 2.4m collected query-product-behavior tuples, and associate the reformulation with the product and behavior, as if it was additional data. We can then re-select tuples with behavior over the same threshold level of activity used to form the local data; now, however, more tuples are above threshold and some new tuples have been introduced. Altogether, this procedure dramatically increases the size of the AL-XMC training corpus, to 16.14m training tuples.

In addition to the local baseline and local+QR reformulation approaches, we compare our data augmentation method to integrative knowledge transfer (IKT) (Pan et al., 2008; Zhuo et al., 2008) from a higher-resource store. To do this, we identify queries in the high-resource store that show strong interaction with a product that is available in both stores. We add those query-product associations to the training set in the target store. Such an approach is of course only possible in a mature ecosystem where previously-established high-resource stores exist.

5 Evaluation

To intrinsically evaluate the impact of fine-tuning data size on reformulation intent preservation, we randomly select 300 QR tuples and determine to what degree intent is preserved during reformulation, using a variety of data conditions to fine-tune T5. We count a reformulation as accurate if it has the same manually judged purchase intent as the input query and a search engine returns a similar set of products for both queries. Table 1 shows that for the reformulation fine-tuned on the 460k pairs obtained as described in Section 3, accuracy is about 87%. To put this in context, Table 1 also shows results for T5 reformulation when fine-tuned on a 130k subset of that data, as well as on larger query reformulation fine-tuning data sets obtained by including query pairs from other high-resource stores. The trend indicates that intent preservation is generally a function of the amount of data used to fine-tune the T5 model. In the rest of this work we use a T5 reformulation model fine-tuned on the 460k pairs obtained as described in Section 3, since the availability of high-resource store data is not guaranteed.

To extrinsically evaluate, we consider the effectiveness of the AL-XMC models when built under different data augmentation conditions. We consider both offline and online evaluation paradigms.

5.1 Offline evaluation

Typically, evaluations are done by computing precision and recall metrics using customer purchases as ground truth. Low-resource stores however, do not have sufficient purchase data and suffer from significant display bias—if a relevant product isn't shown to a customer, they cannot purchase it, resulting in an artificial drop in precision of a new (not deployed) model. Thus, we train crowd-sourced judges using the Toloka platform[5] to evaluate if the products predicted by the AL-XMC model for a particular query are indicative of the query text. We use 1,000 randomly sampled query-product pairs to evaluate the models. Table 2 gives the product accuracy improvement and coverage (average number of products generated per query) for AL-XMC models. AL-XMC models trained using any data-augmentation (local+$*$) significantly outperform the model trained using only local data, both in terms of product accuracy (p-value in a one-sided t-test is < 0.01 for all three results) and coverage. Our QR data augmentation scheme outperforms IKT (local+IKT18) when the size of data augmentation is similar. Using multiple high-resource stores and hand-tuning the parameters for IKT, we can increase the training data by almost 3x to a total size of 47.58m. However, even with this massive data increase (local+IKT48), IKT only achieves a product accuracy comparable to our augmentation scheme. If no high-resource store is available, IKT is not even an option. Query reformulation, on the other hand, only requires information from the

[5]https://toloka.yandex.com/

Training data	Product accuracy improvement	Avg number of products/query	Num training pairs
local	N/A	16.85	0.83m
local+IKT18	13.58%	22.27	18.11m
local+IKT48	19.85%	25.94	47.58m
local+QR (ours)	19.57%	21.08	16.14m

Table 2: Data augmentation method comparison. Product accuracy (proportion of relevant products) improvement measures percent increase from local baseline. Product accuracy numbers use offline crowd sourced evaluations. p-value is < 0.01 for all three data augmentation cases in a one-sided t-test.

Training data	Improvement in SCR	P(Treatment(SCR)> Control(SCR))	Improvement in CRR	P(Treatment(CRR)> Control(CRR))
local+QR	0.26%	0.82	-0.30%	0.15

Table 3: Online A/B test where control is the local model. For Search Click Rate (SCR), positive effect is better, for Customer Reformulation Rate (CRR) negative effect is better.

low-resource store and a language model like T5.

5.2 Online evaluation

For the analysis of a single A/B test, it is common to compute a p-value from the t-statistic. However, in modern industrial settings, a large number of randomized experiments are run every day. In this setting, using only the Null Hypothesis test essentially ignores the information from the whole population of experiments. Stein's paradox (Stein, 1956) states that when estimating multiple parameters, there exist combined estimators more accurate on average than any method that handles the parameters separately. In the case of A/B tests, this means that the true effect of any one experiment can benefit by including the information from prior tests. Also, while the Null Hypothesis test is proper for testing whether the true effect is below or above zero, it is inconvenient to determine the true effect with respect to a loss/utility function. For our evaluations, we use an empirical Bayesian approach for analysis of large-scale experiments proposed by Guo et al. (2020), that uses the Normal-Normal model to determine the posterior probability of a positive return on a loss metric. Adding a risk buffer, we consider our effect positive if the posterior probability of a positive return, i.e., the treatment metric being greater than the control metric, is > 0.66.

We ran a 14 day A/B test on a popular e-commerce site in a low-resource English-speaking store, using the AL-XMC model trained with purchase data augmented with query reformulations as Treatment and the purchase data alone as Control, and observed a significant improvement in business metrics—Search Click Rate (SCR, the proportion of all searches that have at least one click) and Customer Reformulation Rate (CRR, the proportion of all searches where the customer had to reissue the query with different wording). A reduction in the CRR implies that the search returned relevant products in the first query. Table 3 shows a significant increase in SCR and a significant reduction (probability of positive effect < 0.33) in CRR.

6 Discussion

We compare the generated queries to those transferred by IKT48 and find that only 20k of the reformulated queries were not present in the IKT48 set. This indicates that the T5 model is able to generate high fidelity queries that customers are likely to use. In addition, data augmentation with query reformulations is able to achieve the same results as that with IKT48 with only about a third of the data. Thus, the reformulated queries are able to capture the relevant information of the target locale. Although IKT48 contains nearly the same information as QR, it is also noisier in the sense that it transfers queries that are relevant in the source (high-resource) store but may not be relevant in the target low-resource store. This noise necessitates several times more data to achieve the same performance. Model training with the larger IKT data set takes approximately 4 times as long as training with the query reformulations dataset.

7 Related Work

Data augmentation in the e-commerce space has dealt with reformulating queries in several ways.

Kuzi et al. (2016) expand user queries using semantically similar terms according to a learned embedding space, while Wang et al. (2021) use query annotations to identify words to expand queries. Both methods rely on a large amount of natural query reformulation by users to train their models, which we avoid. Zhang et al. (2015) and Wang and Yang (2015) propose synonym or paraphrase replacement reformulation approaches. The noisiness of these approaches, some of which expect significant context, are a bad fit for the product query use case. Other works that leverage data enhancement via model-based generation include Mao et al. (2021), who augment queries in black-box question answering tasks, Sennrich et al. (2016), who generate bilingual parallel data via backtranslation, and Fadaee et al. (2017) who, similar to us, though in a machine translation context, reformulate training data via language model-based generation, in this case focusing on rare word replacement.

8 Conclusion

In this paper, we have presented a method to augment training data for semantic models in low-resource e-commerce stores. Our method is generic enough to be applied as training data augmentation for any model and does not require transfer from high-resource store data. We have shown that augmenting training data using query reformulations improves upon a baseline store-specific AL-XMC semantic matching model in both offline evaluations as well as online business metrics. Our methods increase the training data of a test low-traffic store from 0.83m to 16.14m, resulting in a quality improvement of 19.57% over the baseline model. We also see a significant boost to business metrics in online A/B tests. Next we will explore similar data augmentation techniques for generating multilingual query reformulations, using the mT5 pretrained model (Xue et al., 2021). In addition to low traffic stores, this technique may even be applied to yet-to-be-launched locales where training data is missing completely, by forming pseudo-queries from product descriptions.

9 Ethics Statement

We have performed our research so far only for the English language. Though we believe that similar results can be obtained for non-English languages we have yet to demonstrate this. We only use query and product interaction data for our work. Any identifiable user information is completely stripped before we can access the data. As our method is ultimately used to retrieve a set of products in an e-commerce store, incorrect predictions will not cause harm to the user besides an unsatisfactory experience.

References

Yong-Yeol Ahn, James P. Bagrow, and Sune Lehmann. 2010. Link communities reveal multiscale complexity in networks. *Nature*, 466(7307):761–764.

Leonid Boytsov and Eric Nyberg. 2020. Flexible retrieval with NMSLIB and FlexNeuART. In *Proceedings of Second Workshop for NLP Open Source Software (NLP-OSS)*, pages 32–43, Online. Association for Computational Linguistics.

Kunal Dahiya, Deepak Saini, Anshul Mittal, Ankush Shaw, Kushal Dave, Akshay Soni, Himanshu Jain, Sumeet Agarwal, and Manik Varma. 2021. Deepxml: A deep extreme multi-label learning framework applied to short text documents. In *Proc. 14th ACM Int'l Conf on Web Search and Data Mining*, WSDM '21, page 31–39.

Marzieh Fadaee, Arianna Bisazza, and Christof Monz. 2017. Data augmentation for low-resource neural machine translation. In *Proceedings of the 55th Annual Meeting of the Association for Computational Linguistics (Volume 2: Short Papers)*, pages 567–573, Vancouver, Canada. Association for Computational Linguistics.

F. Richard Guo, James McQueen, and Thomas S. Richardson. 2020. Empirical bayes for large-scale randomized experiments: a spectral approach. *arXiv: Methodology*.

Po-Sen Huang, Xiaodong He, Jianfeng Gao, Li Deng, Alex Acero, and Larry Heck. 2013. Learning deep structured semantic models for web search using clickthrough data. ACM International Conference on Information and Knowledge Management (CIKM).

Thorsten Joachims, Hang Li, Tie-Yan Liu, and ChengXiang Zhai. 2007. Learning to rank for information retrieval (lr4ir 2007). *SIGIR Forum*, 41(2):58–62.

Saar Kuzi, Anna Shtok, and Oren Kurland. 2016. Query expansion using word embeddings. In *Proceedings of the 25th ACM International on Conference on Information and Knowledge Management*, CIKM '16, page 1929–1932, New York, NY, USA. Association for Computing Machinery.

Kenton Lee, Ming-Wei Chang, and Kristina Toutanova. 2019. Latent retrieval for weakly supervised open domain question answering. In *Proceedings of the 57th Annual Meeting of the Association for Computational Linguistics*, pages 6086–6096, Florence, Italy. Association for Computational Linguistics.

Pedro G. Lind, Marta C. González, and Hans J. Herrmann. 2005. Cycles and clustering in bipartite networks. *Physical Review E*, 72(5).

G. Linden, B. Smith, and J. York. 2003. Amazon.com recommendations: item-to-item collaborative filtering. *IEEE Internet Computing*, 7(1):76–80.

Christopher D. Manning, Prabhakar Raghavan, and Hinriche Schütze. 2008. XML retrieval. In *Introduction to Information Retrieval.* Cambridge University Press.

Yuning Mao, Pengcheng He, Xiaodong Liu, Yelong Shen, Jianfeng Gao, Jiawei Han, and Weizhu Chen. 2021. Generation-augmented retrieval for open-domain question answering. In *Proceedings of the 59th Annual Meeting of the Association for Computational Linguistics and the 11th International Joint Conference on Natural Language Processing (Volume 1: Long Papers)*, pages 4089–4100, Online. Association for Computational Linguistics.

Priyanka Nigam, Yiwei Song, Vijai Mohan, Vihan Lakshman, Weitian (Allen) Ding, Ankit Shingavi, Choon Hui Teo, Hao Gu, and Bing Yin. 2019. Semantic product search. In *Proceedings of the 25th ACM SIGKDD*, KDD '19, page 2876–2885.

Sinno Jialin Pan, Dou Shen, Qiang Yang, and James T. Kwok. 2008. Transferring localization models across space. In *Proceedings of the 23rd National Conference on Artificial Intelligence - Volume 3*, AAAI'08, page 1383–1388. AAAI Press.

Colin Raffel, Noam Shazeer, Adam Roberts, Katherine Lee, Sharan Narang, Michael Matena, Yanqi Zhou, Wei Li, and Peter J. Liu. 2020. Exploring the limits of transfer learning with a unified text-to-text transformer. *Journal of Machine Learning Research*, 21(140):1–67.

S. E. Robertson and S. Walker. 1994. Some simple effective approximations to the 2-poisson model for probabilistic weighted retrieval. In *Proceedings of the 17th Annual International ACM SIGIR Conference on Research and Development in Information Retrieval*, SIGIR '94, page 232–241, Berlin, Heidelberg. Springer-Verlag.

Stephen Robertson and Hugo Zaragoza. 2009. *The probabilistic relevance framework: BM25 and beyond.* Now Publishers Inc.

Rico Sennrich, Barry Haddow, and Alexandra Birch. 2016. Improving neural machine translation models with monolingual data. In *Proceedings of the 54th Annual Meeting of the Association for Computational Linguistics (Volume 1: Long Papers)*, pages 86–96, Berlin, Germany. Association for Computational Linguistics.

Yanyao Shen, Hsiang-fu Yu, Sujay Sanghavi, and Inderjit Dhillon. 2020. Extreme multi-label classification from aggregated labels. In *Proceedings of the 37th International Conference on Machine Learning*, ICML'20. JMLR.org.

Charles Stein. 1956. Inadmissibility of the usual estimator for the mean of a multivariate normal distribution. In *Proceedings of the Third Berkeley Symposium on Mathematical Statistics and Probability, Volume 1: Contributions to the Theory of Statistics*, pages 197–206, Berkeley, Calif. University of California Press.

William Yang Wang and Diyi Yang. 2015. That's so annoying!!!: A lexical and frame-semantic embedding based data augmentation approach to automatic categorization of annoying behaviors using #petpeeve tweets. In *Proceedings of the 2015 Conference on Empirical Methods in Natural Language Processing*, pages 2557–2563, Lisbon, Portugal. Association for Computational Linguistics.

Yaxuan Wang, Hanqing Lu, Yunwen Xu, Rahul Goutam, Yiwei Song, and Bing Yin. 2021. Queen: Neural query rewriting in e-commerce. In *The Web Conference 2021, Workshop on Knowledge Management in E-Commerce.*

Linting Xue, Noah Constant, Adam Roberts, Mihir Kale, Rami Al-Rfou, Aditya Siddhant, Aditya Barua, and Colin Raffel. 2021. mT5: A massively multilingual pre-trained text-to-text transformer. In *Proceedings of the 2021 Conference of the North American Chapter of the Association for Computational Linguistics: Human Language Technologies*, pages 483–498, Online. Association for Computational Linguistics.

Xiang Zhang, Junbo Zhao, and Yann LeCun. 2015. Character-level convolutional networks for text classification. In *Proceedings of the 28th International Conference on Neural Information Processing Systems - Volume 1*, NIPS'15, page 649–657, Cambridge, MA, USA. MIT Press.

Hankui Zhuo, Qiang Yang, Derek Hao Hu, and Lei Li. 2008. Transferring knowledge from another domain for learning action models. In *PRICAI 2008: Trends in Artificial Intelligence*, pages 1110–1115, Berlin, Heidelberg. Springer Berlin Heidelberg.

Retrieval Based Response Letter Generation For a Customer Care Setting

Biplob Biswas[1], Renhao Cui[2], and Rajiv Ramnath[1]
[1]Department of Computer Science and Engineering, The Ohio State University
[2]Emplifi
{biswas.102, ramnath.6}@osu.edu, renhao.cui@emplifi.io

Abstract

Letter-like communications (such as email) are a major means of customer relationship management within customer-facing organizations. These communications are initiated on a channel by requests from customers and then responded to by the organization on the same channel. For decades, the job has almost entirely been conducted by human agents who attempt to provide the most appropriate reaction to the request. Rules have been made to standardize the overall customer service process and make sure the customers receive professional responses. Recent progress in natural language processing has made it possible to automate response generation. However, the diversity and open nature of customer queries and the lack of structured knowledge bases make this task even more challenging than typical task-oriented language generation tasks. Keeping those obstacles in mind, we propose a deep-learning based response letter generation framework that attempts to retrieve knowledge from historical responses and utilize it to generate an appropriate reply. Our model uses data augmentation to address the insufficiency of query-response pairs and employs a ranking mechanism to choose the best response from multiple potential options. We show that our technique outperforms the baselines by significant margins while producing consistent and informative responses.

1 Introduction

In modern business operations, customer care services are essential to support customers needing product information, making complaints, and in general, positively addressing their expectations. This support service plays a vital role in ensuring a good customer experience and is a key factor in developing goodwill. While non-specific, general knowledge about a product can now be conveniently retrieved through a web search, the exchange of specific information naturally entails a conversation between the customer and an agent who represents the organization. Traditionally, this task has been carried out by a trained human through chat or email exchanges. However, doing this manually at scale takes an enormous human effort. The process is time-consuming, labor-intensive and error-prone given the massive volume and diversity of customer queries.

Automation of the response generation process can go a long way toward solving this problem. Unfortunately, the rule-based systems that are in existence today struggle to capture the linguistic complexity of typical communications.

Recently, the advent of transformer-based pre-trained language models such as BERT (Devlin et al., 2019), GPT-2 (Radford et al., 2019), T5 (Raffel et al., 2020) has brought about substantial progress in understanding and generating fluent text. Nevertheless, task-oriented dialog (TOD), a process that aims to assist a user to complete a certain task through response generation, is yet to be mastered due to the challenges in producing text that is informative and relevant to the prompt (Zhang et al., 2019; Ko et al., 2019). The task is especially difficult because of the scarcity of annotated datasets needed to train a supervised model.

Furthermore, creating an effective customer feedback system has additional challenges. In the existing and very popular TOD datasets (Rastogi et al., 2020; Wu, 2019), user utterances are usually fact-finding queries annotated with slot labels (e.g. Query: 'Find a park near area51', Slot-Values: {destination: 'park', close_to: 'area51'}). A TOD framework (Young, 2000) first identifies the slots and then uses the slot-value pairs to retrieve facts from a knowledge base to reply. Unfortunately, these frameworks do not realistically address customer-care automation tasks where neither is the user prompt labeled with slot tags nor is there a knowledge base with relevant facts. Fur-

Proceedings of NAACL-HLT 2022: Industry Track Papers, pages 168 - 175
July 10-15, 2022

thermore, a user prompt may not be limited to an inquiry about facts but may also include a complaint, suggestion, compliment, request, etc.

In this work, we factor in these challenges and present a response generation framework that automatically produces and ranks response letters addressing customers' queries or feedback, with a minimally annotated dataset. The contribution of this work is in two areas:

- We propose a retrieve and refine (Weston et al., 2018) based response generation model that is robust, efficient, and generalizable. A retrieval model fetches required knowledge from previous customer-agent letter exchanges and a generator refines the retrieved information to produce a coherent response tailored to the current context. By using historical knowledge retrieval, the model not only circumvents the requirement for an explicit knowledge base or slot-labeled dataset but can also augment and extend such datasets to enable a more diverse generation. In other words, we offer a practical solution.

- A Maximum Mutual Information (MMI) (Li et al., 2016; Zhang et al., 2018) driven approach to rank responses according to their relevance to the query. We also show that the model's loss function itself can indicate the MMI and save us the time and effort of developing yet another "backward" model (Zhang et al., 2020).

Our response generation framework is to be deployed in production as a part of an evolving pipeline for automating the customer service process. It will initially serve as a suggestion system to collect feedback from real human agents and is then expected to progress to enabling increased levels of automation.

2 Dataset

We use two proprietary datasets from the restaurant and adhesive tape industry, named ***DineCare*** (DC) and ***TapeTech*** (TT), consisting of 8448 and 14938 unique email exchanges between customers and agents respectively. Each exchange contains a case id, product and reason codes of the service, the customer query letter, and the human agent's response letter. Examples are included in Table 3. Both product codes and reason codes are alphanumeric strings defined by the corresponding business

DineCare

Items	Train	Validation	Test	All
Samples	5491	1267	1690	8448
Unique Product Code	257	99	138	308
Unique Reason Code	245	168	185	274
Mean Query Token	54	56	55	55
Mean Response Token	48	47	46	47

TapeTech

Items	Train	Validation	Test	All
Samples	8962	2988	2988	14938
Unique Product Code	656	393	371	851
Unique Reason Code	273	211	219	293
Mean Query Token	49	51	50	49
Mean Response Token	74	76	75	75

Table 1: The statistics for the data samples of the DineCare and TapeTech dataset.

and may lack textual description. The reason code stands for the type of customer query; therefore we observe similar responses across queries having the same reason code.

Data Preparation We mask specific personally identifiable or proprietary information elements such as names, email addresses, phone numbers, prices, franchise names, and dates in our dataset with their corresponding generic tokens ("X-email", "X-phone" etc.). This serves two purposes. Firstly, this anonymization protects the privacy of the customers and the organization. Secondly, it forces the model to learn from and generate generic tags while avoiding noise in the form of irrelevant details such as specific names and values.

The average token count of queries in ***DineCare*** and ***TapeTech*** dataset are 55 and 49 respectively. For responses, the mean token counts of the corresponding datasets are 47 and 75. In both cases of query and response, these values are higher than that of a typical live chat. In terms of the type of the customer letters, 52% of *DC* letters are complaints, 33% are inquiries and the rest are of miscellaneous categories. Furthermore, they involve a diverse set of products (308 in DineCare, 851 in TapeTech) and reasons (274 in DineCare, 293 in TapeTech).

Each dataset is randomly divided into training ($\approx$60%), validation ($\approx$20%) and test ($\approx$20%) sets. A summary of the dataset is presented in Table 1. Although the product and reason codes have a long-tailed distribution, samples involving them are present proportionally in each split. However, a fraction (2.5% in DineCare, 3.6% in TapeTech) of the test set contains product or reason codes that are absent in the training set. We retained them because their use helps us to understand the model's resilience in the event of unknown scenarios.

3 Framework

In this section, we first describe a potential baseline approach for response generation and then the retrieval-guided response generation framework.

3.1 Neural Response Generation

We utilize a pre-trained causal language model, GPT-2 (Radford et al., 2019), to train our baseline response generation model. We approach our goal of producing a response for a customer query as a conditional text generation task and hence adopt the pre-trained GPT-2 model to tune the parameters. Given a customer query letter with a token sequence: $q = (x_1, x_2, ..., x_m)$ where $x_i \in V$ for vocabulary V, product code: $d \in D$ and reason code: $s \in S$, the objective of our model is to generate response token sequence: $r = (y_1, y_2, ..., y_n)$ from the same vocabulary, i.e. $y_i \in V$. To this end, we first formulate the conditional probability of the response token sequence by factorizing the distribution using the chain rule:

$$p(r|q, d, s) = \prod_{i=1}^{n} p(y_i|y_{1:i-1}, q, d, s) \quad (1)$$

Equation 2 gives us the negative log-likelihood $\mathcal{L}(E)$ that we want to minimize over a dataset E with parameters θ.

$$\mathcal{L}(E) = -\sum_{j=1}^{|E|} \log p_\theta(y_i|y_{1:i-1}, q, d, s) \quad (2)$$

3.2 History Guided Generation

The GPT-2 baseline model (above) lacks access to factual information while responding to a query. Therefore, it tends to make up a safe or hallucinated reply. For instance, in response to a customer's question regarding a restaurant's service availability, the baseline model is seen to generate "don't know" or "open" although the dataset indicates its closure. To address this issue, a *Retrieve and Refine **(RetRef)*** (Weston et al., 2018) mechanism is employed. The idea is to retrieve valid responses for similar queries used in the recent past and utilize those responses in addition to the query to generate a refined and coherent response.

We split the whole task into three steps: 1. Knowledge Retrieval, 2. Response Generation and 3. Response Ranking. The framework is depicted in Figure 1 and detailed in the following subsections.

3.2.1 Knowledge Retrieval

Given a current customer query (q_c), knowledge can be extracted from agents' past responses (r_p) to similar past queries (q_p). To this end, we first select past conversations having the same reason code as the current one. This intuitively works as candidate generation and reduces our search space for potential knowledge. Then we assign a candidate score, $c = sim(q_c, q_p) + bleu(q_c, q_p)$ to these past query-response pairs where $bleu$ is BLEU-1 score between the corresponding queries and $sim(q_c, q_p) = \cos(E_{q_c}, E_{q_p})$, is cosine similarity between the embedding of the current and of the past query respectively. The embeddings are obtained using sentence-transformer (Reimers and Gurevych, 2019) and can be pre-computed to make the retrieval fast. While training, the similarity between the corresponding responses, $sim(r_c, r_p)$ is also added with a weight, $\gamma < 1$ to ensure that the model finds a relation between them to transfer knowledge (note that this response similarity is not used during testing as the reference response is unknown then). For training we choose (all) responses from candidate pairs that have $c > \tau$, where τ is a hyperparameter. Additional potential candidate responses were used to augment the training instances. We explain their use in the next section.

3.2.2 Response Generation

We use the same GPT-2 baseline model for retrieval-based training and generation. However, for the input to this model, a retrieved response is appended to the beginning of the current query (separated by a special token) as shown in the top-right corner of Figure 1. The objective is to teach the model to generate the reference response utilizing the retrieved knowledge in addition to the query.

Since only one retrieved response is used at a time, having more than one above the threshold ($c > \tau$) allows us to create more training instances with the same query-reference response pair (see Figure 1). In the absence of suitable retrievals, the reference itself is used as a retrieved response to make the model mirror the fetched response.

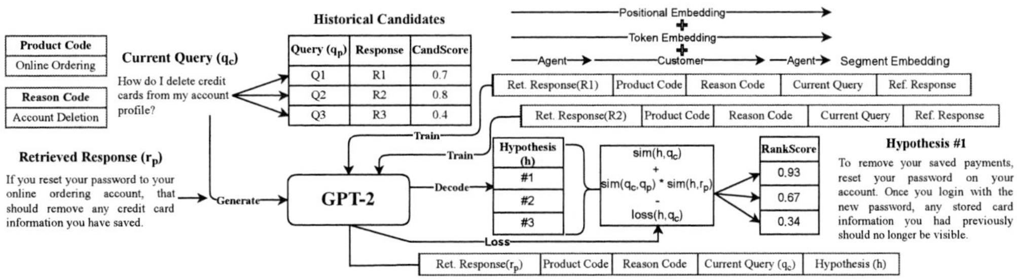

Figure 1: The proposed retrieval based response generation framework.

This technique works like teacher forcing and is intended to avoid ignoring retrievals (as reported in Roller et al. (2021)). In the event of such a scenario during testing, we resort to the baseline model for a generation. We term this mix-model approach ***hybrid*** generation.

Moving on to prompt formation, it has three segments: the retrieved responses from the agent, the current query from the customer followed by the reference response from the agent. Even though the source request and response components are separated by a special token, a model does not have an idea of the author of a token. To address this, we add a segment embedding to the token embedding. The way positional embedding helps the model understand the relative position of the tokens, a segment embedding of the corresponding author is similarly reported to add more meaning to the model (Wolf et al., 2020).

3.3 Response Ranking

Even with the state-of-the-art decoding mechanisms, neural text generation is known to suffer from blandness or inconsistency (Zhang et al., 2019; Ko et al., 2019). Hence, we generate multiple responses using different sampling methods (e.g. top-k, nucleus, etc.) and employ a ranking mechanism to measure the context-awareness of generated responses (by evaluating them as hypotheses of the source query).

Such a hypothesis would indicate stronger correspondence when its probability of producing the query i.e. $p(query|hypothesis)$ is higher. To measure this probability, following the work of DialoGPT (Zhang et al., 2020), we trained an inverse model that considers the reference response as the input and the customer letter as the output. The loss of the model for a pair of queries and hypotheses was used to estimate the $p(query|hypothesis)$ score. The intuition is that a trivial and safe response is likely to appear frequently in different contexts and would usually contain less specific words, causing the inverse model to struggle to retrieve the source query from it, thus resulting in a higher loss. However, comparing the original model loss ($loss(h, q_c)$) with the inverse model loss for each query(q_c)-hypothesis(h) pair, we interestingly found a very high correlation between them. It indicates that we can avoid training an additional inverse model and perform the ranking process using forward loss only.

The final rank score of a hypothesis is computed using the following formula:

$$r_h = sim(h, q_c) - loss(h, q_c) + sim(q_c, q_p) * sim(h, r_p) \quad (3)$$

where $sim(h, q_c)$ indicates similarity between query and hypothesis and $sim(q_c, q_p) * sim(h, r_p)$ takes into account the correspondence between retrieved response(r_p) and hypothesis(h) weighted by the query similarity($sim(q_c, q_p)$). The rationale behind the last product is: a generation that retains knowledge from a good retrieval is likely to offer a better response. Consequently, a higher rank score is expected to indicate better hypothesis quality.

4 Experiment Details

We used a small GPT-2 model of 124M parameters provided by Huggingface (Wolf et al., 2020). Grid search was used to tune the hyper-parameters to the following set of optimal values: {Weight Decay: 0.1, Warm-up steps: 1E2, Gradient Accumulation Steps: 16, Learning rate: 5E-4, Dropout rate: 0.1, Epoch: 5, optimizer: Adam, $\gamma = 0.4$, $\tau = 0.6$}. The training took around 1 hour for the DC dataset and 2.5 hours for the TT dataset on an NVIDIA Tesla V100-SXM2-16GB (GPU device). After training, 4 responses were generated for each query using 4 decoding combinations: 1. (top-k with temperature), 2. (top-p with temperature),

	DineCare						TapeTech					
Method	**S**	**B**	**N**	**M**	**R**	**C**	**S**	**B**	**N**	**M**	**R**	**C**
Baseline	0.59	0.36	4.33	0.25	0.39	2.22	0.84	0.56	6.51	0.38	0.66	3.59
Retrieve Only	0.63	0.34	4.27	0.24	0.38	2.11	0.84	0.53	6.45	0.36	0.64	3.47
RetRef	0.64	0.39	4.57	0.27	0.43	2.50	0.85	0.58	6.75	0.39	0.67	3.82
RetRef+Rank	**0.68±0.02**	**0.40±0.01**	**4.72±0.06**	**0.30±0.02**	**0.47±0.03**	**2.83±0.07**	**0.86±0.01**	**0.61±0.03**	**6.96±0.11**	**0.41±0.01**	**0.69±0.02**	**4.00±0.14**
Hybrid	0.62	0.39	4.51	0.27	0.42	2.43	0.84	0.56	6.61	0.38	0.65	3.58
Hybrid+Rank	0.67	0.40	4.62	0.30	0.46	2.73	0.85	0.59	6.79	0.40	0.67	3.72

Table 2: Test set results of the proposed response generation model on DineCare and TapeTech dataset. Baseline (§3.1) refers to fine-tuned GPT-2 model without knowledge retrieval. Automatic scoring metrics are: Average-SentenceSimilarity (**S**), BLEU-4 (**B**), NIST (**N**), METEOR (**M**), ROUGE-L (**R**) and CIDEr (**C**). Our best model's (*RetRef+Rank*) scores are averaged over 5 runs and have low standard deviation.

3. (top-k,top-p) and 4. (top-k,top-p with temperature) where k=20, p=0.8 and temperature=0.7. For preprocessing and evaluation, we use NLTK and nlg-eval (Sharma et al., 2017).

5 Evaluation

5.1 Retrieval Performance

A higher similarity between retrieved and reference response indicates a better retrieval. Our analysis finds that for 46% of 8382 queries, our retrieval model fetches at least one reference-like (similarity > 0.9) historical response within the top-10 candidates of each retrieval. Within top-5 and top-1 candidates, a retrieval with the above similarity is found in 38% and 21% cases respectively. Our manual evaluation on randomly sampled retrievals finds 49% of the retrieved responses suitable for generation and 20% as somewhat relevant. In the case of retrieval speed, with the pre-computed embeddings of 8448 records, it takes around 70 milliseconds using the aforementioned hardware (in §4) to fetch top-10 candidates of a query from the entire set.

5.2 Generation Quality

The automatic evaluation of all the methods is conducted on the held-out test set with the optimal hyper-parameter setting. The scores are listed in Table 2. Once again, note that the baseline model (§3.1) is a fine-tuned GPT-2 without retrieval and does not employ response ranking. For *Retrieve Only* method we consider only the fetched historical response (without refinement) as a hypothesis. For baseline, *RetRef*, and *Hybrid* method, we consider single hypothesis per query that is produced using the 4th decoding setup (top-k,top-p with temperature) because its corpus-level score is better than other combinations. In ranking enforced versions of *RetRef* and *Hybrid*, for each query, we generate multiple responses using the aforementioned four decoding combinations (§4) and pick one with the highest rank score as the hypothesis for evaluation.

To assess our model, we utilize commonly used metrics such as BLEU (Papineni et al., 2002), NIST (Doddington, 2002), METEOR (Lavie and Agarwal, 2007), ROUGE-L (Lin, 2004), CIDEr (Vedantam et al., 2015) and Average Sentence Similarity. The last metric is our measure of semantic similarity between reference response and hypothesis. For this measure, we use sentence-BERT (Reimers and Gurevych, 2019), a trained Siamese BERT-network to encode a reference and a hypothesis, and then calculate the cosine similarity of the resulting embeddings. The final similarity score is the mean value over the test set.

For both the datasets, our proposed retrieval-based response generation model (*RetRef+Rank*) outperforms all other baselines in all the metrics. Specifically, for *DineCare*, it achieves an improvement over the finetuned GPT-2 baseline model by 15.3% in similarity, 11.1% in BLEU-4, 9% in NIST, 20% in METEOR, 20.5% in Rouge-L and 27.5% in CIDEr. The performance increase with *TapeTech* dataset are 2.4%, 8.9%, 6.9%, 7.9%, 4.5% and 11.4% for the same order of metrics. Knowledge retrieval plays a key role in this rise. On the other hand, without refinement, *Retrieve only* approach yields the worst scores. *Hybrid* version can switch between the baseline and *RetRef* based on the availability of suitable retrieved responses. It was evaluated by including such test cases, and outperformed the baseline model by a significant margin across all metrics and datasets.

To measure the extent to which our model incorporates a retrieved knowledge in the generation, we

Label	Source	Text
DC#1 Inquiry	**Metadata**	Product Code: SERVICE RELATED, Reason Code: GC - PROMO - I
	Input	I just signed up for X-org this morning and have not received my coupon for free pancakes yet. When will I receive it?
	Reference	After signing up, it may take up to 24 hours to receive your initial offer.
	Our model	The day you sign up to create an account, you will be receiving your first email within 24 hours.
DC#2 Suggestion	**Metadata**	Product Code: SERVICE RELATED, Reason Code: OLO - SUGGESTION
	Input	I love your bourbon street foods. ... when ordering online it does not give much options to customize. ... Please try and correct this.
	Reference	We are glad that you suggested these changes to our site! This feedback has been shared with our X-org Online Ordering team.
	Our model	We love hearing from our passionate fans about ways to improve our online ordering. Comments like yours are made available to our Digital Operations team for consideration in future releases. Thank you for your suggestion.
DC#3 Complaint	**Metadata**	Product Code: SERVICE RELATED, Reason Code: GCARD - ORDER - C
	Input	I ordered the X-money gift card today but the 2 X-money bonus cards are not on the invoice or included.
	Reference	We are sorry you did not receive your 2 bonus cards. To make up for this, we will be sending you a X-money digital gift card that you will receive in a separate e-mail.
	Our model	We are sorry to hear you did not receive your bonus card. We will be sending you a X-money digital gift card that you will use on your next visit. You should receive it in a separate e-mail.
TT#4 Inquiry	**Metadata**	Product Code: 31714, Reason Code: USAPPLIC
	Input	I am looking for a duct tape to repair my pontoon boat cover. What tape would you suggest and where can I purchase it from?
	Reference	For your application, we would recommend our T-Rex Waterproof Tape. It is available at X-url; here is the link: X-url.
	Our model	T-Rex Waterproofing Tape would probably be best. You may also find it online on X-url, X-url.
TT#5 Inquiry	**Metadata**	Product Code: L134-P5, Reason Code: GNINGRED
	Input	Can you tell me if your Smooth Top Easy Liner Brand Shelf Liner - Grey Damask contains PVC?
	Reference	The smooth top easy liner is made of PVC coated polyester. Thank you for your inquiry.
	Our model	Our shelf liner is made of PVC coated polyester. Thank you for your inquiry.

Table 3: Sample response generation using our *RetRef+Rank* model

leverage previous work (Weston et al., 2018). Table 4 reports the word-overlap between generated and retrieved responses. For baseline method, overlap is computed between generated and reference response. The results show that our *RetRef+Rank* model retained >70% words from retrieval in 51% and 57% of the test generation of *DineCare* and *TapeTech* dataset respectively. This is a clear improvement over the baseline and the basic *RetRef* model which shows such overlap less frequently.

Human Evaluation Three experts in the field manually assessed the relevance and informativeness of small-scale, randomly selected hypotheses. Relevance measures if a generated response is based on the corresponding product and reason whereas informativeness checks for its information consistency with respect to the reference response (Both scored out of 5). The result shows that responses produced by our *RetRef+Rank* model yield roughly 9% higher relevance (4.05 for DineCare, 4.49 for TapeTech) and 12% better informativeness (3.75 for DineCare, 4.24 for TapeTech) score than the baseline model, and for both the datasets.

5.3 Ablation Study

Apart from the inclusion of retrieved knowledge, two other notable contributors to the performance of the framework are data augmentation and response ranking. Our experiments reveal that the creation of more training instances with multiple candidate responses increases the automatic score by 12% in BLEU-4, 6% in CIDEr, and roughly 2% in other metrics. The role of ranking is also evident from the significant raise of *RetRef+Rank* and *Hybrid+Rank* model score from their base version as shown in Table 2. This can be attributed to the ranker's policy to penalize irrelevant generation while favoring the one that integrates quality retrieval.

	DineCare			TapeTech		
Method	**<30%**	**30-70%**	**>70%**	**<30%**	**30-70%**	**>70%**
Baseline	48%	12%	40%	23%	27%	50%
Retref	42%	12%	46%	21%	25%	54%
RetRef+Rank	34%	15%	51%	17%	26%	57%

Table 4: Word overlap between retrieved and generated response.

5.4 Generation Examples and Discussion

Table 3 shows a few randomly selected generations from both datasets. It suggests that our model's responses are aligned with the type of the customer letter. For instance, letters of type inquiry (DC#1, TT#4, TT#5), suggestion (DC#2), and complaint (DC#3) are responded to accordingly with information, appreciation, and clarification. Secondly, having historical knowledge, our model is not only capable of producing an informed response but also refines that according to the query (DC#1). A few limitations of our model include its inability to verify time-sensitive historical information and handling multiple questions in the same letter. Additionally, any automated offer of a coupon (As shown in DC#3) or other follow-up commitment may put the company at risk. To resolve these issues, a risk or confidence measuring system can be introduced based on which human inspection may be sought before a response is dispatched. We leave this as future work.

6 Related Work

Research in machine-generated response systems originated at least four decades ago. At the end of the last century, Young (2000) introduced a concept of utterance recognizer and response generator for task-oriented dialog (TOD) systems. The past few years have witnessed several response generation models, particularly using neural approaches to conversational AI. Recently, combining the idea of GPT (Radford et al., 2018) and transfer-learning based training scheme, Wolf et al. (2020) produced improved dialog systems. Similarly, Zhang et al. (2020) presented DialoGPT, a tunable large-scale conversational response generation model based on GPT-2 (Radford et al., 2019). For TOD system, Kale and Rastogi (2020) and Du et al. (2020) proposed schema and template guided generation respectively which use slot-value tagged knowledge representations as input. Lately, several works (Weston et al., 2018; Roller et al., 2021; Kim et al., 2020; Lewis et al., 2020) have put forward a retrieve and refine approach to combine plain-text knowledge in conversational response generation. These works have inspired us to adopt similar generation ideas for our task.

7 Conclusion

The study proposes a neural response generation framework to reduce human labor in a real-world customer care setting, where a structured knowledge base is scarce. Our framework extracts knowledge from historical records of conversations to generate an informative response. Our evaluation shows the efficacy of the ranking system and provides evidence for the operational applicability of the framework. We plan to extend the framework with a response validation module for further improvement.

Acknowledgements

We would like to thank all the reviewers for their helpful comments. We are also grateful to Emplifi for their generous support of this research.

References

Jacob Devlin, Ming-Wei Chang, Kenton Lee, and Kristina Toutanova. 2019. BERT: pre-training of deep bidirectional transformers for language understanding. In *Proceedings of NAACL-HLT*, pages 4171–4186.

George Doddington. 2002. Automatic evaluation of machine translation quality using n-gram co-occurrence statistics. In *Proceedings of HLTR*, HLT '02, page 138–145.

Yuheng Du, Shereen Oraby, Vittorio Perera, Minmin Shen, Anjali Narayan-Chen, Tagyoung Chung, Anushree Venkatesh, and Dilek Hakkani-Tur. 2020. Schema-guided natural language generation. In *Proceedings of the 13th International Conference on NLG*, pages 283–295.

Mihir Kale and Abhinav Rastogi. 2020. Template guided text generation for task-oriented dialogue. In *Proceedings of EMNLP*, pages 6505–6520, Online. ACL.

Seokhwan Kim, Mihail Eric, Karthik Gopalakrishnan, Behnam Hedayatnia, Yang Liu, and Dilek Hakkani-Tur. 2020. Beyond domain APIs: Task-oriented conversational modeling with unstructured knowledge access. In *Proceedings of the 21th Annual Meeting of the Special Interest Group on Discourse and Dialogue*, pages 278–289, 1st virtual meeting. Association for Computational Linguistics.

Wei-Jen Ko, Greg Durrett, and Junyi Jessy Li. 2019. Linguistically-informed specificity and semantic plausibility for dialogue generation. In *Proceedings of NAACL-HLT*, pages 3456–3466.

Alon Lavie and Abhaya Agarwal. 2007. Meteor: An automatic metric for mt evaluation with high levels of correlation with human judgments. In *Proceedings of SMT*, StatMT '07, page 228–231.

Patrick Lewis, Ethan Perez, Aleksandra Piktus, Fabio Petroni, Vladimir Karpukhin, Naman Goyal, Heinrich Küttler, Mike Lewis, Wen-tau Yih, Tim Rocktäschel, Sebastian Riedel, and Douwe Kiela. 2020. Retrieval-augmented generation for knowledge-intensive nlp tasks. In *Advances in Neural Information Processing Systems*, volume 33, pages 9459–9474. Curran Associates, Inc.

Jiwei Li, Michel Galley, Chris Brockett, Jianfeng Gao, and Bill Dolan. 2016. A diversity-promoting objective function for neural conversation models. In *Proceedings of NAACL-HLT*, pages 110–119. Association for Computational Linguistics.

Chin-Yew Lin. 2004. ROUGE: A package for automatic evaluation of summaries. In *Text Summarization Branches Out*, pages 74–81, Barcelona, Spain. ACL.

Kishore Papineni, Salim Roukos, Todd Ward, and Wei-Jing Zhu. 2002. Bleu: a method for automatic evaluation of machine translation. In *Proceedings of ACL*, pages 311–318, Philadelphia, Pennsylvania, USA. ACL.

Alec Radford, Karthik Narasimhan, Tim Salimans, and Ilya Sutskever. 2018. Improving language understanding by generative pre-training.

Alec Radford, Jeffrey Wu, Rewon Child, David Luan, Dario Amodei, Ilya Sutskever, et al. 2019. Language models are unsupervised multitask learners. *OpenAI blog*, 1(8):9.

Colin Raffel, Noam Shazeer, Adam Roberts, Katherine Lee, Sharan Narang, Michael Matena, Yanqi Zhou, Wei Li, and Peter J. Liu. 2020. Exploring the limits of transfer learning with a unified text-to-text transformer. *Journal of Machine Learning Research*, 21(140):1–67.

Abhinav Rastogi, Xiaoxue Zang, Srinivas Sunkara, Raghav Gupta, and Pranav Khaitan. 2020. Schema-guided dialogue state tracking task at dstc8.

Nils Reimers and Iryna Gurevych. 2019. Sentence-bert: Sentence embeddings using siamese bert-networks. *arXiv preprint arXiv:1908.10084*.

Stephen Roller, Emily Dinan, Naman Goyal, Da Ju, Mary Williamson, Yinhan Liu, Jing Xu, Myle Ott, Eric Michael Smith, Y-Lan Boureau, and Jason Weston. 2021. Recipes for building an open-domain chatbot. In *Proceedings of the 16th Conference of the European Chapter of the Association for Computational Linguistics: Main Volume*, pages 300–325, Online. Association for Computational Linguistics.

Shikhar Sharma, Layla El Asri, Hannes Schulz, and Jeremie Zumer. 2017. Relevance of unsupervised metrics in task-oriented dialogue for evaluating natural language generation. *CoRR*, abs/1706.09799.

Ramakrishna Vedantam, C. Lawrence Zitnick, and Devi Parikh. 2015. Cider: Consensus-based image description evaluation. In *2015 IEEE Conference on Computer Vision and Pattern Recognition (CVPR)*, pages 4566–4575.

Jason Weston, Emily Dinan, and Alexander Miller. 2018. Retrieve and refine: Improved sequence generation models for dialogue. In *Proceedings of the 2018 EMNLP Workshop SCAI: The 2nd International Workshop on Search-Oriented Conversational AI*, pages 87–92, Brussels, Belgium. Association for Computational Linguistics.

Thomas Wolf, Lysandre Debut, Victor Sanh, Julien Chaumond, Clement Delangue, Anthony Moi, Pierric Cistac, Tim Rault, Rémi Louf, Morgan Funtowicz, Joe Davison, Sam Shleifer, Patrick von Platen, Clara Ma, Yacine Jernite, Julien Plu, Canwen Xu, Teven Le Scao, Sylvain Gugger, Mariama Drame, Quentin Lhoest, and Alexander M. Rush. 2020. Transformers: State-of-the-art natural language processing. In *Proceedings of EMNLP*, pages 38–45.

Chien-Sheng Wu. 2019. Learning to memorize in neural task-oriented dialogue systems.

Steve Young. 2000. Probabilistic methods in spoken dialogue systems. *Philosophical Transactions of the Royal Society A: Mathematical, Physical and Engineering Sciences*, 358.

Yizhe Zhang, Michel Galley, Jianfeng Gao, Zhe Gan, Xiujun Li, Chris Brockett, and Bill Dolan. 2018. Generating informative and diverse conversational responses via adversarial information maximization. In *Proceedings of NeurIPS*, NIPS'18, page 1815–1825.

Yizhe Zhang, Xiang Gao, Sungjin Lee, Chris Brockett, Michel Galley, Jianfeng Gao, and Bill Dolan. 2019. Consistent dialogue generation with self-supervised feature learning. *arXiv preprint arXiv:1903.05759*.

Yizhe Zhang, Siqi Sun, Michel Galley, Yen-Chun Chen, Chris Brockett, Xiang Gao, Jianfeng Gao, Jingjing Liu, and Bill Dolan. 2020. DIALOGPT : Large-scale generative pre-training for conversational response generation. In *Proceedings of ACL*, pages 270–278.

Medical Coding with Biomedical Transformer Ensembles and Zero/Few-shot Learning

Angelo Ziletti* Bayer AG angelo.ziletti@bayer.com

Alan Akbik Humboldt University

Christoph Berns Bayer AG

Thomas Herold areto consulting Gmbh

Marion Legler Bayer AG

Martina Viell Bayer AG

Abstract

Medical coding (MC) is an essential prerequisite for reliable data retrieval and reporting. Given a free-text *reported term* (RT) such as "pain of right thigh to the knee", the task is to identify the matching *lowest-level term* (LLT) –in this case "unilateral leg pain"– from a very large and continuously growing repository of standardized medical terms. However, automating this task is challenging due to a large number of LLT codes (as of writing over 80 000), limited availability of training data for long tail/emerging classes, and the general high accuracy demands of the medical domain. With this paper, we introduce the MC task, discuss its challenges, and present a novel approach called xTARS that combines traditional BERT-based classification with a recent zero/few-shot learning approach (TARS). We present extensive experiments that show that our combined approach outperforms strong baselines, especially in the few-shot regime. The approach is developed and deployed at Bayer, live since November 2021. As we believe our approach potentially promising beyond MC, and to ensure reproducibility, we release the code to the research community.

1 Introduction

Medical coding (MC) is the process of classifying textual descriptions of medical events into standardized alphanumerical terms and codes. An example textual description is "pain of right thigh to the knee" that would need to be classified as an instance of "unilateral leg pain" in the MedDRA (MSSO, Retrieved Jun 24, 2021) ontology (see Table 1 for more examples).

MC allows the consistent documentation of medical records, enabling the analysis of clinical trials, for example facilitating safety data retrieval or detection of adverse drug reactions. Medical codes are also used by health plan, medical billing, and health care providers to make decisions for example about prior authorization requests and claims, impacting how much a patient will pay for medical care in some countries. At Bayer, around 55 000 terms per month need to be manually coded via a "four-eye concept" (proposing/accepting) by highly specialized medical coders, a costly process we seek to (partially) automate.

Problem Statement. However, automating MC faces several challenges: First, the number of target classes is very large and continuously growing, with over 80 000 as of writing. Second, available training data is limited and imbalanced, with few training examples in particular available for long tail and emerging classes. Third, language is non-canonical and domain-specific, with frequent misspellings, non-standard abbreviations, irrelevant text, and specialized vocabulary. Forth, as is standard in the medical domain, very high accuracy requirements apply (see Section 2).

Conceptually, this task may be phrased in two ways: (1) as a standard large-scale multiclass classification task that takes as input a reported term and outputs a distribution over all classes (Chalkidis et al., 2020), or (2) as a matching task that takes as input both a reported term and a candidate class label and makes a binary prediction whether the class matches the term. The latter allows the model to leverage additional information conveyed by the natural language class labels (i.e. allowing the model to learn that the semantics of the class description "unilateral leg pain" and the text "pain of right thigh to the knee" overlap) and has thus been shown work well in few-shot learning set-

Proceedings of NAACL-HLT 2022: Industry Track Papers, pages 176 - 187
July 10-15, 2022 ©2022 Association for Computational Linguistics

Reported term (RT)	Lowest level term (LLT) name	Preferred term (PT) name
on and off lethargy	lethargy	lethargy
scattered indeterminate subcentimeter pulmonary nodules	lung nodule	pulmonary mass
ckd-unknown etiology	chronic kidney disease	chronic kidney disease
elective left fem-pop bypass graft	femoropopliteal artery bypass	peripheral artery bypass
osteomyelitis of the left metatarsal	osteomyelitis of the foot	osteomyelitis
right foot second toe gangrene	gangrene toe	gangrene
worsenin renal function	renal function aggravated	renal impairment
oliguric acute kidney injury/ckd	acute oliguric renal failure	acute kidney injury
urinary tract infection [enterobacter cloacae]	urinary tract infection bacterial	urinary tract infection bacterial
skin defect [no split]	skin disorder	skin disorder
haemangioma th12	spinal haemangioma	haemangioma of bone
pain of right thigh to the knee	unilateral leg pain	pain in extremity

Table 1: Sample medical coding data. *Reported terms* (RT) are short, free-form medical event descriptions that need to be classified into the most suitable *lowest level term* (LLT), from a total of over 80 000 standardized LLTs. Each LLT belongs to a *preferred term* (PT), i.e. a less granular category of classes. For instance "cdk-unknown etiology" should be normalized to "chronic kidney disease".

tings (Halder et al., 2020). It suffers however from scalability issues that prevent practical application to large-scale classification problems.

Contributions. With this paper, we present a novel approach that addresses the above challenges by integrating a classic BERT-based classification approach (Devlin et al., 2019) into a recently proposed few-shot classification approach (Halder et al., 2020). The main idea is to leverage a standard classifier to predict a set of candidate labels which are then separately evaluated by the few-shot learner. We argue that this architecture allows both components to leverage their respective strengths. To summarize, our contributions are as follows:

- We present and discuss the MC task, and discuss its challenges in particular with regards to industry application.
- We present a novel and straightforward approach called XTARS(eXtreme Task-Aware Representation of Sentences) to address this task by combining strengths of large-scale classification and few-shot learning.
- We conduct an extensive experimental evaluation that shows that our proposed approach outperforms very strong baselines. We also evaluate ensemble learning setups and discus results in different confidence brackets.
- Since we believe this approach to be useful beyond the task of MC, and to ensure reproducibility, we make available our implementation to the research community.[1]

The presented approach is deployed since November 2021 at Bayer and is used to generate coding proposals for all clinical trial studies running at the time of writing.

2 Task and Data Sources

The MC input is the textual description of a medical event, known as *reported term* (RT). The goal of MC is to associate a given RT to the most appropriate term from a given ontology.

2.1 MedDRA as target ontology

We leverage the MedDRA (MSSO, Retrieved Jun 24, 2021) ontology, which is organized in a multi-level hierarchy with coarse- and fine-grained classes. The more fine-grained level of the hierarchy is the *lowest level term* (LLT), of which approximately 80 000 distinct classes exist as of writing. A more coarse-grained level is the *preferred term* (PT), of which approximately 26 000 currently exist in MedDRA. Table 1 shows a number of examples for RTs and their corresponding MedDRA LLT and PT names.

MedDRA undergoes frequent releases that include changes to the number of classes or their definitions. As we are required to always use the most current version of MedDRA, our approach needs to be robust with regards to such changes.

[1] `https://github.com/Bayer-Group/xtars-naacl2022`

Data	# of samples	# of classes	samples from classes with ≤10 samples (%, label cardinality)	samples from classes with ≤5 samples (%, label cardinality)
All	293 645	26 893	21.0% 4.96	12.2% 2.81
Train+Val	285 070	26 692	21.1% 4.95	12.3% 2.81
Test (all)	8 575	4 436	18.0% 5.06	10.0% 2.80
Test (top-80%)	6 860	3 495	12.7% 5.84	5.5% 3.11
Test (btm-50%)	4 287	3 126	29.5% 4.71	18.0% 2.72
Test (btm-25%)	1 715	1 455	39.1% 4.05	28.0% 2.55

Table 2: Summary statistics of the medical coding dataset comprising coded and autocoded data, and company synonyms. Augmented data is excluded. Uncertainty from one PubMedBERT model is used for test set splits.

2.2 Training data

We use a number of proprietary data sources to train and evaluate our proposed approach. The first is *coded data*, which are RTs manually linked to LLTs by human experts. The second is *autocoded data* where a simple rule-based system automatically linked those RTs which either are or contain an LLT verbatim. The system has high precision but low recall, with the majority of samples (∼55%) out of autocoder scope, and passed to humans for manual coding. In addition, we use a dataset of *company synonyms* consisting of pairs of medical text descriptions and corresponding LLT. These synonyms are created and maintained by the company MC department. These synonyms define concepts that are more specific than LLTs.

Final training dataset (Table 2). We collect data from these sources for all Bayer active clinical trials as of October 2021. Data processing and augmentation steps are outlined in the Appendix. The final dataset is split into training, validation and test splits.

Summary statistics are presented in Table 2. We observe that in the entire training data set, only 26 893 classes are observed, meaning that a significant portion of MedDRA LLT codes have no training data at all. We further note a significant data imbalance: among the observed classes, 21 187 (78%) have less than 10 samples, with roughly 21% of all samples coming from those classes. We split the test data into three distinct splits that have different uncertainty, as quantified by the predictive entropy (see Section 4.1). Top-80% indicates the 80% more certain data from the test set while btm-50% and btm-25% contain the least certain 50% and 25% of the test set respectively.

3 Method

We frame the MC task as multiclass classification, where each LLT name is treated as a distinct class. Since each LLT belongs to exactly one PT, the PT is then obtained directly from MedDRA. We therefore disregard the label hierarchy in MedDRA, as this results in a simpler model to train and deploy, and it makes the model less dependent on topological changes of the underlying MedDRA ontology[2].

Method overview. As outlined in Section 1, our approach builds on and combines two existing approaches: (1) a default large-scale multiclass prediction approach based on BERT, and (2) a few-shot classification approach. In this section, we first discuss these two baseline approaches and their advantages and drawbacks (Sections 3.1 and 3.2). We then present our XTARS approach in Section 3.3.

3.1 Baseline 1: Multiclass Classification with BERT Ensembles

Our first baseline follows the standard multiclass classification approach based on BERT (Devlin et al., 2019): we add a single softmax classifier as "prediction head" over the text embedding retrieved from the CLS-token of a pre-trained BERT model. The language model and prediction head are jointly fine-tuned using standard parameters (see Appendix for details) to output a distribution of prediction scores for all classes given a single input text. Such approaches have been applied to large-scale multi-label text classification for biomedical data, showing results comparable to more complex and bespoke approaches (Chalkidis et al., 2020).

Deep ensembles. However, deploying a single model is not advisable for a production setting due to the underspecification problem (D'Amour et al., 2020). Models that perform equally well on their training domain can produce widely different results in their deployment domain, especially under dataset shift. This can result in instabilities when

[2]Moreover, Chalkidis et al. (2020) showed that using label hierarchy information in large-scale multilabel classification is on-par or even inferior to transfer learning approaches.

models are deployed in a real-world setting. This is particularly problematic for MC, where consistency is an essential requirement.

To mitigate the underspecification problem we use deep ensembles (Lakshminarayanan et al., 2017). The main idea is to train different models which only differ by a random perturbation (usually the random seed) and then average across these models to increase prediction stability, and possibly performance. As a further advantage, deep ensembles have also shown to produce reliable uncertainty estimates (Lakshminarayanan et al., 2017; Fort et al., 2020), on par with Bayesian deep learning approaches (Gal and Ghahramani, 2016).

3.2 Baseline 2: TARS Few-Shot Classification

Traditional machine learning algorithms do not have access to the natural language definition of the label, but rather to a discrete representation known as encoding (e.g., one-hot encoding). This representation does not preserve any semantic information present in the natural language definition. As a result, the model can learn the class meaning only indirectly, via the samples associated to a given label during learning.

In the few-shot setting, the lack of label semantic is a clear drawback. Inspired by natural language inference, Task-Aware Representation of Sentences (TARS, Halder et al. (2020)) include label semantic by concatenating the input text (e.g., RT) with labels (e.g., LLT name), and then predicting *True* if the label is the correct one, and *False* otherwise (negative classes or samples). They showed that TARS reaches strong results in few-shot and zero-shot settings, but only evaluated on data sets with comparatively small label sets.

Limitations with regards to medical coding. For MC, TARS is confronted with severe scalability issues due to the very large number of classes in MedDRA: During prediction, a distinct forward pass through the model needs to be made to separately evaluate each label candidate. This procedure requires K predictions, where K is the number of possible labels. When K is very large (e.g., $K \sim 80\,000$ for MC with MedDRA), calculating predictions becomes computationally prohibitive.

In addition, the large-scale classification scenario complicates the training procedure. TARS employs a hard-negative sampling technique to sample a set of neg plausible negatives for each labeled data point, sampling with a probability proportional to the cosine similarity between the correct label and the given label. Since the similarity is used as drawing probability for negative labels, in large-scale classification (as in MC), the model will often see negative labels that are "too easy". This hinders learning with ultra-fine-grained labels.

3.3 Proposed Approach: xTARS

We introduce changes to the TARS algorithm that improve on negative sampling for training, and address the complexity issues during predictions. Our approach leverages a default BERT multiclass classification model (see Section 3.1) that must first be separately trained for MC.

Sampling hard negatives in large label sets. To address the above-mentioned issue on sampling difficult negatives in very large label sets, we propose two sampling techniques that we use jointly. The first leverages predictions from the trained BERT classification model. We use its top-5 predictions (or top-4 if the correct class is in the top-5) as negative samples, as these are hard from the point of view of a fully trained standard model.

The second modifies TARS' cosine similarity-based sampling using top-k and softmax rescaling: After computing label similarities, we extract only the top-k similar classes (out of all K classes) to the correct label, and set all others to zero. We choose k to be three times the number of negative samples to be drawn. Finally, we rescale the top-k similarities via temperature-scaled softmax with temperature T. Low (high) T will result in more peaked (broad) distribution. This procedure improves the quality of negative samples (Table 3, cf. *TARS (neg=10)* and *xTARS (neg=10)*), and it is faster (sampling probability vector of k instead of K dimensions, with $k \ll K$) .

Limiting candidate labels during prediction. We address the scalability issues in prediction by first predicting a multiclass distribution with a default BERT model (or deep ensemble). We select the n top-scoring predictions to be used as label candidates for TARS. Through experimentation, we found a good value of n to be 5. This leads to a four-order of magnitude reduction in computational cost (5 vs 80 000) with only a small decrease in accuracy. The obvious drawback is that xTARS cannot predict correctly if the correct label is not in the top-5 BERT candidates; however, the number of candidates can be increased so that a target cumulative accuracy is reached.

Model	LLT Accuracy [%]				PT accuracy [%]			
	All	top-80%	btm-50%	btm-25%	All	top-80%	btm-50%	btm-25%
PubMedBERT (PMB) (single)	$74.9_{0.5}$	$83.9_{0.3}$	$57.3_{0.9}$	$42.1_{1.4}$	$88.9_{0.2}$	$\mathbf{95.8}_{0.1}$	$79.8_{0.3}$	$66.5_{0.6}$
BioBERT (BB) (single)	$74.9_{0.3}$	$83.7_{0.2}$	$56.9_{0.7}$	$42.6_{1.3}$	$88.8_{0.2}$	$\mathbf{95.8}_{0.2}$	$79.7_{0.3}$	$66.2_{0.5}$
sciBERT (SB) (single)	$74.9_{0.1}$	$83.5_{0.1}$	$57.1_{0.5}$	$43.8_{0.7}$	$88.9_{0.1}$	$\mathbf{95.8}_{0.1}$	$79.8_{0.2}$	$66.7_{0.4}$
TARS (neg=2 cos)	$64.9_{1.2}$	$70.3_{1.4}$	$52.2_{0.9}$	$44.6_{0.6}$	$85.5_{0.4}$	$90.7_{0.5}$	$78.3_{0.1}$	$68.6_{0.3}$
TARS (neg=10 cos)	$62.6_{0.8}$	$67.8_{0.9}$	$50.8_{0.4}$	$43.8_{0.7}$	$85.1_{0.1}$	$90.3_{0.1}$	$78.0_{0.3}$	$68.7_{0.2}$
xTARS (neg=10 cos)	$64.9_{0.9}$	$70.4_{1.1}$	$51.9_{0.8}$	$44.5_{0.5}$	$86.1_{0.4}$	$91.4_{0.4}$	$78.7_{0.4}$	$69.3_{0.3}$
xTARS (neg=top-5)	$76.2_{0.4}$	$83.5_{0.6}$	$61.7_{0.4}$	$51.2_{0.4}$	$89.0_{0.1}$	$94.7_{0.2}$	$81.0_{0.1}$	$70.5_{0.2}$
xTARS (neg=top-5+5 cos)	$77.3_{0.2}$	$84.3_{0.2}$	$63.1_{0.1}$	$52.4_{0.4}$	$89.7_{0.05}$	$95.3_{0.05}$	$82.1_{0.1}$	$71.6_{0.3}$
xTARS (neg=top-5+10 cos)	$76.9_{0.7}$	$84.0_{0.7}$	$62.9_{0.5}$	$52.2_{0.6}$	$89.8_{0.3}$	$95.2_{0.3}$	$82.3_{0.3}$	$72.3_{0.1}$
xTARS (neg=top-5+5 cos; T=1)	$\mathbf{77.5}_{0.3}$	$\mathbf{84.4}_{0.3}$	$\mathbf{63.5}_{0.2}$	$\mathbf{53.5}_{0.2}$	$\mathbf{90.0}_{0.05}$	$95.4_{0.1}$	$\mathbf{82.5}_{0.1}$	$\mathbf{72.4}_{0.1}$
PMB (3 models)	77.8	**85.7**	61.2	49.2	90.6	**96.7**	82.6	71.2
BB (3 models)	**77.9**	85.2	**61.5**	**51.0**	**90.7**	96.5	**83.0**	**72.0**
SB (3 models)	**77.9**	85.3	**61.5**	50.8	90.5	96.3	82.5	70.9
PMB+SB+BB (3×3)	79.7	86.2	64.4	55.4	**91.7**	96.7	84.6	74.9
xTARS (PMB+SB+BB, 3×3)	**80.4**	**86.4**	**64.7**	**56.1**	91.6	**96.8**	**84.8**	**75.5**
PMB+SB+BB (3×5)	80.1	86.3	64.9	56.8	92.0	96.8	85.1	76.2

Table 3: Results on the test set. BERT (TARS and xTARS) models are fine-tuned with five (three) different random seeds: average accuracy and standard deviation are reported. Unless otherwise specified, xTARS and TARS are fine-tuned from PubMedBERT. If not specified, $T = 0.01$. m cos indicates that m negative samples are drawn via the cosine similarity procedure (Sec. 3.3); top-5 means that the top-5 (or top-4, if the correct class is in the top-5) BERT predictions are used as negative samples. xTARS ensemble is performed with xTARS (neg=top-5+5 cos; $T = 1$). In bold the highest accuracy for a fixed number of models (i.e. 1, 3, 9).

4 Evaluation

We evaluate our proposed xTARS approach against strong BERT and TARS baselines, both in single-model and ensemble-model setups common to industrial application. Our evaluation tests all approaches in the large-scale multiclass classification scenario of MC, and evaluates the impact of our proposed negative sampling techniques. We also specifically evaluate performance for certain (top-80%) and uncertain samples (btm-50% and btm-25%). The uncertain splits aim at evaluating performance in the few-shot regime (Table 2)[3].

4.1 Experimental setup

Language models and ensembles. We select the top-scoring pre-trained language models for biomedical tasks from the BLURB leaderboard (Gu et al., 2020), namely bioBERT (Lee et al., 2019), PubMedBERT (Gu et al., 2020), and sciBERT (Beltagy et al., 2019). For each training run, we train multiple models which differ only in the random seed initialization, and then perform model ensembling via averaging their classification probabilities (see Appendix for more details).

Estimation of uncertainty. To obtain principled uncertainty estimates, we utilize the concept of predictive entropy which captures the average amount of information contained in the predictive distribution (Gal and Ghahramani, 2016). The larger (smaller) the predictive entropy, the more uncertain (certain) the prediction is. The maximum of the predictive entropy is attained when all prediction probabilities are equal, while it is zero when one probability is equal to one and all the rest are zero.

4.2 Experimental results

Results for both LLT and PT are shown in Table 3. As expected, accuracy is higher across all experiments for PT than for LLT, and lower for less certain predictions. In more detail, we make the following observations:

Strong single-model performance for xTARS. The top 10 rows in Table 3 list the results for single (e.g. non-ensemble) models. We note that all three BERT models (PubMedBERT, BioBERT, sciBERT) score roughly on-par. TARS underperforms BERT when all samples are considered, especially for LLT; gains are marginal even for very uncertain samples (btm-25%). Inclusion of more negative samples (Table 3, cf. *TARS (neg=10 cos)* vs *TARS (neg=2 cos)*) does not improve results.

Our xTARS models on the other hand for

[3]We split by uncertainty instead of class frequency because the uncertainty estimation is also available at prediction time, i.e. during industrial deployment of the model.

the most part significantly outperform all single-model baselines, reaching an LLT accuracy of 77.5 (↑3.6pp from the best single-model BERT) and a PT accuracy of 90 (↑1.1pp).

Impact of different negative sampling techniques. Further analyzing these results, we find that xTARS top-k and softmax rescaling sampling improves performance over TARS (Table 3, cf. *TARS (neg=10)* and xTARS *(neg=10))*, but only slightly. In contrast, inclusion of negative samples from the trained BERT classification model strongly improves performance (↑11.3pp in LLT accuracy), making xTARS outperform all BERT models in the single-model setting. This indicates that hard negatives are needed to learn effectively with large label sets. Combining these two sampling strategies further improves performance.

Impact of model uncertainty. xTARS improves BERT performance overall, with stronger improvements for uncertain samples (↑9.7pp for btm-25%), which is the few-shot regime (Table 2). It also reduces the standard deviation for uncertain samples, suggesting an increased stability on random seed initialization w.r.t. BERT and TARS models in the few-shot regime.

Ensemble results. Ensembling results in performance gains for all models, with stronger gains observed for BERT over xTARS. Model ensembling improve accuracy overall, including uncertain samples. Ensembling models from the same and different language model are both beneficial. Gains flatten with more models (cf. 3→9 vs 9→15).

5 Discussion and practical deployment

Our experimental evaluation shows that xTARS strongly outperforms all other approaches in the single-model setting, and even slightly outperforms other approaches in the ensemble setting.

For model deployment, however, other practical considerations need to be taken into account than just overall accuracy. One drawback of xTARS is that it requires a fully trained multiclass classification BERT model before the model can be trained. As our setup is a continuously running system, and both MedDRA and our training data are constantly expanded, we implemented an automated system for retraining models in regular intervals. Here, we decided on the BERT ensemble setup (3×5) because of its high accuracy and relatively low complexity.

Human verification in running system. After deployment, we perform back-testing to estimate real-world performance: predictions are compared with the label given by the human coder. For a total of 2 452 predictions from the live system, we found a LLT accuracy of 90.9% with 80.3% coverage.

From an industry perspective, this accuracy significantly improves coding efficiency. Human coders are presented with a system proposal which they can simply accept in many cases, leaving only a small portion of data points in which coders need to manually search for the best matching LLT code. For the top-80% most certain samples, nearly all models meet the regulatory requirements of 95% PT accuracy for MC.

6 Related work

Large-scale text classification. The literature focuses on assigning multiple medical codes to the unstructured portion of electronic health records (patient notes or narratives) (Baumel et al., 2018; Mullenbach et al., 2018; Rios and Kavuluru, 2018; Shi et al., 2017; Xie and Xing, 2018; Kim and Ganapathi, 2021). In our case, however, only text snippets relevant to the coding process (i.e. RT) are gathered during the clinical trial data collection process. Each text snippet must be assigned to a single code.

Zero/few-shot learning. Few-shot learning in NLP has been performed mostly via meta-learning (Finn et al., 2017). Meta-learning has been applied for example in machine translation (Gu et al., 2018), sentiment analysis (Yu et al., 2018), and dialog intent classification (Geng et al., 2019). However, these approaches cannot perform zero-shot predictions. Yin et al. (2019) propose to treat zero/few-shot text classification as a textual entailment problem. The input text acts as premise, and labels are used as hypotheses. Halder et al. (2020) adopt a similar idea. Literature on zero/few-shot learning in large-scale text classification for biomedical data is scarce (Chalkidis et al., 2020; Song et al., 2020).

Deployed systems for medical coding. MagiCoder is a rule-based system (Zorzi et al., 2017; Combi et al., 2019) to obtain medical codes from pharmacovigilance reports that scans the input text for terms matching the ontology, and votes the best match. They achieved an average precision (recall) of 69% (70%) on an adverse drug reaction dataset scraped from social media (Yang et al., 2012).

7 Conclusions

In this paper, we introduced the MC task and discussed its challenges. We outlined a MC system based on biomedical transformers deployed in a production environment, and showed that ensembling improves performance. We introduced xTARS, a zero/few-show learning approach, suitable for classification tasks with very large label sets and long-tailed distribution of labels in data points. The main limitation of xTARS is that it requires a (well-performing) BERT model, thus increasing model complexity. We report promising results for xTARS in MC, and release our code to the research community for application to other tasks.

Acknowledgments

We thank Adrian Wrobel and Christoph Brieden for the connection with the MC platform, Hanna Viol for providing subject matter expertise, Tanja Bellaire for the validation process, and Stefanie Neumann and Tim Disselhoff for project management. Alan Akbik is supported by the Deutsche Forschungsgemeinschaft (DFG, German Research Foundation) under Germany's Excellence Strategy – EXC 2002/1 "Science of Intelligence" (project number 390523135) and the DFG Emmy Noether grant "Eidetic Representations of Natural Language" (project number 448414230).

References

Waleed Ammar, Dirk Groeneveld, Chandra Bhagavatula, Iz Beltagy, Miles Crawford, Doug Downey, Jason Dunkelberger, Ahmed Elgohary, Sergey Feldman, Vu Ha, Rodney Kinney, Sebastian Kohlmeier, Kyle Lo, Tyler Murray, Hsu-Han Ooi, Matthew Peters, Joanna Power, Sam Skjonsberg, Lucy Wang, Chris Wilhelm, Zheng Yuan, Madeleine van Zuylen, and Oren Etzioni. 2018. Construction of the literature graph in semantic scholar. In *Proceedings of the 2018 Conference of the North American Chapter of the Association for Computational Linguistics: Human Language Technologies, Volume 3 (Industry Papers)*, pages 84–91, New Orleans - Louisiana. Association for Computational Linguistics.

Tal Baumel, Jumana Nassour-Kassis, Raphael Cohen, Michael Elhadad, and Noemie Elhadad. 2018. Multi-label classification of patient notes: Case study on icd code assignment. In *AAAI Workshops*, pages 409–416.

Iz Beltagy, Kyle Lo, and Arman Cohan. 2019. SciBERT: A pretrained language model for scientific text. In *Proceedings of the 2019 Conference on Empirical Methods in Natural Language Processing and the 9th International Joint Conference on Natural Language Processing (EMNLP-IJCNLP)*, pages 3615–3620, Hong Kong, China. Association for Computational Linguistics.

Ilias Chalkidis, Manos Fergadiotis, Sotiris Kotitsas, Prodromos Malakasiotis, Nikolaos Aletras, and Ion Androutsopoulos. 2020. An empirical study on large-scale multi-label text classification including few and zero-shot labels. In *Proceedings of the 2020 Conference on Empirical Methods in Natural Language Processing (EMNLP)*, pages 7503–7515, Online. Association for Computational Linguistics.

Carlo Combi, Margherita Zorzi, Gabriele Pozzani, Elena Arzenton, and Ugo Moretti. 2019. Normalizing spontaneous reports into meddra: Some experiments with magicoder. *IEEE Journal of Biomedical and Health Informatics*, 23(1):95–102.

Alexander D'Amour, Katherine A. Heller, Dan Moldovan, Ben Adlam, Babak Alipanahi, Alex Beutel, Christina Chen, Jonathan Deaton, Jacob Eisenstein, Matthew D. Hoffman, Farhad Hormozdiari, Neil Houlsby, Shaobo Hou, Ghassen Jerfel, Alan Karthikesalingam, Mario Lucic, Yi-An Ma, Cory Y. McLean, Diana Mincu, Akinori Mitani, Andrea Montanari, Zachary Nado, Vivek Natarajan, Christopher Nielson, Thomas F. Osborne, Rajiv Raman, Kim Ramasamy, Rory Sayres, Jessica Schrouff, Martin Seneviratne, Shannon Sequeira, Harini Suresh, Victor Veitch, Max Vladymyrov, Xuezhi Wang, Kellie Webster, Steve Yadlowsky, Taedong Yun, Xiaohua Zhai, and D. Sculley. 2020. Underspecification presents challenges for credibility in modern machine learning. *CoRR*, abs/2011.03395.

Jacob Devlin, Ming-Wei Chang, Kenton Lee, and Kristina Toutanova. 2019. BERT: Pre-training of deep bidirectional transformers for language understanding. In *Proceedings of the 2019 Conference of the North American Chapter of the Association for Computational Linguistics: Human Language Technologies, Volume 1 (Long and Short Papers)*, pages 4171–4186, Minneapolis, Minnesota. Association for Computational Linguistics.

Chelsea Finn, Pieter Abbeel, and Sergey Levine. 2017. Model-agnostic meta-learning for fast adaptation of deep networks. In *Proceedings of the 34th International Conference on Machine Learning, ICML 2017, Sydney, NSW, Australia, 6-11 August 2017*, volume 70 of *Proceedings of Machine Learning Research*, pages 1126–1135. PMLR.

Stanislav Fort, Huiyi Hu, and Balaji Lakshminarayanan. 2020. Deep ensembles: A loss landscape perspective.

Yarin Gal and Zoubin Ghahramani. 2016. Dropout as a bayesian approximation: Representing model uncertainty in deep learning. In *Proceedings of the 33nd International Conference on Machine Learning, ICML 2016, New York City, NY, USA, June 19-24,*

2016, volume 48 of *JMLR Workshop and Conference Proceedings*, pages 1050–1059. JMLR.org.

Ruiying Geng, Binhua Li, Yongbin Li, Xiaodan Zhu, Ping Jian, and Jian Sun. 2019. Induction networks for few-shot text classification. In *Proceedings of the 2019 Conference on Empirical Methods in Natural Language Processing and the 9th International Joint Conference on Natural Language Processing (EMNLP-IJCNLP)*, pages 3904–3913, Hong Kong, China. Association for Computational Linguistics.

Jiatao Gu, Yong Wang, Yun Chen, Victor O. K. Li, and Kyunghyun Cho. 2018. Meta-learning for low-resource neural machine translation. In *Proceedings of the 2018 Conference on Empirical Methods in Natural Language Processing*, pages 3622–3631, Brussels, Belgium. Association for Computational Linguistics.

Yu Gu, Robert Tinn, Hao Cheng, Michael Lucas, Naoto Usuyama, Xiaodong Liu, Tristan Naumann, Jianfeng Gao, and Hoifung Poon. 2020. Domain-specific language model pretraining for biomedical natural language processing. *CoRR*, abs/2007.15779.

Kishaloy Halder, Alan Akbik, Josip Krapac, and Roland Vollgraf. 2020. Task-aware representation of sentences for generic text classification. In *Proceedings of the 28th International Conference on Computational Linguistics*, pages 3202–3213, Barcelona, Spain (Online). International Committee on Computational Linguistics.

Byung-Hak Kim and Varun Ganapathi. 2021. Read, attend, and code: Pushing the limits of medical codes prediction from clinical notes by machines. In *Proceedings of the 6th Machine Learning for Healthcare Conference*, volume 149 of *Proceedings of Machine Learning Research*, pages 196–208. PMLR.

Balaji Lakshminarayanan, Alexander Pritzel, and Charles Blundell. 2017. Simple and scalable predictive uncertainty estimation using deep ensembles. In *Advances in Neural Information Processing Systems 30: Annual Conference on Neural Information Processing Systems 2017, December 4-9, 2017, Long Beach, CA, USA*, pages 6402–6413.

Jinhyuk Lee, Wonjin Yoon, Sungdong Kim, Donghyeon Kim, Sunkyu Kim, Chan Ho So, and Jaewoo Kang. 2019. BioBERT: a pre-trained biomedical language representation model for biomedical text mining. *Bioinformatics*, 36(4):1234–1240.

Edward Ma. 2019. Nlp augmentation. https://github.com/makcedward/nlpaug.

MedDRA MSSO. Retrieved Jun 24, 2021. Medical dictionary for regulatory activities.

James Mullenbach, Sarah Wiegreffe, Jon Duke, Jimeng Sun, and Jacob Eisenstein. 2018. Explainable prediction of medical codes from clinical text. In *Proceedings of the 2018 Conference of the North American Chapter of the Association for Computational Linguistics: Human Language Technologies, Volume 1 (Long Papers)*, pages 1101–1111, New Orleans, Louisiana. Association for Computational Linguistics.

Anthony Rios and Ramakanth Kavuluru. 2018. Few-shot and zero-shot multi-label learning for structured label spaces. In *Proceedings of the 2018 Conference on Empirical Methods in Natural Language Processing*, pages 3132–3142, Brussels, Belgium. Association for Computational Linguistics.

D. Sculley, Gary Holt, Daniel Golovin, Eugene Davydov, Todd Phillips, Dietmar Ebner, Vinay Chaudhary, Michael Young, Jean-François Crespo, and Dan Dennison. 2015. Hidden technical debt in machine learning systems. In *Advances in Neural Information Processing Systems 28: Annual Conference on Neural Information Processing Systems 2015, December 7-12, 2015, Montreal, Quebec, Canada*, pages 2503–2511.

Haoran Shi, Pengtao Xie, Zhiting Hu, Ming Zhang, and Eric P. Xing. 2017. Towards automated ICD coding using deep learning. *CoRR*, abs/1711.04075.

Congzheng Song, Shanghang Zhang, Najmeh Sadoughi, Pengtao Xie, and Eric P. Xing. 2020. Generalized zero-shot text classification for ICD coding. In *Proceedings of the Twenty-Ninth International Joint Conference on Artificial Intelligence, IJCAI 2020*, pages 4018–4024. ijcai.org.

Pengtao Xie and Eric Xing. 2018. A neural architecture for automated ICD coding. In *Proceedings of the 56th Annual Meeting of the Association for Computational Linguistics (Volume 1: Long Papers)*, pages 1066–1076, Melbourne, Australia. Association for Computational Linguistics.

Christopher C. Yang, Haodong Yang, Ling Jiang, and Mi Zhang. 2012. Social media mining for drug safety signal detection. In *Proceedings of the 2012 International Workshop on Smart Health and Wellbeing*, SHB '12, page 33–40, New York, NY, USA. Association for Computing Machinery.

Wenpeng Yin, Jamaal Hay, and Dan Roth. 2019. Benchmarking zero-shot text classification: Datasets, evaluation and entailment approach. In *Proceedings of the 2019 Conference on Empirical Methods in Natural Language Processing and the 9th International Joint Conference on Natural Language Processing (EMNLP-IJCNLP)*, pages 3914–3923, Hong Kong, China. Association for Computational Linguistics.

Mo Yu, Xiaoxiao Guo, Jinfeng Yi, Shiyu Chang, Saloni Potdar, Yu Cheng, Gerald Tesauro, Haoyu Wang, and Bowen Zhou. 2018. Diverse few-shot text classification with multiple metrics. In *Proceedings of the 2018 Conference of the North American Chapter of the Association for Computational Linguistics: Human Language Technologies, Volume 1 (Long Papers)*, pages 1206–1215, New Orleans, Louisiana. Association for Computational Linguistics.

Margherita Zorzi, Carlo Combi, Gabriele Pozzani, and Ugo Moretti. 2017. Mapping free text into meddra by natural language processing: A modular approach in designing and evaluating software extensions. In *Proceedings of the 8th ACM International Conference on Bioinformatics, Computational Biology,and Health Informatics*, ACM-BCB '17, page 27–35, New York, NY, USA. Association for Computing Machinery.

A Appendix

A.1 Data processing and augmentation

The proposed algorithm maps *reported terms* (RTs) to lower level terms (LLT) in the MedDRA ontology (see main text). This mapping is already available for the coded and autocoded data, and thus these data sources can be readily used.

Data augmentation. The dataset presents a large amount of rare classes: more than 66% of the LLT classes appear less than five times in the data. To mitigate this problem, for each sample belonging to rare LLTs, we perform data augmentation by generating two simulated samples (one word split and one random character change, see Fig. 1). We define LLTs as rare if they have less than ten samples. Data augmentation is performed with the *nlpaug* package (Ma, 2019).

Data from MedDRA and its augmentation. For the MedDRA ontology, we interpret each LLT as RT. For each LLT in the ontology, we generate three RTs: the LLT verbatim, plus two simulated misspelled entries (one word split and one character change), as depicted in Fig. 1. As label, we use the original LLT. This procedure of adding all possible MedDRA LLT via simulated samples enables the algorithm to make predictions encompassing all possible LLTs, including the ones never encountered in the real (autocoded + coded) data.

Company synonyms. Each company synonym is interpreted as RT, and the pair RT/LLT is added to the dataset. We do not augment synonyms because they are very similar to the corresponding LLT, and the LLTs are already augmented directly from the ontology.

Data preprocessing. Data preprocessing is minimal: everything is lowercased and only unique RTs are kept; if multiple RT/LLT pairs are present, the most recent pair is kept.

Split into training, validation, and test set. The last step is to split the data into training, validation, and test set. The most recent 5% of coded data is used as test set. From the remaining coded data, a randomly sampled 10% of the coded data (excluding data augmentation) is used as validation data. The training data comprises all autocoded data, all RT originating from the ontology, the company synonyms, and the remaining coded data ($\sim$ 85%), plus augmented data. Finally, we remove from the training data the augmented samples if their original sample is included in the validation data. This is done to avoid target leakage due to data augmentation, and enforce the independence of the validation data.

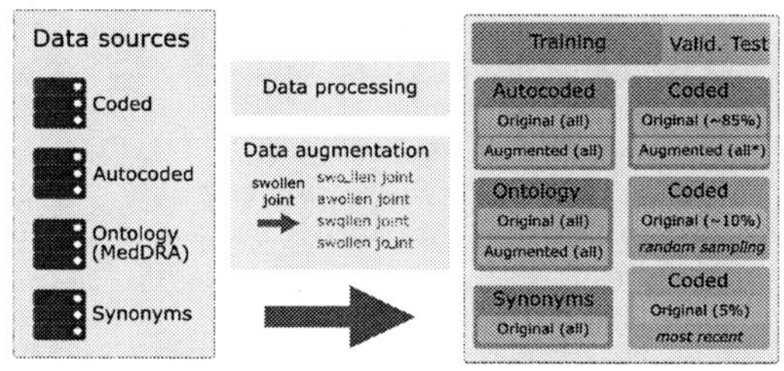

Figure 1: From raw data sources to training, validation, and test data via data processing and data augmentation (BERT models).

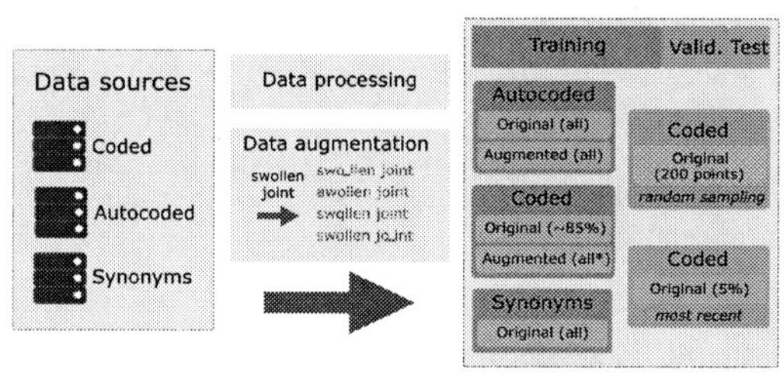

Figure 2: From raw data sources to training, validation, and test data via data processing and data augmentation (TARS and XTARS models). Data coming from the ontology is omitted for computational reasons.

For the XTARS experiments, we train only on coded, autocoded, and synonyms (including augmented data). We omit the ontology data for computational reasons. Still, the XTARS model can in principle predict for all LLTs in MedDRA (including LLTs not included in the training set) because the underlying BERT model is able to propose all LLTs from MedDRA, and the XTARS model is able to make zero-shot predictions. As validation set, we only take 200 samples (instead of the full validation set) because in the current implementation, all possible classes are passed to XTARS for validation during training, resulting in a computational cost of $\sim$ 80 000 prediction for each validation sample. At prediction time, however, only the top-5 candidate classes from the BERT models are passed to XTARS, as outlined in the main text.

A.2 Biomedical language models

From the BLURB leaderboard (Gu et al., 2020), we take the best performing language models for biomedical tasks (as of July 2021):

- **bioBERT**(Lee et al., 2019) is a BERT model trained on a biomedical corpus via a mixed domain pre-training strategy. The starting point is a standard BERT model pretrained on general corpus such as Wikipedia and BookCorpus. From that, the pretraining process is continued using biomedical text, namely PubMed abstracts (PubMed) and PubMedCentral (PMC) full text articles. We use BioBERT v.1.1.

- **PubMedBERT**(Gu et al., 2020) is a BERT model which - in constrast with bioBERT - is pretrained exclusively on biomedical text; specifically, it does not use the BERT weights as initialization, and it builds the vocabulary from scratch based on the biomedical text. The training corpus is also PubMed and PMC. A larger batch size w.r.t. bioBERT (8,192 vs 192) is used in the pretraining process.

- **sciBERT**(Beltagy et al., 2019) is a BERT model which is also pretrained from scratch. Differently from PubMedBERT (and bioBERT), sciBERT is trained on a corpus comprising both computer science (18%) and biomedical papers (82%) from Semantic Scholar (Ammar et al., 2018).

A.3 Details on model training

A.3.1 BERT models

Training is performed on the training set (see Fig. 1) for 20 epochs with Adam optimizer with a learning rate of 1e-4 and batch size of 512. Learning rates of 1e-5 and 5e-5 were also evaluated, but yield a lower performance. The same hyper-parameters are used for each language model. Training a single model takes approximately 7 h on 4 Tesla V100 GPUs. We select the model with the highest accuracy on the validation (holdout) data, and we evaluate the model on the test data.

A.3.2 TARS and xTARS models

Training is performed on the training set (see Fig. 2) for 5 epochs with Adam optimizer with a learning rate of 5e-5 and batch size of 32. Learning rates of 1e-5, 3e-5, 7e-5, and 8e-5 were also evaluated, but yield a lower performance. The same hyper-parameters are used for each language model. Training a single model takes approximately 28 h on 1 Tesla V100 GPUs. We select the model with the highest accuracy on a subset of 200 samples of validation (holdout) data due to computational cost. We evaluate the model on the test data.

A.4 Results on the test set, split by class frequency

Results split by class frequency are presented in Table A1.

A.5 Machine learning solution architecture

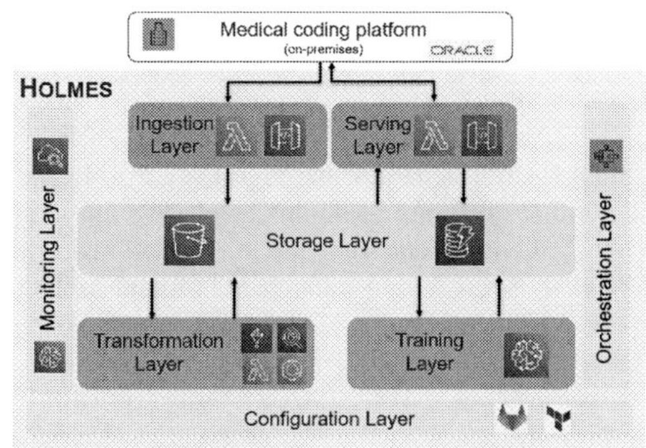

Figure 3: Cloud architecture of the deployed medical coding system outlined in the main text.

Designing and implementing machine learning systems is challenging since they exhibit a different behavior than traditional software systems (Sculley et al., 2015). The cloud architecture of the medical coding (MC) system outlined in the main text (termed Holmes) is organized in separate yet interconnected layers.

Serving layer. It is responsible for receiving RTs from the MC platform, forwarding them to Holmes, and returning the respective predictions.

Ingestion layer. Via the ingestion layer, the MC platform sends all available data needed for model training to Holmes.

Storage layer. In the storage layer we save all data, solutions, and model versions that are received or created by Holmes. It can be considered as the hard-drive of Holmes.

Transformation layer. It handles all steps required to make the data received from the MC platform ready for model training. It implements all pre-processing steps, including data augmentation and split into training, validation, and test data.

Model	LLT Accuracy [%]							
	All	k=0	k=1	k=2	k=3	k=5	k=10	k>=100
PubMedBERT (PMB) (single)	$74.9_{0.5}$	$31.0_{1.8}$	$44.5_{0.8}$	$57.1_{1.3}$	$60.3_{1.8}$	$68.5_{1.7}$	$\mathbf{65.6}_{1.2}$	$84.0_{0.7}$
BioBERT (BB) (single)	$74.9_{0.1}$	$29.2_{1.9}$	$41.8_{1.5}$	$53.5_{1.5}$	$60.0_{2.6}$	$65.9_{2.6}$	$62.5_{1.1}$	$84.4_{0.4}$
sciBERT (SB) (single)	$74.9_{0.3}$	$27.8_{1.7}$	$42.5_{2.5}$	$58.4_{1.3}$	$57.5_{2.2}$	$66.4_{1.1}$	$60.3_{2.4}$	$84.6_{0.8}$
TARS (neg=2 cos)	$64.9_{1.2}$	$\mathbf{44.0}_{1.2}$	$\mathbf{52.3}_{1.9}$	$58.2_{1.2}$	$56.1_{1.3}$	$55.0_{1.9}$	$58.5_{1.7}$	$69.8_{3.0}$
TARS (neg=10 cos)	$62.6_{0.8}$	$39.8_{0.4}$	$47.4_{1.0}$	$53.8_{4.6}$	$56.3_{3.9}$	$52.8_{1.7}$	$52.7_{2.8}$	$66.4_{1.3}$
xTARS (neg=10 cos)	$64.9_{0.9}$	$42.2_{2.3}$	$51.0_{1.2}$	$56.4_{0.7}$	$56.7_{2.5}$	$55.6_{1.2}$	$56.0_{3.5}$	$71.4_{1.6}$
xTARS (neg=top-5)	$76.2_{0.4}$	$37.0_{1.1}$	$48.7_{1.0}$	$57.7_{1.2}$	$64.6_{2.2}$	$67.8_{1.7}$	$63.6_{2.2}$	$83.9_{0.7}$
xTARS (neg=top-5+5 cos)	$77.3_{0.2}$	$37.9_{0.2}$	$47.4_{3.1}$	$\mathbf{59.3}_{2.0}$	$\mathbf{67.4}_{2.0}$	$\mathbf{68.9}_{2.5}$	$63.6_{1.7}$	$84.8_{0.3}$
xTARS (neg=top-5+10 cos)	$76.9_{0.7}$	$38.5_{1.1}$	$48.8_{0.4}$	$\mathbf{59.3}_{0.5}$	$66.1_{0.8}$	$68.8_{1.1}$	$63.3_{1.1}$	$84.6_{0.9}$
xTARS (neg=top-5+5 cos; T=1)	$\mathbf{77.5}_{0.3}$	$37.3_{0.9}$	$48.1_{0.2}$	$59.7_{0.9}$	$64.8_{1.1}$	$67.8_{2.4}$	$\mathbf{65.6}_{0.7}$	$\mathbf{84.9}_{0.3}$
PMB (3 models)	77.8	**33.0**	46.0	60.4	63.4	**70.9**	**68.9**	86.6
BB (3 models)	**77.9**	**33.0**	**47.9**	**64.3**	**65.8**	69.2	65.6	87.0
SB (3 models)	**77.9**	30.8	43.7	57.1	65.2	69.8	64.7	**87.1**
PMB+SB+BB (3×3)	79.7	34.8	49.8	63.2	63.4	**73.8**	**70.6**	**88.2**
xTARS (PMB+SB+BB, 3×3)	**80.4**	**48.9**	**52.6**	**64.8**	**68.3**	71.5	68.9	86.9
PMB+SB+BB (3×5)	80.1	36.2	48.8	64.8	67.1	73.8	68.9	88.5

Table A1: LLT accuracy on the test set. For details on the models, please see Table 3 in the main text. k refers to the number of training samples, excluding augmented data. In this setting, BERT models can perform zero-shot (k=0) predictions because the training set contains augmented samples from the ontology for all categories (see Sec. A.1), even when no real samples are present in the training data (i.e. k=0).

Training layer. It performs model training with data transformed by the transformation layer, and saves the trained models to the storage layer.

Configuration layer. The entire architecture is defined, configured, and created by the configuration layer via infrastructure as code. This allows to install the entire infrastructure via simple scripts.

Monitoring layer. It observes the system and raises alerts if unusual behavior is detected, e.g. requests from unknown IP addresses.

Orchestration layer. It schedules all tasks such as model training or data processing in the right order.

A.6 Graphical user interface of the medical coding platform

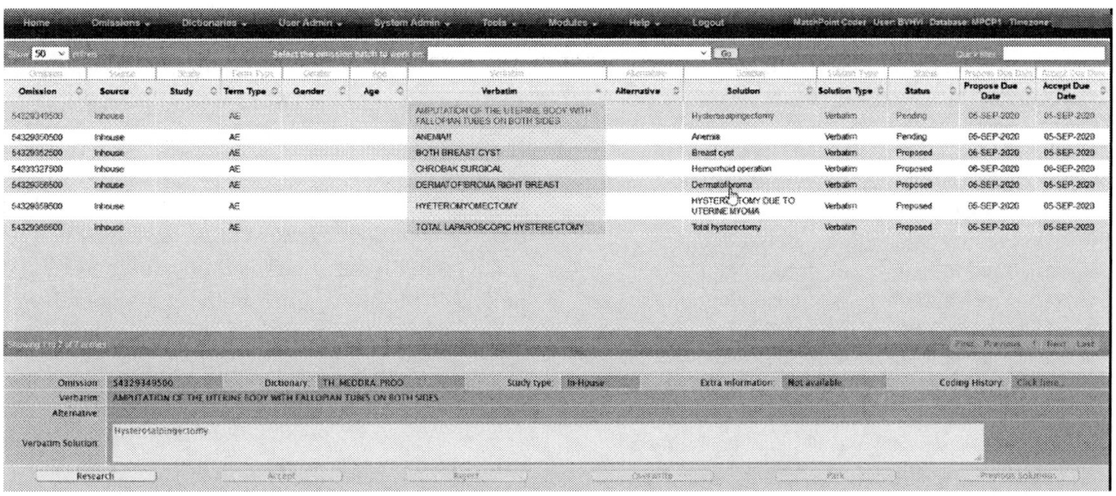

Figure 4: Screenshot of the medical coding platform where the coding solutions proposed by the algorithm described in the main text are shown to medical coders for acceptance or rejection.

Knowledge extraction from aeronautical messages (NOTAMs) with self-supervised language models for aircraft pilots

Alexandre ARNOLD
Fares ERNEZ
Catherine KOBUS
Marion-Cécile MARTIN
Airbus (AI Research)
firstname.lastname@airbus.com

Abstract

During their pre-flight briefings, aircraft pilots must analyze a long list of NOTAMs (NOtice To AirMen) indicating potential hazards along the flight route, sometimes up to 100 pages for long-haul flights. NOTAM free-text fields typically have a very special phrasing, with lots of acronyms and domain-specific vocabulary, which makes it differ significantly from standard English. In this paper, we pretrain language models derived from BERT on circa 1 million unlabeled NOTAMs and reuse the learnt representations on three downstream tasks valuable for pilots: criticality prediction, named entity recognition and translation into a structured language called Airlang. This self-supervised approach, where smaller amounts of labeled data are enough for task-specific fine-tuning, is well suited in the aeronautical context since expert annotations are expensive and time-consuming. We present evaluation scores across the tasks showing a high potential for an operational usability of such models (by pilots, airlines or service providers), which is a first to the best of our knowledge.

1 Introduction

Each upcoming flight requires a preparation phase for the crew. During this phase, the pilots check all the elements concerning the flight, being the meteorological conditions, fuel supply, or safety related notifications. Pilots receive these notifications from the aviation authorities under the form of small text messages, called NOtice To AirMen (NOTAM). It represents a large number of messages to read and process before the flight, sometimes up to 100 pages for long-haul flights, which translates to a long analysis time. The messages are mostly, but not only, written in the English language. However, the phrasing being very special, with a lot of acronyms, technical words and without the usual grammar and syntax rules, the language differs from standard English.

In this paper, we aim to apply the latest advances in Natural Language Processing (NLP) to the aeronautical field leading to more autonomy and less overhead for the pilots. In particular, the use of language models like BERT enables leveraging lots of unlabeled data for pretraining and fine-tuning on downstream tasks with limited amounts of labeled data. Our main contribution is to present a knowledge extraction pipeline adapted to the aeronautical context. We introduce a language model trained from scratch on a large amount of raw NOTAMs, followed by three downstream tasks: criticality prediction, named entity recognition and translation into a structured language called Airlang.

This paper is organised as followed: in Section 2, the NOTAMs are detailed both on the operational and the linguistic side, the problem is defined in Section 3 with a focus on the three downstream tasks. In Section 4, after a brief reminder of the state of the art, we present our approaches and the results of our experiments.

2 NOTAMs in aeronautical context

A NOTAM is a message filled by aviation authorities to alert pilots about potential hazards along a flight route or at a location that could affect the flight. The message can inform about temporary disruptions (from a few hours to one year maximum) on aeronautical infrastructures (for example, closure or limited usage of runway or taxiway in a given airport), about inoperable radio navigational aids, military exercises with resulting airspace restrictions, temporary erections of obstacles near airfields (e.g. cranes), passage of flocks of birds through airspace, etc. An example of a NOTAM message is shown in Figure 1; more details about the fields can be found in Appendix A.

2.1 Operational point of view

During the pre-flight briefing phase, a pilot has to read all NOTAMs relevant for the flight in order to

Proceedings of NAACL-HLT 2022: Industry Track Papers, pages 188 - 196
July 10-15, 2022

```
A1234/06 NOTAMR A1212/06
Q)EGTT/QMXLC/IV/NBO/A/000/999/5129N00028W005
A)EGLL
B)0609050500
C)0704300500
E)DUE WIP TWY B SOUTH CLSD BTN 'F' AND 'R'. TWY 'R' CLSD BTN 'A' AND 'B' AND DIVERTED VIA NEW GREEN CL AND BLUE EDGE LGT. CTN ADZ
```

Figure 1: NOTAM example with its different Q, A, B, C and E fields

guarantee safety.

Reading these NOTAMs is a mandatory task for the pilot but can be long and challenging. First, those short messages are quite cryptic, all written in capitals, with many confusing abbreviations. Second, the number of emitted NOTAMs is growing over time with for example 2 million in 2018 (circa 5500 per day). Some of them are crucial for the flight, but the vast majority are of low importance, which makes the analysis difficult.

NLP techniques can be very helpful in that aeronautical context, typically to rank NOTAMs by criticality and highlight important information in them (like runway and taxiway identifiers). For example, NOTAMs about runway or flight area closure are often more relevant than the ones repeated every day by small airports about strong wind in the area.

```
TWY E(BTN H AND Z)-RESTRICTED DUE TO
CONST RMK/NOT AVBL FOR ACFT WITH MORE
THAN 65M

TWY HOTEL CLSD 283M FROM INTERSECTION
WITH TWY GOLF
```

Figure 2: Example of NOTAMs (E field)

2.2 Linguistic point of view

NOTAMs are composed of multiple fields, some of which contain structured information that is easy to parse with a fixed grammar. In this work we focus on the "E field", which usually contains the most detailed information in an unstructured free-text form. NOTAMs (E field) are quite short text messages and are not written in standard English but rather in a domain-specific language, mainly composed of abbreviations and acronyms from the aeronautical world; an official list of acronyms is maintained by ICAO (International Civil Aircraft Organization).

A strong expertise is required to decode and understand those messages; if, overall, English is the main used language, some authorities use their local language. Two examples of NOTAM content (E field) are shown on figure 2.

The NOTAM language is designed to be concise in order to transmit information in the most efficient way. In order for this language to be understood and written by everyone from the aeronautical world, some guidelines exist and it is strongly encouraged to use the official list of acronyms. Such patterns like "*"RWY XX/YY CLSD"*" (which means that the runway "XX/YY" is closed) appear quite often in the NOTAM corpus but despite the official recommendations, people authoring NOTAMs regularly deviate from them, can make spelling mistakes, etc. The resulting NOTAM language thus presents the same challenges as any natural language and cannot be robustly analyzed with a rule-based system.

3 Problem definition

3.1 Criticality prediction

During the preparation of the flight, the pilot and co-pilot must take note of all these documents introduced above. However, as mentioned before, NOTAMs can be very numerous and may not all be relevant for the flight in question. With the criticality estimation, we aim to highlight the most important messages for the flight, to help the pilot optimize the preparation phase.

3.2 Named entity recognition

As mentioned in Section 2, highlighting the most important and relevant entities can help the pilot digest the NOTAMs and focus on the most insightful parts. This is a typical NLP task called Named Entity Recognition (NER).

One crucial information the pilot needs to know is about the closure of airways (*runway* or *taxiway*)[1]. Sometimes, the closure of an airway is specified with :

- a *geographical* condition : for example, only a given part of the airway is closed

[1] A *runway* is where the aircraft lands/takes-off, whereas a *taxiway* is a road connecting runways to terminals and hangars in an airport

- a *temporal* condition : the airway is closed certain days of the week or at certain time schedules of the day
- an *aircraft* condition : for example, an airway can be closed only to aircraft whose wingspan is larger than a given size
- an *operational* condition : for example, an airway can be closed only for take-off or landing

Similarly, exceptions and reasons can be added to further specify the NOTAM.

3.3 Translation

Pilots and co-pilots are often supported by digital apps provided on the so-called electronic flight bag (EFB), a mobile tablet docked to the aircraft, replacing the physical flight bag that used to contain all flight documents in the past. Beyond giving digital access to the required documents, some of these apps now propose to visualize contextual flight information (e.g. extracted from NOTAMs) in a more digestible format for the pilot, such as maps with visual cues. Such apps typically rely on structured machine-parsable languages like Airlang, synthesizing the most important pieces of information from NOTAMs. Today, the translation from raw NOTAMs to Airlang is generally done manually by multiple humans (in charge of the translation itself or its verification). In this paper, we are investigating the possibility to automate this translation using modern sequence-to-sequence language models. The goal is to accelerate this translation task, potentially reducing the manual effort to the verification part only.

4 Experiments and results

4.1 NOTAM language model pretraining

Significant advances in the NLP field have been made in the recent years thanks to powerful Transformer architectures (Vaswani et al., 2017) and self-supervised pretraining, as introduced by the BERT paper (Devlin et al., 2019) and continued in various derivative work like RoBERTa (Liu et al., 2019) or DeBERTa (He et al., 2020). Due to its characteristics, the NOTAM language can benefit from such state-of-the-art language models.

Following popular practices on BERT models and its variants, the idea is to pretrain a language model on many raw NOTAMs with a dedicated tokenizer (we cannot reuse models available online since there is almost no overlap with standard English), and then fine-tune it for each downstream task introduced in section 3. See Appendix B for architecture details.

We experimented with a few language model variants (RoBERTa and DeBERTa v2, both with 6 layers), each being trained on a dataset of 1.2 million unlabeled NOTAMs, from which the E field (the free text part) was extracted. No other pre-processing was performed on the data.

The RoBERTa models were trained on a corpus tokenized using BPE (Sennrich et al., 2016), whereas the DeBERTa ones were trained using SentencePiece (Kudo and Richardson, 2018) tokenization; both tokenization models has a vocabulary size of 52000.

The language models were trained using the Huggingface *transformers* library [2], using a masked language model objective, during 3 epochs.

4.2 Criticality prediction

The objective is to assign a score to each free-text part of a NOTAM (part E), from 1 = lowest priority to 5 = highest priority. In terms of NLP task, this fine-tuning consists in a sequence-level prediction (classification or regression). We train a regression head that takes as input the output of the classification [CLS] token after passing through the pretrained language model. This pooled embedding reflects the context of the full text as it contains information about all the other tokens of the considered sequence. The classification head is mainly a linear layer.

We choose to cast this task as a regression rather than a classification in order to take into account the ranking of the scores. Indeed, classifying a message to 2 or 5 rather than 1 should not give the same loss value. Therefore, the output of our additional head is of size 1.

The dataset comes from ICAO and is composed of circa 35000 NOTAMs annotated by experts. One of its characteristics is its heterogeneity between the labels : more than 10% of the dataset contains duplicated messages to which different scores have been attributed, sometimes even 1 and 5 for the same NOTAM. This reflects a divergence of views that can come from the pilot's perception or the context of the flight. Moreover, as you can see in Figure 3, NOTAMs with the lowest importance are

[2] https://github.com/huggingface/transformers

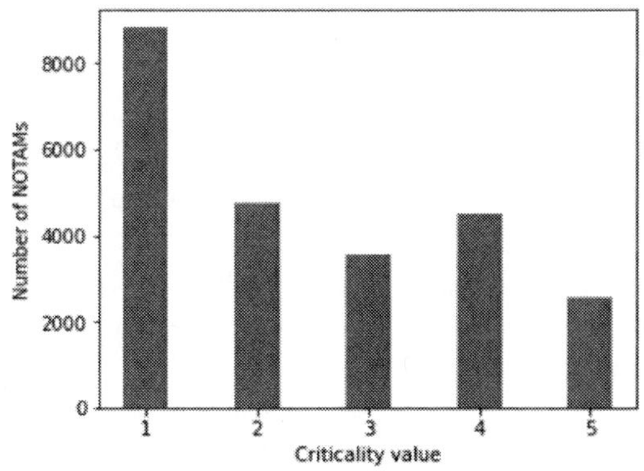

Figure 3: Distribution of the scores in the training set

much more represented than the others.

The dataset is split in 80%-20% between training and testing. By training on this dataset and considering the prediction scores rounded to the nearest integer, we reach a Mean Absolute Error (MAE) of 1.08 in the best case: DeBERTa v2 with hidden size of 768. However, we notice a strong bias towards middle criticality scores with low recalls on the extremes.

To mitigate this point, we can alternatively use a multi-class F1-score as evaluation metric for the best model selection. To tackle the imbalance and heterogeneity problem, we pre-process the dataset by keeping for each NOTAM its most frequently attributed score, followed by an oversampling in order to have the same number of messages for each score in the training set. With these changes, the recall of the lowest and highest criticality NOTAMs are significantly improved (by absolute 28% and 16% respectively). This shows the ability to support the pilot in detecting important NOTAMs, even if it is technically impossible to get perfect predictions on this dataset because of the frequent disagreements between the annotators themselves.

A perspective of improvement would be to calibrate the model with inputs coming from the pilots and human factors team. We may expect that the impact of predicting a low priority when it is actually a high priority message would be larger on the flight's safety than the contrary. An asymmetric loss could then be used during training to reflect these specificities.

4.3 Named entity recognition

NER is the second downstream task studied in this work; it is a classical token classification task that can be implemented by adding, on top of each token's embedding, a linear layer and a softmax to derive the most probable entity tag. The pretrained language model is fine-tuned within this architecture on an annotated dataset.

	Train	**Dev**	**Test**
#NOTAMs	196	50	62
runway	231	56	71
taxiway	385	82	97
closure	187	42	57
condition	211	51	42
exception	25	7	9
reason	81	21	26

Table 1: NER dataset description

An extension of this approach was explored by adding a Conditional Random Field (CRF) on top of the linear layer as detailed in (Souza et al., 2019). The biLSTM-CRF (Lample et al., 2016) used to be the state-of-the-art approach before the emergence of BERT-based models; in a sequence labeling task, CRF maximizes the probability of the whole sequence of decisions, so it can better take context into account instead of making independent predictions.

The dataset consists in a set of 308 NOTAMs that were annotated with the different entities in the IOB format (Ramshaw and Marcus, 1995). In this study, the following list of entities are considered: *runway*, *taxiway*, *closure*, *condition*, *exception* and *reason*. The dataset is rather small but annotation is quite costly since it requires aeronautical expertise. The dataset was respectively split into training, development and test sets as detailed in Table 1.

Three different kinds of models were trained. The baseline model is a layered biLSTM model (Ju et al., 2018); it was already explored in the context of NOTAMs in previous work (Arnold et al., 2019). The layered aspect is interesting to tackle NOTAM entities, which can be nested as shown in Figure 4. Indeed, inside the *closure* clause, there can be mentions of other entities like *runway*, *taxiway* but also of *condition*, *exception* or *reason*.

The other approaches presented in this paper are based on the RoBERTa language model (trained from scratch on NOTAM data), fine-tuned on the NER dataset in two variants: without and with a CRF layer. As entities are nested, a first simple approach consists in training a separate model for each kind of entity; as *runway*, *taxiway* cannot be nested in each other, they are covered by one model.

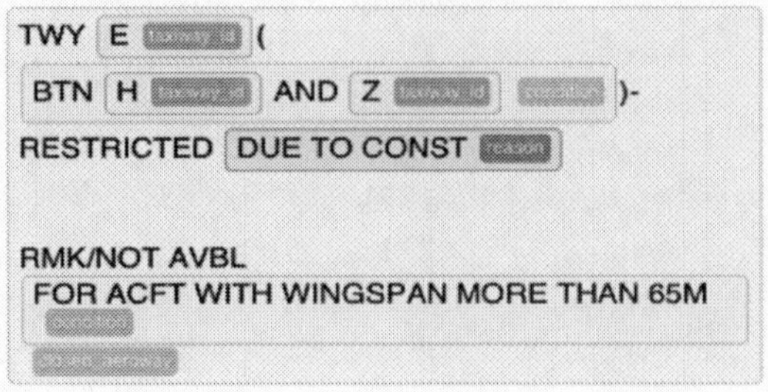

Figure 4: Example of nested entities

Every other entity (*closure*, *condition*, *exception* or *reason*) is covered by its own model.

The results (obtained with the conlleval script [3] with the different models are summed up in Table 2. Using the RoBERTa fine-tuned model without CRF seems to significantly degrade the results globally compared to the biLSTM-CRF baseline on all entities, except for *runway* where the F1-score is improved. The degradation is even more significant for "long-span" entities like *closure* and *reason*. However, the CRF layer seems to boost the F1-scores for all the entities; results are significantly improved compared to the initial baseline. In this context, where entities can have a long span, the CRF layer seems to play a crucial role in this sequence labeling task. Finally, entities like *runway* and *taxiway* reach very high F1-scores; they are the easiest to catch (because often preceded by keywords like "RWY" and "TWY"). The results on other entities are globally lower; they are more difficult to recognize because they have a longer span and are often less represented in the corpus.

As described previously, the RoBERTa fine-tuned models seem to provide good results globally on all the entities but each entity needs its own model due to the nested aspect. This approach is not very efficient both in terms of memory and computing time. This motivated us to explore multitask learning (Caruana, 1997; Collobert and Weston, 2008); the idea is to start with the pretrained RoBERTa model but this time with one dedicated classification head for each entity type. By simultaneously training on all the entities, each task could hopefully benefit from each other. Results are presented in Table 2. The multitask model that handles all the entities at once keep good F1-scores on entities like *runway*, *taxiway* and *closure*, for which we have more examples in the training set, whereas the results are a bit degraded on entities like *condition* and *reason*. The results for *exception* are to be considered carefully because there are too few examples in the training and test sets. This motivated us to train a multitask model only on the *runway*, *taxiway*, *closure* and *condition* entities for which we had at least 200 occurrences in the training set. F1-scores are further improved on *runway*, *taxiway* and *closure* entities. Multitask learning enables recognizing nested entities with a single model, as long as a minimal amount of data is present for each entity type (otherwise, less represented entities tend to penalize the training overall).

4.4 Translation

The last downstream task of interest is the automatic translation from the raw NOTAM text to the Airlang structured language, the latter being parsable by a fixed grammar (see example in Figure 5). This sequence-to-sequence task requires an encoder-decoder model like the original Transformer architecture (Vaswani et al., 2017). For the encoder, we reuse the pretrained model introduced in Section 4.1. For the decoder, we use a similar model (RoBERTa) but initialized from scratch without pretraining because we do not have access to huge amounts of unlabeled Airlang data, as opposed to raw NOTAMs. We then fine-tune the whole encoder-decoder model end-to-end on a dataset of circa 20000 NOTAM-Airlang pairs (translated by human professionals).

NOTAM: `YMMM E1166/20 17JUN0100-17JUN0300 STIRLING AIRSPACE R192ABC ACT (RA2) DUE MILITARY FLYING SFC / FL300`

Airlang: `TIMEDEF DURATION = 17 Jun 2020 1:00 TO 17 Jun 2020 3:00; AREADEF "YM:192A" FL001 TO FL300 ACTIVE DURATION; AREADEF "YM:192B" FL001 TO FL300 ACTIVE DURATION; AREADEF "YM:192C" FL001 TO FL300 ACTIVE DURATION;`

Figure 5: Example of NOTAM translated to Airlang

Although the output sequence is not constrained by any special mechanism, after training we observe that most generated Airlang translations are valid with regard to the grammar underpinning this structured language. As opposed to classical translation tasks where BLEU or ROUGE scores are often used to allow for some flexibility, here the

[3] https://github.com/sighsmile/conlleval/blob/master/conlleval.py

	Layered biLSTM CRF			RoBERTa			RoBERTa CRF			Multitask model			Multitask model w/o *exception/reason*		
Entity	Prec.	Rec.	F1	Prec.	Rec.	F1	Prec.	Rec.	F1	Prec.	Rec.	F1	Prec.	Rec.	F1
runway	95.8	95.8	95.8	97.3	100.0	98.6	98.6	100	**99.3**	98.6	100.0	99.3	98.6	100.0	**99.3**
taxiway	97.7	87.6	92.4	92.6	89.7	91.1	94.9	94.9	**94.9**	95.8	93.8	94.8	96.9	95.9	**96.4**
closure	70.5	78.2	74.1	59.4	74.6	66.1	87.0	72.7	**79.2**	80.8	76.4	78.5	81.8	81.8	**81.8**
condition	55.9	46.3	50.7	30.7	56.1	39.7	63.2	58.5	**60.8**	67.9	46.3	55.1	61.6	58.5	60.1
exception	100.0	33.3	50.0	100.0	22.2	36.4	100.0	33.3	50.0	100.0	22.2	36.4			
reason	87.0	76.9	81.6	73.9	65.4	69.4	91.7	84.6	**88.0**	91.3	80.8	85.7			

Table 2: NER results in terms of Precision, Recall and F1-score

model performance is evaluated (on a test set of circa 5000 NOTAM-Airlang pairs) with a much more conservative metric because of the safety-critical context and the fact that the target language is structured: we consider the percentage of "perfect translations", i.e. the ones matching exactly the ground truth in a case-sensitive way. However we noticed a few tiny variations in this ground truth that are parsed equivalently down the line (optional presence of a white space in certain places, some words that are both valid whether they are capitalized or not, equivalent ways of expressing flight levels like "FL001 TO FLxxx" and "FLxxx AND BELOW"...). So we propose to post-process both the model output and ground truth with simple hard-coded rules to normalize their form, leading to adjusted performance scores which better reflect the actual quality of the translation (see Table 3 for results without/with post-processing using different encoder models).

We note that our system (using the best translation model) is able to produce 84.5% correct translations, which can significantly reduce manual efforts from operational teams providing such services to airlines. To further support these teams by giving a confidence score on these translations, we use gradient boosting (Chen and Guestrin, 2016) to train a classifier in charge of detecting good/bad translations based on various seemingly relevant features (length of the NOTAM, number of occurrences for certain elements like days/months, etc.). As seen in Figure 6, this classifier obtains a AUC score (Area Under Curve) of 0.90, showing a strong ability to distinguish good/bad translations (the business can adapt the threshold to select any point on the curve according to their preferred trade-off between probability of detection vs false alarms).

Encoder model	Hidden size	No post-process	With post-process
RoBERTa	768	74.3%	83.6%
RoBERTa	1536	**78.1%**	**84.5%**
DeBERTa v2	768	78.0%	83.1%
DeBERTa v2	1536	77.3%	82.3%

Table 3: Perfect NOTAM to Airlang translation scores

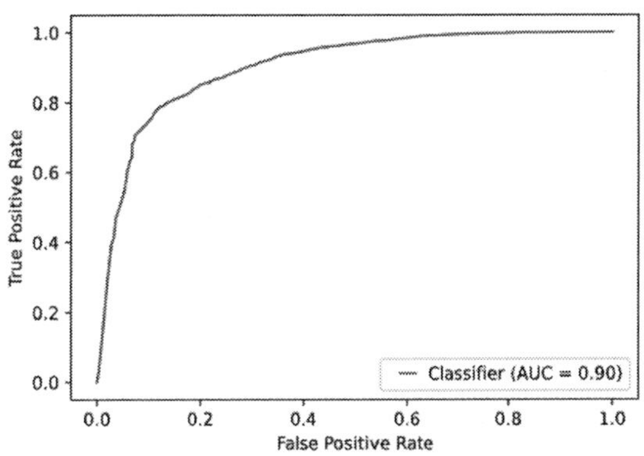

Figure 6: Translation classifier AUC score

5 Conclusion and perspectives

In this work, we presented the use of modern self-supervised language models (derived from BERT) to extract knowledge from NOTAM aeronautical messages. We showed that a single deep learning model pretrained on circa 1 million unlabelled NOTAMs can be efficiently reused on downstream tasks with dedicated fine-tuning. NOTAM criticality prediction can support pilots during their pre-flight briefing by highlighting the most important messages. Furthermore, named entity recognition can be applied to extract relevant parts of NOTAMs (e.g. closed runways/taxiways, specific conditions/exceptions...). Finally, automatic translation to a domain-specific structured language (Airlang) used by pilot apps during flight, can support operational teams providing services to airlines. The evaluation scores on these tasks show a high potential for an operational usability of such models (by pilots, airlines or service providers), which is a first to the best of our knowledge.

In the future, alternative NLP methods such as summarization for NOTAMs could be explored to continue reducing pilots' workload. While the use of deep learning networks (and pretrained language models) enabled increasing accuracy in a lot of NLP downstream tasks, they are known to be overconfident in their predictions. It is an issue in the aviation context given its safety-critical nature, where trust in systems' predictions is key. In that respect, uncertainty quantification methods - such as conformal predictions (Vovk V. and Shafer, 2005)(Angelopoulos and Bates, 2021) - could give a reliable measure of confidence in model's outputs. The robustness of the model could also be assessed through adversarial attacks, as in (Morris et al., 2020). Finally, formal methods could be used for verification and could pave the way to the certification of such deep learning models, required for any use on board.

Ethical considerations

In any safety-critical context like aeronautics, there is an inherent risk associated with the use of automatic methods supporting human operators. This is why our proposed techniques are limited to a responsible use on ground, at least until the underlying models can be certified for in-flight use thanks to rigorous methods from the *Trusted Artificial Intelligence* research field. In any case, such systems are only meant to support human analysis and decision making by decreasing workload, not to replace them.

The NOTAMs collected worldwide and used in this study are public data (accessible via numerous official platforms online). The datasets used for named entity recognition and translation are proprietary and built internally by expert annotators as part of their work (with the permission to be used in our work). The ICAO dataset used for criticality prediction is public and enables research use.

The Huggingface Transformers framework supporting model training in our study is open sourced under the permissive Apache 2.0 license. Every model training mentioned in this paper (RoBERTa and DeBERTa v2 ones) took less than 12 GPU hours for pretraining and for each of the three downstream tasks. The hyperparameters used by these models in our experiments are the default ones from the Transformers library (faithful to the original papers), except when explicitly mentioned (e.g. varying the hidden size).

References

Anastasios N. Angelopoulos and Stephen Bates. 2021. A gentle introduction to conformal prediction and distribution-free uncertainty quantification.

Alexandre Arnold, Gérard Dupont, Catherine Kobus, François Lancelot, and Pooja Narayan. 2019. Interprétation et visualisation contextuelle de NOTAMs (messages aux navigants aériens) (). In *Actes de la Conférence sur le Traitement Automatique des Langues Naturelles (TALN) PFIA 2019. Volume IV : Démonstrations*, pages 639–643, Toulouse, France. ATALA.

Rich Caruana. 1997. Multitask learning. *Machine Learning*, 28(1):41–75.

Tianqi Chen and Carlos Guestrin. 2016. Xgboost: A scalable tree boosting system. In *Proceedings of the 22nd acm sigkdd international conference on knowledge discovery and data mining*, pages 785–794.

Ronan Collobert and Jason Weston. 2008. A unified architecture for natural language processing: Deep neural networks with multitask learning. In *Proceedings of the 25th International Conference on Machine Learning*, ICML '08, page 160–167, New York, NY, USA. Association for Computing Machinery.

Jacob Devlin, Ming-Wei Chang, Kenton Lee, and Kristina Toutanova. 2019. BERT: Pre-training of deep bidirectional transformers for language understanding. In *Proceedings of the 2019 Conference of the North American Chapter of the Association for Computational Linguistics: Human Language Technologies, Volume 1 (Long and Short Papers)*, pages 4171–4186, Minneapolis, Minnesota. Association for Computational Linguistics.

Pengcheng He, Xiaodong Liu, Jianfeng Gao, and Weizhu Chen. 2020. Deberta: Decoding-enhanced bert with disentangled attention. *arXiv preprint arXiv:2006.03654*.

Meizhi Ju, Makoto Miwa, and Sophia Ananiadou. 2018. A neural layered model for nested named entity recognition. In *Proceedings of the 2018 Conference of the North American Chapter of the Association for Computational Linguistics: Human Language Technologies, Volume 1 (Long Papers)*, pages 1446–1459, New Orleans, Louisiana. Association for Computational Linguistics.

Taku Kudo and John Richardson. 2018. SentencePiece: A simple and language independent subword tokenizer and detokenizer for neural text processing. In *Proceedings of the 2018 Conference on Empirical Methods in Natural Language Processing: System Demonstrations*, pages 66–71, Brussels, Belgium. Association for Computational Linguistics.

Guillaume Lample, Miguel Ballesteros, Sandeep Subramanian, Kazuya Kawakami, and Chris Dyer. 2016. Neural architectures for named entity recognition. In *Proceedings of the 2016 Conference of the North American Chapter of the Association for Computational Linguistics: Human Language Technologies*, pages 260–270, San Diego, California. Association for Computational Linguistics.

Yinhan Liu, Myle Ott, Naman Goyal, Jingfei Du, Mandar Joshi, Danqi Chen, Omer Levy, Mike Lewis, Luke Zettlemoyer, and Veselin Stoyanov. 2019. Roberta: A robustly optimized bert pretraining approach.

John Morris, Eli Lifland, Jin Yong Yoo, Jake Grigsby, Di Jin, and Yanjun Qi. 2020. TextAttack: A framework for adversarial attacks, data augmentation, and adversarial training in NLP. In *Proceedings of the 2020 Conference on Empirical Methods in Natural Language Processing: System Demonstrations*, pages 119–126, Online. Association for Computational Linguistics.

Lance Ramshaw and Mitch Marcus. 1995. Text chunking using transformation-based learning. In *Third Workshop on Very Large Corpora*.

Rico Sennrich, Barry Haddow, and Alexandra Birch. 2016. Neural machine translation of rare words with subword units. In *Proceedings of the 54th Annual Meeting of the Association for Computational Linguistics (Volume 1: Long Papers)*, pages 1715–1725, Berlin, Germany. Association for Computational Linguistics.

Fábio Souza, Rodrigo Nogueira, and Roberto Lotufo. 2019. Portuguese named entity recognition using bert-crf.

Ashish Vaswani, Noam Shazeer, Niki Parmar, Jakob Uszkoreit, Llion Jones, Aidan N Gomez, Łukasz Kaiser, and Illia Polosukhin. 2017. Attention is all you need. In *Advances in neural information processing systems*, pages 5998–6008.

Gammerman A. Vovk V. and G. Shafer. 2005. *Algorithmic Learning in a Random World*. Springer.

A Appendix: NOTAM details (ICAO format)

A NOTAM message is structured into 5 or 6 different fields, namely:

- Q field is the Qualifier line; it contains a series of classification tags that the operator is supposed to fill while authoring the NOTAM
- A field is the ICAO indicator of the aerodrome or the FIR (Flight Information Region)
- B field corresponds to the date/time when this NOTAM becomes effective
- C field corresponds to the date/time when the NOTAM ceases to be effective
- D field (optional) can specify a miscellaneous diurnal time for the NOTAM if the hours of effect are less than 24 hours a day
- E field contains the NOTAM text message (the free text part), the part of interest for our study

B Appendix: Model architectures for the three downstream tasks

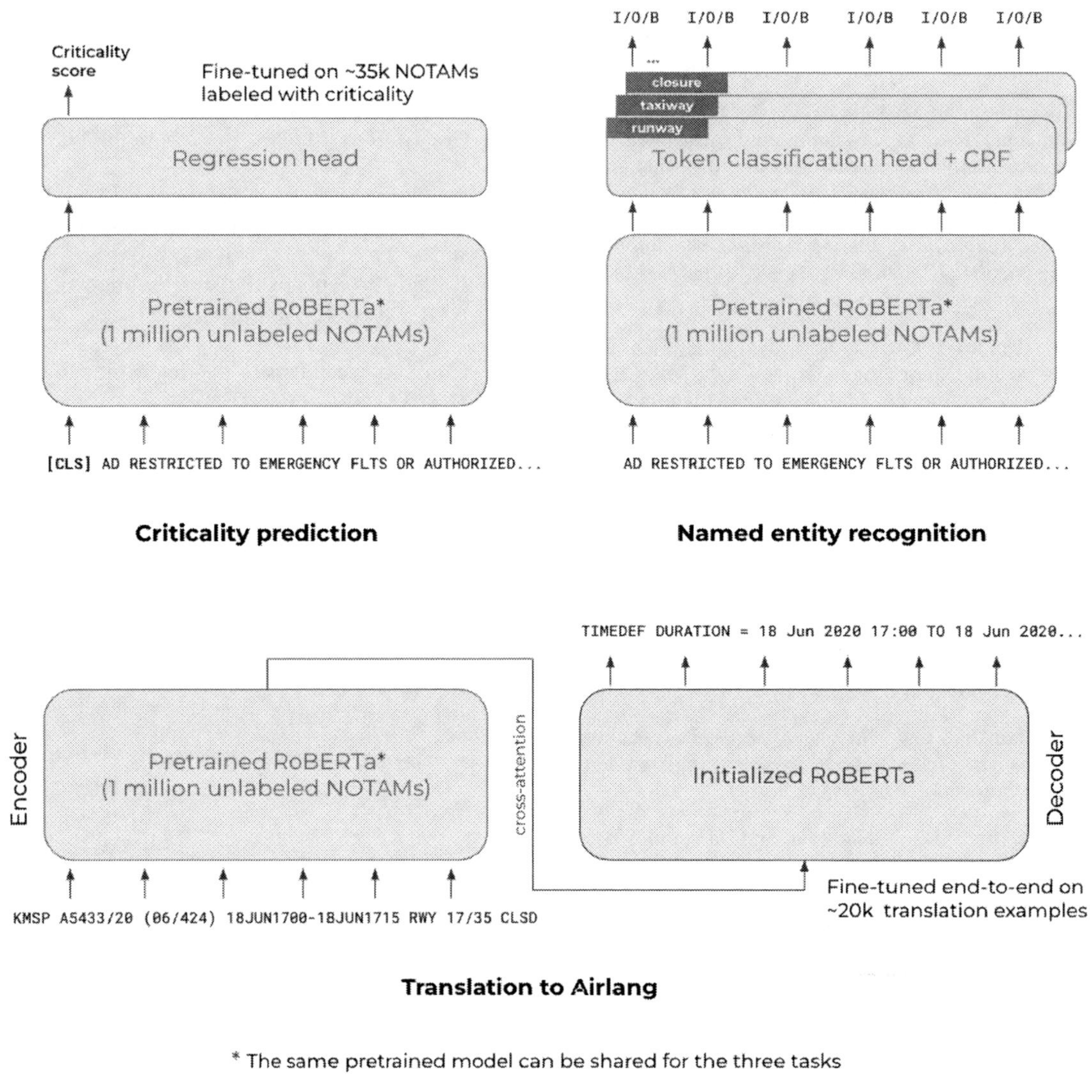

Intent Discovery for Enterprise Virtual Assistants: Applications of Utterance Embedding and Clustering to Intent Mining

Minhua Chen
Interactions LLC
mchen@interactions.com

Badrinath Jayakumar
Interactions LLC
bjayakumar@interactions.com

Michael Johnston*
Amazon Alexa AI
mjohnstn@amazon.com

Eman Mahmoodi
Interactions LLC
smahmoodi@interactions.com

Daniel Pressel
Interactions LLC
dpressel@interactions.com

Abstract

A key challenge in the creation and refinement of virtual assistants is the ability to mine unlabeled utterance data to discover common intents. We develop an approach to this problem that combines large-scale pre-training and multi-task learning to derive a semantic embedding that can be leveraged to identify clusters of utterances that correspond to unhandled intents. An utterance encoder is first trained with a language modeling objective and subsequently adapted to predict intent labels from a large collection of cross-domain enterprise virtual assistant data using a multi-task cosine softmax loss. Experimental evaluation shows significant advantages for this multi-step pre-training approach, with large gains in downstream clustering accuracy on new applications compared to standard sentence embedding approaches. The approach has been incorporated into an interactive discovery tool that enables visualization and exploration of intents by system analysts and builders.

1 Introduction

To build an enterprise virtual assistant capable of providing effective interaction with customers, intent detection – automatically detecting the customer's intent based on their input – is an indispensable component. Large-scale pre-trained language models have shown promising abilities in few-shot classification, and high accuracy intent detection can now be obtained with limited amounts of labeled data (Devlin et al., 2019; Henderson et al., 2020; Vulic et al., 2021). However, there are still situations where no labeled data is available. This situation is commonly encountered when designing a dialogue system for a brand new application. In this case, we would like to identify common intents from any available unlabeled data in the domain, such as call transcripts or chat logs. Also, for deployed applications, intent discovery can be applied to 'no-match' data; that is, utterances that the current system does not handle.

At first glance, the problem of intent discovery from unlabeled data appears similar to text clustering, which is well-studied in the literature. One natural approach for clustering is to use Transformer-based sentence embedding methods (Devlin et al., 2019; Reimers and Gurevych, 2019) to represent each utterance as a fixed-length vector, and then apply standard clustering methods such as K-means to extract intent clusters (Wu and Xiong, 2020; Aharoni and Goldberg, 2020). However, these models are mostly pre-trained on generic data such as Wikipedia or Natural Language Inference (NLI) datasets, which are quite different from typical enterprise customer service data. Hence there is a domain mismatch between the pre-trained model and the downstream application task.

In our experience, enterprise virtual assistant data has several key characteristics. First, utterances are mostly short, containing only a few words. Additionally, they contain some level of noise from Automatic Speech Recognition (ASR) transcriptions. Moreover, the data distribution is affected by the customer service communication channel. For example, there are many calls asking to speak to a live agent in order to bypass the system. Finally, the semantics differ at some points from ordinary language, because of business logic and design constraints. For example, the two utterances "my screen is broken" and "power button not responding" may be treated as containing the same semantic intent of "TECH-SUPPORT", while in common datasets (e.g., NLI), they would likely be considered different.

For these reasons, directly applying a generically pre-trained Transformer encoder (such as BERT (Devlin et al., 2019), or even an adapted model like Sentence-BERT (Reimers and Gurevych, 2019)) may not be optimal for the intent discovery problem. However, in our data lake we have accumu-

*Work completed at Interactions LLC

Proceedings of NAACL-HLT 2022: Industry Track Papers, pages 197 - 208
July 10-15, 2022

lated large amounts of utterance data from a large number of applications across multiple business verticals, all with intent labels either from production understanding models or human annotators. We, therefore, hypothesized that continuing pre-training on our existing virtual assistant data, to obtain a domain-specific utterance encoder, could be beneficial for downstream intent discovery tasks.

We propose a three-step solution (Figure 1) to the intent discovery problem: **1)** Generic Transformer Pre-training, **2)** Domain-adaptive Pre-training, **3)** Downstream Embedding and Clustering.

This approach is related to the don't-stop-pretraining paradigm proposed in (Gururangan et al., 2020), in which a generic Language Model (LM) is adapted to the target domain (or task) through domain (or task) adaptive pre-training. However, a key difference is that we leverage supervised data for the domain-adaptive pre-training in the second step; on the contrary, they only leverage unlabeled data for the continued pre-training. Recently Vulic et al. (2021) proposed ConvFIT where supervised contrastive learning is performed after generic LM pre-training. ConvFIT uses a small amount of labeled data from the same task in the adaptive pre-training step, which can be viewed as supervised task-adaptive pre-training for few-shot learning. In contrast, we use a collection of labeled data across a large number of customer service use cases in the second step, which can be viewed as supervised domain-adaptive pre-training for downstream clustering tasks. Notice that no access to the downstream data is needed for our domain-adaptive pre-training step, which makes our model reusable for new and unseen applications and use cases.

2 The Three-step Approach

2.1 Step 1: Generic Transformer Pre-training

Transformer-based pre-training such as BERT (Devlin et al., 2019) and GPT and its variants (Radford et al., 2018, 2019; Brown et al., 2020) have changed the landscape of natural language processing. Through self-supervised pre-training on large amounts of public data, Transformers can learn many language regularities, from syntax to semantics to even commonsense knowledge (Manning et al., 2020; Tenney et al., 2019). These pre-trained models then serve as excellent starting points for downstream tasks through model fine-tuning. Instead of adopting a publicly available pre-trained model, we pre-trained our own Transformer-based language model from public dialogue data, including three years of Reddit (Al-Rfou et al., 2016; Henderson et al., 2019), online forums, as well as customer reviews and Wikipedia. We use a masked language model (MLM) training loss and train an 8-layer model with eight attention heads and relative positional encoding (Shaw et al., 2018) on full conversations (Pressel et al., 2022), where each turn is demarcated with a special end-of-utterance token. We also place the layer norm at the front of each sub-layer in the Transformer to simplify training and improve performance (Nguyen and Salazar, 2019; Xiong et al., 2020; Wang et al., 2019). We found that, despite its smaller size, our model often outperforms much larger previously created models on many downstream dialogue related tasks, including intent detection, slot-filling, belief state tracking, probing, and few-shot learning. We use this in-house pre-trained model as our starting point for the intent discovery task, and leverage the mead-baseline (Pressel et al., 2018) package for the implementation.

2.2 Step 2: Domain-adaptive Pre-training

The premise of the domain-adaptive pre-training step is that the model can learn from a broad spectrum of existing use cases covering different business verticals so that the adapted encoder is applicable to new previously unseen use cases. To achieve this goal, we drew a balanced amount of (utterance, intent) sample pairs from each of 20 applications in our enterprise virtual assistant database thereby ensuring that applications with larger data volume do not dominate the pre-training data. The applications cover a broad range of verticals including insurance, telecommunications, consumer electronics, financial, retail, travel, and utilities.

Additionally, we note that many of the application models were designed independently, yielding differences in the naming conventions for intent labels across applications, even for intents with the same semantic meaning. For example, the technical-support intent could be named "TECH-SUPPORT" in one application but "TECHNICAL-SERVICE" in another. Consequently, we could not simply merge data from different applications and pre-train one single model. To deal with this problem, we employed a multi-task approach to pre-training where the Transformer encoder is shared between different applications, but the intent classifier is specific for each application. This ensures that varying labels across applications do not compete with each other in the softmax loss.

If we directly use a linear classifier with standard softmax loss for each task, the embeddings (i.e., feature inputs) to the softmax loss will be trained to yield linear discrimination, but may not preserve the distance metrics which are critical for our downstream clustering task. To preserve distance-metrics in the geometry, we replace the standard softmax with cosine softmax, where the logit score inside softmax is computed via the cosine similarity between the embeddings and the classifier weights. The resulting approach has a novel multi-task cosine softmax loss for domain-adaptive pre-training to accommodate the nature of our enterprise virtual assistant data and the downstream clustering task. This is the key contribution of this paper. We will present more details in Section 3.

2.3 Step 3: Downstream Embedding and Clustering

After the model is pre-trained and adapted to our enterprise virtual assistant domain, we can apply it to any new application for intent discovery. We apply the encoder to each utterance from the new application to obtain ℓ_2 normalized utterance embeddings, and run K-means clustering on the embeddings to extract intent clusters.

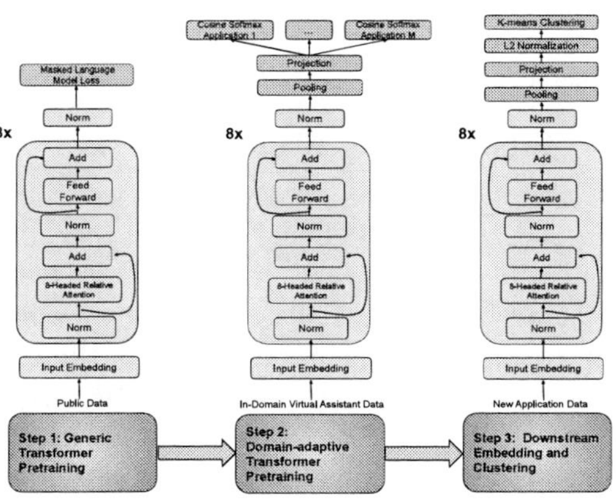

Figure 1: The Three-step Approach

3 Model Description

We describe here the model formulation for Step 2 of our intent discovery pipeline. We collected pre-training data from $M = 20$ applications in our data lake, and for each application m we sample $n^{(m)}$ (utterance, intent) pairs $(\boldsymbol{x}_i^{(m)}, y_i^{(m)})$, $(i = 1, 2, \cdots, n^{(m)})$. Here $\boldsymbol{x}_i^{(m)}$ is a raw utterance from ASR transcription, $y_i^{(m)} \in \{1, 2, \cdots, C^{(m)}\}$ is the intent label for that utterance, the total number of intents $C^{(m)}$ for application m is about 1000, and the number of samples $n^{(m)}$ for application m is around one million.

Our multi-application intent classifier is a multi-task learning model where the utterance encoder is shared across applications but the classifier is built separately for each application. Mathematically the model can be formulated by minimizing the following loss function $L(\boldsymbol{X}, \boldsymbol{Y}) = \sum_{m=1}^{M} \sum_{i=1}^{n^{(m)}} \ell^{(m)} \left(\boldsymbol{h}(\boldsymbol{x}_i^{(m)}), y_i^{(m)} \right)$ where $\boldsymbol{h}$ is the utterance encoder which is shared across applications and initialized from the generic pre-training on public data in Step 1. It consists of the pre-trained Transformer layers followed by mean-pooling to yield a fixed-length representation of the utterance, and a Multilayer Perceptron (MLP) to project it to a desired embedding space. During pre-training we randomly sample a mini-batch of utterances from the pre-training data, pass it through the same Transformer encoder $\boldsymbol{h}$, and then use different classifier heads for different utterances depending on which applications they come from. This multi-task learning approach has been used successfully in the literature to learn sentence embeddings (Liu et al., 2019; Wei et al., 2021). However, our approach differs in its use of the cosine softmax loss in $\ell^{(m)}$ with a distance-metric preserving property as explained below. A standard softmax loss computes the cross-entropy between the intent prediction distribution and the label as follows:

$$\ell^{(m)} \left(\boldsymbol{h}(\boldsymbol{x}_i^{(m)}), y_i^{(m)} \right) = - \sum_{c=1}^{C^{(m)}} 1(c = y_i^{(m)}) \times \log \frac{\exp \left(\boldsymbol{h}(\boldsymbol{x}_i^{(m)})^\top \boldsymbol{\theta}_c^{(m)} \right)}{\sum_{c'=1}^{C^{(m)}} \exp \left(\boldsymbol{h}(\boldsymbol{x}_i^{(m)})^\top \boldsymbol{\theta}_{c'}^{(m)} \right)} \tag{1}$$

where $\boldsymbol{\theta}_c^{(m)}$ is the classifier vector for intent c in application m. However, as discussed in Section 2.2, this loss is not a good option for our downstream intent discovery task. For example, two nearby utterances in the embedding space could belong to different intent classes, if they lie on different sides of the linear boundary. To remedy this, we replace the above standard softmax loss with a cosine softmax loss as follows

$$\ell^{(m)}\left(\boldsymbol{h}(\boldsymbol{x}_i^{(m)}), y_i^{(m)}\right) = -\sum_{c=1}^{C^{(m)}} 1(c = y_i^{(m)}) \times \log \frac{\exp\left(\bar{\boldsymbol{h}}(\boldsymbol{x}_i^{(m)})^\top \bar{\boldsymbol{\theta}}_c^{(m)}/\tau\right)}{\sum_{c'=1}^{C^{(m)}} \exp\left(\bar{\boldsymbol{h}}(\boldsymbol{x}_i^{(m)})^\top \bar{\boldsymbol{\theta}}_{c'}^{(m)}/\tau\right)} \tag{2}$$

Here $\bar{\boldsymbol{h}}(\boldsymbol{x}_i^{(m)}) = \boldsymbol{h}(\boldsymbol{x}_i^{(m)})/\|\boldsymbol{h}(\boldsymbol{x}_i^{(m)})\|$ and $\bar{\boldsymbol{\theta}}_c^{(m)} = \boldsymbol{\theta}_c^{(m)}/\|\boldsymbol{\theta}_c^{(m)}\|$ are normalized unit vectors which will be used as the final embeddings for the utterances and intents, and τ is a pre-defined temperature parameter. Since the cosine similarity is related to the distance metric via $\boldsymbol{v}_1^\top \boldsymbol{v}_2 = -\|\boldsymbol{v}_1 - \boldsymbol{v}_2\|^2/2 + 1$ for ℓ_2 normalized vectors, the cosine softmax pushes the embeddings of the utterances and the corresponding intents to be close to each other, which will yield the distance-metric preserving property we desire. Appendix A.3 's figure visually represents the difference between standard softmax and cosine softmax.

This is the novel multi-task cosine softmax loss we propose in this paper. Notice that both the utterance encoder $\boldsymbol{h}$ and the unnormalized intent embeddings $\boldsymbol{\theta}$ are learned in this domain-adaptive pre-training process, where the Transformer is initialized from generic pre-training in Step 1 and the intent embeddings are initialized randomly as a look-up table. After this Step 2, the adapted utterance encoder, which summarizes all enterprise virtual assistant data characteristics and business logics from multiple existing applications, can then be applied to downstream intent discovery tasks for new applications in Step 3. We also mention alternative modeling approaches in Appendix A.1.

4 Experiments

4.1 Experimental Methodology

To monitor the quality of the domain-adaptive pre-training in Step 2, we randomly select 4% from the supervised pre-training data as a validation set and predict the intent following the multi-task cosine softmax loss proposed in Section 3,

$$\begin{aligned}\tilde{y}_i^{(m)} &= \underset{c\in\{1,2,\cdots,C^{(m)}\}}{\operatorname{argmax}} \log \frac{\exp\left(\bar{\boldsymbol{h}}(\boldsymbol{x}_i^{(m)})^\top \bar{\boldsymbol{\theta}}_c^{(m)}/\tau\right)}{\sum_{c'=1}^{C^{(m)}} \exp\left(\bar{\boldsymbol{h}}(\boldsymbol{x}_i^{(m)})^\top \bar{\boldsymbol{\theta}}_{c'}^{(m)}/\tau\right)} \\ &= \underset{c\in\{1,2,\cdots,C^{(m)}\}}{\operatorname{argmin}} \|\bar{\boldsymbol{h}}(\boldsymbol{x}_i^{(m)}) - \bar{\boldsymbol{\theta}}_c^{(m)}\|^2\end{aligned} \tag{3}$$

which is essentially performing a nearest neighbor intent search in the embedding space. We compare the true intent label $y_i^{(m)}$ with the above predicted intent $\tilde{y}^{(m)}$ to compute the pre-training accuracy for Step 2. The domain-adapted Transformer model achieved an accuracy of 91.5% on this validation set, which demonstrates the consistency of the true intent labels and the high quality of the adapted Transformer model.

However, the ultimate goal of our model is not to test the intent classification accuracy for our existing applications but to perform intent discovery on a new application. It is not possible to directly apply equation (3) for intent discovery, as we do not have the intent embeddings $\bar{\boldsymbol{\theta}}^{(m)}$ for the new application. A natural approach for this problem is to embed all utterances from a new application t using the pre-trained application-independent encoder $\bar{\boldsymbol{h}}(\boldsymbol{x}_i^{(t)})$ and apply a clustering algorithm. Then, we simultaneously identify the centroids as the discovered intent embeddings and the cluster indices as intent predictions. This is the Step 3 in our intent discovery pipeline. For simplicity and a fair comparison with other methods, we use the K-means algorithm to perform clustering on the new application's data,

$$(\tilde{y}_i^{(t)}, \bar{\boldsymbol{\theta}}^{(t)}) = \underset{c_i\in\{1,2,\cdots,K\},\bar{\boldsymbol{\theta}}^{(t)}}{\arg\min} \sum_{i=1}^{n^{(t)}} \|\bar{\boldsymbol{h}}(\boldsymbol{x}_i^{(t)}) - \bar{\boldsymbol{\theta}}_{c_i}^{(t)}\|^2 \tag{4}$$

From equation (4), we can see that we are essentially using an enterprise virtual assistant domain adapted utterance encoder for this clustering problem. We will evaluate the performance of the proposed intent discovery pipeline objectively and subjectively.

4.2 Objective Evaluation

For objective evaluation of the proposed method, we collected four additional existing applications from different business verticals and treated each of them as a "new" candidate application for intent discovery. Notice that these four applications are different from the 20 existing applications used in our Step 2 pre-training. Thus, we ensure that this "new" application simulation process is valid and the evaluation is fair. The details of the four applications are provided in Table 2 in the appendix. The intent distribution for each of the four applications is imbalanced, and about 50% samples of each application contains the top five intents of the application.

Evaluating clustering results is a challenging task, as there might be different (but all valid) ways to partition the data (Färber et al., 2010). In our objective evaluation we choose the production intent label as the ground truth label, as this is the real business model we deployed for the application, and it is consistent with our enterprise virtual assistant pre-training process in Step 2. Inevitably there will be noise in the production intent labels. However, according to our offline human evaluation, the noise level is reasonably low.

For testing application t, we collect samples $(\boldsymbol{x}_i^{(t)}, y_i^{(t)})$ from our data lake, and only leverage the utterance part $\boldsymbol{x}_i^{(t)}$ for intent discovery in Step 3 via equation (4). We then evaluate the intent discovery performance through the standard clustering evaluation metrics (Wagner and Wagner, 2007; Xu et al., 2017), which take the ground truth intent labels $y_i^{(t)}$ and the clustering indices $\tilde{y}_i^{(t)}$ from equation (4) as inputs, and output evaluation scores (the higher the better) to measure the clustering quality. We use the following clustering evaluation metrics: **ACC** (Accuracy with label set alignment), **ARI** (Rand Index Adjusted for chance), **NMI** (Normalized Mutual Information), and **AMI** (Adjusted Mutual Information). **ACC** is defined as $\text{ACC} = \max_g \sum_{i=1}^{n^{(t)}} 1\{y_i^{(t)} = g(\tilde{y}_i^{(t)})\}/n^{(t)}$ where g ranges over all possible one-to-one mappings between cluster indices and ground truth labels. In practice, we use the Hungarian algorithm (Kuhn, 1955) to identify the optimal mapping that produces the best accuracy score. The definition of **ARI**, **NMI** and **AMI** together with training details are available in Appendix A.4 and A.5.

We evaluate the following intent discovery approaches using the above evaluation metrics.

1. **Step 1 + Step 2 + Step 3.** This is the intent discovery procedure we propose in this paper. See Figure 1 for the full pipeline.

2. **Step 1 + Step 2 (Standard) + Step 3.** This approach is similar to Step 1 + Step 2 + Step 3; however, in Step 2 we use the standard softmax loss in equation (1) instead of the cosine softmax loss in equation (2). Consequently, we do not have the ℓ_2 normalization for Step 3 in Figure 1.

3. **Step 2 + Step 3.** In this baseline approach, we skip the generic Transformer pre-training in Step 1 and randomly initialize the Transformer weights to start the enterprise virtual assistant domain adaptive pre-training in Step 2.

4. **Step 1 + Step 3.** In this baseline approach, we only use the utterance encoder pre-trained on generic data for intent discovery, and no enterprise virtual assistant domain adaptation in Step 2 is applied. As a result, we do not have the projection layer and ℓ_2 normalization for Step 3 in Figure 1.

5. **SBERT + Step 3.** In this baseline approach, we directly borrow a publicly available sentence encoder Sentence-BERT model (Reimers and Gurevych, 2019) to replace the $\bar{\boldsymbol{h}}(\boldsymbol{x}_i^{(t)})$ encoder in (4).

6. **DEC.** In this baseline approach, we reimplemented the Deep Embedded Clustering (DEC) algorithm (Xie et al., 2016). Here, the utterance encoder is pre-trained on testing data alone, and it is fine-tuned during the clustering process (Hadifar et al., 2019).

Since we do not know the true number of clusters in advance, we presented **ACC** result with different K values in Figure 2. The results for **ARI**, **NMI**, and **AMI** with different K values are presented in Appendix A.7. From the results, we can make the following observations:

1. The models with domain-adaptive pre-training perform much better than all other methods without domain-adaptive pre-training (including the state-of-the-art Sentence-BERT model) across different testing datasets. The performance improvement can be as high as 20% absolute in clustering accuracy. This performance clearly shows the benefit of domain-adaptive pre-training for downstream clustering tasks.

2. Step 1 + Step 2 (Standard) + Step 3 performs much worse than Step 1 + Step 2 + Step 3 in downstream clustering accuracy, according to Figure 2. This performance gap is expected as pre-training with the standard softmax loss in Step 2 does not induce the distance-metric preserving property, which is important for distance-based clustering such as K-means in downstream tasks.

3. In most cases, Step 2 + Step 3 performs similarly as Step 1 + Step 2 + Step 3, which means that the generic pre-training in Step 1 is not helping much for the downstream clustering task. The reason might be that we already

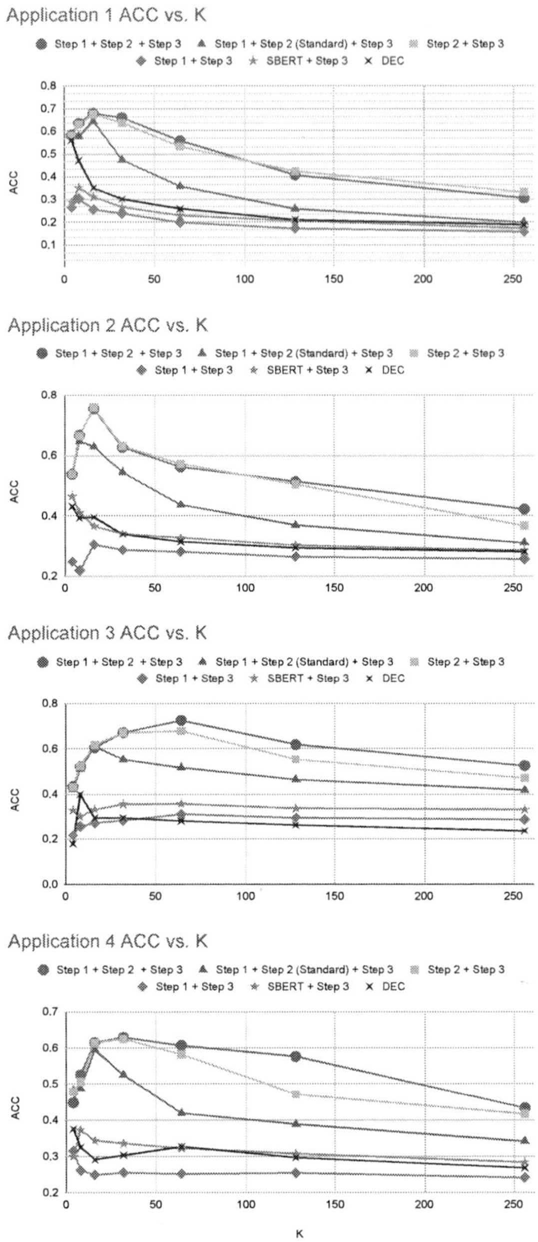

Figure 2: ACC of intent discovery for four applications with $K = [4, 8, 16, 32, 64, 128, 256]$. Resolution of subfigures is automatically adjusted to show differences in the curves, which causes y-axis' scale to be different.

have a large amount of enterprise virtual assistant domain pre-training data in Step 2. As a result, the Transformer initialization from the generic pre-training will not have a lot of impact on the domain-adaptive pre-training result. Nevertheless, we still see that in some instances (e.g., **ACC** curves for Application 4 in Figure 2), Step 2 + Step 3 experienced performance drop compared with Step 1 + Step 2 + Step 3, indicating that the generic pre-training in Step 1 improves the robustness of the model across different domains.

4. In our error analysis, we observe that Step 1 + Step 2 + Step 3 tends to keep semantically similar utterances (e.g., "pay my bill" and "make a payment") into one cluster; however, other methods tend to split semantically similar utterances into multiple clusters. This leads to degradation in performance in other methods. In addition to that, our applications contain Spanish data with low frequency. Interestingly, on Step 1 + Step 2 + Step 3 results, we find that the cluster centroid where Spanish speakers want to speak to a live agent (e.g., "o hablar con un representante") and the cluster centroid where English speakers want to speak to a live agent (e.g., "i need to talk to a representative") are proximal. Such proximity is not well pronounced in other methods.

In summary, the proposed intent discovery pipeline with domain-adaptive pre-training outperforms other methods by a large margin. Hence, by continuing pre-training the Transformer on in-domain enterprise virtual assistant data from multiple existing applications, we can effectively distill the knowledge of enterprise virtual assistant data characteristics and business logic into the Transformer encoder, which provides high-quality utterance embeddings and excellent intent discovery results on unseen applications.

4.3 Intent Discovery Portal

For new applications and for unexpected inputs to a deployed application, we generally do not have labels that can be used for objective evaluation. In order to extract value from the results of semantic embedding on new data we built out an interactive intent discovery portal that enables visualization, interactive inspection of intent clusters, and subjective evaluation. Figure 3 shows the intent discovery user interface. The left panel contains an un-directed graph in which semantic closeness among clusters is represented by graph links in a minimum spanning tree. The graph is interactive and when the user selects a node in the graph, the middle panel shows a list of examples of members of the cluster along with an interactive phrase cloud.

The right panel supports replay of audio (if available) and presents a list of related examples and intents from a large database of existing application data. More details on the intent discovery portal are available in Appendix A.2 and A.6.

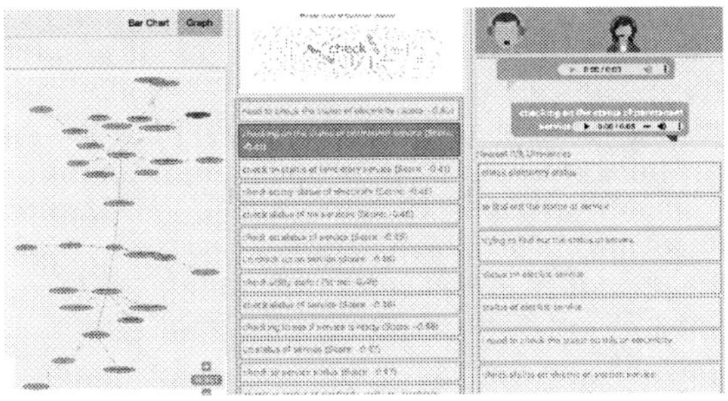

Figure 3: Intent Discovery Portal View.

5 Conclusion

This paper proposed a practical three-step solution to the challenge of intent discovery for virtual assistants. From our experiments, we found that a domain-adaptive pre-training step is essential for achieving good downstream clustering performance. Through supervised pre-training, enterprise virtual assistant data characteristics and associated business logic are all distilled into the resulting utterance encoder. This three-step approach can be viewed as an extension of the don't-stop-pretraining paradigm (Gururangan et al., 2020) to the downstream clustering tasks. We also found that state-of-the-art generic sentence encoders may not yield the best sentence representations to specific industrial applications such as enterprise virtual assistants. A consequence of this domain-adaptive pre-training is that the resulting sentence encoder is no longer generic, hence cannot necessarily be applied to data beyond the domain of enterprise virtual assistants. However, the same methodology could be applied to any enterprise database, so that people can pre-train domain-specific sentence encoders to match their own needs.

Acknowledgements

We would like to thank the anonymous reviewers for their constructive comments. We would also like to thank colleagues at Interactions LLC for their discussions and help on this work, especially Lou Nicotra for all the support on computing infrastructure.

References

Martín Abadi, Paul Barham, Jianmin Chen, Zhifeng Chen, Andy Davis, Jeffrey Dean, Matthieu Devin, Sanjay Ghemawat, Geoffrey Irving, Michael Isard, et al. 2016. Tensorflow: A system for large-scale machine learning. In *12th USENIX symposium on operating systems design and implementation (OSDI 16)*, pages 265–283.

Roee Aharoni and Yoav Goldberg. 2020. Unsupervised domain clusters in pretrained language models. In *Proceedings of the 58th Annual Meeting of the Association for Computational Linguistics*, pages 7747–7763.

Rami Al-Rfou, Marc Pickett, Javier Snaider, Yun-Hsuan Sung, Brian Strope, and Ray Kurzweil. 2016. Conversational contextual cues: The case of personalization and history for response ranking. *arXiv preprint arXiv:1606.00372*.

Tom Brown, Benjamin Mann, Nick Ryder, Melanie Subbiah, Jared D Kaplan, Prafulla Dhariwal, Arvind Neelakantan, Pranav Shyam, Girish Sastry, Amanda Askell, Sandhini Agarwal, Ariel Herbert-Voss, Gretchen Krueger, Tom Henighan, Rewon Child, Aditya Ramesh, Daniel Ziegler, Jeffrey Wu, Clemens Winter, Chris Hesse, Mark Chen, Eric Sigler, Mateusz Litwin, Scott Gray, Benjamin Chess, Jack Clark, Christopher Berner, Sam McCandlish, Alec Radford, Ilya Sutskever, and Dario Amodei. 2020. Language models are few-shot learners. In *Advances in Neural Information Processing Systems*, volume 33, pages 1877–1901.

Ting Chen, Simon Kornblith, Mohammad Norouzi, and Geoffrey Hinton. 2020. A simple framework for contrastive learning of visual representations. In *International conference on machine learning*, pages 1597–1607. PMLR.

Jacob Devlin, Ming-Wei Chang, Kenton Lee, and Kristina Toutanova. 2019. Bert: Pre-training of deep bidirectional transformers for language understanding. In *Proceedings of the 2019 Conference of the North American Chapter of the Association for Computational Linguistics: Human Language Technologies, Volume 1 (Long and Short Papers)*, pages 4171–4186.

Ines Färber, Stephan Günnemann, Hans-Peter Kriegel, Peer Kröger, Emmanuel Müller, Erich Schubert, Thomas Seidl, and Arthur Zimek. 2010. On using class-labels in evaluation of clusterings. In *MultiClust: 1st international workshop on discovering, summarizing and using multiple clusterings held in conjunction with KDD*, page 1.

Suchin Gururangan, Ana Marasović, Swabha Swayamdipta, Kyle Lo, Iz Beltagy, Doug Downey, and Noah A. Smith. 2020. Don't stop pretraining: Adapt language models to domains and tasks. In *Proceedings of the 58th Annual Meeting of the Association for Computational Linguistics*, pages 8342–8360.

Amir Hadifar, Lucas Sterckx, Thomas Demeester, and Chris Develder. 2019. A self-training approach for short text clustering. In *Proceedings of the 4th Workshop on Representation Learning for NLP (RepL4NLP-2019)*, pages 194–199.

Matthew Henderson, Paweł Budzianowski, Iñigo Casanueva, Sam Coope, Daniel Gerz, Girish Kumar, Nikola Mrksic, Georgios P. Spithourakis, Pei hao Su, Ivan Vulic, and Tsung-Hsien Wen. 2019. A repository of conversational datasets. In *Proceedings of the First Workshop on NLP for Conversational AI*, pages 1–10.

Matthew Henderson, Iñigo Casanueva, Nikola Mrkvsi'c, Pei hao Su, Tsung-Hsien, and Ivan Vulic. 2020. Convert: Efficient and accurate conversational representations from transformers. In *Proceedings of the 2020 Conference on Empirical Methods in Natural Language Processing: Findings*, pages 2161–2174.

Prannay Khosla, Piotr Teterwak, Chen Wang, Aaron Sarna, Yonglong Tian, Phillip Isola, Aaron Maschinot, Ce Liu, and Dilip Krishnan. 2020. Supervised contrastive learning. In *Advances in Neural Information Processing Systems*, volume 33, pages 18661–18673.

Harold W Kuhn. 1955. The hungarian method for the assignment problem. *Naval research logistics quarterly*, 2(1-2):83–97.

Xiaodong Liu, Pengcheng He, Weizhu Chen, and Jianfeng Gao. 2019. Multi-task deep neural networks for natural language understanding. In *Proceedings of the 57th Annual Meeting of the Association for Computational Linguistics*, pages 4487–4496.

Christopher D Manning, Kevin Clark, John Hewitt, Urvashi Khandelwal, and Omer Levy. 2020. Emergent linguistic structure in artificial neural networks trained by self-supervision. *Proceedings of the National Academy of Sciences*, 117(48):30046–30054.

Toan Q. Nguyen and Julian Salazar. 2019. Transformers without tears: Improving the normalization of self-attention. *arXiv preprint arXiv:1910.05895*.

Adam Paszke, Sam Gross, Francisco Massa, Adam Lerer, James Bradbury, Gregory Chanan, Trevor Killeen, Zeming Lin, Natalia Gimelshein, Luca Antiga, Alban Desmaison, Andreas Kopf, Edward Yang, Zachary DeVito, Martin Raison, Alykhan Tejani, Sasank Chilamkurthy, Benoit Steiner, Lu Fang, Junjie Bai, and Soumith Chintala. 2019. Pytorch: An imperative style, high-performance deep learning library. In H. Wallach, H. Larochelle, A. Beygelzimer, F. d'Alché-Buc, E. Fox, and R. Garnett, editors, *Advances in Neural Information Processing Systems*, volume 32, pages 8024–8035.

Fabian Pedregosa, Gaël Varoquaux, Alexandre Gramfort, Vincent Michel, Bertrand Thirion, Olivier Grisel, Mathieu Blondel, Peter Prettenhofer, Ron Weiss, Vincent Dubourg, et al. 2011. Scikit-learn: Machine learning in python. *the Journal of machine Learning research*, 12:2825–2830.

Daniel Pressel, Sagnik Ray Choudhury, Brian Lester, Yanjie Zhao, and Matt Barta. 2018. Baseline: A library for rapid modeling, experimentation and development of deep learning algorithms targeting nlp. In *Proceedings of Workshop for NLP Open Source Software (NLP-OSS)*, pages 34–40.

Daniel Pressel, Wenshuo Liu, Michael Johnston, and Minhua Chen. 2022. Lightweight transformers for conversational ai. In *Proceedings of the 2022 Conference of the North American Chapter of the Association for Computational Linguistics: Human Language Technologies: Industry Papers*, page 1.

Alec Radford, Jong Wook Kim, Chris Hallacy, Aditya Ramesh, Gabriel Goh, Sandhini Agarwal, Girish Sastry, Amanda Askell, Pamela Mishkin, Jack Clark, et al. 2021. Learning transferable visual models from natural language supervision. *arXiv preprint arXiv:2103.00020*.

Alec Radford, Karthik Narasimhan, Tim Salimans, and Ilyas Sutskever. 2018. Improving language understanding by generative pre-training. *OpenAI Blog*, page 1.

Alec Radford, Jeff Wu, Rewon Child, David Luan, Dario Amodei, and Ilya Sutskever. 2019. Language models are unsupervised multitask learners. *OpenAI Blog*, page 1.

Nils Reimers and Iryna Gurevych. 2019. Sentence-bert: Sentence embeddings using siamese bert-networks. In *Proceedings of the 2019 Conference on Empirical Methods in Natural Language Processing and the 9th International Joint Conference on Natural Language Processing (EMNLP-IJCNLP)*, pages 3982–3992.

Peter Shaw, Jakob Uszkoreit, and Ashish Vaswani. 2018. Self-attention with relative position representations. In *Proceedings of the 2018 Conference of the North American Chapter of the Association for Computational Linguistics: Human Language Technologies, Volume 2 (Short Papers)*, pages 464–468.

Ian Tenney, Dipanjan Das, and Ellie Pavlick. 2019. Bert rediscovers the classical nlp pipeline. In *Proceedings of the 57th Annual Meeting of the Association for Computational Linguistics*, pages 4593–4601.

Ivan Vulic, Pei hao Su, Sam Coope, Daniel Gerz, Paweł Budzianowski, Iñigo Casanueva, Nikola Mrkvsi'c, and Tsung-Hsien Wen. 2021. Convfit: Conversational fine-tuning of pretrained language models. In *Proceedings of the 2021 Conference on Empirical Methods in Natural Language Processing*, pages 1151–1168.

Silke Wagner and Dorothea Wagner. 2007. *Comparing clusterings: an overview*. Universität Karlsruhe, Fakultät für Informatik Karlsruhe.

Qiang Wang, Bei Li, Tong Xiao, Jingbo Zhu, Changliang Li, Derek F Wong, and Lidia S Chao. 2019. Learning deep transformer models for machine translation. In *Proceedings of the 57th Annual Meeting of the Association for Computational Linguistics*, pages 1810–1822.

Jason Wei, Maarten Bosma, Vincent Y Zhao, Kelvin Guu, Adams Wei Yu, Brian Lester, Nan Du, Andrew M Dai, and Quoc V Le. 2021. Finetuned language models are zero-shot learners. *arXiv preprint arXiv:2109.01652*.

Chien-Sheng Wu and Caiming Xiong. 2020. Probing task-oriented dialogue representation from language models. In *Proceedings of the 2020 Conference on Empirical Methods in Natural Language Processing (EMNLP)*, pages 5036–5051.

Junyuan Xie, Ross Girshick, and Ali Farhadi. 2016. Unsupervised deep embedding for clustering analysis. In *International conference on machine learning*, pages 478–487. PMLR.

Ruibin Xiong, Yunchang Yang, Di He, Kai Zheng, Shuxin Zheng, Chen Xing, Huishuai Zhang, Yanyan Lan, Liwei Wang, and Tieyan Liu. 2020. On layer normalization in the transformer architecture. In *International Conference on Machine Learning*, pages 10524–10533. PMLR.

Jiaming Xu, Bo Xu, Peng Wang, Suncong Zheng, Guanhua Tian, and Jun Zhao. 2017. Self-taught convolutional neural networks for short text clustering. *Neural Networks*, 88:22–31.

A Appendix

A.1 Alternative Models

The cosine softmax loss in (2) is reminiscent of the cosine-similarity based loss used in contrastive learning (Chen et al., 2020; Radford et al., 2021). For example, in OpenAI CLIP (Radford et al., 2021) two modalities (text and image) are aligned in the latent space via a dual-encoder model and a cosine-similarity based loss. The cosine softmax loss we use in equation (2) is also aligning two modalities (utterance and intent). However, since the set of all possible intents for an application is finite and known in advance, we do not need to use the in-batch negative sampling approach as in the contrastive learning loss. Instead we contrast with all possible intents in the denominator of equation (2).

Another alternative approach is supervised contrastive learning (Khosla et al., 2020; Vulic et al., 2021), where the contrastive learning is done using just the utterance modality. In this approach, the positive utterance pair is obtained by sampling utterances with the same intents, while the negative utterance pair is obtained by sampling utterances with different intents. Then the supervised contrastive loss will impose the constrain that embeddings for the positive pair should live nearby and the embeddings for the negative pair should live further apart.

We note that both the multi-model contrastive learning and the supervised contrastive learning are valid modeling approaches for our domain-adaptive pre-training. However, we focus on the cosine softmax loss in equation (2) in this paper due to its simplicity and its straightforward nature, and leave the comparison to the above alternative models in our future work.

Another approach is to use the standard softmax (equation (1)) in Step 2, and then use spectral clustering in Step 3. There are a few issues in this approach. Firstly, the embedding geometry learned with standard softmax is not friendly to downstream clustering tasks. Secondly, there is no guarantee that the spectral embedding step in spectral clustering can infer the right semantic geometry, as no supervised pre-training data is used in Step 3. Lastly, spectral clustering is quite computationally expensive and could not scale to large downstream datasets. Empirically we also observe that this approach is inferior to our proposed approach. In contrast, our proposed approach shifts the heavy-lifting geometric manifold learning task to the cosine softmax (equation (2)) in Step 2, so that K-means is enough for the downstream clustering task.

A.2 Intent Unification and Vector Search

A by-product of the above domain-adaptive pre-training is a mechanism for intent unification across multiple applications. Suppose intent c in application m and intent c' in application m' are semantically similar but named differently. Since the utterances (which are callers' realizations of the intents) associated with these two intents are similar, and they share the same utterance encoder, the embeddings for these utterances will live nearby. This again will drive the intent embeddings for the above two intents close together, according to the multi-task cosine softmax loss function. As a result, after the pre-training, semantically similar intents across applications will live close-by in the embedding space. Hence by simply exploring the intent embedding space through K-means clustering, we could unify intents across applications by grouping semantically related intents together.

Another by-product is vector search for utterances. Since we have learned an utterance encoder specific for the enterprise virtual assistant domain in the Step 2 pre-training, we can embed any new utterance and convert it into a fixed-length vector. Since we already have utterance embeddings and intent embeddings for our pre-training data from the existing applications, for each new utterance or discovered cluster centroid, we can obtain the nearest utterances and intents from the pre-training data via K-nearest neighbor search. These nearest neighbors can be used to help to augment the query utterances or name the discovered intent clusters, which can greatly improve the interpretability of our intent discovery results. A potential risk of this vector search is that private information from our existing applications could be revealed to a new user of our system. Hence, careful considerations are needed when we activate this vector search feature, and all sensitive information should be redacted from the utterance pool used for this K-nearest neighbor search.

A.3 Standard Softmax vs. Cosine Softmax

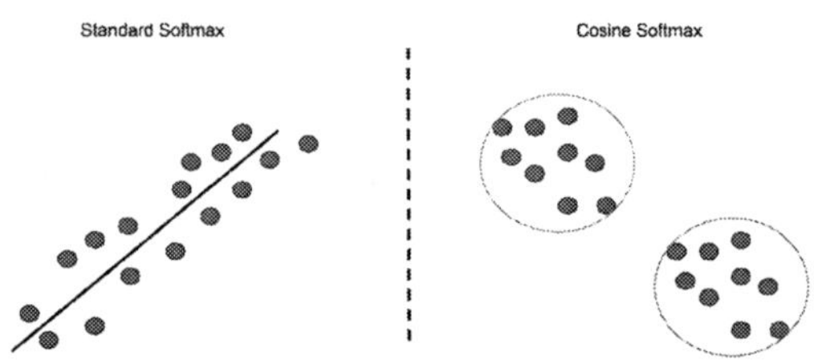

Figure 4: Standard softmax and cosine softmax induce different geometries in the embedding space

A.4 Definition of Clustering Evaluation Metrics

Here are some descriptions for the clustering evaluation metrics. More formal definitions could be found in (Wagner and Wagner, 2007).

ARI: In the Rand Index, we consider all pairs of samples and see how often pairs are grouped consistently under the clustering results and the ground truth labels. In Adjusted Rand Index (ARI), this consistency frequency is adjusted by a base model to correct the impact of consistency by chance.

NMI: The Mutual Information directly measures the correspondence between the clusters and the ground truth classes via a probability measure of common samples between them. This measure is normalized by entropy of the partitions to yield the Normalized Mutual Information (NMI).

AMI: The above Normalized Mutual Information is further adjusted to account for chance and size of the clusters, to yield this Adjusted Mutual Information (AMI) measure.

Hyperparameter	Description	Value
Pooling	Mean pooling layer output before projection (Figure 1)	512
Projection	Projection layer output before cosine softmax (Figure 1)	256
Epochs	Training epochs	3
Softmax	Type of softmax used in loss function (Figure 1)	cosine
Dropout	Layer dropout	0.1
Cosine Temperature (τ)	Cosine softmax temperature (Equation 3)	0.125
Optimizer	Training optimizer	AdamW
Learning Rate	Learning rate for optimizer	1.e-5
Weight Decay	Weight decay for optimizer	1.0e-3
Clip	Gradient clip	1.0
Batch Size	Training batch size	360
Input Length	Maximum input length	64
Layers	Transformer layers	8
Multi-head attention	Number of head in the attention module	8

Table 1: Step 2 Hyperparameters

Name	Business	Samples	Intents	Average words
Application 1	Collections	707907	82	5
Application 2	Power Utility	616145	432	4
Application 3	Insurance	1000000	1830	4
Application 4	Photography	921440	2521	5

Table 2: Testing Applications for Step 3

A.5 Training Details

In this section we provide training details for each Step in the pipeline (Figure 1). For Step 1, we trained using Apache Licensed TensorFlow (Abadi et al., 2016) on a single v3 Tensor Processing Unit (TPU). For best performance on TPUs, we use bucketing based on full conversation lengths, scaling the number of samples for each bucket length so that the number of tokens is constant per batch. We use AdamW with a peak learning rate of 4e-4, a weight decay of 1e-3, and a linear warmup of 10,000 steps followed by cosine decay. For Step 2, hyperparameters are listed in Table 1, and we built our model using open source BSD-licensed PyTorch library (Paszke et al., 2019). Our model has 49 million parameters. The pre-training in Step 2 were conducted on two NVIDIA GeForce 1080Ti GPUs, and it took about 30 hours to finish. For Step 3, we used the open source BSD-licensed scikit-learn library (Pedregosa et al., 2011) for K-means clustering with default hyperparameters. More specifically, we used "k-means++" initialization with multiple runs to make the results more robust. The intent discovery results for downstream applications in Table 2 are reported in Figure 2, Figure 7, Figure 8, and Figure 9 with $K = [4, 8, 16, 32, 64, 128, 256]$.

A.6 Additional Details on Intent Discovery Portal

Figure 5 provides a more detailed view of the graph representation of the automatic intent discovery results from the intent discovery portal. The nodes are automatically labelled with keywords from each cluster determined using TF-IDF, e.g., 'make bill payment pay' for a cluster associated with bill payment. Figure 6 shows an alternative view of the cluster data as a bar chart capturing the relative size of clusters in the data. The different views are interconnected, and the user can select an intent in one and see where it is in the alternate view.

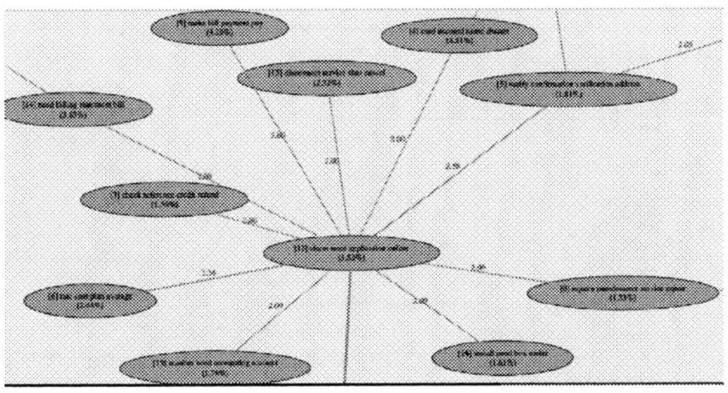

Figure 5: Detail view of the portal zoomed on few nodes in the un-directed graph.

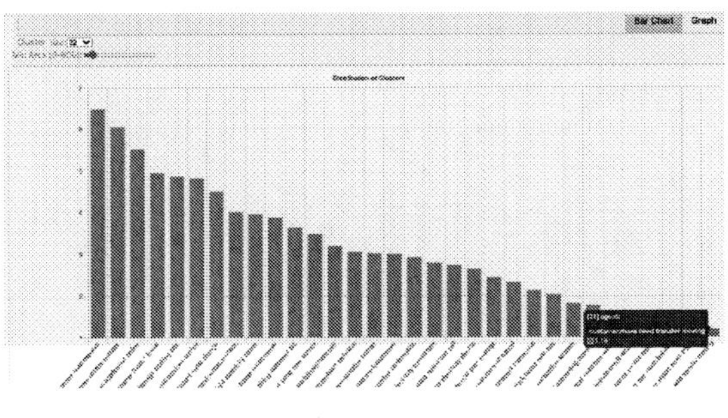

Figure 6: Cluster-size Bar Chart View.

A.7 More Objective Evaluation (ARI, NMI, and AMI) on Testing Applications

Figure 7, Figure 8, and Figure 9 provide **ARI**, **NMI** and **AMI** results on our testing applications.

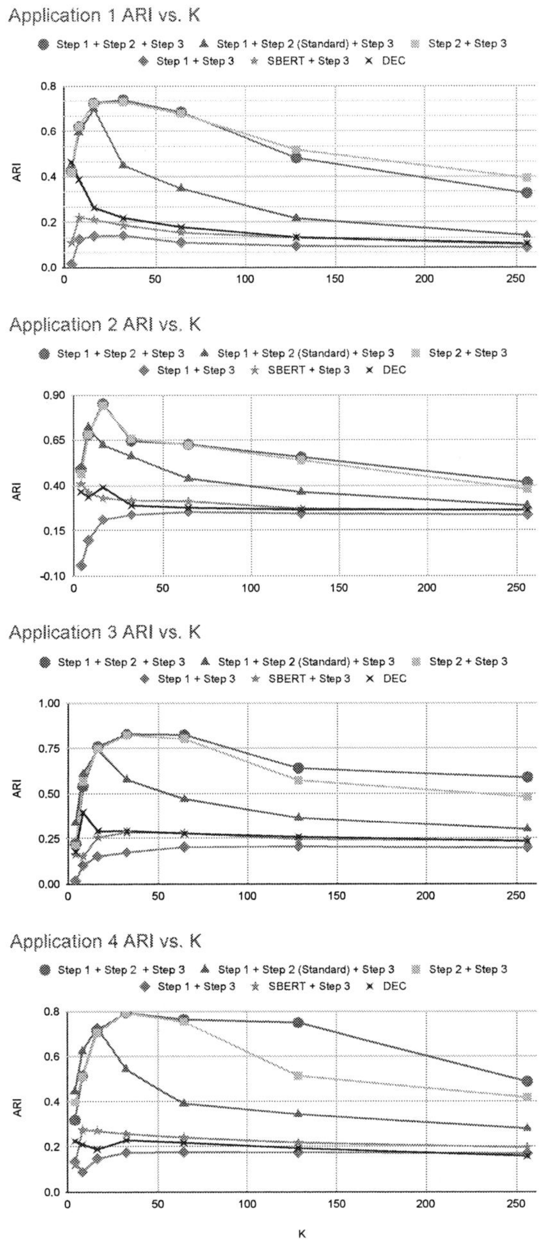

Figure 7: ARI of intent discovery for four applications with $K = [4, 8, 16, 32, 64, 128, 256]$.

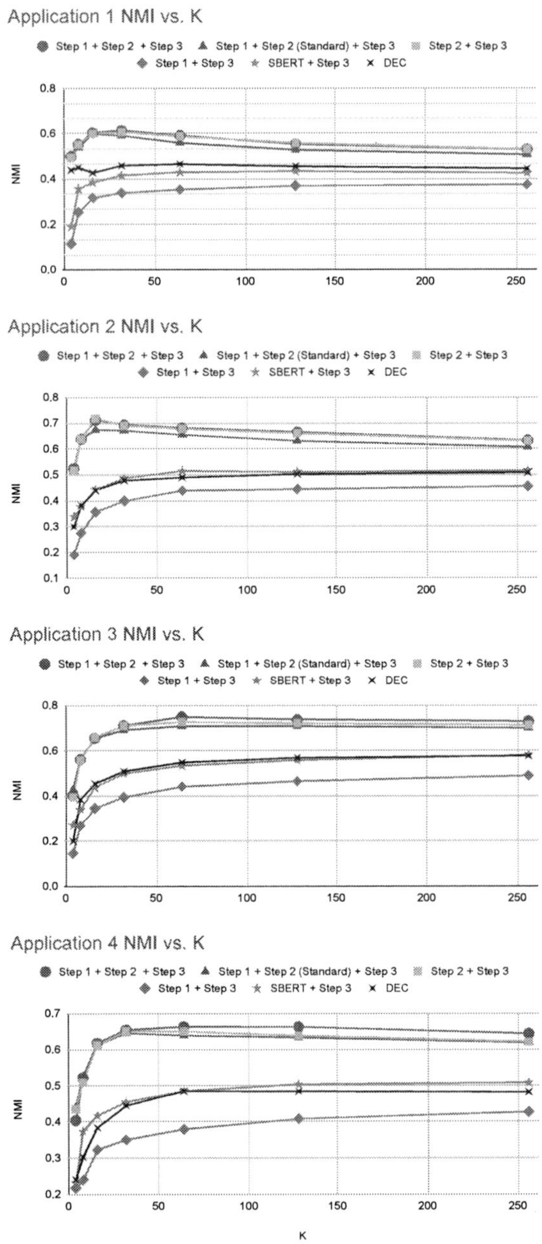

Figure 8: NMI of intent discovery for four applications with $K = [4, 8, 16, 32, 64, 128, 256]$.

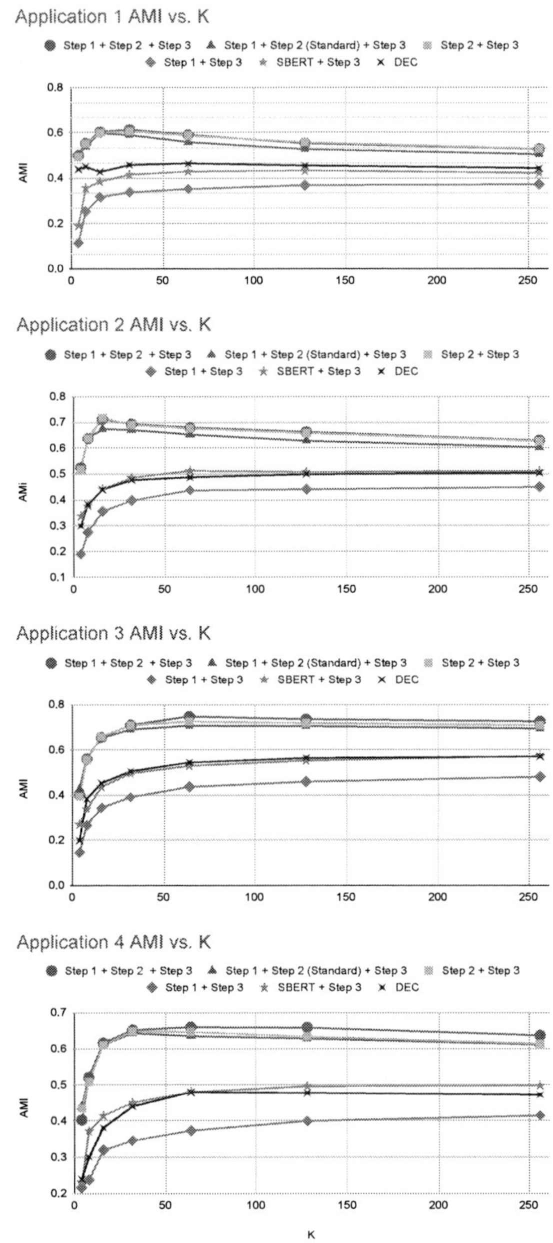

Figure 9: AMI of intent discovery for four applications with $K = [4, 8, 16, 32, 64, 128, 256]$.

ReFinED: An Efficient Zero-shot-capable Approach to End-to-End Entity Linking

Tom Ayoola, Shubhi Tyagi, Joseph Fisher, Christos Christodoulopoulos, Andrea Pierleoni
Amazon Alexa AI
Cambridge, UK
{tayoola, tshubhi, fshjos, chrchrs, apierleo}@amazon.com

Abstract

We introduce ReFinED, an efficient end-to-end entity linking model which uses fine-grained entity types and entity descriptions to perform linking. The model performs mention detection, fine-grained entity typing, and entity disambiguation for all mentions within a document in a single forward pass, making it more than 60 times faster than competitive existing approaches. ReFinED also surpasses state-of-the-art performance on standard entity linking datasets by an average of 3.7 F1. The model is capable of generalising to large-scale knowledge bases such as Wikidata (which has 15 times more entities than Wikipedia) and of zero-shot entity linking. The combination of speed, accuracy and scale makes ReFinED an effective and cost-efficient system for extracting entities from web-scale datasets, for which the model has been successfully deployed. Our code and pre-trained models are available at https://github.com/alexa/ReFinED.

1 Introduction

Entity linking (EL) is the task of recognising mentions of entities in unstructured text documents and linking them to the corresponding entities in a Knowledge Base (KB), such as Wikidata. EL is commonly a first stage in systems for question answering (Wang et al., 2021), automated KB population (Hoffmann et al., 2011), and relation extraction (Baldini Soares et al., 2019).

Currently, EL systems use deep learning methods to learn representations for entities and mentions (Ganea and Hofmann, 2017; Le and Titov, 2018). Initial techniques learned representations from text alone, which relied on entities appearing in similar contexts in the training data and meant models were only able to link mentions to entities that appeared in the training data. This is problematic both as KBs are continuously growing, and as it is infeasible to build an EL dataset containing all entities in a large KB (such as Wikidata with over 90 million entities). The largest public EL dataset is Wikipedia (using internal hyperlinks as labels), which covers just 3% of the entities in Wikidata.

Recent models addressed this problem by producing entity representations from a subset of KB information, e.g., entity descriptions (Wu et al., 2020; Logeswaran et al., 2019) or fine-grained entity types (Onoe and Durrett, 2020; Raiman and Raiman, 2018), allowing linking to entities not present in the training data or added to the KB after training; termed "zero-shot" in the EL literature.[1]

However, existing zero-shot-capable EL approaches are an order of magnitude more computationally expensive than non-zero-shot models (van Hulst et al., 2020) as they either require numerous entity types (Onoe and Durrett, 2020), multiple forward passes of a large-scale model to encode mentions and descriptions (Wu et al., 2020), or regeneration of the input text autoregressively (Cao et al., 2020). This makes large-scale processing expensive and thus makes it difficult to benefit from many advantages of zero-shot EL, e.g. the ability to keep up-to-date with new or updated KBs.

In this paper, we propose an efficient end-to-end zero-shot-capable EL model, ReFinED[2], which uses fine-grained entity types and entity descriptions to perform entity linking or entity disambiguation (ED; where entity mentions are given). We show that combining information from entity types and descriptions in a simple transformer-based encoder yields performance which is stronger than more complex architectures, surpassing state-of-the-art (SOTA) on 4 ED datasets and 5 EL datasets, and improving overall EL performance by 3.7 F1 points on average across 8 datasets. Importantly, ReFinED performs mention detection, fine-grained entity typing, and entity disambiguation for all men-

[1] Note the difference to "zero-shot" in the language-model literature, which refers to using no training data for the task.

[2] ReFinED stands for Representation and Fine-grained typing for Entity Disambiguation.

Proceedings of NAACL-HLT 2022: Industry Track Papers, pages 209 - 220

tions within a document in a single forward pass, making it comparable in terms of inference speed to non-zero-shot models. It is 6 times faster than the most efficient zero-shot-capable baseline (which has 9 F1 points lower performance), and more than 60 times faster than more accurate systems (which come within 3 F1 points of ReFinED's average ED performance).

As opposed to previous EL models which primarily use Wikipedia as the target KB, ReFinED targets Wikidata, which enables it to link to 15 times more entities. This is because prior work uses information (e.g. titles, categories, first sentences) from Wikipedia to perform linking. It is unclear whether prior work could be expanded to Wikidata without a drop in performance because entity descriptions are less informative and there are fewer types per entity (Weikum et al., 2021).

The combination of high accuracy, scalability (with respect to KB size) and fast inference speed makes ReFinED a strong choice for a "web-scale"[3] EL system, in which cost scales approximately linearly with inference speed. We have successfully deployed ReFinED to production in a real-world application and share the lessons learned in Section 6.

Our contributions are as follows:

1. We build a simple and efficient zero-shot capable end-to-end EL model using entity descriptions and entity typing, which outperforms previous approaches on standard-EL datasets by 3.7 F1 points on average.
2. We demonstrate our model is more than 6 times faster than existing low-accuracy zero-shot capable systems, and 60 times faster than higher-accuracy systems, whilst also being capable of disambiguating against Wikidata-scale entity sets. The combination of accuracy, speed and scale makes the model suitable for web-scale information extraction.
3. We release our code and models.

2 Related work

Single architecture for entity linking EL consists of two main tasks, mention detection (MD) and ED. MD involves recognising mentions of entities in text, and ED assigns a KB entity to each mention. We follow (Kolitsas et al., 2018) in training a joint model for MD and ED.

[3]We refer to corpora with more than 1 billion documents as "web-scale".

Entity disambiguation with fine-grained entity typing In Onoe and Durrett (2020) and Raiman and Raiman (2018) ED is formulated as an entity typing problem. A fine-grained entity typing model is trained on a distantly-supervised dataset consisting of over 10k types derived from Wikipedia categories (e.g. movies released in a specific year). The entity typing model is then used to link entities. We extend their approach to Wikidata, by using a subset of Wikidata triples for providing types instead of Wikipedia categories.

Entity disambiguation with entity descriptions Several recent works have used entity descriptions for ED (Wu et al., 2020; Logeswaran et al., 2019). Typically, descriptions are sourced from Wikipedia by joining the entity's title with the first sentence of the Wikipedia article. Entities are ranked by concatenating mention context and entity description, then passing each mention-entity pair to a cross-encoder. Wu et al. (2020) shows a cross-encoder outperforms a bi-encoder, with the latter missing many fine-grained interactions between context and description. In our work, we find that a bi-encoder is sufficient to achieve SOTA performance when combined with fine-grained entity typing, and generalise the approach from Wikipedia (6M entities) to Wikidata (90M entities).[4]

3 Proposed method

3.1 Task Formulation

Given a KB[5] with a set of entities $E = \{e_1, e_2, \ldots, e_{|E|}\}$, let $X = [x_1, x_2, \ldots, x_{|X|}]$ be a sequence of tokens in the document, and $M = \{m_1, m_2, ...m_{|M|}\}$ be a set of entity mentions. The goal of ED is to create a function $\mathcal{M} : M \rightarrow E$ which assigns each mention the correct entity label. In EL, both the mention spans and entity labels need to be predicted. We only consider mentions with a valid gold entity in the KB during evaluation.

3.2 Overview

We propose an end-to-end EL model which is jointly optimised for mention detection, fine-grained entity typing, and entity disambiguation for all mentions within a document in a single forward pass. In this section, we describe the components of our model, depicted in Figure 1.

[4]We replace Wikipedia titles with Wikidata labels, and Wikipedia sentences with Wikidata entity descriptions.

[5]We assume entities in the KB have a textual description and a collection of facts.

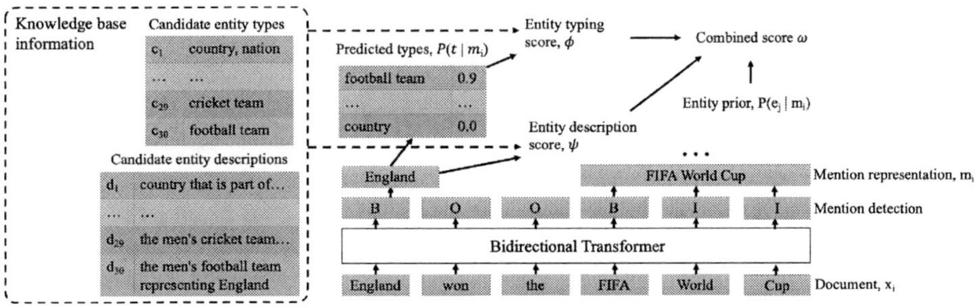

Figure 1: Our model architecture shown for a document with two mentions, *England* and *FIFA World Cup*. The model performs mention detection, entity typing, and entity disambiguation for all mentions in a single pass.

3.3 Context representation

We encode the tokens x_i in the input text document using a Transformer model. We use the contextualised token embeddings from the final layer, denoted as $\mathbf{h_i}$ for the token x_i.[6]

3.4 Mention detection

Entity linking requires entity mentions to be predicted. We encode mentions using the BIO tagging format (Ramshaw and Marcus, 1995) with 3 labels which indicate whether a token is at the beginning, inside of, or outside of a mention. We train a linear layer to perform token classification from the contextualised token embeddings $\mathbf{h_i}$ using cross-entropy loss $\mathcal{L}_m$ with respect to the gold token labels.

3.5 Mention representation

A fixed-length embedding $\mathbf{m_i}$ for each mention m_i is obtained by average pooling the contextualised tokens embeddings of the mention. All mentions M in a document X are encoded in a single forward pass, which improves efficiency relative to previous work that require a forward-pass for each mention (Wu et al., 2020; Orr et al., 2021).

3.6 Entity typing score ϕ

Given a fixed set of types $t \in T$ from a KB, where t is a relation-object pair (r, o) (e.g. (instance of, song)), we predict an independent probability for each type t for each mention by applying a linear layer f_1 followed by a sigmoid activation to the mention embedding $\mathbf{m_i}$. To score mention-entity pairs using predicted types, we calculate the Euclidean distance (L2 norm) between predicted types and the candidate entity's types $\mathbf{c_j}$ binary vector[7]:

$$\phi(e_j, m_i) = \|\sigma(f_1(\mathbf{m_i})) - \mathbf{c_j}\|_2 \tag{1}$$

We follow Onoe and Durrett (2020) by training the entity typing module on distantly-supervised type labels from the gold entity using binary cross-entropy loss $\mathcal{L}_t$. See Appendix A for details on the choice of types T.

3.7 Entity description score ψ

We use a bi-encoder architecture similar to the work of Wu et al. (2020) but modified to encode all mentions m_i in a document simultaneously (as explained in Section 3.5). We represent KB entities as:

[CLS] label [SEP] description [SEP]

where label and description are the tokens of the entity label and entity description in the KB. We use a separate Transformer model (trained jointly with our mention transformer) to encode the representation of KB entities e_j into fixed dimension vectors (description embeddings) $\mathbf{d_j}$ by taking final layer embedding for the [CLS] token. We apply linear layers f_2 and f_3 to the mention embeddings $\mathbf{m_i}$ and entity description embeddings $\mathbf{d_j}$ respectively to project them to a shared vector space. We calculate the dot product between the two projected embeddings to compute the entity scores:

$$\psi(e_j, m_i) = f_2(\mathbf{m_i}) \cdot f_3(\mathbf{d_j}) \tag{2}$$

We train this module using cross-entropy loss $\mathcal{L}_d$, with respect to gold entity label.

3.8 Combined score ω

We compute a combined score ω by applying a linear layer (with output dimension 1) f_4 on top

[6] We use bold letters for vectors throughout our paper, and treat m_i and $\mathbf{m_i}$ as different terms.

[7] We use 1 to indicate the presence of an entity type and 0 the absence of an entity type for our binary vector. Note that a single entity can have multiple entity types.

of the concatenation of entity typing score, entity description score, and a global entity prior $\hat{P}(e|m)$. The global entity prior is obtained from a corpus (Hoffart et al., 2011) or a popularity metric (Diefenbach and Thalhammer, 2018). We include $\hat{P}(e|m)$ to improve results for cases where context is limited (e.g. short question text). In addition, we add a special candidate for the NIL entity with an unnormalised score of 0, which indicates none of the candidate entities are correct.

$$\omega(e_j, m_i) = f_4(\psi(\mathbf{e_j}, \mathbf{m_i}); \phi(\mathbf{e_j}, \mathbf{m_i}); \hat{P}(\mathbf{e_j}|\mathbf{m_i})) \tag{3}$$

We train this module using cross-entropy loss $\mathcal{L}_c$ with respect to the gold entity label.

3.9 Optimisation and inference

We optimise the model using a weighted sum of the module-specific losses with fixed weights, which are tunable hyperparameters. At training time, we use the provided mention spans instead of the predicted mention spans and train mention detection alongside the other tasks:

$$\mathcal{L} = \lambda_1\mathcal{L}_m + \lambda_2\mathcal{L}_t + \lambda_3\mathcal{L}_d + \lambda_4\mathcal{L}_c \tag{4}$$

For EL inference, we use the predicted mention spans and take the KB entity (or NIL) with the highest combined score. For ED inference, we use the provided gold mention spans.

3.10 Zero-shot ED

Our proposed method is able to link to zero-shot (unseen during training) entities because it scores entities based on types and descriptions. New entities can be introduced by updating entity lookups.

4 Experiments

4.1 Entity disambiguation

Non-zero-shot ED We evaluate our model on the ED task using the same experimental setting as previous work (Ganea and Hofmann, 2017; Le and Titov, 2018; Cao et al., 2020). We pretrain on Wikipedia, then use the AIDA-CoNLL dataset (Hoffart et al., 2011) to fine-tune and evaluate. We measure out-of-domain performance on the datasets MSNBC (Cucerzan, 2007), AQUAINT (Milne and Witten, 2008), ACE2004 (Ratinov et al., 2011), WNED-CWEB (CWEB) (Gabrilovich et al., 2013) and WNED-WIKI (WIKI) (Guo and Barbosa, 2018). We report *InKB* micro-F1 (Röder et al., 2018). We also evaluate on AIDA-CoNLL using the candidate list generated by Pershina et al. (2015), known as PPRforNED, for the sake of comparison with previous SOTA results.

Zero-shot ED To compare our method to previous work, we measure zero-shot ED performance using the WikiLinksNED Unseen Mentions dataset (Eshel et al., 2017; Onoe and Durrett, 2020). The dataset contains a diverse set of ambiguous entities spanning multiple domains. We train our model on the provided training data and evaluate accuracy on the test set for seen and unseen (zero-shot) entities.

4.2 Entity linking

Non-zero-shot EL Following previous work (Kolitsas et al., 2018; Cao et al., 2020), we use the GERBIL platform (Röder et al., 2018) to evaluate EL. We evaluate *InKB* micro-F1 with strong matching (predictions must match exactly the gold mention boundaries). Similarly to the non-zero-shot ED experiment, we pretrain on Wikipedia, then use the AIDA-CoNLL dataset for fine-tuning and evaluation. For out-of-domain performance evaluation we use MSNBC (Cucerzan, 2007), OKE-2015, OKE-2016 (Nuzzolese et al., 2015), N3-Reuters-128 (R128), N3-RSS-500 (Röder et al., 2014), Derczynski (Derczynski et al., 2015), KORE50 (Hoffart et al., 2012).

4.3 Inference speed

We compare the computational efficiency of our model to three high-performing EL systems (Wu et al., 2020; Cao et al., 2020; Orr et al., 2021) for which code is available. We benchmark both modes of BLINK (Wu et al., 2020); the bi-encoder (encodes mention and entities independently) and the more accurate cross-encoder (encodes mention and entities jointly).[8] We measure the time to perform end-to-end EL inference on the AIDA-CoNLL test dataset using a single V100 GPU. The dataset consists of 231 documents and 4464 mentions.

4.4 Training details

Candidate generation We follow Le and Titov (2018) by selecting the top-30 candidate entities using entity priors.[9] For training, we only keep 5 candidates, 1 gold candidate, 2 candidates with the highest $\hat{p}(e_j|m_i)$ and 2 random candidates. When the gold entity is not in the candidate list during training, we use NIL as the correct label.

[8] We use a max context length of 128 tokens and pre-computed entity embeddings for the bi-encoder. For the cross-encoder, we use max context length of 32 tokens.

[9] Derived from Wikipedia hyperlink count statistics, YAGO, a large Web corpus and Wikidata aliases.

	Method	AIDA	MSNBC*	AQUAINT*	ACE2004*	CWEB*	WIKI*	Avg.
	Yang et al. (2018)	93.0	92.6	89.9	88.5	<u>81.8</u>	79.2	87.5
	Yang et al. (2019)	93.7	93.8	88.3	90.1	75.6	78.8	86.7
	Fang et al. (2019)	**94.3**	92.8	87.5	<u>91.2</u>	78.5	82.8	87.9
	Wu et al. (2020)†	86.7	90.3	88.9	88.7	**82.6**	86.1	87.2
	Cao et al. (2020)	93.3	<u>94.3</u>	89.9	90.1	77.3	<u>87.4</u>	<u>88.7</u>
	Orr et al. (2021)**	80.9	80.5	74.2	83.6	70.2	76.2	77.6
	ReFinED (Wikipedia)	87.5	**94.4**	**91.8**	**91.6**	77.8	**88.7**	88.6
	ReFinED (fine-tuned)	<u>93.9</u>	94.1	<u>90.8</u>	90.8	79.4	<u>87.4</u>	**89.4**
Ablations	w/o entity priors (Wikipedia)	86.3	93.7	86.0	92.8	76.0	88.3	87.2
	w/o entity types (Wikipedia)	82.2	92.6	91.1	90.1	76.5	87.0	86.6
	w/o descriptions (Wikipedia)	85.7	93.9	89.5	91.2	76.1	84.3	86.8
	w/o pretraining (fine-tuned)	88.2	92.3	86.8	90.6	75.1	74.5	84.6

Table 1: ED InKB micro F1 scores on in-domain and out-of-domain test sets. The best value in **bold** and second best is <u>underlined</u>. †Normalised accuracy is reported. *Out-of-domain datasets. **Result obtained using code released by authors.

Wikipedia pretraining We use Wikidata as our KB (i.e. for entity types and descriptions). To make comparisons reliable, we restrict to the set of entities in English Wikipedia (total of 6.2M). We build a training dataset from the 2021-02-01 dump of Wikipedia and Wikidata and use hyperlinks as entity labels. To increase entity label coverage, we add weak labels to mentions of the article entity (Orr et al., 2021; Broscheit, 2019; Cao et al., 2020).[10] The dataset consists of approximately 100M mention-entity pairs. We use entity labels to generate entity type labels, as in Onoe and Durrett (2020). In addition, we follow Févry et al. (2020) by adding mention labels to unlinked mentions using a named entity recogniser to provide additional mention detection signal.

Model details We divide the documents into chunks of 300 tokens and subsample 40 mentions per chunk during pretraining. The model is trained for 2 epochs on Wikipedia and the transformers are initialised with RoBERTa (Liu et al., 2019) base weights. The description transformer has 2 layers. BERT-style masking (Devlin et al., 2019) is applied to mentions during pretraining. During fine-tuning and evaluation, we increase the sequence length to 512 and set the maximum candidate entities to 30.

5 Results

5.1 Entity disambiguation

Non-zero-shot ED We report *InKB* micro-F1 (with and without fine-tuning on AIDA) and compare it with SOTA ED models in Table 1. Our model performs strongly across all datasets, surpassing the previous average F1 across the 6 datasets by 0.7 F1 points. We observe the model achieves SOTA performance on 4 out of the 6 datasets without fine-tuning, suggesting it is able to learn patterns from Wikipedia that transfer well to other domains. Nonetheless, fine-tuning on the AIDA-CoNLL dataset leads to a substantial improvement (+6.4 F1 points) which can be attributed to the model learning peculiarities of the dataset (e.g. cricket score tables).

The ablations in Table 1 show entity types and entity descriptions are complementary (+2.0 F1 points when combined). This is explained by increased robustness to partially missing entity information (e.g. KB entities without descriptions) and different knowledge being expressed. Entity priors are useful but contribute less than other components of our combined score (Section 3.8). Without priors, F1 falls by 5.0 points on AQUAINT and increases by 1.2 points on ACE2004, which is expected as AQUAINT contains a high proportion of popular entities, and ACE2004 more rare entities. Pretraining has the largest impact on ED performance, particularly on datasets such as WIKI (+12.0 F1) derived from encyclopedia text.

Method	AIDA
Onoe and Durrett (2020)	85.9
Raiman and Raiman (2018)	94.9
Orr et al. (2021)	<u>96.8</u>
ReFinED (Wikipedia)	89.1
ReFinED (fine-tuned)	**97.1**

Table 2: ED accuracy on AIDA-CoNLL using PPRForNED candidates.

Table 2 shows accuracy on the AIDA-CoNLL dataset when we use PPRforNED candidates. ReFinED outperforms purely entity typing approaches

[10]We add weak labels by using simple heuristics such as matching mentions to the page's title.

Method	AIDA	MSNBC*	DER*	K50*	R128*	R500*	OKE15*	OKE16*	Avg.
Hoffart et al. (2011)	72.8	65.1	32.6	55.4	46.4	**42.4**	63.1	0.0	47.2
Kolitsas et al. (2018)	82.4	72.4	34.1	35.2	50.3	38.2	61.9	52.7	53.4
van Hulst et al. (2020)	80.5	72.4	41.1	50.7	49.9	35.0	63.1	58.3	56.4
Cao et al. (2020)	83.7	**73.7**	**54.1**	60.7	46.7	40.3	56.0	50.0	58.2
ReFinED (Wikipedia)	77.8	70.0	49.0	**65.9**	52.6	40.1	**65.0**	**59.5**	60.0
ReFinED (fine-tuned)	**84.0**	71.8	50.7	64.7	**58.1**	42.0	64.4	59.1	**61.9**

Table 3: EL InKB micro F1 scores on in-domain and out-of-domain test sets reported by Gerbil. The best value in **bold** and second best is underlined. *Out-of-domain datasets.

(Raiman and Raiman, 2018; Onoe and Durrett, 2020) by a margin of +2.2% accuracy, due to the addition of entity descriptions.

Zero-shot ED In Table 4, we report ED accuracy on the WikiLinksNED Unseen Mentions test set for seen and unseen entities. Our model outperforms the baseline by 3.0 F1, with, surprisingly, 6.6% higher accuracy for unseen than for seen entities. We find this is partly due to higher top 30 candidate recall for the unseen entity subset (95.0% compared to 91.1% for the seen entity subset) and also because our mention masking strategy reduces the reliance of entities appearing in the training data with similar surface forms. Moreover, ReFinED uses entity types and descriptions to link entities instead of relying on entity memorisation, which means the number of training examples for a given entity will not necessarily correlate with performance. The number of similar entities in the training dataset and the ambiguity of the test examples (Provatorova et al., 2021) will likely have more significant influence on performance.

Method	Seen	Unseen	Total
Cao et al. (2020)	64.3	63.2	63.5
ReFinED	61.6	68.2	66.5

Table 4: ED accuracy on WikiLinksNED Unseen Mentions test.

5.2 Entity linking

EL results are shown in Table 3. ReFinED outperforms other models on all but 3 datasets, often by a considerable F1 point margin (e.g. 7.8 on N3-Reuters-128 and 4.0 on KORE50) and improves the average across all 8 datasets by 3.7 F1 points. EL improves as ED and mention detection can generalise to different datasets due to the model being pretrained on Wikipedia hyperlinks as opposed to only AIDA-CoNLL. We also report results on the ISTEX and WebQSP datasets in Appendix C.

5.3 Inference speed

Table 5 shows the time taken to run inference on the AIDA-CoNLL test dataset, alongside the average ED performance. ReFinED is 6 times faster than the BLINK (Wu et al., 2020) bi-encoder, which also has an average F1 which is 9 points lower. Compared to the higher accuracy systems, ReFinED is 60 times faster than the BLINK cross-encoder, and 140 times faster than the autoregressive approach of Cao et al. (2020). This is because ReFinED uses a single forward pass to jointly encode all mentions and candidate KB entities in the document (512 token chunk), and hence requires $\approx$ 231 forward passes for the full dataset. The bi-encoder model requires $\approx$ 4464 forward passes as mentions are encoded individually, and the cross-encoder baseline requires $\approx$ 90k forward passes as each mention is encoded with each candidate. The autoregressive approach suffers from high computational cost due to the deep decoder, which generates a single token at a time. Also, all baselines require a separate model for MD whereas ReFinED performs end-to-end EL using a single model, which improves efficiency and simplifies model deployment.

Method	Time taken (s)	Avg. ED F1
Cao et al. (2020)	2100	88.7
Wu et al. (2020) bi-encoder	93	80.4
Wu et al. (2020) cross-encoder	917	87.2
Orr et al. (2021)	438	77.6
ReFinED	**15**	**89.4**

Table 5: Time taken in seconds for EL inference on AIDA-CoNLL test dataset.

6 Deployment Details

We have successfully deployed the ReFinED EL model in a real-world application, the aim of which is to populate a KB by extracting facts from unstructured text found on web pages with high precision. The application requires running ReFinED on a billion web pages (in which we link 25 billion mentions) multiple times per year. The scale of this deployment highlighted a number of learning points.

Firstly, the entity linking model must be computationally efficient. The inference speed of ReFinED allows the processing of the billion web pages in 27k machine hours (2 days using 500 instances), on machines with a single T4 GPU. Given availability of cloud compute, the cost of processing the same documents with the models evaluated in Section 5.3 would scale approximately linearly with their inference speeds. That is, the BLINK bi-encoder would require 3000 instances for 2 days, or 500 instances for 12 days, implying a roughly 6-fold increase in cost.

Secondly, the scale of the number of pages also brings with it diversity of domains, meaning the model benefits from linking to a large catalogue of entities (over 90 million) - including zero-shot entities.

Thirdly, we observed that deploying an end-to-end self-contained EL model is easier to horizontally scale and has a lower operational cost than deploying multiple systems for each subcomponent (such as candidate generation).

Finally, in real-world data, unlike in ED datasets, there are a large number of cases where the correct entity does not exist in the KB. This meant that we had to train the model on examples where the correct entity was not in the candidate list to reduce overprediction.

7 Conclusion

We propose a scalable end-to-end EL model which uses entity types and entity descriptions to perform linking. Our model achieves SOTA results for both ED (+0.7 F1 points on average across 6 datasets) and EL (+3.7 F1 points on average across 8 datasets) while being 60 times faster than comparatively accurate baselines. We demonstrate our approach scales well to a KB (Wikidata) 15 times larger than Wikipedia while maintaining competitive performance. The combination of accuracy, speed and scale means the system is capable of being deployed to extract entities from web-scale datasets with higher accuracy and an order of magnitude lower cost than existing approaches.

Acknowledgements

The authors would like to thank Clara Vania, Grace Lee, and Amir Saffari for helpful discussions and feedback. We also thank the anonymous reviewers for valuable comments that improved the quality of the paper.

References

Livio Baldini Soares, Nicholas FitzGerald, Jeffrey Ling, and Tom Kwiatkowski. 2019. Matching the blanks: Distributional similarity for relation learning. In *Proceedings of the 57th Annual Meeting of the Association for Computational Linguistics*, pages 2895–2905, Florence, Italy. Association for Computational Linguistics.

Samuel Broscheit. 2019. Investigating entity knowledge in BERT with simple neural end-to-end entity linking. In *Proceedings of the 23rd Conference on Computational Natural Language Learning (CoNLL)*, pages 677–685, Hong Kong, China. Association for Computational Linguistics.

Nicola De Cao, Gautier Izacard, Sebastian Riedel, and F. Petroni. 2020. Autoregressive entity retrieval. *ArXiv*, abs/2010.00904.

Silviu Cucerzan. 2007. Large-scale named entity disambiguation based on Wikipedia data. In *Proceedings of the 2007 Joint Conference on Empirical Methods in Natural Language Processing and Computational Natural Language Learning (EMNLP-CoNLL)*, pages 708–716, Prague, Czech Republic. Association for Computational Linguistics.

Antonin Delpeuch. 2020. Opentapioca: Lightweight entity linking for wikidata.

Leon Derczynski, Diana Maynard, Giuseppe Rizzo, Marieke van Erp, Niraj Aswani, Raphaël Troncy, and Kalina Bontcheva. 2015. Analysis of named entity recognition and linking for tweets. *Information Processing and Management, Volume 51, N°2, March 2015, Elsevier.* © Elsevier. Personal use of this material is permitted. The definitive version of this paper was published in Information Processing and Management, Volume 51, N°2, March 2015, Elsevier and is available at : http://dx.doi.org/10.1016/j.ipm.2014.10.006.

Jacob Devlin, Ming-Wei Chang, Kenton Lee, and Kristina Toutanova. 2019. BERT: Pre-training of deep bidirectional transformers for language understanding. In *Proceedings of the 2019 Conference of the North American Chapter of the Association for Computational Linguistics: Human Language Technologies, Volume 1 (Long and Short Papers)*, pages 4171–4186, Minneapolis, Minnesota. Association for Computational Linguistics.

Dennis Diefenbach and Andreas Thalhammer. 2018. PageRank and Generic Entity Summarization for RDF Knowledge Bases. In *European Semantic Web Conference , ESWC 2018,*, The Semantic Web 15th International Conference, ESWC 2018, Heraklion, Crete, Greece, June 3–7, 2018, Proceedings, Heraklion, Greece.

Yotam Eshel, Noam Cohen, Kira Radinsky, Shaul Markovitch, Ikuya Yamada, and Omer Levy. 2017. Named entity disambiguation for noisy text. In *Proceedings of the 21st Conference on Computational Natural Language Learning (CoNLL 2017)*, pages 58–68, Vancouver, Canada. Association for Computational Linguistics.

Zheng Fang, Yanan Cao, Qian Li, Dongjie Zhang, Zhenyu Zhang, and Yanbing Liu. 2019. Joint entity linking with deep reinforcement learning. In *The World Wide Web Conference*, WWW '19, page 438–447, New York, NY, USA. Association for Computing Machinery.

Paolo Ferragina and Ugo Scaiella. 2012. Fast and accurate annotation of short texts with wikipedia pages. *IEEE Software*, 29(1):70–75.

Thibault Févry, Nicholas FitzGerald, Livio Baldini Soares, and T. Kwiatkowski. 2020. Empirical evaluation of pretraining strategies for supervised entity linking. *ArXiv*, abs/2005.14253.

Evgeniy Gabrilovich, Michael Ringgaard, and Amarnag Subramanya. 2013. Facc1: Freebase annotation of clueweb corpora. Preprint.

Octavian-Eugen Ganea and Thomas Hofmann. 2017. Deep joint entity disambiguation with local neural attention. In *Proceedings of the 2017 Conference on Empirical Methods in Natural Language Processing*, pages 2619–2629, Copenhagen, Denmark. Association for Computational Linguistics.

Zhaochen Guo and Denilson Barbosa. 2018. Robust named entity disambiguation with random walks. *Semantic Web*, Preprint(Preprint):1–21.

Johannes Hoffart, Stephan Seufert, Dat Ba Nguyen, Martin Theobald, and Gerhard Weikum. 2012. Kore: Keyphrase overlap relatedness for entity disambiguation. In *Proceedings of the 21st ACM International Conference on Information and Knowledge Management*, CIKM '12, page 545–554, New York, NY, USA. Association for Computing Machinery.

Johannes Hoffart, Mohamed Amir Yosef, Ilaria Bordino, Hagen Fürstenau, Manfred Pinkal, Marc Spaniol, Bilyana Taneva, Stefan Thater, and Gerhard Weikum. 2011. Robust disambiguation of named entities in text. In *Proceedings of the 2011 Conference on Empirical Methods in Natural Language Processing*, pages 782–792, Edinburgh, Scotland, UK. Association for Computational Linguistics.

Raphael Hoffmann, Congle Zhang, Xiao Ling, Luke Zettlemoyer, and Daniel S. Weld. 2011. Knowledge-based weak supervision for information extraction of overlapping relations. In *Proceedings of the 49th Annual Meeting of the Association for Computational Linguistics: Human Language Technologies*, pages 541–550, Portland, Oregon, USA. Association for Computational Linguistics.

Diederik P. Kingma and Jimmy Ba. 2015. Adam: A method for stochastic optimization. In *3rd International Conference on Learning Representations, ICLR 2015, San Diego, CA, USA, May 7-9, 2015, Conference Track Proceedings*.

Nikolaos Kolitsas, Octavian-Eugen Ganea, and Thomas Hofmann. 2018. End-to-end neural entity linking. In *Proceedings of the 22nd Conference on Computational Natural Language Learning*, pages 519–529, Brussels, Belgium. Association for Computational Linguistics.

Phong Le and Ivan Titov. 2018. Improving entity linking by modeling latent relations between mentions. In *Proceedings of the 56th Annual Meeting of the Association for Computational Linguistics (Volume 1: Long Papers)*, pages 1595–1604, Melbourne, Australia. Association for Computational Linguistics.

Belinda Z. Li, Sewon Min, Srinivasan Iyer, Yashar Mehdad, and Wen-tau Yih. 2020. Efficient one-pass end-to-end entity linking for questions. In *Proceedings of the 2020 Conference on Empirical Methods in Natural Language Processing (EMNLP)*, pages 6433–6441, Online. Association for Computational Linguistics.

Y. Liu, Myle Ott, Naman Goyal, Jingfei Du, Mandar Joshi, Danqi Chen, Omer Levy, M. Lewis, Luke Zettlemoyer, and Veselin Stoyanov. 2019. Roberta: A robustly optimized bert pretraining approach. *ArXiv*, abs/1907.11692.

Lajanugen Logeswaran, Ming-Wei Chang, Kenton Lee, Kristina Toutanova, Jacob Devlin, and Honglak Lee. 2019. Zero-shot entity linking by reading entity descriptions. In *Proceedings of the 57th Annual Meeting of the Association for Computational Linguistics*, pages 3449–3460, Florence, Italy. Association for Computational Linguistics.

David Milne and Ian H. Witten. 2008. Learning to link with wikipedia. In *Proceedings of the 17th ACM Conference on Information and Knowledge Management*, CIKM '08, page 509–518, New York, NY, USA. Association for Computing Machinery.

Isaiah Onando Mulang', Kuldeep Singh, Chaitali Prabhu, Abhishek Nadgeri, Johannes Hoffart, and Jens Lehmann. 2020. Evaluating the impact of knowledge graph context on entity disambiguation models. *Proceedings of the 29th ACM International Conference on Information & Knowledge Management.*

Andrea Giovanni Nuzzolese, Anna Lisa Gentile, Valentina Presutti, Aldo Gangemi, Darío Garigliotti, and Roberto Navigli. 2015. Open knowledge extraction challenge. In *Semantic Web Evaluation Challenges*, pages 3–15, Cham. Springer International Publishing.

Yasumasa Onoe and Greg Durrett. 2020. Fine-grained entity typing for domain independent entity linking. In *The Thirty-Fourth AAAI Conference on Artificial Intelligence, AAAI 2020, The Thirty-Second Innovative Applications of Artificial Intelligence Conference, IAAI 2020, The Tenth AAAI Symposium on Educational Advances in Artificial Intelligence, EAAI 2020, New York, NY, USA, February 7-12, 2020*, pages 8576–8583. AAAI Press.

L. Orr, Megan Leszczynski, Simran Arora, Sen Wu, Neel Guha, Xiao Ling, and C. Ré. 2021. Bootleg: Chasing the tail with self-supervised named entity disambiguation. *ArXiv*, abs/2010.10363.

Maria Pershina, Yifan He, and Ralph Grishman. 2015. Personalized page rank for named entity disambiguation. In *Proceedings of the 2015 Conference of the North American Chapter of the Association for Computational Linguistics: Human Language Technologies*, pages 238–243, Denver, Colorado. Association for Computational Linguistics.

Vera Provatorova, Samarth Bhargav, Svitlana Vakulenko, and Evangelos Kanoulas. 2021. Robustness evaluation of entity disambiguation using prior probes: the case of entity overshadowing. In *Proceedings of the 2021 Conference on Empirical Methods in Natural Language Processing*, pages 10501–10510, Online and Punta Cana, Dominican Republic. Association for Computational Linguistics.

Jonathan Raiman and O. Raiman. 2018. Deeptype: Multilingual entity linking by neural type system evolution. In *AAAI*.

Lance Ramshaw and Mitch Marcus. 1995. Text chunking using transformation-based learning. In *Third Workshop on Very Large Corpora*.

Lev Ratinov, Dan Roth, Doug Downey, and Mike Anderson. 2011. Local and global algorithms for disambiguation to Wikipedia. In *Proceedings of the 49th Annual Meeting of the Association for Computational Linguistics: Human Language Technologies*, pages 1375–1384, Portland, Oregon, USA. Association for Computational Linguistics.

Michael Röder, Ricardo Usbeck, Sebastian Hellmann, D. Gerber, and A. Both. 2014. N^3 - a collection of datasets for named entity recognition and disambiguation in the nlp interchange format. In *LREC*.

Michael Röder, Ricardo Usbeck, and Axel-Cyrille Ngonga Ngomo. 2018. GERBIL - benchmarking named entity recognition and linking consistently. *Semantic Web*, 9(5):605–625.

Johannes M. van Hulst, Faegheh Hasibi, Koen Dercksen, Krisztian Balog, and Arjen P. de Vries. 2020. Rel: An entity linker standing on the shoulders of giants. In *Proceedings of the 43rd International ACM SIGIR Conference on Research and Development in Information Retrieval*, SIGIR '20, page 2197–2200, New York, NY, USA. Association for Computing Machinery.

Zhiguo Wang, Patrick Ng, Ramesh Nallapati, and Bing Xiang. 2021. Retrieval, re-ranking and multi-task learning for knowledge-base question answering. In *Proceedings of the 16th Conference of the European Chapter of the Association for Computational Linguistics: Main Volume*, pages 347–357, Online. Association for Computational Linguistics.

Gerhard Weikum, Luna Dong, Simon Razniewski, and Fabian Suchanek. 2021. Machine knowledge: Creation and curation of comprehensive knowledge bases.

Thomas Wolf, Lysandre Debut, Victor Sanh, Julien Chaumond, Clement Delangue, Anthony Moi, Pierric Cistac, Tim Rault, R'emi Louf, Morgan Funtowicz, and Jamie Brew. 2019. Huggingface's transformers: State-of-the-art natural language processing. *ArXiv*, abs/1910.03771.

Ledell Wu, Fabio Petroni, Martin Josifoski, Sebastian Riedel, and Luke Zettlemoyer. 2020. Scalable zero-shot entity linking with dense entity retrieval. In *Proceedings of the 2020 Conference on Empirical Methods in Natural Language Processing (EMNLP)*, pages 6397–6407, Online. Association for Computational Linguistics.

Xiyuan Yang, Xiaotao Gu, Sheng Lin, Siliang Tang, Yueting Zhuang, Fei Wu, Zhigang Chen, Guoping Hu, and Xiang Ren. 2019. Learning dynamic context augmentation for global entity linking. In *Proceedings of the 2019 Conference on Empirical Methods in Natural Language Processing and the 9th International Joint Conference on Natural Language Processing (EMNLP-IJCNLP)*, pages 271–281, Hong Kong, China. Association for Computational Linguistics.

Yi Yang, Ozan Irsoy, and Kazi Shefaet Rahman. 2018. Collective entity disambiguation with structured gradient tree boosting. In *Proceedings of the 2018 Conference of the North American Chapter of the Association for Computational Linguistics: Human Language Technologies, Volume 1 (Long Papers)*, pages 777–786, New Orleans, Louisiana. Association for Computational Linguistics.

A Entity Type Selection

Our entity types are formed from Wikidata relation-object pairs and relation-object pairs inferred from the Wikidata subclass hierarchy (for example, (instance of, organisation) can be inferred from (instance of, business)). We only consider types with the following relations: instance of, occupation, country, sport. We select types by iteratively adding types that separate (assuming an oracle type classifier) the gold entity from negative candidates for the most examples in our Wikipedia training dataset.

Type information stored in KBs often varies in granularity between entities (e.g. some capital city entities have the type capital city and others only city), adversely affecting training signal. To mitigate this, we use the class hierarchy to add parent types to entities. This injects class hierarchy information into the model, enabling type granularity to depend on context.

B Training Details

We use the Hugging Face implementation of RoBERTa (Wolf et al., 2019) and optimise our model using Adam (Kingma and Ba, 2015) with a linear learning rate schedule. We ignore the loss from mentions where the gold entity is not in the candidate set. The named-entity recogniser, used to preprocess our Wikipedia training dataset, is a RoBERTa token classification model trained on the AIDA-CoNLL dataset mention boundaries. We add weak entity labels for mentions that match the page's title (or surname for Wikipedia pages about people). We present our main hyperparameters in Table 6. Due to the high computational cost of training the model, we did not conduct an extensive hyperparameter search. Training on Wikipedia took approximately 48 hours on a single machine with 4 V100 GPUs. The model has approximately 154M parameters (123 million in the roberta-base architecture, and 31M for the additional description encoder and output layers).

C Additional results

Wikidata ED experimental setup To measure ED performance on non-Wikipedia entities, we expand our entity set to Wikidata (which has over 90M entities) and evaluate our model on the ISTEX test dataset (Delpeuch, 2020). We add labels and aliases from Wikidata for candidate generation and remove entity priors from our entity scoring (Section 3.8).

Hyperparameter	Value
learning rate	3e-5
batch size	64
max sequence length	300
dropout	0.05
description embeddings dim.	300
# training steps	1M
# candidates	30
# entity types	1400
mention transformer init.	roberta-base
# mention encoder layers	12
description transformer init.	roberta-base
# description encoder layers	2
# description tokens	32
λ_1, λ_2, λ_3, λ_4	(0.01, 1, 0.01, 1)
mention mask prob.	0.7

Table 6: Our model hyperparameters

Wikidata ED results We evaluate ED performance on the ISTEX dataset (which targets Wikidata). Our model outperforms Delpeuch (2020) (92.1 vs 87.0 micro F1) which uses hand-crafted features specifically designed for linking Wikidata entities. This shows that our approach scales to Wikidata and generalises well when there is increased mention ambiguity. Our model performs 0.5 F1 points below the SOTA Mulang' et al. (2020) (92.6 vs 92.1 micro F1) which is likely due to differing candidate entity generation methods.

Entity Linking performance on questions We report results on the WebQSP dataset in Table 7, which shows EL performance on questions. Our model has similar performance to ELQ, which is SOTA on WebQSP and is optimised for questions. Our model is faster than all baselines which can be attributed to using an end-to-end EL model, restricting ED predictions to the predicted mentions only, and using a smaller model (compared to ELQ which uses BERT-large (Devlin et al., 2019)).

Method	WebQSP	#Q/s
TAGME (Ferragina and Scaiella, 2012)	36.1	2.39
BLINK (Wu et al., 2020) (Wikipedia)	80.8	0.80
ELQ (Li et al., 2020) (Wikipedia)	83.9	1.56
ELQ (Li et al., 2020) (fine-tuned)	89.0	1.56
ReFinED (Wikipedia)	84.1	**2.78**
ReFinED (fine-tuned)	**89.1**	**2.78**

Table 7: Entity linking weak matching InKB micro F1 scores on WebQSP EL dataset (Li et al., 2020). #Q/s is number of questions per second for a single CPU.

D Dataset statistics

We present the topic, number of documents and number of mentions for each dataset used for evaluation. The datasets used cover a variety of sources including wikipedia text, news articles, web text and tweets. Note that the performance of the model outside these domains may be significantly different.

Note also that all datasets used are for English only, allowing comparison to previous work. Our method is extendable to any language for which there is an language-specific version of Wikipedia on which the model could be trained. However, we cannot guarantee the accuracy of the model across these languages without further experimentation.

	Topic	Num docs	Num Mentions
AIDA	news	231	4464
MSNBC	news	20	656
AQUAINT	news	50	743
ACE2004	news	57	259
CWEB	web	320	11154
WIKI	Wikipedia	320	6821
WikilinksNED	web	10000	10000

Table 8: Dataset statistics for entity disambiguation datasets

	Topic	Num docs	Num Mentions
AIDA	news	231	4464
MSNBC	news	20	656
DER	tweets	182	242
K50	mixed	50	145
R128	news	128	638
R500	news	500	530
OKE15	Wikipedia	199	1017
OKE16	Wikipedia	254	1402

Table 9: Dataset statistics for entity linking datasets

Lightweight Transformers for Conversational AI

Daniel Pressel
Interactions, LLC
dpressel@interactions.com

Wenshuo Liu
Twitter*
wenshuol@twitter.com

Michael Johnston
Alexa AI, Amazon*
mjohnstn@amazon.com

Minhua Chen
Interactions, LLC
mchen@interactions.com

Abstract

To understand how training on conversational language impacts performance of pre-trained models on downstream dialogue tasks, we build compact Transformer-based Language Models from scratch on several large corpora of conversational data. We compare the performance and characteristics of these models against BERT and other strong baselines on dialogue probing tasks. Commercial dialogue systems typically require a small footprint and fast execution time, but recent trends are in the other direction, with an ever-increasing number of parameters, resulting in difficulties in model deployment. We focus instead on training fast, lightweight models that excel at natural language understanding (NLU) and can replace existing lower-capacity conversational AI models with similar size and speed. In the process, we develop a simple but unique curriculum-based approach that moves from general-purpose to dialogue-targeted both in terms of data and objective. Our resultant models have around 1/3 the number of parameters of BERT-base and produce better representations for a wide array of intent detection datasets using linear and Mutual-Information probing techniques. Additionally, the models can be easily fine-tuned on a single consumer GPU card and deployed in near real-time production environments.

1 Introduction

The development of the Transformer (Vaswani et al., 2017) – a multi-headed attention architecture with high capacity – caused a breakthrough in the pre-training of contextualized representations for text (Radford et al., 2018; Devlin et al., 2019). This architecture can internalize large amounts of information from massive datasets, yielding powerful encoders that can be fine-tuned for various NLP tasks. The generative pre-training (GPT) model (Radford et al., 2018) used a standard language modeling objective, learning to predict the next word in a sequence, and demonstrated the ability of Transformers to learn long distance dependencies – a limitation of previous architectures. BERT (Devlin et al., 2019) later introduced a Masked Language Model (MLM) objective, where a portion of the text is masked out or perturbed, and the model learns to reconstruct those portions, yielding bi-directional representations.

Various datasets have been explored for pre-training including the Toronto BookCorpus (Zhu et al., 2015) and Wikipedia. More recently, much larger datasets have been used including Common Crawl datasets for RoBERTa (Liu et al., 2019b), T5 (Raffel et al., 2020) and others. Larger datasets facilitate more parameters (Kaplan et al., 2020; Raffel et al., 2020) and with so much available data, many recent models range from tens to hundreds of billions of parameters. These large language models (LLMs) exhibit remarkable capabilities for many tasks, but they are massive, difficult to control, and expensive to deploy. [1]

LLMs have yielded improvements over their predecessors, with little architectural modification, primarily by using larger datasets, more capacity, and training longer with more compute. The trend in the literature seems clear – use a denoising or language model objective and train on larger datasets with longer contexts and more capacity to improve NLP performance.

The main approach seems to be "more is better" without much qualification to the type of textual content that is applied. There have been some attempts to qualify the corpora used for pre-training (Mitchell et al., 2019), but attempting to limit what goes into training becomes increasingly difficult as the datasets get larger. For this work, we attempt to target conversational AI, taking into account both

* Work done while the authors were at Interactions

[1] While denoising auto-encoders such as T5 and BERT are not considered proper LMs, they are often lumped under that nomenclature, which we retain for consistency.

Proceedings of NAACL-HLT 2022: Industry Track Papers, pages 221 - 229
July 10-15, 2022 ©2022 Association for Computational Linguistics

model and dataset.

It seems reasonable to assume that some carefully curated data, like Wikipedia, should be broadly useful as it presents related concepts in close proximity with reliable structure. But for our purposes, it also seems desirable to have a large amount of data that is conversational, though its unclear how this data should be structured and how it should be balanced with non-conversational sources. Knowing that task-oriented dialogue systems often have a need to understand domain-specific concepts and proper names, it also seems reasonable to assume that sources such as consumer reviews of products and services might be helpful.

In this work, we attempt to build practical, compact models that excel for conversational AI, especially NLU. We set out to build on data sources that will be particularly useful for dialogue systems, and try to incorporate common-sense architectural modifications that should improve performance on dialogue. We focus our effort on MLM models as most NLU tasks benefit from bi-directionality (Devlin et al., 2019). We also investigate a curriculum that teaches the model a grounded foundation first in generic language, followed by increasingly complex masking over conversational data.

2 Related Work

2.1 Models targeting Dialogue

Several Transformer models have been developed specifically to target dialogue, including ConveRT (Henderson et al., 2020), and later ToD-BERT (Wu et al., 2020). The former was trained from scratch on 3 years of Reddit data (Henderson et al., 2019) using a dual-encoder with a contrastive loss function to predict the second utterance in a paired dialogue turn. ToD-BERT similarly used a contrastive loss head (in conjunction with an MLM head) to predict the next turn of dialogue (again in a dialogue pair). Unlike ConveRT, ToD-BERT was adapted to a very small corpus of only task-oriented dialogue from a pre-trained BERT checkpoint. DialoGPT (Zhang et al., 2020) is a GPT2-adapted (Radford et al., 2019) model using a corpus of conversational data. Unlike our work, they are specifically targeting response generation.

Some dialogue-targeted models have attempted to solve end-to-end task-oriented dialogue with pre-trained Transformers, including SimpleToD (Hosseini-Asl et al., 2020), a model that learns the entire process of NLU, state internalization, NLG and API calls using only a prefix-LM. This model is particularly strong on MultiWoz (Budzianowski et al., 2018), a common task-oriented dialogue benchmark, but the design is ill-suited for real-world system deployment – API calls and NLG are integrated directly into the LM, making the model difficult to adapt, control, and maintain over time. We focus instead on targeting the understanding portion of a dialogue system. As a result, our models can be easily incorporated into modular dialogue management systems.

2.2 Compact models

Distillation (Hinton et al., 2015) is a common technique for creating compact Transformers (Sanh et al., 2019; Jiao et al., 2020). In basic distillation, a larger model (the "teacher") predicts the labels on a dataset and its outputs are treated as the target distribution using the Kullback-Leibler (KL) Divergence against the predictions of a smaller "student" model. During training, the student learns to make similar predictions to the teacher (Beyer et al., 2021).

While we could attempt to train a very large Transformer from scratch and distill to a smaller one in the hopes of improved performance, this would be resource-inefficient. Alternatively, we could adapt an existing off-the-shelf pre-trained model and distill it down, but we are concerned that both the prior pre-training and distillation events could create biases on our models that would limit our ability to understand the impacts of data choices. We decided instead to training compact models from scratch without distillation.

3 Model Description

Our model is an encoder-only Transformer, similar to BERT or RoBERTa, trained primarily on full-context conversational input. Unlike most previous MLMs, our model is trained with relative attention (Shaw et al., 2018). In this approach, relative positional representations are not conditioned on the global position of the token but instead use a local relative offset embedding at every layer as part of the self-attention computation, which we hypothesize makes them more suitable for dialogue applications where the global offset in a conversation is not meaningful. Additionally, we perform layer normalization before each sub-layer and we also after the last Transformer encoder layer (Chen et al., 2018).

We also experiment with a curriculum for our MLM where the initial masking follows BERT but, later in training, switches to masked turn modeling (MTM), where we mask entire turns, token-by-token.

We train eight-layer models with eight attention heads, and a hidden size of 512. We use Byte Pair Encoding (BPE) (Sennrich et al., 2016) with a vocab containing 30,000 lower-case tokens. We also include special tokens including "[CLS]" and "[MASK]" (borrowed from BERT), "<EOS>" for end-of-sentence and "<EOU>" for end-of-utterance. We use fastBPE [2] to train, sampling 2 million posts from Reddit as the BPE corpus.

4 Datasets

In our investigation of sources of data for pre-training targeting conversational AI, we identified several potential source types. We bucket these into three basic categories:

- *foundational:* general purpose data sources, expected to provide a broad basis for pre-training
- *online reviews and customer data*: domain-informative data from single users, drawn primarily from online reviews
- *conversational*: data taken from bulletin boards and online forums capturing interactions between multiple users

We hypothesized that, used together, each data source may provide complementary information that could improve model performance and robustness for a range of dialogue tasks.

4.1 Foundational Data Sources

Dialogue systems, particularly task-oriented ones, are often required to recognize entities, their relations to one another, and to user intent. Wikipedia seems like an especially useful dataset as it makes explicit the relationship between many objects in the world. Words like "Camaro", a type of vehicle manufactured by "Chevrolet", itself a company owned by "General Motors", will all be mentioned in close proximity along with other types of vehicles, and possibly competitors. Thus we get access to a large number of proper-noun concepts and their relationships in the universe. A data source lacking encyclopedic knowledge would be unlikely to be present these primary relationships explicitly (or so thoroughly) across so many domains. Still there are several potential problems with a corpus like Wikipedia. First, the data is written formally in a manner that would rarely be encountered in actual conversations between humans. Second, queries to DBpedia to find concepts in Wikipedia show that certain domains may have quite different coverage from other domains, possibly resulting in inconsistent performance or coverage on a downstream target domain. Third (and this is a problem for any online corpus), the knowledge represented is a snapshot in time. New concepts are introduced often, and old ones may become irrelevant to daily life.

The authors of T5 created a new, large dataset from Common Crawl with broad coverage, which they refer to as "C4" (Raffel et al., 2020). The content of this corpus was subsequently analyzed and documented in (Dodge et al., 2021). Their analysis reveals that the largest sources of data within the cleaned C4 corpus are patents, Wikipedia and news sites. Based on this knowledge, a model trained on C4 would also be expected to have good coverage of concepts and their relations and strong downstream performance on problems with formal language and syntactic structure.

4.2 Online Reviews and Customer Data

We considered online reviews as a potential source of data to acquire world-knowledge useful for targeting specific domains, particularly considering entities and their relationships. For instance, for a food service application, restaurant review sites might provide some background knowledge of food items, their component parts, and in-domain co-reference knowledge. For hospitality applications, we may want to include information telling us about the properties of hotels, bed and breakfasts and resorts, and how they relate to concepts such as location, cleanliness and desirability for consumers.

4.3 Conversational Data Sources

We wished to target pre-training sources considering size and similarity to the content of our target data, including formality and structure of the lexical content. For this work, we decided to focus on English data sources only, as most of the previously available collected corpora and downstream datasets are in English.

[2]https://github.com/glample/fastBPE

We hypothesized that online forums, where users are looking for guidance regarding a product or service, would be closely related to typical task-oriented dialogue problems, and of generally high value. Also, as threads on forums can be updated over years, the lengths of forum conversations can be quite long, which may allow our models to learn rich long-distance relationships. However, even with a large number of forums, the total amount of data collected is fairly small in comparison to other online data sources. We also considered lower-quality sources of conversational data which, though dissimilar from task-oriented dialogue, might capture common discourse aspects over a large number of full conversations. We considered Twitter threads as a possible source, but the conversations tend to be very short and unfocused, and are not easy to capture using the streaming API. On the other hand, recent work has been published on Reddit as a data source (Al-Rfou et al., 2016; Henderson et al., 2019), and the scripts for obtaining this data were previously released (Henderson et al., 2019) and are reproducible with minimal cost. The corpus is quite large, and full conversations are available.

We note that, for all of our conversational data sources, author handles may be mentioned by other users, but no metadata regarding authors, locations nor any other profile information is included in the text corpus. All data collection was limited to the visible textual content of a post.

As we are particularly interested in task-oriented dialogue, we also looked into large available Wizard-of-Oz (WoZ) collected data, but found a limited selection to be available.

For all conversational data sources, we pass entire conversations into the pre-training and we use an end-of-turn marker (<EOU>) to mark new posts within a thread. In most cases its not possible (or probably even useful) to further disentangle the authors.

4.4 Combinations of data

Conversational data sources seem the most directly related to our dialogue pre-training goals. If we only considered that data, we could always provide conversational turn demarcation, and provide full conversations for each sample. We could also focus on objectives that specifically target dialogue data. However, with the non-dialogue data sources, this is not possible. As a result, its not clear how to combine the approaches effectively, or what mixture of the data we should use to support downstream applications.

We were interested in isolating the contributions of the different types of data. We trained two sets of models with slightly different datasets (version 1 and version 2). The version 1 model was trained and used internally for several months before we began work on the version 2 approach.

4.4.1 Version 1: RWD Corpus

For our first pre-training experiments, we used the full Reddit corpus from (Henderson et al., 2019), as well as 2.5 million online threads from publicly available forums, 8.2 million online reviews for restaurants and hotels, and a small amount of task-oriented dialogue (about 160,000 conversations). We determined from early experiments that Wikipedia complemented the Reddit dataset, providing better downstream fine-tuning results, so we also incorporated all of English Wikipedia. We call the resultant corpus "Reddit-Wiki-Dialogues" (RWD).

Table 1 shows a list of the datasets contained in RWD and their sizes.

4.4.2 Version 2: RF Corpus

We were interested in further isolating the impact of models trained only on conversations. While in version 1, models were trained on RWD, which is comprised of various types of data, for version 2 we attempt to better isolate the impact of conversation data only.

We introduce a conversation-only dataset containing Reddit and online forums, which we refer to as "Reddit-Forums" (RF). It does not include online reviews nor Wikipedia, nor does it use any task-oriented dialogue data.

We hypothesized that a model trained only on conversations, which are subjective in nature, might benefit from an initial pre-training with more coverage of broad concepts, so we also explore training in a curriculum that starts with a single epoch of C4 pre-training and continues on the RF corpus.

For version 2, we observed that forum data often contains quotes from previous posters, which are usually expressed in a markdown format like BB-Code [3]. For these quotes, which often juxtapose the post itself, we create additional tokens marking

[3] https://www.bbcode.org/reference.php

Label	Size	Content
Reddit	173GB	700M conversations
Wikipedia	20GB	2.7B tokens
Forums	14GB	2.5M threads
Yelp	3.9GB	6.6MB reviews
TripAdvisor	1.5GB	1.6M reviews
MetalWoz	19MB	37k conversations
DSTC7 (ubuntu)	54MB	105k conversations
DSTC8	18MB	15k conversations

Table 1: RWD Corpus

the beginning and end and rely on the attention mechanism of the Transformer in the same manner we do for end-of-sentence and end-of-turn markers. For version 2, to somewhat offset the loss of the review data and the task-oriented dialogue corpus, we collected another approx. 800k conversations from additional forum sources (yielding a total of approx 3.3M threads).

5 Training Details

We train each model using mead-baseline (Pressel et al., 2018) on a single v3 Tensor Processing Unit (TPU). [4]. To best utilize TPUs, we use bucketing based on full conversation lengths, scaling the number of samples for each bucket length so that the number of tokens is constant per batch. We use AdamW with a peak learning rate of 4e-4, a weight decay of 1e-3, and a linear warm-up of 10,000 steps followed by cosine decay over training to zero.

For version 1, we use a maximum context window of length 256, training for 1 million steps with context windows between 64 and 256 tokens.

For version 2, targeting the RF conversation-only corpus, we use a longer maximum context window of length 1024. For comparison purposes, in version 2, we train separate models using C4 only, C4 followed by RF, and RF only.

From early experiments, we determined that the MTM objective was too difficult to learn from scratch, so for MTM models, we train the first 80% following the masking algorithm for BERT, and we switch to MTM masking for the last 20%.

6 Experiments

We use the SentEval (Conneau and Kiela, 2018) approach to perform linear probing on a several intent detection datasets, including few-shot scenarios. We also perform Mutual Information-based clustering probing experiments.

6.1 Linear Probing Intent Detection

To assess the quality of our representations, we use the linear probing methods from SentEval applied to intent detection, and compare against BERT-base, ToD-BERT and SentenceBERT (Reimers and Gurevych, 2019) (an adaptation of BERT on Natural Language Inference data shown to improve embedding quality) [5]. Our analysis includes several commonly used datasets – Clinc150 (OOS) (Larson et al., 2019), PolyAI Banking77 (Casanueva et al., 2020), and the Heriot-Watt University dataset (Liu et al., 2019a). In addition to the original versions, we use 10-example and 30-example versions for each dataset to attempt understand the few-shot capabilities of our models. We also compare three internally-created intent detection datasets targeting automotive customer service, pizza customer service, and pizza ordering (shown in Table 2).

From our linear probing experiments, we find compelling evidence that our representations have internalized more useful information for dialogue, yielding better general-purpose representations. Both aspects of our training curriculum for RF models improve the overall results. The best model overall starts with C4 and continues pre-training on a conversational dataset (RF) using our MTM objective at the end of training. However, while pre-training with C4 does typically improve our MTM, the RF-only MTM model is still stronger than the version 1 model which contains all three data source types. All of our conversationally pre-trained models exhibit much better performance than the baselines. Interestingly, we observe that

[4] Each run takes 2-3 days, but curriculum branches are run from previous checkpoints, minimizing the total training time

[5] Each of these baselines has 12 heads, 12 layers, and 768 hidden units

our 8-layer, C4-only baseline is similar in performance to BERT and ToD-BERT. This might be due to the much larger size of the training set compared to BERT. Overall, our results clearly demonstrate the importance of conversational pre-training. We find very little difference in the performance of the basic MLM models using RWD versus C4+RF alone, but once coupled with the new MTM objective, the RF corpus shows a clear advantage over RWD for linear probing.

6.2 Mutual Information-based Clustering Intent Detection

In Mutual Information-based Clustering, utterances are clustered using K-means algorithm for various values of K. Then, the Adjusted Mutual Information (ANMI) score is computed between the predicted clustering and intent-based clusterings for the different settings of K (Wu and Xiong, 2020). In that work, the authors show the strength of ToD-BERT, primarily based on strong probing results using the MultiWoz dataset.

We apply the same method and compare against BERT, ToD-BERT and SentenceBERT across Intent Detection datasets. While BERT is a strong baseline for supervised downstream tasks, using Mutual Information-based Clustering, we find that ToD-BERT is significantly better than SentenceBERT which, in turn, produces consistently better representations than BERT. However, despite their much smaller size, our MTM models outperform the others by a large margin, including the MLM-only models trained on the same dataset (Figures 1, 2, 3).

For two of the datasets, the C4+RF models are the best, but for the HWU dataset, the RF-only model is better.

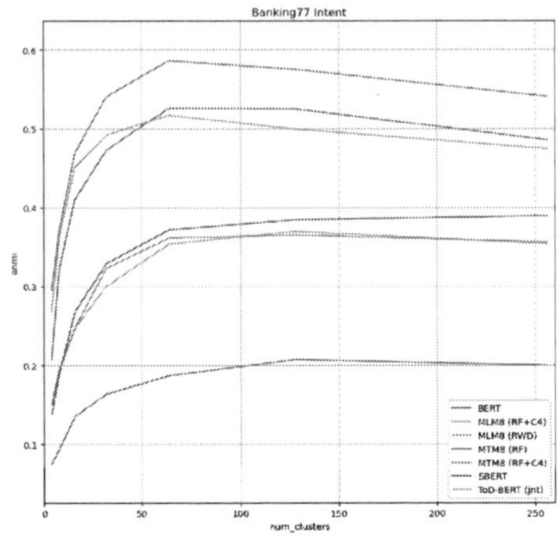

Figure 1: Banking77 Dataset ANMI

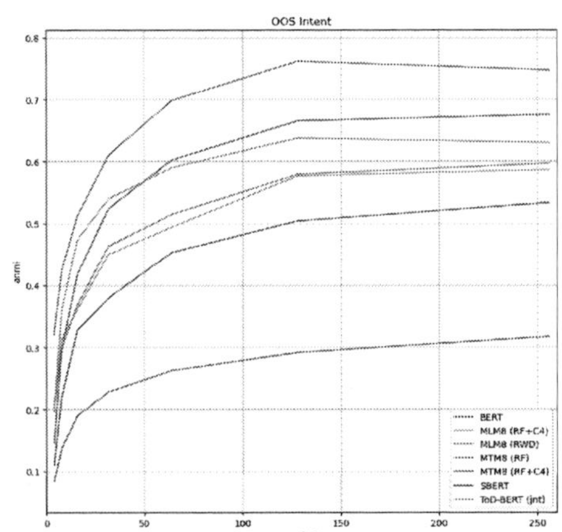

Figure 2: OOS Dataset ANMI

7 Deployment

To support deployment into our Intelligent Virtual Assistant (IVA) environment, we compared fine-tuning of our version 1 models against our production models, which operate on ASR N-best hypotheses and predict multiple outputs, representing intents and entities. For all fine-tuning, we trained on a single NVIDIA GTX1080ti and measured the joint accuracy on a real-world customer care application. We found the new models to be competitive, especially in few-shot environments. Using distillation to a single model from an ensem-

ID	BERT	SBERT	ToD-BERT	RWD48	C4	C4+RF	MTM RF	MTM C4+RF
AutoCS	60.54	53.79	58.98	63.45	61.06	65.52	66.25	**66.36**
PizzaCS	55.06	51.45	54.43	**60.22**	54.34	57.05	58.23	59.13
PizzaOrder	81.44	80.64	80.82	**83.39**	80.91	82.68	81.97	82.06
OOS10	72.24	80.82	79.51	84.47	77.29	84.56	85.76	**88.16**
OOS30	85.49	87.44	85.51	91.27	85.93	91.27	90.53	**91.98**
OOS	90.89	91.98	90.31	94.56	89.84	93.93	93.13	**94.93**
HWU	86.25	85.41	83.18	87.08	82.43	86.80	86.71	**89.03**
HWU10	68.31	70.54	68.96	72.58	65.61	73.42	75.74	**76.39**
HWU30	78.44	79.00	77.51	81.13	76.39	82.53	82.06	**83.36**
Bank	83.80	87.86	84.19	87.99	84.9	87.76	90.42	**90.49**
Bank10	56.14	70.71	65.42	70.42	66.82	71.56	77.27	**78.44**
Bank30	74.84	81.82	76.92	82.37	77.86	82.21	85.00	**85.84**
Avg	74.45	76.79	75.48	79.91	75.28	79.94	81.09	**82.18**

Table 2: Comparison of Model Accuracy by Probing Intent Detection Datasets

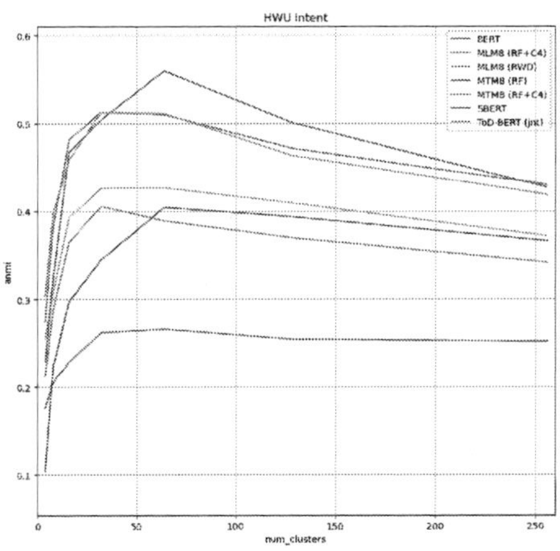

Figure 3: HWU Dataset ANMI

ble of fine-tuned MLM-based models trained on only one week of data (about 100k samples), we were able to match the performance of a production model trained on two months of data (about 650k samples). In many cases, it was also possible to truncate our models during fine-tuning, removing the top 4 layers without significant deterioration of performance. Table 3 shows the joint accuracy and speed results of our ONNX-converted models trained on a production dataset of 1.1 million noisy training samples. We observe that, even after truncating our pre-trained models to only 2 layers, they still perform better than the production system, allowing us to trade off speed and accuracy.

Model	sec/sample	Testing Acc
Production	0.0003s	83.67%
MLM 2-Layers	0.0018s	83.82%
MLM 4-layers	0.0033s	**83.94%**

Table 3: IVA Dataset Speed vs. Accuracy

8 Conclusion

Using a combination of online user conversations and sensible design choices, we are able to provide models that are compact, efficient and perform well for conversational AI. We find that conversational-only pre-training compares favorably to more traditional online data sources, but that combining the two in a curriculum can be advantageous in many cases. Additionally we find that masking whole turns later in training is also particularly helpful for learning good dialogue representations.

In future work, we will compare alternative architectures an a larger number of dialogue-oriented tasks. We are also interested in how model capacity affects downstream performance, particularly for few-shot learning. We also wish to explore the trade-offs between LM pre-training in the conversational domain versus equivalent adaptation using a contrastive loss function as used in (Vulić et al., 2021), and to further isolate the impacts of individual data sources and lexical content.

Acknowledgments

Pre-training was supported with Cloud TPUs from Google's TPU Research Cloud (TRC). TRC is an important program that empowers researchers by giving them access to compute which would otherwise be very prohibitively costly.

References

Rami Al-Rfou, Marc Pickett, Javier Snaider, Yun-Hsuan Sung, Brian Strope, and Ray Kurzweil. 2016. Conversational contextual cues: The case of personalization and history for response ranking. *ArXiv*, abs/1606.00372.

Lucas Beyer, Xiaohua Zhai, Amélie Royer, Larisa Markeeva, Rohan Anil, and Alexander Kolesnikov. 2021. Knowledge distillation: A good teacher is patient and consistent. *ArXiv*, abs/2106.05237.

Paweł Budzianowski, Tsung-Hsien Wen, Bo-Hsiang Tseng, Iñigo Casanueva, Stefan Ultes, Osman Ramadan, and Milica Gašić. 2018. MultiWOZ - a large-scale multi-domain Wizard-of-Oz dataset for task-oriented dialogue modelling. In *Proceedings of the 2018 Conference on Empirical Methods in Natural Language Processing*, pages 5016–5026.

Iñigo Casanueva, Tadas Temčinas, Daniela Gerz, Matthew Henderson, and Ivan Vulić. 2020. Efficient intent detection with dual sentence encoders. In *Proceedings of the 2nd Workshop on Natural Language Processing for Conversational AI*, pages 38–45.

Mia Xu Chen, Orhan Firat, Ankur Bapna, Melvin Johnson, Wolfgang Macherey, George Foster, Llion Jones, Mike Schuster, Noam Shazeer, Niki Parmar, Ashish Vaswani, Jakob Uszkoreit, Lukasz Kaiser, Zhifeng Chen, Yonghui Wu, and Macduff Hughes. 2018. The best of both worlds: Combining recent advances in neural machine translation. In *Proceedings of the 56th Annual Meeting of the Association for Computational Linguistics (Volume 1: Long Papers)*, pages 76–86.

Alexis Conneau and Douwe Kiela. 2018. Senteval: An evaluation toolkit for universal sentence representations. *arXiv preprint arXiv:1803.05449*.

Jacob Devlin, Ming-Wei Chang, Kenton Lee, and Kristina Toutanova. 2019. Bert: Pre-training of deep bidirectional transformers for language understanding. In *Proceedings of the 2019 Conference of the North American Chapter of the Association for Computational Linguistics: Human Language Technologies, Volume 1 (Long and Short Papers)*, pages 4171–4186.

Jesse Dodge, Maarten Sap, Ana Marasović, William Agnew, Gabriel Ilharco, Dirk Groeneveld, Margaret Mitchell, and Matt Gardner. 2021. Documenting large webtext corpora: A case study on the colossal clean crawled corpus. In *Proceedings of the 2021 Conference on Empirical Methods in Natural Language Processing*, pages 1286–1305.

Matthew Henderson, Paweł Budzianowski, Iñigo Casanueva, Sam Coope, Daniel Gerz, Girish Kumar, Nikola Mrksic, Georgios P. Spithourakis, Pei hao Su, Ivan Vulic, and Tsung-Hsien Wen. 2019. A repository of conversational datasets. *ArXiv*, abs/1904.06472.

Matthew Henderson, Iñigo Casanueva, Nikola Mrkvsi'c, Pei hao Su, Tsung-Hsien, and Ivan Vulic. 2020. Convert: Efficient and accurate conversational representations from transformers. In *Proceedings of the 2020 Conference on Empirical Methods in Natural Language Processing: Findings*, pages 2161–2174.

Geoffrey E. Hinton, Oriol Vinyals, and Jeffrey Dean. 2015. Distilling the knowledge in a neural network. *ArXiv*, abs/1503.02531.

Ehsan Hosseini-Asl, Bryan McCann, Chien-Sheng Wu, Semih Yavuz, and Richard Socher. 2020. A simple language model for task-oriented dialogue. *ArXiv*, abs/2005.00796.

Xiaoqi Jiao, Yichun Yin, Lifeng Shang, Xin Jiang, Xiao Chen, Linlin Li, Fang Wang, and Qun Liu. 2020. Tinybert: Distilling bert for natural language understanding. *ArXiv*, abs/1909.10351.

Jared Kaplan, Sam McCandlish, T. J. Henighan, Tom B. Brown, Benjamin Chess, Rewon Child, Scott Gray, Alec Radford, Jeff Wu, and Dario Amodei. 2020. Scaling laws for neural language models. *ArXiv*, abs/2001.08361.

Stefan Larson, Anish Mahendran, Joseph J. Peper, Christopher Clarke, Andrew Lee, Parker Hill, Jonathan K. Kummerfeld, Kevin Leach, Michael A. Laurenzano, Lingjia Tang, and Jason Mars. 2019. An evaluation dataset for intent classification and out-of-scope prediction. In *Proceedings of the 2019 Conference on Empirical Methods in Natural Language Processing and the 9th International Joint Conference on Natural Language Processing (EMNLP-IJCNLP)*, pages 1311–1316.

Xingkun Liu, Arash Eshghi, Pawel Swietojanski, and Verena Rieser. 2019a. Benchmarking natural language understanding services for building conversational agents. In *IWSDS*, pages xxx–xxx.

Yinhan Liu, Myle Ott, Naman Goyal, Jingfei Du, Mandar Joshi, Danqi Chen, Omer Levy, Mike Lewis, Luke Zettlemoyer, and Veselin Stoyanov. 2019b. Roberta: A robustly optimized bert pretraining approach. *arXiv preprint arXiv:1907.11692*.

Margaret Mitchell, Simone Wu, Andrew Zaldivar, Parker Barnes, Lucy Vasserman, Ben Hutchinson, Elena Spitzer, Inioluwa Deborah Raji, and Timnit Gebru. 2019. Model cards for model reporting. In *Proceedings of the Conference on Fairness, Accountability, and Transparency*, page 220–229.

Daniel Pressel, Sagnik Ray Choudhury, Brian Lester, Yanjie Zhao, and Matt Barta. 2018. Baseline: A library for rapid modeling, experimentation and development of deep learning algorithms targeting nlp. In *Proceedings of Workshop for NLP Open Source Software (NLP-OSS)*, pages 34–40.

Alec Radford, Karthik Narasimhan, Tim Salimans, and Ilyas Sutskever. 2018. Improving language understanding by generative pre-training. *OpenAI Blog*, page 1.

Alec Radford, Jeff Wu, Rewon Child, David Luan, Dario Amodei, and Ilya Sutskever. 2019. Language models are unsupervised multitask learners. *OpenAI Blog*, page 1.

Colin Raffel, Noam M. Shazeer, Adam Roberts, Katherine Lee, Sharan Narang, Michael Matena, Yanqi Zhou, Wei Li, and Peter J. Liu. 2020. Exploring the limits of transfer learning with a unified text-to-text transformer. *ArXiv*, abs/1910.10683.

Nils Reimers and Iryna Gurevych. 2019. Sentence-bert: Sentence embeddings using siamese bert-networks. In *Proceedings of the 2019 Conference on Empirical Methods in Natural Language Processing and the 9th International Joint Conference on Natural Language Processing (EMNLP-IJCNLP)*, pages 3982–3992.

Victor Sanh, Lysandre Debut, Julien Chaumond, and Thomas Wolf. 2019. Distilbert, a distilled version of bert: smaller, faster, cheaper and lighter. *ArXiv*, abs/1910.01108.

Rico Sennrich, Barry Haddow, and Alexandra Birch. 2016. Neural machine translation of rare words with subword units. In *Proceedings of the 54th Annual Meeting of the Association for Computational Linguistics (Volume 1: Long Papers)*, pages 1715–1725.

Peter Shaw, Jakob Uszkoreit, and Ashish Vaswani. 2018. Self-attention with relative position representations. In *Proceedings of the 2018 Conference of the North American Chapter of the Association for Computational Linguistics: Human Language Technologies, Volume 2 (Short Papers)*, pages 464–468.

Ashish Vaswani, Noam Shazeer, Niki Parmar, Jakob Uszkoreit, Llion Jones, Aidan N Gomez, Łukasz Kaiser, and Illia Polosukhin. 2017. Attention is all you need. In *Advances in neural information processing systems*, pages 5998–6008.

Ivan Vulić, Pei-Hao Su, Samuel Coope, Daniela Gerz, Paweł Budzianowski, Iñigo Casanueva, Nikola Mrkšić, and Tsung-Hsien Wen. 2021. ConvFiT: Conversational fine-tuning of pretrained language models. In *Proceedings of the 2021 Conference on Empirical Methods in Natural Language Processing*, pages 1151–1168.

Chien-Sheng Wu, Steven C.H. Hoi, Richard Socher, and Caiming Xiong. 2020. TOD-BERT: Pre-trained natural language understanding for task-oriented dialogue. In *Proceedings of the 2020 Conference on Empirical Methods in Natural Language Processing (EMNLP)*, pages 917–929.

Chien-Sheng Wu and Caiming Xiong. 2020. Probing task-oriented dialogue representation from language models. In *Proceedings of the 2020 Conference on Empirical Methods in Natural Language Processing (EMNLP)*, pages 5036–5051.

Yizhe Zhang, Siqi Sun, Michel Galley, Yen-Chun Chen, Chris Brockett, Xiang Gao, Jianfeng Gao, Jingjing Liu, and Bill Dolan. 2020. DIALOGPT : Large-scale generative pre-training for conversational response generation. In *Proceedings of the 58th Annual Meeting of the Association for Computational Linguistics: System Demonstrations*, pages 270–278.

Yukun Zhu, Ryan Kiros, Richard S. Zemel, Ruslan Salakhutdinov, Raquel Urtasun, Antonio Torralba, and Sanja Fidler. 2015. Aligning books and movies: Towards story-like visual explanations by watching movies and reading books. *2015 IEEE International Conference on Computer Vision (ICCV)*, pages 19–27.

NER-MQMRC: Formulating Named Entity Recognition as Multi Question Machine Reading Comprehension

Anubhav Shrimal[1] **Avi Jain**[2*] **Kartik Mehta**[3†] **Promod Yenigalla**[1]

[1]Retail Business Services, Amazon
[2]Product Graph, Amazon
[3]Amazon Search, Amazon
{shrimaa, jainav, kartim, promy}@amazon.com

Abstract

NER has been traditionally formulated as a sequence labeling task. However, there has been recent trend in posing NER as a machine reading comprehension task (Wang et al., 2020; Mengge et al., 2020), where entity name (or other information) is considered as a question, text as the context and entity value in text as answer snippet. These works consider MRC based on a single question (entity) at a time. We propose posing NER as a multi-question MRC task, where multiple questions (one question per entity) are considered at the same time for a single text. We propose a novel BERT-based multi-question MRC (NER-MQMRC) architecture for this formulation. NER-MQMRC architecture considers all entities as input to BERT for learning token embeddings with self-attention and leverages BERT-based entity representation for further improving these token embeddings for NER task. Evaluation on three NER datasets show that our proposed architecture leads to average 2.5 times faster training and 2.3 times faster inference as compared to NER-SQMRC framework based models by considering all entities together in a single pass. Further, we show that our model performance does not degrade compared to single-question based MRC (NER-SQMRC) (Devlin et al., 2019) leading to F1 gain of +0.41%, +0.32% and +0.27% for AE-Pub, Ecommerce5PT and Twitter datasets respectively. We propose this architecture primarily to solve large scale e-commerce attribute (or entity) extraction from unstructured text of a magnitude of 50k+ attributes to be extracted on a scalable production environment with high performance and optimised training and inference runtimes.

1 Introduction

Named Entity Recognition (NER) is the task of locating and classifying entities mentioned in unstructured text into predefined categories such as names of people, organizations and locations. It is a crucial component of many applications, such as web search, relation extraction (Yu et al., 2019) and e-commerce attribute extraction (Zheng et al., 2018; Mehta et al., 2021). Traditionally, NER has been posed as a sequence labeling task (Ma and Hovy, 2016; Zheng et al., 2018; Devlin et al., 2019) where each token is assigned a single tag class. We term these sequence labeling approaches as NER-SL. Recently, there has been interest in posing NER as a machine reading comprehension task (Wang et al., 2020; Mengge et al., 2020; Xu et al., 2019). Specifically, NER is posed as a question answering problem, where text is considered context, entity name (or some variant) is considered question and entity value mentioned in text is considered as answer snippet. We term these approaches as Single Question Machine Reading Comprehension (NER-SQMRC) as they involve asking a single question (or entity) at a time. We argue that both NER-SL and NER-SQMRC have their merits and demerits, e.g. NER-SQMRC incorporates entity name for better representation and can be easily extended to new entities without re-training and NER-SL requires single scoring pass for extracting all entities from a given text. We pose NER as a multi-question MRC problem, where multiple questions (one question per entity) are asked at the same time and propose a novel architecture (NER-MQMRC) for this formulation. We summarize the merits and demerits of these three formulations in Table 1 considering below factors:

- **Entity scaling**: Ability to scale for new entities without retraining.
- **Multi-entity scoring**: Ability to extract all entities from a given text in a single forward pass.
- **Faster runtime**: Extracting multiple entities together in a single pass leads to faster training and inference as compared to considering single entity in a pass.

*work done as part of Retail Business Services, Amazon
†work done as part of India Machine Learning, Amazon

Proceedings of NAACL-HLT 2022: Industry Track Papers, pages 230 - 238
July 10-15, 2022 ©2022 Association for Computational Linguistics

- **Using entity information**: Leveraging entity information (such as entity name) for learning better representations.

Property	NER-SL	NER-SQMRC	NER-MQMRC
Entity scaling	✗	✓	✓
Multi-entity Scoring	✓	✗	✓
Faster runtime	✓	✗	✓
Entity information	✗	✓	✓

Table 1: Comparing different attribute extraction approaches based on various factors.

As summarized in Table 1, our proposed NER-MQMRC architecture combines the best of NER-SL and NER-SQMRC. NER-MQMRC considers extraction of multiple entities based on multiple questions on same text, and is novel in three ways - 1) Token representations are learnt to incorporate information of all the entities, unlike using single entity as in (Wang et al., 2020; Mengge et al., 2020). 2) We introduce leveraging BERT-based entity representations for further improving token representations for NER task. 3) Our architecture leads to faster training and inference. E.g. scoring of five entities can be done using a single forward pass with our NER-MQMRC as compared to five passes required earlier with NER-SQMRC based models (Devlin et al., 2019; Wang et al., 2020; Mengge et al., 2020). Experiments on three NER datasets establish the effectiveness of NER-MQMRC architecture. NER-MQMRC achieves 2.5x faster training and 2.3x faster inference as compared to single question based MRC (NER-SQMRC) framework based models by considering multiple entities together in training and inference. Further, we show performance boost over SOTA NER-SQMRC (Devlin et al., 2019), obtaining +0.41%, +0.32% and +0.27% F1 improvements for AE-Pub, Ecommerce5PT and Twitter datasets respectively. Rest of the paper is organized as follows. We describe our proposed NER-MQMRC architecture in Section 2. We discuss our experimental setup in Section 3 followed by results in Section 4. We discuss the industry impact of our work in Section 5 and summarize the paper in Section 6.

2 NER as a Multi-Question MRC task

2.1 Problem definition and dataset construction

Given an input sequence $X = \{x_1, x_2, ..., x_n\}$, where n denotes the length of the sequence, the objective in NER task is to find and label tokens in X that represent entity $y \in Y$, where Y is a predefined list of all possible entities (e.g., BRAND, COLOR, etc). Under the NER-SQMRC framework, the model is given a question q_i asking about i^{th} entity and the model has to extract a text span x_{start_i,end_i} from X which are tokens corresponding to the ith entity. For NER-MQMRC framework, the model is given a list of k questions $Q = \{q_1, q_2, ..., q_k\}$ and the model has to extract the text spans $\{(x_{start_1,end_1}), (x_{start_2,end_2}), ..., (x_{start_k,end_k})\}$ from X corresponding to each of the k entities. We use BERT for Question Answering (Devlin et al., 2019) as our NER-SQMRC baseline implementation (refer Appendix A.1).

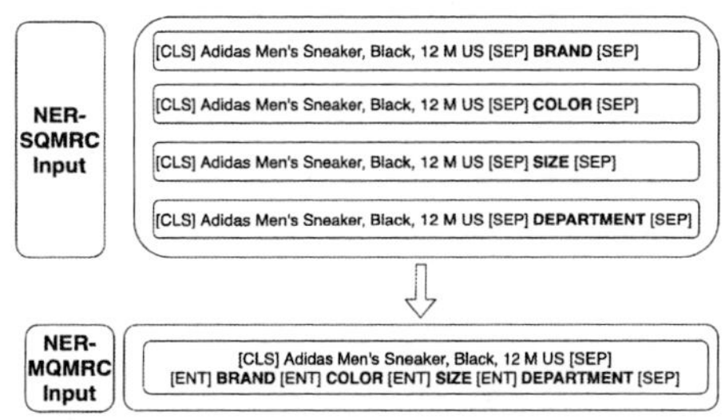

Figure 1: Data Input format for NER-SQMRC and NER-MQMRC model architectures.

Figure 1 shows data input format for both NER-SQMRC and NER-MQMRC. Similar to conventional Question Answering, training data for NER-SQMRC consists of (text, single-entity-question, entity spans from text) triplets. For a dataset with k entities, training data consists of k samples for each text, each sample having question for one entity. However, for NER-MQMRC, training data consists of a single sample for each text, having k questions (one question per entity). Hence, NER-SQMRC formulation requires dealing with larger size training data (k times more samples) with same information as compared to NER-SL and NER-MQMRC. Similarly, during inference, NER-SQMRC requires performing k evaluations for the same text to get text span for each entity, whereas NER-MQMRC requires only a single evaluation for all entities.

2.2 Model Details

Figure 2 shows our proposed NER-MQMRC architecture. We build NER-MQMRC on top of BERT architecture (Devlin et al., 2019) by customizing BERT input and modifying the output layer as described in this section.

2.2.1 NER-MQMRC input

BERT has been trained to take a pair of sentences separated by a special token *[SEP]* as input, and use E_A and E_B segment embeddings respectively for tokens of each sentence. For NER-MQMRC, we concatenate the input text and questions of all entities separated by *[SEP]* (refer Figure 1). Questions of each entity are further separated by a special token *[ENT]*, which we add to the BERT vocabulary. We use E_A segment embeddings for input text and E_B segment embeddings for all question tokens. Output embedding learned corresponding to each *[ENT]* token is considered as embedding representation for the entity adjacent to that *[ENT]* token.

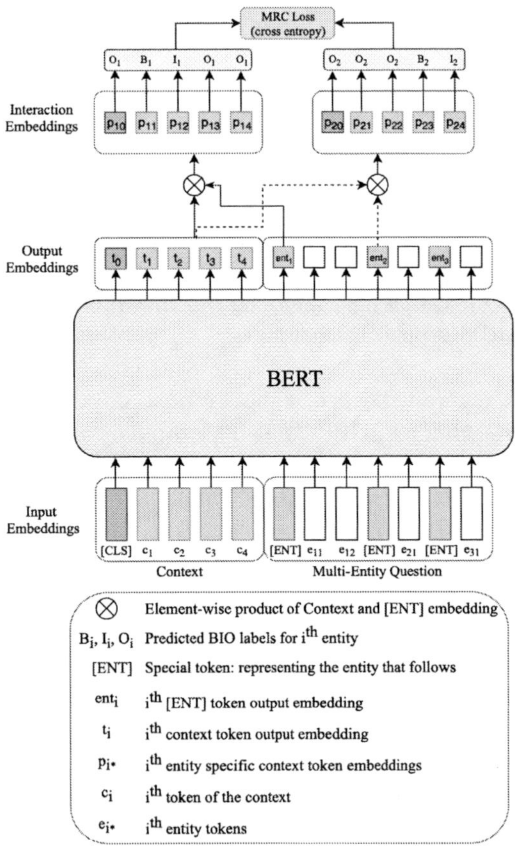

Figure 2: NER-MQMRC model architecture.

2.2.2 Entity specific representation and span selection

As discussed, the ith *[ENT]* token output embedding (ent_i) represents the ith entity in the question. We hypothesize that using ent_i to attend to the context token's output embeddings, $T = \{t_1, t_2, ..., t_n\}$, will help the model find the answer span for entity i. We use entity embeddings to transform the common context representations (T) to entity specific token representations. We consider extraction of each entity as a separate task and use element-wise product of token and entity embeddings to obtain entity specific representations for each token (refer Figure 2). More formally, we perform an element-wise product of token embeddings T with ent_i to get i^{th} entity specific token representations $P_i = \{p_{i1}, p_{i2}, ..., p_{in}\}$.

These entity specific representations are then fed into a separate token-level dense layer, W_{bio}, to get the BIO format label prediction for each token w.r.t. the entity as shown in equation 1, where t_j represents embedding for j^{th} token and ent_i represents embedding for i^{th} entity. Examples with no entity mention are modelled by setting the label for *[CLS]* token as B tag for that entity. For each token and entity pair, loss is calculated using cross entropy loss (L^{ce}) between predicted and actual label. For each sample, total loss, L_{total} (refer equation 2), is average (with equal weightage) of loss for all k entities and n tokens pairs.

$$label_j = \arg\max(softmax(W_{bio}(t_j \odot ent_i))) \quad (1)$$

$$L_{total} = \frac{1}{k \cdot n} \sum_{i=1}^{k} \sum_{j=1}^{n} L_{i,j}^{ce} \quad (2)$$

2.3 Discussion

Our proposed formulation is generic and can be used with other pre-trained architectures (such as XLNET, RoBERTa) instead of BERT for feature extraction. In recent years, there has been incremental advancements to the MRC framework such as the use of knowledge distillation loss as a regularizer and no-answer loss (Wang et al., 2020) to achieve better performance than (Devlin et al., 2019); NER-MQMRC framework can also easily integrate such ideas to get better performance and we keep this to be explored as a future work since in this paper we want to show the effectiveness of NER-MQMRC framework over NER-SQMRC framework with similar setup for both the frameworks. We use BIO label prediction to allow multiple value predictions for an entity from the text, though we also experimented with single (start, end) span index prediction as output labels similar to (Wang et al.,

	Train Data			Test Data		
Dataset	SQMRC	MQMRC	Reduction(%)	SQMRC	MQMRC	Reduction(%)
Ecommerce5PT	981,076	290,698	**70.37**	32,062	4,967	**84.51**
AE-Pub	88,460	39,888	**54.91**	22,005	17,393	**20.96**
Twitter	11,997	3,999	**66.67**	9,768	3,256	**66.67**

Table 2: Reduction in dataset size due to single-entity to multi-entity question transformation.

2020) but has the limitation of predicting only a single answer span.

3 Experimental Setup

3.1 Datasets

Experiments were performed on three NER datasets described below.

AE-Pub (Xu et al., 2019) is a dataset for E-commerce attribute extraction collected from AliExpress Sports & Entertainment category. This dataset is designed to pose E-commerce attribute extraction as a question answering problem and contains over 110k triplets (text, attribute, value) and 2.7k unique attributes. Even though the number of attributes is large, any given text in the dataset has no more than 13 attributes. Train and test dataset is created in an automated manner using distant supervision.

Ecommerce5PT is a 33 attributes (size, material, color, etc.) dataset extracted from five different product types from Amazon catalogue. The train data is constructed in a similar way as AE-Pub using distant supervision. The train data quality is improved using automated gazetteer and matching heuristics (refer Appendix A.2). Unlike AE-pub, test data is constructed with manual audit, thus leading to better quality test data.

Twitter (Zhang et al., 2018) is an English NER dataset based on tweets. We use the setup similar to (Mengge et al., 2020), using textual information queries (refer Appendix A.5) and making entity detection on PER, LOC and ORG.

3.1.1 Datasets transformation

As discussed earlier, NER-MQMRC leads to reduced train and test data size as compared to NER-SQMRC (Table 2). We observe a median of 3, 2 and 3 entities per question in training data of Ecommerce5PT, AE-Pub and Twitter datasets respectively, leading to similar data reduction for NER-MQMRC training. Appendix A.4 elaborates on the distribution of entities per question for NER-MQMRC for each of these datasets. For fair comparison, one should use all entities of a sample while evaluating NER-SL, NER-SQMRC and NER-MQMRC approaches. We use this setup for Ecommerce5PT and Twitter datasets. However, AE-Pub dataset contains only few entities of each sample. We follow setup used in (Xu et al., 2019) for AE-Pub evaluation.

3.2 Experiments

In this section we detail the various experiments to evaluate our proposed solution, NER-MQMRC, on aspects such as operational performance (training and inference runtime), NER task, limited data setting (few shot) and NER-MQMRC model specific analysis.

Training and Inference Runtime: We compare how much time does NER-SQMRC and NER-MQMRC take to do one pass over the complete train data (1 epoch) as well as for inference on complete test data. For a fair comparison, the models are run on the same machine and under the same conditions.

Named Entity Recognition: We evaluate models for the task of extracting entities from a given text. For NER-SL models (Mehta et al., 2021; Ma and Hovy, 2016), input is a text in which tokens are to be tagged with entity BIO labels (B-PER, I-LOC, etc.). For NER-SQMRC models (Devlin et al., 2019; Wang et al., 2020; Xu et al., 2019), input is a text and a corresponding single entity question, whereas, for our proposed NER-MQMRC models, input is a text and a multi-entity question (section 2.1). The output for each model (NER-SL, NER-SQMRC and NER-MQMRC) are BIO labels for each token in the text. We use micro average precision (P), recall (R) and F_1 as evaluation metrics and use Exact Match criteria (Rajpurkar et al., 2016) to compute the scores.

Few-shot Learning: We analyze the performance as the number of data samples seen during training are reduced. We perform this analysis using Ecommerce5PT dataset and compare with Multi-task NER architecture (Mehta et al., 2021).

Context-Entity Interaction: Element-wise product operation is applied over entity embedding and token output embeddings to get entity specific token embeddings. As the operation performed is important to filter information, in this experiment we explore the effects of using different operations other than using element-wise product.

Impact of entity ordering: We evaluate the impact on model performance due to the order in which en-

EcommerceSPT			
methods	P(%)	R(%)	F1(%)
Multi-task NER (Mehta et al., 2021) (single model)	**91.62**	62.47	74.29
Multi-task NER (Mehta et al., 2021) (5 model ensemble)*	88.90	77.20	82.60
BERT-Tagger (Devlin et al., 2019)	88.43	77.51	82.61
NER-SQMRC (Devlin et al., 2019)	87.92	81.18	84.42
NER-MQMRC	87.52	**82.14**	**84.74**
AE-Pub			
methods	P(%)	R(%)	F1(%)
SUOpenTag (Xu et al., 2019)	79.85	70.57	74.92
AVEQA (Wang et al., 2020)	86.11	**83.94**	**85.01**
NER-SQMRC (Devlin et al., 2019)	85.08	83.19	84.13
NER-MQMRC	**86.18**	82.97	84.54
Twitter			
methods	P(%)	R(%)	F1(%)
BiLSTM-CRF (Ma and Hovy, 2016)	-	-	65.32
CoFEE-MRC (Mengge et al., 2020)	75.89	71.93	73.86
NER-SQMRC (Devlin et al., 2019)	**80.37**	76.90	78.59
NER-MQMRC	77.79	**79.96**	**78.86**

$*$ Five individual models were trained and evaluated, one for each product type
AVEQA (Wang et al., 2020) uses no-answer and distillation loss as regularizers

Table 3: Performance comparison on various NER datasets.

tities are mentioned in a question as NER-MQMRC is formulated as a multi-entity question.

4 Results

4.1 Operational Performance – training and inference runtime

Figure 3 shows the relative training and inference time of NER-MQMRC and NER-SQMRC on all three datasets. We observe that NER-MQMRC leads to an average 2.5 times faster training and 2.3 times faster inference due to performing single forward pass for all entities, as compared to NER-SQMRC which requires a separate forward pass for each entity. The runtime improvement depends on how many entities are grouped together in the dataset for each text. NER-MQMRC inference runtime on AE-Pub is only 5% faster than NER-SQMRC as only 20.96% reduction happened in test dataset size after data transformation (Table 2).

4.2 NER Task Performance

Table 3 shows comparison of our proposed model with baselines on multiple NER datasets. Based on evaluation on three NER datasets, our proposed

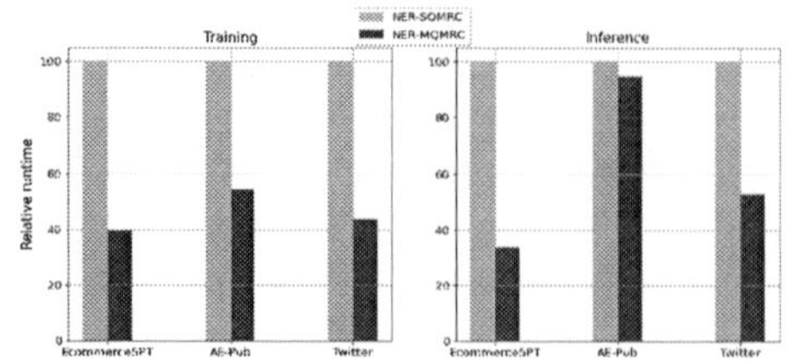

Figure 3: Comparison of operational metrics.

model outperforms NER-SQMRC (Devlin et al., 2019) achieving F1 gain of +0.41%, +0.32% and +0.27% for AE-Pub, Ecommerce5PT and Twitter datasets respectively. A single NER-MQMRC model outperforms ensemble of five Multi-task NER models (one for each product type) by +2.14% F1 and helps in avoiding model proliferation by having a single model instead of a different model for each product type for Ecommerce5PT dataset. NER-MQMRC outperforms BERT-Tagger (Devlin et al., 2019) by +2.13% which uses BERT for NER as a tagging task (NER-SL). For AE-Pub, NER-MQMRC has 0.47% lower F1 compared to AVEQA (Wang et al., 2020), which is due to the additional No-answer and Distillation loss components in AVEQA. Note that NER-MQMRC is agile and such modules can be easily integrated to it as well.

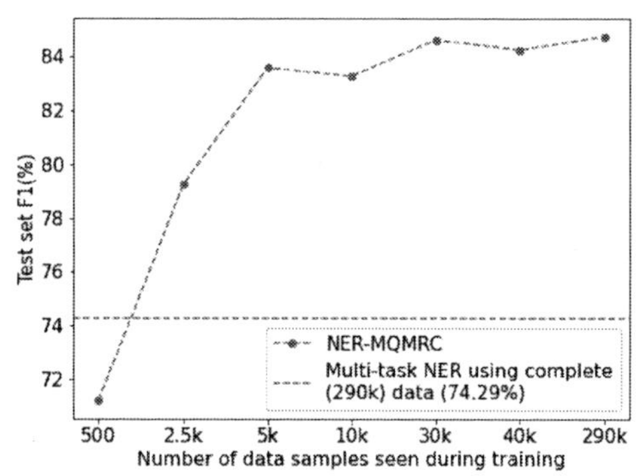

Figure 4: Performance with less training data on Ecommerce5PT.

4.3 Evaluation in limited data setting – Few-shot Learning

Figure 4 shows the performance of NER-MQMRC with lesser data availability during training. NER-MQMRC is able to perform better than Multi-Task NER model trained on complete Ecommerce5PT data (290k samples) with as low as 2.5k samples

Operation Name	Formula	P(%)	R(%)	F1(%)
layer_sum	$P_i = W_1(T) + W_2(ent_i)$	79.07	11.46	20.02
difference	$P_i = T - ent_i$	85.99	20.70	33.36
layer_product_relu	$P_i = relu(W_1(T)) * relu(W_2(ent_i))$	74.80	79.57	77.11
layer_product_tanh	$P_i = tanh(W_1(T)) * tanh(W_2(ent_i))$	76.68	78.49	77.58
max	$P_i = max(T, ent_i)$	76.87	**80.79**	78.78
element-wise product	$P_i = T * ent_i$	77.79	79.96	78.86
layer_product	$P_i = W_1(T) * W_2(ent_i)$	**78.87**	79.66	**79.26**

W_1, W_2 are linear weight matrices
T is the context vector of shape (n, dim) where n is the context length
ent_i is the entity vector of shape $(dim,)$ for the ith entity
P_i is the ith entity specific context vector of shape (n, dim)
$*, +, -$ and max are element-wise product, sum, difference and max operations respectively

Table 4: Effect of different operations to attend context vectors using entity vector.

during training. NER-MQMRC is able to perform even with few samples for training because of the natural language understanding a pre-trained BERT model possesses. The performance further increases with increase in dataset size. For Multi-task NER model we observed the F1 further dropped from 74.29% to 54.49% when trained with 40k data samples.

4.4 NER-MQMRC Specific Experiments

4.4.1 Context Entity Interaction Operations

We experimented with a list of different operations to get better entity specific context embeddings on Twitter dataset. As shown in Table 4, *layer_product* operation performed the best with 79.26% F1. Operations such as element-wise *sum* and *difference* performed poorly in generating good quality entity specific context embeddings because they did not amplify the context vector features by large magnitudes which helps the classification layer better differentiate whereas *product* operation amplified the feature magnitudes.

4.4.2 Effects of entity ordering in a question

We observe that keeping the same ordering of entities in a question while training, leads to deterioration in F1 if the entities are then shuffled during inference (-12.33% on average). This is likely due to model giving more weightage to relative entity position while learning the entity representations and not focusing on the entity name (or entity question). Shuffling the order of entities during training alleviates this issue and leads to robust results for any order of entities during evaluation.

5 Industry Impact

Cost saving: Our production pipeline uses AWS p2.8xlarge compute instance for model training which costs $7.2/hour. Training a single NER-SQMRC model takes 17 hours whereas our proposed NER-MQMRC model takes 7 hours which saves $72 per model training i.e. reducing the model training cost by an average of 58.82%. Training multiple such models leads to large cost savings for production systems.

Faster model runtime: Due to the faster training and inference capabilities of NER-MQMRC, our production systems are deployed faster and are able to serve 2.3 times more inference requests per minute improving the model throughput.

Model proliferation reduction: The NER-SL based production systems need to deploy multiple models as they are not able to perform at scale with the increase in the number of attributes in the e-commerce catalogue due to the increase in output label space. NER-MQMRC alleviates this issue as the output label space remains constant (3 for BIO labels) and a single model can be trained for 50k+ number of attributes.

Better performance: From our experiments we show that NER-MQMRC performs better than NER-SL and NER-SQMRC framework models.

6 Conclusion

In this paper, we formulated NER as a multi question MRC task (NER-MQMRC). Experimental evaluation on three NER datasets shows that our proposed NER-MQMRC model handles multiple entities together and leads to faster training and inference as compared to single question MRC formulation and improves performance over SOTA NER-SQMRC model (Devlin et al., 2019), establishing the effectiveness of our proposed model.

References

Jacob Devlin, Ming-Wei Chang, Kenton Lee, and Kristina Toutanova. 2019. BERT: Pre-training of deep bidirectional transformers for language understanding. In *Proceedings of the 2019 Conference of the North American Chapter of the Association for Computational Linguistics: Human Language Technologies, Volume 1 (Long and Short Papers)*, pages 4171–4186, Minneapolis, Minnesota. Association for Computational Linguistics.

Xuezhe Ma and Eduard Hovy. 2016. End-to-end sequence labeling via bi-directional LSTM-CNNs-CRF. In *Proceedings of the 54th Annual Meeting of the Association for Computational Linguistics (Volume 1: Long Papers)*, pages 1064–1074, Berlin, Germany. Association for Computational Linguistics.

Kartik Mehta, Ioana Oprea, and Nikhil Rasiwasia. 2021. LATEX-numeric: Language agnostic text attribute extraction for numeric attributes. In *Proceedings of the 2021 Conference of the North American Chapter of the Association for Computational Linguistics: Human Language Technologies: Industry Papers*, pages 272–279, Online. Association for Computational Linguistics.

Xue Mengge, Bowen Yu, Zhenyu Zhang, Tingwen Liu, Yue Zhang, and Bin Wang. 2020. Coarse-to-Fine Pretraining for Named Entity Recognition. In *Proceedings of the 2020 Conference on Empirical Methods in Natural Language Processing (EMNLP)*, pages 6345–6354, Online. Association for Computational Linguistics.

Pranav Rajpurkar, Jian Zhang, Konstantin Lopyrev, and Percy Liang. 2016. SQuAD: 100,000+ questions for machine comprehension of text. In *Proceedings of the 2016 Conference on Empirical Methods in Natural Language Processing*, pages 2383–2392, Austin, Texas. Association for Computational Linguistics.

Qifan Wang, Li Yang, Bhargav Kanagal, Sumit Sanghai, D. Sivakumar, Bin Shu, Zac Yu, and Jon Elsas. 2020. Learning to extract attribute value from product via question answering: A multi-task approach. In *KDD '20: The 26th ACM SIGKDD Conference on Knowledge Discovery and Data Mining, Virtual Event, CA, USA, August 23-27, 2020*, pages 47–55. ACM.

Thomas Wolf, Lysandre Debut, Victor Sanh, Julien Chaumond, Clement Delangue, Anthony Moi, Pierric Cistac, Tim Rault, R'emi Louf, Morgan Funtowicz, and Jamie Brew. 2019. Huggingface's transformers: State-of-the-art natural language processing. *ArXiv*, abs/1910.03771.

Huimin Xu, Wenting Wang, Xin Mao, Xinyu Jiang, and Man Lan. 2019. Scaling up open tagging from tens to thousands: Comprehension empowered attribute value extraction from product title. In *Proceedings of the 57th Annual Meeting of the Association for Computational Linguistics*, pages 5214–5223, Florence, Italy. Association for Computational Linguistics.

Bowen Yu, Zhenyu Zhang, Tingwen Liu, Bin Wang, Sujian Li, and Quangang Li. 2019. Beyond word attention: Using segment attention in neural relation extraction. In *Proceedings of the Twenty-Eighth International Joint Conference on Artificial Intelligence, IJCAI 2019, Macao, China, August 10-16, 2019*, pages 5401–5407. ijcai.org.

Qi Zhang, Jinlan Fu, Xiaoyu Liu, and Xuanjing Huang. 2018. Adaptive co-attention network for named entity recognition in tweets. In *Proceedings of the Thirty-Second AAAI Conference on Artificial Intelligence, (AAAI-18), the 30th innovative Applications of Artificial Intelligence (IAAI-18), and the 8th AAAI Symposium on Educational Advances in Artificial Intelligence (EAAI-18), New Orleans, Louisiana, USA, February 2-7, 2018*, pages 5674–5681. AAAI Press.

Guineng Zheng, Subhabrata Mukherjee, Xin Luna Dong, and Feifei Li. 2018. Opentag: Open attribute value extraction from product profiles. In *Proceedings of the 24th ACM SIGKDD International Conference on Knowledge Discovery & Data Mining, KDD 2018, London, UK, August 19-23, 2018*, pages 1049–1058. ACM.

A Appendix

A.1 NER as Single Question MRC

Figure 5 shows our baseline NER-SQMRC architecture. We use BERT for Question Answering (Devlin et al., 2019) as our NER-SQMRC baseline implementation. The model is given a question q_i asking about i^{th} entity and the model has to extract a text span x_{start_i,end_i} from X which are tokens corresponding to the ith entity. The question component of the input in NER-SQMRC comprises of a single entity of interest to be extracted. The context token embeddings derived from the forward pass of the BERT model are then used to extract the text span corresponding to the entity from the context. For a text with five entities the NER-SQMRC model will need to perform five forward pass through the model to extract the text spans for each of the five entities.

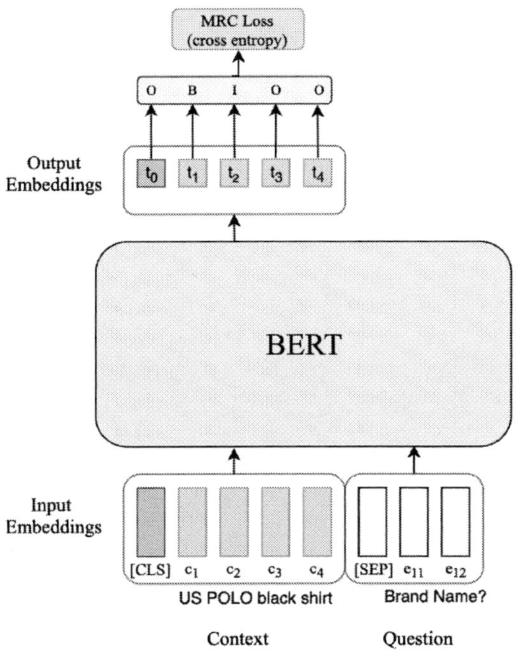

Figure 5: NER-SQMRC model architecture.

A.2 Ecommerce5PT training data generation

Catalogue attribute values can be noisy (e.g. having junk value or missing value) and leads to noisy training annotations with distant supervision. In this section we explain the strategies employed to create better quality training data for Ecommerce5PT dataset.

A.2.1 Automated Gazetteer

Using gazetteers in distant supervision can improve the quality of training annotations (especially for attributes which have limited set of valid values). As part of the data tagging step, the catalogue backend values for an attribute are read to create the gazetteer values using the most frequently occurring attribute values. Elbow method is used to determine the threshold for selecting values for the gazetteer. The training data is then created leveraging the backend attribute values and gazetteer values in distant supervision.

A.2.2 Other Heuristics

The backend catalogue value sometimes contains a different variation of the attribute value than what is present in the context. For example, context is "US Polo t-shirt for Men" whereas the backend value for the attribute *target-audience* is "Man". Such cases will not be tagged using exact match in distant supervision. Custom heuristics such as pluralizing the text (Men, Mens, Men's, etc.), removing or adding "s", lower casing the text and normalizing attributes such as converting "XXXXL" to "4XL" for *size* attribute are added to improve the training data quality.

A.3 Implementation Details

In this section we discuss the dataset creation and model training hyper-parameters details to replicate our results.

During training, we explicitly add no answers for entities that do not have a span in a given text to make the model learn to predict *[CLS]* if no valid answer is present for an entity. We do not make any additions to AE-Pub since it already has no answers added for certain entities. For Ecommerce5PT we add 60% no answers at random and for Twitter and CoNLL we add all no answers for each entity that is not present in that text.

For our implementation of NER-SQMRC and NER-MQMRC, we use the transformers library (Wolf et al., 2019). We use variants of pre-trained BERT model for all our experiments. We use *base-cased* variant for Twitter and *base-uncased* variant for AE-Pub and Ecommerce5PT, keeping our evaluation fairly comparable to existing literature. We use the output layer of single (start, end) span index for AE-Pub dataset similar to (Wang et al., 2020) instead of BIO label. Furthermore, we don't do any dataset specific preprocessing or specific hyperparameter tuning. We use batch size of 32, and a learning rate of 1e-5. We train our models for 20 epochs, choosing the best epoch based on results on the dev set. We make use of AWS compute (ml.p3.8xlarge) instances to run our experiments.

A.4 Entities per question

Figure 6 shows the distribution of number of entities in a question for different datasets. It can be seen from the figure the number of entities in a question greater than 1 are frequent in these datasets which is inefficient for SQMRC type models since they require one forward pass per entity for the same text. We found that Ecommerce5PT and AE-Pub datasets have as many as 12 and 13 attributes for a single text respectively. For Twitter we add all the entities in the question as the dataset has only 3 attributes.

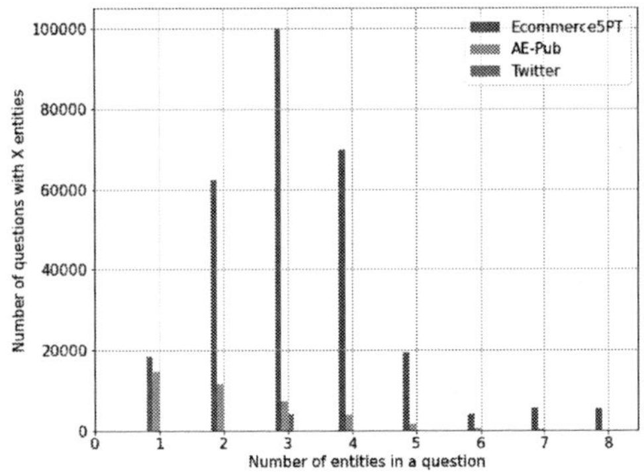

Figure 6: Distribution of number of entities per question in train splits of NER datasets.

Entity Label	Query
PER	People, persons, including fictional
ORG	Companies, agencies, institutions, organizations
LOC	Places, countries, continents, mountain ranges, water bodies

Table 5: Queries used to replace entity label in a question for Twitter.

A.5 Queries

BERT model has natural language understanding capabilities due to large corpus pre-training. This knowledge can be levaraged in MRC to ask better questions. We use a entity description as question instead of entity name in the question so that better representations can be learned by the model. For Twitter we use the language queries in Table 5. For Twitter dataset, only *PER*, *ORG* and *LOC* entity label queries are used because we follow the dataset creation guidelines as stated in (Mengge et al., 2020) where *OTHERS* entity label is ignored.

What Do Users Care About? Detecting Actionable Insights from User Feedback

Kasturi Bhattacharjee[1], **Rashmi Gangadharaiah**[1], **Kathleen McKeown**[1,2], **Dan Roth**[1,3]

[1]AWS AI Labs
[2]Columbia University
[3]University of Pennsylvania
{kastb, rgangad, mckeownk, drot}@amazon.com

Abstract

Users often leave feedback on a myriad of aspects of a product which, if leveraged successfully, can help yield useful insights that can lead to further improvements down the line. Detecting actionable insights can be challenging owing to large amounts of data as well as the absence of labels in real-world scenarios. In this work, we present an aggregation and graph-based ranking strategy for unsupervised detection of these insights from real-world, noisy, user-generated feedback. Our proposed approach significantly outperforms strong baselines on two real-world user feedback datasets and one academic dataset.

1 Introduction

Collecting vast amounts of user feedback on products and services is a common practice these days for a multitude of companies. This can prove to be a rich resource for product owners to improve the quality of their product offerings, correct failures and gauge the general performance of their product from both implicit and explicit signals that might be present in the feedback. However, in most cases, including the one we address in this work, the feedback is unstructured and voluminous, and can therefore remain underutilized for the most part. In our particular use-case, we receive thousands of textual feedback daily on average [1], and it is time-consuming and laborious for product owners to manually extract actionable insights from them.

Users leave feedback on a variety of aspects they experience in the course of using the product (Table 1). These consist of functionalities they find useful (*calculate total size*), issues they encounter when attempting to perform an action (*scroll sideways*), requests around enabling certain features (*sort by Date Modified*), and so on. In this work, our goal is to capture short informative phrases, or ***themes*** which reflect *actionable* insights in the feedback. In capturing these actionable insights, we wish to focus on desired actions that users want to be able to carry out (e.g. *scroll* sideways).

User Feedback Examples
loved the new calculate total size!
Please let me sort by Date Modified
Why can't I scroll sideways on my mac specifically in the new console?

Table 1: Feedback examples from real-world (internal) datasets that illustrate user issues and feature requests when performing an action (underlined).

Owing to the influx of this data in large amounts, and the cost of annotations, it often remains *unlabeled.* Therefore, in this work, we present an *unsupervised* framework to detect actionable insights from such data. In order to capture these insights from an aggregated view of the data, we propose the following two-step approach: a) *aggregating* similar feedback such that each cluster represents coherent insights; b) *detecting themes* from clusters that are pertinent to actionable insights. For instance, in Figure 1, the red cluster consists of feedback expressing users' need to be able to download several files at one time, for which a *possible* theme could be *download files*. As seen in these examples, the desired themes may consist of non-contiguous tokens appearing in text and typically contain a verb mentioning the action. Prior work (see Section 2) uses keyphrase extraction which extracts contiguous words within a noun phrase and thus, cannot capture the kind of actionable insights we find in our data. We utilize unsupervised clustering algorithms for the aggregation step, and a graph-based ranking strategy for the theme detection step.

[1] We take our responsibility to protect customer content extremely seriously. For this research, we followed Amazon's Customer Content policy guidelines.

Proceedings of NAACL-HLT 2022: Industry Track Papers, pages 239 - 246
July 10-15, 2022

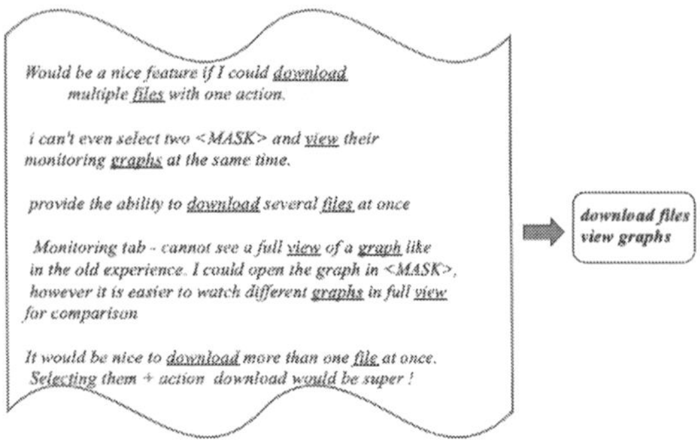

Figure 1: Our pipeline is illustrated above. User feedback documents are first grouped into various clusters. Here, two clusters (blue and red), each representing different insights are shown. For each cluster, we automatically identify a "theme" (right part of the figure) that concisely captures the desired actions expressed in the cluster, e.g. *download files* for the red cluster; *view graphs* for the blue cluster. *<MASK>* tokens are inserted to maintain anonymity when displaying the examples above.

Contributions of the paper:

- We propose a novel approach of identifying actionable user insights in an unsupervised manner. We do so by framing the problem as a clustering and cluster theme detection problem.
- Our approach is unique in the utilization of graph-based ranking in the identification of cluster themes, especially focused on capturing actions that users want to perform.
- We find our method to significantly outperform baselines on two real-world datasets and one academic dataset.

2 Related Work

There is limited work that focuses on uncovering insights from *real-world* user feedback data. Most of the work involves labeled academic datasets, requiring approaches that involve some form of supervision. For instance, Lin et al. (2012) involves a weakly supervised joint sentiment-topic model that detects sentiment and topic simultaneously from text, applied to two labeled academic datasets. Approaches that are unsupervised (Qiu et al., 2021; Liu et al., 2010) are largely based on Latent Dirichlet Allocation (LDA) (Blei et al., 2003), which yields distribution of unigrams as topics. Although Qiu et al. (2021) adopt an unsupervised strategy, it has not been explored on user feedback data. These approaches are not directly applicable to our problem setting since we require short phrases focusing on the performance of an *action* by the user.

Approaches such as TextRank (Kazemi et al., 2020), SingleRank (Wan and Xiao, 2008), ExpandRank (Wan and Xiao, 2008), TopicRank (Bougouin et al., 2013), TopicalPageRank (Sterckx et al., 2015), PositionRank (Florescu and Caragea, 2017), Bi-LSTM-CRF Sequence Labeling (Alzaidy et al., 2019), FACE (Chau et al., 2020), and MultipartiteRank (Boudin, 2018) have been applied to the task of key phrase extraction from documents as opposed to theme detection from clusters. For cluster-labeling, there has been work around using keyword extraction from clusters, utilizing WordNet synsets to expand the keywords, followed by a selection procedure to assign the final label (Poostchi and Piccardi, 2018; Chang and McKeown, 2019). None of these approaches focus on the extraction of short *actionable* phrases, a.k.a. *themes*, as is our use case. In most of these approaches, candidate key phrases are assumed to appear in contiguous positions in a document and are concatenated to form phrases. As described earlier (Figure 1), it is unrealistic to make such assumptions on real-world user feedback data and our proposed approach considers non-contiguous candidate phrases as well.

3 Data

Split	# of samples	# of samples per intent
Train	15K	100
Dev	3K	20
Test	4.5K	30

Table 2: CLINC150 Data Statistics

In this work, we use two internal unlabeled datasets containing user feedback in English on two product offerings. The feedback collection pipeline has opt-in and opt-out mechanisms in place to allow the user to decide whether their data can be used for further analysis. User-specific information has been removed from these datasets for privacy and confidentiality reasons. These datasets vary in content based on the specific product they contain feedback about, and in the number of feedback documents contained in each. We refer to them as **Prod$_1$** and **Prod$_2$**. **Prod$_1$** received orders of magnitude more feedback than **Prod$_2$**. For exploration purposes we sampled about 10K documents for **Prod$_1$** and 1.5K documents for **Prod$_2$**. In addition,

Intent Label	Document
find phone	*i need your help finding my lost phone*
book hotel	*i'm inquiring about the availability of a room that fits 10 people from monday to tuesday in manhattan*
schedule maintenance	*please find someone who specializes in cars, my check engine light has turned on*

Table 3: Examples with various intent labels from **CLINC150** Dataset. **Note that labels are utilized merely for evaluation purposes.**

we conduct evaluations and report results on an intent classification dataset - **CLINC150** (CC 3.0) (Larson et al., 2019; Zhang et al., 2020) that contains English utterances labeled with one of 150 intents, thereby containing *document-level* labels. The data contains utterances from 10 domains, e.g. Banking, Travel, Kitchen & Dining etc. Table 3 contains utterance examples. The intent labels in this data (e.g. *find phone, book hotel, schedule maintenance, etc.*) are similar in form to the cluster themes we aim to discover from our product feedback data, which makes it a good candidate for evaluating our approach. We obtain proxy ground-truth labels (details in Section 5.3) from the data to evaluate and report metrics on this dataset. **Note that the labels were used for the sole purpose of evaluation and not training, since the real-world use case is in an unsupervised setting.** We use the same train/dev/test splits provided with this dataset, statistics of which are reported in Table 2.

4 Methodology

In this section, we describe our proposed approach for extracting themes that help in discovering insights from user-generated text (outlined in Figure 2). In order to discover coherent emerging insights from the vast amounts of user-generated data, we first aggregate semantically similar feedback using clustering algorithms, and extract a *representative set* of documents per cluster. This is described in Section 4.1. Thereafter, themes for these clusters are generated as detailed in Section 4.2. The entire pipeline is unsupervised.

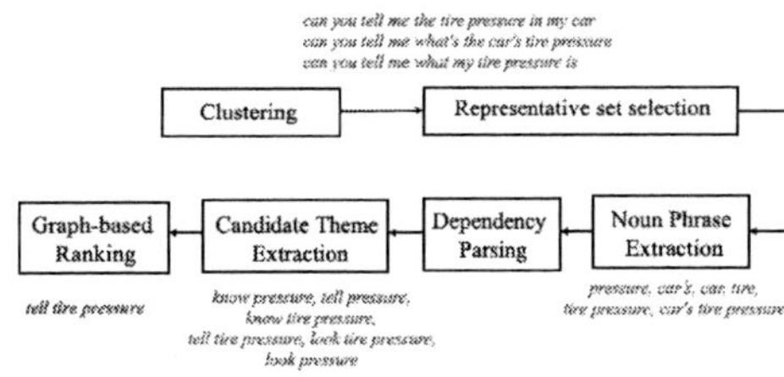

Figure 2: Outline of proposed approach.

4.1 Document Aggregation & Representative Set Selection

Documents are embedded using Sentence-BERT (SBERT) (Reimers and Gurevych, 2019), which we find to capture semantic similarity well even for our internal datasets. k-means (MacQueen et al., 1967) is selected as our clustering approach of choice. Additionally, we explore the use of DNN-based clustering approaches such as Deep Embedded Clustering (**DEC**) (Xie et al., 2016) which has been shown to outperform k-means for a few academic text classification datasets (e.g. REUTERS (Lewis et al., 2004)). When applied to our real-world user-generated text, we find DEC to perform well on the larger dataset, Prod_1 but not on the smaller dataset Prod_2 (Table 4), while k-means performs well across both datasets. Thus, for the remainder of the paper, we report results using k-means as the clustering strategy.

Based on the hypothesis that the centroid of a cluster is representative of the overall cluster itself, we rank documents based on their proximity to the centroid for each cluster. 10 documents closest to the centroid per cluster are subsequently considered for cluster label detection. We chose 10 documents as it provided a good balance between having good representative members of the cluster while also ensuring that we have very few noisy cluster members, if any. Henceforth, we refer to these as the **representative set** of a cluster.

4.2 Unsupervised Cluster Theme Identification

Here, we describe the procedure for cluster theme identification. As previously mentioned, our themes could consist of non-contiguous tokens. We begin by extracting candidate themes using a dependency parsing approach, followed by a graph-based ranking strategy to assign a theme per cluster.

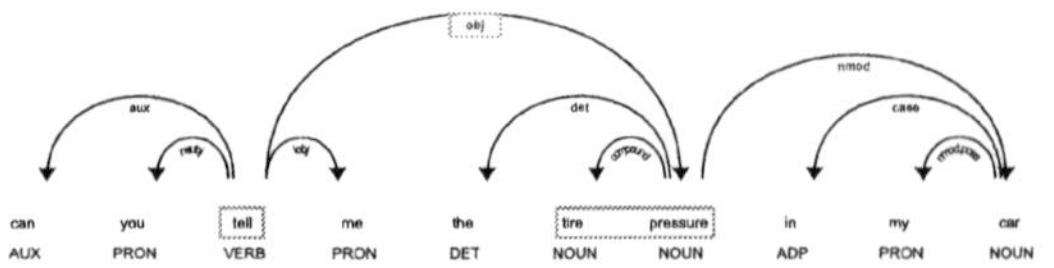

Figure 3: Example of dependency parsing output on CLINC150 utterance.

4.2.1 Cluster Theme Candidate Extraction

- **Noun Phrase Extraction:** Nouns, Proper Nouns and Noun Phrases are extracted from the representative set per cluster. All pronouns that occur in the beginning/end of noun phrases are removed, e.g. *my check engine light* converted to *check engine light*. This is done to capture more generic noun phrases. Those that occur > 2 times throughout the ranked set are retained.
- **Dependency Parsing:** We run a Dependency Parser and extract all verbs for which any of the above selected set of nouns and noun phrases are a *nominal subject* or *object*. For instance in Fig. 3, *tire pressure* is an object for verb *tell.*
- **Candidate Theme Extraction:** Phrases of the form <VERB, NOUN> are thus constructed. For cases where the Noun is part of a previously selected noun phrase, we expand the phrases to <VERB, NP>. These act as *candidate themes* for a given cluster.

4.2.2 Graph-based Ranking for Theme Identification

Graph-based ranking algorithms are often employed in approaches for unsupervised document summarization to measure the importance of a sentence for inclusion in a summary (Erkan and Radev, 2004; Zheng and Lapata, 2019). We apply a similar approach for cluster theme detection. Inspired by these approaches, we construct a graph per cluster, where the nodes consist of the candidate themes and the edge weights capture the semantic similarity between pairs of themes, obtained using cosine similarity between SBERT embeddings of corresponding themes. We then use a graph-based ranking strategy, PageRank (Brin and Page, 1998) and assign the phrase with the highest rank as the cluster theme.

5 Experiments

In this Section, we describe the experimental details of the pipeline, and provide details on the baselines we compare with.

5.1 Data Processing

Since user-generated text tends to be noisy in nature, we preprocess our internal datasets beforehand. This includes converting to lowercase, removing URLs, special characters, and removing text consisting only of digits. For CLINC150, the only pre-processing performed is to replace underscores in the intent labels with spaces, i.e. *book_hotel* converted to *book hotel*, since the generated themes are of a similar form.

5.2 Baselines

We use two baselines to compare with, which are described below.

Poostchi and Piccardi (P&P) This work proposes an approach for cluster labeling by leveraging word embeddings and the synonymy and hypernymy relations in the WordNet (Miller, 1995) lexical ontology. Similar to Chang and McKeown who adapt this method for their clusters, we perform the following steps for each of our clusters. We extract keywords using RAKE (Rose et al., 2010) from the representative set per cluster, to ensure a fair comparison with our methodology. Hypernyms of the component words (restricted to Nouns) of these keywords are obtained, expanded by synonyms (via *synsets*, WordNet's synonym sets). We use *CentHyp* - the best strategy as per Poostchi and Piccardi, to assign the final cluster label. This selects hypernyms that are most central w.r.t. the centroid of the cluster. SBERT embeddings are used for this purpose, to ensure a fair comparison with our approach. Since we could not find offical code for this work, we used our own implementation.

Random baseline We also compare with a random baseline in which the cluster theme is selected at random from the generated set of cluster themes using our proposed approach (Section 4.2.1).

Dataset	Mean Accuracy Score (Human Eval)	
	k-means	DEC
$Prod_1$	90.0	80.0
$Prod_2$	65.0	45.0

Table 4: k-means and DEC clustering algorithms compared on the internal datasets. Annotators provide a score of 0 or 1 to the clusters, based on whether they agree with the quality. Average accuracy per annotator is computed. Scores reported in this table are an average of the annotator scores.

5.3 Evaluation Strategies & Metrics Reported

CLINC150 For this dataset, we leverage the document-level intent labels to generate a *proxy* groundtruth label per cluster. The same representative set (as in Section 4.1) is selected per cluster and the cluster theme is determined by a majority vote over the intent labels of these documents. For the rare case where there is no clear majority, we consider the label of the centroid to be the cluster label. We compute METEOR (Denkowski and Lavie, 2014) and BERTScore (Zhang et al., 2019) metrics w.r.t. the model outputs and proxy labels for our baselines as well as the proposed approach.

Data	Method	METEOR	BERTScore
Dev	P&P	21.30 ±0.69	0.8892 ±0.0033
	Random	21.12 ±0.27	0.8921 ±0.0021
	Ours	**25.79** ±0.55	**0.8962** ±0.0023
Test	P&P	20.94 ±1.37	0.8912 ±0.0034
	Random	19.59 ±1.47	0.8955 ±0.0023
	Ours	**25.31** ±0.69	**0.9026** ±0.0018

Table 5: Mean and standard deviation for METEOR and BERTScores reported for the proposed approach (Ours) against baselines, P&P (Poostchi and Piccardi) and Random on CLINC150, for 3 runs.

Internal Datasets Since $Prod_1$ and $Prod_2$ do not contain labels either on the document or cluster level, we utilize human annotations to evaluate the efficacy of our methodology w.r.t. the baselines. We employ 2 internal annotators who are presented with the cluster themes generated on both datasets, and the representative set of documents per cluster that the themes were detected from. An annotator votes 1 if they completely agree with the cluster theme, 0 if they completely disagree. The final scores are an average of the scores of both annotators. IAA (Cohen's kappa) score is 0.72.

5.4 Modeling Details

We use Stanford Stanza (Qi et al., 2020) for POS tagging and dependency parsing, and scikit-learn's (Pedregosa et al., 2011) k-means implementation for clustering. Using input number of clusters to be the same as the number of intent labels $k = 150$

Dataset	Method	Human Evaluation Score
$Prod_1$	P&P	32.89
	Random	29.70
	Ours	**72.60**
$Prod_2$	P&P	16.67
	Random	8.00
	Ours	**40.00**

Table 6: Performance of the proposed approach (Ours) against baselines, P&P (Poostchi and Piccardi) and Random on our internal datasets.

yields the best results for CLINC150. For our internal datasets, $k = 150$ for $Prod_1$ and $k = 25$ for $Prod_2$ are used. For PageRank, we use networkx's (Hagberg et al., 2008) package, with maximum number of iterations set to 100. CPU-based computing instances are used for both baselines and our methodology.

(Proxy) Cluster Theme	Baseline (P&P) Prediction	Our Prediction
pay bill	electric bill	**pay bill**
calendar	check	**check calendar**
meeting schedule	today	**schedule meeting**
insurance change	insurance policy	**update insurance policy**
shopping list	**shopping list**	buy milk
change accent	**change**	change voice

Table 7: Comparing cluster theme predictions from P&P (Poostchi and Piccardi) & our approach on CLINC150 test set. Themes in bold are those that are qualitatively most similar to the proxy cluster theme.

6 Results

Model performance on CLINC150 Table 5 illustrates the performance of the baseline models and our proposed approach on the dev and test splits of the CLINC150 dataset, over 3 experimental runs.

Dev set: Statistical significance tests conducted show that on the dev set, our methodology significantly outperforms random baseline on METEOR

Representative set of documents per cluster	P&P	Ours
- The new monitoring tab is very poor. It doesn't show enough data and you can't click on graphs to get detailed views. *- I cannot see the monitoring of 2 <MASK> <MASK> side by side. Unreliable reporting of metrics, graphs are sometime unavailable.* *- i can't even select two <MASK> and view their monitoring graphs at the same time.*	detailed view	**view graphs**
- Need to see the <MASK> alarms setup per <MASK> like before instead of loosing this functionality in a new <MASK>. *- I miss the alarm status ""button"" that shows all alarms connected to <MASK> <MASK>* *- On the new <MASK> dashboard all alarms connected to <MASK> <MASK> do not show as it does in the old console. On the old console you get a direct view if any of your <MASK> has any issues while we on the new get that there are no alarms for the <MASK>.*	alarms	**shows alarms**

Table 8: Comparing cluster themes from the baseline P&P method (Poostchi and Piccardi, 2018) vs ours. The documents are in ascending order of proximity to centroid. Text in bold highlights themes that best capture the action being performed by a user.

score by 4.67 points on average (p-value 0.0004). On mean BERTScore, we outperform the random baseline by 0.0041 points (p-value 0.1449). Compared with (Poostchi and Piccardi, 2018), we find our methodology to yield a significantly better performance on METEOR score - an increase of 4.49 points (p-value 0.003). Further, we outperform Poostchi and Piccardi (2018) on BERTScore by 0.007 points (p-value 0.148).

Test set: We significantly outperform both baselines - random and Poostchi and Piccardi (2018), by 5.72 points (p-value 0.0076) and 4.37 points (p-value 0.0159) respectively, on METEOR score. Performance gains obtained using our method over both baselines for BERTScore are also statistically significant - an increase of 0.0071 points (p-value 0.0293) w.r.t. random baseline and that of 0.0114 points (p-value 0.0132) w.r.t. Poostchi and Piccardi (2018).

Model performance on Internal datasets Table 6 demonstrates the significant boost in performance our proposed approach provides over the baselines, as measure by human evaluation scores. We find our approach to outperform both baselines by a large margin for both datasets. On $Prod_1$, we improve upon the random baseline by 42.9 points and upon Poostchi and Piccardi (2018) by 39.71 points. For $Prod_2$, we obtain an improvement of 32 points w.r.t. the random baseline and 23.33 points as compared to Poostchi and Piccardi (2018).

Error Analysis In Tables 7 and 8, we present examples comparing the cluster theme predictions from Poostchi and Piccardi (2018) with ours on the CLINC150 test set, and our internal datasets, respectively. Our method is able to yield more descriptive phrases as cluster themes, that help capture the action being performed. In comparison, the baseline captures shorter and less descriptive phrases. For instance, our method generates themes such as ***pay bill*** and ***update insurance policy*** on clusters from the CLINC150 test set, where the corresponding baseline themes are *electric bill* and *insurance policy*, respectively. Similarly, for a cluster from the internal dataset ($Prod_1$), the theme assigned by our proposed approach is ***show alarms***, whereas the theme detected by the baseline method is *alarms*.

7 Conclusion & Future Work

This work addresses the problem of discovering actionable insights from unlabeled real-world user feedback data, in an unsupervised fashion. Data is clustered into groups containing coherent insights, followed by theme detection per cluster using a graph-based ranking approach. Experiments conducted on two real-world user feedback datasets as well as an academic dataset show our proposed approach to significantly outperform baselines by a large margin. In the future, we would expand the scope of our work to datasets with other characteristics and distributions (e.g. review datasets) to study the applicability of our approach to those use-cases. Further, we would explore the use of generative models to obtain abstractive themes from data.

References

Rabah Alzaidy, Cornelia Caragea, and C. Lee Giles. 2019. Bi-lstm-crf sequence labeling for keyphrase extraction from scholarly documents. In *The World Wide Web Conference*, WWW '19, page 2551–2557, New York, NY, USA. Association for Computing Machinery.

David M. Blei, Andrew Y. Ng, and Michael I. Jordan. 2003. Latent dirichlet allocation. *J. Mach. Learn. Res.*, 3(null):993–1022.

Florian Boudin. 2018. Unsupervised keyphrase extraction with multipartite graphs. In *Proceedings of the 2018 Conference of the North American Chapter of the Association for Computational Linguistics: Human Language Technologies, Volume 2 (Short Papers)*, pages 667–672, New Orleans, Louisiana. Association for Computational Linguistics.

Adrien Bougouin, Florian Boudin, and Béatrice Daille. 2013. TopicRank: Graph-based topic ranking for keyphrase extraction. In *Proceedings of the Sixth International Joint Conference on Natural Language Processing*, pages 543–551, Nagoya, Japan. Asian Federation of Natural Language Processing.

Sergey Brin and Lawrence Page. 1998. The anatomy of a large-scale hypertextual web search engine. *Computer networks and ISDN systems*, 30(1-7):107–117.

Serina Chang and Kathleen McKeown. 2019. Automatically inferring gender associations from language. *arXiv preprint arXiv:1909.00091*.

Hung Chau, Igor Labutov, Khushboo Thaker, Daqing He, and Peter Brusilovsky. 2020. Automatic concept extraction for domain and student modeling in adaptive textbooks. *International Journal of Artificial Intelligence in Education*, pages 1 – 27.

Michael Denkowski and Alon Lavie. 2014. Meteor universal: Language specific translation evaluation for any target language. In *Proceedings of the EACL 2014 Workshop on Statistical Machine Translation*.

Günes Erkan and Dragomir R Radev. 2004. Lexrank: Graph-based lexical centrality as salience in text summarization. *Journal of artificial intelligence research*, 22:457–479.

Corina Florescu and Cornelia Caragea. 2017. PositionRank: An unsupervised approach to keyphrase extraction from scholarly documents. In *Proceedings of the 55th Annual Meeting of the Association for Computational Linguistics (Volume 1: Long Papers)*, pages 1105–1115, Vancouver, Canada. Association for Computational Linguistics.

Aric Hagberg, Pieter Swart, and Daniel S Chult. 2008. Exploring network structure, dynamics, and function using networkx. Technical report, Los Alamos National Lab.(LANL), Los Alamos, NM (United States).

Ashkan Kazemi, Verónica Pérez-Rosas, and Rada Mihalcea. 2020. Biased textrank: Unsupervised graph-based content extraction.

Stefan Larson, Anish Mahendran, Joseph J Peper, Christopher Clarke, Andrew Lee, Parker Hill, Jonathan K Kummerfeld, Kevin Leach, Michael A Laurenzano, Lingjia Tang, et al. 2019. An evaluation dataset for intent classification and out-of-scope prediction. *arXiv preprint arXiv:1909.02027*.

David D Lewis, Yiming Yang, Tony Russell-Rose, and Fan Li. 2004. Rcv1: A new benchmark collection for text categorization research. *Journal of machine learning research*, 5(Apr):361–397.

Chenghua Lin, Yulan He, Richard Everson, and Stefan Ruger. 2012. Weakly supervised joint sentiment-topic detection from text. *IEEE Transactions on Knowledge and Data Engineering*, 24(6):1134–1145.

Zhiyuan Liu, Wenyi Huang, Yabin Zheng, and Maosong Sun. 2010. Automatic keyphrase extraction via topic decomposition. In *Proceedings of the 2010 Conference on Empirical Methods in Natural Language Processing*, pages 366–376, Cambridge, MA. Association for Computational Linguistics.

James MacQueen et al. 1967. Some methods for classification and analysis of multivariate observations. In *Proceedings of the fifth Berkeley symposium on mathematical statistics and probability*, volume 1, pages 281–297. Oakland, CA, USA.

George A. Miller. 1995. Wordnet: A lexical database for english. *Commun. ACM*, 38(11):39–41.

F. Pedregosa, G. Varoquaux, A. Gramfort, V. Michel, B. Thirion, O. Grisel, M. Blondel, P. Prettenhofer, R. Weiss, V. Dubourg, J. Vanderplas, A. Passos, D. Cournapeau, M. Brucher, M. Perrot, and E. Duchesnay. 2011. Scikit-learn: Machine learning in Python. *Journal of Machine Learning Research*, 12:2825–2830.

Hanieh Poostchi and Massimo Piccardi. 2018. Cluster labeling by word embeddings and WordNet's hypernymy. In *Proceedings of the Australasian Language Technology Association Workshop 2018*, pages 66–70, Dunedin, New Zealand.

Peng Qi, Yuhao Zhang, Yuhui Zhang, Jason Bolton, and Christopher D. Manning. 2020. Stanza: A Python natural language processing toolkit for many human languages. In *Proceedings of the 58th Annual Meeting of the Association for Computational Linguistics: System Demonstrations*.

John Xi Qiu, Adam Faulkner, and Aysu Ezen Can. 2021. Towards theme detection in personal finance questions.

Nils Reimers and Iryna Gurevych. 2019. Sentence-bert: Sentence embeddings using siamese bert-networks. *arXiv preprint arXiv:1908.10084.*

Stuart Rose, Dave Engel, Nick Cramer, and Wendy Cowley. 2010. Automatic keyword extraction from individual documents. *Text mining: applications and theory*, 1:1–20.

Lucas Sterckx, Thomas Demeester, Johannes Deleu, and Chris Develder. 2015. Topical word importance for fast keyphrase extraction. In *Proceedings of the 24th International Conference on World Wide Web*, WWW '15 Companion, page 121–122, New York, NY, USA. Association for Computing Machinery.

Xiaojun Wan and Jianguo Xiao. 2008. Single document keyphrase extraction using neighborhood knowledge. In *Proceedings of the 23rd National Conference on Artificial Intelligence - Volume 2*, AAAI'08, page 855–860. AAAI Press.

Junyuan Xie, Ross Girshick, and Ali Farhadi. 2016. Unsupervised deep embedding for clustering analysis. In *International conference on machine learning*, pages 478–487. PMLR.

Jian-Guo Zhang, Kazuma Hashimoto, Wenhao Liu, Chien-Sheng Wu, Yao Wan, Philip S Yu, Richard Socher, and Caiming Xiong. 2020. Discriminative nearest neighbor few-shot intent detection by transferring natural language inference. *arXiv preprint arXiv:2010.13009.*

Tianyi Zhang, Varsha Kishore, Felix Wu, Kilian Q Weinberger, and Yoav Artzi. 2019. Bertscore: Evaluating text generation with bert. *arXiv preprint arXiv:1904.09675.*

Hao Zheng and Mirella Lapata. 2019. Sentence centrality revisited for unsupervised summarization. *arXiv preprint arXiv:1906.03508.*

CTM - A Model for Large-Scale Multi-View Tweet Topic Classification

Vivek Kulkarni
Twitter Cortex
vkulkarni@twitter.com

Kenny Leung
Twitter Cortex
kennyleung@twitter.com

Aria Haghighi
Twitter Cortex
ahaghighi@twitter.com

Abstract

Automatically associating social media posts with topics is an important prerequisite for effective search and recommendation on many social media platforms. However, topic classification of such posts is quite challenging because of (a) a large topic space (b) short text with weak topical cues and (c) multiple topic associations per post. In contrast to most prior work which only focuses on post classification into a small number of topics (10-20), we consider the task of large-scale topic classification in the context of Twitter where the topic space is 10 times larger with potentially multiple topic associations per Tweet. We address the challenges above by proposing a novel neural model, CTM that (a) supports a large topic space of 300 topics and (b) takes a holistic approach to tweet content modeling – leveraging multi-modal content, author context, and deeper semantic cues in the Tweet. Our method offers an effective way to classify Tweets into topics at scale by yielding superior performance to other approaches (a relative lift of **20%** in median average precision score) and has been successfully deployed in production at Twitter.

1 Introduction

On many social media platforms like Twitter, users find posts that they are interested in through two mechanisms: (a) search and (b) recommendation. Both mechanisms typically use the topics associated with posts to identify potential candidates that are displayed to the user. Therefore, automatically associating a post with topics is important for effective search and recommendation. Furthermore, due to the diverse nature of social media content, for such topic association to be useful in practice, it is important to (a) support classification into a large number of topics (potentially hundreds or thousands of topics) and (b) allow for a post to have multiple topics or no topic at all.

Traditionally, there has been a long line of work on classifying documents (like news articles, movie reviews etc.) into topics (Borko and Bernick, 1963; Balabanovic and Shoham, 1995; Joachims, 1998; Tsutsumi et al., 2007; Yang et al., 2014; Adhikari et al., 2019). Additionally, there have been attempts to leverage known label hierarchy to perform hierarchical classification of documents. Most of these approaches learn a model per node of the hierarchy with potentially some form of hierarchy-based regularization in-order to assign labels to a document at each level in the label taxonomy (Koller and Sahami, 1997; Gopal and Yang, 2013; Rojas et al., 2020). With the rise of social media platforms, researchers noted that classification of social media content poses several unique challenges (Chang et al., 2015). First, such posts can be very short and noisy with very weak cues provided by the linguistic context (Baldwin et al., 2013). Second, content may be multi-modal with associated images, videos, and hyperlinks. Approaches for classifying documents tend to ignore this multi-modal nature (Chang et al., 2015). Several works do explore classification of social media posts (like Tweets) (Lee et al., 2011; Genc et al., 2011; Tao et al., 2012; Stavrianou et al., 2014; Selvaperumal and Suruliandi, 2014; Cordobés et al., 2014; Kataria and Agarwal, 2015; Chang et al., 2015; Li et al., 2016b,c,d; Ive et al., 2018; Kang et al., 2019; Gonzalez et al., 2021). However, all of these works suffer from one or more limitations: (a) support only a few topics (an order of 10 topics) (b) model only the text, ignore multi-modal content, deeper semantic-cues and (c) do not support multiple labels per post.

In this paper, we address all of the above limitations in the context of Tweet classification. We propose CTM (Concept Topic Model), a Tweet topic classification model that (a) supports classification into 300 topics (10 times larger than prior work) (b) incorporates rich content like media, hyperlinks,

Proceedings of NAACL-HLT 2022: Industry Track Papers, pages 247 - 258
July 10-15, 2022 ©2022 Association for Computational Linguistics

author features, entity features thus moving beyond shallow Tweet text features and (c) supports multiple topics to be associated per Tweet. Our method offers an effective way to classify Tweets into topics at scale and is superior in performance to other approaches yielding a significant relative lift of **20%** in median average precision score. CTM has been successfully deployed at Twitter where online A/B experiments have also shown increased engagement and improved customer experience.

2 Related Work

Early works on Tweet classification used bag-of-words features constructed from Tweet text and classifiers like Rocchio classifiers, logistic regression, and support-vector machines (Lee et al., 2011; Genc et al., 2011; Tao et al., 2012; Stavrianou et al., 2014; Selvaperumal and Suruliandi, 2014). Follow-up work investigated using increasingly rich features for topic classification including graph-based features of term-co-occurrence graphs, hyperlink information, and distributed representations derived from deep learning models (Cordobés et al., 2014; Kataria and Agarwal, 2015; Li et al., 2016a,b,c,d; Ive et al., 2018; Kang et al., 2019; Gonzalez et al., 2021).

However, one notes at-least one of the following limitations in all of the above works: (a) focus on a very small number of topics ($5-20$) (b) do not support multiple topic labels per Tweet (c) do not consider or discuss how to model content beyond the raw Tweet text (d) do not capture label constraints. A sole exception to some of the above limitations is the work of Yang et al. (2014) which performs large-scale Tweet topic classification focusing on 300 topic labels in a real-time setting using only n-gram based features derived from the Tweet text, but ignores other cues. We revisit their large-scale setting after a decade and propose a vastly improved model for large-scale Tweet topic classification modeling Tweets holistically.

3 Data

Similar to Yang et al. (2014), we consider a set of 300 popular Twitter Topics [1]. While Yang et al. (2014) construct data by only using weak labels obtained from a rule-based system using keyword matches, we employ both high precision human-labeled annotations and weakly-labeled data from a rule-based system using keyword matches [2] to construct the following datasets:

- **Human Labeled Data (HCOMP Dataset)**: We closely follow the procedure outlined by Yang et al. (2014) which first samples Tweets based on topic priors to obtain Tweets that are weakly relevant to a topic, and then seeks label confirmation from trained human annotators. Specifically, we consider Tweets originating from users that are known to tweet mostly about a given topic (for example: Tweets authored by CNN are almost certainly about the "News" topic). We collect 100K such Tweets with at-least 200 Tweets per topic. We then sought label confirmation from trained human annotators with each Tweet-topic pair being independently rated by 3 annotators and use a majority vote to determine the final labels (see Appendix for details). Finally, we create training, validation, and test splits of this dataset disjoint at both the Tweet and the user level.[3]
- **Weakly Labeled Data (WLD Dataset)**: We also construct a large-scale data-set of weakly labeled Tweets (**WLD** dataset) for task-specific pre-training (see Section 4). Specifically, we use the rule-based system to obtain a random sample of 250 million weakly labeled Tweets that is disjoint from the **HCOMP** dataset both in terms of time-span and Tweets.
- **Chatter Data (CHT Dataset)**: To ensure that our model does not incorrectly assign topics to what is termed "Twitter chatter" – Tweets that are largely about daily status updates, greetings and clearly non-topical content, we closely follow Yang et al. (2014) and construct a dataset of weakly labeled non-topical Tweets by sampling Tweets that trigger none of the topical rules in the rule-based system. We verify that a random sample ($N = 150$) (denoted by **CHT-test**) are indeed non-topical through independent human annotators which we set-aside for model evaluation. The remaining portion also user-disjoint ($N = 100000$) is used as training data.

4 Models and Methods

Problem Formulation. We formulate our problem as one of standard multi-label classification.

[1] We focus on only English Tweets. See the Appendix for the full list of topics considered.

[2] See the Appendix for a brief description of this rule-based system for yielding weak labels.

[3] We do this because as we will see later, we use author level features in our model.

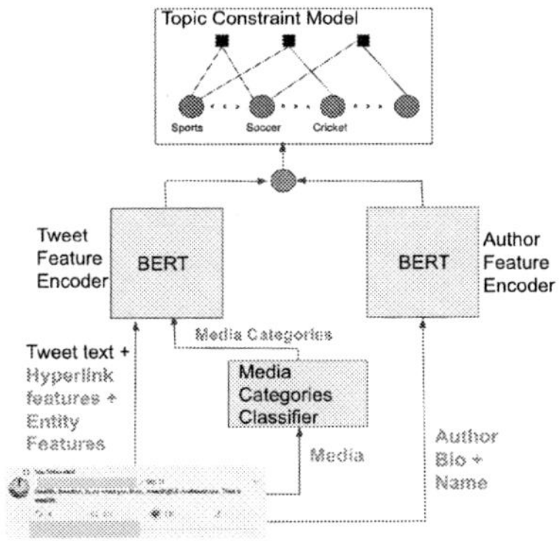

Figure 1: **Overview of our CTM model for large-scale topic classification of Tweets**. Our model consists of 3 components: (a) a Tweet feature encoder encoding Tweet features (b) an Author feature encoder encoding author features thus capturing author-topic affinity and (c) a constraint model that encourages the topic scores to respect prior constraints.

Formally, let $\mathcal{S}$ denote the given set of topics. Given $\boldsymbol{X}$, a set of Tweet features and a set of topics $\boldsymbol{L} \in 2^{\mathcal{S}}$, we seek to model $\Pr(\boldsymbol{L}|\boldsymbol{X})$. We encode the topic labels $\boldsymbol{L}$ as a binary vector $\boldsymbol{Y}$ of length $|\mathcal{S}|$ using multi-hot encoding. We consider a simple approach to multi-label classification[4] – a neural architecture parameterized by $\boldsymbol{\Theta}$ that outputs a vector $\hat{\boldsymbol{Y}}$ of length $|\mathcal{S}|$ where $\hat{\boldsymbol{Y}}_i \in [0, 1]$ is the probability of the Tweet belonging to topic i.

Model Overview. CTM has three components:

- **Tweet Feature Encoder**: This component encodes features of the Tweet holistically. Specifically, it encodes the Tweet text, hyperlink features, named entity mention features, as well as features of associated media. This encoder outputs a vector of topic logits (one for each topic) based on these input features which we denote by $\hat{\boldsymbol{Y}}^t$.
- **Author Feature Encoder**: This component encodes author features like the author name and biography which may be indicative of the author's affinity to certain topics. This encoder outputs a vector of topic logits (one for each topic) based on these input features which we denote by $\hat{\boldsymbol{Y}}^a$. $\hat{\boldsymbol{Y}}^a$ is combined with $\hat{\boldsymbol{Y}}^t$ via a element-wise addition to yield the combined topic logits – $\hat{\boldsymbol{Y}}^c$ which can be converted to probability scores using a sigmoid transformation.
- **Topic Constraint Model**: The topic constraint model encourages the predictions to reflect known constraints among the topic labels. For example, Tweets about "Soccer" are almost certainly also about "Sports" but very unlikely to also be about "Basketball". We encode such pre-specified label constraints in the output space via a factor-graph. Performing inference on the factor-graph re-calibrates the raw probabilities given by $\hat{\boldsymbol{Y}}^c$ to better reflect the output label constraints yielding the final predicted probabilities for each topic $\hat{\boldsymbol{Y}}^f$.

4.1 Tweet Feature Encoder

The Tweet feature encoder is a standard BERT encoder with a linear classification head where all layers are trainable. Each individual Tweet feature is modeled as follows:

- **Tweet Text**: We simply pass the Tweet text as an input string to BERT after standard preprocessing (case-folding, stripping hyperlinks and user mentions).
- **Hyperlink Features**: For each hyperlink in the Tweet text, we obtain the raw HTML content of the web-page being referenced, and extract the web-page title and the first 100 characters of the web-page description. These features are simply concatenated with the Tweet text using a pre-defined separator token.
- **Media**: To incorporate topical cues from any attached media (images, gifs, and videos), we obtain media annotations for the given media. These media annotations are broad categories that summarize the content of the media. We then simply concatenate all of these media annotations to the current input string using a pre-defined token as a delimiter. The media annotations themselves are predicted by a media-annotations classifier that learns to assign each media to zero or more categories from a set of pre-defined categories. [5]
- **Entity Features**: Noting that mentions of named entities provide strong topical cues, we extract such mentions in the Tweet text using an off-the-shelf Twitter NER model (Mishra et al., 2021) and link each extracted named entity to their entry in WIKIDATA where available. We use the WIKIDATA descriptions of each linked entity as addi-

[4] We largely consider a flat classification setting given the absence of well-defined, comprehensive and highly agreed-upon topic taxonomy for Twitter topics, and also because this formulation is better aligned with model deployment constraints.

[5] See the Appendix for details on the media categories classifier.

tional inputs to the Tweet feature encoder. As an example, this enables CTM to infer that Tweets which mention "Steve Waugh" are likely about "Cricket".

Pretraining the Tweet Feature Encoder. Noting that the weights of the standard BERT encoder are not reflective of the domain of Tweets and may represent a poor initialization point during subsequent finetuning, we pretrain the BERT encoder on the task of predicting topics using the **WLD** dataset only using the raw Tweet text as the input feature. As we will show empirically, this large-scale pretraining improves generalization performance by better adapting the model to Twitter data.

4.2 Author Feature Encoder

The author feature encoder is also identical to a standard BERT encoder with a linear classification head, with all layers being trainable. We use the following features of the author (all of which are simply concatenated together as input to BERT): (a) **Author Biography**: We use the self-reported publicly available author-profile description of the author posting the Tweet. (b) **Author Name**: We also use the author's display name. We hypothesize that all of these features may be indicative of the topics that the author likely tweets about. For example, an author name containing the string "FashionNews" strongly suggests that Tweets made by that author will likely be about Fashion.

4.3 Topic Constraint Model

The topic constraint model encodes output label constraints in the topic prediction and captures correlations among topics. We encode such dependencies via a factor graph. Given a vector of topic predictions (probabilities) $\hat{\boldsymbol{Y}}^c$, for each topic T_i, we associate a discrete binary random variable with that topic v_i, and a corresponding unary factor with potential function f_i such that $f_i(0) = 1.0 - \hat{\boldsymbol{Y}}_i^c$ and $f_i(1) = \hat{\boldsymbol{Y}}_i^c$. For every constraint between a pair of topics (i, j), we construct a binary factor with potential function $\phi_{i,j}(v_i, v_j)$. This potential function encodes the compatibility between prediction scores for topic i and topic j. Domain experts can craft their own potential functions to reflect positive or negative compatibility between topic pairs or alternatively even learn these from correlation data. CTM considers two types of constraints:

- **Broader Topic Inclusion**: If a Tweet is about a specific topic c, then it is very likely that the Tweet is also about topic p where p subsumes topic c. Other cases are a "don't-care". For example, if a Tweet is about "Basketball", it is almost certainly about "Sports". We use the following potential matrix[6] for encoding this type of constraint:

p \ c	0	1
0	0.5	0.0
1	0.5	10.0

- **Topic Pair Exclusion**: At-most one among topic a and b can be active at any time. For example, it is very unlikely to have a Tweet which is about both Cricket and Basketball. We use the following potential matrix for encoding this type of constraint:

a \ b	0	1
0	0.5	0.5
1	0.5	0

After constructing a factor graph encoding the specified output constraints, we perform belief propagation[7] on the factor graph to obtain the final marginal probabilities $\hat{\boldsymbol{Y}}^f$ which reflect the encoded output constraints. In our experiments, we impose the above constraint types on specific topics falling under (and including) the broad topics of Sports, Music, Animation, Science, Animals, Anime & Manga.

5 Experiments

5.1 Quantitative Evaluation

Baselines and Evaluation Setup. We consider two baselines: (a) A bag-of-words logistic regression (LR) model – our best-effort attempt to reproduce the decade old setup of Yang et al. (2014) and (b) a standard BERT model using only the Tweet text thus replacing logistic regression in (a) with a current state of the art deep-learning model. We train all models on the training data set using class weighted binary cross entropy loss, and evaluate them on the two held-out test sets:

- **HCOMP Test Set**: We evaluate model performance on the held out test split from the **HCOMP** dataset. We report the median average precision score over all topics. We consider the average precision score, since unlike the F1 score, it summarizes model performance over all operating thresholds.

[6] The potential matrices are not necessarily unique and other equivalent matrices may exist.

[7] See the Appendix for more details on this procedure.

- **CHT Test Set**: In order to measure the ability of our models to effectively reject assigning topics to "non-topical" Tweets (chatter), we evaluate our models on the held-out chatter test set. Here, we report the number of predictions made by the model over a given probability threshold (lower scores are better).

We perform a systematic feature ablation study of our proposed CTM model to quantify the effect of feature sets considered. Table 1 shows the results of our evaluation where model suffixes represent different ablation settings. Note that our full model significantly outperforms the logistic regression and BERT baselines (**Median APS**: 67.0 vs 54.8) and yields a relative improvement of **20%** thus underscoring the effectiveness of our approach. We also make the following additional observations:

- **Including non-topical tweets in training improves performance of rejecting chatter** Note that including non-topical tweets in the training data improved the performance of the BERT baseline on the **CHT** dataset (from **254** to **135** where lower is better).
- **Media features have a focused impact.** Adding media annotations overall does not affect the median average precision score significantly (compare row **CTM-A**: 54.4 to row above: 54.8). However, we observe that many tweets in the evaluation may not contain media annotations. When we restricted our evaluation to only the tweets containing media, we observed a significant improvement where the corresponding average precision scores are **71.0 vs 58.4** respectively. By further computing per-topic performance improvement due to media annotations, we note that media features significantly boost the performance of Automotive, US national news, Anime, and Movies which indeed tend to be media rich, suggesting their focused impact.
- **Large-scale pretraining of feature encoders boosts overall performance.** We observe that pre-training the encoders on domain (and task) specific data is very effective (row **CTM-B** vs **CTM-A:Median APS – 56.7 vs 54.4**).
- **Hyperlink features have a focused impact.** Similar to media features, we observe that hyperlink features have a negligible overall impact (see row **CTM-C:Median APS – 57.2 vs 56.7**). However as with media features, when we restricted our evaluation to only those instances with hyperlinks we indeed observe a significant performance gain where the corresponding scores are **92.67 vs 83.4**. Similar to our analysis of media features, a per-topic improvement analysis reveals that hyperlink features most improve the performance on Travel, Movies, Gaming, and US national news which tend to be hyperlink heavy.
- **Author features significantly boost overall performance.** Author features yield the most benefit overall (see row **CTM-D:Median APS – 63.3 vs 57.2**) thus reaffirming the importance of user-level modeling in NLP tasks.
- **Entity features also significantly boost overall performance.** Similar to author features, the entity features also significantly improve overall performance (see row **CTM-E:Median APS – 66.5 vs 63.3**). Drilling down, we noted that entity linking features most improve the performance on Rap, American football, K-pop, Entertainment News, and Cricket – all topics whose Tweets are likely to mention sport players, movie stars, and musicians that are suggestive of the topic.
- **The constraint model significantly boosts the performance of the relevant topics.** Including the constraint model very slightly improves the median average precision score (**CTM-F:Median APS 67.0 vs 66.5**). This is expected because the constraint model only affects topics for which constraints were included. Looking at the performance on this subset of topics, we note a significant increase in the average precision score (by as much as **20** points) due to reduction in constraint violations – especially violations of the broader topic inclusion constraint (see Table 2).[8]

5.2 Qualitative Evaluation

In addition to evaluating our CTM quantitatively, we also inspected the model predictions qualitatively to identify instances which (a) reveal the benefits of holistic tweet modeling and (b) highlight challenging cases. Table 3 shows a few instances that illustrate the benefit of holistically modeling Tweet content. Note that in "Power hitter joins #yellowstorm", only the attached media (which displays a cricket apparel) is indicative of the topic. Similarly, our model correctly predicts that "Re-

[8]This slight degradation on CHT is due to error propagation of high confidence false positives which occurs to respect the constraints.

	Setting	Median APS ↑	CHT ↓
LR(baseline) (Yang et al., 2014)	Tweet text (trained on only HCOMP)	33.0	108
BERT(baseline)	Tweet text (trained on only HCOMP)	54.5	254
BERT (baseline)	Tweet text (trained on HCOMP + CHT)	54.8	135
CTM-A	Tweet text + media annotation (trained on HCOMP + CHT)	54.4	121
CTM-B	CTM-A + pretraining	56.7	107
CTM-C	CTM-B + Hyperlink features	57.2	101
CTM-D	CTM-C + Author features	63.3	75
CTM-E	CTM-D + Entity Linking features	66.5	80
CTM-F (Full model)	CTM-E + Constraint model	67.0	90

Table 1: **Performance of CTM on the test sets.** The median APS is the median average precision on the **HCOMP** test set (*higher is better*, $N = 10000$) where as **CHT** column shows the number of model predictions exceeding a probability score of 0.9 (noting robustness to other thresholds) on the **CHT** test set (*lower is better*). CTM significantly outperforms baselines and demonstrates the effectiveness of modeling content beyond the immediate Tweet text.

Topic	APS (w/o constraint model)	APS (with constraint model)
Animation	0.64	0.71
Animals	0.88	0.91
Anime & manga	0.66	0.84
Music	0.41	0.70
Sports	0.69	0.89
Science	0.44	0.63

Table 2: **Performance improvements due to the constraint model.** The constraint model yields significant improvements on broader topics (as large as 20 points). Performance on narrower topics do not change significantly.

Tweet Content	Predicted Label	Helpful feature
In times of trouble, regression models come to me, speaking words of wisdom	Data Science	Tweet text
Power hitter joins #yellowstorm `att:Attached media of cricket bat and gloves`	Cricket	Media Annotations
Cameras in USC vs UT stopped working, so it is a podcast now	American Football	Author Bio
Revealed: Australia's stars set to be pulled from IPL `URL to fox.sports domain`	Cricket	Hyperlink
cody ko and noel miller are just ...	Digital creators	Entity features

Table 3: A few examples of correct model predictions that illustrate the benefit of different feature sets. Tweets are paraphrased to protect user privacy.

Tweet Content	Predicted Label	Error Reason
In life, you have not seen your best days, you have not run your best race ...	Running	Metaphor
Cheerleading the mob is not going to save ...	Cheerleading	Metaphor
I am going to have very large drink tonight not sure if whisky or cyanide	Food	Sarcasm or Irony
I need my **** ate	Food	NSFW sense
This is a thread 1/5...	No topic	Conversation thread

Table 4: A few challenging cases for our model. Tweets are paraphrased to protect user privacy.

vealed: Australia's stars set to be pulled from IPL" is about "Cricket" by leveraging topical cues extracted from the linked website's content. Finally, CTM correctly infers that the Tweet referencing "Cody Ko and Noel Miller" is about "Digital Creators" by leveraging named entity cues. Finally, we also noted a few systematic failure modes (see Table 4). In particular, our model does not pick up on (a) metaphorical usage of topical words like "running" or "cheer-leading" (b) sarcasm and irony (c) NSFW senses of certain topical phrases (d) topical content in conversational threads since this requires modeling conversational context.

5.3 Online Evaluation

Finally, we also evaluated CTM online by performing an A/B test comprising of 25 million users in each bucket. To summarize the results of the A/B test briefly, we observed that CTM relatively increased: (a) the size of the topic Tweet inventory online by about 4%. This translates to about 600K additional topical Tweets daily that could be surfaced to users based on their topical interests to improve their user experience. (b) precision by 5%

and (c) user engagement by 5.5%. In a nut-shell, our online experiments suggested that CTM significantly improves the user experience of the Topics product surface in Twitter and has consequently been deployed in production.

6 Conclusion

We revisited the problem of large scale Tweet topic classification posed by Yang et al. (2014) and proposed a model for classifying Tweets into a large set of 300 topics with improved performance. In contrast to prior work we take a holistic approach to modeling Tweets and model not only the immediate Tweet text, but also associated media, hyperlinks, author context, entity mentions, and incorporate domain knowledge expressed as topic constraints in a principled manner. Our model showed significantly increased engagement and improved customer experience in several online A/B experiments, and it has been deployed into production at Twitter with millions of active users. Finally, while our model and approach has been restricted to Tweet classification, our proposed methods and observations may benefit other social media platforms seeking to classify content into a large number of topics effectively.

Ethical Considerations

This paper and the data used within was reviewed as part of Twitter's standard privacy and legal review processes. No data has been publicly released in relation to this paper. While there is a possibility that the model could be misused, we do not anticipate any new or increased risks over those already present in established prior work and prior models on topic classification.

Acknowledgments

We would like to acknowledge the contributions of Inom Mirzaev, Chenguang Yu, Laleh Soltan Ghoraie, Kovas Boguta, Jun Ng, Andy Aitken, Olivia Ifrim, Shubhanshu Mishra, Sneha Mehta, Aman Saini, Sijun He, Wayne Krug, and Ali Mollahosseini in supporting this work. We would also like to thank the anonymous reviewers for their comments and suggestions.

References

Ashutosh Adhikari, Achyudh Ram, Raphael Tang, and Jimmy Lin. 2019. Docbert: Bert for document classification. *arXiv preprint arXiv:1904.08398*.

Marko Balabanovic and Yoav Shoham. 1995. Learning information retrieval agents: Experiments with automated web browsing. In *On-line Working Notes of the AAAI Spring Symposium Series on Information Gathering from Distributed, Heterogeneous Environments*, pages 13–18.

Timothy Baldwin, Paul Cook, Marco Lui, Andrew MacKinlay, and Li Wang. 2013. How noisy social media text, how diffrnt social media sources? In *Proceedings of the Sixth International Joint Conference on Natural Language Processing*, pages 356–364.

Emily M Bender and Batya Friedman. 2018. Data statements for natural language processing: Toward mitigating system bias and enabling better science. *Transactions of the Association for Computational Linguistics*, 6:587–604.

Harold Borko and Myrna Bernick. 1963. Automatic document classification. *Journal of the ACM (JACM)*, 10(2):151–162.

Shuo Chang, Peng Dai, Jilin Chen, and Ed H Chi. 2015. Got many labels? deriving topic labels from multiple sources for social media posts using crowdsourcing and ensemble learning. In *Proceedings of the 24th International Conference on World Wide Web*, pages 397–406.

Héctor Cordobés, Antonio Fernández Anta, Luis F Chiroque, Fernando Pérez, Teófilo Redondo, and Agustín Santos. 2014. Graph-based techniques for topic classification of tweets in spanish. *International Journal of Interactive Multimedia and Artificial Intelligence*.

Yegin Genc, Yasuaki Sakamoto, and Jeffrey V Nickerson. 2011. Discovering context: classifying tweets through a semantic transform based on wikipedia. In *International conference on foundations of augmented cognition*, pages 484–492. Springer.

Jose Angel Gonzalez, Lluís-F Hurtado, and Ferran Pla. 2021. Twilbert: Pre-trained deep bidirectional transformers for spanish twitter. *Neurocomputing*, 426:58–69.

Siddharth Gopal and Yiming Yang. 2013. Recursive regularization for large-scale classification with hierarchical and graphical dependencies. In *Proceedings of the 19th ACM SIGKDD international conference on Knowledge discovery and data mining*, pages 257–265.

Julia Ive, George Gkotsis, Rina Dutta, Robert Stewart, and Sumithra Velupillai. 2018. Hierarchical neural model with attention mechanisms for the classification of social media text related to mental health. In *Proceedings of the Fifth Workshop on Computational*

Linguistics and Clinical Psychology: From Keyboard to Clinic, pages 69–77.

Thorsten Joachims. 1998. Text categorization with support vector machines: Learning with many relevant features. In *European conference on machine learning*, pages 137–142. Springer.

Jaeyong Kang, HongSeok Choi, and Hyunju Lee. 2019. Deep recurrent convolutional networks for inferring user interests from social media. *Journal of Intelligent Information Systems*, 52(1):191–209.

Saurabh Kataria and Arvind Agarwal. 2015. Supervised topic models for microblog classification. In *2015 IEEE International Conference on Data Mining*, pages 793–798. IEEE.

Daphne Koller and Mehran Sahami. 1997. Hierarchically classifying documents using very few words. Technical report, Stanford InfoLab.

Kathy Lee, Diana Palsetia, Ramanathan Narayanan, Md Mostofa Ali Patwary, Ankit Agrawal, and Alok Choudhary. 2011. Twitter trending topic classification. In *2011 IEEE 11th International Conference on Data Mining Workshops*, pages 251–258. IEEE.

Quanzhi Li, Sameena Shah, Mohammad Ghassemi, Rui Fang, Armineh Nourbakhsh, and Xiaomo Liu. 2016a. Using paraphrases to improve tweet classification: Comparing wordnet and word embedding approaches. In *2016 IEEE International Conference on Big Data (Big Data)*, pages 4014–4016. IEEE.

Quanzhi Li, Sameena Shah, Xiaomo Liu, Armineh Nourbakhsh, and Rui Fang. 2016b. Tweet topic classification using distributed language representations. In *2016 IEEE/WIC/ACM International Conference on Web Intelligence (WI)*, pages 81–88. IEEE.

Quanzhi Li, Sameena Shah, Xiaomo Liu, Armineh Nourbakhsh, and Rui Fang. 2016c. Tweetsift: Tweet topic classification based on entity knowledge base and topic enhanced word embedding. In *Proceedings of the 25th ACM International on Conference on Information and Knowledge Management*, pages 2429–2432.

Quanzhi Li, Sameena Shah, Armineh Nourbakhsh, Xiaomo Liu, and Rui Fang. 2016d. Hashtag recommendation based on topic enhanced embedding, tweet entity data and learning to rank. In *Proceedings of the 25th ACM International on Conference on Information and Knowledge Management*, pages 2085–2088.

Shubhanshu Mishra, Sijun He, and Luca Belli. 2020. Assessing demographic bias in named entity recognition. *arXiv preprint arXiv:2008.03415*.

Shubhanshu Mishra et al. 2021. Improved multilingual language model pretraining for social media text via translation pair prediction. In *Proceedings of the Seventh Workshop on Noisy User-generated Text (W-NUT 2021)*, pages 381–388, Online. Association for Computational Linguistics.

Kervy Rivas Rojas, Gina Bustamante, Arturo Oncevay, and Marco A Sobrevilla Cabezudo. 2020. Efficient strategies for hierarchical text classification: External knowledge and auxiliary tasks. *arXiv preprint arXiv:2005.02473*.

Mark Sandler, Andrew Howard, Menglong Zhu, Andrey Zhmoginov, and Liang-Chieh Chen. 2018. Mobilenetv2: Inverted residuals and linear bottlenecks. In *Proceedings of the IEEE conference on computer vision and pattern recognition*, pages 4510–4520.

P Selvaperumal and A Suruliandi. 2014. A short message classification algorithm for tweet classification. In *2014 International Conference on Recent Trends in Information Technology*, pages 1–3. IEEE.

Anna Stavrianou, Caroline Brun, Tomi Silander, and Claude Roux. 2014. Nlp-based feature extraction for automated tweet classification. *Interactions between Data Mining and Natural Language Processing*, 145.

Ke Tao, Fabian Abel, Claudia Hauff, and Geert-Jan Houben. 2012. What makes a tweet relevant for a topic? In *# MSM*, pages 49–56. Citeseer.

Kimitaka Tsutsumi, Kazutaka Shimada, and Tsutomu Endo. 2007. Movie review classification based on a multiple classifier. In *Proceedings of the 21st pacific Asia conference on language, information and computation*, pages 481–488.

Shuang-Hong Yang, Alek Kolcz, Andy Schlaikjer, and Pankaj Gupta. 2014. Large-scale high-precision topic modeling on twitter. In *Proceedings of the 20th ACM SIGKDD international conference on Knowledge discovery and data mining*, pages 1907–1916.

A Appendix

A.1 Details Regarding Off the Shelf Components Used in CTM

A.1.1 Media Annotations Classifier

The media annotations classifier takes as input an image and classifies the image into one or more of 45 media categories listed in Table 5. The classifier is essentially a standard MOBILENET V2 model (Sandler et al., 2018) further fine-tuned on a human-labeled curated dataset of 100K images from Twitter. The operating threshold of the media classifier is set to achieve a precision of about 90% on each topic.[9]

A.1.2 Twitter Named Entity Recognizer

The Twitter NER model is a standard bi-directional LSTM with a CRF layer and detects mentions of persons, places, organizations, and products in a Tweet. The model has been trained on 100K human annotated labeled tweets (Mishra et al., 2020) and has a precision of 85% with a recall of 70% on a held-out test set. We link the extracted mention to a potential WikiData candidate as follows: (a) we first construct a set of potential WikiData entity candidates - the set of all entities whose label or alias has a match with the extracted mention (b) link the mention to the top entity candidate obtained by sorting the candidate set in descending order of page view count as the primary key breaking ties using page rank as the secondary key. We use this approach as an expedient choice noting that more sophisticated entity linking approaches can be used.

A.1.3 Rule Based System for Generating Weakly Labeled Examples.

We employ a rule-based system consisting of tens of thousands of rules based on key-words to generate weakly labeled examples. All rules are manually curated and added by domain experts and data specialists.

A.2 Hyper-parameter Tuning

As is standard practice, we use the validation set ($N = 10000$) to perform hyper-parameter tuning. We explored several hyper-parameter settings for the baseline models namely Logistic Regression and BERT to make baseline comparisons strong and compare CTM against only the best performing baseline settings. In particular, we explored training for different epochs ($1 - 10$) for the BERT baseline. For the logistic regression baseline, we also tried various settings for the maximum number of iterations of the optimizer ($100 - 1000$) as well as various values for the strength of the L2 regularizer ($C = [0, 1, 10, 100]$).

For our proposed model CTM, we did not do any specific hyper-parameter tuning and just trained all models for 5 epochs using 1 A100 GPU.

A.3 Details on the Human Labeled Annotation Task

In this section, we briefly describe the human annotation task used for obtaining topic label confirmation used in the construction of the **HCOMP** dataset. Each annotator is shown a Tweet, topic pair and asked to judge whether the topic is relevant to the Tweet or not. The instructions are:

Task: In this task, you will be shown a tweet and a topic and asked whether the tweet is 'relevant' for a topic.

Topics:You will be asked to determine if a tweet is relevant for a given topic. A "Topic" is a potential subject of conversation that can be identified with a commonly held definition, where mass interest in the subject is not likely to be temporary, e.g. 'Comedy' or 'Knitting' is a topic as it is non-subjective and has a commonly held definition. Purely social tweets like "are you doing okay?" or personal remarks like "I'm having a bad day" are not topical. A Tweet can be popular without being topical.

Question: The primary question you will be asked is "Is this tweet about a topic?", the possible responses are: Yes - This tweet is primarily about this topic. Somewhat - This tweet is related to this topic, but it is not a primary topic of this tweet. No - This tweet is unrelated to this topic. Unsure - I don't understand this tweet.

Guidelines: You will first want to make sure you understand the presented topic. If you are unfamiliar with the topic presented in this question, please click on the topic which will take you to a Google search result page. Feel free to click on a few links (news articles or a Wikipedia page) to familiarize yourself with the topic. When elements of the tweet can I use to make a judgment? It can sometimes be challenging to tell what a tweet is about from tweet text alone. In order to determine what the tweet is about you may need to do the following: Look at replies of a tweet, which might provide additional context by clicking on the tweet. (NOTE: If you can understand the tweet by relying just on the body or author of the tweet, it is fine to not designate replies as being used to make a judgment.) Google phrases in the tweet text if you are unfamiliar with a mentioned entity or phrase that will help you understand the tweet. Look at the image, video, or click on any link (including a hashtag) associated with the Tweet, since it may be commenting on this media. If the media is primarily about the topic, the tweet is as well. Look at the tweet author's name, profile, public timeline, or linked website if it helps disambiguate tweet content. (NOTE: Please don't use the author alone in making determination, without some other element of the tweet.)

[9]For videos, and GIF's each frame is analyzed by the model with the prediction scores being aggregated using the max operator.

Each HIT was judged by 3 independent highly reliable annotators. Finally, we noted that two-way (majority) agreement rate was 86%, unanimous agreement was 66% and the topic precision overall was 70% (with "somewhat" ratings being counted towards a precision error).

A.4 Data Statement

Here, we outline other aspects of our data as per recommendations outlined in (Bender and Friedman, 2018).

SUMMARY – We collect a set of Tweet, topic pairs focusing on only English Tweets which we use for predictive modeling and evaluation.

CURATION RATIONALE – The rationale for the setup used in data collection was primarily driven by our task (large scale topic classification) and the need for data to a build a predictive model. The size of the data collected was thus influenced by task, available budget, and time available.

LANGUAGE VARIETY - The tweets were restricted to English only and are from the time range between September 2020 and May 2021. More fine-grained information is not available.

SPEAKER DEMOGRAPHIC – We do not have any demographic information of the users in this data. One would expect the demographic information to be similar to the demographics of Twitter users around the time of data collection.

ANNOTATOR DEMOGRAPHIC – Human Annotators are primarily native English speakers. No other information is available.

TEXT CHARACTERISTICS – Tweets are short, informal and have at-most 280 characters. Tweets are generally meant to be engaged with by other Twitter users.

A.5 Details on Belief Propagation

In this section, we provide more details on the procedure of belief propagation used in the topic constraint model component. In belief propagation, messages are alternately passed between variable nodes and factor nodes (until convergence is achieved or a finite number of iterations is completed). A message is simply a vector μ where the individual components denote the probability of the random variable taking a specific value $x \in \{0, 1\}$. The message from a variable v to neighboring factor f on taking a specific value x is given by the following equation:

$$\mu_{v \longrightarrow f}(x) \propto \prod_{g \in \mathcal{N}(v) \setminus f} \mu_{g \longrightarrow v}(x) \quad (1)$$

, where g belongs to the set of factor nodes connected to v excluding f. Similarly, the message from a factor node f to the variable v on the variable taking a specific value x is given by the following:

$$\mu_{f \longrightarrow v}(x) \propto \sum_{\mathbf{x}:\mathbf{x}_v = x} \phi(\mathbf{x}) \prod_{u \in \mathcal{N}(f) \setminus v} \mu_{u \longrightarrow f}(\mathbf{x}_u) \quad (2)$$

, where u belongs to the set of variable nodes connected to f excluding v.

Finally, after convergence (or a finite number of iterations), the updated marginal probability of variable v taking on a value x is given by $\Pr(v = x) \propto \prod_{g \in \mathcal{N}(v)} \mu_{g \longrightarrow v}(x)$.

App Screenshots	Entertainment Events	Pets
Arts and Crafts	Food	Piercing
Auto Racing	American Football	Running
Automotive	Gambling	Single Person
Baseball	Gaming	Skateboarding
Basketball	Golf	Skiing
Beauty, Style and Fashion	Hockey	Smoking
Boxing	Home and Garden	Pharmaceuticals and Healthcare
Captioned Images	Infographics, Text and Logos	Snowboarding
Comics, Animation and Anime	Martial Arts	Soccer
Cricket	Multiple People	Swimming
Crowds and Protests	Nature and Wildlife	Tennis
Currency	Weapons	Travel
Cycling	Other	TV Broadcasts
Drinks	Performance Arts	Weather and Natural Disasters

Table 5: List of 45 media categories that make up the label space of the media classifier.

2D animation	Country music	Horses	Rock climbing
3D animation	Cricket	Hotels	Rodeo
Accounting	Cruise travel	Houston	Roleplaying games
Action and adventure films	Cult classics	Independent films	Romance books
Adventure travel	Curling	Indie rock	Rowing
Advertising	Cybersecurity	Information security	Rugby
Agriculture	Cycling	Interior design	Running
Air travel	Dance	Internet of things	Sailing
Alternative rock	Darts	Investing	Saxophone
American football	Data science	J-pop	Sci-fi and fantasy
Animals	Databases	Jazz	Sci-fi and fantasy films
Animated films	Dating	Jewelry	Science
Animation	Digital creators	Job searching and networking	Science news
Animation software	Documentary films	Judo	Screenwriting
Anime	Dogs	K-hip hop	Sculpting
Anime & manga	Drama films	K-pop	Sharks
Antiques	Drawing and illustration	Kaiju	Shoes
Archaeology	Drums	Knitting	Shopping
Architecture	EDM	Lacrosse	Skateboarding
Art	Economics	Language learning	Skiing
Artificial intelligence	Education	Latin pop	Skin care
Arts& culture	Electronic music	MMA	Small business
Arts & culture news	Entertainment	Makeup	Sneakers
Arts and crafts	Entertainment news	Marine life	Snooker
Astrology	Environmentalism	Marketing	Soap operas
Astronauts	Esports	Martial arts	Soccer
Athletic apparel	Europe travel	Mathematics	Soccer stats
Augmented reality	Everyday style	Men's boxing	Soccer transfers
Australian rules football	Experimental music	Men's golf	Soft rock
Auto racing	Famous quotes	Men's style	Softball
Automotive	Fantasy baseball	Motorcycle racing	Space
Aviation	Fantasy basketball	Motorcycles	Sporting goods
Backpacking	Fantasy football	Movie news	Sports
Badminton	Fantasy sports	Movies	Sports news
Ballet	Fashion	Movies & TV	Sports stats
Baseball	Fashion and beauty	Museums	Startups
Basketball	Fashion business	Music	Storyboarding
Beauty	Fashion magazines	Music festivals	Street art
Biographies and memoirs	Fashion models	Music industry	Streetwear
Biology	Fast food	Music news	Supernatural
Biotech and biomedical	Fiction	Music production	Surfing
Birdwatching	Fighting games	Musicals	Swimming
Black Lives Matter	Figure skating	Mystery and crime books	Table tennis
Blues music	Financial services	National parks	Tabletop gaming
Board games	Fintech	Nature	Tabletop role-playing games
Bollywood dance	Fishing	Nature photography	Tattoos
Bollywood films	Fitness	Netball	Tech news
Bollywood music	Folk music	Nonprofits	Technology
Bollywood news	Food	Olympics	Television
Books	Food inspiration	Online education	Tennis
Bowling	Futurology	Open source	Theater
Boxing	Game development	Opera	Theme parks
Brazilian funk	Gaming	Organic	Thriller films
Business & finance	Gaming news	Organic foods	Track & field
Business media	Gardening	Outdoor apparel	Trading card games
Business news	Genealogy	Outdoors	Traditional games
Business personalities	Geography	Painting	Travel
C-pop	Geology	Parenting	Travel guides
Careers	Golf	Pets	Travel news
Cartoons	Graduate school	Philosophy	Triathlon
Cats	Grammy Awards	Photography	US national news
Cheerleading	Graphic design	Physics	Veganism
Chemistry	Guitar	Podcasts & radio	Vegetarianism
Chess	Gymnastics	Poker	Venture capital
Classic rock	Hair care	Pop	Video games
Classical music	Halloween films	Pop Punk	Visual arts
Cloud computing	Handbags	Pop rock	Volleyball
Cloud platforms	Hard rock	Progressive rock	Watches
College life	Health news	Psychology	Weather
Combat sports	Heavy metal	Punjabi music	Web development
Comedy	Historical fiction	Punk	Weddings
Comedy films	History	R&B and soul	Weight training
Comics	Hockey	Rap	Women's boxing
Computer programming	Home & family	Reality TV	Women's golf
Concept Art	Home improvement	Reggae	Women's gymnastics
Construction	Horoscope	Reggaeton	World news
Cooking	Horror films	Road trips	Wrestling
Cosplay	Horse racing and equestrian	Rock	Yoga

Table 6: List of topics making up our topic space.

Developing a Production System for Purpose of Call Detection in Business Phone Conversations

Elena Khasanova, Pooja Hiranandani, Shayna Gardiner,
Cheng Chen, Xue-Yong Fu, Simon Corston-Oliver
Dialpad Canada Inc
1100 Melville St #400
Vancouver, BC, Canada, V6E 4A6
{elena.khasanova,phiranandani,sgardiner}@dialpad.com
{cchen,xue-yong,scorston-oliver}@dialpad.com

Abstract

For agents at a contact centre receiving calls, the most important piece of information is the reason for a given call. An agent cannot provide support on a call if they do not know why a customer is calling. In this paper we describe our implementation of a commercial system to detect *Purpose of Call* statements in English business call transcripts in real time. We present a detailed analysis of types of Purpose of Call statements and language patterns related to them, discuss an approach to collect rich training data by bootstrapping from a set of rules to a neural model, and describe a hybrid model which consists of a transformer-based classifier and a set of rules by leveraging insights from the analysis of call transcripts. The model achieved 88.6 F1 on average in various types of business calls when tested on real life data and has low inference time. We reflect on the challenges and design decisions when developing and deploying the system.

1 Introduction

The Purpose of Call as we define it is similar to a thesis statement in an argument: it introduces the speaker's intent, the broad theme or topic of a conversation, any key entities, and relevant relationships between them. The Purpose of Call statement might also include a linguistic signpost – an indication to the listener that the utterance is intended to convey the purpose of the speaker's call.

For instance:

I'm *calling because* [signpost] I'm trying to open *one of the programs* [entity] on *my computer* [entity] and *it's not opening* [relation] so I'm hoping I can *get some assistance* [intent] with that. [1]

Purpose of Call statements in a contact centre setting are usually uttered by the customer in inbound calls, and by the agent in outbound calls. The Purpose of Call is typically stated near the beginning of the call, is often stated in a single utterance, and does not contain extra information. Atypically, we may sometimes see the Purpose of Call occurring in the middle of a conversation, occurring across several utterances, being implicit, or being uttered by a call recipient rather than a call initiator.

The models described below have been implemented in the Dialpad Contact Center product and are running in production. The Purpose of Call is extracted from an automatic speech recognition (ASR) generated transcript in near-realtime and displayed in a dashboard used by call center supervisors to monitor calls taking place. The dashboard shows information about the caller and the agent, the duration of the call, the Purpose of Call, and customer sentiment. A separate analytics component clusters the Purpose of Call from all calls in a call center during a time period to provide insights about trends and anomalies, customer pain points, and common problems and knowledge gaps among agents. Additional use-cases include showing the Purpose of Call in a summary of prior calls with a customer, and including the Purpose of Call in summaries of the conversation. The utterance segment containing the Purpose of Call is highlighted in the call transcript and the call recording to be easily accessible to agents and call center supervisors. These use-cases are summarized in Figure 1. The Purpose of Call feature is used to help call center managers to navigate to relevant sections of conversations to identify areas to coach sales and support agents and sample relevant calls. Through customer education, we emphasize that the feature should not be used for automated evaluation of agent performance.

There are a few challenges that arise when building an automatic system to detect Purpose of Call.

Diversity of Purpose of Call statements. This type of detection system should be an open-class

[1] In contrast, statements such as *I'm calling to ask a question* are not considered Purpose of Call expressions even though they contain relevant signposting language because there are no entities an agent or a customer can relate to.

Proceedings of NAACL-HLT 2022: Industry Track Papers, pages 259 - 267
July 10-15, 2022 ©2022 Association for Computational Linguistics

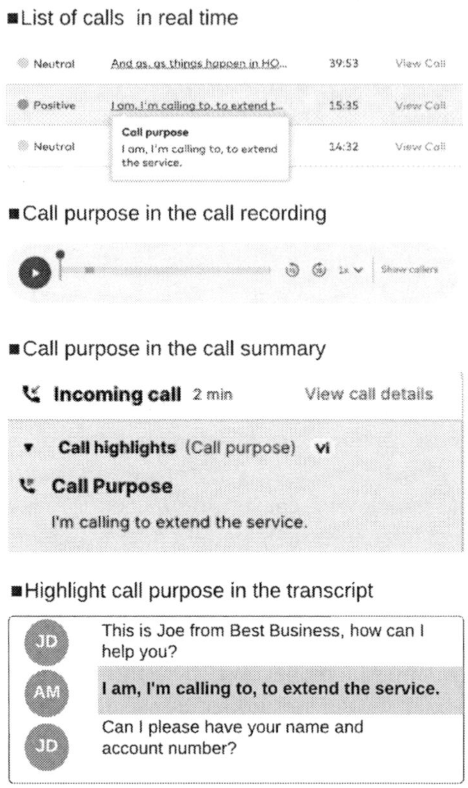

Figure 1: An illustration of the applications of Purpose of Call

system, since call purposes vary across different domains, industries, and types of calls.

Robustness to noise. There are challenges related to the fact that Purpose of Call extraction relies on the output of an ASR system. There are two sources of noise in the ASR transcripts: language production issues such as false starts, dysfluencies, filled pauses, inconsistency in conversational turn-taking (Cailliau and Cavet, 2013; Dutrey et al., 2014; Żelasko et al., 2019; Clavel et al., 2013) as well as their representation in the ASR system and recognition errors due to acoustic noise.

Limitations in training data. Existing intent detection datasets do not reflect real world settings (e.g. they do not distinguish the Purpose of Call from other intent-like statements, and are limited to a subset of domains). Manually annotating data (e.g. using crowd-sourced annotators) raises privacy concerns since annotators must have access to a full conversation transcript in order to find the best Purpose of Call. Annotation is a complex task that requires highly trained annotators, and is expensive and time-consuming because annotators must consider the larger context of the conversation to make a judgment.

Computational efficiency. The need for the system to extract the Purpose of Call statement in real time imposes constraints on memory consumption, latency, and inference speed.

This paper describes an end-to-end system to extract a Purpose of Call statement from the transcript of a business telephone call. Our contributions are three-fold:

1. Data analysis: we present a detailed analysis of language patterns and other features involved in call purpose detection;

2. Data: we describe a process to overcome a lack of training data by bootstrapping a deep learning model from a knowledge-engineered model and discuss the heuristics for developing such a model;

3. System: we describe optimizations that were done in an online commercial system to identify Purpose of Call statements in near-realtime (within three seconds of an utterance being transcribed). To evaluate the effectiveness of our approach, we examine the actual output of our production system.

2 Related work

The concept of a Purpose of Call statement has its roots in the Conversation Analysis framework (Schegloff and Sacks, 1973; Sacks et al., 1974). Within this framework, which combines perspectives from Linguistics and Sociology, a conversation is understood to be composed of turn-taking utterances, with each "turn" being indicated via linguistic and paralinguistic cues. Conversational turns often form adjacency pairs such as question-answer pairs or offer-acceptance/refusal pairs. There are other key aspects of a conversation as well. For instance, a conversation is likely to end after a linguistic cue known as a "closing" is given; likewise, there is usually a linguistic indicator that a conversation is being initiated: an opening (Schegloff and Sacks, 1973; Sacks et al., 1974; Pomerantz and Fehr, 2011). Most work analyzing telephone conversation openings within the framework of Conversation Analysis has been conducted on English, but similar patterns have been observed in other languages, including German and Farsi (Taleghani-Nikazm, 2002).

Within a contact center environment, the Purpose of Call is, like openings and closings, an integral aspect of the conversation (i.e. call) between customer and support agent. We propose that a Purpose of Call is a particular conversational feature that is necessary in contact center calls, and is distinct from the call opening, the body of the call, and the call closing.

The first 120 seconds of a customer support call are predictive of that call's outcome (Takeuchi et al., 2007; Hall et al., 2014). The Purpose of Call statement typically occurs within this timeframe, so highlighting a Purpose of Call in real time could provide agents with additional support in meeting customer needs.

3 Methodology

We formulate the Purpose of Call detection task as a binary classification problem. Each call, after being transcribed by the ASR system, is represented as a sequence of utterances, which may consist of one or more sentences. The division into utterances is based on acoustic features such as silent pauses and the length of a speech fragment.

For a given utterance, we determine the probability that the utterance is the Purpose of Call statement for that particular call. We impose the following constraints on this task: (i) For a given call, there is only one most probable Purpose of Call. (ii) Only calls with two call sides (agent and customer) are considered, which excludes multiparty business conversations. (iii) The model should make a prediction as the call is ongoing and therefore will not have access to the full conversation.

Due to the lack of available annotated data representing the concept of Purpose of Call, we followed an iterative approach to develop the model, consisting of three steps: (1) Computational Linguists on-staff conducted extensive linguistic analysis of transcripts to identify the characteristics of Purpose of Call statements. (2) We then implemented a knowledge-engineered approach to identify these Purpose of Call statements. (3) We bootstrapped from the knowledge-engineered solution, using it to label training data for a transformer-based approach. We select a transformer-based model as it is the current state-of-the-art in sequence classification and is known to have better generalization power than rule-based models.

We evaluate the performance using F1, Precision, and Hit rate, i.e. the number of calls in which a Purpose of Call was detected out of all available calls. We measure Hit rate in calls at least 30 seconds long, based on the observation that shorter calls may not include any content (e.g. because the caller hung up before starting the conversation). The model is tested on an automatically obtained validation set that represents 10% (18K utterances) of the training data, a manually annotated gold test set of 13215 utterances from 909 calls, and unlabeled samples from 600 real-life calls.

3.1 System Overview

The production system to detect a Purpose of Call utterance is a hybrid model consisting of three parts (see Figure 2).

The Selection model, or outer model, inputs an utterance, the previous context of the conversation, and the probabilities of previously detected Purpose of Call events. It consists of two sets of rules: (1) empirically derived filters that determine whether an incoming utterance is a candidate for a Purpose of Call and should be processed by the inner model, a successful candidate is within 180 seconds and 30 utterances in the call, and is between 4 and 150 tokens long; (2) rules that combine and compare scores from the inner model and set various thresholds for different linguistic types of call purpose statements (i.e. the utterances containing signposting language typically receive higher scores than other types and need a higher bar). Every time a new utterance qualifies to be a Purpose of Call, it is dynamically updated in the user interface. (See Appendix B for an example of a Selection rule.)

The Scoring model, or inner model, is implemented as a multiclass classification model which performs inference on a single utterance. We fine-tuned a transformer-based model for classification on proprietary labeled data. The model assigns to an utterance probabilities of it being a *call purpose*, *question*, or *negative* (not a *call purpose* or a *question*). The *question* class represents *question_response* pattern (see Table 1) and is used to boost probabilities of utterances that would otherwise be of the *negative* class.

The Simplification model. The utterance with the highest score is stripped of information that is irrelevant to the purpose of the call (e.g. *greetings, pleasantries, introductions, technical problems*). It consists of a small set of common expressions (many of which are reused from the knowledge-engineered model) to exclude from utterances and reduces the length of Purpose of Call utterances by 7.8% on average. 49% of utterances undergo

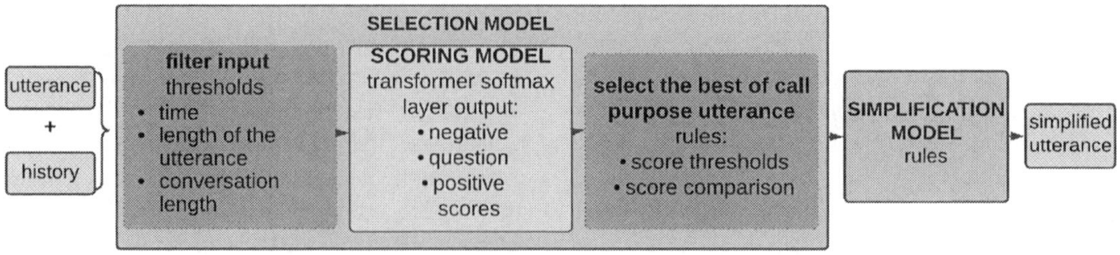

Figure 2: Purpose of Call Detection System Architecture

simplification with precision of 96%.

3.2 Model Development

The model development process consists of three main stages: data analysis and feature selection, designing a knowledge-engineered model informed by the insights from the data, and bootstrapping a transformer based model from the rule-based system. In this section, we discuss these stages.

3.2.1 Data Research and Feature Selection

We manually analyzed a sample of 2000 call transcripts across several dimensions, which are outlined below.

1. **Inbound vs. outbound calls**:
   In *outbound* call center calls (40.8%), the call initiator and the side that utters the Purpose of Call is usually an agent; in *inbound* calls (59.2%), it is a customer, with some exceptions. 55.3% of all Purpose of Call statements are uttered by the customer.

2. **Place**: the Purpose of Call is uttered within the first 40 seconds in a majority of calls (73.8%), in the middle in a minority of calls (10.7%), and towards the end in a handful of (mainly short) calls. The *mean* time of occurrence is 29.9 seconds, *std*=19.1, *median*=25.5 seconds. The *maximum* time is 180 seconds.

3. **Speaker role**:
   The *call initiator* utters the Purpose of Call in the vast majority of cases in the form of a *statement*; in returned or scheduled calls, the Purpose of Call can be uttered by a *call recipient* in the form of a *guess, assumption or inquiry*.

4. **Domain**: There are three main types of call center calls:
   Sales calls: commonly characterized by the Purpose of Call *not* being stated explicitly in one utterance, but gradually being revealed during the course of the call. Agents often spend a longer time building rapport, so utter the purpose later in the call compared to support calls. 74% of Purpose of Call statements still occur within the first 40 seconds. Outbound calls are prevalent. 48% of Purpose of Call statements are uttered by customers.
   Support calls: inbound calls are prevalent, the Purpose of Call is introduced early in the conversation. In fact, 56% of Purpose of Call statements are in the very first utterance, accompanied by a *greeting*, and 63% of the statements occur within the first 50 seconds. 62% of Purpose of Call statements are uttered by customers.
   General business calls: may include support and sales calls as well as other communications, both formal and informal. The Purpose of Call is often implied (e.g. a conversation between colleagues, transfers from a chat to a call, with the purpose of the conversation being known by both parties). 84% occur within the first 45 seconds, and 59% are uttered by customers.

5. **Length distribution**: Purpose of Call utterances range in length from 4 to 224 tokens, with the *mean*=45.5, *std*=29.9, *median*=37, and 75% being under 59 tokens.

6. **Language patterns**: We identified several language markers associated with Purpose of Call statements in Table 1.

Approximately 7% of calls in this sample do not contain an explicit Purpose of Call statement. Instead, the participants in the call appear to already have the context necessary to understand the call purpose.

Pattern	%	Description	Example
call_purpose_phrases	32.7	explicit declarations of the Purpose of Call typically signposted with lexical cues containing *purpose* and *call* and their synonyms	*The **reason for my call** is I moved to a new address, so I need to change it on my profile.*
desire_phrases	31.7	expressions of volition, desire or need	*Hi, I **need** a refund for my order.*
question_response	15.8	responses to an agent's prompt	*- **How can I help you?** / - I received a message that my order has been delayed.*
greetings	9.1	long statements of at least 30 word tokens that follow a *greeting* and occur within the first 6 utterances in the conversation	*Hey, this is Christine. There is a police report, it was next to you guys why you heard it <...>*
problem_phrases	4.4	express problems and concerns	*I'm having an issue with the delivery.*
update	5.8	updates and announcements	***I have an update** on your passport status.*
continuation	0.4	questions preceded by a signpost in the same utterance or a subsequent one from the same speaker	*Hi, I'm calling because I **have a question**. / Do you accept new patients?*

Table 1: Language patterns in Purpose of Call statements

3.2.2 Knowledge-Engineered Model

As outlined in Section 1, collecting labeled data for Purpose of Call extraction is a challenging task. Therefore, to obtain a representative sample of training data, we first implemented a knowledge-based model that takes into account the following parameters: *utterance length* in tokens, the *order* of an utterance in the conversation, the *history* including several preceding utterances, and the presence or absence of *language patterns* summarized in Table 1 and implemented using regular expressions syntax (see Appendix A for an example). In total, stemming from the analysis in Section 3.2.1, 8 rules (56 regex patterns) to detect call purpose candidates and 6 rules (55 regex patterns) to filter out negative statements were developed. The model reached a precision of 90.8% and hit rate of 77% on average across three domains (see Table 4).

Further, we conducted error analysis by manually labelling the output of the production system on a random sample of 1000 calls. After human review, we determined that 3% of calls did not contain an identifiable Purpose of Call and could be considered true negatives, while 20% were false negatives. 40% of these false negatives can be attributed to ASR errors. 27.6% of false negatives include cases with the Purpose of Call being known prior to the conversation (e.g. from shared knowledge, logged information, or in return calls) and therefore not considered by the model, 9.1% correspond to specific industries (e.g. transportation) underrepresented in the data used in the analysis, and 44.7% were caused by the limitations of the rules (note that these groups of false negatives intersect, hence the percentages do not add up to 100%). False positives were mainly related to the lack of morphological flexibility in the rules and speech dysfluencies. In 6.2% of calls, several utterances were legitimate Purpose of Call statements and the one selected by the model was not the best one. These findings motivated the need for a transformer-based model that was more forgiving of ASR noise, had better generalization power, and was more responsive to changes in the data.

3.2.3 Transformer-Based Model

Training Data Collection. Since the knowledge-engineered model achieved high precision, we could rely on its output to train a deep learning model. The dataset consists of English language utterances obtained from business calls in a variety of industries, with accompanying metadata such as timestamps for each token, call side, and call id. See Appendix C and 3.2.1 for detailed statistics. We randomly sampled one million utterances between February 6, 2020 and February 22, 2021, allowing only those that meet the requirements for a Purpose of Call candidate in 3.1. The utterances were divided into two sets: (1) those from the calls with a Purpose of Call hit (likely to be a true positive), (2) utterances from calls with no hit (may contain false negatives). With a series of patterns, we filtered out utterances that are likely to be false positives based on error analysis in 3.2.2. Further, we sampled several datasets of 180K utterances with varying label and language pattern distributions in order to experimentally find the best configuration (see Appendix C). A train, development, and validation split of 80/10/10% of data was used in each experiment. In addition, we created a golden dataset of 909 manually labeled calls, with the utterances organized chronologically within the call and limited to up to 30 utterances per call. This sample comprises 13215 utterances.

Training Details. We employ the DistilBERT (Sanh et al., 2019) model, trained for classification with multimodal features. We combine text features with numerical and binary features, utterance *start time* and *call side* respectively, which have proven to be useful in the knowledge-engineered model, and pass on a gated summation of the transformer output with these features to the classification layer, following the approach in (Gu and Budhkar, 2021). This configuration outperformed other base models [2] [3], combinations of multimodal features, and combining mechanisms outlined in (Gu and Budhkar, 2021). The model architecture is shown in Figure 3. We implement a data-driven iterative fine-tuning process with extensive error analysis and data resampling. See Appendix D for details.

3.3 Model Deployment

Since the model was to operate in a near-realtime environment as a call is ongoing, optimising for inference time was a dominant consideration during model design. The model would perform inference on one CPU core. The model would need to accommodate the time taken to transcribe voice to text and properly format and punctuate the transcription, many of these tasks being accomplished by other deep learning models.

Optimizations include: (i) Having the Selection

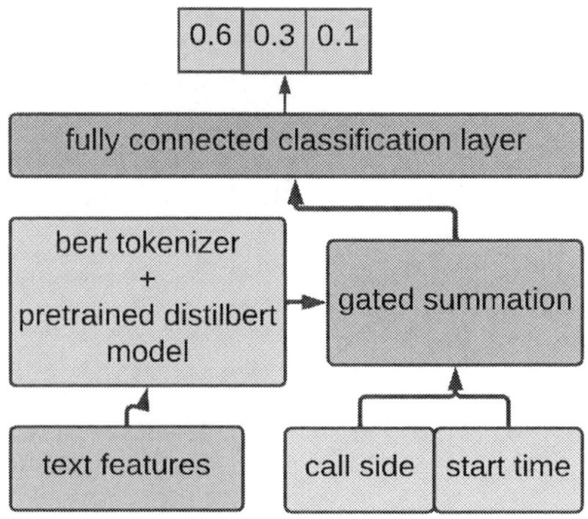

Figure 3: Multimodal Transformer based scoring model

model that uses input features to filter utterances, thereby reducing the number of utterances that were attended to by the transformer model. These features include utterance count number and utterance start time, both of which should be below a threshold determined by experimenting with different parameter values in the knowledge-engineered model. (ii) Incorporating numerical and binary features into the deep learning model - adding signals beyond lexical features allowed us to use a lower capacity BERT variant with faster inference time. (iii) Capping input length to an empirically derived ceiling further reduced memory consumption and inference time.

The system was deployed in containers[4] with 1 CPU and maximum 1GB memory per instance. The average inference time at the 95th percentile is 0.51 seconds, which meets the requirements of our production system for near-realtime deployments to complete inference in under 3 seconds.

4 Evaluation

Table 2 shows full results of the comparative evaluation of the knowledge-engineered and the hybrid models on business calls in three domains.

Qualitative analysis was conducted on the gold set: real life user data of 600 samples, and 200 calls with missed hits. False positives mainly correspond to signposting language without mention of the actual Purpose of Call, and indicate the model's overreliance on lexical features. The model was found to be accurate in assigning utterances to classes, but not always sensitive to the difference between a

[2]https://huggingface.co/microsoft/DialoGPT-small

[3]https://huggingface.co/DeepPavlov/bert-base-cased-conversational

[4]https://cloud.google.com/kubernetes-engine

Domain	Model	Precision	Hit Rate	F1
Support	rules	93.5	80.0	86.2
	hybrid	91.0	90.4	90.7
General	rules	90.0	74.2	81.3
	hybrid	89.0	85.6	87.3
Sales	rules	88.5	78.7	83.5
	hybrid	87.0	88.9	87.9
Avg	rules	90.6	77.6	83.6
	hybrid	89.6	88.3	88.6

Table 2: Comparative evaluation of knowledge-engineered (here *rules*) and hybrid models for Purpose of Call detection.

valid and *the best* Purpose of Call. This can be addressed by introducing more contrastive examples in training data. Missed hits include cases initially excluded from the sample such as Purpose of Call stated across several utterances, and multiple Purpose of Call statements of equal importance. A synthesis of several utterances instead of selecting only one of them might be useful in such cases.

5 Conclusion

This paper discusses the development and deployment of a hybrid system to detect a Purpose of Call statement in business call transcripts for the English language in near-realtime settings. We introduce the concept of the Purpose of Call, provide in-depth analysis of real life data, and discuss overcoming the absence of available training data by bootstrapping from a knowledge-engineered model to a deep learning one. Both the knowledge-engineered and hybrid models demonstrate high precision and hit rate, with the hybrid model showing better performance while maintaining computational efficiency.

6 Ethics Statement

Data. The conversational data is presented in the form of individual utterances with sensitive data such as personal identifiable information removed. No crowdsourced annotation has been conducted, and access to the data was available only to a small number of in-house Scientists.

Use. The Purpose of Call feature is used by call center managers to identify areas to coach sales and support agents. It is recommended to not use this feature for automated evaluation of agent performance. Incorrect Purpose of Call prediction may provide unsatisfactory user experience for the managers as they sample calls but does not present any risk of negative impact for the agents.

Licensing. We follow the licensing requirements accordingly while using external tools such as HuggingFace [5] and Multimodal-Toolkit (Gu and Budhkar, 2021) libraries.

References

Frédérik Cailliau and Ariane Cavet. 2013. Mining automatic speech transcripts for the retrieval of problematic calls. In *CICLing*.

Chloé Clavel, Gilles Adda, Frédérik Cailliau, Martine Garnier-Rizet, Ariane Cavet, Géraldine Chapuis, Sandrine Courcinous, Charlotte Danesi, Anne-Laure Daquo, Myrtille Deldossi, Sylvie Guillemin-Lanne, Marjorie Seizou, and Philippe Suignard. 2013. Spontaneous speech and opinion detection: mining call-centre transcripts. *Language Resources and Evaluation*, 47:1089–1125.

Camille Dutrey, Chloé Clavel, Sophie Rosset, Ioana Vasilescu, and Martine Adda-Decker. 2014. A CRF-Based Approach to Automatic Disfluency Detection in a French Call-Centre Corpus. In *15th Annual Conference of the International Speech Communication Association (Interspeech'14)*, pages 2897–2901, Singapour, Singapore. International Speech Communication Association (ISCA).

Ken Gu and Akshay Budhkar. 2021. A package for learning on tabular and text data with transformers. In *Proceedings of the Third Workshop on Multimodal Artificial Intelligence*, pages 69–73, Mexico City, Mexico. Association for Computational Linguistics.

Judith Hall, Phil Verghis, William Stockton, and Jin Goh. 2014. It takes just 120 seconds: Predicting satisfaction in technical support calls. *Psychology and Marketing*, 31.

Anita Pomerantz and B.J. Fehr. 2011. Conversation analysis: An approach to the analysis of social interaction. *Discourse studies: A multidisciplinary introduction*, pages 165–190.

Harvey Sacks, Emanuel A. Schegloff, and Gail Jefferson. 1974. A simplest systematics for the organization of turn-taking for conversation. *Language*, 50(4):696–735.

Victor Sanh, Lysandre Debut, Julien Chaumond, and Thomas Wolf. 2019. Distilbert, a distilled version of BERT: smaller, faster, cheaper and lighter. *CoRR*, abs/1910.01108.

Emanuel Schegloff and Harvey Sacks. 1973. Opening up closings. *Semiotica*, 8:289–327.

Hironori Takeuchi, L Venkata Subramaniam, Tetsuya Nasukawa, and Shourya Roy. 2007. Automatic identification of important segments and expressions for

[5] https://huggingface.co/

mining of business-oriented conversations at contact centers. In *Proceedings of the 2007 Joint Conference on Empirical Methods in Natural Language Processing and Computational Natural Language Learning (EMNLP-CoNLL)*, pages 458–467, Prague, Czech Republic. Association for Computational Linguistics.

Carmen Taleghani-Nikazm. 2002. A conversation analytical study of telephone conversation openings between native and nonnative speakers. *Journal of Pragmatics*, 34:1807–1832.

Piotr Żelasko, Jan Mizgajski, Mikołaj Morzy, Adrian Szymczak, Piotr Szymański, Łukasz Augustyniak, and Yishay Carmiel. 2019. Towards better understanding of spontaneous conversations: Overcoming automatic speech recognition errors with intent recognition.

A Appendix: Example Rule in a Knowledge-Engineered Model

An utterance is a Purpose of Call if:

- It contains signposting phrases expressing a problem such as *I'm having a problem, There is an issue, I'm having a hard time, I'm trying ... and it's not working*,
- It occurs within the first 10 utterances
- It is at least 12 tokens long

Example: *I got a really big problem here. When I log in, it asks for some pin, and I really, I can't use it. So there's obviously an issue here and can you help me with it?*.

B Appendix: Example Selection model heuristics

Combine the *positive* score for an utterance with the maximum *question* score of the two preceding utterances in another call side. If it passes a threshold and is the biggest score so far, this utterance is a Purpose of Call.

C Appendix: Data Statistics

Total number of calls: 86310
Total number of utterances: 180 000
Industry distribution: see Table 3.

Industry	%
Technology	25.1
IT, Consulting	15.5
Professional, Business Support Services	14.1
Travel	11.4
Health and Wellness	5.6
Real Estate	5.1

Table 3: Industry distribution in training data: top 6 types

Label distribution: A key factor in training the model was determining the right distribution of labels and language patterns. The classes in our problem are naturally imbalanced: since only one utterance per call is a valid Purpose of Call, the vast majority of utterances are of the *negative* class. In a random sample, only 4.7% utterances are *positive* hits, and only 1.9% are *questions*. If the data is sampled randomly, the model is likely to overfit to the *negative* class. Sampling uniformly may reduce the number of complex instances in favor of the ones easier for the model to learn. A set of experiments were conducted to determine the distribution of classes with the goal of optimizing accuracy of the Purpose of Call class predictions. We determined the optimal distribution of classes as follows: 42.5% *positive*, 42.5% *negative*, 15% *question* utterances (corresponds to the share of this pattern in real data). All utterances came from calls with a positive hit, which minimized the chance of false negatives in the training data.

Language patterns distribution: From the error analysis and experiments, we determined the optimal distribution of language patterns within the *positive* class:

- 30% *call_purpose_phrases*
- 30% *desire_phrases*
- 20% *problem_phrases*
- 20% *other patterns*

Other aspects of the data are the same as described in 3.2.1.

D Appendix: Training details

Parameters: The pretrained *distilbert-base-cased* model we use has 6 layers, 768 hidden units, 12 attention heads and 65M parameters and is available through Multimodal-Toolkit (Gu and Budhkar, 2021). We run all fine-tuning experiments on a Google Cloud VM n1-standard-8 instance with 496GB disk size and 1 NVIDIA Tesla K80 GPU. The maximum time for a single experiment was 8 GPU hours. We truncate text input to a maximum 150 tokens since most relevant statements fall into this category. We set the train and eval batch size to

32 and 64 respectively, and use AdamW optimizer with default parameters. We fine-tune the model for 4 epochs with a learning rate of 5e-05, weight decay of 0.01 and 500 warm up steps. The hyper-parameters were obtained from experiments using an in-house tuning tool implementing grid search algorithm. For fine-tuning on small subsets (4K) of data collected through error analysis, we repeat the training process for 12 epochs and a learning rate of 9e-05.

Relevant features: Besides the text features, we experimented with two extra features that have proven to be useful in the knowledge-engineered model: the *start time* of the utterance and the *call side*. We also experimented with several mechanisms to combine the numerical and categorical features with textual data using Multimodal-Toolkit (Gu and Budhkar, 2021). The results are presented in Table 4.

Feature	P	HR	F1	PP
text only	0.891	0.891	0.891	0.894
text + start time	0.948	0.948	0.948	0.944
text + call side	0.948	0.948	0.948	0.946
all	0.949	0.949	0.949	0.957

Table 4: Comparing model performance using tabular features *start time* and *call side*. P-Precision, HR-Hit rate, PP - precision in *positive* class. The results are reported for a single run using concatenation to combine features.

Adversarial Text Normalization

Joanna Bitton
Meta AI
jbitton@fb.com

Maya Pavlova
University of Waterloo
mspavlova@uwaterloo.ca

Ivan Evtimov
Meta AI
ivanevtimov@fb.com

Abstract

Text-based adversarial attacks are becoming more commonplace and accessible to general internet users. As these attacks proliferate, the need to address the gap in model robustness becomes imminent. While retraining on adversarial data may increase performance, there remains an additional class of character-level attacks on which these models falter. Additionally, the process to retrain a model is time and resource intensive, creating a need for a lightweight, reusable defense. In this work, we propose the *Adversarial Text Normalizer*, a novel method that restores baseline performance on attacked content with low computational overhead. We evaluate the efficacy of the normalizer on two problem areas prone to adversarial attacks, *i.e.* Hate Speech and Natural Language Inference. We find that text normalization provides a task-agnostic defense against character-level attacks that can be implemented supplementary to adversarial retraining solutions, which are more suited for semantic alterations.

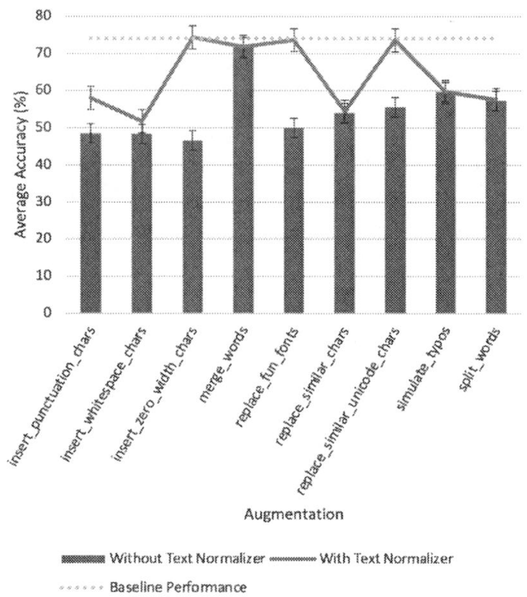

Figure 1: This figure showcases that text normalization is able to restore baseline scores on the Learning From The Worst (LFTW) test set for several augmentation types. The model scores in this graph are the averaged scores across all five LFTW models. To see the raw evaluation results, view Table 4 in the Appendix.

1 Introduction

Natural language processing (NLP) models help preserve the integrity of discourse in online social networks by detecting hate speech, misinformation, and other content that violates community policies (Halevy, 2020). In these application scenarios, classifiers operate under significantly more adversarial conditions than in the standard paradigm of model development. Users often post content that is heavily altered in order to induce worst-case errors, dramatically reducing model performance relative to a standard test set. Recent research in machine learning has made strides towards building robust models to defend against sophisticated adversaries. Nevertheless, our experience and experiments show that models remain vulnerable to many simple and intuitive attacks.

One such class of highly-effective attacks are *syntactic attacks*, which include adding punctuation and spacing, replacing fonts, and inserting zero-width characters. Attackers commonly employ these methods with little or no expert knowledge of machine learning algorithms, and constitute a large proportion of practical threats to natural language processing models deployed in industry. In our experiments on state-of-the-art robust NLP models, such attacks can decrease a model's performance by more than half. Thus, these text-based attacks remain a serious and unaddressed problem for the at-scale deployment of language models in integrity areas.

The literature has proposed methods to improve adversarial robustness by retraining models on

Proceedings of NAACL-HLT 2022: Industry Track Papers, pages 268 - 279
July 10-15, 2022 ©2022 Association for Computational Linguistics

"hard" and adversarial examples (Nie et al., 2020; Vidgen et al., 2021) but we observe several open challenges with applying these approaches. First, as our experiments demonstrate, even state-of-the-art models trained on multiple iterations of adversarial data continue to lack robustness to easily accessible syntactic attacks. For example, in Figure 2, inserting zero-width characters reduces a hate speech classification model's accuracy to less than 15%. Second, these approaches are not amenable to quick iteration. Whenever a new adversarial attack becomes more prevalent, a model developer would need to collect new data or create synthetic examples of such attacks, retrain the model, and redeploy it. This costs time, computational resources and has an environmental impact (Wu et al., 2021).

To address these outstanding issues, we propose a novel lightweight and easily extensible method for recovering model performance in the face of adversaries who perform syntactic attacks. Our key insight is that many adversarial modifications can be undone before they even reach the model with little computational overhead. From a machine learning perspective, this can be thought of as restoring the distribution of inference-time inputs to the original distribution on which the model was trained. From a computer security perspective, this method is analogous to sanitizing the inputs to programs so as to make the input safe for further processing. In this work, we present the design and implementation of a system called the *Adversarial Text Normalizer* (ATN), that achieves this goal. This iterative approach produces a defense mechanism that can be applied at scale in a lightweight fashion to ensure robust model performance.

An important principle in computer security is that defense mechanisms should be evaluated against adaptive adversaries (Petitcolas, 2011), *i.e.* those that can adjust their techniques to actions by the defender. Therefore, we also partner with red teaming experts skilled at creating novel adversarial inputs to classical computer systems to conduct an adaptive evaluation of the ATN. Our text normalizer can provide sufficient robustness gains even in the face of such adaptive adversaries.

Our contributions are as follows:

- We design and implement a system for undoing syntactic attacks on textual models called the Adversarial Text Normalizer.
- We conduct an adaptive attacker red teaming exercise to evaluate the ATN's performance against skilled human adversaries.
- Through extensive experiments on three different benchmarks, we evaluate the performance of the ATN and conclude that it successfully recovers the original performance of a model when faced with syntactic attacks.

2 Related Work

Several papers have introduced benchmarks for adversarial attacks on NLP systems. Attacks focused on preserving semantic content and grammar (Jin et al., 2020; Alzantot et al., 2018; Iyyer et al., 2018) have been shown to be effective against state-of-the-art models at the cost of requiring a greater understanding of the sentence structure and task context. In contrast, Eger and Benz (2020) propose a benchmark of character level, orthographic perturbations as more realistic attacks in general applications, attributing the success of their high performance attacks to large out-of-vocabulary rates and disruption to tokenization. Other work (Eger et al., 2019; Boucher et al., 2021) investigates the replacement of characters with visually similar embedding spaces and the insertion of zero-width characters, noting the effectiveness of those methods against NLP models but marginal effect on human legibility – especially when perturbing key offensive words. For such targeted attacks, (Rodriguez and Rojas-Galeano, 2018) use a simple string matching algorithm to filter obfuscated and negated key words (Rojas-Galeano, 2017), focusing on a limited list of target vocables on each pass.

Our work focuses on the implementation of text normalization as a computationally inexpensive and reusable solution to mitigate a range of highly accessible but effective adversarial text attacks such as character insertions, replacements, and censorship. Concurrent work in the NLI domain has addressed the bias in model performance on classic test sets and adversarial user attacks through iterative human-and-model-in-the-loop (Nie et al., 2020) data generation and model training. Similarly, Vidgen et al. (2021) proposed a complementary approach with the amalgamation of targeted annotator samples including challenging perturbations to generate adversarial data for hate speech classification. Both works explored leveraging domain-experienced annotator resources to progressively train more robust models with each successive iteration. Other works on small text perturbations such as adversarial typos, have proposed the use of robust token-level encodings (Jones et al., 2020) and preceding word recognition models (Pruthi et al., 2019) as reusable systems that are trained once and then reused across models and tasks. In this work we explore a more lightweight, systematic correction layer that does not require training to create model and task-agnostic defenses.

3 Methodology

3.1 Models and Datasets

We identify two natural language tasks with significant importance to industrial applications and adversarial pressure. First, hate speech classification is the problem of detecting statements that are likely to cause harm and inject toxicity in online discourse. It has now become standard practice for providers of services where people can post comments and discuss content to employ hate speech classification models. These models are set up as binary classification models that output a score for the "hatefulness" of a given input statement. Second, Natural Language Inference (NLI) has been adapted for the detection of misinformation (Nie et al., 2020). In this setting, NLI models aim to flag statements that do not receive support from reputable sources or directly contradict information in them. Thus, a model is given access to a set of support statements and a "hypothesis" and it outputs a 3-way classification from among "supported," "not supported," and "not enough information." In the cases of "supported" or "not supported," the model also outputs the statement that supports or refutes the hypothesis.

Since both tasks are the subject of adversarial pressure, there have been several proposed approaches to robustifying models trained on them. Most notably, the Dynalab (Vidgen et al., 2021) approach proactively samples "hard" examples by asking human raters to conceive inputs that challenge the model. Researchers then retrain the models and repeat the process for several rounds. This paradigm helps achieve a large increase in robustness through the rounds, so we evaluate our approaches on those models as the benchmark for state-of-the-art robust performance.

For Hate Speech, we utilize the HateCheck (Röttger et al., 2021) dataset (2,563 examples) and the Learning from the Worst (LFTW) (Vidgen et al., 2021) test set (4,120 examples). The performance of state-of-the-art models

Problem Area	Model	# Parameters
Hate Speech	LFTW	125,000,000
Adversarial NLI	DeBERTa	140,000,000
Adversarial NLI	RoBERTa	125,000,000
Adversarial NLI	T5	220,000,000
Adversarial NLI	BERT	109,000,000
Adversarial NLI	ALBERT	17,000,000

Table 1: The models, associated problem areas, and number of parameters used in our evaluations. All LFTW models, from rounds 1-4 and more, have an identical number of parameters since they are all RoBERTa models.

trained on adversarial data from Learning from the Worst (LFTW) were compared with and without the addition of the text normalizer on both baseline and augmented versions of the dataset. Additionally, we chose to evaluate NLI models on the test sets from all three rounds of Adversarial NLI (Nie et al., 2020) (1,000, 1,000, and 1,200 examples respectively). We assessed the performance of these baseline, augmented, and normalized datasets on five model architectures trained on SNLI (Bowman et al., 2015), MNLI (Williams et al., 2018), FEVER (Thorne et al., 2018) and all three rounds of Adversarial NLI. To see which models we evaluate on, please review Table 1. We specifically choose models already trained on adversarial datasets to assess opportunities for improvement beyond retraining.

3.2 Attacks

To attack the aforementioned datasets, we use the open-source augmentation library AugLy (Papakipos and Bitton, 2022) to simulate various text-based adversarial attacks commonly used on social media platforms. We focus on using character-level attacks as opposed to attacks that can potentially add, remove, or change full words in the text, to avoid perturbations in the semantic meaning. The specific augmentations selected for the analysis are listed in Table 2.

In addition to the synthetically generated attacks, we collected 98 samples of hate speech text which were adversarially created and modified by individuals in a cybersecurity Red Team. In the first half of the session, participants were tasked with creating their own attacks based off of their prior knowledge of text-based attacks seen online. In the second half of the session, they were given direct access to the code implementation for the text nor-

Augmentation	Output Text	Normalized Text
None	This is augmented text	This is augmented text
`insert_punctuation_chars`	Th.i.s ,is ...a.ug;m!en't?ed, ,te!x.t	This ,is ...augmented, ,text
`insert_whitespace_chars`	T h i s is a u g m e n t e d text	This is augmented text
`insert_zero_width_chars`	This is augmented text	This is augmented text
`merge_words`	Thisis augmented text	Thisis augmented text
`replace_fun_fonts`	This is aͦuͦgͦmͦeͦnͦtͦeͦdͦ text	This is augmented text
`replace_similar_chars`	Th!s is @ugmented tex7	Th!s is @ugmented tex7
`replace_similar_unicode_chars`	Thī§ is augméņtεD text	This is augmented text
`simulate_typos`	This is augmentde texht	This is augmentde texht
`split_words`	Th is is augment ed text	Th is is augment ed text

Table 2: Examples of augmentations generated using the open-source library AugLy (Papakipos and Bitton, 2022), leveraged in the analysis for adversarial attacks on the text datasets, and their normalized counterparts. Note that while the output of `insert_zero_width_chars` appears visually identical to the original sentence, there are actually zero-width unicode characters embedded throughout the entire string. We include augmentations that are not covered by the normalizer (such as `merge_words`) in our evaluations to showcase that our method does not further corrupt unknown attack types.

malizer and were tasked to bypass it using targeted attacks.

Many of the attacks created were similar to the attacks of `insert_punctuation_chars`, `replace_fun_fonts`, `simulate_typos`, `replace_similar_unicode_chars`, and `replace_similar_chars`. The adversaries also created letter repetition attacks, i.e. "helllloooooo", censored violating text, and replaced words with emojis.

3.3 Adversarial Text Normalizer

The text normalizer is an isolated correction unit that can be placed in front of models to target character-level attacks for various NLP tasks. The normalizer is designed to be used as a preprocessing step prior to text tokenization. For optimal computational efficiency, the operator is written in torchscript, and can process approximately 77 examples per second on a server with an Intel(R) Xeon(R) CPU E5-2680 v4 @ 2.40GHz processor. This operator was incorporated into the PyTorch model as a customizable data transform. The algorithm relies on sophisticated string manipulation as a targeted defense against known adversarial attacks, and is easily scaled up to support additional attacks as the adversarial environment progresses.

Currently, the text normalizer supports removing three overarching categories of text attacks:

1. **Character insertion**: addition of characters such as punctuation marks, whitespaces, Unicode characters, emojis, and more to separate characters in a word with the intent to disrupt proper tokenization. This category includes augmentation methods such as `insert_punctuation_chars`, `insert_whitespace_chars`, and `insert_zero_width_chars`.
2. **Character replacement**: substitution of standard Latin characters with visually similar characters from other languages or Unicode characters with the intent of obfuscation. This category includes augmentation methods such as `replace_fun_fonts`, `replace_similar_chars`, and `replace_similar_unicode_chars`.
3. **Censorship of violating words**: replacement of letters in violating words with punctuation characters to avoid explicit content. For instance "kill" could be censored as "k***", "k!ll", "k#*!" and more.

To undo the effects of a character insertion attack such as `insert_punctuation_chars`, the text is first split by whitespaces to identify 'words'. For each word, we then determine how many extraneous punctuation characters have been inserted, ignoring punctuation marks at the beginning and end, as such additions do not segment the word to disrupt tokenization. If the amount of punctuation characters is below a set threshold or the word resembles a URL, we do not modify the word and add it to our normalized string. Otherwise, we replace the superfluous punctuation with spaces, strip the string of excessive whitespace, and concatenate consecutive single character entities together.

For character replacement attacks, we predefined multiple mappings between Unicode characters and their keyboard character pairs, and performed a string search method to reverse the replacement.

As for censorship attacks, a list of common user-censored toxic terms were identified prior based on flagged user content. For each toxic term, a regex for the censorship pattern was defined such that the first and last letters of the word remain constant but any of the letters in between can be replaced by punctuation characters - maintaining the same length as the original, uncensored word. For every match found, we replace the censored string with its uncensored pair accordingly.

4 Evaluation

In this section, we examine the performance of Hate Speech and Natural Language Inference (NLI) models with respect to the original, the augmented, and normalized datasets to evaluate the efficacy of the text normalizer. All evaluations were conducted using Dynabench (Ma et al., 2021), in which AWS ECR models are deployed as endpoints and Batch Transform jobs are run on AWS Sagemaker to get dataset predictions. We roughly spent 38.36 CPU hours on model inference (no GPUs were used).

4.1 Hate Speech

To assess performance on adversarial hate speech data, we evaluated on five models from the Learning from the Worst (LFTW) (Vidgen et al., 2021) paper that were previously retrained on varying amounts of "rounds" of adversarial hate speech data collection.

4.1.1 Learning from the Worst

We first evaluate on the test set from Learning from the Worst. Figure 1 showcases these results. Overall, the text normalizer maintains or improves initial performance on all augmented datasets and the baseline. Across all models, normalizing the `insert_zero_width_chars`, `replace_similar_unicode_chars`, and `replace_fun_fonts` augmentations resulted in the most significant performance gains, with a maximum of a **32.18%** increase. In between, normalizing `insert_punctuation_chars` and `insert_whitespace_chars` had increases of at most 11.95%. For the LFTW R3 model, normalizing the whitespace text resulted in a 1.27% loss in performance. This may be due to the fact that not every whitespace character in the AugLy augmentation is removed by the normalizer. As expected, other augmentations that aren't covered by the normalizer did not see any substantial gains or losses in performance. To view the raw model scores, see Table 4 in the Appendix.

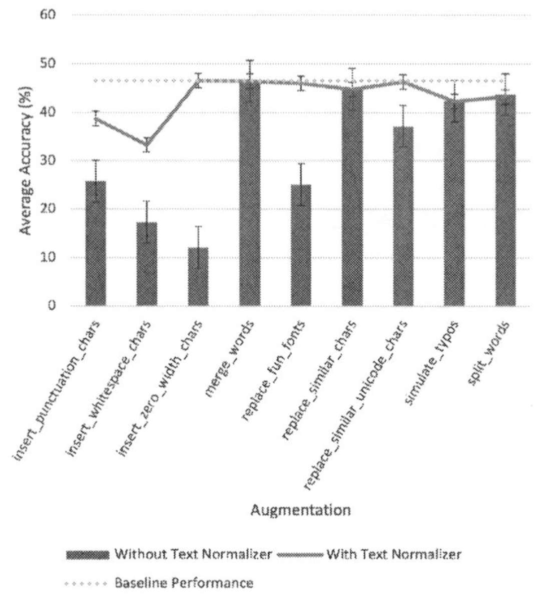

Figure 2: This figure showcases the results of evaluating Hate Speech models against the baseline, augmented, and normalized HateCheck datasets. The model scores in this graph are the averaged scores across all five LFTW models. To see the raw evaluation results, view Table 5 in the Appendix.

4.1.2 HateCheck

In addition to evaluating on the LFTW test set, we also evaluated on an out-of-distribution dataset, HateCheck. Figure 2 displays these results. The trends observed in the LFTW test set overall have agreement with the HateCheck results. However, in this case, there were no losses in performance for normalized augmentations covered by our method. The largest performance gain was **48.89%** by normalizing `insert_zero_width_unicode_chars`, and the smallest performance gain was 6.1% by normalizing `insert_punctuation_chars`. To see the raw evaluation results, please review Table 5 in the Appendix.

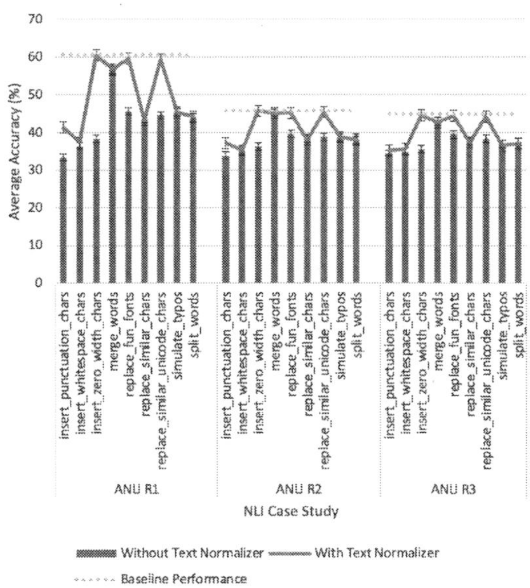

Figure 3: This figure contains the results of evaluating ANLI models against the baseline, augmented, and normalized rounds 1-3 test sets. The model scores in this graph are the averaged scores across all five models. To see the raw evaluation results, view Tables 6, 7, and 8 in the Appendix.

4.1.3 Red Team Attacks

Lastly, we evaluated the LFTW models on the Red Team dataset tasked to bypass the text normalizer. The baseline scores across all models averaged at 39.52% and the normalized scores averaged at 41.32%. In comparison to the synthetically-augmented text, applying the normalizer resulted in a less drastic increase in performance. This difference can be attributed to the fact that a significant amount of the data was attacked similarly to `replace_similar_chars` and `simulate_typos`, two augmentations not covered by our defenses. To view the raw model scores, see Table 3 in the Appendix.

4.2 Natural Language Inference

To validate our results in another problem space, we evaluated on five Natural Language Inference (NLI) models previously trained on a collection of adversarial and benign NLI datasets. We evaluated the models on the baseline, augmented, and normalized ANLI test sets from rounds 1-3.

Overall, the results from the ANLI experiments align with the previous insights discussed in the Hate Speech task. The `replace_fun_fonts`, `insert_zero_width_chars`, and `replace_similar_unicode_chars` attacks were the most performant, followed by `insert_punctuation_chars`, `insert_whitespace_chars`, and finally the non-covered attack types. The largest gain, **29.1%**, was made by normalizing `insert_zero_width_unicode_chars` in the ANLI R1 test set. To view the raw model scores, see Tables 6, 7, and 8 in the Appendix.

5 Discussions

Retraining models on adversarial data has been proposed as a mitigation method for adversarial attacks (Vidgen et al., 2021; Nie et al., 2020). Its benefits are that it's relatively simple to implement, shown to be effective (Goodfellow et al., 2015), and doesn't affect model throughput once deployed. However, if a new adversarial attack were to be discovered on a system, the turnaround time for deploying a robust model can be quite long. A developer would need to (1) gather and annotate or systematically generate the attacked data (2) retrain the model (3) redeploy the model. Steps (1) and (2) could be highly nontrivial depending on the attack type and model size. In addition, there can also be a significant monetary and environmental cost in retraining a large model (Wu et al., 2021).

On the other hand, text normalization allows a developer to move fast. Instead of collecting data, an engineer would simply need to write one additional function to reverse said attack and test it. In addition, it's lightweight and there is no need to retrain, as this is a text preprocessing step. However, text normalization cannot handle every attack type. Text normalization is best suited to mitigate character-level attacks that do not change the semantic meaning of the text, *i.e.* syntactic attacks.

Another important consideration is that text normalization *does* affect real-time performance. A balance must be found between intelligently mitigating attacks and compute. In our use case, we limited the normalizer to sophisticated string manipulation, as anything more would result in too much compute. Hence, it becomes less feasible to build defenses that require knowledge or understanding of words, etc.

Thus, we recommend the best way to mitigate adversarial attacks is to use a combination of text normalization and retraining. Specifically, retraining should be used for semantic adversarial attacks, and adversarial text normalization for syntactic adversarial attacks. Despite all the models evaluated on being retrained on adversarial data, they were still vulnerable to character-level text attacks. However, together with the text normalizer, we were able to increase performance and even return to baseline performance at times. This study is meant to show that text normalization in general is a viable approach to mitigating syntactic text-based attacks. This is certainly not the final method, and we hope researchers extend this work to support multilingual text.

6 Conclusion

We proposed a new method to mitigate text-based adversarial attacks, called the Adversarial Text Normalizer. We evaluated the performance of models retrained on adversarial data with and without the ATN. Our experiments show that text normalization and retraining should be used together in order to maintain baseline performance against a broad range of adversaries.

Acknowledgements

The authors would like to thank Adina Williams, Tristan Thrush, and Kushal Tirumala for their support in running experiments with the Dynabench platform. The authors would also like to thank Luke Zettlemoyer, Caner Hazirbas, and Stefan Hermanek for helpful discussions on the work in this paper. Finally, the authors extend their gratitude to Aaron Grattafiori, Tom Ravenscroft, Adi Ajit, Aimee Couglin, Athena Cheung, Ben Actis, Christopher Korban, Greg Prosser, Hamza Kwisaba, James Burton, Jayson Grace, Martin Vigo, Nat Hirsch, Ryan Hall, Sasha Hanganu, Tom Hebb, and Vlad Ionescu for participating in the evaluation of the Adversarial Text Normalizer.

Impact Statement

Risks from the Work

Our work is meant to reduce risk to online discourse by enabling NLP models to function robustly in an adversarial setting. We acknowledge that releasing this work might enable stronger attacks against some systems, but we believe it is important to discuss these defenses publicly for two reasons. First, other practitioners and researchers can benefit from our findings in building stronger defenses. Second, the history of security and cryptographic research clearly demonstrates that robust systems are built only when they go through ongoing attack/defend iteration cycles. To that end, we hope that our work informs the next steps in building robust NLP systems. As with any NLP system and computer technology, we acknowledge robustness may be at odds with safety when the models defended with our mechanism are themselves used for nefarious purposes.

Use of Scientific Artifacts

In this work, we made heavy use of the Dynabench platform (Kiela et al., 2021; Ma et al., 2021) and the models trained on data collected with it. We worked closely with the creators of the platform and the models, and they were always fully aware of our intentions. The Dynabench platform has been released under the MIT license: `https://github.com/facebookresearch/dynabench/blob/main/LICENSE`. We also used the Adversarial NLI, HateCheck, and Learning from the Worst datasets. Each of those do not contain identifying information and only associate a pseudonymous annotator ID with each example. We verified this manually by looking at samples from the datasets. The HateCheck and Learning from the Worst datasets contain offensive language as part of the nature of the task they were set up for. All datasets are in English and were created by English-speaking authors and annotators in the United States.

Humans Involved in the Research

We did not employ annotators or perform human subject experiments. We engaged with a partner team in a collegial capacity to expand our insights into the adversarial text normalizer and we discuss those findings here for the benefit of the broader research community.

References

Moustafa Alzantot, Yash Sharma, Ahmed Elgohary, Bo-Jhang Ho, Mani Srivastava, and Kai-Wei Chang. 2018. Generating natural language adversarial examples. In *Proceedings of the 2018 Conference on Empirical Methods in Natural Language Processing*, pages 2890–2896, Brussels, Belgium. Association for Computational Linguistics.

Nicholas Boucher, Ilia Shumailov, Ross Anderson, and Nicolas Papernot. 2021. Bad characters: Imperceptible nlp attacks. *arXiv preprint arXiv:2106.09898*.

Samuel R. Bowman, Gabor Angeli, Christopher Potts, and Christopher D. Manning. 2015. A large annotated corpus for learning natural language inference. In *Proceedings of the 2015 Conference on Empirical Methods in Natural Language Processing*, pages 632–642, Lisbon, Portugal. Association for Computational Linguistics.

Steffen Eger and Yannik Benz. 2020. From hero to zéroe: A benchmark of low-level adversarial attacks. In *Proceedings of the 1st Conference of the Asia-Pacific Chapter of the Association for Computational Linguistics and the 10th International Joint Conference on Natural Language Processing*, pages 786–803, Suzhou, China. Association for Computational Linguistics.

Steffen Eger, Gözde Gül Şahin, Andreas Rücklé, Ji-Ung Lee, Claudia Schulz, Mohsen Mesgar, Krishnkant Swarnkar, Edwin Simpson, and Iryna Gurevych. 2019. Text processing like humans do: Visually attacking and shielding NLP systems. In *Proceedings of the 2019 Conference of the North American Chapter of the Association for Computational Linguistics: Human Language Technologies, Volume 1 (Long and Short Papers)*, pages 1634–1647, Minneapolis, Minnesota. Association for Computational Linguistics.

Ian J. Goodfellow, Jonathon Shlens, and Christian Szegedy. 2015. Explaining and harnessing adversarial examples. In *3rd International Conference on Learning Representations, ICLR 2015, San Diego, CA, USA, May 7-9, 2015, Conference Track Proceedings*.

Alon Y. Halevy. 2020. Preserving integrity in online social media. In *KDD '20: The 26th ACM SIGKDD Conference on Knowledge Discovery and Data Mining, Virtual Event, CA, USA, August 23-27, 2020*, page 3601. ACM.

Mohit Iyyer, John Wieting, Kevin Gimpel, and Luke Zettlemoyer. 2018. Adversarial example generation with syntactically controlled paraphrase networks. In *Proceedings of the 2018 Conference of the North American Chapter of the Association for Computational Linguistics: Human Language Technologies, Volume 1 (Long Papers)*, pages 1875–1885, New Orleans, Louisiana. Association for Computational Linguistics.

Di Jin, Zhijing Jin, Joey Tianyi Zhou, and Peter Szolovits. 2020. Is bert really robust? a strong baseline for natural language attack on text classification and entailment. *Proceedings of the AAAI Conference on Artificial Intelligence*, 34(05):8018–8025.

Erik Jones, Robin Jia, Aditi Raghunathan, and Percy Liang. 2020. Robust encodings: A framework for combating adversarial typos. In *Proceedings of the 58th Annual Meeting of the Association for Computational Linguistics*, pages 2752–2765, Online. Association for Computational Linguistics.

Douwe Kiela, Max Bartolo, Yixin Nie, Divyansh Kaushik, Atticus Geiger, Zhengxuan Wu, Bertie Vidgen, Grusha Prasad, Amanpreet Singh, Pratik Ringshia, Zhiyi Ma, Tristan Thrush, Sebastian Riedel, Zeerak Waseem, Pontus Stenetorp, Robin Jia, Mohit Bansal, Christopher Potts, and Adina Williams. 2021. Dynabench: Rethinking benchmarking in NLP. In *Proceedings of the 2021 Conference of the North American Chapter of the Association for Computational Linguistics: Human Language Technologies*, pages 4110–4124, Online. Association for Computational Linguistics.

Zhiyi Ma, Kawin Ethayarajh, Tristan Thrush, Somya Jain, Ledell Yu Wu, Robin Jia, Christopher Potts, Adina Williams, and Douwe Kiela. 2021. Dynaboard: An evaluation-as-a-service platform for holistic next-generation benchmarking. In *Advances in Neural Information Processing Systems*.

Yixin Nie, Adina Williams, Emily Dinan, Mohit Bansal, Jason Weston, and Douwe Kiela. 2020. Adversarial NLI: A new benchmark for natural language understanding. In *Proceedings of the 58th Annual Meeting of the Association for Computational Linguistics*, pages 4885–4901, Online. Association for Computational Linguistics.

Zoe Papakipos and Joanna Bitton. 2022. Augly: Data augmentations for robustness.

Fabien A. P. Petitcolas. 2011. *Kerckhoffs' Principle*, pages 675–675. Springer US, Boston, MA.

Danish Pruthi, Bhuwan Dhingra, and Zachary C. Lipton. 2019. Combating adversarial misspellings with robust word recognition. In *Proceedings of the 57th Annual Meeting of the Association for Computational Linguistics*, pages 5582–5591, Florence, Italy. Association for Computational Linguistics.

Nestor Rodriguez and Sergio Rojas-Galeano. 2018. Shielding google's language toxicity model against adversarial attacks.

Sergio Rojas-Galeano. 2017. On obstructing obscenity obfuscation. *ACM Trans. Web*, 11(2).

Paul Röttger, Bertie Vidgen, Dong Nguyen, Zeerak Waseem, Helen Margetts, and Janet Pierrehumbert. 2021. HateCheck: Functional tests for hate speech detection models. In *Proceedings of the 59th Annual Meeting of the Association for Computational Linguistics and the 11th International Joint Conference on Natural Language Processing (Volume 1: Long Papers)*, pages 41–58, Online. Association for Computational Linguistics.

James Thorne, Andreas Vlachos, Christos Christodoulopoulos, and Arpit Mittal. 2018. FEVER: a large-scale dataset for fact extraction and VERification. In *Proceedings of the 2018 Conference of the North American Chapter of the Association for Computational Linguistics: Human Language Technologies, Volume 1 (Long Papers)*, pages 809–819, New Orleans, Louisiana. Association for Computational Linguistics.

Bertie Vidgen, Tristan Thrush, Zeerak Waseem, and Douwe Kiela. 2021. Learning from the worst: Dynamically generated datasets to improve online hate detection. In *Proceedings of the 59th Annual Meeting of the Association for Computational Linguistics and the 11th International Joint Conference on Natural Language Processing (Volume 1: Long Papers)*, pages 1667–1682, Online. Association for Computational Linguistics.

Adina Williams, Nikita Nangia, and Samuel Bowman. 2018. A broad-coverage challenge corpus for sentence understanding through inference. In *Proceedings of the 2018 Conference of the North American Chapter of the Association for Computational Linguistics: Human Language Technologies, Volume 1 (Long Papers)*, pages 1112–1122, New Orleans, Louisiana. Association for Computational Linguistics.

Carole-Jean Wu, Ramya Raghavendra, Udit Gupta, Bilge Acun, Newsha Ardalani, Kiwan Maeng, Gloria Chang, Fiona Aga Behram, James Huang, Charles Bai, Michael Gschwind, Anurag Gupta, Myle Ott, Anastasia Melnikov, Salvatore Candido, David Brooks, Geeta Chauhan, Benjamin Lee, Hsien-Hsin S. Lee, Bugra Akyildiz, Maximilian Balandat, Joe Spisak, Ravi Jain, Mike Rabbat, and Kim Hazelwood. 2021. Sustainable AI: environmental implications, challenges and opportunities. *CoRR*, abs/2111.00364.

Model	Red Team	Normalized
LFTW R1	32.41	35.95
LFTW R2	40.61	41.32
LFTW R3	39.88	41.32
LFTW R4	42.01	43.68
All LFTW	42.69	44.32

Table 3: Hate Speech Case Study Results by Model: Red Team Dataset

Appendix

A AugLy Augmentation Generation

To augment the hate speech and natural language inference datasets, we chose random parameters for each augmentation for every piece of text. The ranges we used for every parameter are listed below. Since multiple AugLy augmentations accept as input the same parameters, we do not break this down by augmentation type (the same value was used across all augmentations). The following ranges were inputted into `random.uniform()` and lists of options were inputted `random.choice()`:

- **`aug_p`**: (0.3, 1.0)
- **`aug_word_p`**: (0.3, 1.0)
- **`aug_char_p`**: (0.1, 0.4)
- **`granularity`**: ["char", "word", "all"]
- **`vary_fonts`**: [True, False]

B Raw Data: Hate Speech and Natural Language Inference Analyses

Here, we provide the full evaluation results with exact numbers broken down by attack type and model.

Augmentation	LFTW R1	LFTW R2	LFTW R3	LFTW R4	All LFTW
baseline	57.79	70.03	81.20	81.09	80.27
normalized	58.04	70.08	81.24	81.21	80.27
insert_punctuation_chars	43.34	50.48	48.53	49.23	50.74
normalized	50.83	58.48	60.48	63.40	56.43
insert_whitespace_chars	43.05	51.97	53.65	46.89	45.84
normalized	48.83	52.97	52.38	52.50	52.05
insert_zero_width_chars	35.04	50.73	51.04	48.96	46.87
normalized	58.37	70.23	81.29	81.14	80.38
merge_words	56.47	68.74	77.67	78.27	77.30
normalized	56.67	68.83	77.73	78.30	77.10
replace_fun_fonts	42.23	50.08	55.75	51.10	50.43
normalized	58.11	70.67	80.42	80.01	78.91
replace_similar_chars	52.43	56.21	52.39	52.36	56.17
normalized	52.48	56.76	53.00	52.76	56.19
replace_similar_unicode_chars	47.65	56.16	56.26	58.06	59.34
normalized	58.20	70.15	80.25	80.04	79.08
simulate_typos	53.95	60.48	61.61	59.93	61.81
normalized	53.99	60.55	61.34	60.31	61.74
split_words	52.45	55.74	59.27	58.36	60.22
normalized	52.38	56.38	59.32	58.77	60.82

Table 4: Hate Speech Case Study Results: LFTW

Augmentation	LFTW R1	LFTW R2	LFTW R3	LFTW R4	All LFTW
baseline	36.48	47.78	49.23	49.35	49.45
normalized	36.45	47.73	49.29	49.37	49.47
insert_punctuation_chars	13.18	35.05	32.52	30.09	18.09
normalized	28.19	41.15	40.78	44.67	38.95
insert_whitespace_chars	11.19	15.72	29.63	15.41	14.96
normalized	20.60	34.48	45.57	33.01	32.57
insert_zero_width_chars	0.00	21.28	30.50	8.37	0.58
normalized	36.45	47.73	49.29	49.37	49.47
merge_words	37.03	47.99	48.72	49.16	49.15
normalized	37.32	47.92	48.75	49.17	49.08
replace_fun_fonts	16.38	27.04	32.68	27.43	21.95
normalized	36.12	46.32	48.83	49.29	49.38
replace_similar_chars	33.86	47.63	47.57	47.77	47.09
normalized	34.10	47.47	47.46	47.80	47.05
replace_similar_unicode_chars	22.61	39.35	41.07	42.68	40.06
normalized	36.42	47.26	49.12	49.29	49.45
simulate_typos	32.46	44.16	42.84	46.49	45.88
normalized	32.57	43.81	42.79	46.44	45.75
split_words	33.76	47.19	44.11	47.21	46.49
normalized	33.20	46.44	43.58	47.00	46.04

Table 5: Hate Speech Case Study Results: HateCheck

Augmentation	RoBERTa	T5	BERT	ALBERT	DeBERTa
baseline	62.10	58.90	53.80	63.00	65.00
normalized	61.80	58.90	54.00	62.90	65.00
insert_punctuation_chars	32.40	32.70	32.60	34.40	34.60
normalized	40.40	38.80	41.20	39.90	46.40
insert_whitespace_chars	36.40	38.50	40.20	33.60	33.20
normalized	38.00	39.80	39.50	34.60	35.10
insert_zero_width_chars	35.50	34.30	53.80	31.90	36.20
normalized	61.80	58.70	54.00	62.80	65.30
merge_words	60.10	57.20	48.00	58.30	59.90
normalized	60.00	57.30	48.10	58.50	59.70
replace_fun_fonts	40.00	50.10	36.40	62.30	39.10
normalized	60.50	58.50	51.80	63.10	64.00
replace_similar_chars	45.30	44.20	39.60	44.00	44.70
normalized	43.80	43.80	40.50	43.80	44.60
replace_similar_unicode_chars	44.30	42.10	38.20	53.40	44.90
normalized	61.00	58.00	52.40	62.00	63.60
simulate_typos	46.70	44.20	42.90	45.00	48.10
normalized	46.80	44.20	42.90	44.90	47.70
split_words	45.50	42.90	41.40	44.30	46.60
normalized	45.80	42.80	41.60	43.70	47.10

Table 6: Natural Language Inference Case Study Results: ANLI R1

Augmentation	RoBERTa	T5	BERT	ALBERT	DeBERTa
baseline	46.50	46.80	44.80	46.50	44.50
normalized	46.20	46.80	44.90	46.60	44.40
insert_punctuation_chars	35.40	34.10	31.80	34.20	34.10
normalized	35.60	36.10	37.90	38.50	38.00
insert_whitespace_chars	35.30	36.70	35.50	33.90	34.40
normalized	33.60	36.50	35.80	34.80	35.30
insert_zero_width_chars	35.10	34.20	44.80	33.40	34.10
normalized	46.30	46.70	44.90	46.60	44.30
merge_words	45.60	46.60	46.70	44.30	42.80
normalized	45.50	46.60	46.60	44.50	42.50
replace_fun_fonts	36.70	42.20	35.90	46.40	36.80
normalized	44.80	45.90	44.80	46.30	44.00
replace_similar_chars	38.00	37.90	37.50	39.60	38.80
normalized	38.20	37.60	36.20	39.40	38.60
replace_similar_unicode_chars	39.40	38.30	36.90	42.00	37.60
normalized	46.00	46.20	44.30	46.20	44.40
simulate_typos	38.40	39.10	39.00	37.70	39.40
normalized	38.30	38.90	39.30	37.70	39.70
split_words	38.00	38.30	36.80	37.40	39.50
normalized	38.30	38.20	36.10	38.40	39.80

Table 7: Natural Language Inference Case Study Results: ANLI R2

Augmentation	RoBERTa	T5	BERT	ALBERT	DeBERTa
baseline	45.58	44.83	44.00	44.17	45.83
normalized	45.08	44.83	43.67	43.58	45.33
insert_punctuation_chars	35.17	33.50	34.58	33.67	35.17
normalized	35.75	36.58	33.92	33.92	36.00
insert_whitespace_chars	33.67	35.17	36.33	34.33	34.92
normalized	34.75	36.25	37.33	35.00	35.00
insert_zero_width_chars	34.42	32.25	44.00	32.08	35.00
normalized	45.08	44.83	43.83	43.75	45.33
merge_words	43.42	44.58	41.42	40.33	44.92
normalized	42.83	44.58	41.42	40.00	44.42
replace_fun_fonts	38.08	40.92	37.08	44.25	37.50
normalized	45.33	44.92	43.58	43.58	44.83
replace_similar_chars	40.00	37.08	36.92	36.83	37.00
normalized	38.83	37.42	36.42	36.75	37.17
replace_similar_unicode_chars	38.67	38.00	36.17	41.17	37.67
normalized	44.58	45.00	43.08	43.58	44.67
simulate_typos	35.92	36.83	36.83	37.75	38.00
normalized	35.50	36.67	36.00	37.00	37.50
split_words	38.50	38.50	37.08	37.75	35.67
normalized	37.50	38.17	36.42	37.33	35.75

Table 8: Natural Language Inference Case Study Results: ANLI R3

Constraint-based Multi-hop Question Answering with Knowledge Graph

Sayantan Mitra, Roshni Ramnani and **Shubhashis Sengupta**
Accenture Labs, Bengaluru
{sayantan.a.mitra, roshni.r.ramnani, shubhashis.sengupta}@accenture.com

Abstract

The objective of a Question-Answering system over Knowledge Graph (KGQA) is to respond to natural language queries presented over the KG. A complex question answering system typically addresses one of the two categories of complexity: questions with constraints and questions involving multiple hops of relations. Most of the previous works have addressed these complexities separately. Multi-hop KGQA necessitates reasoning across numerous edges of the KG in order to arrive at the correct answer. Because KGs are frequently sparse, multi-hop KGQA presents extra complications. Recent works have developed KG embedding approaches to reduce KG sparsity by performing missing link prediction. In this paper, we tried to address multi-hop constrained-based queries using KG embeddings to generate more flexible query graphs. Empirical results indicate that the proposed methodology produces state-of-the-art outcomes on three KGQA datasets.

1 Introduction

Multi-relational graph, also known as Knowledge Graph (KG) comprises of a large number (often, millions) of entities and relations represented in the form of triplets (entity -> relation -> entity). Some of the most widely used KGs include DBPedia (Lehmann et al., 2015), Freebase [1], YAGO (Suchanek et al., 2007), KENSHO[2] and NELL (Mitchell et al., 2018). In the recent years, Knowledge Graph question answering (KGQA) has emerged as a significant research field (Sun et al., 2018; Zhang et al., 2018; Bordes et al., 2014). Given a natural language question, a KGQA system derives the right answer by analyzing the question and mapping it to the underlying KG.

Early works of KGQA mainly focused on simple questions containing single relations (Yang et al., 2014; Hao et al., 2017; Dong et al., 2015). However, in the real world, questions are often complex and recent work focuses on addressing these complexities. The complexities in KGQA can broadly be divided into two types: (1) **Constraint based:** Single-relation questions with constraints. For example, in this query *"when did the 7th harry potter book come out?"* there is only one relation, *"published in"* between the answer entity and the entity, *"harry potter book"* but there is also a constraint *"7th"* which needs to be addressed. To handle these kind of questions, query graph generation methods have been proposed (Yih et al., 2015; Bao et al., 2016; Luo et al., 2018). These methods first identify the 1-hop paths and then apply constraints on them. (2) **Multi-hop based:** Questions with multi-hop answers. For example, consider this query *"What language is spoken where the capital city is Brussels?"* the answer is associated with entity *"Brussels"* through two hops of relations, namely, *"capital of"* and *"language spoken"*. For addressing such multi-hop questions, it is important to consider longer paths. One of the main challenges is increasing search space. It is important to restrict the multi-hop relations to be considered, otherwise the search space can grow exponentially with the length of the relation paths. For example, Chen et al. (2019) and Lan et al. (2019) proposed to consider only the best matching relations instead of all relations when extending a relation path. However, there exists little work to address both types of complexities together.

In this paper, we address both types of complex question answering - with constraints as well as multi-hop relations - together. We propose an embedding based graph query generation method by allowing longer relation paths. Instead of adding constraints after complete generation of all probable paths, we apply constraints on partial paths

[1] https://developers.google.com/freebase

[2] https://www.kaggle.com/kenshoresearch/kensho-derived-wikimedia-data

Proceedings of NAACL-HLT 2022: Industry Track Papers, pages 280 - 288
July 10-15, 2022 ©2022 Association for Computational Linguistics

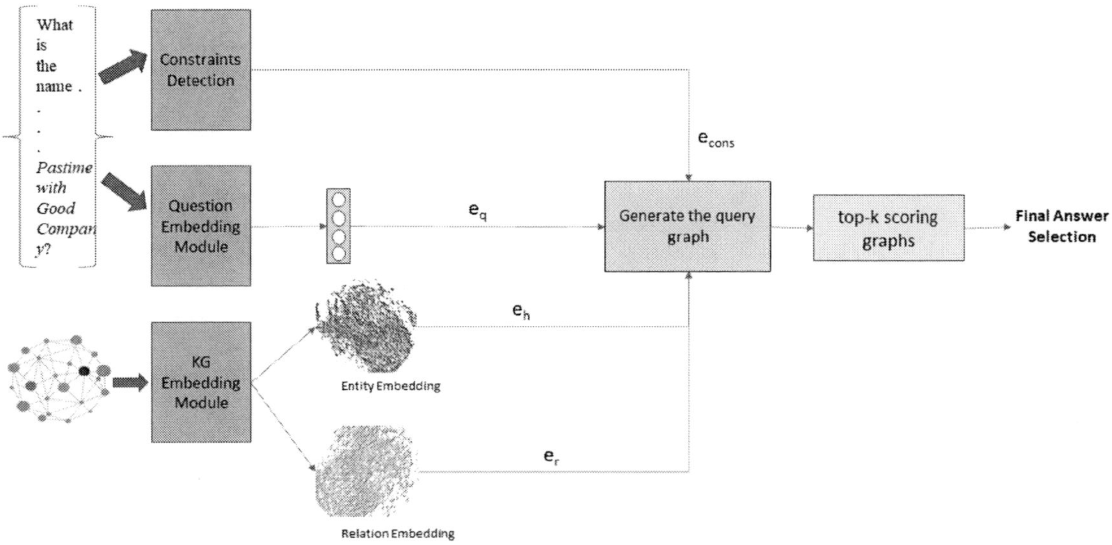

Figure 1: Overall representation of the proposed method for constraint based Multi-hop KGQA. It has five components: (1) KG Embedding Module which learns embeddings of all the entities and relations present in the KG, (2) Question Embedding Module which learns embedding for the given question, (3) Constraint Module for identifying constraints in the question (4) Graph Query Generation Module which generates the relevant query graphs based on the question, and (5) The fifth module selects top-k graphs and generates the final answer. Graph embeddings help our proposed method to effectively handle KG sparsity.

and explore the next path segments. This helps to lessen the query search space effectively. For the ComplexWebQuestions dataset, which has more number of complex questions; our method outperforms SOTA in terms of Prec@1 and F1. On other benchmark datasets as well our proposed approach achieves SOTA results. The overall representation of our proposed model is presented in Figure 1. We make the following contributions in this paper:

1. Our proposed method combines embeddings with query graphs to address constraint based multi-hop complex questions. To the best of our knowledge, this is the first attempt of combining embeddings with query graph to address all types of complex questions.

2. The proposed method leverages the requirement of answer selection from a pre-specified local neighborhood - an auxiliary constraint.

2 Related Work

2.1 Knowledge Graph Question Answering

Previous works (Li et al., 2018) used TransE (Bordes et al., 2013) graph embedding method to answer factoid based questions. However, it is a simple question answering method which works with 1-hop questions and furthermore, it requires ground-truth labeling for each question. Yih et al. (2015) and Bao et al. (2016) in their works used query graph based approaches to answer the questions. Yang et al. (2015) uses embedding based approach to co-related natural language questions to its corresponding logic forms. Different methodologies proposed in (Hao et al., 2017; Lukovnikov et al., 2017; Yin et al., 2016; Dai et al., 2016; Dong et al., 2015) use neural networks based approach. These neural networks are trained to learn a scoring function and rank the candidate answers based on these scores. There are other works (Mohammed et al., 2018; Ture and Jojic, 2017) which have formulated the QA task as a classification problem by using relations as a label. These approaches are not easily extendable to multi-hop settings.

2.2 Knowledge Graph Embedding

Real world KGs have the following limitations: (1) Most of them are often incomplete (Wang et al., 2017); (2) Real-world data is frequently dynamic and constantly changing(Cai et al., 2018). Therefore, KG completion is often formulated as the link-prediction problem(Arora, 2020). In the recent years, a lot of research has gone into link predictions in Knowledge Graphs using KG embeddings.

TransE (Bordes et al., 2013) generates high dimensional embeddings for entities in real space

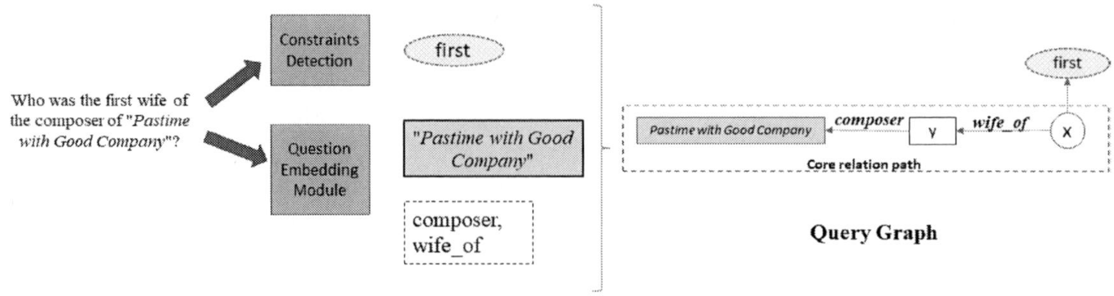

Figure 2: Constraint(s), topic entity and relations are detected for the given question. Assuming we start from the topic entity *"Pastime with Good Company"*, the core relation path is the path linking topic entity to the variable **X**. Here, only one constraint (*"first"*) is present, represented by shaded ellipse.

and TransE (Bordes et al., 2013) embeds entities in high-dimensional real space and translates between the head and tail entities. DistMult (Yang et al., 2015) and RESCAL (Nickel et al., 2011) construct KG embeddings by learning a score function that contains a bi-linear product of the vectors of the head and tail entities, as well as a relation matrix. These models, however, only consider each individual fact and neglect intrinsic relationships, thus cannot capture deeper semantics for better embedding. ComplEx (Trouillon et al., 2016), first presents complex vector space, which is capable of capturing both symmetric and antisymmetric relations. It uses tensor factorization to generate embeddings of relations and entities in complex space. The complex vectors can retain the benefit of dot product, that is linearity in both space and time complexity. This motivated us to use this embedding in our present work. RotatE (Sun et al., 2019) creates entity embeddings by projecting them in complex space, and relations are represented as complex plane rotations. InteractE (Vashishth et al., 2020) is an improvement over ConvE (Dettmers et al., 2018) method by increasing feature interaction. These models have high time complexity.

3 Background

3.1 Knowledge Graph

A knowledge graph is a set of triples represented by (h, r, t), where $r \in \mathcal{R}$ is the relation and $h, t \in \mathcal{E}$ are subject and object respectively. Here, $\mathcal{R}$ and $\mathcal{E}$ represents set of relations and entities respectively.

3.2 Link Prediction

Given an incomplete knowledge graph, the task of the link prediction is to predict the valid unknown links. This task is achieved by KG embedding models which assign a score $s = \phi(h, r, t) \in \mathcal{R}$ to the predicted links and validate whether the link is true. The goal of this model is to predict the missing links correctly.

3.3 Knowledge Graph Embeddings

Complex Embedding (Trouillon et al., 2016) is a latent factorization method that learns a large variety of symmetric and anti-symmetric relations in complex space. The complex vectors can retains the benefit of dot product, that is linearity in both space and time complexity. This motivated us to use this embedding in our present work. It is used to generate entity and relation embeddings in knowledge graphs. Given $h, t \in \mathcal{E}$ and $r \in \mathcal{R}$ the complex embedding generates $e_h, e_r, e_t \in \mathbb{C}^d$ and defines a scoring function:

$$\phi(h, r, t) = Re(\sum_{k=1}^{d} e_h^{(k)} e_r^{(k)} \bar{e}_t^{(k)}) \qquad (1)$$

For all correct triplets $\phi(h, r, t) > 0$ and for others $\phi(h, r, t) < 0$. Re stands for the real part of the complex numbers.

3.4 Graph Query

For a given question Q, the task of the KGQA is to find an answer a such that $a \in \mathcal{E}$.

In Figure 2, we show the query graph (Bao et al., 2016; Yih et al., 2015; Luo et al., 2018) for the input question *Who was the first wife of the composer of "Pastime with Good Company"?* A query graph broadly have four parts: (i) A **grounded entity**, a head/ topic entity (for e.g *"Pastime with Good Company"*) which is explicitly mentioned in the question. It is represented by a shaded recatangle in Fig 2; (ii) A **lambda variable** (**X** in Figure 2) is the actual answer to the input question; (iii) An **existential entity**, intermediate node/nodes (**y** in Figure 2) between grounded entity and lambda variable; and (iv) An **aggregation function** (*argmin/count*) is the constraint imposed on the lambda variable. In Fig 2, *first* is the constraint on the **lambda variable**, it is internally mapped to *argmin* (described under Section 4.6). The edges of the graph represent the relations $r \in \mathcal{R}$. The **core relation path** is the path connecting the **topic entity** to the **lambda variable** X.

4 Method

4.1 Problem Statement

For a given natural language question q having relations r ($r \in \mathcal{R}$), entities e_h ($e_h \in \mathcal{E}$) and zero/more constraint(s), the task is to identify the answer e_t, where $e_t \in \mathcal{E}$. As an external knowledge source, Knowledge graph $\mathcal{G}$ is used. It is the set of available facts represented by triples $\mathcal{K}$, where $\mathcal{K} \subseteq \mathcal{E} \times \mathcal{R} \times \mathcal{E}$. Here, $\mathcal{R}$ is set of relations and $\mathcal{E}$ is set of entities.

4.2 Overview of the Proposed Method

Our proposed method uses graph embeddings to answer complex questions. It begins by learning a KG representation in the embedding space. For a given question, it then learns the question embedding and also identifies the topic entities. For relation extraction, we use the training questions and their answers to learn the linking model. For learning the temporal constraints and superlative linking, we simply use regular expressions and a superlative word list(Luo et al., 2018) . The superlative words are manually mapped to the aggregation functions: *argmin* & *argmax*. Finally it combines these embedding and constraints to predict the answer.

4.3 KG Embedding Module

For KG embedding we used complex embeddings (Trouillon et al., 2016) for all $h, t \in \mathcal{E}$ and all $r \in \mathcal{R}$ such that $e_h, e_r, e_t \in \mathbb{C}^d$. The entity embeddings are used to learn a triple scoring function between topic entity, question and answer entity. The selected triplets are used to generate the query graphs. The entity and relation embeddings learned here are kept fixed and used for fine-tuning subsequent steps. For our work we have used latest dump of Freebase[3] as our Knowledge graph for all the datasets.

[3]https://developers.google.com/freebase/

4.4 Question Embedding Module

This module is used to map the natural language questions to a fixed dimension vector $e_q \in \mathbb{C}^d$. We have used ROBERTa[4] (Liu et al., 2019) model to generate q into vector of dimension 768. The generated vector is passed through three fully-connected linear layers with ReLU activation and a dropout of 0.1 in each layer and finally projected to a complex space $\mathbb{C}^d$.

For a question q, topic entity $h \in \mathcal{E}$ and set of answers $\mathcal{A} \subseteq \mathcal{E}$, the question embedding is learned such that

$$\phi(e_h, e_q, e_a) > 0 \; \forall a \in \mathcal{A} \tag{2}$$

$$\phi(e_h, e_q, e_{\bar{a}}) < 0 \; \forall \bar{a} \notin \mathcal{A} \tag{3}$$

where, ϕ is defined in equation 1 and e_h, e_a are entity embeddings. The model is learned by minimizing the binary cross entropy loss between the $sigmoid$ of the scores and the target answer labels. When the entities are large we do label smoothing.

4.5 Relation matching

For relation matching we learn a scoring function $S_r(r, q)$ similar to PullNet (Sun et al., 2019) and rank the relations $r \in \mathcal{R}$ for question q. Let $\bar{q} = \{< s > w_1, w_2 \ldots w_{|q|} < /s >\}$, word sequence in question q and h_r be the relation embedding, then the scoring function is defined as follows:

$$h_q = ROBERTa(\bar{q}) \tag{4}$$

$$S_r(r, q) = sigmoid(h_q^T h_r) \tag{5}$$

$ROBERTa(.)$ returns the last hidden layer output of ROBERTa model. We select those relations where $S_r > 0.5$ it is denoted as $\mathcal{R}_a$.

4.6 Query Graph Generation

After extracting the entities and relation(s) in the previous steps, the constraint(s) are detected and are manually mapped to the aggregation functions by the method described under Section 4.2. To generate the query graph g, $\{extend, aggregate\}$ actions are applied. An **extend** action extends the core path by one or more relation in $\mathcal{R}$. An **aggregate** action attaches the detected aggregation

[4]The pre-trained ROBERTa base model could be found at https://huggingface.co/models?search=roberta

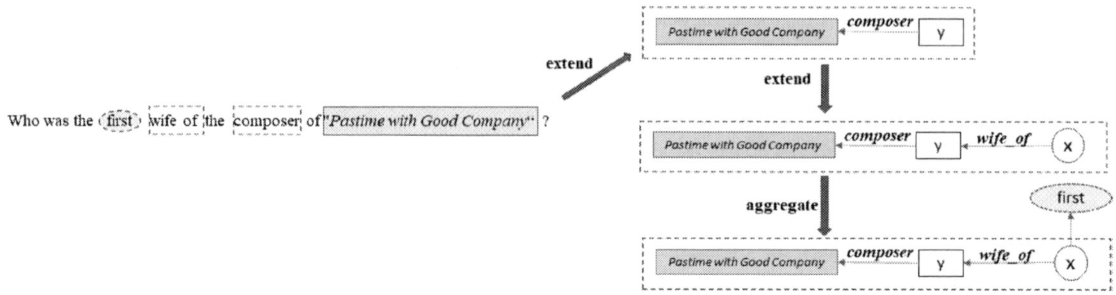

Figure 3: Examples of the Query Graph generation by extend and aggregate actions.

function to either a **lambda variable** or an existential variable.

In Figure 3, we start with the ground entity *"Pastime with Good Company"* and apply **extend** action to find the temporal entity **y** (here it is Henry VIII) connected by the relation *"composer"*. As there is no constraint attached with the above relation, we again apply **extend** action and find the *"lambda variable"* attached with **y** with the relation *"wife_of"*. Here, the constraint *"first"* is associated with this relation and is mapped to the aggregation function *argmin*. We apply this constraint on the *"lambda variable"* (**X**) and select the final answer (here the answer is Catherine of Aragon).

We start with **extend** action, then apply **aggregate** action, this significantly reduces the search space. We repeat the steps till we generate the query graph.

4.7 Answer Selection Module

Sometimes, the previous step may generate a set of query graphs instead of a single graph. In that case we select the best answer by this module. Let $\mathcal{R}_g$ represent the set of relations for each query graph g. We also have a set of relations $\mathcal{R}_a$ extracted from equation 5. For g, we calculate a relation score as:

$$RelScore_g = |\mathcal{R}_a \cap \mathcal{R}_g| \qquad (6)$$

We combine $RelScore_g$ with Complex score to find the answer entity:

$$e_{ans} = \arg\max_{a' \in \mathcal{N}_g} \phi(e_h, e_q, e_{a'}) + \gamma * RelScore_g$$

Here, γ is a tunable parameter. We select the entity with highest score (e_{ans}) as the answer.

5 Experiments

In this section, we first describe the datasets used for evaluating our method and the SOTA models. Finally we describe the results, ablation study and error analysis.

Question Type	CWQ	WQSP
1-hop w/o cons.	0.10%	71.30%
1-hop w/ cons.	35.90%	28.20%
2-hop w/o cons.	33.50%	0.0%
2-hop w/ cons.	30.50%	0.50%

Table 1: Statistics for CWQ and WQSP datasets. *cons.* stands for constraints.

5.1 Datasets

We evaluate our method on the following datasets: WebQuestions Semantic Parses (WQSP)(Yih et al., 2015), ComplexQuestions (CQ) (Bao et al., 2016) and ComplexWebQuestions (CWQ) (Talmor and Berant, 2018). In Table 1, we have listed the statistics for each dataset. CQ dataset does not provide ground truth query graphs so we could not collect similar statistics. It has been observed that major questions are 1-hop in CQ dataset.

Method	CWQ (Prec@1 / F1)	WQSP (F1)	CQ (F1)
Yih et al. (2015)	NA	69.0	NA
Luo et al. (2018)	NA	NA	40.9
Bao et al. (2016)	NA	NA	42.8
Lan et al. (2019)	39.3/36.5	67.9	NA
Bhutani et al. (2019)	40.8/33.9	60.3	NA
Chen et al. (2019)	30.5/29.8	68.5	35.3
Ansari et al. (2019)	NA	72.6	NA
Lan and Jiang (2020)	44.1/40.4	74.0	43.3
Proposed Method	46.3/41.9	77.8	45.9

Table 2: Comparison of the results between our proposed method and other state of the art methods.

5.2 Results

We compare the results of our proposed model with the following existing works. We first compare with the methods which use staged graph query but cannot handle multi-hop questions (Yih et al., 2015; Bao et al., 2016; Luo et al., 2018). Next, we compare with the method proposed by Lan et al. (2019), it handles constraints and consider multi-hop but does not use any strategy to reduce the search space. We further compare with (Chen et al., 2019), which does not handle constraint but uses beam search with a beam size of 1 to handle multi-hop questions. Bhutani et al. (2019) uses a strategy to decompose complex questions into simple questions and achieved SOTA results on CWQ dataset in terms of Prec@1. Ansari et al. (2019) proposed a method which generates query programs from question token by token. Finally, we compare our method with Lan and Jiang (2020), their method handles both multi-hop and constrained based complex question and uses beam search with beam size 3 to reduce the search space.

The overall comparison results with the SOTA models in shown in Table 2. From the table we can see that our model outperforms other methods on CWQ dataset in terms of both Prec@1 and F1. Our models shows an improvement of 2.2% in terms of Prec@1 and 1.5% in terms of F1 compared to the best SOTA model. This validates our claim that our proposed method can effectively handle the complex questions with both constraints and multiple hops. In WQSP dataset, the percentage of constrained based questions are low specially for multi hops (0.5% only, shown in Table 1). For this reason, our model not only outperforms all other SOTA models but also displays around 74% F1 score which is highest in comparison to other two datasets (CWQ and CQ). CQ dataset contains only single hop constrained based questions. In this dataset also our model outperforms other models in terms of F1 by 2.5%. This shows the effectiveness of our model in terms of handling only constraint based question. Overall the results in Table 2 shows the robustness and efficiency of our proposed model.

Method	CWQ (Prec@1 / F1)
SOTA	44.1 / 40.4
w GRU	43.3 / 38.6
w/o extend	26.4 / 22.8
w/o connect	36.8 / 32.3
w/o aggregate	43.8 / 39.5
Freebase-50 (avg.)	27.7 / 22.8
TransE	43.8 / 39.8
TransH	44.5 / 40.8

Table 3: Ablation study on CWQ dataset.

5.3 Ablation Study

We performed ablation study to better understand our model. To show that the performance of our model is not mainly due to use of ROBERTa (Liu et al., 2019) we replaced it with simple GRU model and conducted the experiments. The results in Table 3 shows that GRU based version of our methodology shows comparable results with SOTA in terms of both Prec@1 and F1. This verifies that performance of our method is not mainly because of the use of ROBERTa. To show the importance of each actions in the query graph, we have created three variants of our proposed method by eliminating one of the actions from each of them. From the results in Table 3, we can see that aggregate action has the least effect among the three and extend action have the most effect on the performance of the proposed method. The best answer is obtained when all the three actions are used together. To show the effectiveness of the KG embedding module we have randomly removed 50% of the relations from the KG (Freebase) and created a new KG Freebase-50 and then execute our algorithm on this new KG. We reported this step 10 times and reported the average results of our model in Table 3 in terms of Prec@1 and F1. From the results we can see that with the reduced KG our model performs similar to that of the *w/o extend* approach. This shows that our model is able to predict the missing links correctly but failed to apply constraints effectively due to sparse KG.

Further, to show the effect of embedding model on our proposed method, we have created two new variants of our proposed model using TransE (Bordes et al., 2013) and TransH(Wang et al., 2014) KG embeddings. The results are shown in Table 3. From the Table it can be seen that both the models produce comparable results with respect to SOTA models. This shows that the performance of our proposed method is not mainly dependent on the type of KG embeddings used.

6 Conclusion

In this paper, we propose an embedding based query graph generation method to address complex questions (constrained multiple hops queries). Often KGs are incomplete or sparsely populated, and this poses additional challenges for complex KGQA methods. By using KG embedding, the proposed methodology effectively address this KG sparsity problem by predicting missing links without the use of secondary corpus. By strategically incorporating constraints into the query graphs, we are able to restrict the search space. Experiments showed that our proposed method outperforms all other SOTA methods on all the datasets (CWQ, WQSP and CQ). In future, we would like include a module to handle abbreviation errors.

References

Ghulam Ahmed Ansari, Amrita Saha, Vishwajeet Kumar, Mohan Bhambhani, Karthik Sankaranarayanan, and Soumen Chakrabarti. 2019. Neural program induction for kbqa without gold programs or query annotations. In *Proceedings of the Twenty-Eighth International Joint Conference on Artificial Intelligence, IJCAI-19*, pages 4890–4896. International Joint Conferences on Artificial Intelligence Organization.

Siddhant Arora. 2020. A survey on graph neural networks for knowledge graph completion. *CoRR*, abs/2007.12374.

Junwei Bao, Nan Duan, Zhao Yan, Ming Zhou, and Tiejun Zhao. 2016. Constraint-based question answering with knowledge graph. In *Proceedings of COLING 2016, the 26th International Conference on Computational Linguistics: Technical Papers*, pages 2503–2514, Osaka, Japan. The COLING 2016 Organizing Committee.

Nikita Bhutani, Xinyi Zheng, and H V Jagadish. 2019. Learning to answer complex questions over knowledge bases with query composition. In *Proceedings of the 28th ACM International Conference on Information and Knowledge Management*, CIKM '19, page 739–748, New York, NY, USA. Association for Computing Machinery.

Antoine Bordes, Sumit Chopra, and Jason Weston. 2014. Question answering with subgraph embeddings. In *Proceedings of the 2014 Conference on Empirical Methods in Natural Language Processing (EMNLP)*, pages 615–620, Doha, Qatar. Association for Computational Linguistics.

Antoine Bordes, Nicolas Usunier, Alberto Garcia-Duran, Jason Weston, and Oksana Yakhnenko. 2013. Translating embeddings for modeling multi-relational data. In *Advances in Neural Information Processing Systems*, volume 26. Curran Associates, Inc.

HongYun Cai, Vincent W. Zheng, and Kevin Chen-Chuan Chang. 2018. A comprehensive survey of graph embedding: Problems, techniques, and applications. *IEEE Transactions on Knowledge and Data Engineering*, 30(9):1616–1637.

Zi-Yuan Chen, Chih-Hung Chang, Yi-Pei Chen, Jijnasa Nayak, and Lun-Wei Ku. 2019. UHop: An unrestricted-hop relation extraction framework for knowledge-based question answering. In *Proceedings of the 2019 Conference of the North American Chapter of the Association for Computational Linguistics: Human Language Technologies, Volume 1 (Long and Short Papers)*, pages 345–356, Minneapolis, Minnesota. Association for Computational Linguistics.

Zihang Dai, Lei Li, and Wei Xu. 2016. CFO: Conditional focused neural question answering with large-scale knowledge bases. In *Proceedings of the 54th Annual Meeting of the Association for Computational Linguistics (Volume 1: Long Papers)*, pages 800–810, Berlin, Germany. Association for Computational Linguistics.

Tim Dettmers, Pasquale Minervini, Pontus Stenetorp, and Sebastian Riedel. 2018. Convolutional 2d knowledge graph embeddings. In *Proceedings of the AAAI Conference on Artificial Intelligence*, volume 32.

Li Dong, Furu Wei, Ming Zhou, and Ke Xu. 2015. Question answering over Freebase with multi-column convolutional neural networks. In *Proceedings of the 53rd Annual Meeting of the Association for Computational Linguistics and the 7th International Joint Conference on Natural Language Processing (Volume 1: Long Papers)*, pages 260–269, Beijing, China. Association for Computational Linguistics.

Yanchao Hao, Yuanzhe Zhang, Kang Liu, Shizhu He, Zhanyi Liu, Hua Wu, and Jun Zhao. 2017. An end-to-end model for question answering over knowledge base with cross-attention combining global knowledge. In *Proceedings of the 55th Annual Meeting of the Association for Computational Linguistics (Volume 1: Long Papers)*, pages 221–231, Vancouver, Canada. Association for Computational Linguistics.

Yunshi Lan and Jing Jiang. 2020. Query graph generation for answering multi-hop complex questions from knowledge bases. In *Proceedings of the 58th Annual Meeting of the Association for Computational Linguistics*, pages 969–974, Online. Association for Computational Linguistics.

Yunshi Lan, Shuohang Wang, and Jing Jiang. 2019. Multi-hop knowledge base question answering with an iterative sequence matching model. In *2019 IEEE International Conference on Data Mining (ICDM)*, pages 359–368.

Jens Lehmann, Robert Isele, Max Jakob, Anja Jentzsch, Dimitris Kontokostas, Pablo N. Mendes, Sebastian Hellmann, Mohamed Morsey, Patrick van Kleef, Sören Auer, and Christian Bizer. 2015. Dbpedia – a large-scale, multilingual knowledge base extracted from wikipedia. *Semantic Web*, 6:167–195. 2.

Dingcheng Li, Jingyuan Zhang, and Ping Li. 2018. Representation learning for question classification via topic sparse autoencoder and entity embedding. In *2018 IEEE International Conference on Big Data (Big Data)*, pages 126–133.

Yinhan Liu, Myle Ott, Naman Goyal, Jingfei Du, Mandar Joshi, Danqi Chen, Omer Levy, Mike Lewis, Luke Zettlemoyer, and Veselin Stoyanov. 2019. RoBERTa: A Robustly Optimized BERT Pretraining Approach. *arXiv e-prints*, page arXiv:1907.11692.

Denis Lukovnikov, Asja Fischer, Jens Lehmann, and Sören Auer. 2017. Neural network-based question answering over knowledge graphs on word and character level. In *Proceedings of the 26th International Conference on World Wide Web*, WWW '17, page 1211–1220, Republic and Canton of Geneva, CHE. International World Wide Web Conferences Steering Committee.

Kangqi Luo, Fengli Lin, Xusheng Luo, and Kenny Zhu. 2018. Knowledge base question answering via encoding of complex query graphs. In *Proceedings of the 2018 Conference on Empirical Methods in Natural Language Processing*, pages 2185–2194, Brussels, Belgium. Association for Computational Linguistics.

T. Mitchell, W. Cohen, E. Hruschka, P. Talukdar, B. Yang, J. Betteridge, A. Carlson, B. Dalvi, M. Gardner, B. Kisiel, J. Krishnamurthy, N. Lao, K. Mazaitis, T. Mohamed, N. Nakashole, E. Platanios, A. Ritter, M. Samadi, B. Settles, R. Wang, D. Wijaya, A. Gupta, X. Chen, A. Saparov, M. Greaves, and J. Welling. 2018. Never-ending learning. *Commun. ACM*, 61(5):103–115.

Salman Mohammed, Peng Shi, and Jimmy Lin. 2018. Strong baselines for simple question answering over knowledge graphs with and without neural networks. In *Proceedings of the 2018 Conference of the North American Chapter of the Association for Computational Linguistics: Human Language Technologies, Volume 2 (Short Papers)*, pages 291–296, New Orleans, Louisiana. Association for Computational Linguistics.

Maximilian Nickel, Volker Tresp, and Hans-Peter Kriegel. 2011. A three-way model for collective learning on multi-relational data. In *Proceedings of the 28th International Conference on International Conference on Machine Learning*, ICML'11, page 809–816, Madison, WI, USA. Omnipress.

Fabian M. Suchanek, Gjergji Kasneci, and Gerhard Weikum. 2007. Yago: A core of semantic knowledge. In *Proceedings of the 16th International Conference on World Wide Web*, WWW '07, page 697–706, New York, NY, USA. Association for Computing Machinery.

Haitian Sun, Tania Bedrax-Weiss, and William Cohen. 2019. PullNet: Open domain question answering with iterative retrieval on knowledge bases and text. In *Proceedings of the 2019 Conference on Empirical Methods in Natural Language Processing and the 9th International Joint Conference on Natural Language Processing (EMNLP-IJCNLP)*, pages 2380–2390, Hong Kong, China. Association for Computational Linguistics.

Haitian Sun, Bhuwan Dhingra, Manzil Zaheer, Kathryn Mazaitis, Ruslan Salakhutdinov, and William Cohen. 2018. Open domain question answering using early fusion of knowledge bases and text. In *Proceedings of the 2018 Conference on Empirical Methods in Natural Language Processing*, pages 4231–4242, Brussels, Belgium. Association for Computational Linguistics.

Zhiqing Sun, Zhi-Hong Deng, Jian-Yun Nie, and Jian Tang. 2019. RotatE: Knowledge Graph Embedding by Relational Rotation in Complex Space. *arXiv e-prints*, page arXiv:1902.10197.

Alon Talmor and Jonathan Berant. 2018. The web as a knowledge-base for answering complex questions. In *Proceedings of the 2018 Conference of the North American Chapter of the Association for Computational Linguistics: Human Language Technologies, Volume 1 (Long Papers)*, pages 641–651, New Orleans, Louisiana. Association for Computational Linguistics.

Théo Trouillon, Johannes Welbl, Sebastian Riedel, Éric Gaussier, and Guillaume Bouchard. 2016. Complex embeddings for simple link prediction. In *Proceedings of the 33rd International Conference on International Conference on Machine Learning - Volume 48*, ICML'16, page 2071–2080. JMLR.org.

Ferhan Ture and Oliver Jojic. 2017. No need to pay attention: Simple recurrent neural networks work! In *Proceedings of the 2017 Conference on Empirical Methods in Natural Language Processing*, pages 2866–2872, Copenhagen, Denmark. Association for Computational Linguistics.

Shikhar Vashishth, Soumya Sanyal, Vikram Nitin, Nilesh Agrawal, and Partha Talukdar. 2020. Interacte: Improving convolution-based knowledge graph embeddings by increasing feature interactions. In *Proceedings of the 34th AAAI Conference on Artificial Intelligence*, pages 3009–3016. AAAI Press.

Quan Wang, Zhendong Mao, Bin Wang, and Li Guo. 2017. Knowledge graph embedding: A survey of approaches and applications. *IEEE Transactions on Knowledge and Data Engineering*, 29(12):2724–2743.

Zhen Wang, Jianwen Zhang, Jianlin Feng, and Zheng Chen. 2014. Knowledge graph embedding by translating on hyperplanes. In *Proceedings of the Twenty-Eighth AAAI Conference on Artificial Intelligence*, AAAI'14, page 1112–1119. AAAI Press.

Min-Chul Yang, Nan Duan, Ming Zhou, and Hae-Chang Rim. 2014. Joint relational embeddings for knowledge-based question answering. In *Proceedings of the 2014 Conference on Empirical Methods in Natural Language Processing (EMNLP)*, pages 645–650, Doha, Qatar. Association for Computational Linguistics.

Min-Chul Yang, Do-Gil Lee, So-Young Park, and Hae-Chang Rim. 2015. Knowledge-based question answering using the semantic embedding space. *Expert Systems with Applications*, 42(23):9086–9104.

Wen-tau Yih, Ming-Wei Chang, Xiaodong He, and Jianfeng Gao. 2015. Semantic parsing via staged query graph generation: Question answering with knowledge base. In *Proceedings of the 53rd Annual Meeting of the Association for Computational Linguistics and the 7th International Joint Conference on Natural Language Processing (Volume 1: Long Papers)*, pages 1321–1331, Beijing, China. Association for Computational Linguistics.

Wenpeng Yin, Mo Yu, Bing Xiang, Bowen Zhou, and Hinrich Schütze. 2016. Simple question answering by attentive convolutional neural network. In *Proceedings of COLING 2016, the 26th International Conference on Computational Linguistics: Technical Papers*, pages 1746–1756, Osaka, Japan. The COLING 2016 Organizing Committee.

Yuyu Zhang, Hanjun Dai, Zornitsa Kozareva, Alexander J. Smola, and Le Song. 2018. Variational reasoning for question answering with knowledge graph. In *Proceedings of the Thirty-Second AAAI Conference on Artificial Intelligence, (AAAI-18), the 30th innovative Applications of Artificial Intelligence (IAAI-18), and the 8th AAAI Symposium on Educational Advances in Artificial Intelligence (EAAI-18), New Orleans, Louisiana, USA, February 2-7, 2018*, pages 6069–6076. AAAI Press.

Fast Bilingual Grapheme-To-Phoneme Conversion

Hwa-Yeon Kim , Jong-Hwan Kim , Jae-Min Kim
NAVER Corp., South Korea
{hwayeon.kim, jhwan.kim, kjm.kim} @navercorp.com

Abstract

Autoregressive transformer (ART)-based grapheme-to-phoneme (G2P) models have been proposed for bi/multilingual text-to-speech systems. Although they have achieved great success, they suffer from high inference latency in real-time industrial applications, especially processing long sentence. In this paper, we propose a fast and high-performance bilingual G2P model. For fast and exact decoding, we used a non-autoregressive structured transformer-based architecture and data augmentation for predicting output length. Our model achieved better performance than that of the previous autoregressive model and about 2700% faster inference speed.

1 Introduction

Speech synthesis has been applied in various real-world services, such as AI speaker, car navigation guidance and news article-reading services in each language. Grapheme-to-phoneme (G2P) module convert text to phonemes in text-to-speech (TTS) system. G2P conversion has been studied in various ways, including rules, dictionaries, statistical-based methods (Deri and Knight, 2016) and neural network-based methods (Yolchuyeva et al., 2021; Sun et al., 2019a; Kim et al., 2021; Choi et al., 2021). Currently, monolingual G2P research is the most conducted, although recently bilingual or multilingual G2P research is also being actively performed (Clematide and Makarov, 2021; Yu et al., 2020; Bansal et al., 2020; Gautam et al., 2021). Most of the proposed models with high performance are based on autoregressive transformers (A.Vaswani et al., 2017) in both monolingual and multilingual G2P. However, these models suffer from high inference latency, which is sometimes unacceptable for real-time TTS applications that generate long speech synthesis sounds, such as news sentences. A previous study (Kim et al., 2021) used a simple model structure with a few features and batch inference for fast inference speed; however, there were limitations in specific language characteristics.

In this paper, we propose a high-performance bilingual G2P model that has an fast inference speed that enables real-time service. For an efficient expression for each language, byte-level representation input and a language index are used as the main inputs, and for fast decoding, the transformer model is based on a non-autoregressive structured decoder. Because the length of the estimated output used in the non-autoregressive structured decoder has a great impact on the G2P accuracy, a sub-network and a data augmentation technique are used to better infer the output length. In addition, we experimented with the difference between training the whole input unit (sentence) and the tokenized unit.

We conducted experiments for different language systems, such as European which have a small number of graphemes and East Asian ones which have a large number of graphemes. We chose two languages for bilingual G2P model; English and Korean. Experimental results showed that, despite significantly losing speed, our non-autoregressive transformer-conditional random field (NART-CRF) based G2P model achieved better performance than those of previous ART models. When it is applied to an actual service system, in addition to the speed and high accuracy applicable to real-world TTS applications, it is possible to generate the phonemes of several languages with one model.

2 Related work

2.1 Multilingual G2P

Recent works propose various methods for multilingual natural language processing (NLP) tasks such as machine translation (Aharoni et al., 2019; Zhang et al., 2020) and language model (Pires et al., 2019). A few multilingual G2P studies are also in

Proceedings of NAACL-HLT 2022: Industry Track Papers, pages 289 - 296
July 10-15, 2022 ©2022 Association for Computational Linguistics

progress. The benchmarks for multilingual g2p is provides and utilized various G2P models : A neural transducer system using an imitation learning paradigm (Ashby et al., 2021), studies building an ensemble of several different sequence models (Vesik et al., 2020; Gautam et al., 2021; Clematide and Makarov, 2021). Meanwhile, there is a neural multilingual G2P model with byte-level input representation (Yu et al., 2020). On this wise, most of the autoregressive sequence models are used to learn phonemes of various languages. But, the autoregressive factorization makes the inference process hard to be parallelized as the results are generated token by token sequentially. Therefore, these models have limitations in applying them to real-world processing services, especially dealing with long sentence, because the inference time increases linearly with the length of the generated phoneme output.

2.2 Fast decoding

For various tasks, the transformer (A.Vaswani et al., 2017) model achieve good performance. However, the autoregressive method suffer from high inference latency. Therefore, there are several studies to solve this problem. Since decoding takes a high inference latency, the deep-encoder and shallow-decoder architecture is proposed and it improve the inference speed (Kasai et al., 2021). For parallelism, the non-autoregressive sequence models are proposed and applied it to the machine translation and speech synthesis (Gu et al., 2018; Sun et al., 2019b). The non-autoregressive sequence models improve the inference speed; however, they cannot get results as good as their autoregressive counterparts that generate each token in the target sentence independently. To decode token co-occurrence be guaranteed, a structured inference module is incorporated in the non-autoregressive decoder to directly model the multi-modal distribution of phoneme sequences (Sun et al., 2019b). In this study, we follow the structure (Sun et al., 2019b) to apply G2P task and achieve great performance.

3 The proposed model

This section describes the proposed model for fast bilingual G2P conversion. The overall structure of the model is shown in Figure 1.

3.1 Byte-level representation input and sentence/token-level input

Following the method of Yu et al. (2020), the proposed model uses an input with a byte-level representation for the efficient representation of multiple languages. Each character is expressed at the byte level based on the UTF-8 encoding. This expression can reduce the size of the input vocabulary, and the byte-level vocabulary cardinality is constrained to be equal to or smaller than 256. In this study, two experiments were performed: processing of the entire sentence as the input, and tokenizing of the sentence and processing of each token as one batch.

Processing of the entire sentence as the input : The input sentence encoded at the byte level and the language index of the input are used as the inputs to the model. Using the entire sentence as the input is good for inferring the correct pronunciation sequence according to the meaning because it learns by considering the context of the entire sentence together. On the other hand, if the dataset is divided by language, as in this experiment, it is necessary to separate and process the language-mixed sentences for each language when inferring the pronunciation sequence.

Processing of the input token unit : First, a given input sentence is divided into tokens using an appropriate tokenizer for the language. In the case of Korean and English, a tokenizer that separates the space-delimited orthographic words (tokens) was used in this study. Here, in the case of Korean, there is a point to be particularly careful about. The pronunciation of the first syllable or the last syllable of a token may change depending on whether the tokens are read after a break or not. Therefore additional features were needed to connect the separated tokens naturally in the final G2P results. Following the method of Kim et al. (2021), we used the phonological phrasing information between tokens. Moreover, for the first and last syllables of token to be naturally connected with each front/next token, information on the ending or beginning of the part to be connected is required. For example, for the input as shown in the Figure 2, each token's input elements in the input sentence are as follows: A language index, a input token x_t to be converted to a byte-level representation (part *a*), two phonological phrasing information on both sides of the token (part *b*), a last *jaso* (orthographic phoneme segments) in front token x_{t-1} (part *c*) and a first

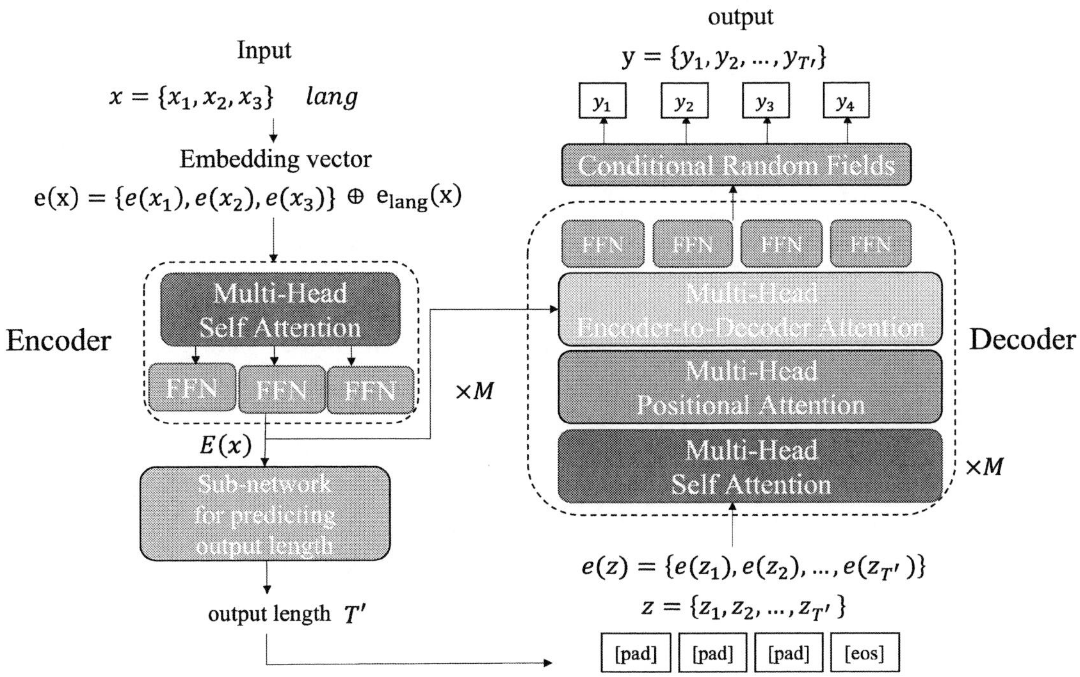

Figure 1: The overview of proposed model

~ 모바일^c < *clitic* >^{b} 앱을^a < *ap* >^{b} 통^d 해서 ~

(Means : through the mobile app)

Language index = Korean

Figure 2: The example of composition for each token in a sentence

jaso in next token x_{t+1} (part *d*). They are concatenated with each token, and the entire token in the sentence is composed of one batch, so that it learns and infers at once. In this way, if it is configured in token units, it is not necessary to separate the language-mixed sentences for each language and compose the input, and it is possible to infer faster with relatively short input and output lengths. On the other hand, tokenizers for each language are required, and there is a limit for including context information rather than the entire sentence unit.

3.2 Transformer-based structured decoding model for G2P conversion

The model design follows the NART architecture with CRFs. For more information on the model, see A.Vaswani et al. (2017); Gu et al. (2018); Sun et al. (2019b).

NART-based model : Like in the ART model, the encoder of our model takes the embeddings of the input tokens and their additional features as the input and generates a contextual representation. Following the decoder in NART-CRF, the decoder independently decodes each pronunciation token given a sequence length T' and a decoder input z. It also uses the padding symbol "<pad>" followed by the end-of-sentence symbol "<eos>" as the decoder input. The transformer model utilizes multi-head self-attention and multi-head encoder-decoder attention. In contrast to the ART model, multi-head positional attention in the decoder is also used to model local word orders within a sentence or a token. In our model, each decoder layer refers to the output of each encoder layer with the same depth. It follows the model architecture of Yu et al. (2020) and performs better than the existing architecture in our experiment. The position-wise feedforward network consists of a two-layer linear transformation with a ReLU activation function and is applied after using multi-head attention in both the encoder and the decoder.

Structured inference module: Like in Sun et al. (2019b), a linear-chain CRF is incorporated into the decoder part to model richer structural dependencies. The CRF module can be jointly trained end to end with neural networks using a negative log-likelihood loss L_{CRF}. In the context of G2P

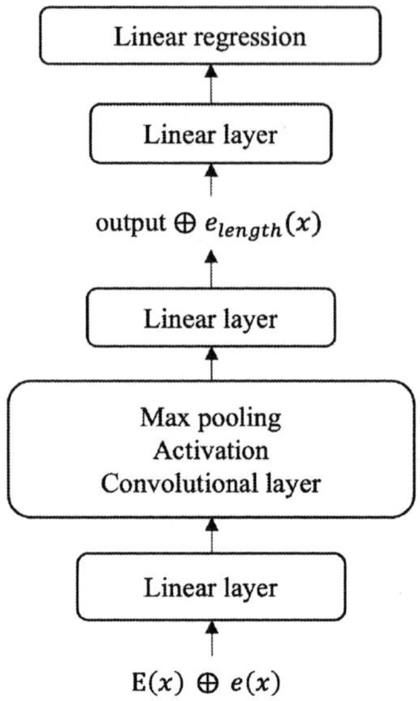

Figure 3: The sub-network for predicting and using output length

conversion, we use a "phoneme" for the decoder output and decode its highest scoring sequence.

3.3 Predicting output length for decoder

In the NART-CRF structure, an input of a specific length is used as the input z of the decoder. The length of this input has a great influence on inferring the final output of the model. Through several experiments, we realized that it is not easy to predict the exact output length using only the encoder output. Even if it is long or short by a small number such as 1 or 2, the pronunciation sequence can be generated incorrectly, which greatly affects the performance. So, while adding a layer or sub-network to predict the output length T', we applied a data augmentation technique that can supplement the decoding process despite incorrect prediction values.

Sub-network for predicting the output length In the G2P task, the prediction of the input and output lengths of the decoder has a greater effect on the overall accuracy than that in the machine translation task (Sun et al., 2019b). We added a sub-network to infer the phoneme sequence length exactly, as shown in Figure 3. The sub-network follows the model proposed in Yang et al. (2020); however, it differs in the prediction of an output length that is continuous in nature using linear regression rather than softmax at the end of the model.

Data augmentation As mentioned above, the length of the sentence is very important in the phoneme sequence of the G2P model. Therefore, even if the sentence length is incorrectly predicted, it should still be used to generate a phoneme sequence with the correct length. Thus, we trained model to guess correctly actual output length by padding by the length that exceeds the actual length even in a sequence that is a little longer than the actual output length. To this end, data augmentation was performed by pairing an output with an output length of 1 or 2 longer in addition to the existing dataset and filled with a padding tag with an existing input.

Joint training with regression loss: Our training loss L is the sum of the CRF negative log-likelihood loss L_{CRF} and the mean square error (MSE) of the sub-network as loss L_{length}. :

$$L = L_{CRF} + L_{length} = -\log P(y|x) + (T - T')^2 \quad (1)$$

4 Experiments

4.1 Experimental settings

We collected scripts of domains used in real-world services and constructed a Korean and English G2P dataset by labeling it from speech. A voice actor read a Korean or English script naturally, and taggers dictated the phonological phrasing information and pronunciations exactly as they heard them. We used 20,000 sentences in each language for training and 200 samples in each language for testing. Each sentence consisted of an average of 12.45 tokens (words in English and *Eojoel* in Korean) and the average length of output for each token is 5 and the maximum is 29. The phonological phrasing information used in this model is mainly composed of the intonation phrase (IP), accent phrase (AP), clitic, and end of sentence (sb). IP refers to reading with a pause, and AP refers to a delimitation. The size of input vocabulary of bilingual was 110 and the number of phonemes was 42 in Korean and 39 in English. We used the default network architecture of the original base transformer (A.Vaswani et al., 2017), which consists of a four-layer encoder and a four-layer decoder.

4.2 Inference

In the training process, to generate an accurate phoneme sequence, we performed data augmentation so that the pad was filled even when a length

exceeding the actual length was predicted. In fact, the model predicted a length that was a few smaller or longer than the actual output length. So, we bias the predicted length so that the decoder's input is made longer than the actual output length in most cases. It is intended that the pad will eventually be filled in to generate a phoneme sequence of the correct length.
We evaluate the average per-sentence decoding latency with a single NVIDIA Tesla V100 GPU for the ART-G2P and our models to measure the speedup.

4.3 Evaluation

The evaluation metrics used in the experiment were the phoneme error rate (PER), accuracy (Acc) and accuracy of length (L-Acc). PER, as used in the evaluation of the G2P model performance (Yu et al., 2020) , is the Levenshtein distance between the predicted phoneme sequences and the reference phoneme sequences, divided by the number of phonemes in the reference pronunciation. Acc is the percentage of sentences in which the predicted phoneme sequence exactly matches the reference pronunciation. L-Acc is the percentage of length in which the predicted phoneme sequence exactly matches the reference pronunciation sequence's length.

4.4 Results : ART vs NART

Table 1 shows the performance of the ART (Yu et al., 2020) and the proposed G2P model with a sentence- or token-level input. While ART-G2P shows high accuracy, the inference time is very long. When time was measured for each area, the average encoding and decoding time was 40/66ms, but since ART continuously decodes as much as the output length, the time increases linearly as much as the output length. On the other hand, the proposed NART-CRF based model trained at sentence-level showed about 22 times faster speed than ART-G2P; but, it was less accurate than ART-G2P. The model trained in token unit showed higher accuracy with about 27 times faster inference speed, confirming that it is a fast and accurate model structure.
It is analyzed that the proposed model has outperforms ART in the Korean dataset, because it refers to the phonological phrasing information. In the case of the proposed model, the token-level showed higher performance in both languages because the shorter input length is more advantageous in predicting the output length. When looking at the distribution of the difference between the actual length and the predicted length, in the case of sentence units, there was a large deviation, which caused a lot of errors.

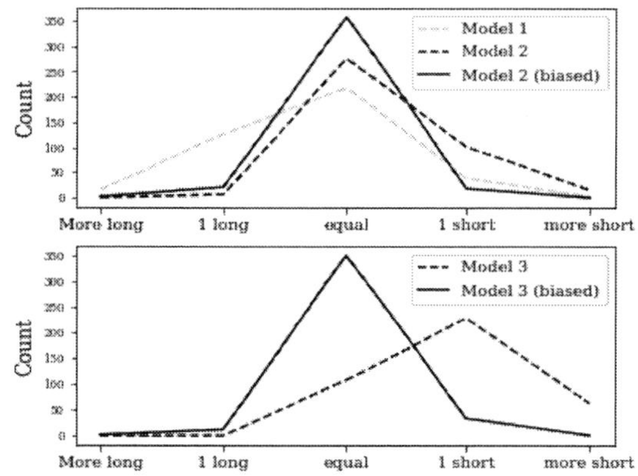

Figure 4: Results with predicted output length (biased or not)

4.5 Ablation study about augmentation

The Table 2 is an ablation study showing whether the method described in Section 3.3 is effective. The compared models are three models trained at sentence-level : *Model 1* incorporating regression layer for predicting output length in NART-CRF, *Model 2* trained with data augmentation in the same structure as Model1, *Model 3* incorporating sub-network for predicting output length and trained with data augmentation. Figure 4 shows how much the predicted sentence length differs from the actual sentence length. Looking at the sentence length prediction result of Model 1, it is inferred a lot with approximations around the actual sentence length, so the sentence length accuracy is only 54.5%. Model 2 has a slightly higher value for accurately predicting the length than Model 1. Through this, it can be seen that data augmentation is effective in accurately predicting the length of a sentence by filling the "<pad>" tag even in sentences that are longer than the actual length. However, since data augmentation was performed only in cases of be longer, there are still cases in which it is not applied for shorter than actual length. Therefore we used the predicted sentence length with a bias of 2, and actually showed a big increase in performance. In the case of Model 3, the accuracy of length was very low at 27% because the sentence length was often predicted shorter than the actual length, but when the sentence length was

Model	Language	Acc (%)	PER (%)	Inference time (ms/sent)
ART-G2P	Merged	83.25	0.62	3830
	English	92.50	0.43	
	Korean	74.00	0.82	
Sentence-level NART-CRF G2P	Merged	81.00	0.64	177.15 (×22)
	English	84.50	0.72	
	Korean	77.50	0.56	
Token-level NART-CRF G2P	Merged	**87.75**	**0.43**	**140** (×27)
	English	**93.00**	**0.38**	
	Korean	**82.50**	**0.49**	

Table 1: The table shows results of the ART-G2P and proposed NART-CRF G2P models with sentence and token level training. We evaluate accuracy, PER of model and inference time in each language.

Model	Acc (%)	PER (%)	L-Acc (%)
Model 1 ; NART-CRF	48.75	2.91	54.5
Model 2 ; NART-CRF + augm	63.75	1.48	69.0
Model 2 + biased	**81.50**	0.80	**89.5**
Model 3 ; NART-CRF w/subNN + augm	24.50	4.22	27.0
Model 3 + biased	81.00	**0.64**	**87.8**

Table 2: The Ablation study about data augmentation and bias

biased during inference, the length prediction accuracy increased significantly. In fact, looking at the generated result, when the actual sentence length is 14 and the biased inference sentence length is 17, the pronunciation sequence is generated as $y = \{y_0, y_1, ..., y_{13}, pad, pad, pad\}$. If "<pad>" tags are deleted in post-processing, the inference result and the correct answer were matched. The proposed method of biasing the sentence length predicted in inference and data augmentation make predict the correct length through an additional decoding process even at the predicted length as an approximation of the actual sentence length. The proposed method of biasing the sentence length predicted in inference and data augmentation make predict the correct length through an additional decoding process even at the predicted length as an approximation of the actual sentence length.

4.6 In real-time TTS application

We applied it to the industrial TTS system. In our system, bilingual TTS attempts to generate a pronunciation sequence based on a specific language for an input with mixed languages. To this end, numbers and symbols are normalized based on a specific language, and each language goes through processing such as estimation of phonological phrasing information for each language. In bilingual G2P, the phoneme sequence is generated with the grapheme processed for each language for the input with mixed languages and then connect the results.

We utilized the Open Neural Network Exchange (ONNX) [1] to apply to a TTS system running in a CPU environment[2]. ONNX is an open-source machine-independent format and widely used for exchanging neural network models. First, our model implemented in tensorflow was exported to ONNX format, and inference was performed using Onnxruntime [3]. Onnxruntime is a cross-platform inference and training machine-learning accelerator. It performs hardware acceleration through graph optimization, graph partition and then distributed runner.

We applied our model to a real-time processing system and inferred at an average speed of $40ms/sent$ for 1000 sentences. In addition, we measured the Real Time Factor (RTF) when only the monolingual G2P module used in the existing system was changed to our model. As our Unit-selection Text-to-Speech (UTS) system, it is judged that real-time processing is possible only when the volume of processing is less than 0.1RT. When 500 sentences

[1] https://github.com/onnx/onnx

[2] Intel(R) Xeon(R) Silver 4114 CPU @ 2.20GHz (40 cores)

[3] https://onnxruntime.ai

were processed for each language, 0.026 to 0.037 RTx for Korean and 0.033 to 0.057 RTx for English were measured, confirming that real-time processing was possible.

5 Conclusion

In this study, a structure of a NART-CRF was proposed for fast bilingual G2P with real-time processing. For bilingual, input of byte representation was used, and additional sub-network and data augmentation techniques were used for accurate output length inference. The proposed model showed higher accuracy than the existing ART-G2P and at the same time showed about 27 times faster inference speed. In addition, when applied to an industrial TTS system, the speed was improved to a level capable of real-time processing.

In future work, we will study a model with contextual information or representation of language model to solve some error cases caused by lack of context. Furthermore, we will experiments with fast "multilingual" G2P by expanding the language types to Chinese, Japanese, and European languages. As a result of testing two different language system (i.e. European and East Asian), It is expected that expansion of languages, which others in same language group, will be possible. Additionally, considering the accents and tones used in languages such as English and Chinese, and training on an unbalanced dataset remain issues to be resolved.

References

Roee Aharoni, Melvin Johnson, and Orhan Firat. 2019. Massively multilingual neural machine translation. In *proc. Annual Conference of the North American Chapter of the Association for Computational Linguistics*.

Lucas F.E. Ashby, Travis M. Bartley, Simon Clematide, Luca Del Signore, Cameron Gibson, Kyle Gorman, Yeonju Lee-Sikka, Peter Makarov, Aidan Malanoski, Sean Miller, Omar Ortiz, Reuben Raff, Arundhati Sengupta, Bora Seo, Yulia Spektor, and Winnie Yan. 2021. Results of the second sigmorphon shared task on multilingual grapheme-to-phoneme conversion. In *proc. The Seventeenth SIGMORPHON Workshop on Computational Research in Phonetics, Phonology, and Morphology*, pages 115–125.

A.Vaswani, N.Shazeer, N.Parmar, J.Uszkoreit, L.Jones, A.N. Gomez, L. Kaiser, and I. Polosukhin. 2017. Attention is all you need. In *proc. The 31st Conference on Neural Information Processing Systems (NIPS 2017)*.

Shubham Bansal, Arijit Mukherjee, Sandeepkumar Satpal, and Rupeshkumar Mehta. 2020. On improving code mixed speech synthesis with mixlingual grapheme-to-phoneme model. In *proc. INTERSPEECH 2020*, pages 2957–2961.

Eunbi Choi, Hwa-Yeon Kim, Jong-Hwan Kim, and Jae-Min Kim. 2021. Label embedding for chinese grapheme-to-phoneme conversion. In *proc. INTERSPEECH 2021*.

Simon Clematide and Peter Makarov. 2021. Cluzh at sigmorphon 2021 shared task on multilin- gual grapheme-to-phoneme conversion: variations on a baseline. In *proc. The 18th SIGMORPHON Workshop on Computational Research in Phonetics, Phonology, and Morphology*.

A. Deri and K. Knight. 2016. Grapheme-to-phoneme models for (almost) any language. In *proc. the 54th Annual Meeting of the Association for Computational Linguistics*.

Vasundhara Gautam, Wang Yau Li, Zafarullah Mahmood, Frederic Mailhot, Shreekantha Nadig, Riqiang Wang, and Nathan Zhang. 2021. Avengers, ensemble! benefits of ensembling in grapheme-to-phoneme prediction. In *proc. The 18th SIGMORPHON Workshop on Computational Research in Phonetics, Phonology, and Morphology*.

Jiatao Gu, James Bradbury, Caiming Xiong, Victor OK Li, and Richard Socher. 2018. Non-autoregressive neural machine translation. In *proc. The Sixth International Conference on Learning Representations*.

Jungo Kasai, Nikolaos Pappas, Hao Peng, James Cross, and Noah A. Smith. 2021. Deep encoder, shallow decoder: Reevaluating non-autoregressive machine translation. In *proc. The Ninth International Conference on Learning Representations*.

Hwa-Yeon Kim, Jong-Hwan Kim, and Jae-Min Kim. 2021. Nn-kog2p: A novel grapheme-to-phoneme model for korean language. In *proc. 2021 International Conference on Acoustics, Speech, and Signal Processing (ICASSP)*.

Telmo Pires, Eva Schlinger, and Dan Garrette. 2019. How multilingual is multilingual bert? In *proc. the 57th Annual Meeting of the Association for Computational Linguistics*.

H. Sun, X. Tan, J. Gan, H. Liu, S. Zhao, T. Qin, and T. Liu. 2019a. Token-level ensemble distillation for grapheme-to-phoneme conversion. In *proc. INTERSPEECH 2019*.

Zhiqing Sun, Zhuohan Li, Haoqing Wang, Di He, Zi Lin, and Zhi-Hong Deng. 2019b. Fast structured decoding for sequence models. In *proc. The 33rd Conference on Neural Information Processing Systems (NeurIPS 2019)*, pages 2957–2961.

Kaili Vesik, Muhammad Abdul-Mageed, and Miikka Silfverberg. 2020. One model to pronounce them all: Multilingual grapheme-to-phoneme conversion with a transformer ensemble. In *proc. The 17th SIGMORPHON Workshop on Computational Research in Phonetics, Phonology, and Morphology*, pages 146–152.

Zijian Yang, Yingbo Gao, Weiyue Wang, and Hermann Ney. 2020. Predicting and using target length in neural machine translation. In *proc. the 1st Conference of the Asia-Pacific Chapter of the Association for Computational Linguistics and the 10th International Joint Conference on Natural Language Processing*.

S. Yolchuyeva, G. Németh, and B. Gyires-Tóth. 2021. Transformer based grapheme-to-phoneme conversion. In *proc. INTERSPEECH 2019*.

Mingzhi Yu, Hieu Duy Nguyen, Alex Sokolov, Jack Lepird, Kanthashree Mysore Sathyendra, Samridhi Choudhary, Athanasios Mouchtaris, and Siegfried Kunzmann. 2020. Multilingual grapheme-to-phoneme conversion with byte representation. In *proc. ICASSP*, pages 33–40.

Biao Zhang, Philip Williams, Ivan Titov, and Rico Sennrich. 2020. Improving massively multilingual neural machine translation and zero-shot translation. In *proc. the 58th Annual Meeting of the Association for Computational Linguistics*.

Knowledge Extraction From Texts Based on Wikidata

Anastasia Shimorina **Johannes Heinecke** **Frédéric Herledan**

Orange, Lannion, France

firstname.lastname@orange.com

Abstract

This paper presents an effort within our company of developing knowledge extraction pipeline for English, which can be further used for constructing an entreprise-specific knowledge base. We present a system consisting of entity detection and linking, coreference resolution, and relation extraction based on the Wikidata schema. We highlight existing challenges of knowledge extraction by evaluating the deployed pipeline on real-world data. We also make available a database, which can serve as a new resource for sentential relation extraction, and we underline the importance of having balanced data for training classification models[1].

1 Introduction

Knowledge extraction aims at discovering semantic information from texts using a knowledge representation schema. This discovered information is used to build a knowledge base (KB), which is a useful resource for structured information. KBs can play an important role in many tasks and systems: domain question-answering systems, recommender systems, natural language generation systems, search result enhancement, and many others.

Entreprise knowledge bases have recently gained a lot of attention (Singhal, 2012; Liu et al., 2019a; Song et al., 2019; Dong et al., 2020). They allow to transform heterogeneous data, both public and private, into knowledge representations, which are effectively used for specific applications.

In this paper, we report on a preliminary step for building a company-specific KB, namely how to extract knowledge from texts in the form of (*subject, relation, object*) triples . We develop a system consisting of several components: entity detection and linking, coreference resolution, and relation extraction (RE). For the first two components we use off-the-shelf tools, whereas for RE we develop our own module. Our RE module is based on Wikidata (Vrandečić and Krötzsch, 2014), the existing KB, which contains many pre-defined relations. With the goal to cover as many relations from Wikidata as possible, we create a database, which merges several datasets for RE and distributes them in a standardised format. We make use of this database to create different training scenarios for the RE task and show how balancing existing RE datasets impacts the task performance. We finally evaluate our knowledge extraction system on our company's internal data by human evaluation. Our system is deployed and is intended to be used on real-world data within the company.

Since we apply state-of-the-art NLP techniques, it is equally interesting to see the limitations of current approaches witnessed by our evaluation.

To summarise, the main contributions of this paper are the following:

- We provide insights based on real-world texts coming from industry, which allow to benchmark state-of-the-art systems on real-world data.
- We construct a database with cleaned and homogeneous datasets for sentence-based relation extraction from English texts.
- We train several models for the relation extraction task based on different training data and show how dataset balancing affects the task.
- We discuss some positive and negative results: what did and did not work in a real-life scenario.

2 Related Work

The literature on Information/Knowledge Extraction is incredibly vast (Martinez-Rodriguez et al., 2020). There exist many approaches for information extraction from raw texts. Here we describe

[1]The relation extraction database is available here: https://github.com/Shimorina/relation-extraction-db-wikidata

Proceedings of NAACL-HLT 2022: Industry Track Papers, pages 297 - 304
July 10-15, 2022 ©2022 Association for Computational Linguistics

text	The abbreviation GDPR stands for "General Data Protection Regulation". The GDPR governs the processing of personal data within the territory of the European Union. ...
triples	(GDPR$_{Q1172506}$, instance of$_{P31}$, abbreviation$_{Q102786}$)
	(General Data Protection Regulation$_{Q1172506}$, short name$_{P1813}$, GDPR$_{Q1172506}$)
	(GDPR$_{Q1172506}$, main subject$_{P921}$, personal data$_{Q3702971}$)
	(GDPR$_{Q1172506}$, applies to jurisdiction$_{P1001}$, European Union$_{Q458}$)

Table 1: The beginning of text from the internal wiki page "GDPR", and triples which correspond to the text. Wikidata IDs are given after subjects, objects, and relations. In the example all entities are linked to Wikidata, however it is not always possible.

different approaches for RE, the main subtask of information extraction.

We can differentiate between binary and n-ary relation extraction (Bach and Badaskar, 2007), which link two or more entities respectively. For triple extraction, most of research work concentrates on binary relation extraction (Sakor et al., 2020), however there are also approaches based on n-ary relation extraction, or semantic parsing, where different semantic formalisms are used. Frame Semantics, PropBank, Discourse Representation Structures, Abstract Meaning Representations were used to extract triples from texts (Gangemi et al., 2017; Fossati et al., 2018; Mihindukulasooriya et al., 2020).

Another important difference in RE approaches is the use of an open or closed relation set. A closed, pre-defined set of relations is targeted in relation classification systems, where either a custom pool of relations is used (Gábor et al., 2018) or the set is defined by an underlying KB, such as Wikidata, Freebase, DBpedia, etc. The paradigm opposite to closed RE is Open Information Extraction (Etzioni et al., 2008, OpenIE). OpenIE aims at extracting domain-independent relations from large corpora without using a predefined schema. OpenIE systems may extract redundant information due to lexical variations in texts, so while using this paradigm for knowledge extraction, a process called canonicalisation is used to reconciliate their output with a given KB (Lin et al., 2020).

We adopt the knowledge extraction approach with binary RE on a closed set of relations from Wikidata. We hope that this choice will allow us to facilitate entreprise-specific KB construction in the future.

3 Data

Our company has an internal wiki in English where different terms are explained. Those terms can belong to some general knowledge (e.g., *climate change, Agile software development*) or can be specific to the company. The wiki terms span over several areas: from human resources, marketing, legal affairs to computer science and information technology. Those wiki documents, while having valuable information for the company, represent unstructured text with no linguistic annotation; they sometimes exhibit some information overlap or they can have related term descriptions span over several pages not linked between each other. An example of the beginning of such document describing a general term is displayed in Table 1. The length of a document is variable: it can range from several to a few hundred sentences.

Our motivation to explore internal documents is as follows: we would like to represent the information in a structured way, that would allow reasoning and better understanding of the company knowledge. Moreover, a potential KB may serve in different downstream applications developed in the company: question answering, task-oriented dialogue, knowledge management.

We chose Wikidata as our initial KB schema because of its steady growth within last years and increased community participation. The Wikidata schema may be eventually refined to better suit our needs in the future. For instance, we might add new relations, not yet defined in Wikidata.

4 Approach Overview

We aim to extract RDF (Resource Description Framework) triples in the form *(subject, relation, object)* from text.

We develop a classical pipeline for triple extraction: sentence splitting, entity detection and linking, coreference resolution, and relation classification.

1. Text is preprocessed and is split into sentences with pySBD (Sadvilkar and Neumann, 2020).

dataset	# instances	# R types	% neg.	human checks	license
FewRel (Han et al., 2018)	56,000	80	0%	yes	MIT
T-REx (Elsahar et al., 2018)	12,081,023	652	0%	no	CC BY-SA 4.0
DocRED (Yao et al., 2019)	778,914	96	0%	no (yes*)	MIT
WikiFact (Goodrich et al., 2019)	33,628,338	934	92%	no	CC BY 4.0
Wiki20m (Han et al., 2020)	738,463	81	60%	no	MIT
WebRED (Ormandi et al., 2021)	107,819	385	54%	yes	CC BY 4.0
our database (DB)	47,390,557	1,022	66%	yes/no	CC BY-SA 4.0

Table 2: Summary of the datasets used in the database. R types is a number of relation types including P0 and NA; neg. is a percentage of negative examples, i.e. examples with no relation detected or unknown relation; human checks correspond to whether some human checks were carried out to construct a dataset. *The large part of DocRED is collected using distant supervision; 2.68% of the dataset instances were verified by humans.

2. Entities are detected and linked to Wikidata IDs with GENRE (Cao et al., 2021). We chose GENRE because it identifies common nouns as well as proper nouns and links them to Wikidata. Common noun identification was important for our case, since the texts under consideration often describe common noun terms rather than named entities, such as geographical locations, persons, which frequently are the target of other popular named entity recognisers. GENRE is also able to identify entities without linking them to Wikidata. That feature was useful for us while handling texts about company-specific named entities and abbreviations.

3. Coreference is resolved with neuralcoref from HuggingFace[2].

4. For each pair of entities (e_1, e_2) present in a sentence, a Wikidata relation is predicted using our relation classifier. It predicts whether a relation exists, and if yes, which one.

The desired output of the pipeline is shown in Table 1.

While for the steps 1-3, we used off-the-shelf libraries, for relation extraction we developed an in-house solution, which is described in Section 5.

5 Relation Extraction

RE is a notoriously difficult task because relations, as compared to entities, are not often expressed explicitly, i.e. it is hard to find a precise verbal expression. Moreover, relations can be expressed in many different ways in a text. RE usually works well when it covers a limited set of well-defined relations. We, on the other hand, have no explicit relations, defined on our data. Our goal is to explore texts to possibly find some relations coming from the external closed set (Wikidata).

Relations in Wikidata are numerous. There are around 9,500 relations as of January 2022[3]. However, most of them are not exploitable in ordinary texts, since a lot of them are about some ID numbers in different catalogues and libraries, e.g. IMDb ID (P345), Swiss parliament ID (P1307), etc. We estimate that about 1,500-2,000 relations can be usable in everyday texts. To explore relations in Wikidata, we use available datasets for RE that are based on Wikidata relations. It means that we could not use other popular datasets for RE such as NYT (Riedel et al., 2010) or TACRED (Zhang et al., 2017), since they use other knowledge bases.

5.1 Database

Within the RE task modelling, our goal was to have as many relations from Wikidata as possible to increase the probability to find relations in our data. The issue with most datasets for RE is that relation types are few. So we proceeded to create a database (DB)—a common resource where several RE datasets are merged.

We preprocessed 6 existing datasets to adapt them to sentence-based RE (see Table 2): FewRel (Han et al., 2018), T-REx (Elsahar et al., 2018), DocRED (Yao et al., 2019), WikiFact (Goodrich et al., 2019), Wiki20m (Han et al., 2020), and WebRED (Ormandi et al., 2021). Initially these datasets were developed for different purposes and with different methods. Most of them were collected using

[2] https://github.com/huggingface/neuralcoref

[3] https://www.wikidata.org/w/index.php?title=Special:ListProperties

instance	relation	label
SUBJ{Under Pressure} is a 1981 song by Queen and OBJ{David Bowie}.	P676	lyrics by
Official figures showed there were 25 million baptised Anglicans in OBJ{England} and SUBJ{Wales}.	P0	no relation

Table 3: Examples of database instances where the subject and object are marked with special symbols in the text. Labels correspond to Wikidata relation labels.

distant supervision (Mintz et al., 2009), afterwards some of them were verified by humans. After merging those datasets, we obtain a dataset with 1,022 unique Wikidata relation types including the relation 'P0' (called negative relation), which means "the absence of relation" between the designated subject and object, and 'NA', which defines an unknown relation. The main advantage of the created DB is to have a homogeneous dataset where an instance is a sentence with a subject and an object identified and a relation between them (see examples in Table 3). Apart from this main information, the DB stores some additional features that were available in the original datasets, e.g. Wikidata IDs for subjects and objects, a source document for the sentence, etc. If training/validation/test split was provided for a dataset, we did not include test splits in the DB to reduce possible overuse of test data by future users. We also ensure that datasets coming from the same research groups do not have an overlap by deleting duplicate items.

The DB is easy and fast to query to obtain a sample of desired data: for example, choosing the instances that were verified by humans, choosing the instances expressing a particular relation, etc. We hope that the DB will serve the community by providing an easy access to RE datasets standardised for the sentence-based RE task. We will make it available upon acceptance.

5.2 Training Data

While most RE datasets were collected automatically, WebRED presents a cleaned dataset with the most relation coverage, so we use it as a main source for training and testing our RE models. We also know that around 50% of examples are negative examples in WebRED, i.e. examples with 'P0', so we paid special attention to that while constructing our training data. We used four collections of training data to develop different models for the RE component of our pipeline:

1. **WebRED**. It is the original dataset, called WebRED$_{H2+1}$ in Ormandi et al. (2021). The training data contains 383 relations (classes) for relation classification; there are 2 classes less than shown in Table 2 because they happened to appear only in the validation part.

2. **WebRED-balanced**. WebRED, as it is also often the case with other RE datasets, is largely imbalanced: 30 most frequent relation types cover more than 90% instances in the dataset. So for each relation that has less than 500 examples we tried to add more examples from other corpora present in the DB to reach 500 examples per relation if possible. This training data has 385 classes. After adding the underrepresented relations, 30 most common relation types account for 43% of instances in the dataset.

3. **DB-500**. In this case we aim to explore all the relation types present in the DB. For each relation (including P0 but excluding NA), we choose 500 training examples from different datasets, preferably choosing in the first place from the datasets where human annotation was present. However, a relation can still have less than 500 examples for training if there are not enough examples in the DB. This training data has 1,013 classes. From 1,022 relations present in the DB (Table 2), we removed NA and 8 Wikidata relations that existed in Wikidata during the time of dataset creation but that were subsequently removed from Wikidata.

4. **DB-500+neg**. As we test our approach on WebRED development data where negative examples constitute more than a half of the dataset, we add all the P0 examples from WebRED to DB-500. This training set equally has 1,013 classes.

Number of training instances for each training set is shown in Table 4. In what follows, we do not compare our results to the numbers reported in Ormandi et al. (2021), since the published dataset is different from the one used in their paper due to

training data	# examples	# classes	F1	P	R	F1*	P*	R*
WebRED	97,037	383	80.47	80.48	80.47	72.87	71.79	73.99
WebRED-balanced	215,937	385	85.65	85.90	85.39	80.02	77.86	82.30
DB-500	205,331	1,013	49.60	51.81	47.58	51.17	41.84	65.85
DB-500+neg	249,532	1,013	69.14	69.88	68.42	53.70	65.06	45.71

Table 4: Classification results on WebRED validation data. Classes include the P0 relation. F1: micro F1; P: precision; R: recall. * negative examples were removed from the evaluation data. When training with 5 random seeds, the standard deviation in the range of 0.14-0.59 was observed for the scores.

copyright[4].

5.3 Experimental Setup

Computational experiments. We treated RE as a multi-class classification problem where one relation must be predicted given a set of all possible relations. We fine-tune RoBERTa$_{\text{LARGE}}$ (Liu et al., 2019b) by adding a softmax classification layer, and we use the training data described in Section 5.2. Each training instance has special symbols around subject and object entities (see examples in Table 3). We use the simpletransformers library[5], which in its turn is built on the HuggingFace Transformers library (Wolf et al., 2020). The models are fine-tuned with the AdamW optimiser (Loshchilov and Hutter, 2019), with a learning rate of 0.00004, and a batch size of 32 for three epochs. Models were trained on two GPUs (GeForce GTX 1080 Ti); training time ranged from three to seven hours depending on the size of training data.

Evaluation was done on WebRED development data, which has 10,782 instances. We did not use WebRED test data, since we think of continuing our model development.

Human evaluation. We assessed the performance on our unlabeled data (see Section 3) with one human annotator. We focused on entity detection and linking, and RE. For entity recognition, one of the authors of the paper examined 52 first paragraphs of the wiki documents, where 550 entities and 457 linked entities were tagged by GENRE. For RE, the annotator examined 100 relations predicted by the model trained on DB-500+neg with the highest probability scores (more than 0.94). The relations were assessed on a 3-point scale (1: "bad", 2: "not sure; ambiguous case", 3: "good").

[4]See Ormandi et al. (2021) and https://github.com/google-research-datasets/WebRED

[5]https://github.com/ThilinaRajapakse/simpletransformers

6 Results

6.1 Entity Detection and Linking

	F1	P	R
Entity Detection	0.78	0.83	0.74
Entity Linking	0.71	0.79	0.64

Table 5: Manual evaluation. Micro F1, precision, recall for entity detection and linking on our data.

Manual evaluation of entity detection and linking based on GENRE without any fine-tuning on our data showed quite satisfying performance (Table 5). Entity detection reaches F1 of 0.78 with high precision of 0.83. Entity linking performs a bit worse with F1 of 0.71 and precision of 0.79. We conjecture that this relatively good performance may be due to the resemblance of our data (factual documents) to Wikipedia texts, which were used for training of the entity recogniser.

6.2 RE on WebRED Validation Data

Table 4 presents the results of the classification task. Models fine-tuned with WebRED show higher scores due to the lower number of classes. The highest micro F1 (85.65) is achieved with the balanced version of WebRED. Overall, all the metrics are higher for WebRED-balanced, which suggests that simply adding more examples for underrepresented classes could help notably increase overall performance. Models learned on DB have more classes to predict, hence lower scores comparing to WebRED-based fine-tuning. F1 drastically drops to 49.60 in the case of DB-500. DB-500+neg shows better results for all metrics as compared to DB-500; this finding highlights the importance of accounting for the majority negative class present in the evaluation data.

The performance without the negative examples, which represent more than 50% of the evaluation

sentence	relation	label	human ann.
Venture capitalists refers to specialized SUBJ{professional} OBJ{investors} who generally invest the money of institutional investors in early-stage startups.	P425	field of this occupation	bad
The Kaya equation was developed by SUBJ{Yoichi Kaya}, a Japanese energy economist, in his book OBJ{"Environment, Energy, and Economy: Strategies for Sustainability."}.	P800	notable work	good
Civil liberties refer to all OBJ{individual} and SUBJ{collective} rights and freedoms guaranteed by the State and regulated and protected by law.	P461	opposite of	not sure

Table 6: Human annotation of model predictions for the RE task.

data, is also shown (marked with *). We can see that in the case of WebRED the performance drops from 80.47 to 72.87 as measured by F1; the drop in WebRED-balanced is twice less — 5 points — due to the more balanced nature of the training data. Naturally, DB-500, being the dataset without a negative majority class, does not yield any drop: on the contrary, F1 increases from 49.60 to 51.17. DB-500+neg where a large set of negative examples were added exhibits the opposite trend: F1 goes down from 69.14 to 53.70.

Precision was a little bit higher than recall in the negative example evaluation setting (P vs. R); however, without the negative examples (P* vs. R*), recall was higher for WebRED, WebRED-balanced, and DB-500. In the case of DB-500+neg, precision is 65.06 while recall is lower (45.71).

6.3 RE on Real-World Data

Despite evaluating the relations with high probability scores, the human evaluation results are less confident: 70% of examples were tagged as "bad", 19% as "good", and 11% as "not sure; ambiguous case". Some examples of model prediction along with human ratings are shown in Table 6. Most of the examples annotated as "bad" are connected to entity detection, which was not pertinent for RE, as in the case of the first example in Table 6. Annotating an example as "not sure" usually means that the relation is not explicitly conveyed in a sentence, and it is hard to say whether it is present or not (see the third example). Overall, we witness that RE is a much more difficult task than entity detection and linking for existing methods when they are applied to the data that was never seen during training.

6.4 Final Pipeline and Time-Task Distribution

The described pipeline of knowledge extraction from text is deployed within our company and can be executed on any corpus of texts. It is hosted on a virtual machine with 4 CPU and 32 Gb of RAM, and all the pipeline components are ran on CPU. The time of response is not immediate, but in our use case we do not consider it important. To develop the pipeline, we spent most of the time working with data rather than developing models. Here is the approximate time-task distribution:

- 3 weeks: overall design (understanding the task and the needs, related work review, pipeline conception, looking at our data)
- 1 week: entity detection/linking and coreference
- 5 weeks: RE data preparation (search for corpora, collect, clean, prepare)
- 3 weeks: RE model development
- 1 week: entity detection/linking and RE evaluation
- 3 weeks: final pipeline deployment (code cleaning/refactoring, dockerisation, API, documentation)

7 Conclusion

In this paper we presented the pipeline for knowledge extraction from text based on Wikidata. We showed its utility on real-world data coming from our company's internal wiki. While entity detection and linking tools perform well on unseen data, RE still presents significant challenges. We developed the database for sentence-based RE with a large coverage of Wikidata relations, which we hope will be useful for the community. We also showed that balancing training data is crucial for good performance in RE.

In future work, we plan to improve the current pipeline, especially the RE component. We envisage several possible ways that can be explored: integrating syntactic parsing for better entity detection, using insights from semantic parsing to better represent sentence structure, and annotating some part of our data and using it for fine-tuning.

References

Nguyen Bach and Sameer Badaskar. 2007. A review of relation extraction. *Literature review for Language and Statistics II*, 2:1–15.

Nicola De Cao, Gautier Izacard, Sebastian Riedel, and Fabio Petroni. 2021. Autoregressive entity retrieval. In *International Conference on Learning Representations*.

Xin Luna Dong, Xiang He, Andrey Kan, Xian Li, Yan Liang, Jun Ma, Yifan Ethan Xu, Chenwei Zhang, Tong Zhao, Gabriel Blanco Saldana, Saurabh Deshpande, Alexandre Michetti Manduca, Jay Ren, Surender Pal Singh, Fan Xiao, Haw-Shiuan Chang, Giannis Karamanolakis, Yuning Mao, Yaqing Wang, Christos Faloutsos, Andrew McCallum, and Jiawei Han. 2020. *AutoKnow: Self-Driving Knowledge Collection for Products of Thousands of Types*, page 2724–2734. Association for Computing Machinery, New York, NY, USA.

Hady Elsahar, Pavlos Vougiouklis, Arslen Remaci, Christophe Gravier, Jonathon Hare, Frederique Laforest, and Elena Simperl. 2018. T-REx: A large scale alignment of natural language with knowledge base triples. In *Proceedings of the Eleventh International Conference on Language Resources and Evaluation (LREC 2018)*, Miyazaki, Japan. European Language Resources Association (ELRA).

Oren Etzioni, Michele Banko, Stephen Soderland, and Daniel S Weld. 2008. Open information extraction from the web. *Communications of the ACM*, 51(12):68–74.

Marco Fossati, Emilio Dorigatti, and Claudio Giuliano. 2018. N-ary relation extraction for simultaneous t-box and a-box knowledge base augmentation. *Semantic Web*, 9(4):413–439.

Kata Gábor, Davide Buscaldi, Anne-Kathrin Schumann, Behrang QasemiZadeh, Haïfa Zargayouna, and Thierry Charnois. 2018. SemEval-2018 task 7: Semantic relation extraction and classification in scientific papers. In *Proceedings of The 12th International Workshop on Semantic Evaluation*, pages 679–688, New Orleans, Louisiana. Association for Computational Linguistics.

Aldo Gangemi, Valentina Presutti, Diego Reforgiato Recupero, Andrea Giovanni Nuzzolese, Francesco Draicchio, and Misael Mongiovì. 2017. Semantic web machine reading with fred. *Semantic Web*, 8(6):873–893.

Ben Goodrich, Vinay Rao, Peter J. Liu, and Mohammad Saleh. 2019. Assessing the factual accuracy of generated text. In *Proceedings of the 25th ACM SIGKDD International Conference on Knowledge Discovery & Data Mining*, KDD '19, page 166–175, New York, NY, USA. Association for Computing Machinery.

Xu Han, Tianyu Gao, Yankai Lin, Hao Peng, Yaoliang Yang, Chaojun Xiao, Zhiyuan Liu, Peng Li, Jie Zhou, and Maosong Sun. 2020. More data, more relations, more context and more openness: A review and outlook for relation extraction. In *Proceedings of the 1st Conference of the Asia-Pacific Chapter of the Association for Computational Linguistics and the 10th International Joint Conference on Natural Language Processing*, pages 745–758, Suzhou, China. Association for Computational Linguistics.

Xu Han, Hao Zhu, Pengfei Yu, Ziyun Wang, Yuan Yao, Zhiyuan Liu, and Maosong Sun. 2018. FewRel: A large-scale supervised few-shot relation classification dataset with state-of-the-art evaluation. In *Proceedings of the 2018 Conference on Empirical Methods in Natural Language Processing*, pages 4803–4809, Brussels, Belgium. Association for Computational Linguistics.

Xueling Lin, Haoyang Li, Hao Xin, Zijian Li, and Lei Chen. 2020. Kbpearl: A knowledge base population system supported by joint entity and relation linking. *Proc. VLDB Endow.*, 13(7):1035–1049.

Danyang Liu, Ting Bai, Jianxun Lian, Xin Zhao, Guangzhong Sun, Ji-Rong Wen, and Xing Xie. 2019a. News graph: An enhanced knowledge graph for news recommendation. In *Proceedings of the Second Workshop on Knowledge-aware and Conversational Recommender Systems, co-located with 28th ACM International Conference on Information and Knowledge Management, KaRS@CIKM 2019, Beijing, China, November 7, 2019*, volume 2601 of *CEUR Workshop Proceedings*, pages 1–7. CEUR-WS.org.

Yinhan Liu, Myle Ott, Naman Goyal, Jingfei Du, Mandar Joshi, Danqi Chen, Omer Levy, Mike Lewis, Luke Zettlemoyer, and Veselin Stoyanov. 2019b. Roberta: A robustly optimized bert pretraining approach.

Ilya Loshchilov and Frank Hutter. 2019. Decoupled weight decay regularization. In *7th International Conference on Learning Representations, ICLR 2019, New Orleans, LA, USA, May 6-9, 2019*. OpenReview.net.

Jose L Martinez-Rodriguez, Aidan Hogan, and Ivan Lopez-Arevalo. 2020. Information extraction meets the semantic web: a survey. *Semantic Web*, 11(2):255–335.

Nandana Mihindukulasooriya, Gaetano Rossiello, Pavan Kapanipathi, Ibrahim Abdelaziz, Srinivas Ravishankar, Mo Yu, Alfio Gliozzo, Salim Roukos, and Alexander Gray. 2020. Leveraging semantic parsing for relation linking over knowledge bases. In *The Semantic Web – ISWC 2020*, pages 402–419, Cham. Springer International Publishing.

Mike Mintz, Steven Bills, Rion Snow, and Daniel Jurafsky. 2009. Distant supervision for relation extraction without labeled data. In *Proceedings of the Joint Conference of the 47th Annual Meeting of the ACL and the 4th International Joint Conference on Natural Language Processing of the AFNLP*, pages

1003–1011, Suntec, Singapore. Association for Computational Linguistics.

Robert Ormandi, Mohammad Saleh, Erin Winter, and Vinay Rao. 2021. Webred: Effective pretraining and finetuning for relation extraction on the web.

Sebastian Riedel, Limin Yao, and Andrew McCallum. 2010. Modeling relations and their mentions without labeled text. In *Proceedings of the 2010 European Conference on Machine Learning and Knowledge Discovery in Databases: Part III*, ECML PKDD'10, page 148–163, Berlin, Heidelberg. Springer-Verlag.

Nipun Sadvilkar and Mark Neumann. 2020. PySBD: Pragmatic sentence boundary disambiguation. In *Proceedings of Second Workshop for NLP Open Source Software (NLP-OSS)*, pages 110–114, Online. Association for Computational Linguistics.

Ahmad Sakor, Kuldeep Singh, Anery Patel, and Maria-Esther Vidal. 2020. *Falcon 2.0: An Entity and Relation Linking Tool over Wikidata*, page 3141–3148. Association for Computing Machinery, New York, NY, USA.

Amit Singhal. 2012. Introducing the knowledge graph: things, not strings.

Dezhao Song, Frank Schilder, Shai Hertz, Giuseppe Saltini, Charese Smiley, Phani Nivarthi, Oren Hazai, Dudi Landau, Mike Zaharkin, Tom Zielund, Hugo Molina-Salgado, Chris Brew, and Dan Bennett. 2019. Building and querying an enterprise knowledge graph. *IEEE Transactions on Services Computing*, 12(3):356–369.

Denny Vrandečić and Markus Krötzsch. 2014. Wikidata: A free collaborative knowledgebase. *Commun. ACM*, 57(10):78–85.

Thomas Wolf, Lysandre Debut, Victor Sanh, Julien Chaumond, Clement Delangue, Anthony Moi, Pierric Cistac, Tim Rault, Remi Louf, Morgan Funtowicz, Joe Davison, Sam Shleifer, Patrick von Platen, Clara Ma, Yacine Jernite, Julien Plu, Canwen Xu, Teven Le Scao, Sylvain Gugger, Mariama Drame, Quentin Lhoest, and Alexander Rush. 2020. Transformers: State-of-the-art natural language processing. In *Proceedings of the 2020 Conference on Empirical Methods in Natural Language Processing: System Demonstrations*, pages 38–45, Online. Association for Computational Linguistics.

Yuan Yao, Deming Ye, Peng Li, Xu Han, Yankai Lin, Zhenghao Liu, Zhiyuan Liu, Lixin Huang, Jie Zhou, and Maosong Sun. 2019. DocRED: A large-scale document-level relation extraction dataset. In *Proceedings of the 57th Annual Meeting of the Association for Computational Linguistics*, pages 764–777, Florence, Italy. Association for Computational Linguistics.

Yuhao Zhang, Victor Zhong, Danqi Chen, Gabor Angeli, and Christopher D. Manning. 2017. Position-aware attention and supervised data improve slot filling. In *Proceedings of the 2017 Conference on Empirical Methods in Natural Language Processing*, pages 35–45, Copenhagen, Denmark. Association for Computational Linguistics.

AIT-QA: Question Answering Dataset over Complex Tables in the Airline Industry

Yannis Katsis[1], **Saneem Chemmengath**[1], **Vishwajeet Kumar**[1], **Samarth Bharadwaj**[2*], **Mustafa Canim**[1], **Michael Glass**[1], **Alfio Gliozzo**[1], **Feifei Pan**[3], **Jaydeep Sen**[1], **Karthik Sankaranarayanan**[1], **Soumen Chakrabarti**[4]

[1] IBM Research [2] Microsoft [3] Rensselaer Polytechnic Institute [4] IIT Bombay

yannis.katsis@ibm.com, saneem.cg@in.ibm.com, vishk024@in.ibm.com, sabharadwaj@microsoft.com, mustafa@us.ibm.com, mrglass@us.ibm.com, gliozzo@us.ibm.com, panf2@rpi.edu, jaydesen@in.ibm.com, kartsank@in.ibm.com, soumen.chakrabarti@gmail.com

Abstract

Table Question Answering (Table QA) systems have been shown to be highly accurate when trained and tested on open-domain datasets built on top of Wikipedia tables. However, it is not clear whether their performance remains the same when applied to domain-specific scientific and business documents, encountered in industrial settings, which exhibit some unique characteristics: (a) they contain tables with a much more complex layout than Wikipedia tables (including hierarchical row and column headers), (b) they contain domain-specific terms, and (c) they are typically not accompanied by domain-specific labeled data that can be used to train Table QA models.

To understand the performance of Table QA approaches in this setting, we introduce AIT-QA; a domain-specific Table QA test dataset. While focusing on the airline industry, AIT-QA reflects the challenges that domain-specific documents pose to Table QA, outlined above. In this work, we describe the creation of the dataset and report zero-shot experimental results of three SOTA Table QA methods. The results clearly expose the limitations of current methods with a best accuracy of just 51.8%. We also present pragmatic table pre-processing steps to pivot and project complex tables into a layout suitable for the SOTA Table QA models. Finally, we provide data-driven insights on how different aspects of this setting (including hierarchical headers, domain-specific terminology, and paraphrasing) affect Table QA methods, in order to help the community develop improved methods for domain-specific Table QA.

1 Introduction

The tabular data format is commonly used in digital documents such as PDFs and HTMLs to store semi-structured information (Canim et al., 2019; Zhang and Balog, 2018; Pasupat and Liang, 2015). Due to the rich content found in tables, many works have looked into extracting information out of tables (Burdick et al., 2020) and leveraging it for various NLP tasks, such as answering questions over tables (Cafarella et al., 2009; Sun et al., 2019; Shraga et al., 2020a,b). The quality of answers depends on first, high quality extraction of tables out of documents (aka *Table Extraction*); second, retrieval of relevant tables for a given natural language question or keyword query (aka *Table Retrieval*); and finally, identification of the relevant cells over the retrieved tables (aka *Table QA*). Most recently, transformer-based pre-trained architectures such as TaBERT (Yin et al., 2020), TaPas (Herzig et al., 2020), and RCI (Glass et al., 2021) have been proposed to tackle the Table QA task by identifying table cells containing the answer to a given question. These models have been shown to exhibit very high accuracy in Table QA. However, the results are based on training and testing the proposed techniques on *open in-domain* datasets, built on top of Wikipedia tables, such as the WikiTableQuestions (Pasupat and Liang, 2015) and WikiSQL (Zhong et al., 2017) datasets.

Based on our experience in designing and implementing industrial table processing approaches (Burdick et al., 2020), open-domain web tables typically exhibit much simpler structures than the ***complex table structures*** found in *domain-specific* scientific or business documents. For instance, consider the sample question-table pair from our proposed airline dataset shown in Figure 1. The table contains both column headers and row headers (i.e., descriptors of columns and rows, respectively) and both of them are hierarchical in nature. Moreover, answering a question often requires reasoning on such complex column/row header hierarchies. For instance, finding the requested main-

* Work done while author was working at IBM.

Proceedings of NAACL-HLT 2022: Industry Track Papers, pages 305 - 314
July 10-15, 2022 ©2022 Association for Computational Linguistics

Question: What was the reported mainline RPM for American Airlines in 2017 ?

Hierarchical column headers

Hierarchical row headers

	Year Ended December 31,		
	2017	2016	2015
Mainline			
Revenue passenger miles (millions) [a]	201,351	199,014	199,467
Available seat miles (millions) [b]	243,806	241,734	239,375
Passenger load factor (percent) [c]	82.6	82.3	83.3
Yield (cents) [d]	14.52	14.02	14.56
Passenger revenue per available seat mile (cents) [e]	11.99	11.55	12.13
Operating cost per available seat mile (cents) [f]	12.96	11.94	12.03
Aircraft at end of period	948	930	946
Fuel consumption (gallons in millions)	3,579	3,596	3,611
Average aircraft fuel price including related taxes (dollars per gallon)	1.71	1.41	1.72
Full-time equivalent employees at end of period	103,100	101,500	98,900
Total Mainline and Regional			
Revenue passenger miles (millions) [a]	226,346	223,477	223,010
Available seat miles (millions) [b]	276,493	273,410	268,736
Passenger load factor (percent) [c]	81.9	81.7	83.0

Figure 1: Question-table pair in AIT-QA, showing the complex structure of tables in the dataset. The cell containing the answer is shown in blue and its hierarchical column/row headers are shown in orange and green, respectively

line Revenue Passenger Miles (RPMs) (which are contained in the blue cell) requires understanding that the cell has two hierarchical row headers "Mainline" and "Revenue passenger miles" (shown in green). Ignoring row headers or not reasoning on the row header hierarchy may lead to wrong results. For instance, if we simply searched for cells with a flat row header containing "Revenue Passenger Miles", we may mistakenly return value 226,346 appearing further down the table (which corresponds to the RPMs of *total* operations, instead of the requested *mainline* operations). In contrast, web tables in open-domain Table QA datasets, such as WikiTableQuestions or WikiSQL, exhibit significantly simpler structures. Such tables do not contain row headers and only have a single column header, closely resembling relational database tables.

Moreover, while open-domain datasets capture common entities, such as locations, person names, etc, which often appear in Wikipedia articles, they typically lack ***domain-specific vocabulary*** that one encounters in scientific or business documents (such as the "Revenue Passenger Miles" above).

Finally, from a deployment point of view, when clients bring their own domain-specific documents, they typically ***do not provide domain-specific labeled data*** to train Table QA models. This comes in contrast to existing Table QA evaluations on open-domain data, where tested models are first trained using large amounts of open-domain training data.

Based on the above, domain-specific Table QA exhibits major differences from open-domain settings: Domain-specific documents include *more complex table structures* and *specialized vocabulary*, and are *not accompanied by domain-specific labeled data.*

To understand whether existing Table QA approaches support these settings, we create AIT-QA; a domain-specific Table QA dataset, where tables are extracted from financial documents in the airline industry. The majority of the tables exhibit a complex structure, including hierarchical row and column headers, as well as airline-specific terminology. Finally, we build the dataset as a test set to reflect the lack of domain-specific labeled data and encourage works on zero/few-shot learning. To the best of our knowledge, this is the first Table QA dataset that includes and explicitly encodes such complex table layouts and domain-specific table contents. Our experiments with three state-of-the-art Table QA models show that existing models struggle to support this setting, yielding an accuracy of at most 51.8%. We hope that this dataset and associated insights will help the community better support domain-specific Table QA in the future.

This work makes the following contributions:

A complex and domain-specific Table QA dataset called *AIT-QA (Airline Industry Table QA)*, created by human annotators based on 10-K financial reports of major airline companies. The questions are created based on the content of tables appearing in the 10-K reports, as well as KPIs (Key Performance Indicators); i.e., important metrics tracked by analysts in the airline industry. The dataset has been made publicly available under a CDLA-Sharing-1.0 license at `https://github.com/IBM/AITQA`.

Experimental evaluation of state-of-the-art Table QA models on AIT-QA, demonstrating that high performance on open-domain datasets does not

Dataset	Year	Table only	Wikipedia	Hierarchical Column Headers	Hierarchical Row Headers
WikiTableQuestions (Pasupat and Liang, 2015)	2015	✓	✓	✗	✗
TabMCQ (Jauhar et al., 2016)	2016	✓	✗ (Science Exam)	✗	✗
WikiSQL (Zhong et al., 2017)	2017	✓	✓	✗	✗
FeTaQA (Nan et al., 2022)	2021	✓	✓	✗	✗
HybridQA (Chen et al., 2020)	2020	✗	✓	✗	✗
OTT-QA (Chen et al., 2021)	2021	✗	✓	✗	✗
TAT-QA (Zhu et al., 2021)	2021	✗	✗ (Finance)	✗	✗
AIT-QA (this work)	2021	✓	✗ (Airlines)	✓	✓

Table 1: Comparison of AIT-QA to other Table QA datasets

guarantee similar performance on domain-specific datasets containing complex tables, further motivating the need for a domain-specific Table QA dataset.

A novel data pre-processing technique for existing Table QA models, which improves their performance on datasets with complex table structures. This is achieved by translating complex table structures (incl. hierarchical row and column headers) to simpler structures resembling the structure of the tables on which such approaches have been trained.

2 Related Work

Prior work on leveraging tables to answer questions studied two tasks: (a) *Table retrieval*; i.e., given a corpus of tables, identify the table containing the answer to a question, and (b) *Table QA*; i.e., given a single table containing the answer, find this answer. We next discuss datasets for Table QA, which is the focus of this work.

The most commonly used Table QA datasets include WikiTableQuestions (Pasupat and Liang, 2015), WikiSQL (Zhong et al., 2017), and TabMCQ (Jauhar et al., 2016). Out of them, the first two are based on Wikipedia. The third, contains manually-curated general knowledge tables created from the Regents 4th-grade exam. While it is domain-specific, the included tables have a very peculiar structure (with table rows containing entire natural language sentences that have been split into columns), which in our experience is not representative of tables appearing in most domains. Recently, Nan et al. (2022) proposed FeTaQA; another Wikipedia-based dataset but with answers that are long free-form sentences (instead of short answers found in prior datasets).

Finally, the last couple of years saw the introduction of three multi-hop QA datasets: *HybridQA* (Chen et al., 2020), *OTT-QA* (Chen et al., 2021), and *TAT-QA* (Zhu et al., 2021). In these datasets finding an answer requires reasoning not only on tables but across both tables and associated text. Out of them, HybridQA and OTT-QA are both based on Wikipedia. On the other hand, TAT-QA, is based on data extracted from financial reports, making it the most similar to our proposed AIT-QA dataset.

However, while the TAT-QA paper mentions complex table structures (including row headers), the resulting dataset does not include explicit annotations of row and column headers (not to mention hierarchies thereof). Without explicit annotations of such headers, not only is it hard to understand the complexity of the included tables (e.g., the Appendix of (Zhu et al., 2021) points to the absence of column header hierarchies in TAT-QA), but it also makes it harder to understand the effect of table complexity on the performance of Table QA algorithms. Instead, our proposed AIT-QA treats hierarchical column and row headers as first-class citizens and is to the best of our knowledge the first *domain-specific* Table QA dataset that contains *explicit annotations of complex table structures, including hierarchical row and column headers.* Table 1 summarizes the discussed Table QA datasets.

3 Dataset

We next outline the process followed to generate AIT-QA, from data acquisition and preparation to question annotation and table header identification.

Data Acquisition. AIT-QA is based on 10-K forms; comprehensive annual reports that publicly traded companies file with the U.S. Securities and Exchange Commission (SEC). For this dataset, we focused on the airline industry and retrieved recent 10-K forms of all 5 airlines included in the Standard & Poor's 500 (S&P 500) stock market index[1]. Covered airlines include: Alaska Air Group (ALK), American

[1] https://en.wikipedia.org/wiki/List_of_S%26P_500_companies

Airlines Group (AAL), Delta Air Lines Inc. (DAL), Southwest Airlines (LUV), and United Airlines Holdings (UAL). The 10-K forms were downloaded through the publicly accessible SEC EDGAR online system[2] in HTML form.

Data Preparation and Cleaning. While the downloaded 10-K forms encode tables using standard HTML tags, the tables are formatted with human consumption in mind. As such, table rows/columns/cells are used for the table to be neatly rendered on the screen and/or paper and they do not always correspond to the table's logical structure. In particular, we found that tables often contain extraneous rows/columns (introduced to allow for more space between table elements). Moreover, the contents of a single logical cell are often split into multiple physical cells, to allow for better vertical alignment of the information within a table. For instance, cells containing a currency symbol and negative monetary amounts such as $(1,234), are often split into three physical cells | $ | (1,234 |) | so that the currency symbols and numbers align with other similar contents across rows. To separate these formatting decisions from the logical structure of the table, we post-processed the downloaded HTML files to remove extraneous rows/columns and merge back components of logical cells originally split into multiple cells. Processing was done through a combination of scripts and manual error correction.

Question Annotation. The cleaned 10-K forms were given to 8 co-authors of this paper to generate question-answer pairs over tables appearing on the forms. To capture questions of particular interest to domain experts in the domain, while ensuring a diversity of question topics, we asked annotators to provide two types of questions:

KPI-driven questions: These are questions that inquiry about Key Performance Indicators (KPIs), which are metrics of particular interest to analysts in the airline industry. Annotators were provided with a list of KPIs along with common synonyms to ensure that the questions capture not only the topic of interest but also use the correct vocabulary. Then they were instructed to search the document for mentions of KPIs within tables and create corresponding questions. Thirteen KPIs were used in total, each with three variants, depending on whether it referred to the airlines' mainline, regional, or total operations.

Table-driven questions: While KPI-driven questions capture common metrics tracked by analysts, they can be limiting for two reasons: First, there is a small number of KPIs and second, given their domain importance, they often appear within a small set of tables. Hence, limiting ourselves to such questions would lead to a non-diverse dataset. To avoid this issue, annotators were asked to also provide questions that inquired about other concepts appearing within the input tables. To create such questions, annotators browsed through the tables in the documents and wrote questions that could be answered by them.

After an initial set of question-answer pairs was collected, annotators were also asked to generate paraphrases. While creating paraphrased questions, annotators were given access to the set of question-answer pairs collected in earlier stages and asked to pick a subset of questions to paraphrase. This leads to the second major dimension along which questions in AIT-QA can be classified: ***Original questions*** (Questions collected during the initial annotation) and ***Paraphrased questions*** (Questions generated as paraphrases of original questions).

Finally, in all stages of the annotation process, annotators were asked to keep track of additional metadata indicating whether a question relied on the hierarchy of row headers to be answered. A question relies on the hierarchy of row headers when in order to be unambiguously answered, one has to consult not only the row header that appears on the same row as the answer, but also row headers appearing on higher levels of the hierarchy. For instance, the question in Figure 1 depends on the row header hierarchy, as ignoring the hierarchy may lead to an incorrect answer, as explained in the introduction. Based on these metadata, questions in the dataset can be differentiated across a third dimension into: ***Row header hierarchy questions*** (Questions whose answer relies on the row header hierarchy) and ***No row header hierarchy questions*** (Questions whose answer does not rely on the row header hierarchy).

For each question-answer pair, annotators provided the question, the table cell where the answer appears, as well as metadata indicating the classification of the question along the three aforementioned dimensions. For the first version of the dataset, we focus on *lookup* questions - i.e., questions where the answer appears within table cells and does not require aggregate operations (such as min/max/sum/count) to be returned (Glass et al., 2021), leaving the expansion of the dataset with aggregate questions as future work. Annotation was carried out using a custom-built Table QA annotation tool (see Appendix A for more details). Finally, the collected question-answer pairs

[2]https://www.sec.gov/edgar.shtml

Question Type	Count (%)
KPI-driven questions	145 (28%)
Table-driven questions	370 (72%)
Original questions	439 (85%)
Paraphrased questions	76 (15%)
Row header hierarchy questions	146 (28%)
No row header hierarchy questions	369 (72%)

Table 2: Breakdown of questions across 3 dimensions

and associated metadata were subsequently reviewed by other annotators to verify their validity and correct minor issues, such as typos or associated metadata.

Hierarchical Column/Row Header Identification. To identify column and row headers of tables, we leveraged Table Understanding technology incorporated in IBM Watson Discovery[3]. Table Understanding allows among others identifying for each body (i.e., non-header) cell, the set of column headers and row headers that describe the cell[4]. Table Understanding also supports column and row header hierarchies, as described above. The identified header hierarchies are included as part of the dataset so that they can be leveraged by Table QA models.

Dataset Statistics. The resulting test dataset consists of 515 questions generated out of 116 tables. These tables were chosen from 13 10-K forms of the 5 considered airlines filed for years between 2017 and 2019. Table 2 shows the breakdown of questions along the three aforementioned dimensions.

4 Experimental Evaluation

To analyze the effect of AIT-QA's domain-specific complex tables to existing Table QA approaches, we next provide a comprehensive evaluation of state-of-the-art Table QA models on it.

4.1 Experimental Setting

We evaluate three Table QA systems - **RCI** (Glass et al., 2021), **TaBERT** (Yin et al., 2020), and **TaPaS** (Herzig et al., 2020) - selected as representing SOTA Table QA approaches of different architectures.

TaBERT employs an encoder-decoder approach, utilizing a BERT (Devlin et al., 2019) encoder and LSTM decoder, which generates intermediate logical forms which - when executed over tables - yield the answer (Liang et al., 2017). In contrast, TaPaS (Herzig et al., 2020) and RCI (Glass et al., 2021) both treat Table QA as a classification problem. However, TaPas considers tables as a whole, while RCI splits them into rows and columns and carries out inference on them separately. In all three systems, tables and questions are encoded using transformers (Vaswani et al., 2017).

To test whether high Table QA performance reported on open-domain tables translates to the domain-specific AIT-QA dataset, all three Table QA models are pre-trained on the larger WikiSQL (Zhong et al., 2017) train split and tested on AIT-QA without any hyper-parameter tuning. To set up the baselines, we use the source code and instructions of the respective authors (see Appendix B).

4.2 Transforming Table Structures

Existing table QA models are based on open-domain web tables. They assume that the input tables contain flat column headers (i.e., a single row of column headers) and no row headers. Therefore, none of the existing baselines are built for handling complex column or row header hierarchies seen in AIT-QA. Thus, we experiment with table transformation operations to maximize these baselines' performance on AIT-QA.

Base transformations are first performed on AIT-QA tables to render the tables compatible to the models: (1) Row headers are added as the first column of the table as regular body cells. We use the dummy text 'header' as the column header of the new column. (2) Header hierarchies are flattened by concatenating parent header text with children text. Note that these transformations are designed to help the baseline models perform better than if we ran them on the raw table. For instance, when converting the table of Figure 1, the cell on the left of the blue cell will contain the concatenated row header hierarchy (i.e., 'Mainline passenger revenue miles (millions)'). This should help the models (which are not built to recognize row header hierarchies) perform better on AIT-QA.

Transposing tables. However, after running the models, we observed that there was further room for improvement. In particular, we observed that in many tables in AIT-QA, row headers contain more information than column headers. For example, in Figure 1, row headers contain the metric names, which are arguably more descriptive than the column headers containing the year information. Based on this intuition, we experimented with transposing the headers, so that row headers become column headers (which

[3]https://www.ibm.com/cloud/watson-discovery

[4]https://cloud.ibm.com/docs/discovery-data?topic=discovery-data-understanding_tables

Version	TaBERT	TaPaS	RCI
Base	33.20	49.32	40.58
All T	33.39	43.88	48.54
Partial T	33.98	46.80	51.84

(a) Accuracy of Table QA on different transformations of the tables in AIT-QA (**Base** = No transpose, **All T** = All transpose, **Partial T** = Partial Transpose).

Data subset	TaBERT	TaPaS	RCI
Overall accuracy	33.98	49.32	51.84
KPI-driven	41.37	48.26	60.00
Table-driven	31.08	50.0	48.64
Row header hierarchy	21.92	47.26	45.89
No row header hierarchy	38.75	50.39	54.20

(b) Accuracy of Table QA models on slices of AIT-QA

Table 3: Accuracy of Table QA models on AIT-QA

the models are trained to pay more attention to) and vice versa. During this process body cells are appropriately transposed as well. This led to three versions of AIT-QA data: (1) *Base:* without transposing tables, (2) *All transpose:* With all tables transposed, and (3) *Partial transpose:* Transposing tables that have more characters in row headers than column headers. Table 3a depicts the accuracy of baseline models on each dataset version. Interestingly, RCI and TaBERT benefit from transposing, while the performance of TaPas declines. For our analysis below, we pick for each model the version of the data that yields the highest performance.

4.3 Analyzing Baseline Performance on AIT-QA's Dimensions

The first row of Table 3b shows the overall accuracy of the baselines on AIT-QA. Performance is relatively low ranging from 34% (for TaBERT) to 49% / 52% (for TaPaS / RCI, respectively). For reference, the accuracy of the models on the dev split of the WikiSQL dataset is significantly higher, ranging from 70.5% (for TaBERT) to 89.2% / 89.8% (for TaPaS / RCI, respectively). This verifies our intuition that open-domain datasets do not reflect the intricacies of domain-specific use cases, which was the main motivation for the creation of AIT-QA.

To gain further insights on how domain vocabulary, table structure, and question phrasing affect the performance of Table QA models, we next evaluate the models on the three dimensions of our dataset:

KPI-driven vs Table-driven. Table 3b shows the performance of the baselines on KPI-driven vs Table-driven questions. As shown, accuracy is always higher for the former than the latter. While identifying the reason behind this is beyond the scope of this paper (being related to the promising area of explainability of AI models), there are two factors that may be potentially contributing: First, KPIs are limited in number and often easily differentiable from other terms in the tables, which may help baselines identify the right answer. Second, KPI-driven questions were formed by having a KPI in mind and searching for the corresponding term in the document. In contrast, table-driven questions were formed by looking at a table and trying to form a question. As a result, it is much more common to find distorted utterances of row/column headers in table-driven questions, making it harder for the baseline to identify the correct answer.

Paraphrase	TaBERT	TaPaS	RCI
All correct	25.00	38.88	33.33
Any correct	29.17	30.55	34.72
All wrong	45.83	30.55	31.94

Table 4: Percentage of paraphrased question sets that are (a) all correctly answered, (b) at least one correctly and another one incorrectly answered, and (c) all incorrectly answered by each baseline

Row Header Hierarchy vs No Row Header Hierarchy. One of the key challenges associated with AIT-QA are row/column header hierarchies. While we tried to help the baselines (which have not built with complex header structures in mind) deal with hierarchies (see table transformations in Section 4.2), this implicit treatment of headers has two important limitations: (1) the explicit hierarchical information is lost and (2) in some cases, transformations may add noise into a row/column. Therefore, it is not surprising that questions that depend on row header hierarchies negatively affect the performance of all baselines and cause an average drop of ~10 percentage points (see Table 3b). This indicates that additional work is needed to make Table QA models better leverage row header hierarchies.

Paraphrasing. Paraphrasing is an important aspect of Table QA systems. AIT-QA contains 76 paraphrased questions, which can be grouped into 72 paraphrased question sets (i.e., sets that include the original questions and all its paraphrases). To study the effect of paraphrasing, we computed for each approach the percentage of question sets for which (1) all questions were answered correctly (referred to as *All Correct*), (2) at least one question was answered correctly and another incorrectly (*Any Correct*), and (3) all questions in the set were answered incorrectly (*All Wrong*).

Table 4 shows the resulting percentages for all baselines. For instance, for RCI the percentages for (1) / (2) / (3) are ~33% / 35% / 32%, respectively. Out of the three categories, especially interesting is the 2nd category, as it represents questions that are supported when phrased in one way but not supported when phrased in a different way. With almost 30-35% of question sets in this category, Table QA systems seem to be very sensitive to question phrasing; another area that would benefit from additional work.

5 Conclusion

Table QA systems have shown high performance on existing Wikipedia-based datasets with simple tables. To understand whether they perform as well on domain-specific datasets commonly encountered in the industry, we created AIT-QA; the first Table QA dataset that explicitly captures domain-specific tables with complex structure, including column and row header hierarchies. Our experiments show the deficiency of SOTA Table QA approaches in this setting. We hope that this work and dataset encourage the community to consider new Table QA approaches that can support such complexity, so that Table QA methods can more effectively support domain-specific scientific and business use cases.

References

Doug Burdick, Marina Danilevsky, Alexandre V. Evfimievski, Yannis Katsis, and Nancy Xin Ru Wang. 2020. Table extraction and understanding for scientific and enterprise applications. *Proc. VLDB Endow.*, 13(12):3433–3436.

Michael J. Cafarella, Alon Halevy, and Nodira Khoussainova. 2009. Data integration for the relational web. *Proc. VLDB Endow.*, 2(1):1090–1101.

Mustafa Canim, Cristina Cornelio, Arun Iyengar, Ryan Musa, and Mariano Rodriguez-Muro. 2019. Schemaless queries over document tables with dependencies. *CoRR*.

Wenhu Chen, Ming wei Chang, Eva Schlinger, William Wang, and William Cohen. 2021. Open question answering over tables and text. *Proceedings of ICLR 2021*.

Wenhu Chen, Hanwen Zha, Zhiyu Chen, Wenhan Xiong, Hong Wang, and William Yang Wang. 2020. HybridQA: A dataset of multi-hop question answering over tabular and textual data. In *Findings of the Association for Computational Linguistics: EMNLP 2020*, pages 1026–1036, Online. Association for Computational Linguistics.

Jacob Devlin, Ming-Wei Chang, Kenton Lee, and Kristina Toutanova. 2019. BERT: Pre-training of deep bidirectional transformers for language understanding. In *Proceedings of the 2019 Conference of the North American Chapter of the Association for Computational Linguistics: Human Language Technologies, Volume 1 (Long and Short Papers)*, pages 4171–4186, Minneapolis, Minnesota. Association for Computational Linguistics.

Michael Glass, Mustafa Canim, Alfio Gliozzo, Saneem Chemmengath, Vishwajeet Kumar, Rishav Chakravarti, Avi Sil, Feifei Pan, Samarth Bharadwaj, and Nicolas Rodolfo Fauceglia. 2021. Capturing row and column semantics in transformer based question answering over tables. In *Proceedings of the 2021 Conference of the North American Chapter of the Association for Computational Linguistics: Human Language Technologies*, pages 1212–1224, Online. Association for Computational Linguistics.

Jonathan Herzig, Pawel Krzysztof Nowak, Thomas Müller, Francesco Piccinno, and Julian Eisenschlos. 2020. TaPas: Weakly supervised table parsing via pre-training. In *Proceedings of the 58th Annual Meeting of the Association for Computational Linguistics*, pages 4320–4333, Online. Association for Computational Linguistics.

Sujay Kumar Jauhar, Peter Turney, and Eduard Hovy. 2016. Tabmcq: A dataset of general knowledge tables and multiple-choice questions.

Chen Liang, Jonathan Berant, Quoc Le, Kenneth D. Forbus, and Ni Lao. 2017. Neural symbolic machines: Learning semantic parsers on Freebase with weak supervision. In *Proceedings of the 55th Annual Meeting of the Association for Computational Linguistics (Volume 1: Long Papers)*, pages 23–33, Vancouver, Canada. Association for Computational Linguistics.

Linyong Nan, Chiachun Hsieh, Ziming Mao, Xi Lin, Neha Verma, Rui Zhang, Wojciech Kryściński, Hailey Schoelkopf, Riley Kong, Xiangru Tang, Mutethia Mutuma, Benjamin Rosand, Isabel Trindade, Renusree Bandaru, Jacob Cunningham, Caiming Xiong, and Dragomir Radev. 2022. FeTaQA: free-form table question answering. *Transactions of the Association for Computational Linguistics*, 10(0).

Panupong Pasupat and Percy Liang. 2015. Compositional semantic parsing on semi-structured tables. In *Proceedings of the 53rd Annual Meeting of the Association for Computational Linguistics and the 7th International Joint Conference on Natural Language Processing (Volume 1: Long Papers)*, pages 1470–1480, Beijing, China. Association for Computational Linguistics.

Roee Shraga, Haggai Roitman, Guy Feigenblat, and Mustafa Canim. 2020a. *Ad Hoc Table Retrieval Using Intrinsic and Extrinsic Similarities*, page 2479–2485. Association for Computing Machinery, New York, NY, USA.

Roee Shraga, Haggai Roitman, Guy Feigenblat, and Mustafa Canim. 2020b. Web table retrieval using multimodal deep learning. In *Proceedings of the 43rd International ACM SIGIR Conference on Research and Development in Information Retrieval*, SIGIR '20, page 1399–1408, New York, NY, USA. Association for Computing Machinery.

Yibo Sun, Zhao Yan, Duyu Tang, Nan Duan, and Bing Qin. 2019. Content-based table retrieval for web queries. *Neurocomputing*, 349:183–189.

Ashish Vaswani, Noam Shazeer, Niki Parmar, Jakob Uszkoreit, Llion Jones, Aidan N Gomez, Łukasz Kaiser, and Illia Polosukhin. 2017. Attention is all you need. In *Advances in Neural Information Processing Systems*, volume 30. Curran Associates, Inc.

Pengcheng Yin, Graham Neubig, Wen-tau Yih, and Sebastian Riedel. 2020. TaBERT: Pretraining for joint understanding of textual and tabular data. In *Proceedings of the 58th Annual Meeting of the Association for Computational Linguistics*, pages 8413–8426, Online. Association for Computational Linguistics.

Shuo Zhang and Krisztian Balog. 2018. Ad hoc table retrieval using semantic similarity. In *Proceedings of the 2018 World Wide Web Conference*, WWW '18, page 1553–1562, Republic and Canton of Geneva, CHE. International World Wide Web Conferences Steering Committee.

Victor Zhong, Caiming Xiong, and Richard Socher. 2017. Seq2SQL: Generating structured queries from natural language using reinforcement learning. *CoRR*, abs/1709.00103.

Fengbin Zhu, Wenqiang Lei, Youcheng Huang, Chao Wang, Shuo Zhang, Jiancheng Lv, Fuli Feng, and Tat-Seng Chua. 2021. TAT-QA: A question answering benchmark on a hybrid of tabular and textual content in finance. In *Proceedings of the 59th Annual Meeting of the Association for Computational Linguistics and the 11th International Joint Conference on Natural Language Processing (Volume 1: Long Papers)*, pages 3277–3287, Online. Association for Computational Linguistics.

A Annotation Tool

To generate the question-answer pairs, annotators employed a custom-built Table QA annotation tool, a screenshot of which is shown in Figure 2. Using the tool, annotators can create question-answer pairs by (a) entering the question and its classification along the three dimensions of the dataset on the top of the screen and (b) selecting the table cell that contains the answer. As an annotator specifies questions, these are displayed in blue boxes above the tables containing the corresponding answers to allow for easier inspection. Finally, a counter of annotations is provided on the left side of the screen to allow annotators to keep track of their progress.

B Implementation Details for Baseline Table QA Models

To aid in reproducability, we next provide details on the codebases and processes used to create the state-of-the-art Table QA models employed in the experiments described in Section 4. As part of the experiments, we evaluate three Table QA systems: RCI (Glass et al., 2021), TaBERT (Yin et al., 2020), and TaPaS (Herzig et al., 2020), all pre-trained on the larger WikiSQL[5] (Zhong et al., 2017) train split. In all cases we use the original source code released by the respective authors, pretrained weights along with details in their papers, for setting up all baseline models. In particular:

- For TaBERT (Yin et al., 2020), we use the pre-trained BERT released on the official GitHub repository[6] with semantic parser MAPO[7]. TaBERT is trained for 10 epochs on 4 Nvidia Tesla v100s with a batchsize of 10, number of explore samples as 10 and all other hyperparameters kept exactly the same as (Yin et al., 2020).

- For RCI (Glass et al., 2021), we use the code released with the paper[8] to train the model for 2 epochs on 2 Tesla v100s, with learning rate 2.5e-5 and batch size 128. All the hyperparameters are kept the same as described in Section A.2 of (Glass et al., 2021).

- For TaPaS (Herzig et al., 2020), we use the model[9] trained on the WikiSQL dataset from the official GitHub repository[10].

[5] https://github.com/salesforce/WikiSQL

[6] https://github.com/facebookresearch/TaBERT

[7] Source code available at https://github.com/pcyin/pytorch_neural_symbolic_machines

[8] https://github.com/IBM/row-column-intersection/

C Ethical Considerations

The main goal of this work is to (a) inform the research community of the challenges that state-of-the-art Table QA approaches face when applied to domain-specific settings, and (b) provide resources (including the dataset and the insights in Section 4) to help address these challenges. As a result, we believe that this work has the potential to bring Table QA research closer to the real needs of users interested in getting answers to questions over tables found in domain-specific business and scientific documents, as commonly encountered in industrial settings.

While using the AIT-QA dataset for the above purpose, it is important to understand that the dataset represents a single domain/use case and may not be entirely representative of other domains/use cases. Based on our experience, the complex tabular structures encoded in AIT-QA (incl. column and row hierachies) are representative of structures found in many other scientific and business documents (e.g., medical papers with tables containing the results of clinical trials, licensing agreements with tables describing details of the agreement, etc.). However, other domains may have their own peculiarities (e.g., different vocabulary or specific table templates). As a result, even though AIT-QA can be used to get a first indication of the performance of a Table QA system in a domain-specific setting, we encourage the research community to also look at additional domains/use cases, as each one may have its own unique characteristics and associated challenges.

Including several domain-specific datasets in the evaluation of Table QA systems can also help ensure that when we design such systems, we take into account the needs of diverse sets of potential users and avoid introducing unwanted bias. As a concrete example, we believe that more work should be done in multi-lingual settings, as most Table QA datasets (including AIT-QA) focus on documents and questions written in English.

[9] https://storage.googleapis.com/tapas_models/2020_08_05/tapas_wikisql_sqa_masklm_large_reset.zip

[10] https://github.com/google-research/tapas

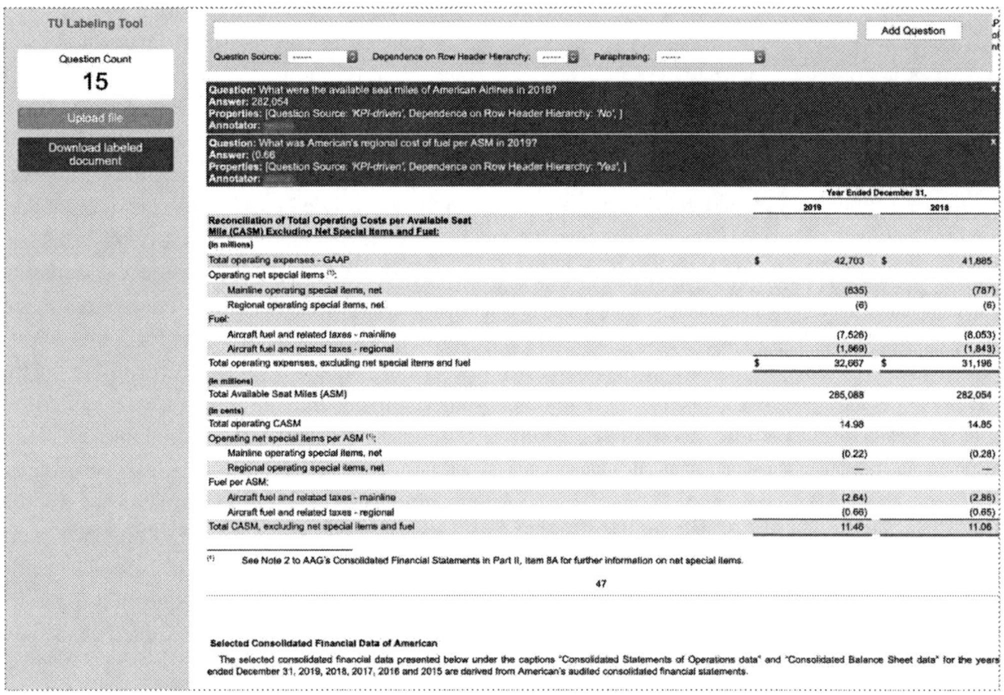

Figure 2: Screenshot of annotation tool used to create AIT-QA

Parameter-efficient Continual Learning Framework in Industrial Real-time Text Classification System

Tao Zhu, Zhe Zhao [*], Weijie Liu, Jiachi Liu, Yiren Chen, Weiquan Mao, Haoyan Liu, Kunbo Ding, Yudong Li, and Xuefeng Yang
Tencent Research, Beijing, China
{mardozhu, nlpzhezhao, jagerliu, jiachiliu, yirenchen, weiquanmao, haoyanliu, karlding, yudongli, ryanxfyang}@tencent.com

Abstract

Catastrophic forgetting is a challenge for model deployment in industrial real-time systems, which requires the model to quickly master a new task without forgetting the old one. Continual learning aims to solve this problem; however, it usually updates all the model parameters, resulting in extensive training times and the inability to deploy quickly. To address this challenge, we propose a parameter-efficient continual learning framework, in which efficient parameters are selected through an offline parameter selection strategy and then trained using an online regularization method. In our framework, only a few parameters need to be updated, which not only alleviates catastrophic forgetting, but also allows the model to be saved with the changed parameters instead of all parameters. Extensive experiments are conducted to examine the effectiveness of our proposal. We believe this paper will provide useful insights and experiences on developing deep learning-based online real-time systems.

1 Introduction

In industry, many text-related applications have enjoyed a superior performance boost from the emerging of pre-trained language models, such as word2vec (Mikolov et al., 2013a,b; Zhao et al., 2017) , ELMo (Peters et al., 2018), GPT (Radford et al., 2018, 2019), and BERT (Devlin et al., 2019; Liu et al., 2019; Sun et al., 2019). However, when a fine-tuned model needs to be updated to master a new task swiftly, it usually loses the ability to handle previous tasks. This phenomenon is known as catastrophic forgetting (French, 1999), and it poses a significant issue in industrial settings.

Continual learning aims to incrementally expand acquired knowledge for future learning (Chen and Liu, 2018), and mitigate the impact of catastrophic forgetting in the meantime. Existing continual learning methods usually use data replay (Rebuffi et al., 2017b), parameter isolation (Rusu et al., 2016; Fernando et al., 2017), and regularization (Kirkpatrick et al., 2017; Li and Hoiem, 2017) to make models adapt to new tasks without catastrophic forgetting. However, these approaches lack research on implementing continual learning in industrial scenarios, where endowing models with continual learning capabilities meets numerous practical constraints. For time constraints, when new data or tasks arrive, the model should be launched in minutes or even seconds, which is common in time-sensitive scenarios, e.g., blocking certain rumors content. For space constraints, the strong demand for tracing tasks makes it necessary to save every model once it is changed. So for the current large-scale pre-trained models, storage becomes an industrial challenge with the increase of new tasks.

To solve these industrial challenges, we propose a parameter-efficient continual learning framework based on an offline parameter selection strategy. The framework consists of two parts, i.e., offline calculation and online training. In the offline calculation part, all the parameters that are important to the old task are selected to be fixed, while the remaining parameters are employed to learn the new task. Since in a real industrial scenario, the arrival of a new task will have an interval of hours or even days, we can make full use of this interval to advance the selection of parameters. During the online training phase, the model is parameter-efficiently trained on a new task within a small set of parameters and further combines multiple regularization-based methods (Kirkpatrick et al., 2017; Li and Hoiem, 2017) to overcome catastrophic forgetting. To alleviate storage costs, we only save the modified parameters for each snapshot. Extensive experiments demonstrate that our framework can maintain the old task performance while learning a new task quickly. Our implementa-

*Corresponding author.

Proceedings of NAACL-HLT 2022: Industry Track Papers, pages 315 - 323

tion is based on UER-py pre-training toolkit[1] (Zhao et al., 2019).

The main contributions of this paper can be summarized as follows:

- We are the first to explore continual learning with only a few model parameters, and show that updating 0.1% parameters of BERT can achieve competitive performance.
- We propose a parameter-efficient continual learning framework that solves issues in real-world industrial settings by utilizing parameter-efficient-based offline parameter selection strategies and regularization-based online training methods.
- Extensive experiments on a real-world domain incremental text classification task verify the effectiveness of our proposed framework.

2 Related Work

2.1 Continual Learning

The major challenge of continual learning is catastrophic forgetting (McCloskey and Cohen, 1989; French, 1999), which occurs when optimizing for a new task causes performance degradation on a task learned previously. Methods designed to mitigate catastrophic forgetting mainly fall into three categories: replay methods, parameter isolation methods, and regularization-based methods (Delange et al., 2021).

Replay methods explicitly retrain on a subset of stored old task samples while training on new tasks. Instead of selecting samples at random, Rebuffi et al. (2017b) incorporated the Herding technique (Welling, 2009) to choose samples that best approximate the mean feature vector of a class, and it is widely used in Castro et al. (2018), Wu et al. (2019), Hou et al. (2019), Zhao et al. (2020), Mi et al. (2020a,b). Ramalho and Garnelo (2019) proposed to store samples that the model is least confident. However, replay methods exploit samples from old tasks, which will slow down the online training. To meet the time constraint, they are not used in our framework.

Parameter isolation methods dedicate different model parameters to each task, which are divided in two directions. One is growing a new branch network for a new task, while freezing previous task parameters (Rusu et al., 2016; Xu and Zhu, 2018). The other one is masking out parameters of previous task during new task training, which is imposed either at parameters level (Fernando et al., 2017; Mallya and Lazebnik, 2018), or unit level (Serra et al., 2018). Parameter isolation is unsuitable for usage in industrial scenario. It is difficult to keep track of the model's scale if the number of used parameters is continually accumulated as the number of tasks increases.

Regularization-based methods add an additional regularization term in the loss function, which will consolidate previous knowledge when learning on new data (Delange et al., 2021). Elastic weight consolidation (EWC) (Kirkpatrick et al., 2017) is a well-known regularization-based method, which introduces network parameter uncertainty in the Bayesian framework. LwF (Li and Hoiem, 2017) is another regularization method, using the previous model to infer current data and taking the outputs as soft labels to mitigate forgetting and transfer knowledge.

2.2 Parameter-efficient Training

Training a model with a few parameters is useful in many applications. Not only does the model have the potential to achieve better performance, but also disk space can be saved by only saving the updated parameters for each task. Recent work has shown that it is possible to update only a small subset of the model's parameters during training. This kind of work could heavily alleviate storage and deployment communication requirements . For example, Adapters (Houlsby et al., 2019; Rebuffi et al., 2017a; Bapna et al., 2019) introduce additional trainable parameters into a pre-trained model in the form of small task-specific modules while the rest of the model's parameters are kept fixed. Many works like Diff Pruning (Guo et al., 2020) and BitFit (Ben Zaken et al., 2021) have shown that it is possible to update only a small subset of the model's parameters during training, which can alleviate storage and communication requirements. Xu et al. (2021) and Sung et al. (2021) even show a acceptable performance on random selection of parameters. Therefore, we choose to perform parameter-efficient training on continual learning to quickly master a new task while avoid catastrophic forgetting.

3 Methodology

We introduce a parameter-efficient continual learning framework, as shown in figure 1. Our frame-

[1]https://github.com/dbiir/UER-py/

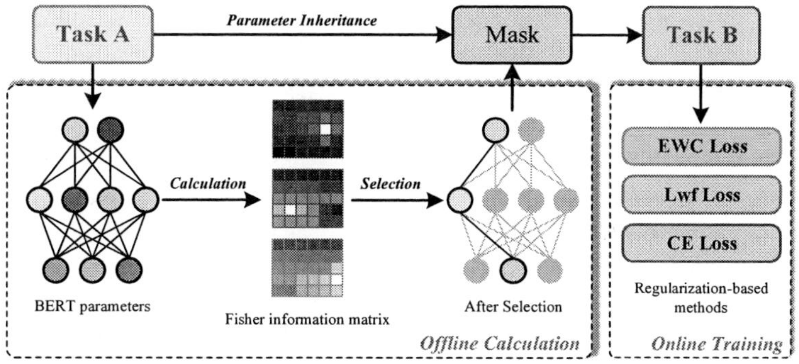

Figure 1: The overall architecture of the parameter-efficient continual learning framework.

work is divided into two components. The first is offline computation, which makes use of the interval between tasks to evaluate the data and select the parameters that are crucial to old tasks. These parameters are kept fixed in the new task. The other part is online training. In this stage, we utilize parameter-efficient training to perform new task training on the parameters that are not fixed. In addition, we introduce some well-known regularization-based methods in our framework for further improvement.

3.1 Offline calculation

The goal of offline calculation is to select the subset of parameters that are (in some sense) the most important to all of the old tasks, and fix them. Therefore, we make full use of the interval between tasks to review the previous training data, and calculate the parameters that are important to the previous tasks in the latest model (snapshot). These parameters will be fixed in the new task, and the remaining parameters will participate in the training.

As for the method of measuring the importance of parameters, we consider the indicator of how much changing the parameter will impact the model's output. The Fisher information is particularly well suited to identifying the highly relevant subset of parameters for previous tasks. It serves as an useful tool for estimating how much information a random variable contains about a parameter of the distribution (Tu et al., 2016). The Fisher information assumes that the more important the parameter towards the target task, the higher value it conveys. Formally, the Fisher information for the parameter θ_i is as follows:

$$F(\theta_i) = \frac{1}{|D|} \sum_{j=1}^{|D|} \left(\frac{a\partial \log p\left(y_j | x_j; \theta\right)}{\partial \theta_i} \right)^2 \quad (1)$$

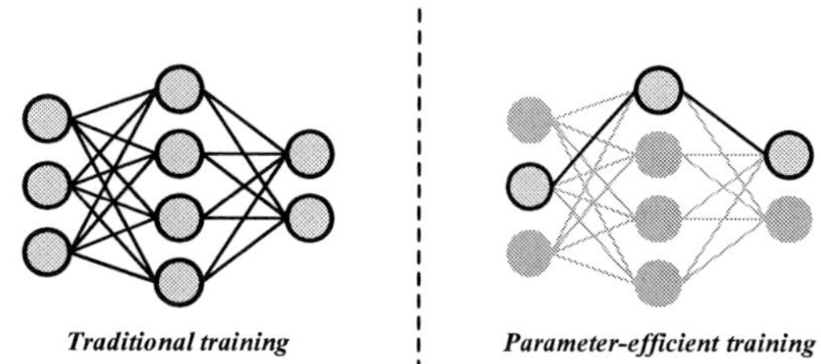

Figure 2: Illustration of parameter-efficient training.

where D denotes the task-specific training data, x and y denote the input and the output respectively.

3.2 Parameter-efficient Online training

Given the important parameters selected in offline stage, we use the remaining parameters for online training. Updating subset of the parameters can avoid catastrophic forgetting to some extent and largely decrease the storage space required by the snapshot. In addition, we combine the parameter-efficient training with two typical regularization-based continual learning methods. The combination of multiple orthogonal techniques can further improve the performance of our system. The overview optimization objective is as follows:

$$L(\theta^*) = L_{CE}(\theta^*) + L_{regul-based}(\theta^*), \theta^* \in S_\theta \quad (2)$$

where S_θ are parameters selected from the offline calculation stage, which have small Fisher values. L_{CE} denotes the cross-entropy loss, and $L_{regul-based}$ denotes regularization-based method loss.

3.2.1 Parameter-efficient learning

As shown in figure 2, in traditional training setting (left), all of the model's parameters are updated. But in our online training (right), we only train a few parameters, and most of the parameters are fixed according to the result of offline calculation to avoid forgetting old tasks. In general, the model will be easy to forget old tasks while learning new tasks, if more parameters are updated. Therefore, in our framework, we choose to perform parameter-efficient training on parameters that are not important to previous tasks, which are not fixed. Refer to previous experience (Ben Zaken et al., 2021; Xu et al., 2021), we chose a layer-wise strategy to select important parameters. We fixed the parameters from large to small (Fisher information) in a certain proportion at each layer.

On the other hand, updating a small number of parameters is beneficial for storage purpose and rapid deployment. Sometimes we need to deploy our model on thousands of servers. So the model size needs to be as small as possible (around 1.2 GB for BERT-Large 400 MB for BERT-Base). Our framework only needs to store the values and indices denoting the position of the updated parameters. Our experimental results demonstrate that only 0.1% trainable parameters of the original model can achieve competitive performance.

3.2.2 Regularization-based method

EWC and LwF are two representative approaches for preventing catastrophic forgetting in neural networks. They respectively add restrictions on model parameters and output activation. The two methods are orthogonal and we combine them as follows:

$$L_{regul-based}(\theta) = \lambda_1 L_{EWC}(\theta) + \lambda_2 L_{LwF}(\theta) \tag{3}$$

Elastic Weight Consolidation (EWC) (Kirkpatrick et al., 2017) introduces network parameter uncertainty in the Bayesian framework. Intuitively, this approach consists of a $L2$ penalty on the difference between the parameters for the old θ_i^* (i denotes the indexes of the parameters) and the new θ_i. It uses the diagonal of the Fisher information matrix F_i (2) to weight different parameters. The EWC loss (4) slows down the learning process of task-relevant parameters, which contains knowledge learned previously.

$$L_{EWC}(\theta) = \sum_i F_i(\theta_i - \theta_i^*)^2 \tag{4}$$

From formula (4), we can see that if most of the parameters are fixed, it is equivalent to reducing the EWC loss, which is beneficial to preventing catastrophic forgetting.

Learning without forgetting (LwF) (Li and Hoiem, 2017) is another method for continual learning. Before training the new task, network outputs for the new task data are recorded, which is denoted by y'_o. It will be subsequently used during training to distill prior task knowledge. LwF employs a variant of knowledge distillation. In our framework, we use $L2$ (5) loss to regulate the outputs:

$$L_{LwF}(\theta) = \sum_k (y_o - y'_o)^2 \tag{5}$$

4 Experiment

In this section, we empirically verify the effectiveness and efficiency of our framework under the setting of incremental text classification tasks in the industrial scenarios.

4.1 Dataset & Implementation Details

In the experiments, we utilize the Amazon Reviews dataset (He and McAuley, 2016) to examine our method, which is widely used in text classification tasks. The original dataset contains 142.8 million product reviews collecting from 29 different domains. To be consistent with our industrial scenario, we firstly create a reduced dataset by randomly selecting 10000 pieces of data from 12 domains as the base task, 6000 of which are used as training set, 2000 as validation set, 2000 as test set. In the incremental learning session, we construct 17 subsequent tasks with 300 examples for training, 100 for validation and 100 for test from the rest domains.

We adopt the BERT-Base model (Devlin et al., 2019) and the BERT default uncased vocabulary. All runs use the AdamW optimizer[2] (Kingma and Ba, 2014; Devlin et al., 2019) with 5 epochs, 32 batch size and 0.1 dropout rate. For the base task, we set learning rate as 2e-5. For the incremental tasks, we set learning rate as 2e-3, λ_1 as 0.35 and λ_2 as 1. Based on offline calculation results, we only pick up 0.1% parameters to participate in each training process. Our experiments are conducted in Intel(R) Xeon(R) CPU E5-2699 v4 at 2.20GHz, 2 Nvidia Tesla P40 GPU with 24 GB of RAM.

[2] https://www.fast.ai/2018/07/02/adam-weight-decay/

Order ↓ ~ Method →	EWC	LwF	EWC&LwF	PE-rand	PE-*	Lower Bound	Upper Bound
I	47.39	47.6	45.76	**50.6**	50.46	45.14	51.59
II	48.54	47.95	48.3	51.35	**51.63**	45.81	53.18
III	40.44	45.23	42.11	45.42	**49.51**	38.29	51.1
IV	43.27	45.16	41.04	42.07	**46.8**	41.27	54.78
Average Acc	44.91	46.49	43.30	47.36	**49.6**	42.63	52.66

Table 1: Main result of text classification (above) averaged accuracy score respectively (see Appendix A for the dataset orderings).

4.2 Models

We compare our proposed models with the a series of baseline methods in our experiments:

- lower-bound: a standard classification model is fine-tuned on the individual task without any continual learning strategy, which can be considered as the lower-bound method.
- upper-bound: a model is trained on all tasks simultaneously, which can be considered as the upper-bound method since it has access to the whole dataset.
- EWC & LwF: Two classical regularization-based methods for continual learning.
- PE-rand: Our proposal model is trained by randomly choosing some parameters and keeping them unchanged during online training stage, instead of using the offline calculation strategy.
- PE-*: Our continual learning framework, including offline calculation and parameter-efficient online training.

4.3 Results

The models are trained on the current training set and evaluated on the union of all the test sets. To ensure the robustness of the task ordering, we evaluate our methods on the four different orderings (chosen randomly), which are shown in Appendix A.

Table 1 provides a summary of our main results. We report the micro-averaged accuracy for the classification task. The lower bound is trained in the current task without using any continual learning strategy to overcome catastrophic forgetting, while the upper bound is trained on all data after the new task comes, which can be considered multi-task method. There is a significant gap between the lower bound and the upper bound, which illustrates the need for continual learning. As the classical CL methods, EWC and LwF outperform the standard model without any specific continual learning, but still suffer from catastrophic forgetting in the order IV. It can be seen that our proposed PE-* achieves a better performance than EWC, LwF and their combination. This is because most of the parameters in BERT are fixed, which is equivalent to posing a strict regularization to the parameters to prevent catastrophic forgetting while using the remaining parameters to learn new tasks. Compared to PE-rand, PE-* has a better average accuracy, which verifies the importance of parameter selections. Although the random selection method outperforms PE-* in order I, it is difficult to obtain a suitable set of parameters in most cases for models to learn new tasks while maintaining previous knowledge.

Moreover, according to the principles of EWC and LwF, the former records the initial model parameters, and the latter records the data features of new tasks. As the training progresses, their regular loss terms especially $L_{EWC}(\theta)$ will get bigger and bigger in model like BERT-Base with 110M parameters. What's more, in real industrial scenarios, each new task may have different suitable hyper parameters. We do not have time to do grid search of the best hyper parameters, so λ_{EWC} and λ_{LwF} may not be optimal solutions. This results in an unbalanced ratio of $L(\theta)$ to $L_{EWC}(\theta)$ and $L_{LwF}(\theta)$, where $L(\theta)$ may much smaller than $L_{EWC}(\theta)$ and $L_{LwF}(\theta)$. Therefore, as the number of tasks increases, the training of new tasks will become more and more difficult with the same set of hyper-parameters. However, the previous tasks have not been fully learned. This problem accumulates gradually in regularization-based method and leads to results that are not as good as our method (PE-*) which just handles a very small amount parameters.

Figure 3 shows the accuracy of model on the first task test set as the model are trained on more tasks. The figure illustrates how well each model retains its previously acquired knowledge as it learns new knowledge. We can see that our framework is con-

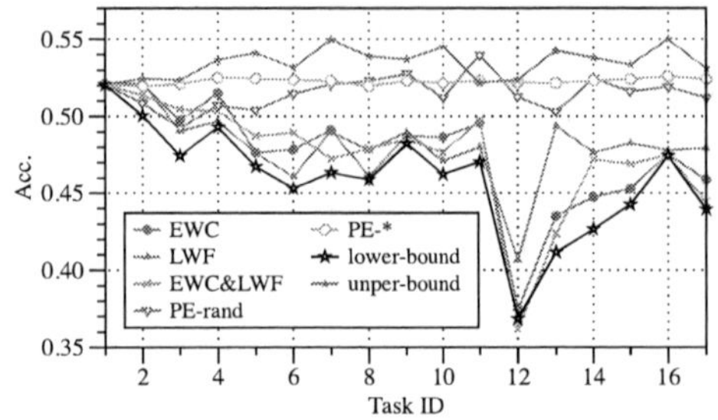

Figure 3: Performance on the first task test examples of order I during training as training progresses.

Reserved Percent	Order1	Order2	Order3	Order4
0.50%	**50.46**	**51.63**	**49.51**	46.8
1.00%	50.04	51.63	49.05	**47.34**
5.00%	45.11	48.61	46.44	44.43
10.00%	39.08	38.36	34.38	37.61

Table 2: The effect of layer-wise parameter reserved percentage on accuracy.

sistently better and more stable compared to other methods.

4.4 Parameter-efficient Strategy

Figure 4 shows the weight map of Fisher information. It can be seen that in the BERT model, the parameters of the embedding-layer have little effect on our classification task. Most of the important parameters are concentrated in the transformer block layer, and the importance of the attention layer is higher than that of the feed forward layer. In addition, according to our statistics, we found that 13%(about 14M) of the parameters' Fisher information is 0, and most of them are in embedding-layer.

In our experiments, we found that the parameters to be fixed cannot be determined simply in order of magnitude. According to (Jawahar et al., 2019), BERT encodes rich linguistic information in different transformer blocks. Therefore, refer to previous experience (Ben Zaken et al., 2021; Xu et al., 2021), we chose a layer-wise strategy to select important parameters. We fixed the parameters from large to small in a certain proportion at each layer of the model. To this end, each layer has parameters for new tasks to learn.

4.5 Model Size

We set layer-wise parameter reserved for new task to different values, 0.5%, 1%, 5% and 10%, and the percent of parameters fixed for old task are 99.5%, 99%, 95% and 90%. The advantage of our parameter-efficient continual learning becomes more pronounced at extreme sparsity rates. In Table 2, we report the accuracy across different task orders and reserved rates. We can observe that the more parameters fixed, the better the effect on alleviating catastrophic forgetting.

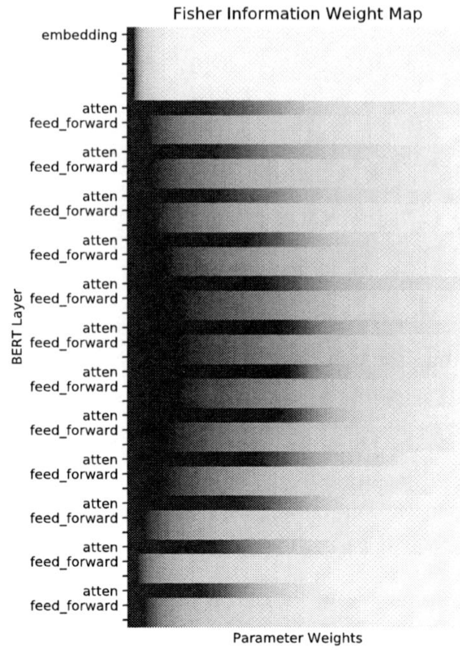

Figure 4: Calculating the model Fisher information by review old tasks, where dark colors are weighted more than light colors. The layers of BERT are ordered from bottom to top (i.e. the embedding layer is shown at the top).

Method	Acc	Saved Parameters	Saved model size
EWC	47.49	110B	421MB
LwF	47.95	110B	421MB
EWC&LwF	48.65	110B	421MB
PE-*	**51.63**	0.1B	1.2MB

Table 3: Comparison of storage costs.

In the above experiments, we only trained 0.1% of the parameters in the BERT model. We use the sparse-matrix method to store the model, and only store the index and value each time, occupying about 1.2 Mb of space, which is 0.3% of the entire model, as shown in Table 3. Parameter-efficient strategy greatly saves network bandwidth and storage requirements.

5 Conclusion

This paper introduces a parameter-efficient continual learning framework, which is designed for real-time incremental learning system. In offline stage, the framework identifies the parameters that are less important to the old tasks. By updating these parameters in online training stage, the model is able to learn new tasks in short time without forgetting the old ones. Furthermore, we surprisingly find that decent results can be achieved by only training a small subset of parameters (e.g. 0.1%). This observation enables us to largely decrease the storage of the snapshot, which is important for the system requiring frequent update.

References

Ankur Bapna, Naveen Arivazhagan, and Orhan Firat. 2019. Simple, scalable adaptation for neural machine translation. *arXiv preprint arXiv:1909.08478*.

Elad Ben Zaken, Shauli Ravfogel, and Yoav Goldberg. 2021. Bitfit: Simple parameter-efficient fine-tuning for transformer-based masked language-models. *arXiv e-prints*, pages arXiv–2106.

Francisco M Castro, Manuel J Marín-Jiménez, Nicolás Guil, Cordelia Schmid, and Karteek Alahari. 2018. End-to-end incremental learning. In *Proceedings of the European conference on computer vision (ECCV)*, pages 233–248.

Zhiyuan Chen and Bing Liu. 2018. Lifelong machine learning. *Synthesis Lectures on Artificial Intelligence and Machine Learning*, 12(3):1–207.

Matthias Delange, Rahaf Aljundi, Marc Masana, Sarah Parisot, Xu Jia, Ales Leonardis, Greg Slabaugh, and Tinne Tuytelaars. 2021. A continual learning survey: Defying forgetting in classification tasks. *IEEE Transactions on Pattern Analysis and Machine Intelligence*.

Jacob Devlin, Ming-Wei Chang, Kenton Lee, and Kristina Toutanova. 2019. Bert: Pre-training of deep bidirectional transformers for language understanding. In *Proceedings of the 2019 Conference of the North American Chapter of the Association for Computational Linguistics: Human Language Technologies, Volume 1 (Long and Short Papers)*, pages 4171–4186.

Chrisantha Fernando, Dylan Banarse, Charles Blundell, Yori Zwols, David Ha, Andrei A Rusu, Alexander Pritzel, and Daan Wierstra. 2017. Pathnet: Evolution channels gradient descent in super neural networks. *arXiv preprint arXiv:1701.08734*.

Robert M French. 1999. Catastrophic forgetting in connectionist networks. *Trends in cognitive sciences*, 3(4):128–135.

Demi Guo, Alexander M Rush, and Yoon Kim. 2020. Parameter-efficient transfer learning with diff pruning. *arXiv preprint arXiv:2012.07463*.

Ruining He and Julian McAuley. 2016. Ups and downs: Modeling the visual evolution of fashion trends with one-class collaborative filtering. In *proceedings of the 25th international conference on world wide web*, pages 507–517.

Saihui Hou, Xinyu Pan, Chen Change Loy, Zilei Wang, and Dahua Lin. 2019. Learning a unified classifier incrementally via rebalancing. In *Proceedings of the IEEE/CVF Conference on Computer Vision and Pattern Recognition*, pages 831–839.

Neil Houlsby, Andrei Giurgiu, Stanislaw Jastrzebski, Bruna Morrone, Quentin De Laroussilhe, Andrea Gesmundo, Mona Attariyan, and Sylvain Gelly. 2019. Parameter-efficient transfer learning for nlp. In *International Conference on Machine Learning*, pages 2790–2799. PMLR.

Ganesh Jawahar, Benoît Sagot, and Djamé Seddah. 2019. What does BERT learn about the structure of language? In *Proceedings of the 57th Annual Meeting of the Association for Computational Linguistics*, pages 3651–3657, Florence, Italy. Association for Computational Linguistics.

Diederik P Kingma and Jimmy Ba. 2014. Adam: A method for stochastic optimization. *arXiv preprint arXiv:1412.6980*.

James Kirkpatrick, Razvan Pascanu, Neil Rabinowitz, Joel Veness, Guillaume Desjardins, Andrei A Rusu, Kieran Milan, John Quan, Tiago Ramalho, Agnieszka Grabska-Barwinska, et al. 2017. Overcoming catastrophic forgetting in neural networks. *Proceedings of the national academy of sciences*, 114(13):3521–3526.

Zhizhong Li and Derek Hoiem. 2017. Learning without forgetting. *IEEE transactions on pattern analysis and machine intelligence*, 40(12):2935–2947.

Yinhan Liu, Myle Ott, Naman Goyal, Jingfei Du, Mandar Joshi, Danqi Chen, Omer Levy, Mike Lewis, Luke Zettlemoyer, and Veselin Stoyanov. 2019. Roberta: A robustly optimized bert pretraining approach. *arXiv preprint arXiv:1907.11692*.

Arun Mallya and Svetlana Lazebnik. 2018. Packnet: Adding multiple tasks to a single network by iterative pruning. In *Proceedings of the IEEE conference on Computer Vision and Pattern Recognition*, pages 7765–7773.

Michael McCloskey and Neal J Cohen. 1989. Catastrophic interference in connectionist networks: The sequential learning problem. In *Psychology of learning and motivation*, volume 24, pages 109–165. Elsevier.

Fei Mi, Lingjing Kong, Tao Lin, Kaicheng Yu, and Boi Faltings. 2020a. Generalized class incremental learning. In *Proceedings of the IEEE/CVF Conference on Computer Vision and Pattern Recognition Workshops*, pages 240–241.

Fei Mi, Xiaoyu Lin, and Boi Faltings. 2020b. Ader: Adaptively distilled exemplar replay towards continual learning for session-based recommendation. In

Fourteenth ACM Conference on Recommender Systems, pages 408–413.

Tomas Mikolov, Kai Chen, Greg Corrado, and Jeffrey Dean. 2013a. Efficient estimation of word representations in vector space. *arXiv preprint arXiv:1301.3781*.

Tomas Mikolov, Ilya Sutskever, Kai Chen, Greg S Corrado, and Jeff Dean. 2013b. Distributed representations of words and phrases and their compositionality. *Advances in neural information processing systems*, 26.

Matthew E Peters, Mark Neumann, Mohit Iyyer, Matt Gardner, Christopher Clark, Kenton Lee, and Luke Zettlemoyer. 2018. Deep contextualized word representations. In *Proceedings of the 2018 Conference of the North American Chapter of the Association for Computational Linguistics: Human Language Technologies, Volume 1 (Long Papers)*, pages 2227–2237.

Alec Radford, Karthik Narasimhan, Tim Salimans, and Ilya Sutskever. 2018. Improving language understanding by generative pre-training.

Alec Radford, Jeffrey Wu, Rewon Child, David Luan, Dario Amodei, Ilya Sutskever, et al. 2019. Language models are unsupervised multitask learners. *OpenAI blog*, 1(8):9.

Tiago Ramalho and Marta Garnelo. 2019. Adaptive posterior learning: few-shot learning with a surprise-based memory module. *arXiv preprint arXiv:1902.02527*.

Sylvestre-Alvise Rebuffi, Hakan Bilen, and Andrea Vedaldi. 2017a. Learning multiple visual domains with residual adapters. *arXiv preprint arXiv:1705.08045*.

Sylvestre-Alvise Rebuffi, Alexander Kolesnikov, Georg Sperl, and Christoph H Lampert. 2017b. icarl: Incremental classifier and representation learning. In *Proceedings of the IEEE conference on Computer Vision and Pattern Recognition*, pages 2001–2010.

Andrei A Rusu, Neil C Rabinowitz, Guillaume Desjardins, Hubert Soyer, James Kirkpatrick, Koray Kavukcuoglu, Razvan Pascanu, and Raia Hadsell. 2016. Progressive neural networks. *arXiv preprint arXiv:1606.04671*.

Joan Serra, Didac Suris, Marius Miron, and Alexandros Karatzoglou. 2018. Overcoming catastrophic forgetting with hard attention to the task. In *International Conference on Machine Learning*, pages 4548–4557. PMLR.

Yu Sun, Shuohuan Wang, Yukun Li, Shikun Feng, Xuyi Chen, Han Zhang, Xin Tian, Danxiang Zhu, Hao Tian, and Hua Wu. 2019. Ernie: Enhanced representation through knowledge integration. *arXiv preprint arXiv:1904.09223*.

Yi-Lin Sung, Varun Nair, and Colin A Raffel. 2021. Training neural networks with fixed sparse masks. *Advances in Neural Information Processing Systems*, 34.

Ming Tu, Visar Berisha, Martin Woolf, Jae-sun Seo, and Yu Cao. 2016. Ranking the parameters of deep neural networks using the fisher information. In *2016 IEEE International Conference on Acoustics, Speech and Signal Processing (ICASSP)*, pages 2647–2651. IEEE.

Max Welling. 2009. Herding dynamical weights to learn. In *Proceedings of the 26th Annual International Conference on Machine Learning*, pages 1121–1128.

Yue Wu, Yinpeng Chen, Lijuan Wang, Yuancheng Ye, Zicheng Liu, Yandong Guo, and Yun Fu. 2019. Large scale incremental learning. In *Proceedings of the IEEE/CVF Conference on Computer Vision and Pattern Recognition*, pages 374–382.

Ju Xu and Zhanxing Zhu. 2018. Reinforced continual learning. *arXiv preprint arXiv:1805.12369*.

Runxin Xu, Fuli Luo, Zhiyuan Zhang, Chuanqi Tan, Baobao Chang, Songfang Huang, and Fei Huang. 2021. Raise a child in large language model: Towards effective and generalizable fine-tuning. *arXiv preprint arXiv:2109.05687*.

Bowen Zhao, Xi Xiao, Guojun Gan, Bin Zhang, and Shu-Tao Xia. 2020. Maintaining discrimination and fairness in class incremental learning. In *Proceedings of the IEEE/CVF Conference on Computer Vision and Pattern Recognition*, pages 13208–13217.

Zhe Zhao, Hui Chen, Jinbin Zhang, Wayne Xin Zhao, Tao Liu, Wei Lu, Xi Chen, Haotang Deng, Qi Ju, and Xiaoyong Du. 2019. Uer: An open-source toolkit for pre-training models. In *Proceedings of the 2019 Conference on Empirical Methods in Natural Language Processing and the 9th International Joint Conference on Natural Language Processing (EMNLP-IJCNLP): System Demonstrations*, pages 241–246.

Zhe Zhao, Tao Liu, Shen Li, Bofang Li, and Xiaoyong Du. 2017. Ngram2vec: Learning improved word representations from ngram co-occurrence statistics. In *Proceedings of the 2017 conference on empirical methods in natural language processing*, pages 244–253.

A Task order

We use the following task orders (chosen randomly) for text classification:

- Kindle_Store → Arts_Crafts_and_Sewing → Electronics → Magazine_Subscriptions → Pet_Supplies → Sports_and_Outdoors → Prime_Pantry → Office_Products

→ Movies_and_TV → Automotive → CDs_and_Vinyl → Gift_Cards → Digital_Music → Clothing_Shoes_and_Jewelry → Home_and_Kitchen → Software → Grocery_and_Gourmet_Food

- Pet_Supplies → Gift_Cards → Electronics → Prime_Pantry → Office_Products → Digital_Music → Magazine_Subscriptions → Home_and_Kitchen → CDs_and_Vinyl → Grocery_and_Gourmet_Food
- Digital_Music → Arts_Crafts_and_Sewing → Office_Products → Magazine_Subscriptions → Kindle_Store → Software → Automotive → Prime_Pantry → Grocery_and_Gourmet_Food → Movies_and_TV → Electronics → Home_and_Kitchen → Pet_Supplies → CDs_and_Vinyl → Clothing_Shoes_and_Jewelry → Gift_Cards
- Magazine_Subscriptions → Sports_and_Outdoors → Digital_Music → Electronics → Prime_Pantry → CDs_and_Vinyl → Grocery_and_Gourmet_Food → Home_and_Kitchen → Software → Arts_Crafts_and_Sewing → Clothing_Shoes_and_Jewelry → Pet_Supplies → Office_Products → Kindle_Store → Gift_Cards

Self-Aware Feedback-Based Self-Learning in Large-Scale Conversational AI

Pragaash Ponnusamy* **Clint Solomon Mathialagan***
Gustavo Aguilar **Chengyuan Ma** **Chenlei Guo**
Amazon Alexa
{ponnup,matclint,gustalas,mchengyu,guochenl}@amazon.com

Abstract

Self-learning paradigms in large-scale conversational AI agents tend to leverage user feedback in bridging between what they say and what they mean. However, such learning, particularly in Markov-based query rewriting systems have far from addressed the impact of these models on future training where successive feedback is inevitably contingent on the rewrite itself, especially in a continually updating environment. In this paper, we explore the consequences of this inherent lack of self-awareness towards impairing the model performance, ultimately resulting in both Type I and II errors over time. To that end, we propose augmenting the Markov Graph construction with a superposition-based adjacency matrix. Here, our method leverages an induced stochasticity to reactively learn a locally-adaptive decision boundary based on the performance of the individual rewrites in a bi-variate beta setting. We also surface a data augmentation strategy that leverages template-based generation in abridging complex conversation hierarchies of dialogs so as to simplify the learning process. All in all, we demonstrate that our self-aware model improves the overall PR-AUC by 27.45%, achieves a relative defect reduction of up to 31.22%, and is able to adapt quicker to changes in global preferences across a large number of customers.

1 Introduction

Large-scale conversational AI systems such as Alexa, Google, Siri etc. serve millions of users daily all over the planet, who speak diverse languages and have a myriad of regional preferences. These models need to be constantly updated with new data to adapt to changing customer behavior and trends. Data curation processes that rely solely on human annotations cannot possibly scale to sustain the rapid update pace of these systems. Therefore, quite naturally, these AI agents have increased their reliance on explicit and implicit feedback from customer interactions to automate the learning process while limiting manual annotation efforts selectively only to auditing and quality control purposes.

In such feedback-based self-learning systems where new streams of data are being funneled in to continually update the system, the mere presence of the ML model itself inevitably impacts future training data. This is rather evident with query rewriting models where the reformulated query becomes intertwined with the original utterance to the extent where the successive feedback in the customer-system interaction paths become contingent on the rewrite. Here, we show that as these models continue to be updated without accounting for this unintended interference, they tend to learn false equivalencies between the original requests and rewrites, thereby impeding their own self-learning capabilities.

In this work, we build upon an absorbing Markov Chain model to make the model self-aware i.e. it can distinguish between customer requests and system rewrites, and adapt its decision boundary based on the quality of the rewrites. Note that the system can also be an ensemble of heterogeneous agents proposing different reformulations for the same query. The self-learning Markov model does not require any agent specific information and rather treats them all as a single entity. Thus, this work can be integrated into any conversational AI system to enable self-learning at a system-level without major changes to the rest of the architecture.

2 Related Work

Query rewriting techniques, particularly in the form of suggestive disambiguation have been extensively employed in online search systems (Jansen et al., 2009; Antonellis et al., 2008; He et al., 2016; Riezler and Liu, 2010), so as to increase recall and im-

* Equal contribution

Proceedings of NAACL-HLT 2022: Industry Track Papers, pages 324 - 333
July 10-15, 2022 ©2022 Association for Computational Linguistics

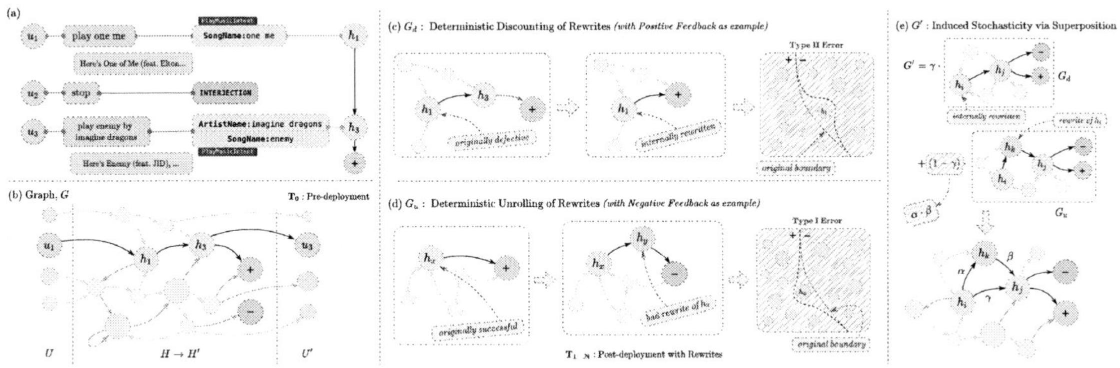

Figure 1: A general walk-through for motivating a meta-state augmented Graph: Beginning with the original construction of chains in **(a)** where utterances, U are projected into the hypothesis space, H before being encoded into the absorbing Markov model in **(b)** showing how a target rewrite in U' is resolved given a source in U. Thereafter, upon deployment, the effect of continuing to model the Graph as before i.e. by discounting the presence of rewrites, G_d in **(c)** and choosing to always unroll the internal rewrites as an externalized state, G_u in **(d)**, both lead to Type II and I errors respectively. Note that the decision boundaries over discrete spaces here are to illustrate the nature of mis-classifications. Naturally, in attempt to balance these two categories of error, a superposition of G_d and G_u is constructed in **(e)** wherein the rewrites act as meta-states that induce stochasticity within the Graph, G'.

prove click-through rates. Naturally, conversational AI systems have also adopted similar techniques to reduce customer defects (Sodhi et al., 2021; Hao et al., 2020; Su et al., 2019; Rastogi et al., 2019; Roshan-Ghias et al., 2020; Yuan et al., 2021; Fan et al., 2021). To the best of our knowledge, none of them address feedback issues that arise from model-in-the-loop environments.

Previous work has analyzed biases and noises in the feedback loop of machine learning models, particularly in recommendation systems (Chaney et al., 2018; Mansoury et al., 2020; Sun et al., 2019; Mehrabi et al., 2021; Lim et al., 2015; Saito et al., 2020). Khritankov (2021); Sculley et al. (2015); Amodei et al. (2016) delve into the effects of unwanted feedback loops that can lead to AI system instability. These works do not consider misplaced attribution of the feedback itself, which is exacerbated in query-rewriting systems.

In Ponnusamy et al. (2020), customer interactions are modeled as an absorbing chain Markov model, and the candidate that is most likely to result in a successful absorbing state is predicted as the rewrite. This work does not address the equivalence conflation problem that occurs over time in such a setup. We update the Markov formulation to enable self-awareness and resolve the ambiguity in feedback attribution.

In Shi et al. (2021), the Markov model is leveraged as a recall layer that produces candidates which are re-ranked by a self-learning neural model that relies on negative user feedback. While there is not much information on the performance of the recall layer, their neural ranking mechanism is richly augmented with common sense and various user preferences. They do not mention any degradation of the Markov model over time but it is possible that the enriched re-ranker could be compensating for this. In contrast, our work solves the issue within the self-learning Markov model itself as opposed to deferring it to a downstream model. This has the added benefit of accelerating the rate of self-learning.

3 Dataset

To extract the chains of successive customer interactions for the eventual Graph, we first pre-process about 90 days of de-identified time-series utterance data from a representative sample of customers worldwide to construct our dataset of sessions, $\mathcal{D}$. Here, conceptually speaking, each such session represents a time-delimited snapshot of a particular customer's conversation history. To illustrate this, consider the session in Figure 1(a) that encapsulates a series of consecutive utterances which follows a customer interjecting with a "*stop*" and following up with a rephrase of their original request to play the song "*Enemy*". Note that in practice, to maximize the consistency of a conversational goal, the time delay between consecutive turns is heuristically bounded.

Now, while the vast majority of interactions are

indeed stateless, there are those which trigger dialogs so as to solicit the user to disambiguate. This inevitably creates conversational hierarchies that span multiple turns. To ground this, consider the dialog in Figure 2(a) where the system is unable to fulfill the initiating request without first clarifying which playlist to add the song to. To address this complexity and improve the overall intelligibility of the corresponding session, such multi-turn dialogs are abridged by connecting the initiating turn with a synthetic one as shown in Figure 2(c). This is accomplished via template-based DAGs (*the construction of which is explored with greater detail in the Appendix Section 8.1*) wherein the resolved entities towards the end of the corresponding dialog are passed through to generate the synthetic utterance e.g. the DAG in Figure 2(b) is fed with "**SongName:**escape", "**ArtistName:**enrique iglesias", and "**PlaylistName:**kacey's" so as to surface the eventual synthesized utterance, "*add escape by enrique iglesias to kacey's playlist*".

4 Self-Aware Markov Model

Much akin to the original formulation of the Markov model by Ponnusamy et al. (2020), which we henceforth regard as our baseline, our dataset of ordered linear sequence of utterances is first projected into the hypothesis space, H e.g. the utterance "*play one me*" is mapped with the aid of the system's NLU component to the hypothesis, "**Music|PlayMusicIntent|SongName:**one me". Thereafter, they are each terminated with an absorbing state. The union of these disjoint chains tantamount to our Markov Graph, $G = (V, E)$ where $V = H \cup S$ represents the set of all transient and absorbing states respectively, while $E = V \times V$, naturally corresponds to the set of edges. In a more canonical form, the Graph can be represented via the transition matrix $\mathbf{A}$:

$$\mathbf{A} = \begin{bmatrix} \mathbf{Q} & \mathbf{S} \\ \mathbf{0} & \mathbf{I_2} \end{bmatrix} \tag{1}$$

where $\mathbf{Q} \in \mathbb{R}^{|H| \times |H|}$ is the sub-matrix of transition probabilities between transient states such that its (i, j)-th element corresponds to the probability of some source transition state, h_i transitioning to some target transition state, h_j in a single step or mathematically speaking, $q_{i,j} = P(h_j|h_i)$. The sub-matrix $\mathbf{S} \in \mathbb{R}^{2 \times |H|}$ refers to the immediate absorption probabilities of the corresponding transient states i.e. $\mathbf{S} = [\mathbf{s}^+, \mathbf{s}^-]$.

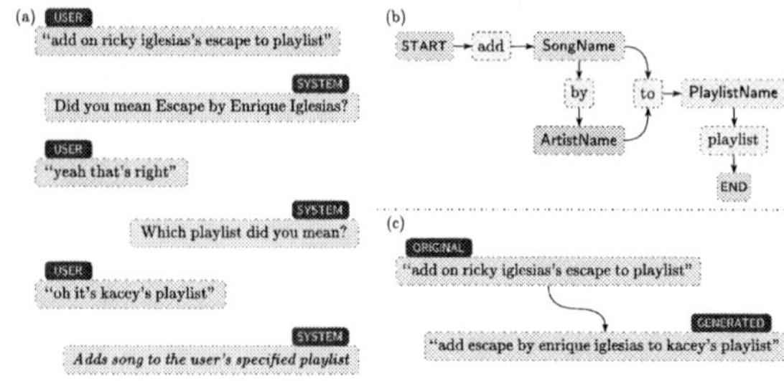

Figure 2: Dialog abridging via template-based DAG with (a) being the original dialog, (b) the extracted template graph, and (c) original with the synthesized utterance.

Now, with $\mathbf{Q}$ being a square matrix[1] whose norm, $\|\mathbf{Q}\| < 1$, the *fundamental matrix* of the Markov model, $\mathbf{N}$ as formulated in Definition 11.3 by Grinstead and Snell (2012) is therefore given by $\mathbf{N} = \sum_{n=0}^{\infty} \mathbf{Q}^n = \left(\mathbf{I}_{|\mathcal{H}|} - \mathbf{Q}\right)^{-1}$ where $\mathbf{Q}^n$ refers to the transition probability sub-matrix $\mathbf{Q}$ after exactly n steps. The *fundamental matrix*, $\mathbf{N}$ is leveraged in resolving the Markov model so as to surface rewrite candidates. Specifically, for a given initial transient state, h_i, a particular target transient state, h_t would be classified as a potential candidate should it be both *reachable* by h_i and conditioned on h_i, it leads to a higher chance of success. Mathematically speaking, this optimization objective can be expressed as $\Phi_\infty(h_t) > \Phi_\infty(h_i)$ where $\Phi_k(h_j)$ refers to the probability of reaching a successful absorbing state, s^+ from h_i via another state h_j that is at most k hops away i.e.:

$$\Phi_k(h_j) = P(s^+|h_j) \cdot \mathbf{N}_{i,j} \tag{2}$$

Here, by identifying the initial transient states that have at least one relatively more successful target transient state and thereby learning a measure of equivalency between states in the hypothesis space, H, the model is effectively able to partition H into those that require reformulation i.e. the defective sub-space, H^- and those that don't i.e. the successful sub-space, H^+. This nature of automatic partitioning leads the model to predict *rewritability* $\hat{y}$ of a given h_i as follows:

$$\hat{y}(h_i) = \mathbb{1}\left\{ \left(\underset{h \in H}{\arg\max}\, \Phi_\infty(h) \right) \neq h_i \right\} \tag{3}$$

[1] As every atomic chain in the Graph is terminated with an absorbing state, these terminal states are guaranteed to always be reachable by any given source transient state, thus ensuring their convergence i.e. $\lim_{n \to \infty} \mathbf{Q}^n = \mathbf{0}$.

4.1 Decision Boundary Degeneracy

Upon deployment however, the very presence of rewrites can significantly destabilize the Graph and impair the integrity of its learned partitioning. To ground this, consider, in the absence of any rewrite, a commonly misrecognized utterance, *"play theme"* (u_1) is followed up with rephrases of *"play team"*, *"play the song team by lorde"*, etc. Now, when the first Markov model $G_d^{(0)}$ is trained initially at T_0 (Figure 1b), it learns to rewrite u_1 to *"play team by lorde"* (r_1). Once deployed, as the Markov model continually learns from customer feedback, u_1 becomes more and more successful than it actually is, since r_1 is not explicitly modeled. Conceptually, this **deterministic discounting** deforms the decision boundary around u_1, resulting in a Type II error (Figure 1c). Such a misclassification will eventually shed the rewrite, forcing the graph to revert to $G_d^{(0)}$. This increases the rephrases to u_1 as previously observed at T_0 and as it gathers sufficient defect statistics, the pattern would repeat, resulting in an unstable oscillatory system that struggles to maintain a consistent decision boundary.

One way of solving the above problem, is to account for rewrites by always including them in the original interaction chain. While this might alleviate the Type II error described above, we show that this limits the system's capability to handle defective rewrites. Imagine a case where a successful utterance, say *"play la da dee"* is followed up by a defective system rewrite *"play lady"* (Figure 1d). This may arise due to a number of reasons such as epistemic or systemic errors, multi-agent interaction, etc. as it is the nature of any statistical model. This process of **deterministic unrolling**, which presumes rewrites to have some degree of latent intent equivalency with the original utterance, would cause the original hypothesis to become more and more defective than it actually is, resulting in a Type I error. To recover the original intent, the customers would need to rephrase following the defective rewrite e.g. *"play la da dee by cody simpson"* or some external guardrail mechanism would need to intervene. Yet again, the Graph will be slow to adapt the decision boundary in response to a Type I error or even worse, may completely fail to recover.

4.2 Meta-State Augmentation

A natural way to balance out these Type I and II errors and thereby maximizing the eventual precision and recall of the rewrites would to be to learn to unroll the rewrite should it improve the customer experience and discount it otherwise. This form of adaptive preservation and suppression of rewrites gives rise to a probabilistic decision making process where the rewrites act as a kind of meta-states that induce stochasticity within the Graph. Conceptually speaking, this is equivalent to both G_d and G_u being in a state of superposition as shown in Figure 1(e) where in the event that a particular transient state, h_i is both rewritten to h_k and followed-up by h_j, a meta-state triplet (MST) is formed. In more robust terms, each of these MSTs within the Graph are comprised of a *viability* edge, (h_i, h_k), a *succeeding* edge, (h_k, h_j), and a *discounting* edge, (h_i, h_j) and are uniquely parameterized by their own set of probabilistic values, namely in this case, α_{ik}, β_{kj}, and γ_{ij} respectively so as to allow the Graph to truly be locally adaptive in its learning. To that extent, we first construct a superposition-based transition matrix $\mathbf{A}'$ by updating the probabilities as below:

$$\begin{aligned} \mathbf{A}' &= (\boldsymbol{\lambda} \circ \mathbf{C})^\top \mathbf{D}^{-1} \\ \boldsymbol{\lambda} &= \boldsymbol{\alpha} \circ \mathbf{J}^{(\alpha)} + \boldsymbol{\beta} \circ \mathbf{J}^{(\beta)} + \boldsymbol{\gamma} \circ \mathbf{J}^{(\gamma)} + \mathbf{J}^{(\epsilon)} \end{aligned} \tag{4}$$

where $\mathbf{C} \in \mathbb{Z}_{0+}^{|V|\times|V|}$ such that $\mathbf{C}_{xy}$ refers to the co-occurrence count of the directed edge $e_{xy} = (h_x, h_y)$ in the superposition Graph, G' and $\mathbf{D}$ is the diagonal matrix whose entries are row-wise sum of the matrix $\mathbf{C}$ i.e. $\mathrm{diag}(\mathbf{D}) = (\boldsymbol{\lambda} \circ \mathbf{C}) \cdot \mathbf{1}$. The entries $\mathbf{J}_{xy}^{(\alpha)}$, $\mathbf{J}_{xy}^{(\beta)}$ and $\mathbf{J}_{xy}^{(\gamma)}$ on the other hand, are the ratios of e_{xy} occurring as either a *viability*, *succeeding* or *discounting* edge respectively. $\mathbf{J}_{xy}^{(\epsilon)}$, however, is the complementary ratio of e_{xy} not being a part of any MST. As a matter of completeness, it's worth noting here that $\boldsymbol{\alpha}, \boldsymbol{\beta}, \boldsymbol{\gamma}, \mathbf{J}^{(\cdot)} \in [0,1]^{|V|\times|V|}$ such that $\mathbf{J}_{xy}^{(\alpha)} + \mathbf{J}_{xy}^{(\beta)} + \mathbf{J}_{xy}^{(\gamma)} + \mathbf{J}_{xy}^{(\epsilon)} = 1$. Consequently, this modified transition matrix is then used in resolving the Markov Graph as before, to generate rewrite candidates.

4.3 Meta-State Triplet Parameters

In order to adaptively preserve or suppress the rewrites, the weights on the *viability* edges, α should reflect the performance of rewriting. As such, for a given *viability* edge e_{xy} we compare the interaction quality (IQ), as scored by a neural dialog model (Gupta et al., 2021) of the population where h_x was not rewritten, X against that where h_x was rewritten to h_y, $Y|X = W$. Now, suppose that the probability of success in each of these populations follows Beta distributions i.e. $p_X \sim \text{Beta}(a_x, b_x)$ and $p_W \sim \text{Beta}(a_w, b_w)$. Then, leveraging the beta bi-variate hypothesis testing model as formalized by Miller (2015), the probability that rewriting is comparatively better is given by:

$$P(p_W > p_X) = 1 - \int_0^1 f(p_X, p_W) \cdot d_{p_X}$$

$$f(p_X, p_W) = \frac{p_X^{a_x - 1}(1 - p_X)^{b_x - 1}}{B(a_x, b_x)} \cdot I_{p_X}(a_w, b_w)$$

where, B is the beta function and I, the regularized incomplete beta function. Thereafter, α_{xy} is computed as a variant of $P(p_X > p_Y)$ by leveraging different probability arguments depending on support sufficiency for both p_X and p_Y as detailed in the appendix.

Then, while α reflects the rewrite quality via historical statistics, the weights on the *succeeding* edge, $\beta = \alpha^\rho$ are designed to maintain the semantic connectivity between the rewrite and the succeeding states. Here, we rely on Levenshtein ratio to score on both the grapheme and phoneme levels so as to compute a relevance measure, $\rho \in [0, 1]$. Intuitively speaking, it allows the α-β flow to be dampened in the event the rewrite is followed up with a semantically similar rephrase, indicating that it may not have quite achieved the customer's true intent. In a complementary fashion, the weight of the *discounting* edge $\gamma = 1 - \alpha \cdot \beta$ acts as a response whose magnitude correspond to how much the corresponding rewrite in its MST needs to be suppressed. Thus, the locally adaptive Markov model is **self-aware** to be able to tailor the decision boundary so as to surgically maximize the precision and recall over the space of rewrites.

5 Experiments

We build an evaluation dataset of request-rewrite pairs annotated by a cascaded labeling pipeline comprising of an interaction quality model, NLU scores and manual verification. This fundamentally enables us to surface, for a given request, u, both the set of rewrites which significantly improve the customer experience, $\mathbf{r}_u^+$ and the set that significantly worsen, $\mathbf{r}_u^-$ to collectively yield our core evaluation dataset, $\mathcal{D}_e$. Then, for any given request, we further define its *rewritability*, i.e. a binary label which indicates whether a particular request, u, should at all be rewritten, as $y_u = \mathbb{1}(|\mathbf{r}_u^+| > 0)$.

We benchmark our self-aware Markov model variant $\mathcal{M}_s$ against the baseline $\mathcal{M}_b$ (Ponnusamy et al., 2020) [2] and measure the gains introduced by our template-based generation strategy on both model variants, denoted by the subscript $+g$. Specifically, we measure their performance on the evaluation set $\mathcal{D}_e$ over three tasks, namely their ability to **partition** the requests based on their predicted *rewritability*, learn the optimal rewrite for a given request i.e. **equivalence learning**, and react to changing customer preferences i.e **reactivity rate**.

5.1 Partitioning

The automatic partitioning task is a binary classification problem where the ground truth label y_u is compared against the model prediction (Equation 3). We observe that the self-aware models significantly improve precision and recall compared to their baseline counterparts as shown in Table 1. Here, it is worth mentioning that the consistent significant gain in recall with template-based generation enabled is in part due to a strong correlating property between the need for rewriting and the need for disambiguation, which otherwise would have been lost due to the local Markov property.

Model	$\mathcal{M}_{b+g}$	$\mathcal{M}_s$	$\mathcal{M}_{s+g}$
Precision	+0.0961	**+0.1808**	+0.1688
Recall	+0.1724	+0.4674	**+0.5110**
Accuracy	+0.0606	+0.1922	**+0.2047**
F_1	+0.2555	+0.5547	**+0.5834**

Table 1: Partitioning metrics measured as improvement over $\mathcal{M}_b$

5.2 Equivalence Learning

Once the requests are partitioned, the performance of the model in selecting rewrites i.e. its ability to optimally learn *equivalencies* for those in $\mathcal{H}^-$ are evaluated. To this end, we compare the score of the models (Φ_∞ from Equation 2) against the ground truth annotations in D_e i.e. whether a given rewrite candidate makes the customer experience significantly better (+1) or worse (-1). The precision-recall curves are then obtained as in Figure 3. The

[2]To the best of our knowledge, this is a novel space where widely peer-reviewed work on continual adaptive self-learning systems are few and far between. As such, this Markov-based baseline which has already shown to outperform a pointer-generator LSTM is chosen given its already established production impact.

self-aware models exhibit much better precision vs. recall trade-offs and have significantly higher areas under the curve. To highlight, the template augmented self-aware model $\mathcal{M}_{s+g}$ improves the PR-AUC by **27.45%** relative to $\mathcal{M}_{b+g}$.

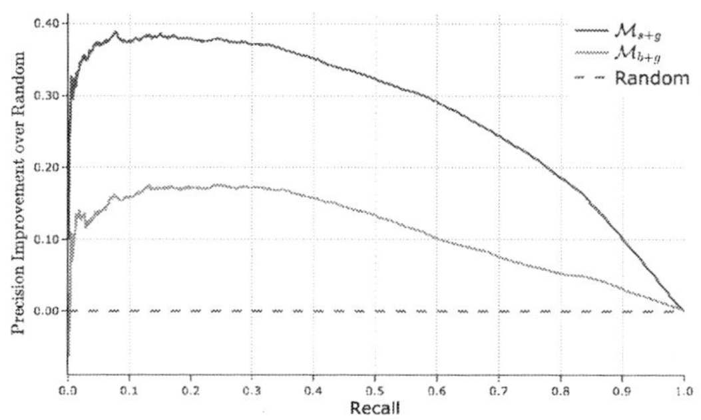

Figure 3: Precision-Recall Characteristics of Equivalence Learning.

5.3 Reactivity Rate

A key paradigm in designing large-scale AI solutions is the adaptability of the system to changing customer preferences. In the query rewriting domain, this quality can be expressed via the rate at which the top rewrite candidate changes over time i.e. the *reactivity rate*. Figure 4 shows the distribution of reactivity rate for common requests across the graph over a 30 day time period. The

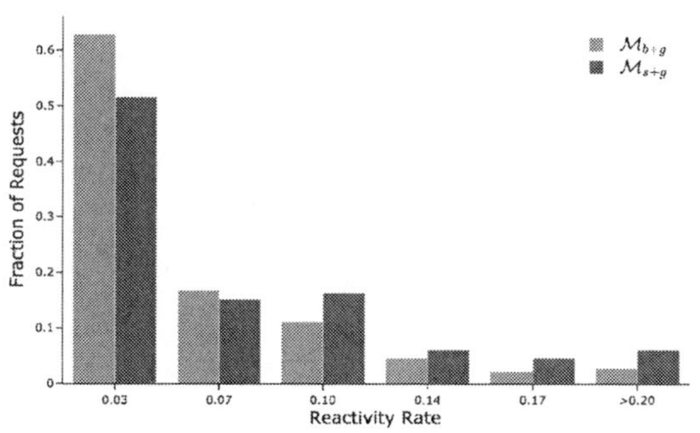

Figure 4: Reactivity Rate Distribution.

self-aware model exhibits higher reactivity as seen by the right shift in the distribution with respect to the baseline. To study the impact on performance over time, we compare the relative change in F_1 scores of the models $\Delta F_1^{(t)} = \frac{F_1^{(t)}}{F_1^{(0)}} - 1$ where, $F_1^{(t)}$ is the F_1 score of the given model at a given timestamp t on the equivalence learning task. It can be seen from Figure 5 that the self-aware model shows relative increase in the score over time, whereas the baseline is subject to a degradation in performance. Thus the higher reactivity rate of self-awareness is correlated to increased self-learning with the models adapting to customer feedback.

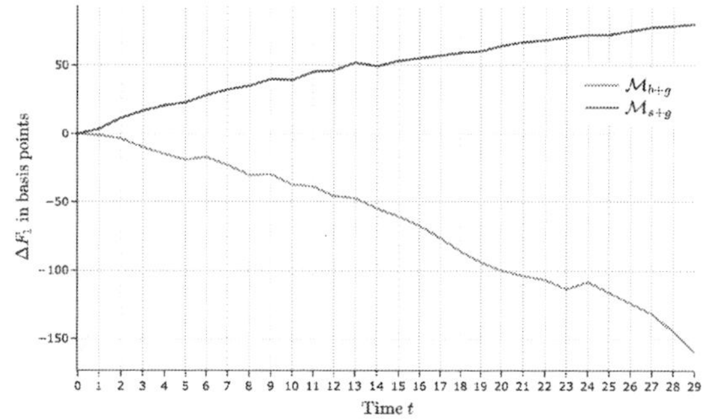

Figure 5: Relative change in F_1 score over time t. Note that for every timestamp, both models were retrained with new customer feedback.

5.4 Online Performance

With our approach for template-based generation being inherently scalable across languages and our self-aware Markov Graph naturally being language agnostic, we successfully deployed the model across 11 locales spanning 6 languages worldwide. To facilitate the models' ability to be continually adaptive, they are refreshed daily with new customer feedback. After nearly 6 weeks of in-depth A/B testing in production, we observed a strongly significant reduction (i.e. achieving a p-value of ≤ 0.0001) in defects experienced by the customers compared to the baseline (see Table 2) with a relative defect reduction of up to **31.22%**.

6 Deployment

In similar fashion to the well-established architecture of modern conversational AI systems (Gao et al., 2018), Alexa follows suit in which the user-spoken audio is first transcribed into an utterance text by an automatic speech recognition (ASR) system and thereafter has its domain, intent and entities inferred by the natural language understanding (NLU) system. However, with the presence of our reformulation engine as shown in Figure 6 below, the utterance text is intercepted so as to vend out a rewrite by means of an online database-backed lookup system before being funneled through to NLU. Thereafter, the resulting interpretation in context of the active dialog is leveraged to execute the corresponding action and respond back to the user.

Language	Defect Reduction	Example Request	Example Rewrite
English	25.78%	play tokyo take out	OLD: play tokyo **takedown** NEW: play **towkyo takeout by michael giacchino**
French	31.22%	mets la chanson le dimanche à bamako	OLD: mets **le** dimanche à bamako NEW: **joue la album dimanche** à bamako **par amadou**
Italian	23.98%	metti campioni del mondo	OLD: **metti la** canzone campioni del mondo NEW: **riproduci** canzone **italia** campione del mondo **di gigione**
German	22.73%	spiel sun goes down von lenas x.	OLD: spiel sun goes down von lil nas **you** NEW: spiel sun goes down von lil nas **x**.
Spanish	28.06%	reproducir feliz cumpleaños de alejandro fernández	OLD: **pon las mañanitas con** alejandro fernández NEW: reproduce **las mañanitas** de alejandro fernández
Portuguese	26.21%	toca mulher chorona	OLD: toca mulher chorona de **corpo e alma** NEW: tocar mulher chorona de **trio parada bruta**

Table 2: Online Performance of $\mathcal{M}_{s+g}$ with Qualitative Examples.

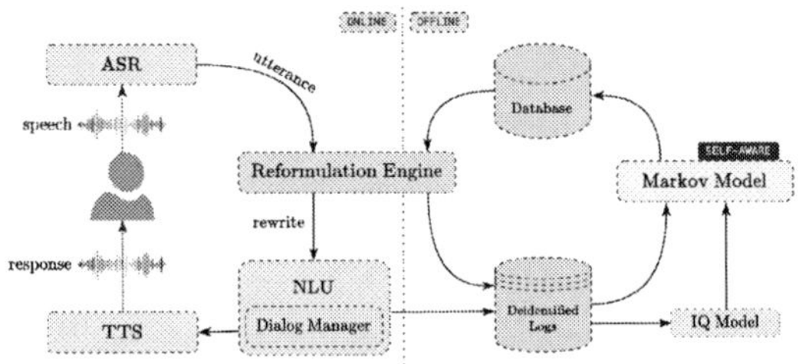

Figure 6: System Architecture

Within the offline data cycle, the de-identified logs are enriched with defect predictor labels by the interaction quality (IQ) model before being collectively used to train the self-aware Markov model. The resulting rewrites surfaced by the Markov model are successively uploaded to the aforementioned online database. It is worth noting here that the offline data cycle in entirely is executed on a daily cadence so as to ensure the overall reactivity of the system. In contrast to the baseline Markov Graph, training the self-aware model incurs a rather moderate ($\sim 8.33\%$) computational overhead due to the additional α computation and the increased amount of edges.

7 Conclusion

In this work, we address one of the key hurdles to the achieving self-learning in continuously updated feedback based systems, namely the deformation of the partitioning decision boundary due to lack of self-awareness. To overcome this degradation in Markov-based query rewriting models, we propose a superposition-based model that continually and reactively learns locally-adaptive decision boundaries, maximizing its precision and recall over time. Our proposed strategies show significant improvements in self-learning tasks and overcome long-term performance degradation. That being said, its dependence on sufficient statistical evidence for rewrite quality renders it subject to volatility with regard to tail or highly personalized rewrites, which we discuss further in the Appendix.

References

Dario Amodei, Chris Olah, Jacob Steinhardt, Paul Christiano, John Schulman, and Dan Mané. 2016. Concrete problems in ai safety. *arXiv preprint arXiv:1606.06565*.

Ioannis Antonellis, Hector Garcia-Molina, and Chi-Chao Chang. 2008. Simrank++: Query rewriting through link analysis of the clickgraph (poster). In *Proceedings of the 17th International Conference on World Wide Web*, WWW '08, page 1177–1178, New York, NY, USA. Association for Computing Machinery.

Allison J. B. Chaney, Brandon M. Stewart, and Barbara E. Engelhardt. 2018. How algorithmic confounding in recommendation systems increases homogeneity and decreases utility. In *Proceedings of the 12th ACM Conference on Recommender Systems*, RecSys '18, page 224–232, New York, NY, USA. Association for Computing Machinery.

Xing Fan, Eunah Cho, Xiaojiang Huang, and Chenlei Guo. 2021. Search based self-learning query rewrite system in conversational ai.

Jianfeng Gao, Michel Galley, and Lihong Li. 2018. Neural approaches to conversational ai.

Charles Miller Grinstead and James Laurie Snell. 2012. *Introduction to probability*. American Mathematical Soc.

Saurabh Gupta, Xing Fan, Derek Liu, Benjamin Yao, Yuan Ling, Kun Zhou, Tuan-Hung KPham, and Chenlei Guo. 2021. Robertaiq: An efficient framework for automatic interactionquality estimation of dialogue systems.

Jie Hao, Linfeng Song, Liwei Wang, Kun Xu, Zhaopeng Tu, and Dong Yu. 2020. Robust dialogue utterance rewriting as sequence tagging. *arXiv preprint arXiv:2012.14535*.

Yunlong He, Jiliang Tang, Hua Ouyang, Changsung Kang, Dawei Yin, and Yi Chang. 2016. Learning to rewrite queries. CIKM '16, page 1443–1452, New York, NY, USA. Association for Computing Machinery.

Bernard J Jansen, Danielle L Booth, and Amanda Spink. 2009. Patterns of query reformulation during web searching. *Journal of the american society for information science and technology*, 60(7):1358–1371.

Anton Khritankov. 2021. Hidden feedback loops in machine learning systems: A simulation model and preliminary results. *Lecture Notes in Business Information Processing*, page 54–65.

Daryl Lim, Julian McAuley, and Gert Lanckriet. 2015. Top-n recommendation with missing implicit feedback. In *Proceedings of the 9th ACM Conference on Recommender Systems*, pages 309–312.

Masoud Mansoury, Himan Abdollahpouri, Mykola Pechenizkiy, Bamshad Mobasher, and Robin Burke. 2020. *Feedback Loop and Bias Amplification in Recommender Systems*, page 2145–2148. Association for Computing Machinery, New York, NY, USA.

Ninareh Mehrabi, Fred Morstatter, Nripsuta Saxena, Kristina Lerman, and Aram Galstyan. 2021. A survey on bias and fairness in machine learning. *ACM Comput. Surv.*, 54(6).

Evan Miller. 2015. https://www.evanmiller.org/bayesian-ab-testing.html.

Pragaash Ponnusamy, Alireza Roshan Ghias, Chenlei Guo, and Ruhi Sarikaya. 2020. Feedback-based self-learning in large-scale conversational ai agents. 34:13180–13187.

Pushpendre Rastogi, Arpit Gupta, Tongfei Chen, and Mathias Lambert. 2019. Scaling multi-domain dialogue state tracking via query reformulation. In *Proceedings of the 2019 Conference of the North American Chapter of the Association for Computational Linguistics: Human Language Technologies, Volume 2 (Industry Papers)*, pages 97–105, Minneapolis, Minnesota. Association for Computational Linguistics.

Stefan Riezler and Yi Liu. 2010. Query rewriting using monolingual statistical machine translation. *Computational Linguistics*, 36(3):569–582.

Alireza Roshan-Ghias, Clint Solomon Mathialagan, Pragaash Ponnusamy, Lambert Mathias, and Chenlei Guo. 2020. Personalized query rewriting in conversational ai agents.

Yuta Saito, Suguru Yaginuma, Yuta Nishino, Hayato Sakata, and Kazuhide Nakata. 2020. Unbiased recommender learning from missing-not-at-random implicit feedback. WSDM '20, page 501–509, New York, NY, USA. Association for Computing Machinery.

D. Sculley, Gary Holt, Daniel Golovin, Eugene Davydov, Todd Phillips, Dietmar Ebner, Vinay Chaudhary, Michael Young, Jean-François Crespo, and Dan Dennison. 2015. Hidden technical debt in machine learning systems. In *Advances in Neural Information Processing Systems*, volume 28. Curran Associates, Inc.

Chen Shi, Yuxiang Hu, Zengming Zhang, Liang Shao, and Feijun Jiang. 2021. *User Feedback and Ranking In-a-Loop: Towards Self-Adaptive Dialogue Systems*, page 2046–2050. Association for Computing Machinery, New York, NY, USA.

Sukhdeep S. Sodhi, Ellie Ka-In Chio, Ambarish Jash, Santiago Ontañón, Ajit Apte, Ankit Kumar, Ayooluwakunmi Jeje, Dima Kuzmin, Harry Fung, Heng-Tze Cheng, Jon Effrat, Tarush Bali, Nitin Jindal, Pei Cao, Sarvjeet Singh, Senqiang Zhou, Tameen Khan, Amol Wankhede, Moustafa Alzantot, Allen Wu, and Tushar Chandra. 2021. Mondegreen: A post-processing solution to speech recognition error correction for voice search queries. In *Proceedings of the 27th ACM SIGKDD Conference on Knowledge Discovery & Data Mining*, KDD '21, page 3569–3575, New York, NY, USA. Association for Computing Machinery.

Hui Su, Xiaoyu Shen, Rongzhi Zhang, Fei Sun, Pengwei Hu, Cheng Niu, and Jie Zhou. 2019. Improving multi-turn dialogue modelling with utterance rewriter. In *Proceedings of the 57th Annual Meeting of the Association for Computational Linguistics*, pages 22–31, Florence, Italy. Association for Computational Linguistics.

Wenlong Sun, Sami Khenissi, Olfa Nasraoui, and Patrick Shafto. 2019. Debiasing the human-recommender system feedback loop in collaborative filtering. In *Companion Proceedings of The 2019 World Wide Web Conference*, WWW '19, page 645–651, New York, NY, USA. Association for Computing Machinery.

Siyang Yuan, Saurabh Gupta, Xing Fan, Derek Liu, Yang Liu, and Chenlei Guo. 2021. Graph enhanced query rewriting for spoken language understanding system. In *ICASSP 2021 - 2021 IEEE International Conference on Acoustics, Speech and Signal Processing*, pages 7997–8001.

8 Appendix

8.1 Template-Based Generation

While most interactions are single-turn, i.e. closed-form requests that are information complete, there are nonetheless dialogs that serve to disambiguate the user's intention. Such multi-turn interactions introduce conversational hierarchies, rendering each subsequent dialog turn contextually and cumulatively dependent on all its preceding turns. To ground this, consider the pair of requests – "*set an alarm for tomorrow*" and "*set an alarm for seven a. m.*". While the latter is informationally sufficient for the system to take the requisite action, the former in contrast remains ambiguous and warrants multiple turns. Under Markov conditions where the conditional distributions are entirely uni-variate, such hierarchies are not simultaneously observed by the model and fundamentally prevent it from providing an optimal rewrite.

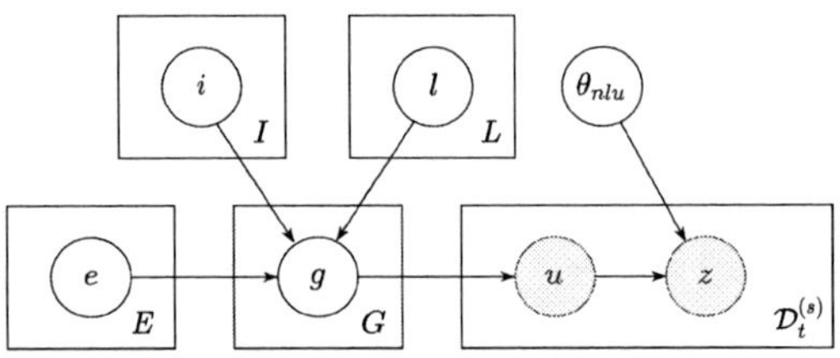

Figure 7: Plate notation summarizing the relationship between intents I, languages L, entity sets E, the corresponding templates G and the consequent utterances and confidences in the single-turn training dataset, $\mathcal{D}_t^{(s)} = \{(u,z)^{(1)}, \ldots, (u,z)^{(k)}\}$.

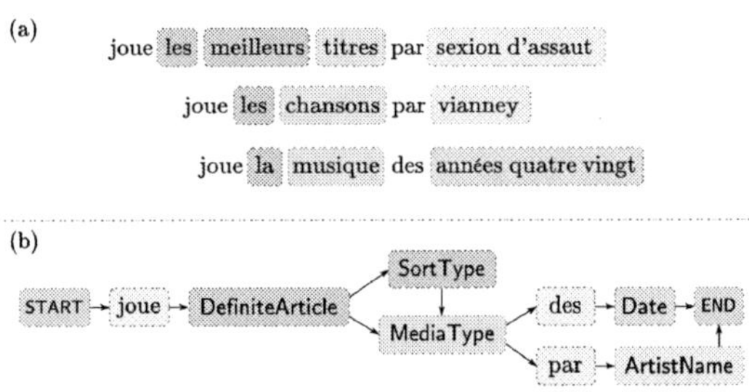

Figure 8: Template DAG extraction via NER and POS tagging with (a) showing multiple utterances with their entities and articles in colored boxes, and (b) representing the DAG for those utterances.

To address the limitation of the local Markov property in multi-turn dialogs, we introduce a synthetic utterance generation strategy that abridges the aforementioned hierarchy into a mere pair of turns. We define the single-turn training dataset $\mathcal{D}_t^{(s)}$ as described in the plate notation in Figure 7. We form the dataset of utterances u by sampling from a distribution of templates that are conditioned on entity sets, languages, and user intents. These templates are obtained by leveraging NER and POS tagging results from NLU, as shown in Figure 8a. Note, however, that a template g leads to utterances that are not enforced to follow a proper grammatical form—potentially reflecting a low NLU confidence z. Thus, for a specific entity set e, an intent i, and a language l, we determine the most plausible template g^* by maximizing the expected value of the NLU confidence z:

$$g^* = \underset{g \sim p_{g|e,i,l}}{\arg\max}\, E[z \mid g] \tag{5}$$

where $p_{g|e,i,l}$ denotes the sampling probability for the template g conditioned on its corresponding entity type, language, and intent. Once we have the set of templates for a given language and intent, we convert each template into a token chain and unify nodes across chains to form a single graph (see Figure 8b). Although this graph is constructed from high-quality templates, it may contain cycles that prevent a proper synthetic utterance generation. Therefore, we factorize the graph into multiple directed acyclic graphs (DAGs). We identify and break cycles using depth-first search to ensure directedness while preserving the syntactic integrity of the original linguistic structures. This process results in multiple DAGs that account for all the original valid paths.

When generating synthetic utterances, we extract the entities from a multi-turn dialog and obtain the template g^* that maximizes the overlap between its entity types e and the DAG nodes N_g:

$$\underset{g^* \in G^*_{(i,l)}}{\arg\max}\, |e \cap N_{g^*}| \tag{6}$$

where $G^*_{(i,l)}$ is the set of optimal templates that defines the DAG and (i,l) denotes a common intent and language across those templates. Once the path has been determined, we replace the entities in template $g^*_{(i,l)}$ with their corresponding values and resolve the entity articles, if applicable. It is possible, however, that the algorithm may not necessarily find a satisfactory path among the DAGs defined from $G^*_{(i,l)}$. In such cases, we abridge the entire dialog to merely retain the first turn of the dialog. Additionally, our algorithm is only executed when the multi-turn dialog has a successful conversion (i.e., the user's request was satisfied). In the event of an unsuccessful dialog or an abrupt end (e.g. "*no*", "*stop*"), we terminate the dialog with an interjectory utterance. Figure 2 describes the high-level process of compressing a multi-turn dialog into a single-turn dialog.

8.2 Meta-State Augmentation

The weight α is chosen in a hierarchical fashion as follows. We select the first α from the successive preference relation, $\alpha_c \succ \alpha_g \succ \alpha_e$ whose confidence interval widths given by Wilson's method for both the utterance and rewrite are lesser than η. Here, the Wilson's score interval is computed with a significance of 89% CI and η was calibrated via cross-validation to an optimal value of 0.588. Each of the α_c, α_g and α_e is defined by the following probability arguments,

$$\alpha_c = P(p_{W|c} > p_{X|c})$$
$$\alpha_g = P(p_W > p_X)$$
$$\alpha_e = P(p_{W_e} > p_{X_e})$$

where α_c relies on the supporting statistics for a given customer, c while α_g extends that statistic globally across all customers in the data. Unlike α_c and α_g, however, we determine α_e by the distributions of entity changes between the utterance and the rewrite. Given the entity set e, along with their corresponding changes between the original and its rewrite (e.g., **ArtistName** added, **SongName** changed, etc.), we compute α_{e_i} for every entity $e_i \in e$ and retrieve the maximum absolute deviation as α_e:

$$\alpha_e = \max_{e_i \in e} |\alpha_{e_i} - 0.5| \tag{7}$$

We choose the maximum absolute deviation because it linearly provides a sense of dispersion without overly weighting values as in other formulations (e.g., standard deviation). More importantly, Equation 7 defines α_e based on a single most-dispersed α_{e_i} value, which can lead to either suppress (i.e. low dispersion) or encourage (i.e. high dispersion) the $\alpha\beta$-path.

8.3 Risks and Limitations

In order to be locally adaptive i.e. decisively unroll or discount a particular rewrite when warranted so, the learning of the Graph hinges on its ability to determine the *viability* i.e. the α value of the said rewrite—the performance of which is squarely correlated with that of the IQ model and thereby inheriting the model's limitations in its overall precision and recall. That being said, the Graph does internally rely on its collaborative filtering ability to regularize the model's decision while external guard-rail mechanisms are also in place to further mitigate the impact of this dependency.

Another matter of concern here would be the requisite for sufficient statistics when computing α, which becomes a limiting factor for highly tail or personalized rewrites, where the Graph would essentially struggle to learn a consistent decision boundary given a high entropy of plausible rewrite alternatives, resulting in its equivalency learning to be entirely contingent on the more prevalent cohort within each learning cycle. In practice however, this is far from being a considerable issue as the over-arching system takes on a multi-stage hierarchical approach that permits other personalized agents to act in lieu of the Graph, while maintaining the Graph's role for its more confident set of customer cohorts.

Conversely speaking, should there be a significantly widespread rewrite that abruptly becomes defective, the Graph would inevitably require a substantial or quite possibly, an equally voluminous source of negative feedback to counter the highly successful prior. This in turn could subject a vast number of customers to a bad experience for a considerable amount of time that ultimately drives down the engagement. As clear of a risk this is in a deployed application setting, a veritable solution here would be to adopt a sense of recency-weighting in constructing the Graph's adjacency matrix, which stands as a worthwhile future effort. In the meantime however, we rely on external gating mechanisms that refresh far more often than the Graph to aid in mitigating the overall severity of such an issue.

Fast and Light-Weight Answer Text Retrieval in Dialogue Systems

Hui Wan
IBM Research AI
hwan@us.ibm.com

Siva Sankalp Patel
IBM Research AI
siva.sankalp.patel@ibm.com

J. William Murdock
IBM Watson
murdockj@us.ibm.com

Saloni Potdar
IBM Watson
potdars@us.ibm.com

Sachindra Joshi
IBM Research AI
jsachind@in.ibm.com

Abstract

Dialogue systems can benefit from being able to search through a corpus of text to find information relevant to user requests, especially when encountering a request for which no manually curated response is available. The state-of-the-art technology for neural dense retrieval or re-ranking involves deep learning models with hundreds of millions of parameters. However, it is difficult and expensive to get such models to operate at an industrial scale, especially for cloud services that often need to support a big number of individually customized dialogue systems, each with its own text corpus. We report our work on enabling advanced neural dense retrieval systems to operate effectively at scale on relatively inexpensive hardware. We compare with leading alternative industrial solutions and show that we can provide a solution that is effective, fast, and cost-efficient.

1 Introduction

Dialogue systems such as Amazon Lex, IBM Watson Assistant, or Microsoft Azure Bot Service operate mainly through intent detection. A subject matter expert (SME) creates a dialogue system by defining a fixed set of intents that a user might have and provides scripted responses for each of them. Machine learning models are adopted to identify the user intent and route to the corresponding dialogue nodes and responses. It usually takes a considerable amount of human curated data to train an intent detection model. Adding features or content to a dialogue system would require adding new intents and training the model all over again.

To alleviate such limitations, an alternative approach to enabling the same user experience is to have a system automatically search through a corpus of text to find relevant responses to each user request. One motivation behind this approach is to replace the intent detection, so to make it flexible, quicker, and easier to set up and maintain a dialogue system, because the SME does not need to enumerate all the intents they expect a user to have. Applying text retrieval in such a system can also complement intent detection: intent detection can handle the anticipated user needs and text search can handle unanticipated requests. In either case, the value of the text retrieval depends critically on how accurate it is. Another big advantage of the text retrieval approach is that it could provide reasonable accuracy even when there is little or no labeled training data.

A popular line of text retrieval methods is matching sparse terms and weighing those matches by how frequent they are in the document being found and how infrequent they are in the corpus. For example, BM25 (Robertson et al., 1995) is an extremely popular algorithm of this sort that provides an excellent balance between accuracy and computational cost. However, in the recent years, research has shown that neural network solutions can provide superior accuracy to sparse term matching approaches like BM25. In particular, neural dense retrieval approaches such as DPR (Karpukhin et al., 2020) and ColBERT (Khattab and Zaharia, 2020; Khattab et al., 2021) have achieved outstanding results in retrieval and re-ranking even at zero-shot setting, and further boosted accuracy when in-domain training data is available.

Neural dense retrievers achieve high accuracy but usually involve models with hundreds of millions of parameters and require long training time. However, in real-world scenarios, a cloud service sometimes supports many different deployed dialogue applications at the same time, hence needs to be able to process requests for all of those applications at the same time. This can be extremely expensive if each application has a model that demands an enormous amount of memory and/or processing power when handling requests. A practical system needs to be able to balance the benefits of a sophisticated model with the costs of running it. Furthermore, dialogue system administrators want

Proceedings of NAACL-HLT 2022: Industry Track Papers, pages 334 - 343
July 10-15, 2022 ©2022 Association for Computational Linguistics

to be able to add training data to an existing, deployed system and start getting improved results quickly.

We explore various approaches to addressing these requirements, including scaling techniques such as distilled encoders and dimension reduction, self-directed iterative learning and asynchronous learning. We conduct thorough experiments on our datasets to benchmark these approaches, and show that we have emerging technology that achieves accuracy that is competitive with state-of-the-art research solutions with substantially less expensive resource requirements.

2 Related Work

In Information Retrieval (IR), popular relevancy algorithms such as TF-IDF and BM25 (Robertson et al., 1995) match keywords with an inverted index and compute relevancy using heuristic functions. Together with pre-processing methods such as stemming and removal of curated stop words, sparse-term-based retrieval works fairly well without training, and is widely adopted in real world applications.

Dense passage retrieval (Karpukhin et al., 2020; Khattab and Zaharia, 2020; Khattab et al., 2021; Xiong et al., 2021; Luan et al., 2021; Santhanam et al., 2021) has gained a lot of attention lately with applications extending beyond retrieval tasks into areas including open-domain question answering, language model pre-training, fact checking, dialogue generation (e.g., RAG (Lewis et al., 2020), REALM (Guu et al., 2020), MultiDPR (Maillard et al., 2021), KILT (Petroni et al., 2021), ConvDR (Yu et al., 2021), RocketQA (Qu et al., 2021)). In dense passage retrieval, the query q and each passage p are separately encoded into dense vectors, and relevance is modeled via similarity functions such as dot-product. Recent works improve efficiency and effectiveness of single-vector dense retrieval systems, including model distillation (Hofstätter et al., 2020; Lin et al., 2021), hard negative sampling (Xiong et al., 2021; Zhan et al., 2021), etc..

Another line of related work is cross-encoder document ranking (MacAvaney et al., 2019; Dai and Callan, 2019; Nogueira and Cho, 2019). Query–document pairs are concatenated and sent through Transformer-based encoders, an additional layer on top of the encoded representation is adopted to produce a relevance score of the document to the query, which is then used for ranking.

Arora et al. (2020) and Qi et al. (2021) benchmark intent detection models on intent detection datasets such as CLINC150 (Larson et al., 2019) where sufficient training examples exist for each intent. On the other hand, our use case focuses on the scenarios where answer text is available but training examples are insufficient.

3 Task and Baselines

The task we are dealing with is a real-world use case of answer text retrieval in an FAQ dialogue system.

Formally, we have a corpus P of answer text snippets (passages). For each answer text passage p in P, we have a limited number of associated example queries Q_p. The system is expected to retrieve the most relevant answer text passage for each incoming user query q. It needs to deliver a good latency, and work well when the size of Q_p is small, i.e., when there are not many training examples available. Most importantly, the resource consumption must be kept low.

To address the use case, we start with two leading industrial solutions as baselines:

- One approach is to map each answer text p as a class c_p, and train a classifier on $\{(c_p, q_p)$ for each p and each q_p in $Q_p\}$ to predict the incoming queries. With the recently ubiquitous large pre-trained language models such as BERT (Devlin et al., 2019) and RoBERTa (Liu et al., 2019), classifiers equipped with both hand-crafted features and neural embedding features are very powerful and deliver decent predictions when there are enough training examples. However, obtaining large amounts of high-quality training data is expensive. Often there is little or no training data.

- Sparse-term-based retrieval (e.g., BM25) on the answer text is another natural approach to address the task without the demand for training data. It has the advantage of having minimal resources requirement. On the other hand, it could not well leverage training data when it is available.

The two aforementioned approaches each have their own strength. The classifier approach leverages query examples and machine learning, while the sparse-term-based retrieval approach utilizes answer text but not query examples, and does not involve training. We seek to get the benefits from both approaches. One option is to capture the cross-attention between query q and each candidate passage p by feeding $\langle q, p \rangle$ pair to a Transformer-based encoder and learn over the encoded output (MacAvaney et al., 2019; Dai and Callan, 2019; Nogueira and Cho, 2019). However, due to the need to cross-encode the incoming query together with each passage, this approach requires more computation by orders of magnitude and is not practical for our task setting.

Dense passage retrieval methods (Karpukhin et al., 2020; Khattab and Zaharia, 2020; Santhanam et al., 2021; Luan et al., 2021; Humeau et al., 2020; MacAvaney et al., 2020; Xiong et al., 2021) have gained a lot of attention lately and achieved state of the art results on various retrieval and ranking datasets. Dense retrievers are efficient compared to other neural methods such as transformer-based cross-encoder models: passages are encoded and indexed offline, at inference time only the query needs to be encoded once; also they leverage ANN (approximate nearest neighbor) algorithms to efficiently search for relevant dense vectors. Dense retrievers are effective compared to traditional sparse-term-based IR methods such as BM25: They are not restricted by rigid keyword matching; They use transformers to encode both the queries and the passages, and benefit from transfer learning from large retrieval/re-ranking datasets. Being effective and efficient, neural dense retrievers make an ideal solution for our task setting and requirements.

4 Approach

We first briefly overview the work in neural dense retrieval and talk about the gaps from practical usage in Section 4.1. In the remainder of Section 4, we explain our efforts applying dense passage retrieval to the task and further reducing response time, memory footprint, and training time.

4.1 Neural Dense Retrieval Preliminaries

In dense passage retrieval, q and p are separately encoded. All the passages can be encoded and indexed offline. During inference time, only the query needs to be encoded; ANN (approximate nearest neighbor) search libraries such as FAISS (Johnson et al., 2017) are used to efficiently search for the most relevant passage.

In single-vector retrieval models such as DPR (Karpukhin et al., 2020) and BERT Siamese/Dual Encoder (Luan et al., 2021), the query and passages are separately encoded into single vectors, models are trained with the objective of mapping the relevant passage vector close to the query vector, and pushing the irrelevant passage vectors far away from the query vector. During inference time, ANN search is used to retrieve directly for the passage vectors closest to the query vector. Several other systems leverage multi-vector representations and attention-based re-ranking, including Poly-encoders (Humeau et al., 2020), PreTTR (MacAvaney et al., 2020), etc..

In late interaction models such as ColBERT (Khattab and Zaharia, 2020; Khattab et al., 2021; Santhanam et al., 2021), the query and passages are separately encoded to obtain query token vectors and passage token vectors. These models adopt token-decomposed scoring, e.g. the sum of maximum-similarity (SumMaxSim) scores to query vectors are used to model the relevance of passages. During training, models are trained with the objective of maximizing the SumMaxSim scores of relevant passage and minimizing those of irrelevant passages. During inference time, the passage tokens closest to query tokens are fetched, and then the relevant passages are re-ranked based on the SumMaxSim scores.

We experimented with two of the most popular dense retrieval models, DPR and ColBERT. As effective as they are, they still consume more computing resources and take longer response time than required in our real-world use case of hosting thousands of customized systems. Also, in our use case, dialogue system administrators want to reduce the time to fine-tune neural retrieval models on custom training data.

4.2 Dense Retrieval Scaled for Practical Usage

For practical usage we implemented improvement features into ColBERT code: 1) for encoder, add flexible accommodation for various transformer types and models in the Huggingface model hub; 2) new improved batcher and training loop logic by epochs, flexible shuffling and checkpoint saving.

We benchmark DPR and ColBERT on our datasets, and experiment reducing response time and memory footprint at retrieval time as follows.

Distilled transformer encoder We pre-train ColBERT model on the Natural Questions (NQ) dataset (Kwiatkowski et al., 2019) from multiple small-size or distilled transformers models including Electra (Clark et al., 2020), TinyBERT (Jiao et al., 2020), DistilBERT (Sanh et al., 2019) and DistilRoBERTa. After comparing the memory footprint, the retrieval time, and the retrieval accuracy, we chose to use TinyBERT (Jiao et al., 2020) with 4 layers and 312 hidden dimensions[1].

Dimension reduction (Khattab and Zaharia, 2020; Santhanam et al., 2021) showed that a ColBERT model with quantized and reduced-dimension vectors could perform comparably to the standard model on big retrieval/ranking benchmarks while greatly reducing the space requirement for saving the final representations. For our use case on the small retrieval datasets, we explored using smaller dimensions for the vector representations in ColBERT. In our experiments, however, reduced dimension models yield much lower accuracy.

Shorter query length We decrease the maximum query length in DPR from 256 to 32, reducing the response time of DPR by 80%. As this length still fits the majority of the queries in our task setting, the effect to accuracy is very tiny and could be neglected.

4.3 Self-directed Iterative Learning

Dense retrieval training data consists of $\langle q, p^+, p^- \rangle$ triples, where q is the query, p^+ is a positive (relevant) passage, and p^- is a negative (irrelevant) passage. Dense neural retrieval models learn from such triples to effectively map query token representations and relevant answer text token representations together, and push irrelevant (token) representations away. While forming training triples, one straightforward way is using all the negative passages to make sure not missing any useful training data. However, this results in long training time. Sampling from BM25 top ranked passages is a widely used approach to select negative passages. However, this introduces a data bias and limit the model's learning ability (Luan et al., 2021). An alternative approach is to choose negatives passages from those highly ranked by the model from the previous training iteration. This allows each iteration of the training to learn from negative examples for which the previous model did not do well (Simo-Serra et al., 2015; Wu et al., 2017).

To be more specific, given a trained ColBERT model CKPT, we take a query q from training data, and get CKPT's top m ranked passages

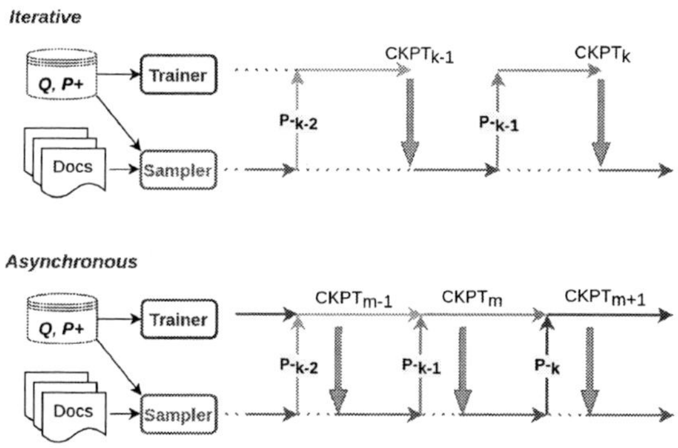

Figure 1: Iterative learning strategy 4.3 and asynchronous learning strategy 4.4.

$(p_1, ..., p_m)$ for q, suppose the positive passage is p_i, we take each negative passage ranked higher than p_i to form the new batch of training triples $\langle q, p_i, p_1 \rangle, ... \langle q, p_i, p_{i-1} \rangle$. When $i = 1$, i.e., the model gave the right prediction, we still include several randomly sampled triples, so as to avoid over-fitting on a few difficult queries.

With the self-directed triple curation, we explore an iterative learning strategy as illustrated in Figure 1. In each iteration, the Sampler module and the Trainer module work together as follows. In each iteration, first, Sampler uses a recently trained model checkpoint $\mathtt{CKPT_{k-1}}$ to update the representation of documents in the corpus and refresh the ANN index, then from the refreshed ANN index fetch the top ranked negatives P^-_{k-1} for training queries Q to produce training triples together with P^+. Then, Trainer uses the triples generated by Sampler to train a new model checkpoint $\mathtt{CKPT_k}$. In each iteration, only the negative examples that are "hard" for the current model are used to form the training triples, thus we achieve effective and focused training with reduced time. Note that similar strategy was adopted by Khattab et al. (2021) by training two more stages after the initial ColBERT model. We make the further exploration by automatically continuing the iterations until the model reached certain accuracy on training queries.

4.4 Asynchronous Learning

During the iterative learning in Section 4.3, the Trainer and Sampler wait for each other's output to proceed to next round. This causes overhead and wasted resources. To alleviate that, we adopt the asynchronous learning approach as described in ANCE (Xiong et al., 2021) and let the Trainer and Sampler work asynchronously without waiting on each other, as depicted in Figure 1. To be

[1]https://huggingface.co/huawei-noah/TinyBERT_General_4L_312D

Dataset	HRFAQ	MEDFAQ
# docs	186	87
# words / doc	35.4	31.4
# training queries	5433	862
# words / train query	8.8	4.9
# test queries	1174	462
# words / test queries	6.6	4.5

Table 1: Dataset statistics.

specific, while Sampler is curating the new batch, the Trainer does not wait but continues training on the old batch of training triples. After generating a batch of training triples, the Sampler always fetches the latest model checkpoint and starts creating a new batch. Note that the implementation in ANCE (Xiong et al., 2021) is on BERT Siamese/Dual Encoder (Luan et al., 2021). As far as we know, our implementation is the first on ColBERT model.

4.5 Ensemble

With the scaling efforts in Section 4.2, we achieve a neural dense retriever with a latency comparable to neural-embedding-based SVM and BM25. This makes it practical to ensemble the two systems with the neural dense retrieval system. We ensemble a neural-embedding-based SVM classifier and neural retrieval in scenarios where training data is available, and ensemble BM25 and neural retrieval in scenarios where training data is unavailable.

5 Experiments

5.1 Datasets

For our experiments, we obtain datasets from real-world dialogue systems. We create datasets from an HR policy FAQ bot (denoted by HRFAQ) and a medical group portal FAQ bot (denoted by MEDFAQ), both in English. Each dialogue system dataset consists of intents, intent examples, dialogue node graphs and response texts created by subject-matter experts. For each dataset, we created a test set of queries and ground truth responses by sampling the real-world chat logs from the deployed dialogue system. The task is measured by Match@1 score in results tables, which is the percentage of test queries for which the top system result is correct. Table 1 shows the dataset statistics. Note that the datasets are not big and the queries are generally short. The challenge in scaling comes mainly from trying to support many such systems at once in the same cloud.

5.2 Experimental Settings

For the sparse-term-based retrieval baseline, we use BM25 (Robertson et al., 1995) as implemented in ElasticSearch[2], with lower-casing, stemming and stop-word removal.

For the neural-embedding-based classifier, we train a one vs all SVM classifier with sophisticated pre-processing, hand-crafted n-gram features, and neural word/sentence embeddings based on Transformers with 512-dimension vectors[3]. We also train a classifier with answer text added as training queries, denoted by " NSVM w/ text", as opposed to "NSVM" which does not use answer text hence has no 0-shot numbers.

For DPR experiments, we use the Facebook research DPR repository[4]. The DPR full model before fine-tuning is downloaded from the DPR repository (March 2021 release). The DPR$_{tiny}$ model before fine-tuning is pre-trained on the triples created from Natural Questions (NQ) dataset (Kwiatkowski et al., 2019), also obtained from the same repository. "DPR(S)" stands for shorter query setting.

For ColBERT experiments, our code is built on top of the v0.2 version of ColBERT code[5], which is in PyTorch and uses Huggingface Transformers[6]. We implemented the code for iterative learning and asynchronous learning in PyTorch. For real-world usage we also implemented improvement features into ColBERT code as described in Section 4.2.

The ColBERT full model before fine-tuning is provided by the authors of ColBERT. The ColBERT$_{tiny}$ model before fine-tuning is pre-trained on triples created from Natural Questions (NQ) dataset (Kwiatkowski et al., 2019) as specified in ColBERT (Khattab et al., 2021).

For CPU environment inferencing, all models and data/indices reside locally on a CPU machine with four Intel® Core™ i7-8650U CPUs. Neural models are trained on a single NVIDIA V100 GPU in a computing cluster environment unless otherwise stated.

Hyper-parameters and other detailed settings are included in Appendix.

[2]http://www.elastic.co/elasticsearch/

[3]We refrain from giving more details because this is a commercial product.

[4]http://github.com/facebookresearch/DPR

[5]http://github.com/stanford-futuredata/ColBERT

[6]http://github.com/huggingface/transformers

System	Size	Mem	Time
BM25	–	–	4.6ms
NSVM	1.1G	2.9G	10ms
DPR	836M	2.5G	267ms
ColBERT	419M	2.4G	59ms
DPR(S)	836M	2.5G	45ms
DPR_{tiny}(S)	110M	0.6G	5ms
ColBERT_{tiny}	55M	1.7G	10ms

Table 2: Inference latency and resources usage of different systems on HRFAQ dataset in CPU environment. Latency is for single query and includes pre-processing time. DPR and ColBERT model sizes do not include optimizer variables.

5.3 Experiments and Results

Resources Consumption Table 2 compares the resource usage and response times of different systems during inference (retrieval). Full Neural models have high memory consumption and consume a lot of disk space because of millions of parameters in the neural networks. The smaller dense retrieval models, as scaled in Section 4.2, are able to reduce both footprints and inference latency drastically.

Choosing Distilled Base Models We conduct further benchmarking on ColBERT models based on different distilled language models[7] including DistilBERT_{base}, $\text{DistilRoBERTa}_{base}$, $\text{Electra}_{small,discriminator}$, TinyBERT_{4L-312} and TinyBERT_{6L-768}. We pre-train a ColBERT model from each of these transformer models, and test on the 0-shot setting of the HRFAQ dataset. An alternative approach would be to distill from fully trained ColBERT models using the corresponding distillation algorithms, which we leave for future work. All models are pre-trained on the NQ dataset at a batch size of 192 for 40k steps, except Electra and DistilRoBERTa are trained for 80k steps because of their lower accuracy at 40k steps. The results suggest that the general pre-training before ColBERT training does impact generalization performance of the ColBERT models. Specifically, larger models, e.g., $\text{DistilRoBERTa}_{base}$, do not always result in better generalization, and starting from TinyBERT_{4L-312} appears to be a good choice considering efficiency and accuracy. We use TinyBERT_{4L-312} as the distilled base model in the remainder of the paper and denote it by $tiny$. The full models trained from BERT_{base} are sub-scripted by $full$.

[7]All models downloaded from Huggingface model hub `https://huggingface.co/models`.

System	Size	Mem	Time	M@1
DistilBERT	254M	2.3G	26ms	35.0
DistilRoBERTa	314M	3.8G	32ms	32.3
TinyBERT_{6L-768}	256M	2.1G	27ms	35.3
TinyBERT_{4L-312}	55M	1.7G	10ms	36.3
Electra	52M	1.7G	18ms	29.5

Table 3: Inference latency, resources usage, and accuracy of different ColBERT models on HRFAQ dataset in a CPU environment.

	HRFAQ	0-shot	1 ex/doc	3 ex/doc
1	BM25	29.2	–	–
2	NSVM	–	23.2(4.4)	43.3(3.6)
3	NSVM w/ text	10.4	27.5(3.7)	46.0(3.5)
4	DPR_{full}	29.9	42.3(2.6)	53.5(2.2)
5	ColBERT_{full}	38.9	47.8(1.8)	53.6(2.3)
6	DPR_{tiny}(S)	25.7	37.8(2.9)	46.2(4.1)
7	ColBERT_{tiny}	36.3	42.4(1.7)	50.7(2.0)
8	Ensemble(1,7)	**39.0**	**47.4(1.8)**	53.4(2.2)
9	Ensemble(3,7)	30.4	45.0(2.3)	**55.4(2.0)**

Table 4: Match@1 scores on HRFAQ test set. For k ex/doc experiments: we take 10 random seeds; for each random seed, sample k training queries per answer text, train a model; finally report avg(std) of the 10 models. Scores in bold are best in efficient setting.

Fine-tuning Accuracy Tables 4 and 5 show results or HRFAQ and MEDFAQ. ColBERT_{full} is the most accurate single system especially in 0-shot setting, which is consistent with results from research papers. With more training examples, DPR catches up in accuracy, showing that retrieval methods based on single vector similarity instead of token vector late interactions is at disadvantage transferring to 0-shot use cases, but performs nicely with some training examples. It is worth noting that, ColBERT_{tiny} shows only a small degradation from ColBERT_{full} on HRFAQ, presenting a nice trade-off between accuracy and efficiency in real-world industry use cases. In MEDFAQ, there is a bigger drop in accuracy from ColBERT_{full} to ColBERT_{tiny}. This may be a result of MEDFAQ's vocabulary and content being more distant from the NQ data used for pre-training, since medical vocabulary tends to be highly specialized. In 1-shot and 3-shot settings where the models are trained with 1 or 3 examples per answer, ColBERT_{tiny} is more competitive for MEDFAQ.

Ensembling We take a linear combination of 0-shot BM25 predictions and ColBERT_{tiny} predictions with heuristic weight 0.3:1, and a 10:1 combination of SVM predictions and ColBERT_{tiny} predictions, since the scores from the SVM classifier

	MEDFAQ	0-shot	1 ex/doc	3 ex/doc
1	BM25	25.1	–	–
2	NSVM	–	39.7(5.1)	60.0(6.4)
3	NSVM w/ text	22.5	41.4(4.9)	58.6(4.7)
4	DPR_{full}	37.0	58.5(3.7)	67.2(2.2)
5	ColBERT_{full}	45.2	57.6(2.5)	67.7(1.7)
6	DPR_{tiny}(S)	25.5	44.7(5.0)	56.9(4.1)
7	ColBERT_{tiny}	26.6	47.1(4.0)	60.4(4.4)
8	Ensemble(1,7)	28.6	47.5(4.2)	60.4(4.1)
9	Ensemble(3,7)	**29.9**	**51.3(7.0)**	**63.3(5.0)**

Table 5: Match@1 scores on MEDFAQ test set. Details same as Table 4.

HRFAQ	1 ex/doc		3 ex/doc	
ColBERT_{tiny}	Time	M@1	Time	M@1
All neg	475s	42.4(1.7)	1374s	50.7(2.0)
BM25 Guided	37s	37.1(1.7)	85s	39.4(2.1)
Iterative	104s	44.0(2.1)	226s	49.4(1.6)
Asynchronous	78s	43.0(2.1)	200s	49.3(1.9)

Table 6: Training time and Match@1 scores of different training strategies. Scores avg(std) on 10 randomly sampled training sets.

are in a higher magnitude. As shown in the second parts of Tables 4 and Table 5, there is a nice boost from both systems being ensembled, showing ensembling to be a feasible and effective approach to further increase the accuracy.

Self-guided Iterative / Asynchronous Learning Table 6 compares the retrieval results and training time efficiency of one-pass training with all negatives, one-pass training with BM25 guided negatives, iterative learning, and asynchronous learning. We use ColBERT_{tiny} for this comparison. For BM25 guided and iterative/asynchronous learning, negative examples are curated as described in Section 4.3, from top 20 model-guided predictions. Models are trained for 10 epochs in the one-pass experiments, and 5 rounds of 6 epochs each in the iterative and asynchronous learning experiments. The results demonstrate that, with iterative self-guided sampling of negative passages, ColBERT models can achieve results competitive to the models trained on complete data within 20% training time. The M@1 score of `All neg` is slightly lower at 1-shot, likely due to the mismatch of randomly sampled training examples and the testset.

Summary Although with resources consumptions higher than BM25, dense passage retrieval with scaling techniques could deliver higher accuracy than BM25 and neural embedding based classifiers with similar latency, thus makes a great solution for our use case.

6 Conclusion

We report on our work on enabling advanced neural dense retrieval systems to operate effectively at scale on relatively inexpensive hardware. On our real-world use case and datasets from dialogue systems, we show that we can provide a solution that achieves accuracy that is competitive with state-of-the-art research solutions with substantially less expensive resource requirements and shorter response time.

References

Gaurav Arora, Chirag Jain, Manas Chaturvedi, and Krupal Modi. 2020. HINT3: Raising the bar for intent detection in the wild. In *Proceedings of the First Workshop on Insights from Negative Results in NLP*, pages 100–105, Online. Association for Computational Linguistics.

Kevin Clark, Minh-Thang Luong, Quoc V. Le, and Christopher D. Manning. 2020. Electra: Pre-training text encoders as discriminators rather than generators. In *International Conference on Learning Representations (ICLR)*.

Zhuyun Dai and Jamie Callan. 2019. Deeper text understanding for ir with contextual neural language modeling. *Proceedings of the 42nd International ACM SIGIR Conference on Research and Development in Information Retrieval*.

Jacob Devlin, Ming-Wei Chang, Kenton Lee, and Kristina Toutanova. 2019. BERT: Pre-training of deep bidirectional transformers for language understanding. In *Proceedings of the 2019 Conference of the North American Chapter of the Association for Computational Linguistics: Human Language Technologies, Volume 1 (Long and Short Papers)*, pages 4171–4186, Minneapolis, Minnesota. Association for Computational Linguistics.

Kelvin Guu, Kenton Lee, Zora Tung, Panupong Pasupat, and Ming-Wei Chang. 2020. Realm: Retrieval-augmented language model pre-training. *arXiv preprint arXiv:2002.08909*.

Sebastian Hofstätter, Sophia Althammer, Michael Schröder, Mete Sertkan, and Allan Hanbury. 2020. Improving efficient neural ranking models with cross-architecture knowledge distillation.

Samuel Humeau, Kurt Shuster, Marie-Anne Lachaux, and Jason Weston. 2020. Poly-encoders: Architectures and pre-training strategies for fast and accurate multi-sentence scoring. In *International Conference on Learning Representations (ICLR)*.

Xiaoqi Jiao, Yichun Yin, Lifeng Shang, Xin Jiang, Xiao Chen, Linlin Li, Fang Wang, and Qun Liu. 2020. TinyBERT: Distilling BERT for natural language understanding. In *Findings of the Association for Computational Linguistics: EMNLP 2020*, pages 4163–4174, Online. Association for Computational Linguistics.

Jeff Johnson, Matthijs Douze, and Hervé Jégou. 2017. Billion-scale similarity search with gpus. *arXiv preprint arXiv:1702.08734*.

Vladimir Karpukhin, Barlas Oguz, Sewon Min, Patrick Lewis, Ledell Wu, Sergey Edunov, Danqi Chen, and Wen-tau Yih. 2020. Dense passage retrieval for open-domain question answering. In *Proceedings of the 2020 Conference on Empirical Methods in Natural Language Processing (EMNLP)*, pages 6769–6781, Online. Association for Computational Linguistics.

Omar Khattab, Christopher Potts, and Matei Zaharia. 2021. Relevance-guided supervision for OpenQA with ColBERT. *Transactions of the Association for Computational Linguistics*, 9:929–944.

Omar Khattab and Matei Zaharia. 2020. Colbert: Efficient and effective passage search via contextualized late interaction over bert. In *Proceedings of the 43rd International ACM SIGIR Conference on Research and Development in Information Retrieval*, pages 39–48.

Tom Kwiatkowski, Jennimaria Palomaki, Olivia Redfield, Michael Collins, Ankur Parikh, Chris Alberti, Danielle Epstein, Illia Polosukhin, Jacob Devlin, Kenton Lee, Kristina Toutanova, Llion Jones, Matthew Kelcey, Ming-Wei Chang, Andrew M. Dai, Jakob Uszkoreit, Quoc Le, and Slav Petrov. 2019. Natural questions: A benchmark for question answering research. *Transactions of the Association for Computational Linguistics*, 7:452–466.

Stefan Larson, Anish Mahendran, Joseph J. Peper, Christopher Clarke, Andrew Lee, Parker Hill, Jonathan K. Kummerfeld, Kevin Leach, Michael A. Laurenzano, Lingjia Tang, and Jason Mars. 2019. An evaluation dataset for intent classification and out-of-scope prediction. In *Proceedings of the 2019 Conference on Empirical Methods in Natural Language Processing and the 9th International Joint Conference on Natural Language Processing (EMNLP-IJCNLP)*, pages 1311–1316, Hong Kong, China. Association for Computational Linguistics.

Patrick Lewis, Ethan Perez, Aleksandra Piktus, Fabio Petroni, Vladimir Karpukhin, Naman Goyal, Heinrich Küttler, Mike Lewis, Wen-tau Yih, Tim Rocktäschel, Sebastian Riedel, and Douwe Kiela. 2020. Retrieval-augmented generation for knowledge-intensive nlp tasks. In *Advances in Neural Information Processing Systems*, volume 33, pages 9459–9474. Curran Associates, Inc.

Sheng-Chieh Lin, Jheng-Hong Yang, and Jimmy Lin. 2021. In-batch negatives for knowledge distillation with tightly-coupled teachers for dense retrieval. In *Proceedings of the 6th Workshop on Representation Learning for NLP (RepL4NLP-2021)*, pages 163–173, Online. Association for Computational Linguistics.

Yinhan Liu, Myle Ott, Naman Goyal, Jingfei Du, Mandar Joshi, Danqi Chen, Omer Levy, Mike Lewis, Luke Zettlemoyer, and Veselin Stoyanov. 2019. Roberta: A robustly optimized BERT pretraining approach. *CoRR*, abs/1907.11692.

Yi Luan, Jacob Eisenstein, Kristina Toutanova, and Michael Collins. 2021. Sparse, dense, and attentional representations for text retrieval. *Transactions of the Association for Computational Linguistics*, 9:329–345.

Sean MacAvaney, Franco Maria Nardini, Raffaele Perego, Nicola Tonellotto, Nazli Goharian, and Ophir Frieder. 2020. Efficient document re-ranking for transformers by precomputing term representations. In *Proceedings of the 43rd International ACM SIGIR Conference on Research and Development in Information Retrieval*, page 49–58, New York, NY, USA. Association for Computing Machinery.

Sean MacAvaney, Andrew Yates, Arman Cohan, and Nazli Goharian. 2019. Cedr: Contextualized embeddings for document ranking. *Proceedings of the 42nd International ACM SIGIR Conference on Research and Development in Information Retrieval*.

Jean Maillard, Vladimir Karpukhin, Fabio Petroni, Wen-tau Yih, Barlas Oguz, Veselin Stoyanov, and Gargi Ghosh. 2021. Multi-task retrieval for knowledge-intensive tasks. In *ACL/IJCNLP (1)*, pages 1098–1111. Association for Computational Linguistics.

Rodrigo Nogueira and Kyunghyun Cho. 2019. Passage re-ranking with bert. *arXiv preprint arXiv:1901.04085*.

Fabio Petroni, Aleksandra Piktus, Angela Fan, Patrick Lewis, Majid Yazdani, Nicola De Cao, James Thorne, Yacine Jernite, Vladimir Karpukhin, Jean Maillard, Vassilis Plachouras, Tim Rocktäschel, and Sebastian Riedel. 2021. KILT: a benchmark for knowledge intensive language tasks. In *Proceedings of the 2021 Conference of the North American Chapter of the Association for Computational Linguistics: Human Language Technologies*, pages 2523–2544, Online. Association for Computational Linguistics.

Haode Qi, Lin Pan, Atin Sood, Abhishek Shah, Ladislav Kunc, Mo Yu, and Saloni Potdar. 2021. Benchmarking commercial intent detection services with practice-driven evaluations. In *Proceedings of the 2021 Conference of the North American Chapter of the Association for Computational Linguistics: Human Language Technologies: Industry Papers*, pages 304–310, Online. Association for Computational Linguistics.

Yingqi Qu, Yuchen Ding, Jing Liu, Kai Liu, Ruiyang Ren, Wayne Xin Zhao, Daxiang Dong, Hua Wu, and

Haifeng Wang. 2021. RocketQA: An optimized training approach to dense passage retrieval for open-domain question answering. In *Proceedings of the 2021 Conference of the North American Chapter of the Association for Computational Linguistics: Human Language Technologies*, pages 5835–5847, Online. Association for Computational Linguistics.

Stephen E. Robertson, Steve Walker, Susan Jones, Micheline Hancock-Beaulieu, and Mike Gatford. 1995. Okapi at TREC-3. In *Overview of the Third Text REtrieval Conference (TREC-3)*, pages 109–126. National Institute of Standards and Technology (NIST).

Victor Sanh, Lysandre Debut, Julien Chaumond, and Thomas Wolf. 2019. DistilBERT, a distilled version of BERT: smaller, faster, cheaper and lighter. In *5th Workshop on Energy Efficient Machine Learning and Cognitive Computing @ NeurIPS 2019*.

Keshav Santhanam, Omar Khattab, Jon Saad-Falcon, Christopher Potts, and Matei Zaharia. 2021. Colbertv2: Effective and efficient retrieval via lightweight late interaction.

Edgar Simo-Serra, Eduard Trulls, Luis Ferraz, Iasonas Kokkinos, Pascal Fua, and Francesc Moreno-Noguer. 2015. Discriminative learning of deep convolutional feature point descriptors. In *Proceedings of the IEEE International Conference on Computer Vision*, pages 118–126.

Chao-Yuan Wu, R. Manmatha, Alexander J. Smola, and Philipp Krähenbühl. 2017. Sampling matters in deep embedding learning. In *2017 IEEE International Conference on Computer Vision (ICCV)*, pages 2859–2867.

Lee Xiong, Chenyan Xiong, Ye Li, Kwok-Fung Tang, Jialin Liu, Paul N. Bennett, Junaid Ahmed, and Arnold Overwijk. 2021. Approximate nearest neighbor negative contrastive learning for dense text retrieval. In *International Conference on Learning Representations*.

Shi Yu, Zhenghao Liu, Chenyan Xiong, Tao Feng, and Zhiyuan Liu. 2021. Few-shot conversational dense retrieval. In *Proceedings of the 44th International ACM SIGIR Conference on Research and Development in Information Retrieval*, page 829–838, New York, NY, USA. Association for Computing Machinery.

Jingtao Zhan, Jiaxin Mao, Yiqun Liu, Jiafeng Guo, Min Zhang, and Shaoping Ma. 2021. Optimizing dense retrieval model training with hard negatives. In *Proceedings of the 44th International ACM SIGIR Conference on Research and Development in Information Retrieval*, page 1503–1512, New York, NY, USA. Association for Computing Machinery.

	HRFAQ	0-shot	1 ex/doc	3 ex/doc
1	BM25	41.3	-	-
2	NSVM	-	35.2(4.9)	58.3(3.1)
3	NSVM w/ text	18.7	42.8(2.5)	61.9(1.9)
4	DPR_{full}	43.9	58.1(2.7)	67.2(1.6)
5	ColBERT_{full}	53.7	62.5(1.0)	67.1(1.8)
6	DPR_{tiny}(S)	37.0	52.8(1.7)	61.0(2.3)
7	ColBERT_{tiny}	45.3	56.4(1.8)	65.2(1.1)
8	Ensemble(1,7)	**49.6**	59.2(1.5)	66.8(1.1)
9	Ensemble(3,7)	45.6	**60.0(1.8)**	**69.1(1.4)**

Table 7: Match@3 scores on HRFAQ testset. For k ex/doc experiments: we take 10 random seeds; for each random seed, sample k training queries per answer text, train a model; finally report avg(std) of the 10 models.

A Appendix

A.1 Hyper-parameters

Hyper-parameters for ColBERT:

```
NQ pre-training batch_size: 192
tuning batch_size: 32
tuning num_epochs: 10
doc_maxlen: 180
mask-punctuation: true
amp: true
learning_rate: 3e-06
weight_decay: 0.0
adam_eps: 1e-8
similarity: l2
dimension: 128
query_maxlen: 32
doc_maxlen: 128
```

Hyper-parameters for DPR:

```
NQ pre-training batch_size: 144
Full model tuning batch_size: 27
Tiny model tuning batch_size: 80
NQ pre-train warmup_steps: 1237
tuning warmup_steps: 100
NQ pre-train num_train_epochs: 40
tuning num_train_epochs: 100
learning_rate: 2e-5
weight_decay: 0.0
adam_eps: 1e-8
adam_betas: (0.9, 0.999)
max_grad_norm: 2.0
hard_negatives: 1
other_negatives: 0
```

A.2 More Results

Match@3 scores could be found in Table 7 and Table 8.

	MEDFAQ	0-shot	1 ex/doc	3 ex/doc
1	BM25	37.2	-	-
2	NSVM	-	53.9(7.1)	68.9(6.1)
3	NSVM w/ text	33.5	55.5(4.6)	70.6(6.4)
4	DPR_{full}	47.4	72.8(2.7)	78.7(1.6)
5	$ColBERT_{full}$	61.7	74.1(2.0)	79.8(1.4)
6	DPR_{tiny}(S)	35.3	56.3(4.7)	70.7(3.6)
7	$ColBERT_{tiny}$	38.5	62.7(3.0)	73.1(3.0)
8	Ensemble(1,7)	**41.8**	63.6(3.0)	73.8(3.3)
9	Ensemble(3,7)	40.26	**63.7(5.8)**	**74.4(4.8)**

Table 8: Match@3 scores on MEDFAQ testset. For k ex/doc experiments: we take 10 random seeds; for each random seed, sample k training queries per answer text, train a model; finally report avg(std) of the 10 models.

A.3 Licenses and Potential Risks

The licenses of ColBERT code and DPR code can be found at `https://github.com/stanford-futuredata/ColBERT/blob/master/LICENSE` and `https://github.com/facebookresearch/DPR/blob/main/LICENSE`, respectively. The license of ElasticSearch can be found at `https://github.com/elastic/elasticsearch/blob/7.16/licenses/ELASTIC-LICENSE-2.0.txt`. The neural embedding based SVM classifier is part of commercial products owned by our organization.

We ran the experiments on our own extracted datasets for solely research exploration purpose, and we did not distribute or use the code or data to make any profit. The datasets are small to check / anonymize. We use them solely for benchmarking purpose, and strictly protected access to the datasets to only a couple of co-authors.

Our work is exploring the efficient and effective approaches of text retrieval on answer text corpus curated by chat-bot administrators. The use case is how to present the most matching answer text to users, where the answer text itself is created and closely administered by chat-bot administrators. The scope of this paper does not cover research on how to filter offensive content. On the other hand, our work does not generate any new text, hence does not create risks to users.

BLINK with Elasticsearch for Efficient Entity Linking in Business Conversations

Md Tahmid Rahman Laskar, Cheng Chen, Aliaksandr Martsinovich, Jonathan Johnston, Xue-Yong Fu, Shashi Bhushan TN, Simon Corston-Oliver
Dialpad Canada Inc.
1100 Melville St #400
Vancouver, BC, Canada, V6E 4A6
{tahmid.rahman,cchen,aliaksandr.martsinovich,jonathan}@dialpad.com
{xue-yong,sbhushan,scorston-oliver}@dialpad.com

Abstract

An Entity Linking system aligns the textual mentions of entities in a text to their corresponding entries in a knowledge base. However, deploying a neural entity linking system for efficient real-time inference in production environments is a challenging task. In this work, we present a neural entity linking system that connects the product and organization type entities in business conversations to their corresponding Wikipedia and Wikidata entries. The proposed system leverages Elasticsearch to ensure inference efficiency when deployed in a resource limited cloud machine, and obtains significant improvements in terms of inference speed and memory consumption while retaining high accuracy.

1 Introduction

Companies that offer VoIP telephony products with built-in speech and natural language processing features aim to assist the customer support agents with information relevant to the content of their conversations with the customers. To be useful, such assistance should be provided in near real-time of the triggering utterance. In this paper, we demonstrate how we build a near real-time entity linking system at Dialpad[1] to link the entities in business phone transcripts to a knowledge base to provide more semantically-informed assistance.

The entity linking task is usually comprised of three steps: (i) detect the mentions in the given text, (ii) generate a list of candidate entities relevant to each mention, and finally (iii) link each mention to its most relevant entry in the knowledge base (Ravi et al., 2021). Note that entity linking systems used in production should provide the optimum performance in terms of both inference speed and memory consumption while being used within a limited computational budget. Since there are millions of entities stored in a knowledge base, the scaling issue is a major concern while developing a real-time entity linking system.

The goal of this research is to develop a neural entity linking system to efficiently link *product* and *organization* type entities in business phone conversations to their respective entries in a knowledge base for information extraction. For that purpose, we present an extended version of the state-of-the-art neural entity linker, the BLINK model (Wu et al., 2020). Though BLINK was originally proposed for entity linking on Wikipedia, we extend it for entity linking on Wikidata[2] since unlike Wikipedia, the Wikidata knowledge base contains information related to the entities in a structured way. Thus, it allows effective extraction of relevant information for each entity. More importantly, for production deployment, we also introduce several new techniques that significantly reduce the memory requirements, computational resource usage, and the inference speed of BLINK. More concretely, our major contributions are stated below:

- We tackle the computational complexities in BLINK by saving all pre-trained entity embeddings in Elasticsearch[3] and propose a word matching technique to retrieve the candidate entities faster. We also present an approach to pre-compute the linking between the Wikipedia page of each entity to its respective Wikidata page to reduce the runtime latency.
- Extensive experiments show that our entity linking system significantly reduces the inference time and memory requirements while retaining high accuracy in a computationally inexpensive machine. We also successfully deploy our entity linking system in a 10GB RAM machine (without GPU) whereas the original model requires a machine in our server having 60 GB RAM for inference.

[1] https://www.dialpad.com/

[2] https://www.wikidata.org/

[3] https://www.elastic.co/elasticsearch/

Proceedings of NAACL-HLT 2022: Industry Track Papers, pages 344 - 352
July 10-15, 2022

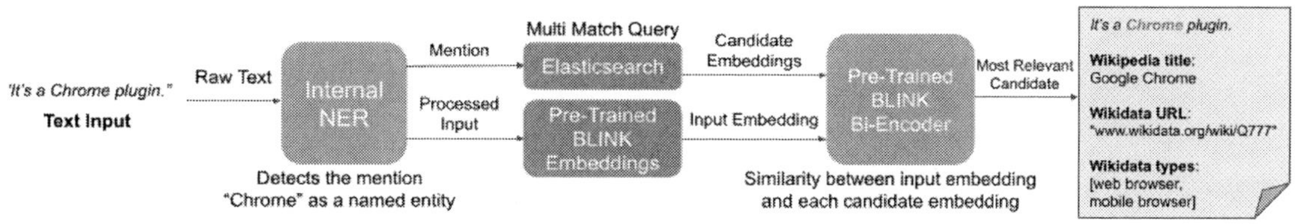

Figure 1: The Proposed Entity Linking System. First, our Internal NER model detects the mention in the given text. Then we retrieve a list of candidate entities with their embeddings from Elasticsearch. At the same time, we generate the contextualized representation of the input text using the pre-trained BLINK embeddings. Afterward, we utilize the pre-trained BLINK Bi-Encoder to determine the entity that is the most relevant among the candidates and finally we extract information related to that entity from our knowledge base in Elasticsearch.

2 Related Work

Prior work on entity linking mostly focused on linking named entities to unstructured knowledge bases like Wikipedia, whereas the amount of work that used a structured knowledge base like Wikidata is very limited (Shen et al., 2014; Sakor et al., 2020). Though other knowledge bases like DBpedia (Auer et al., 2007) or YAGO (Fabian et al., 2007) have also been studied, the utilization of Wikidata as the knowledge base to extract relevant information has gained lots of attention recently (Lin et al., 2021; Möller et al., 2021).

Detecting mentions (i.e., entities) in the given text (Huang et al., 2015; Akbik et al., 2018) is an important step for entity linking. In recent years, utilizing the neural network architecture for mention detection has been extensively studied (Wu et al., 2020; Onoe and Durrett, 2020a). More recently, the impressive success of the transformer architecture (Vaswani et al., 2017; Devlin et al., 2019; Yamada et al., 2020) in a wide range of natural language processing tasks has also inspired researchers to apply transformer models for the entity recognition (Lin et al., 2021) step in entity linking (Ravi et al., 2021), which results in obtaining superior performance over the previously used recurrent neural network-based models (Peters et al., 2018).

For the candidate generation step in entity linking, early work mostly utilized various non-neural network approaches such as TF-IDF or alias tables (Wu et al., 2020), whereas more recent work utilized dense embeddings learnt via pre-trained transformers to retrieve the relevant candidates (Wu et al., 2020; Onoe and Durrett, 2020b). However, there is an important limitation while generating the candidates via pre-trained embeddings. For instance, the state-of-the-art neural entity linking model BLINK (Wu et al., 2020) loads the pre-trained embeddings of all entities in Wikipedia into memory. Thus, it becomes inapplicable for deployment in production scenarios where the requirement is to ensure lower memory consumption. In this paper, we address this issue via storing the pre-trained embeddings in Elasticsearch. Moreover, we introduce new techniques that pre-compute the linking between Wikipedia and Wikidata to ensure efficient information retrieval, while also optimize the pre-trained models to meet the goal of deploying the proposed system in a limited computational resource setting.

3 System Overview

To develop the entity linking system, we adopt BLINK, a neural entity linker that uses the transformer-based BERT model (Vaswani et al., 2017; Devlin et al., 2019) and trains it on Wikipedia. BLINK connects each mention in a given text with its respective Wikipedia page based on the overall context. Since Wikipedia contains textual data in an unstructured format, it is difficult to extract information from it. Thus, we connect BLINK with a structured knowledge base, Wikidata, to extract information about product and organization type entities. Note that we store our knowledge base as well as the embedding representation of each entity in Elasticsearch. Moreover, we replace the Flair Named Entity Recognition (NER) model (Akbik et al., 2019) originally used by BLINK with an NER model (we denote it as **Internal NER**) trained on transcripts of business phone conversations using DistilBERT (Sanh et al., 2019).

We show our entity linking system in Figure 1. At first, the input text is processed by the NER model to detect the mention. Then, we generate the representation for the input text using the pre-trained BLINK embeddings, while we retrieve the relevant candidates with their embeddings from

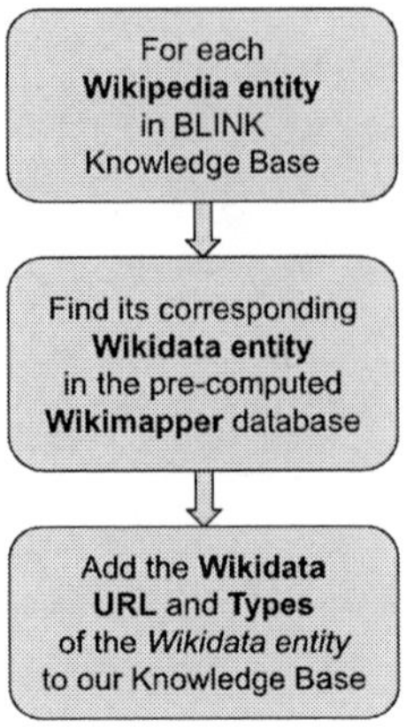

Figure 2: Precomputing Wikipedia to Wikidata Linking.

```
"query":{
        "multi_match":
        {
                "query": mention,
                "fields": [title^2, description],
        }
}
```

Figure 3: Our Multi Match Query in Elasticsearch.

Elasticsearch using the Multi Match Query[4] feature of Elasticsearch. Finally, the embedding representations of the input text and the candidates are sent to the pre-trained BLINK Bi-Encoder to select the most relevant candidate. Below, we first demonstrate our proposed entity linking system: ***BLINK with Elasticsearch***, followed by describing how we deploy our proposed system in production.

3.1 BLINK with Elasticsearch

The original BLINK model requires about 25GB RAM to load all pretrained embeddings into memory. In our proposed system, we instead store these embeddings in an external database. To do so, we store all entity embeddings as dense vectors[5] in our knowledge base in a remote Elasticsearch server along with saving textual information, such as Wikipedia title, description, URL, and etc. of each entity. This allows the model to only load the top K candidate embeddings into the memory that are most relevant to the mention in a given utterance. As mentioned earlier, the BLINK model was trained over Wikipedia, while our goal is to utilize Wikidata for information extraction. Thus, we need to map the Wikipedia URL of each entity to its Wikidata URL such that we can utilize Wikidata to extract relevant information. Below, we first describe how we add Wikidata URL of each entity to our knowledge base. Then, we demonstrate how we retrieve the relevant candidates from our knowledge base.

3.1.1 Pre-computing Wikipedia to Wikidata Linking

We pre-compute the mapping between Wikipedia and Wikidata using the Wikimapper[6] API and add the Wikidata URL of each entity to our knowledge base in Elasticsearch (see Figure 2). This allows our entity linking system to reduce the runtime latency. Note that during the pre-computation step, other information from Wikidata for each entity can also be added to the knowledge base (for our case, we add the *instance of* property as the entity type).

3.1.2 Multi Match Query for Candidate Retrieval

We find that the whole word or subword(s) in the product or organization type entity names usually appear in the Wikipedia *title* and *description* fields. Thus, to retrieve the most relevant candidates, we utilize the *multi match query* feature of Elasticsearch for each entity mention in the input text and apply it to the *title* and *description* fields in our knowledge base (see Figure 3). For *multi match query*, we give more weight to the *title* field to make it two times more important than the *description* field. In this way, we retrieve the top $k = 250$ candidates from Elasticsearch and send to the BLINK Bi-Encoder to select the most relevant entity.

3.2 Model Deployment

We deploy our entity linking system in containers[7] in a Kubernetes[8] cluster with 2 CPUs and 10GB RAM. The deployed system architecture is shown in Figure 4. For production deployment, we also apply some optimization techniques to reduce the size of the pre-trained Bi-Encoder, as well as our knowledge base. We describe these below.

[4]https://www.elastic.co/guide/en/elasticsearch/reference/current/query-dsl-multi-match-query.html

[5]https://www.elastic.co/guide/en/elasticsearch/reference/current/dense-vector.html

[6]https://github.com/jcklie/wikimapper

[7]https://cloud.google.com/kubernetes-engine

[8]https://kubernetes.io/

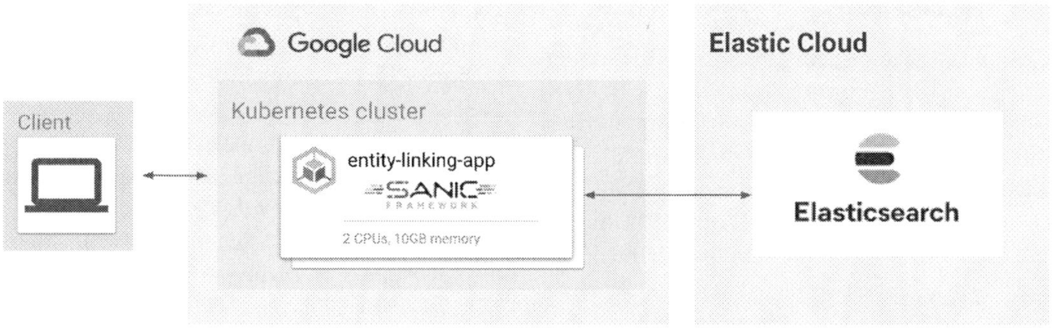

Figure 4: Deployed System Architecture.

3.2.1 Pre-trained Bi-Encoder Optimization

We noticed that the binary file of the pre-trained BLINK Bi-Encoder had two type of tensors: one for context encoding (for the input representation), and the other for the candidate encoding. However, the candidate encoding is only required during the training phase and it is not required during the inference stage since all the candidate embeddings are already stored in our knowledge base in Elasticsearch. Thus, we remove the unnecessary candidate encoding tensors from the binary file which results in reducing the file size from 2.5GB to 1.2GB (50% reduced space) to improve memory efficiency.

3.2.2 Knowledge Base Optimization

The original version of the pre-trained BLINK model (Wu et al., 2020) learns the embedding representations of 59,03,527 Wikipedia entities. In total, the size of these pre-computed embeddings is about 23GB. As our goal is to detect the *Product* and *Organization* type entities in business conversational data, we apply some filtering techniques to optimize the knowledge base such that it mostly contains the entities that are relevant to our NER system. In order to do that, we utilize the *Instance Of* property in Wikidata of each entity and remove entities that are of *Person, Disambiguation, Location, etc*. In this way, the size of the Knowledge base is reduced from 23GB to 12GB (about 50% reduced space), while the total number of entities has been reduced from 59,03,527 to 27,84,042.

4 Experimental Details

In this section, we demonstrate the datasets used in our experiments and the implementation details.

4.1 Datasets

To demonstrate the effectiveness of our proposed approach, we conduct a series of experiments on seven academic datasets as well as on a sample of 287 utterances collected from business conversation data. Below, we describe these datasets.

4.1.1 Business Conversation Dataset

As our goal is to develop an entity linking system that can link entities in conversational data from business domains, we sample some real world business phone conversation transcripts. After data collection, we use domain experts (in-house scientists) to annotate the utterances to label the mentions (i.e., product and organization type entities). Our annotated business conversation data consists of 287 utterances that we use in our experiment for evaluation.

4.1.2 Academic Datasets

Since our goal is to develop an entity linking system to extract information for product and organization type entities, at first we pre-process the academic datasets such that our model only links product and organization type entities during experiments. Similar to the original BLINK model (Wu et al., 2020), we also did not leverage the training data and only used the test data of each dataset for zero-shot entity linking. In our experiment, we use the AIDA-YAGO2-CONLL dataset (testa and testb) from Hoffart et al. (2011) that contains newswire articles from the Reuters Corpus; the ACE 2004, AQUAINT, and MSNBC datasets from (Guo and Barbosa, 2018) that were constructed from news articles; and the WNED-CWEB (Guo and Barbosa, 2018) and the WNED-WIKI (Gabrilovich et al., 2013) datasets that were constructed from CWEB and Wikipedia respectively.

4.2 Implementation

Recall that instead of using the Flair NER model (Akbik et al., 2019) used by the original BLINK model, we train an NER model on phone transcripts as our goal is to build the entity linking model for real world business conversation data. For this purpose, we adopt the pre-trained DistilBERT model (Sanh et al., 2019) and fine-tune it on a business conversational dataset collected from some phone transcripts in Dialpad that contains 516124 training samples (16124 instances were annotated by humans while 500k instances were pseudo labels generated by the pre-trained LUKE NER model (Yamada et al., 2020)). There were also 2292 human annotated samples in the validation set while 4497 human annotated samples in the test set. We use the HuggingFace[9] library (Wolf et al., 2020) to implement the distilbert-base-cased[10] model and utilize it for the sequence labeling task with the following hyperparameters: *learning rate = 2e-5, total number of epoch = 15,* and *batch size = 32*. To implement the BLINK model for inference, we use its original source code[11].

5 Results and Discussions

We denote our entity linking model that utilizes Multi Match Query (MMQ) on Elasticsearch (ES) as **BLINK + ES$_{MMQ}$**. Here, we first discuss its performance on our business conversation data. Then we conduct experiments on some academic datasets to demonstrate its generalized effectiveness.

5.1 Performance on Business Conversation Data

Below, we present some baselines that we use to compare the performance of our proposed model.

BLINK + PWB: This model adopts the original BLINK model for entity linking on Wikipedia and utilizes Pywikibot[12](PWB) for linking between Wikipedia and Wikidata.

BLINK$_{FAISS}$ + PWB: This model is similar to the above but utilizes the approximate nearest neighbour search using FAISS (Johnson et al., 2021).

BLINK + ES$_{CS}$: This model is similar to our proposed model but uses the Cosine Similarity (CS) feature of Elasticsearch instead of MMQ to retrieve the candidate entities.

For this experiment, we use the following evaluation metrics, **(i) average inference time:** *it refers to how much time it takes on average per utterance for entity linking,* (ii) **accuracy:** *it computes the correctness of linking the named entities to the Wikidata knowledge base,* (iii) **memory:** *it refers to the RAM configuration of the Machine that had to be used to run the model in Google Cloud Platform (GCP)*[13] .

Since the utilization of GPUs significantly increases the computational cost, we did not leverage any GPU in our experiments to mimic the production environment. We show our experimental results in Table 1 and find that our proposed model significantly reduces the inference time while achieving high accuracy. Moreover, we were able to run our proposed model in GCP on an *n1-standard-4* machine having 15GB RAM with 4 CPUs whereas BLINK models with Pywikibot had to be run on an *n1-standard-16* machine having 60GB RAM with 16 CPUs (we failed to run the model for inference due to memory leaks in other *n1-standard* machines in GCP that had less RAM).

From Table 1, we also observe that the performance of BLINK + ES$_{CS}$ model is the poorest among all models. One possible explanation behind this could be because the BLINK model did not leverage cosine similarity during its training phase and so zero-shot cosine similarity between the embedding of the candidate entity and the input embedding for candidate entity retrieval led to poorer accuracy. Moreover, we observe that the cosine similarity between embeddings is also very slow in comparison to MMQ. Furthermore, we find that our Internal NER is more effective than the Flair NER (about 46%) and combining it with the MMQ leads to the highest accuracy score of 93.03.

5.2 Performance on Academic Datasets

In this section, we further analyze the performance of our proposed **BLINK + ES$_{MMQ}$** model via conducting experiments on seven academic datasets. We particularly conduct this experiment to investigate the generalized effectiveness of multi match query. For this analysis, we use the **BLINK + ES$_{CS}$** model as the baseline where cosine similar-

[9]https://github.com/huggingface

[10]https://huggingface.co/distilbert-base-cased/blob/main/config.json

[11]https://github.com/facebookresearch/BLINK

[12]https://www.mediawiki.org/wiki/Manual:Pywikibot

[13]https://cloud.google.com/

Model	NER	Avg. Inf. Time	Accuracy	Memory
BLINK + PWB	Flair	2.45	62.72	60 GB
$\text{BLINK}_{\text{FAISS}}$ + PWB	Flair	2.34	60.28	60 GB
BLINK + PWB	Internal	2.79	91.64	60 GB
$\text{BLINK}_{\text{FAISS}}$ + PWB	Internal	2.71	88.50	60 GB
BLINK + ES_{CS}	Internal	13.93	75.96	15 GB
BLINK + ES_{MMQ}	**Internal**	**1.76**	**93.03**	**15 GB**

Table 1: Experimental Results on a sample of 287 utterances. Here, "Avg. Inf. Time" refers to "Average Inference Time in seconds per utterance", "Memory" refers to the RAM configuration of the Machine that was used. Moreover, we refer the DistilBERT model fine-tuned on phone conversational transcripts as the "Internal" NER model.

Datasets	BLINK + ES_{CS}	BLINK + ES_{MMQ}	Total Instances
AIDA-YAGO2-CONLL (testa)	**67.83**	62.84	3407
AIDA-YAGO2-CONLL (testb)	63.74	**65.64**	3425
ACE 2004	75.12	**82.95**	217
AQUAINT	**76.96**	76.46	599
MSNBC	71.50	**79.02**	386
WNED-CWEB	54.98	**61.15**	8834
WNED-WIKI	70.07	**74.10**	5617

Table 2: Experimental Results on academic datasets based on Cosine Similarity (CS) vs Multi Match Query (MMQ). Here, we use Accuracy as the evaluation metric.

ity has been used instead of multi match query. As our goal is to deploy our model in a limited computational resource setting to ensure less memory consumption, we only use the models in this experiment that can be run in a machine that do not require more than 16GB RAM. For this reason, we use the models that leverage Elasticsearch instead of Pywikibot (we have already demonstrated in our previous experiment on business conversation data how our proposed method is more effective in terms of both accuracy and efficiency than other baseline models that utilized Pywikbot).

We show the results of our experiments in Table 2 to find that in 5 out of 7 datasets, our proposed method that uses multi match query instead of cosine similarity outperforms its counterparts. The only two datasets where our model could not outperform the baseline are the AIDA-YAGO2-CONLL dataset (testa) and the AQUAINT dataset where cosine similarity outperforms multi match query by 7.94% and 0.65% respectively. In other datasets, our proposed **BLINK + ES_{MMQ}** model outperforms the **BLINK + ES_{CS}** model by 2.98%, 10.42%, 10.52%, 11.22%, and 5.75% in AIDA-YAGO2-CONLL (testb), ACE 2004, MSNBC, WNED-CWEB, and WNED-WIKI datasets respectively. Furthermore, we find during our experiments that our proposed method outperforms its counterpart in terms of inference speed in all 7 datasets (on average, 8 times faster). These findings further validate the effectiveness of our proposed **BLINK + ES_{MMQ}** model for real world deployment in computationally limited resource settings.

Top K	Avg. Inf. Time	Accuracy
K = 100	1.53	89.55
K = 250	1.76	93.03
K = 500	2.30	94.08

Table 3: Case study results on our business conversation data by varying the value to retrieve the top K candidates. Here, "Avg. Inf. Time" refers to "Average Inference Time in Seconds per utterance",

So far, we discuss the effectiveness of our entity linking system in terms of both accuracy and efficiency based on extensive experiments in business conversation data, as well as in benchmark academic datasets. Below, we conduct a case study to analyze how the top K candidates retrieval from Elasticsearch impacts the overall performance.

5.3 Case Study

For the case study (see Table 3), we conduct experiments with some additional values of K for candidate retrieval to investigate its effect on accuracy and inference speed. For that purpose, in addition to the original value of $K = 250$ for the

Model	Avg. Inf. Time	Accuracy
BLINK + ES_{MMQ}	1.76	93.03
without BLINK	0.55	74.22

Table 4: Ablation test results on our business conversation data. Here, "Avg. Inf. Time" refers to "Average Inference Time in Seconds per utterance",

BLINK + ES_{MMQ} model, we use the following values: $K = 100$ and $K = 500$. We find that even though reducing the value of K to 100 for candidate retrieval leads to a faster inference speed, the accuracy is decreased by 3.74%. Moreover, increasing the value of K to 500 provides an opposite impact, as it improves the accuracy by 1.13% but makes the candidate retrieval speed slower by taking more than 2 seconds per utterance. This trade-off implies that the retrieval value for K can be tuned based on the requirement.

5.4 Ablation Study

To further investigate the effectiveness of our proposed approach of combining BLINK with Elasticsearch via leveraging MMQ for candidate retrieval, we do an ablation test. In our ablation test, we remove BLINK and only utilize the MMQ of Elasticsearch to retrieve the most relevant candidate. In this way, only one top matched candidate entity is retrieved from Elasticsearch. The result of our experiment is given in Table 4.

From Table 4, we observe that even though removing BLINK led to a great improvement in terms of the inference speed, there is a significant drop in accuracy (by 20.22%). This makes the model without BLINK inapplicable in production scenarios where the requirement is to ensure high accuracy.

6 Conclusion

In this paper, we introduce an efficient, scalable version of the BLINK model and extend it for entity linking on Wikidata. With extensive experiments, we show that our proposed system is usable for production environments within a limited budget setting since it significantly reduces memory requirements, computing resource usage, as well as the inference time while retaining high accuracy. We also effectively deploy our proposed entity linking system in a 10GB RAM machine without using any GPU for near real-time inference. In the future, we will investigate how to make our entity linking system more efficient such that it can give inference in real-time (e.g., within one second). Moreover, we will study how different BERT-based (Sanh et al., 2019; Devlin et al., 2019; Liu et al., 2019; Lan et al., 2019) sentence similarity models (Garg et al., 2019; Laskar et al., 2020a,b, 2021) for candidate retrieval can impact the performance, while also exploring different techniques such as dimensionality reduction (Wang et al., 2016) to optimize the space used in Elasticsearch as well as the computing resource requirements.

7 Ethics Statement

The business phone conversational data used for entity linking experiments is annotated by the inhouse Scientists for which the annotations were acquired for individual utterances. Whereas to annotate the conversation dataset to train our internal NER model, Appen was used (`https://appen.com/`) for data annotation and the annotators were provided with adequate compensation (above minimum wages). There is a data retention policy available for all users so that data will not be collected if the user is not consent to data collection. To protect user privacy, sensitive data such as personally identifiable information (e.g., credit card number, phone number) were removed while collecting the data. Since our model is doing classification to link the named entities to their corresponding entries in a publicly available knowledge base for information extraction, incorrect predictions will not cause any harm to the user besides an unsatisfactory experience. We also maintain the licensing requirements accordingly while using different tools, such as Wikidata, WikiMapper, PyWikiBot, Elasticsearch, HuggingFace, BLINK, etc.

Acknowledgements

We gratefully appreciate the reviewers for their excellent review comments that helped us to improve the quality of this paper.

References

Alan Akbik, Tanja Bergmann, Duncan Blythe, Kashif Rasul, Stefan Schweter, and Roland Vollgraf. 2019. FLAIR: an easy-to-use framework for state-of-the-art NLP. In *Proceedings of the 2019 Conference of the North American Chapter of the Association for Computational Linguistics: Human Language Technologies, NAACL-HLT 2019, Minneapolis, MN, USA, June 2-7, 2019, Demonstrations*, pages 54–59. Association for Computational Linguistics.

Alan Akbik, Duncan Blythe, and Roland Vollgraf. 2018. Contextual string embeddings for sequence labeling. In *Proceedings of the 27th International Conference on Computational Linguistics, COLING 2018, Santa Fe, New Mexico, USA, August 20-26, 2018*, pages 1638–1649. Association for Computational Linguistics.

Sören Auer, Christian Bizer, Georgi Kobilarov, Jens Lehmann, Richard Cyganiak, and Zachary Ives. 2007. Dbpedia: A nucleus for a web of open data. In *The semantic web*, pages 722–735. Springer.

Jacob Devlin, Ming-Wei Chang, Kenton Lee, and Kristina Toutanova. 2019. BERT: pre-training of deep bidirectional transformers for language understanding. In *Proceedings of the 2019 Conference of the North American Chapter of the Association for Computational Linguistics: Human Language Technologies, NAACL-HLT 2019, Minneapolis, MN, USA, June 2-7, 2019, Volume 1 (Long and Short Papers)*, pages 4171–4186. Association for Computational Linguistics.

MS Fabian, Kasneci Gjergji, WEIKUM Gerhard, et al. 2007. Yago: A core of semantic knowledge unifying wordnet and wikipedia. In *16th International World Wide Web Conference, WWW*, pages 697–706.

Evgeniy Gabrilovich, Michael Ringgaard, and Amarnag Subramanya. 2013. Facc1: Freebase annotation of clueweb corpora, version 1 (release date 2013-06-26, format version 1, correction level 0).

Siddhant Garg, Thuy Vu, and Alessandro Moschitti. 2019. Tanda: Transfer and adapt pre-trained transformer models for answer sentence selection. *arXiv preprint arXiv:1911.04118*.

Zhaochen Guo and Denilson Barbosa. 2018. Robust named entity disambiguation with random walks. *Semantic Web*, 9(4):459–479.

Johannes Hoffart, Mohamed Amir Yosef, Ilaria Bordino, Hagen Fürstenau, Manfred Pinkal, Marc Spaniol, Bilyana Taneva, Stefan Thater, and Gerhard Weikum. 2011. Robust disambiguation of named entities in text. In *Proceedings of the 2011 Conference on Empirical Methods in Natural Language Processing*, pages 782–792.

Zhiheng Huang, Wei Xu, and Kai Yu. 2015. Bidirectional LSTM-CRF models for sequence tagging. *CoRR*, abs/1508.01991.

Jeff Johnson, Matthijs Douze, and Hervé Jégou. 2021. Billion-scale similarity search with gpus. *IEEE Trans. Big Data*, 7(3):535–547.

Zhenzhong Lan, Mingda Chen, Sebastian Goodman, Kevin Gimpel, Piyush Sharma, and Radu Soricut. 2019. Albert: A lite bert for self-supervised learning of language representations. *arXiv preprint arXiv:1909.11942*.

Md Tahmid Rahman Laskar, Enamul Hoque, and Jimmy Xiangji Huang. 2021. Domain adaptation with pre-trained transformers for query focused abstractive text summarization. *arXiv preprint arXiv:2112.11670*.

Md Tahmid Rahman Laskar, Enamul Hoque, and Xiangji Huang. 2020a. WSL-DS: Weakly supervised learning with distant supervision for query focused multi-document abstractive summarization. In *Proceedings of the 28th International Conference on Computational Linguistics*, pages 5647–5654.

Md Tahmid Rahman Laskar, Xiangji Huang, and Enamul Hoque. 2020b. Contextualized embeddings based transformer encoder for sentence similarity modeling in answer selection task. In *Proceedings of the 12th Language Resources and Evaluation Conference*, pages 5505–5514.

Bill Yuchen Lin, Wenyang Gao, Jun Yan, Ryan Moreno, and Xiang Ren. 2021. Rockner: A simple method to create adversarial examples for evaluating the robustness of named entity recognition models. In *Proceedings of the 2021 Conference on Empirical Methods in Natural Language Processing*, pages 3728–3737.

Yinhan Liu, Myle Ott, Naman Goyal, Jingfei Du, Mandar Joshi, Danqi Chen, Omer Levy, Mike Lewis, Luke Zettlemoyer, and Veselin Stoyanov. 2019. Roberta: A robustly optimized bert pretraining approach. *arXiv preprint arXiv:1907.11692*.

Cedric Möller, Jens Lehmann, and Ricardo Usbeck. 2021. Survey on english entity linking on wikidata. *arXiv preprint arXiv:2112.01989*.

Yasumasa Onoe and Greg Durrett. 2020a. Fine-grained entity typing for domain independent entity linking. In *The Thirty-Fourth AAAI Conference on Artificial Intelligence, AAAI 2020, The Thirty-Second Innovative Applications of Artificial Intelligence Conference, IAAI 2020, The Tenth AAAI Symposium on Educational Advances in Artificial Intelligence, EAAI 2020, New York, NY, USA, February 7-12, 2020*, pages 8576–8583. AAAI Press.

Yasumasa Onoe and Greg Durrett. 2020b. Interpretable entity representations through large-scale typing. In *Proceedings of the 2020 Conference on Empirical Methods in Natural Language Processing: Findings*, pages 612–624.

Matthew E. Peters, Mark Neumann, Mohit Iyyer, Matt Gardner, Christopher Clark, Kenton Lee, and Luke Zettlemoyer. 2018. Deep contextualized word representations. In *Proceedings of the 2018 Conference of the North American Chapter of the Association for Computational Linguistics: Human Language Technologies, Volume 1 (Long Papers)*, pages 2227–2237, New Orleans, Louisiana. Association for Computational Linguistics.

Manoj Prabhakar Kannan Ravi, Kuldeep Singh, Isaiah Onando Mulang, Saeedeh Shekarpour, Johannes

Hoffart, and Jens Lehmann. 2021. CHOLAN: A modular approach for neural entity linking on wikipedia and wikidata. In *Proceedings of the 16th Conference of the European Chapter of the Association for Computational Linguistics: Main Volume, EACL 2021, Online, April 19 - 23, 2021*, pages 504–514. Association for Computational Linguistics.

Ahmad Sakor, Kuldeep Singh, Anery Patel, and Maria-Esther Vidal. 2020. Falcon 2.0: An entity and relation linking tool over wikidata. In *CIKM '20: The 29th ACM International Conference on Information and Knowledge Management, Virtual Event, Ireland, October 19-23, 2020*, pages 3141–3148. ACM.

Victor Sanh, Lysandre Debut, Julien Chaumond, and Thomas Wolf. 2019. Distilbert, a distilled version of BERT: smaller, faster, cheaper and lighter. *CoRR*, abs/1910.01108.

Wei Shen, Jianyong Wang, and Jiawei Han. 2014. Entity linking with a knowledge base: Issues, techniques, and solutions. *IEEE Transactions on Knowledge and Data Engineering*, 27(2):443–460.

Ashish Vaswani, Noam Shazeer, Niki Parmar, Jakob Uszkoreit, Llion Jones, Aidan N. Gomez, Lukasz Kaiser, and Illia Polosukhin. 2017. Attention is all you need. In *Advances in Neural Information Processing Systems 30: Annual Conference on Neural Information Processing Systems 2017, December 4-9, 2017, Long Beach, CA, USA*, pages 5998–6008.

Yasi Wang, Hongxun Yao, and Sicheng Zhao. 2016. Auto-encoder based dimensionality reduction. *Neurocomputing*, 184:232–242.

Thomas Wolf, Julien Chaumond, Lysandre Debut, Victor Sanh, Clement Delangue, Anthony Moi, Pierric Cistac, Morgan Funtowicz, Joe Davison, Sam Shleifer, et al. 2020. Transformers: State-of-the-art natural language processing. In *Proceedings of the 2020 Conference on Empirical Methods in Natural Language Processing: System Demonstrations*, pages 38–45.

Ledell Wu, Fabio Petroni, Martin Josifoski, Sebastian Riedel, and Luke Zettlemoyer. 2020. Scalable zero-shot entity linking with dense entity retrieval. In *Proceedings of the 2020 Conference on Empirical Methods in Natural Language Processing, EMNLP 2020, Online, November 16-20, 2020*, pages 6397–6407. Association for Computational Linguistics.

Ikuya Yamada, Akari Asai, Hiroyuki Shindo, Hideaki Takeda, and Yuji Matsumoto. 2020. LUKE: deep contextualized entity representations with entity-aware self-attention. In *Proceedings of the 2020 Conference on Empirical Methods in Natural Language Processing, EMNLP 2020, Online, November 16-20, 2020*, pages 6442–6454. Association for Computational Linguistics.

Q2R: A Query-to-Resolution System for Natural-Language Queries

Shiau Hong Lim
IBM Research, Singapore
shonglim@sg.ibm.com

Laura Wynter
IBM Research, Singapore
lwynter@sg.ibm.com

Abstract

We present a system for document retrieval that combines direct classification with standard content-based retrieval approaches to significantly improve the relevance of the retrieved documents. Our system exploits the availability of an imperfect but sizable amount of labeled data from past queries. For domains such as technical support, the proposed approach enhances the system's ability to retrieve documents that are otherwise ranked very low based on content alone. The system is easy to implement and can make use of existing text ranking methods, augmenting them through the novel Q2R orchestration framework. Q2R has been extensively tested and is in use at IBM.

1 Introduction

A document retrieval system typically solves a text ranking problem defined as follows: given a query x, a relevance score $s(x, y)$ is computed for each document y in the target collection $\mathcal{D}$. Thus, the text ranking problem can be equivalently cast as a relevance-based binary classification problem (Lin et al., 2020), where for each (x, y) pair, the label is either "relevant" or "not-relevant". A learned probabilistic model can be used to provide the score where $s(x, y) \propto \Pr(\text{relevant}|x, y)$.

Typically, computing the relevance score $s(x, y)$ involves using the content of each document y. For example, the keyword-based approach BM25 (Robertson and Zaragoza, 2009) employs sparse bag-of-words representations of the query x and the content y, $f_q(x)$ and $f_d(y)$, and then $s(x, y)$ is given by the inner product $\langle f_q(x), f_d(y)\rangle$.

Modern deep learning approaches learn a parametric classifier $s_\theta(x, y)$ that takes as input the concatenated content of x and y. Such approaches may be computationally costly since $s_\theta(x, y)$ needs to be evaluated for every $y \in \mathcal{D}$. A two-stage approach is typically employed where a small $\mathcal{D}' \subset \mathcal{D}$ is first retrieved through a fast keyword-based method, then re-ranked with $s_\theta(x, y)$. An alternative to this approach is to learn a dense-representation (e.g. Reimers and Gurevych (2019)) for both f_q and f_d and compute $s(x, y) = \xi(f_q(x), f_d(y))$ where ξ is easy to compute (e.g. the dot product) and $f_d(y)$ can be pre-computed for every $y \in \mathcal{D}$. For simple ξ, the top-scoring documents can be easily retrieved via approximate nearest-neighbors (ANN) techniques. The latter is appealing for real-world applications due to its computational advantage.

While content-based methods have proven effective for general-purpose document ranking and are in widespread use, there are circumstances where using the content of the target documents is less effective. A primary example is when the document content is technical and queries are structurally and linguistically different. Consider the medical domain where documents concern medical treatments. Queries may describe symptoms experienced, which need not be included in a database of treatments. The availability of labeled examples that map symptoms to treatment plans motivates mapping queries from the labeled pairs to the best treatment documents. The same occurs in other domains such as information technology (IT), law, etc. For these technical domains, where such curated historical data often exists, we propose an approach based on direct classification that relies on learning a classifier from the queries themselves to the identity of the target document, without the need for the content of the target documents. The proposed method is complementary to content-based approaches. Hence, to cover potential new queries where similar labeled examples do not exist, we provide an ensemble paradigm, called the Q2R Orchestrator – Q2R stands for "Query-to-Resolution" – to obtain the best of both worlds.

In the proposed approach, each document $y \in \mathcal{D}$ is viewed as a class. We thus have a multiclass classification problem with $|\mathcal{D}|$ classes. In prac-

Proceedings of NAACL-HLT 2022: Industry Track Papers, pages 353 - 361
July 10-15, 2022 ©2022 Association for Computational Linguistics

tice, $|\mathcal{D}|$ can be huge and is likely to increase with time. Therefore, a parametric method for learning a classifier may not be a good fit. We thus propose a nonparametric approach based on kernel K-nearest-neighbors (KNN), which readily handles a growing set of documents, $\mathcal{D}$, and requires only occasional re-tuning.

The KNN approach takes the similarity between a new query x and past queries x' in the training set, rather than the contents of the documents y. In addition to bypassing the problem of using long document content, this approach allows retrieving documents not reachable through content alone. This ability is valuable in application domains such as technical support, where the content may not be well-represented in pretrained language models. The effectiveness of the KNN approach is, however, limited by the availability of labeled training examples and their coverage in terms of the "reachable" documents in $\mathcal{D}$. The Q2R Orchestrator thus combines highly accurate results from KNN for queries where labeled training data is sufficiently similar with a standard content-based retrieval system, for non-similar queries, through a learned orchestrator. Empirically we show that the resulting system benefits from both components.

The three main contributions of Q2R are as follows: (i) Q2R adds a direct classification component to document retrieval based on kernel KNN that enhances the ability to retrieve relevant documents. (ii) Q2R makes use of a labeled data set to train a symmetric query-to-query similarity metric for the kernel KNN, which enhances considerably the system performance, and (iii) Q2R blends the results from the KNN and content-based retrieval methods through an optimized orchestrator.

2 Related Work

For a survey on text ranking, especially modern transformer-based approaches, we refer the reader to Lin et al. (2020). The majority of text-ranking approaches, driven by publicly available datasets such as those from TREC (Voorhees, 2004) and more recently MS MARCO (Nguyen et al., 2016), are content-based. These approaches range from keyword-based, such as BM25 (Robertson and Zaragoza, 2009), to the recent BERT-based (Devlin et al., 2019) models such as re-ranking (Nogueira and Cho, 2019; Dai and Callan, 2019; MacAvaney et al., 2019; Li et al., 2020) and full-ranking with dense-representations (Reimers and Gurevych, 2019; Karpukhin et al., 2020; Khattab and Zaharia, 2020; Xiong et al., 2021).

In terms of ensembling multiple document retrieval approaches, the recent focus has been on the computational cost, where faster techniques are used to pre-filter the large document pool, to be re-ranked by computationally more expensive but more accurate techniques. A good example is the work by Ganhotra et al. (2020), which combines a series of traditional IR techniques with neural approaches.

While content-based approaches benefit greatly from models pre-trained with large corpora, they are at a disadvantage in specialized domains involving technical support documents. In such domains, the "resolution" documents given a query need not have a high relevance score based on the content alone. Document expansion techniques can play a role but often fall short as compared to direct classification, as we demonstrate in this work. To the best of our knowledge, there are no existing works that combine a content-based approach with direct classification as proposed in this work.

The proposed Q2R Orchestrator learns a separate classifier to choose results from either the content-based or the direct classification approaches. Traditional fusion techniques (Fox and Shaw, 1994; Vogt and Cottrell, 1999; Aslam and Montague, 2001) can be used here and in some settings may further improve the retrieval performance. We leave this as possible future work.

3 Method

3.1 Kernel KNN

A key component of Q2R is direct classification through kernel KNN. Let $\mathcal{Z} = \{(x_1, y_1), (x_2, y_2) \ldots, (x_N, y_N)\}$ be the training set of query-document pairs, where x_i is the text of a query and y_i the identifier of the document that was matched to each query in a curated dataset. We emphasize that y_i here refers to the document *identity* only, and not its content. Note that there may be more than one historical document y_i for any given historical query x_i. Furthermore, there are often many examples $x_i, x_j, x_i \neq x_j$ with the same document label $y_i = y_j$; this motivates the use of a kernel-weighted voting paradigm. For now, we assume that a feature function f is given and $f(x) \in \Phi$ is defined for each x, where Φ is a finite-dimensional Euclidean space.

The kernel KNN is a generative model for classification where the class conditional distributions $p(X|Y)$ are represented by a mixture:

$$p(X=x|Y=y) = \frac{1}{|\mathcal{Z}_y|} \sum_{(x',y')\in\mathcal{Z}_y} \psi\left(f(x) - f(x')\right)$$

where $\mathcal{Z}_y = \{(x', y') \in \mathcal{Z} : y' = y\}$ and $\psi : \Phi \to \mathbb{R}$ is a *kernel* function, with the following properties:

$$\psi(u) \geq 0, \int_{\Phi} \psi(u) du = 1.$$

A frequently used, smooth kernel function is the Gaussian kernel $\psi(u) \propto \exp\{-\frac{\|u\|^2}{2}\}$.

Given a query x, classification is done based on the posterior, given by:

$$\begin{aligned}
&p(Y = y|X = x) \\
&\propto p(X = x|Y = y)p(Y = y) \\
&= \left(\frac{1}{|\mathcal{Z}_y|} \sum_{(x',y')\in\mathcal{Z}_y} \psi\left(f(x) - f(x')\right)\right) \left(\frac{|\mathcal{Z}_y|}{N}\right) \\
&\propto \sum_{(x',y')\in\mathcal{Z}_y} \psi\left(f(x) - f(x')\right).
\end{aligned}$$

In practice, the computation of the posterior $p(Y|X)$ is restricted to only the K nearest neighbors of x in the feature space Φ. Let $\mathcal{Z}^K(x) \subset \mathcal{Z}$ be the set of K nearest neighbors of x in Φ based on $f(x)$ and $\mathcal{Z}_y^K(x) = \mathcal{Z}^K(x) \cap \mathcal{Z}_y$, then the kernel KNN relevance score between x and y is defined as

$$s^K(x, y) := \sum_{(x',y')\in\mathcal{Z}_y^K(x)} \psi\left(f(x) - f(x')\right). \quad (1)$$

Here, K is a hyperparameter that is optimized using a separate validation set. The feature function f plays a critical role and is optimized through metric learning on $\mathcal{Z}$ (Section 3.2). Notice that the relevance score s^K between a query x and a document y as defined in (1) depends only on the features of x (the query) and x' (training queries) and never on the contents of the document y.

3.2 Metric Learning

Q2R improves the relevance score s^K in (1) by fixing the kernel ψ and optimizing the feature function f through metric learning. Assume that f is parameterized by $\theta \in \Theta$, and denote the particular instance f_θ. In general, Θ can be a space of neural networks, and f_θ can range from linear to very complex nonlinear mappings.

The objective is to find f such that $f(x)$ is close to $f(x')$ if both (x, y) and (x', y) are in $\mathcal{Z}$. In other words, queries that have the same answers should be close to each other in the feature space. We use the triplet loss (2), a widely used objective function for metric learning (Weinberger and Saul, 2009; Schroff et al., 2015).

The idea is to create a set $\mathcal{T}$ of "triplets" (x_a, x_p, x_n) from $\mathcal{Z}$. Each triplet contains an anchor example x_a, a positive example x_p that belongs to the same class as x_a and a negative example x_n that belongs to a different class. Given $\mathcal{T}$, we find:

$$\begin{aligned}
\theta^* = \arg\min_{\theta\in\Theta} &\sum_{(x_a,x_p,x_n)\in\mathcal{T}} \max\{0, 1 + \\
&\|f_\theta(x_a) - f_\theta(x_p)\| - \|f_\theta(x_a) - f_\theta(x_n)\|\}.
\end{aligned} \quad (2)$$

For large $\mathcal{Z}$, the number of triplets can be huge. We propose an iterative sampling approach similar to that in Xiong et al. (2021) to optimize f_θ as follows:

1. Initialize θ randomly.
2. Set $\mathcal{T} \leftarrow \emptyset$.
3. For each $(x, y) \in \mathcal{Z}$,
   (a) Sample (x', y') from $\mathcal{Z}_y - \{(x, y)\}$ with weight $\psi(f_\theta(x) - f_\theta(x'))$; let $x_p \leftarrow x'$.
   (b) Sample (x'', y'') from $\mathcal{Z} - \mathcal{Z}_y$ with weight $\psi(f_\theta(x) - f_\theta(x''))$; let $x_n \leftarrow x''$.
   (c) Let $x_a \leftarrow x$, add (x_a, x_p, x_n) to $\mathcal{T}$.
4. Solve (2) for θ^*; let $\theta \leftarrow \theta^*$.
5. Evalute f_θ on validation set. Stop if no improvement after sufficiently many iterations.
6. Otherwise, go to step 2.

In Step 3, note that both the positive and the negative examples are sampled based on their similarities to the anchor example, preferring the more similar ones. Empirically we find that this approach performs better than always choosing a "hard" triplet i.e. picking the most dissimilar positive examples and the most similar negative examples. One reason could be that positive examples form clusters that are far from each other and including such distant examples in the triplet may actually harm the learning process.

Dataset	# URLs	# Training	# Validation	# Test
Twitter	3585	9622	493	472
Telco	1214	31,096	3859	3732
IBM	149,729	433,369	24,082	22,143

Table 1: Specifications of the Data Sets

Step 3 can be repeated for each $(x, y) \in \mathcal{Z}$ to produce multiple triplets. In our implementation, for each anchor, we sample one triplet using the weighted distribution as described above and another triplet using uniform weights. For large $\mathcal{Z}$, one can use a subset of $\mathcal{Z}$ in Step 3. For general neural networks, (2) can be solved using stochastic gradient descent or its variants on minibatches from $\mathcal{T}$.

3.3 The Q2R Orchestrator

As noted in Section 3.1, the content of a document y is never used in the direct classification approach via kernel KNN, only its identity. This relies on the presence of a sufficient number of labeled examples (x, y) in $\mathcal{Z}$ for each $y \in \mathcal{D}$. In practice, this will be possible for some, but not all, y, especially when the collection of documents, $\mathcal{D}$, is large. To provide answers to previously unseen, or under-represented documents in $\mathcal{Z}$, Q2R makes use of a standard content-based retrieval approach in conjunction with the kernel KNN method. This is done through the Q2R Orchestrator.

Suppose that s^C is the relevance score for a content-based approach while s^K is the relevance score for kernel KNN described above. Suppose that the objective is to return the top R documents. For a given query x, let $\mathcal{Y}^C = \{y^C_{(1)} \cdots y^C_{(R)}\} \subset \mathcal{D}$ be the top R documents based on s^C and respectively $\mathcal{Y}^K = \{y^K_{(1)} \cdots y^K_{(R)}\} \subset \mathcal{D}$ the top R documents based on s^K. The question of interest is formulated as a binary decision: decide whether to select $\mathcal{Y}^C$ or $\mathcal{Y}^K$ as the set of results to provide to the user. The Q2R Orchestrator thus trains a binary classifier to make this decision. For efficiency we use a linear classifier trained using logistic regression. To construct the training set, we identify examples in the validation set where the ground truth is contained in $\mathcal{Y}^C$ or $\mathcal{Y}^K$, but not both. The input features for the classifier include minimally $(s^C(x, y^C_{(1)}), \ldots, s^C(x, y^C_{(R)}),$ $s^K(x, y^K_{(1)}), \ldots, s^K(x, y^K_{(R)}))$, and may include other features such as confidence intervals.

4 Experiments

4.1 Data Sets

We focus on the task of natural-language retrieval of technical documents. We evaluate the proposed method along with baseline methods on datasets in which labeled examples are available.[1] In particular, we use the Twitter and Telco datasets described in Ganhotra et al. (2020) along with an IBM dataset.

The Twitter dataset is publicly available. It contains 10,587 labeled examples. Each example consists of a sequence of dialog messages and a URL document as the answer label. The set is split $90\%/5\%/5\%$ for train/validation/test, respectively. The Telco set contains 38,687 examples, with an $80\%/10\%/10\%$ train/validation/test split. The IBM set is an order of magnitude larger than the Telco set with a $90\%/5\%/5\%$ train/validation/test split. Table 1 summarizes the data sets used in our experiments.

4.2 Models

Q2R allows for virtually any content-based method to be used in conjunction with the kernel KNN component. Furthermore, thanks to the availability of training examples, the content-based approach itself can be improved by augmenting the content of the documents with the labeled examples using text from the corresponding training examples (Amitay et al., 2005). We show that this augmentation improves considerably the performance of the content-based approaches.

Here, as a baseline content-based method, we use BM25 (Robertson and Zaragoza, 2009). The variant wherein each document $y \in \mathcal{D}$ is augmented with text from $\{x : (x, y) \in \mathcal{Z}^{\text{Train}}\}$ is referred to as *BM25-aug*. We also include results obtained using the information retrieval method proposed by Ganhotra et al. (2020) (IRC, short for IR-Cascade) as well as ESIM (Chen et al., 2017). In addition, we examine a number of content-based

[1]The documents in the IR data sets Robust04 and MS MARCO are not sufficiently well-covered by the training set for use with Q2R.

methods based on Sentence-BERT (Reimers and Gurevych, 2019). We fine-tuned a pretrained DistilBERT model (Sanh et al., 2019) on our data sets using the triplet loss. To deal with long documents, we use a similar technique as in Dai and Callan (2019). We evaluate the following variants:

- SBERT-First (SB-F): Only the beginning of each document is used, up to the maximum sequence length of the model.
- SBERT-MaxP (SB-M): Each document is segmented into overlapping sliding windows. For training, each sub-document is assumed relevant. For evaluation, the maximum relevance score over all sub-documents is used.
- SBERT-aug-MaxP (SB-aug): SBERT-MaxP with augmented content as described above.

For our proposed KNN-based direct-classification component, we use kernel KNN with the following similarity metrics:

- (BOW) A simple TF-IDF weighted bag-of-words (BOW) representation for $f(\cdot)$ and $\psi(u) \propto 1 - \frac{1}{2}\|u\|^2$. Each feature vector $f(x)$ is normalized such that $\|f(x)\| = 1$, in which case it is straightforward to see that $\psi(f(x) - f(x')) = \langle f(x), f(x')\rangle$.
- (LinNet) We use (2) to train a linear transformation (LinNet) that maps the BOW vectors to a low-dimensional space. The feature dimension is a hyperparameter optimized on a validation set. We use dimension 200 throughout. For ψ we use the Gaussian kernel.
- (Transformers) For $f(x)$, fine-tune a pretrained transformer architecture using (2). We use DistilBERT (Sanh et al., 2019) (labeled KNN-DB) and MPNET (Song et al., 2020) (labeled KNN-MP), both with final 768-dimensional feature vectors. For ψ, we again use the Gaussian kernel.

For the kernel KNN models, we use a validation set to select the number of neighbors, $K \in \{5, 10, 20, 40, 80, 160, 320, 640\}$. The nearest-neighbor search can be done via an index by approximate-KNN (Malkov and Yashunin, 2020), and is as such nearly as fast as BM25.

	MRR	Recall@ 1	3	5
Content-based				
BM25	0.079	0.051	0.087	0.114
BM25-aug	0.498	0.403	0.561	0.629
IRC	0.498	0.417	0.547	0.606
ESIM	0.380	0.261	0.460	0.519
SB-F-0	0.030	0.015	0.028	0.042
SB-M-0	0.028	0.013	0.028	0.042
SB-aug-0	0.299	0.220	0.333	0.409
SB-F	0.449	0.375	0.489	0.545
(A) SB-M	0.482	0.384	0.536	0.598
(B) SB-aug	0.546	0.449	0.600	**0.663**
Kernel KNN (ours)				
BOW	0.477	0.409	0.525	0.568
LinNet	0.504	0.441	0.559	0.619
(C) KNN-DB	0.542	0.462	0.612	**0.661**
Q2R Orchestrator (ours)				
(A)+(C)	**0.557**	0.466	**0.621**	**0.665**
(B)+(C)	**0.552**	**0.473**	0.608	0.657

Table 2: Results on the Twitter set

4.3 Results

The results for the Twitter set are shown in Table 2, in terms of both the Mean Reciprocal Rank (MRR) as well as Recall@R for $R \in \{1, 3, 5\}$. The results reported in Ganhotra et al. (2020) were obtained by restricting the answer set to URLs from the same company/domain; here we use the full URL set, making the problem more challenging.

For the content-based approach, document-expanded BM25-aug and IRC far outperform vanilla BM25. Also included are results for the three "SB-x-0" variants, which use the pretrained DistilBERT model without any fine-tuning on the Twitter training set. Again, we see that augmentation makes a huge difference. The best-performing content-based approach is the fine-tuned SB-aug. The KNN classification methods based on bag-of-words perform similarly to the content-based methods but are outperformed by KNN-DB. Finally, it is clear that combining both approaches with the Q2R orchestrator results in the best performance.

Table 3 shows a breakdown of the results based on training-set coverage of the ground truth URLs. For each test query, we use the term "training coverage" to refer to the number of training examples that share the same ground truth URL. In classifier terms this is equivalent to the size of the training

Training coverage	0	1-9	10-55	56-338	339+
# Test queries	96	93	100	91	92
Content-based					
BM25	0.075	0.131	0.160	0.021	0.001
BM25-aug	0.046	0.373	0.531	0.815	0.749
IRC	0.022	0.354	0.507	0.711	0.917
ESIM	0.063	0.149	0.371	0.559	0.776
SB-F	0.144	0.363	0.453	0.417	0.884
(A) SB-M	**0.149**	0.351	0.447	0.577	0.904
(B) SB-aug	0.089	**0.382**	0.612	0.782	0.884
Kernel KNN (ours)					
BOW	0.000	0.268	0.420	0.817	0.913
LinNet	0.000	0.311	0.485	0.863	0.891
(C) KNN-DB	0.000	0.269	**0.656**	**0.879**	0.923
Q2R Orchestrator (ours)					
(A)+(C)	0.090	0.313	0.608	0.859	**0.937**
(B)+(C)	0.069	0.368	0.602	0.815	**0.930**

Table 3: MRR by training coverage on Twitter set. Training coverage of 0 means documents not in training set.

	MRR	Recall@		
		1	3	5
Content-based				
BM25	0.033	0.012	0.034	0.049
BM25-aug	0.337	0.201	0.408	0.510
(A) IRC	0.444	0.294	0.532	0.633
ESIM	0.458	0.299	0.554	0.658
(B) IRC+E	0.481	0.327	0.596	**0.691**
SB-F	0.428	0.280	0.519	0.616
SB-M	0.432	0.287	0.524	0.612
SB-aug	0.420	0.284	0.511	0.596
Kernel KNN (ours)				
BOW	0.484	0.346	0.569	0.656
(C) LinNet	0.496	0.370	0.599	0.665
KNN-DB	0.454	0.321	0.546	0.627
(D) KNN-MP	0.493	0.360	0.591	0.661
Q2R Orchestrator (ours)				
(A)+(C)	0.496	0.371	0.598	0.664
(A)+(D)	**0.510**	0.372	0.603	0.676
(B)+(D)	**0.515**	**0.381**	**0.623**	**0.694**

Table 4: Results on the Telco set

set with the same label. Training coverage of 0 means no such document was in the training set.

Naturally, for kernel KNN classification, we expect higher recall performance for queries with larger training coverage. This can be observed in Table 3 for all kernel-KNN models which far outperform on queries with coverage more than 10. On the other hand, kernel KNN has 0-recall for documents with 0 coverage since no neighbors could vote for such documents. The content-based approaches are able to perform on such queries. Q2R benefits from both approaches, performing well on queries with both high and low training coverage.

MRR	Train	Validation	Test
SB-F	0.498	0.433	0.428
SB-M	0.506	0.438	**0.432**
SB-aug	0.841	0.430	0.420

Table 5: Investigating Sentence-BERT performance on the Telco set.

Table 4 shows the results for the Telco set. The Telco set breakdown by training coverage is provided in the Appendix in Table 8. We see that among content-based approaches, the BERT-based approaches are no longer superior. Interestingly, SB-aug performs worse than SB without augmentation. Table 5 reveals that even though the final model is picked based on the validation-set results, there may be overfitting on the training set. Amongst the KNN models, LinNet performs the best overall, slightly better than the transformer-based model. However, the breakdown in Table 8 shows that each excels in different subsets of test queries. Q2R, combining IRC and KNN-MP results in better performance than combining IRC and LinNet.

Train. coverage	0	1-2	3-4	5-9	10-18	19-36	37-71	72-163	164-467	471+
# Test queries	2457	2649	1576	2255	2243	2170	2191	2194	2204	2204
Content-based										
(A) COMBL	**0.166**	**0.118**	0.108	0.093	0.088	0.078	0.079	0.080	0.071	0.060
BM25	0.111	0.087	0.089	0.076	0.069	0.068	0.075	0.074	0.067	0.048
(B) BM25-aug	0.077	0.100	**0.128**	**0.164**	**0.198**	0.225	0.294	0.303	0.302	0.262
(C) IRC	0.002	0.070	0.110	0.143	0.187	0.221	0.290	0.340	0.404	0.418
Kernel KNN (ours)										
BOW	0.000	0.024	0.058	0.103	0.154	0.200	0.295	0.357	0.465	0.647
(D) LinNet	0.000	0.032	0.069	0.115	0.190	**0.246**	**0.351**	**0.412**	**0.519**	**0.689**
Q2R Orchestrator (ours)										
(A)+(D)	0.050	0.052	0.081	0.117	0.188	0.241	0.345	0.409	**0.513**	**0.683**
(B)+(D)	0.012	0.039	0.073	0.116	0.189	**0.245**	**0.349**	**0.412**	**0.517**	**0.686**
(C)+(D)	0.000	0.032	0.070	0.115	0.190	**0.246**	**0.351**	**0.413**	**0.519**	**0.688**
(A)+(D) W.	0.139	0.100	0.104	0.116	0.148	0.177	0.247	0.306	0.401	0.578
(B)+(D) W.	0.073	0.097	0.122	**0.158**	**0.199**	0.228	0.304	0.341	0.394	0.515

Table 6: MRR by training coverage on the IBM set. Coverage of 0 means documents not in training set.

	MRR	Recall@ 1	3	5
Content-based				
(A) COMBL	0.095	0.060	0.107	0.134
BM25	0.077	0.044	0.086	0.113
(B) BM25-aug	0.204	0.131	0.234	0.287
(C) IRC	0.216	0.153	0.247	0.291
Kernel KNN (ours)				
BOW	0.228	0.162	0.256	0.311
(D) LinNet	0.260	0.186	0.298	0.352
Q2R Orchestrator (ours)				
(A)+(D)	**0.266**	**0.194**	**0.306**	**0.358**
(B)+(D)	0.261	0.186	0.299	0.353
(C)+(D)	0.260	0.186	0.298	0.351
(A)+(D) W.	0.231	0.168	0.266	0.315
(B)+(D) W.	0.242	0.162	0.273	0.327

Table 7: Results on the IBM set

Finally, Tables 6 and 7 show the results on the large IBM dataset. LinNet is the best-performing model for the kernel KNN. The transformer-based models are too computationally-costly and are not considered competitive; in addition, the transformer-based model results are inferior to those presented in the table. For content-based approaches on the IBM set, we include an alternative to BM25, based on keyword enrichment, labeled COMBL.

One important observation for this dataset is that the KNN models significantly outperform the content-based approaches in terms of overall average performance. This results in a significantly unbalanced training set for the orchestrator, where most examples would favor choosing the KNN results. The Q2R orchestrator can thus be trained using a weighted loss such that examples where the content-based model should be selected are given more weight. We tag this weighted version with "W." in the tables. Observe that the unweighted hybrid methods perform the best overall, but from Table 6 we see that the weighted version gives a more balanced performance across queries with different levels of training coverage.

5 Conclusion

We presented the Q2R system aimed at providing relevant documents in response to technical queries in natural language. The key novelty in this system is its use of both content-based document retrieval techniques as well as the proposed kernel KNN approach, which taps into the available labeled data from historical queries. Our experimental results show that content-based document retrieval and the kernel KNN approach complement each other; Q2R is able to take advantage of both. The system has been deployed at IBM on various applications that involve natural language queries and has shown encouraging performance improvement over existing systems. Potential future enhancements include more sophisticated sampling procedures for the metric-learning, as well as new fusion approaches for the orchestrator.

References

Einat Amitay, Adam Darlow, David Konopnicki, and Uri Weiss. 2005. Queries as anchors: Selection by association. In *Proceedings of the Sixteenth ACM Conference on Hypertext and Hypermedia*, HYPERTEXT '05, page 193–201, New York, NY, USA. Association for Computing Machinery.

Javed A Aslam and Mark Montague. 2001. Models for metasearch. In *Proceedings of the 24th annual international ACM SIGIR conference on Research and development in information retrieval*, pages 276–284.

Qian Chen, Xiaodan Zhu, Zhen-Hua Ling, Si Wei, Hui Jiang, and Diana Inkpen. 2017. Enhanced LSTM for natural language inference. In *Proceedings of the 55th Annual Meeting of the Association for Computational Linguistics (Volume 1: Long Papers)*, pages 1657–1668, Vancouver, Canada. Association for Computational Linguistics.

Zhuyun Dai and Jamie Callan. 2019. Deeper text understanding for ir with contextual neural language modeling. In *Proceedings of the 42nd International ACM SIGIR Conference on Research and Development in Information Retrieval*, SIGIR'19, page 985–988, New York, NY, USA. Association for Computing Machinery.

Jacob Devlin, Ming-Wei Chang, Kenton Lee, and Kristina Toutanova. 2019. BERT: Pre-training of deep bidirectional transformers for language understanding. In *Proceedings of the 2019 Conference of the North American Chapter of the Association for Computational Linguistics: Human Language Technologies, Volume 1 (Long and Short Papers)*, pages 4171–4186, Minneapolis, Minnesota. Association for Computational Linguistics.

Edward A Fox and Joseph A Shaw. 1994. Combination of multiple searches. *NIST special publication SP*, 243.

Jatin Ganhotra, Haggai Roitman, Doron Cohen, Nathaniel Mills, R. Chulaka Gunasekara, Yosi Mass, Sachindra Joshi, Luis A. Lastras, and David Konopnicki. 2020. Conversational document prediction to assist customer care agents. In *Proceedings of the 2020 Conference on Empirical Methods in Natural Language Processing, EMNLP 2020, Online, November 16-20, 2020*, pages 349–356. Association for Computational Linguistics.

Vladimir Karpukhin, Barlas Oguz, Sewon Min, Patrick Lewis, Ledell Wu, Sergey Edunov, Danqi Chen, and Wen-tau Yih. 2020. Dense passage retrieval for open-domain question answering. In *Proceedings of the 2020 Conference on Empirical Methods in Natural Language Processing (EMNLP)*, pages 6769–6781, Online. Association for Computational Linguistics.

Omar Khattab and Matei Zaharia. 2020. *ColBERT: Efficient and Effective Passage Search via Contextualized Late Interaction over BERT*, page 39–48. Association for Computing Machinery, New York, NY, USA.

Canjia Li, Andrew Yates, Sean MacAvaney, Ben He, and Yingfei Sun. 2020. Parade: Passage representation aggregation for document reranking. *arXiv preprint arXiv:2008.09093*.

Jimmy Lin, Rodrigo Nogueira, and Andrew Yates. 2020. Pretrained transformers for text ranking: Bert and beyond. *arXiv preprint arXiv:2010.06467*.

Sean MacAvaney, Andrew Yates, Arman Cohan, and Nazli Goharian. 2019. Cedr: Contextualized embeddings for document ranking. In *Proceedings of the 42nd International ACM SIGIR Conference on Research and Development in Information Retrieval*, SIGIR'19, page 1101–1104, New York, NY, USA. Association for Computing Machinery.

Y. A. Malkov and D. A. Yashunin. 2020. Efficient and robust approximate nearest neighbor search using hierarchical navigable small world graphs. *IEEE Transactions on Pattern Analysis and Machine Intelligence*, 42(04):824–836.

Tri Nguyen, Mir Rosenberg, Xia Song, Jianfeng Gao, Saurabh Tiwary, Rangan Majumder, and Li Deng. 2016. Ms marco: A human generated machine reading comprehension dataset.

Rodrigo Nogueira and Kyunghyun Cho. 2019. Passage re-ranking with bert. *arXiv preprint arXiv:1901.04085*.

Nils Reimers and Iryna Gurevych. 2019. Sentence-BERT: Sentence embeddings using Siamese BERT-networks. In *Proceedings of the 2019 Conference on Empirical Methods in Natural Language Processing and the 9th International Joint Conference on Natural Language Processing (EMNLP-IJCNLP)*, pages 3982–3992, Hong Kong, China. Association for Computational Linguistics.

Stephen Robertson and Hugo Zaragoza. 2009. The probabilistic relevance framework: Bm25 and beyond. *Found. Trends Inf. Retr.*, 3(4):333–389.

Victor Sanh, Lysandre Debut, Julien Chaumond, and Thomas Wolf. 2019. Distilbert, a distilled version of bert: smaller, faster, cheaper and lighter. *ArXiv*, abs/1910.01108.

Florian Schroff, Dmitry Kalenichenko, and James Philbin. 2015. Facenet: A unified embedding for face recognition and clustering. In *CVPR*, pages 815–823. IEEE Computer Society.

Kaitao Song, Xu Tan, Tao Qin, Jianfeng Lu, and Tie-Yan Liu. 2020. Mpnet: Masked and permuted pre-training for language understanding. In *Advances in Neural Information Processing Systems*, volume 33, pages 16857–16867. Curran Associates, Inc.

Christopher C Vogt and Garrison W Cottrell. 1999. Fusion via a linear combination of scores. *Information retrieval*, 1(3):151–173.

Ellen M. Voorhees. 2004. Overview of the trec 2004 robust retrieval track. In *In Proceedings of the Thirteenth Text REtrieval Conference (TREC2004)*, page 13.

Kilian Q. Weinberger and Lawrence K. Saul. 2009. Distance metric learning for large margin nearest neighbor classification. *J. Mach. Learn. Res.*, 10:207–244.

Lee Xiong, Chenyan Xiong, Ye Li, Kwok-Fung Tang, Jialin Liu, Paul N. Bennett, Junaid Ahmed, and Arnold Overwijk. 2021. Approximate nearest neighbor negative contrastive learning for dense text retrieval. In *International Conference on Learning Representations*.

A Appendix: Privacy

Since our training data includes past queries, it is important to remove all sensitive or personal information from the raw text before using them for training. We employ both automated masking and filtering followed by manual human tagging (for truly sensitive queries) as a preprocessing step in our data preparation pipeline.

B Appendix: Additional Experiment Details

All our models are trained using single-GPU (NVidia V100) 16-core machines with 128GB RAM. The total training time for each model varies from a few minutes (Twitter set, BM25) to a few days (larger BERT-based models).

For bag-of-words models, we trim the vocabulary by removing rare words and stop words, to 2000, 5600 and 54,000 words respectively for Twitter, Telco and IBM data sets.

Our BERT-based models use pretrained DistilBERT ('distilbert-base-nli-mean-tokens') (model size 253MB) and MPNET ('all-mpnet-base-v2') (model size 418MB).

For most results, the variance due to approximate-NN is small so we omitted them. For results based on neural-network training, we report averages based on at least 3 runs.

C Appendix: Additional Results

In Table 8 we present the Telco set breakdown results by training coverage.

Training coverage	0-59	63-213	216-1557	2009-2388	4165
# Test queries	757	759	887	786	543
Content-based					
BM25	0.07	0.05	0.03	0.01	0.00
BM25-aug	0.17	0.31	0.40	0.37	0.47
IRC (A)	**0.24**	**0.44**	0.56	0.41	0.58
ESIM	0.17	0.31	0.54	0.59	0.75
IRC+E (B)	0.17	0.36	0.58	0.61	0.75
SB-F	0.22	0.30	0.47	0.50	0.72
SB-M	0.23	0.30	0.48	0.56	0.64
SB-aug	0.21	0.31	0.48	0.52	0.63
Kernel KNN (ours)					
BOW	0.15	0.28	0.52	**0.70**	0.87
LinNet (C)	0.15	0.35	0.56	0.63	**0.89**
KNN-DB	0.11	0.29	0.52	0.60	0.83
KNN-MP (D)	0.15	0.35	0.61	0.65	0.77
Q2R Orchestrator (ours)					
(A)+(C)	0.17	0.37	0.55	0.60	**0.88**
(A)+(D)	0.21	0.42	0.62	0.60	0.75
(B)+(D)	0.15	0.37	**0.63**	0.68	0.80

Table 8: MRR by training coverage on Telco set. Training coverage of 0 means documents not in training set.

Identifying Corporate Credit Risk Sentiments from Financial News

Noujoud Ahbali*, **Xinyuan Liu***, **Albert Aristotle Nanda***
Jamie Stark, Ashit Talukder, Rupinder Paul Khandpur
Moody's Analytics, 7 World Trade Center, New York, NY 10007, USA
`{noujoud.ahbali, xinyuan.liu, albert.nanda jamie.stark, ashit.talukder, rupinder.khandpur}@moodys.com`

Abstract

Credit risk management is one central practice for financial institutions, and such practice helps them measure and understand the inherent risk within their portfolios. Historically, firms relied on the assessment of default probabilities and used the press as one tool to gather insights on the latest credit event developments of an entity. However, due to the deluge of the current news coverage for companies, analyzing news manually by financial experts is considered a highly laborious task. To this end, we propose a novel deep learning-powered approach to automate news analysis and credit adverse events detection to score the credit sentiment associated with a company. This paper showcases a complete system that leverages news extraction and data enrichment with targeted sentiment entity recognition to detect companies and text classification to identify credit events. We developed a custom scoring mechanism to provide the company's credit sentiment score (CSS^{TM}) based on these detected events. Additionally, using case studies, we illustrate how this score helps understand the company's credit profile and discriminates between defaulters and non-defaulters.

1 Introduction

Motivation. Historically, financial institutions performed credit risk management with techniques based on two different approaches (Chatterjee, 2015). The first approach is structural models, based on (Black and Scholes, 1973) and (Merton, 1974), which use the company's assets and liabilities to derive its probability of default. The second approach is default intensity models, also called reduced form models, developed by (Jarrow and Turnbull, 1995) and (Grundke and Riedel, 2004), which measure the default event as a statistical process, a random event following Poisson law, without considering the company's assets or liabilities.

*These authors contributed equally to this work

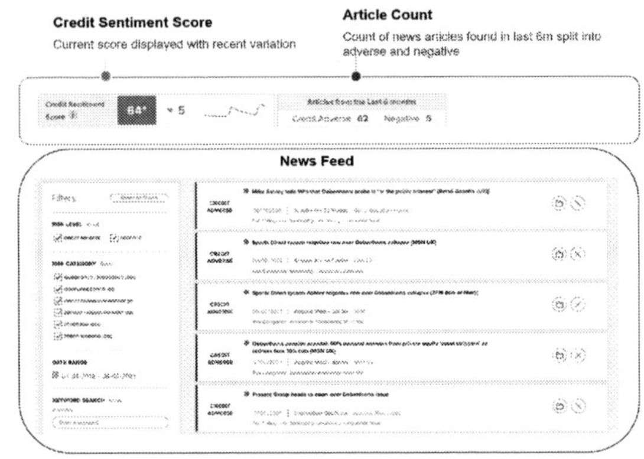

Figure 1: A screenshot of our deployed application.

These historic methods focus primarily on assessing the probability of default, which is useful in credit risk management. However, they are not designed to gain insights about a company's credit overall situation or identify the negative and credit adverse events the company has experienced or is likely to experience. This task falls under the responsibility of financial experts who may rely on news to identify such events, but this activity is considered highly tedious and time-consuming. Moreover, companies are increasingly covered in the press and journalists nowadays not only report facts, but go beyond in their analysis by making predictions, releasing warnings as well as establishing connections between companies.

Challenges. Most of the available news data is unannotated and un-exploitable at its initial state, which requires a significant entry effort for machine learning experiments. Furthermore, machine learning experiments in credit risk management has shown to boost accuracy in the default risk measure ('Oskarsd'ottir and Bravo, 2021) to show the effect of news sentiment on that same metric (Elena, 2020) or to focus on a single event prediction - credit downgrade in (Tran-The, 2020). However, none tackles news analysis automation and uses

Proceedings of NAACL-HLT 2022: Industry Track Papers, pages 362 - 370
July 10-15, 2022 ©2022 Association for Computational Linguistics

deep learning for credit event detection.

Our Goals. In order to derive explainable knowledge about a company's credit risk, we propose automating news analysis and identifying signals of negative and credit adverse events for companies. Such a method enables us to score the negative credit sentiment of companies. Our approach is a complete deployed application as shown in Figure 1. The enrichment pipeline starts with news collection (in English). It outputs a credit sentiment score (CSS) for companies based on the severity, recency, and volume of negative and credit adverse events detected from financial news articles. The custom Natural Language Processing (NLP) based pipeline's hallmarks include automated ingestion & filtering for finance-domain news articles, target-specific entity sentiment extraction. This pipeline allows high-precision content filtering and classification of the negative and credit adverse events mentioned in news articles (classified into five risk categories).

Our Contributions. The key contributions of this paper are:

- A novel, data-driven approach to detecting credit adverse events with targeted-entity sentiments
- A custom credit scoring methodology for companies from news, traditionally performed by financial experts.
- Extensive experimentation on real-world data on which our modeling approach performs well: including studies for defaulters VS non-defaulters and analysis of the discriminatory power of CSS between defaulters and non-defaulters.

2 Related Work

2.1 Aspect-Level Sentiment Analysis

When scientists prepare fine-grained sentiment models, they usually tackle the tasks of Aspect-based sentiment analysis (ABSA) (Do et al., 2019) and Targeted ABSA (TABSA) (Ma et al., 2018), where the latter considers the sentiment regarding a specific entity. Researchers have added context-dependencies to pretrained self-attention based language models called QACG-BERT (Wu and Ong, 2021) to improve the performance better. A mutual learning framework is used to take advantage of unlabeled data to assist the aspect-level sentiment-controllable review generation, consisting of a generator and a classifier that utilize confidence mechanism and reconstruction reward to enhance each other (Chen et al., 2021).

2.2 Deep Learning in Text Sentiment Analysis

A RNN model with LSTM units is trained based on Glove Embeddings of 400K words to predict the polarity (i.e., positive or negative sentiment) of the news (Souma et al., 2019). Moreover, an ensemble of CNN (Kim, 2014), LSTM (Hochreiter and Schmidhuber, 1997) and GRU (Chung et al., 2014) and a classical supervised model based on Support Vector Regression (SVR) is constructed which performs impressively on Microblog (Twitter and StockTwits) and news headlines datasets (Akhtar et al., 2017). Researchers have found that CNN is an effective model for predicting the sentiment of authors in the StockTwits dataset, among other models of logistic regression, doc2vec, and LSTM (Sohangir et al., 2018). A BERT model for the financial domain (FinBERT) pre-trained on a financial corpus and fine-tuned for sentiment analysis has shown promising results (Araci, 2019).

2.3 Machine Learning in Credit Risk

A study has shown that tree-based models are more stable than the models based on multilayer artificial neural networks in predicting loan default probability with structural features of financial conditions of a company (Addo et al., 2018). In addition, researchers have provided further evidence that regardless of the number of features used, boosted models outperform Linear Models, Decision Trees, and Neural Networks (Torrent et al., 2020). Further studies have stated that deep learning lends itself particularly well to analyzing textual data, but the improvement on numerical data is limited compared to traditional data mining models (Mai et al., 2019). Regarding Micro, Small, and Medium Enterprise (mSME) credit risk modeling, deep learning models, including the BERT model, appear to be robust concerning the quality of the text and therefore suitable for partly automating the mSME lending process because of their power to predict default based on textual assessments provided by a lender (Stevenson et al., 2021). In this study (Tran-The, 2020) a more NLP-focused approach is taken, using a combination of topic modeling and sentiment lexicons.

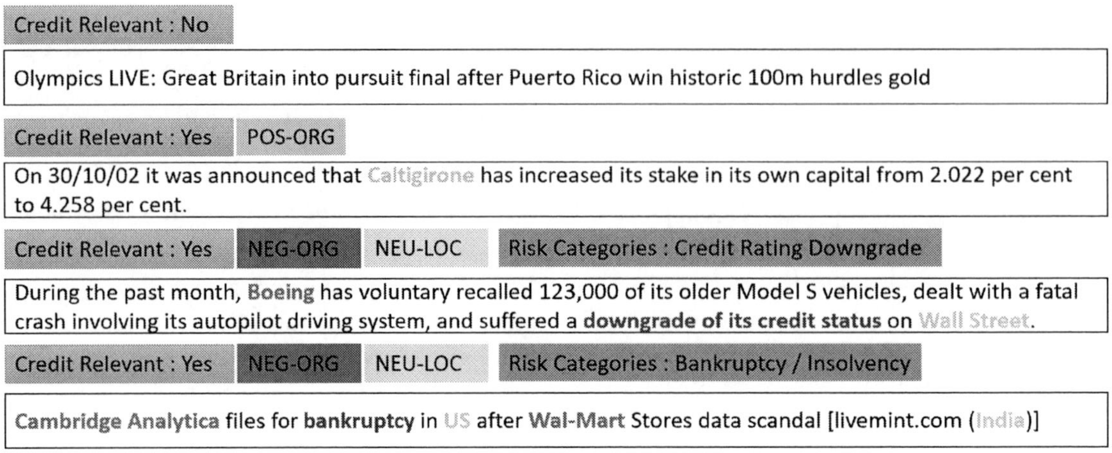

Figure 2: Annotated sentences by Credit Relevance, Target Entity Sentiment and Risk Categorization models.

3 Our Approach

In this section, we discuss different components of our scalable NLP pipeline that can ingest and infer English news from a news data source (Moody's Analytics NewsEdge [1]) that has over 170M articles, with an average of 150K news articles daily volume. To efficiently process large volumes of data, we have designed a data funnel process.

We have a credit relevance model at the head of the funnel, which helps discard irrelevant documents, viz. sports/technology-related articles. This model filters out 70% of the incoming documents. Next, the Target Entity Sentiment (TES) model extracts and tags all the entities in a document with Positive, Negative, and Neutral sentiment polarity, respectively. Following this step, the Risk Categorization model then classifies each sentence in the article into appropriate risk categories (discussed later in this section). In Figure 2 we illustrate different examples of sentences as annotated by each model.

3.1 News Enrichment Pipeline

In the pipeline, news articles are enriched with the output of the three following models.

Credit Relevance Model. We define credit-relevant news as any news story that contains business & finance-related topics which mention one or more corporate entities. We trained a binary relevance classification model using news data to identify relevant news. We leveraged the Reuters [2] news topics classification system, where we mapped Reuters codes into two classes: (1) in-domain (such as Merger/Acquisition, Sales, and promotions) and (2) out-of-domain (such asArt, Sports). In Table 1 we show the label distribution in both the train and test sets for the model.

After the text pre-processing (removal of Html links, numbers, and stop words removed), it was used with TF-IDF weighted features (Aizawa, 2003). Due to the train set size of over 30 Million articles, we chose a linear Support Vector Machine (SVM) model, trained with stochastic gradient descent (SGD) in out-of-core learning (Benczúr et al., 2018) setup.

Label	Train set	Test set
Relevant	13,323,062	3,291,751
Not Relevant	10,442,654	2,647,689
Total	23,765,716	5,939,440

Table 1: Distribution of annotated dataset for Credit Relevance model.

Target Entity Sentiment Model. The raw documents are first split into sentences using syntok [3] and then on each sentence a pre-trained WordPiece tokenizer (Schuster and Nakajima, 2012) is applied. Finally, each sentence is represented as $\{t_1, t_2, \ldots\}$ and the corresponding case tags $\{t_1^c, t_2^c, \ldots\}$. Token case tags used in the model are described in Table 2. Then given this sequence $\{t_1, t_2, \ldots\}$, we feed it to pre-trained Electra Base model[4] (Clark

[1] https://newsedge.com/

[2] https://liaison.reuters.com/tools/topic-codes

[3] https://github.com/fnl/syntok

[4] https://huggingface.co/google/electra-base-discriminator

Case Label	Description
AU	All letters in the token are upper-case
AL	All letters in the token are lower-case
IU	Only the initial letter of the token is upper-case
NU	All characters are digits(0-9)
MN	Most of the characters are digits
SN	Token has a digit

Table 2: Token case tags.

et al., 2020) to obtain contextual embeddings for each token $\{e_1, e_2, \ldots\}$. As shown in Figure 3, the contextualized embeddings are concantened with case embeddings $\{e_1^c, e_2^c, \ldots\}$ and fed to a linear layer to obtain the labels $\{\hat{y_1}, \hat{y_2}, \ldots\}$. To compute the loss, we used masked cross-entropy. And a dropout layer for regularization was added as well. The network was optimized using AdamW (Loshchilov and Hutter, 2019) optimizer.

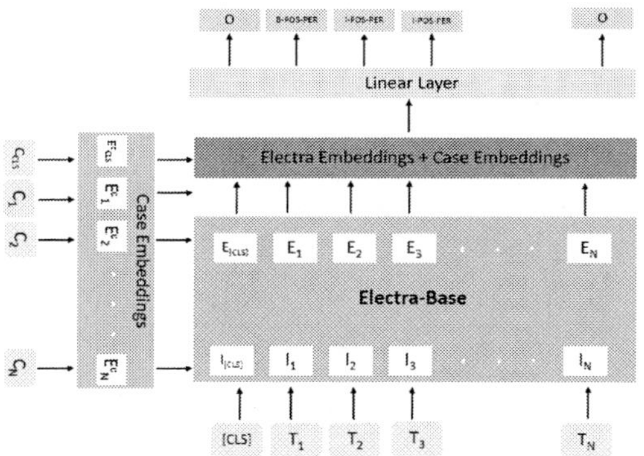

Figure 3: Architecture of Target Entity Sentiment Model.

To annotate data, each sentence was shown to 5 analysts, and those with majority consensus were selected; those with no clear majority were discarded. In Table 3 we show the overall distribution of labels across our final annotated dataset of 9,859 unique sentences, with an 80:20 split for training and evaluating the model.

Named Entity	Count	NEU	POS	NEG
PER	3585	67.92%	7.62%	24.46%
ORG	9020	63.47%	15.42%	21.11%
LOC	3824	92.89%	3.53%	3.58%
MONEY	2138	100%	0.00%	0.00%
MISC.	3020	92.29%	4.17%	3.54%

Table 3: Distribution of annotated dataset for Target Entity Sentiment model.

Risk Categorization Model. With similar pre-processing steps as inputs to the TES model, we trained a multi-label classification model, with an pre-trained Electra base model[5] (Clark et al., 2020), followed by convolutional layers (Kim, 2014) and a linear layer. We also used dropout to reduce over-fitting and a sigmoid layer to generate the final prediction output. The final tuned hyperparameters for the model are listed in Table 7 in Appendix. We trained the model with different model architectures and hyperparameters over 30 epochs in each model training iteration and saved the best epoch on the test set. Our team of 4 annotators (among the paper's authors) was engaged in data labeling and cross-review activities for more than 60 hours to build the dataset. A tagging guideline was first discussed and agreed upon with explicit definitions of the seven labels. The risk categories labels and examples are listed in Table 4. Around 7000 sentences were collected and labeled according to the tagging guidelines to form the train and test sets (using stratified sampling). The distribution of labels in the train and test sets are listed in Table 8 in Appendix.

Credit Risk Scoring Model. Each company is scored daily using credit adverse news articles for the company, as tagged by Risk Categorization Model.

Step 1: For each date, we calculate the category weights w_{cat}^{date} over a fixed window of days. This is done by counting the number of articles in each category and using an exponential decay so more recent counts have more weights, as shown in Formula 1.

$$w_{cat}^{date} = \sum_{i=from}^{date} \text{count}_{cat}^{i} * e^{(date-i)/k} \quad (1)$$

where:

$from$ = start date of the fixed window used for the calculations

count_{cat}^{i} = count of all articles found for a given category (cat) on day (i)

k = decay constant

Step 2: For each date, we calculate the category scores $score_{cat}^{date}$ by transforming the weights using a sigmoid function, which has the effect of capping the weight and also ensuring that only one or two articles mentioned will have limited impact.

[5]https://huggingface.co/google/electra-base-discriminator

Risk Category	Definitions	Example Sentences	Fixed Score
Bankruptcy / Insolvency	Proceedings of bankruptcy, insolvency or foreclosure, mentions of restructuring, administration or refinancing due to liquidity issues.	The British firm filed for Chapter 7 bankruptcy protection late Thursday.	100
Default / Missed Payments	Any mention of unpaid debts by a entity or the prospect of default for an entity.	Levitt home-building unit gets loan default notices.	75
Credit Rating Downgrade	Downgrades from rating organizations.	Standard Chartered's Shares Plunge 7% After Fitch Downgrade.	30
Profit Warning	Revenue, sales or EPS fall.	Carillion has been fighting for survival after contract delays and a drop in new business led to three profit warnings last year.	20
Compliance Issue	Any kind of financial crime, investigations, lawsuits, or violations.	TransAtlantic Petroleum Announces Notice of Noncompliance With NYSE MKT Continued Listing Standards.	2.5
Other Risk	Any type of company or credit relevant risks not covered in one of the five risk categories above.	On June 28, 2017, Southern Company and its subsidiary, Mississippi Power, suspended operations involving the coal gasifier portion of the Kemper County energy facility.	0
Not Relevant	Any text that is not evolved with credit risk.	Marks & Spencer to issue its first junk bond after reporting its first loss since joining the stock market in 1926.	0

Table 4: Risk Categories definitions with examples and weights in entity scoring

We multiply by a fixed score for that category as described in equation 2.

$$\text{score}_{cat}^{date} = \text{fixed}_{cat}/(1 + e^{-m*(w_{cat}^{date}-c)}) \quad (2)$$

where:

m = steepness of sigmoid function
c = number of articles needed to reach the midpoint of sigmoid function
fixed_{cat} = fixed score for a given risk category

The more severe the credit event is, the higher the fixed score is, as shown in Table 4.

Step 3: The Credit Sentiment Score at date t is the maximum category scores:

$$CSS^{date} = max(\text{score}_{cat}^{date}) \quad (3)$$

Our scoring function has an exponential decay which recognizes that news has a lasting value and impact during a specific period. It is reactive to the latest news as it weights recent news higher than older ones. The risk scores in the Credit Risk Scoring model are calculated via heuristics, as we do not have enough training data for a supervised approach. The fixed category score of each risk category in the Credit Risk Scoring model is shown in Table 4.

4 Evaluation

This section regroups the models evaluation as well as examples of case studies conducted on real-world data.

The Baseline. A simplified set of baseline models consists of three event relevance (binary classification) models instead of the multi-label classification model in the Risk Categorization model: Bankruptcy, Default, and Adverse News. This baseline method was actually in the earliest version of CSS^{TM} product, where we only considered the two most severe credit risk events: Bankruptcy and Default, in addition to a general class of less severe events called Adverse News. Bankruptcy and Default models handle bankruptcy and default-related events, respectively, while the Adverse News model deals with other credit events such as credit rating downgrade and illiquidity.

$$(C * m_t + \sum_{i=1}^{n} \text{article}_i^T)/(C + n) \quad (4)$$

where:

C = average number of articles per day in the last 10 days
m_t = historical daily score mean in last 10 days
n = number of articles in day t
article_i^T = i-th article score on day t

Each model outputs a score representing the prediction confidence about the underlying event from 0 to 100 for the input paragraph. The Bankruptcy and Default models are LSTM models (Hochreiter and Schmidhuber, 1997). And the Adverse News model is an LSTM model with attention mechanisms (Bahdanau et al., 2015) as these events are usually not as explicitly mentioned in the articles as the Bankruptcy and Default events.

These three classes are only present in the baseline, and we have added new risk categories (as shown in Table 4) for our latest version of the Risk Categorization Model. During the inference stage, each article is split into paragraphs fed to the three event relevance models. The paragraph score is the maximum score of the three relevance models, and the article score is the maximum score of all the paragraph scores within the article. Since Bankruptcy events are the most severe events while Adverse News are the least severe ones, we have applied weightings to the article scores of the three events with 100%, 75%, and 50%, respectively. At the company level, related articles are scored and are aggregated using a bayesian averaging, as shown in equation 4, to generate the company's daily sentiment score.

Models Evaluation. In Table 5 we show the classification report for the Credit Relevance Model on the test set (an overall F1-Score of 87%). As re-

	Precision	Recall	F1	Support
Not Relevant	86%	86%	86%	2647689
Relevant	89%	89%	**89%**	3291751

Table 5: Credit Relevance results.

ported in Table 6 (detailed report in Table 10 in Appendix), the overall F1-Score of Target Sentiment Model on the test set is 77%, which shows best performance for ORG (Organization), the most relevant entity for our purpose. As reported in Table 6

	Precision	Recall	F1	Support
TES	76%	79%	77%	5391
RiskCat	83%	82%	83%	2146

Table 6: Performance (micro average) results for Targeted Entity Sentiment (TES) and Risk Categorization (RiskCat) model results.

(detailed report in Table 9 in Appendix), the overall F1-Score of Risk Categorization Model on the test set is 83%. We also notice better results for three of the four major credit events in the Credit Risk Scoring Model (Bankruptcy/ Insolvency, Credit Rating Downgrade, and Profit Warning).

The weights of risk categories in the Credit Risk Scoring model indicate the importance of the related credit events. That analyzes a company's creditworthiness. It coincides with the fact that we have better classification results in the Risk Categorization Model for the credit events that contribute with higher weights in the Credit Risk Scoring Model. As for Default / Missed Payments risk, its performance is close to the average performance.

To validate that our scoring model picks up credit adverse events for more than 6000 companies, we collect 40,000 negative articles over two years (2016 -2018) and corresponding default dates of defaulters. Of these companies, 1192 experienced a severe credit event (Bankruptcy/Insolvency or Default/Missed Payments), and the remaining became our control group. We refer to the former as defaulters and the latter as non-defaulters. We further filtered companies based on their newsworthiness to keep the ones with at least an article per month on average. In the end, the defaulters' group contains 1166 companies, whereas the non-defaulters have 3009 companies.

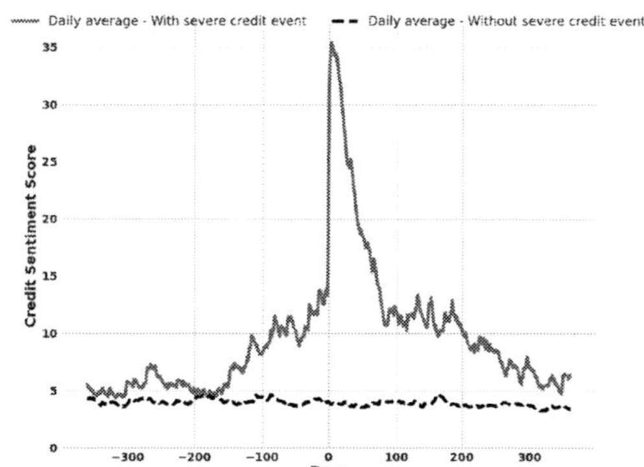

Figure 4: CSS Comparison between defaulters and non-defaulters

In Figure 4 we show the daily average CSS of the companies a year before and after the credit event (represented as the "0" date on X-axis). For comparison, we show the average score for the control group. The event dates for non-defaulters are chosen randomly during the same period as defaulters. The average CSS moves away from the long-term average towards the credit event. At around three months before the credit event and until five months afterward, the score is around two times compared to the non-defaulters average. The peak of the defaulters after default events is around 35 after taking the average within the defaulters' group. However, not around 80 as in an individual company when a default event happens. Still, in Figure 4 we clearly distinguish defaulters and non-defaulters around default events by their average credit sentiment scores.

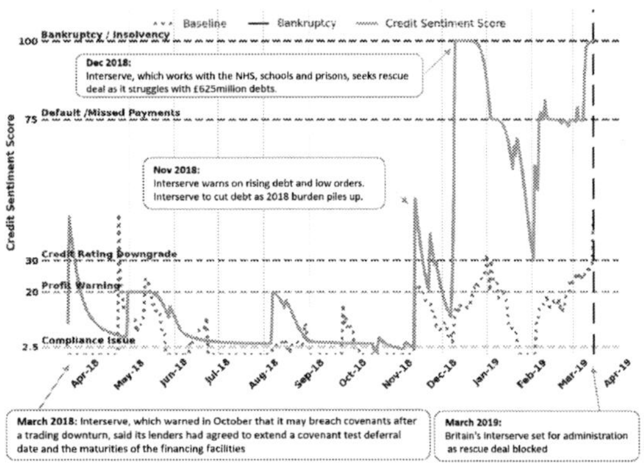

Figure 5: CSS and Baseline - INTERSERVE PLC.

Additionally, to validate the discriminatory power of CSS to identify the default and non-defaulting companies, we ran the following statistical tests. With *Kolmogorov–Smirnov* test (Massey Jr, 1951), we observed the Credit Sentiment Scores of the two groups (defaulters and non-defaulters) were statistically different, with a confidence level of 95%. Meanwhile, a *Mann–Whitney U* test (Nachar, 2008) showed that the probability of a defaulter's score is more significant than a non-defaulter's score (both selected randomly from the two groups) is statistically higher than 50%, with a confidence level of 95%.

Case Studies. To illustrate, we compared our CSS model to the baseline for defaulters and non-defaulters. As shown in Figure 5, CSS for Interserve PLC reacted to an early credit adverse signal (driven by Profit Warning and Default/Missed Payments) stronger compared to the baseline a year before the company was set for administration. Later, the news picked up a strong Bankruptcy / Insolvency signal as the company was seeking a rescue deal before it was set into administration.

In another example, in Figure 6 we show a consistently low CSS (as expected for the company as it is a non-defaulter company) compared to the baseline. This result is due to the baseline system

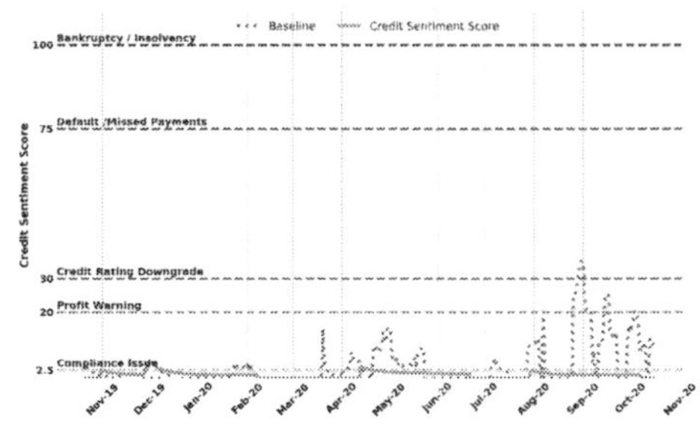

Figure 6: CSS and Baseline - AIR LEASE.

noise, as the articles often mention Air Lease's partners going into liquidation and insolvency issues. The result also shows that misclassifications on the paragraph level are way noisier than at the sentence level. A paragraph may have multiple sentences which refer to different companies with different sentiments in different contexts.

5 Conclusion

In this paper, we have designed, implemented, and deployed a deep-learning/NLP-powered application. This application can assist credit analysts in processing large amounts of news data and detecting and understanding the negative and credit averse events for companies. The pipeline utilizes various machine learning and deep learning models for data filtering, entity recognition sentiment analysis, and text classification.

As validated by the case studies and the modeling evaluation, the output sentiment score can distinguish between defaulted and non-defaulted companies. Since we only expose the CSS product instead of the complete models to the public, we will guarantee the truthiness of our in-house news source so that the system cannot be misused by publishing fake news.

We plan to use credit sentiment score as a signal to predict future credit events in future work. For example, given a company's credit sentiment score of a certain level, the probability that the target company will have some credit events within a certain period. We could also explore the sentiment analysis for positive credit events, aggregate company level scores into industry or region level, or focus on entities other than companies.

References

Peter Martey Addo, Dominique Guegan, and Bertrand Hassani. 2018. Credit risk analysis using machine and deep learning models. *Risks*, 6(2):38.

Akiko Aizawa. 2003. An information-theoretic perspective of tf–idf measures. *Information Processing Management*, 39(1):45–65.

Md Shad Akhtar, Abhishek Kumar, Deepanway Ghosal, Asif Ekbal, and Pushpak Bhattacharyya. 2017. A multilayer perceptron based ensemble technique for fine-grained financial sentiment analysis. In *Proceedings of the 2017 Conference on Empirical Methods in Natural Language Processing*, pages 540–546, Copenhagen, Denmark. Association for Computational Linguistics.

Dogu Araci. 2019. Finbert: Financial sentiment analysis with pre-trained language models. *ArXiv preprint*, abs/1908.10063.

Dzmitry Bahdanau, Kyunghyun Cho, and Yoshua Bengio. 2015. Neural machine translation by jointly learning to align and translate. In *3rd International Conference on Learning Representations, ICLR 2015, San Diego, CA, USA, May 7-9, 2015, Conference Track Proceedings*.

András A. Benczúr, Levente Kocsis, and Róbert Pálovics. 2018. Online machine learning in big data streams.

Fischer Black and Myron Scholes. 1973. The pricing of options and corporate liabilities. *Journal of Political Economy*, 81(3):637–54.

Somnath Chatterjee. 2015. *Modelling credit risk*. Number 34 in Handbooks. Centre for Central Banking Studies, Bank of England.

Huimin Chen, Yankai Lin, Fanchao Qi, Jinyi Hu, Peng Li, Jie Zhou, and Maosong Sun. 2021. Aspect-level sentiment-controllable review generation with mutual learning framework. *Proceedings of the AAAI Conference on Artificial Intelligence*, 35(14):12639–12647.

Junyoung Chung, Caglar Gulcehre, Kyunghyun Cho, and Yoshua Bengio. 2014. Empirical evaluation of gated recurrent neural networks on sequence modeling. In *NIPS 2014 Workshop on Deep Learning, December 2014*.

Kevin Clark, Minh-Thang Luong, Quoc V. Le, and Christopher D. Manning. 2020. ELECTRA: pretraining text encoders as discriminators rather than generators. In *8th International Conference on Learning Representations, ICLR 2020, Addis Ababa, Ethiopia, April 26-30, 2020*. OpenReview.net.

Hai Ha Do, PWC Prasad, Angelika Maag, and Abeer Alsadoon. 2019. Deep learning for aspect-based sentiment analysis: a comparative review. *Expert Systems with Applications*, 118:272–299.

Makeeva Elena. 2020. News sentiment in bankruptcy prediction models: Evidence from russian retail companies. , 14(4):7–18.

Peter Grundke and Karl O. Riedel. 2004. Pricing the risks of default: A note on madan and unal. *Review of Derivatives Research*, 7(2):169–173.

Sepp Hochreiter and Jürgen Schmidhuber. 1997. Long short-term memory. *Neural computation*, 9(8):1735–1780.

Robert Jarrow and Stuart M Turnbull. 1995. Pricing derivatives on financial securities subject to credit risk. *Journal of Finance*, 50(1):53–85.

Yoon Kim. 2014. Convolutional neural networks for sentence classification. In *Proceedings of the 2014 Conference on Empirical Methods in Natural Language Processing (EMNLP)*, pages 1746–1751, Doha, Qatar. Association for Computational Linguistics.

Ilya Loshchilov and Frank Hutter. 2019. Decoupled weight decay regularization. In *7th International Conference on Learning Representations, ICLR 2019, New Orleans, LA, USA, May 6-9, 2019*. OpenReview.net.

Yukun Ma, Haiyun Peng, and Erik Cambria. 2018. Targeted aspect-based sentiment analysis via embedding commonsense knowledge into an attentive LSTM. In *Proceedings of the Thirty-Second AAAI Conference on Artificial Intelligence, (AAAI-18), the 30th innovative Applications of Artificial Intelligence (IAAI-18), and the 8th AAAI Symposium on Educational Advances in Artificial Intelligence (EAAI-18), New Orleans, Louisiana, USA, February 2-7, 2018*, pages 5876–5883. AAAI Press.

Feng Mai, Shaonan Tian, Chihoon Lee, and Ling Ma. 2019. Deep learning models for bankruptcy prediction using textual disclosures. *European journal of operational research*, 274(2):743–758.

Frank J Massey Jr. 1951. The kolmogorov-smirnov test for goodness of fit. *Journal of the American statistical Association*, 46(253):68–78.

Robert Merton. 1974. On the pricing of corporate debt: The risk structure of interest rates. *Journal of Finance*, 29(2):449–70.

Nadim Nachar. 2008. The mann-whitney u: A test for assessing whether two independent samples come from the same distribution. *Tutorials in Quantitative Methods for Psychology*, 4.

Mar'ıa 'Oskarsd'ottir and Cristi'an Bravo. 2021. Multilayer network analysis for improved credit risk prediction. *Omega*, 105:102520.

Mike Schuster and Kaisuke Nakajima. 2012. Japanese and korean voice search. In *2012 IEEE International Conference on Acoustics, Speech and Signal Processing (ICASSP)*, pages 5149–5152. IEEE.

Sahar Sohangir, Dingding Wang, Anna Pomeranets, and Taghi M Khoshgoftaar. 2018. Big data: Deep learning for financial sentiment analysis. *Journal of Big Data*, 5(1):1–25.

Wataru Souma, Irena Vodenska, and Hideaki Aoyama. 2019. Enhanced news sentiment analysis using deep learning methods. *Journal of Computational Social Science*, 2(1):33–46.

Matthew Stevenson, Christophe Mues, and Cristi'an Bravo. 2021. The value of text for small business default prediction: A deep learning approach. *European Journal of Operational Research*.

Neus Llop Torrent, Giorgio Visani, and Enrico Bagli. 2020. Psd2 explainable ai model for credit scoring. *ArXiv preprint*, abs/2011.10367.

Tam Tran-The. 2020. Modeling institutional credit risk with financial news. *ArXiv preprint*, abs/2004.08204.

Zhengxuan Wu and Desmond C Ong. 2021. Context-guided bert for targeted aspect-based sentiment analysis. In *Proceedings of the AAAI Conference on Artificial Intelligence*.

6 Appendix

6.1 Risk Categories Model

Risk Categorization model final set of hyperparameters are shown in Table 7.

Hyperparameter	Value
Best Epochs	13
Max Length of Input Text	300
Train Batch Size	8
Test Batch Size	16
Initial Learning Rate*	1e-05
Dropout	0.7

* A learning rate scheduler is implemented to decrease the learning rate in later epochs to better converge and reduce overfitting

Table 7: Tuned Hyperparameters in Risk Categorization Model.

Risk Category	Train set	Test set
Profit Warning	688	329
Bankruptcy / Insolvency	853	372
Compliance Issue	326	161
Default / Missed Payments	596	309
Credit Rating Downgrade	426	204
Other Risk	1347	544
Not Relevant	596	227
Total	4832	2146

Table 8: Distribution of annotated dataset for Risk Categories model.

In Table 8 we show the distribution of the model's annotated dataset (train and test sets) along with the detailed classification report on the test set in Table 9.

Labels	Precision	Recall	F1-Score	Support
Profit Warning	**86%**	**89%**	**87%**	**329**
Bankruptcy / Insolvency	**93%**	**94%**	**94%**	**372**
Compliance Issue	81%	60%	69%	161
Default / Missed Payment	**79%**	**83%**	**81%**	**309**
Credit Rating Downgrade	**95%**	**95%**	**95%**	**204**
Other Risk	75%	76%	75%	544
Not Relevant	79%	68%	73%	227
Micro Avg	83%	82%	83%	2146
Macro Avg	84%	81%	82%	2146

Table 9: Detailed Risk Categories results.

6.2 Target Entity Sentiment Model

The primary entity label that our pipeline relies on is - *Organization* (Org) as our focus is on corporate entities. Accurately discerning the sentiment polarity (Pos, Neg, Neu) of these target Organizations is an essential requirement of the pipeline, and in the Table 10 we highlight the F1 score on these three classes.

Entity Type	Precision	Recall	F1-Score	Support
Money	94%	96%	95%	502
Neg Loc	57%	32%	41%	25
Neg Misc	36%	30%	33%	30
Neg Org	**66%**	**70%**	**68%**	**514**
Neg Per	72%	67%	69%	220
Neu Loc	85%	89%	87%	890
Neu Misc	71%	76%	73%	676
Neu Org	**74%**	**79%**	**77%**	**1612**
Neu Per	78%	80%	79%	518
Pos Loc	46%	24%	32%	25
Pos Misc	44%	44%	44%	27
Pos Org	**66%**	**69%**	**67%**	**298**
Pos Per	54%	70%	61%	54
Micro Avg	76%	79%	77%	5391
Macro Avg	65%	64%	64%	5391

Table 10: Detailed Targeted Sentiment results.

Author Index

Association for Computational Linguistics
209 N. Eighth Street
Stroudsburg, Pennsylvania 18360

ISBN 978-1-7138-5619-1